INSIDERS' GUIDE® TO RENO AND LAKE TAHOE

HELP US KEEP THIS GUIDE UP TO DATE

Every effort has been made by the author and editors to make this guide as accurate and useful as possible. However, many things can change after a guide is published—phone numbers change, facilities come under new management, etc.

We would love to hear from you concerning your experiences with this guide and how you feel it could be improved and be kept up to date. While we may not be able to respond to all comments and suggestions, we'll take them to heart and we'll also make certain to share them with the author. Please send your comments and suggestions to the following address:

The Globe Pequot Press
Reader Response/Editorial Department
P.O. Box 480
Guilford, CT 06437

Or you may e-mail us at:

editorial@GlobePequot.com

Thanks for your input, and happy travels!

INSIDERS' GUIDE® SERIES

INSIDERS' GUIDE® TO RENO AND LAKE TAHOE

FIFTH EDITION

JEANNE LAUF WALPOLE

INSIDERS' GUIDE®

GUILFORD, CONNECTICUT

AN IMPRINT OF THE GLOBE PEQUOT PRESS

The prices and rates in this guidebook were confirmed at press time. We recommend, however, that you call establishments before traveling to obtain current information.

To buy books in quantity for corporate use
or incentives, call **(800) 962–0973**
or e-mail **premiums@GlobePequot.com.**

INSIDERS' GUIDE®

A previous edition of this book was published by Falcon Publishing Inc. in 1999.

Text design: LeAnna Weller Smith
Maps created by XNR Productions Inc. © Morris Book Publishing, LLC

ISSN: 1535-8305
ISBN-13: 978-0-7627-4190-8
ISBN-10: 0-7627-4190-2

Manufactured in the United States of America
Fifth Edition/First Printing

CONTENTS

CONTENTS

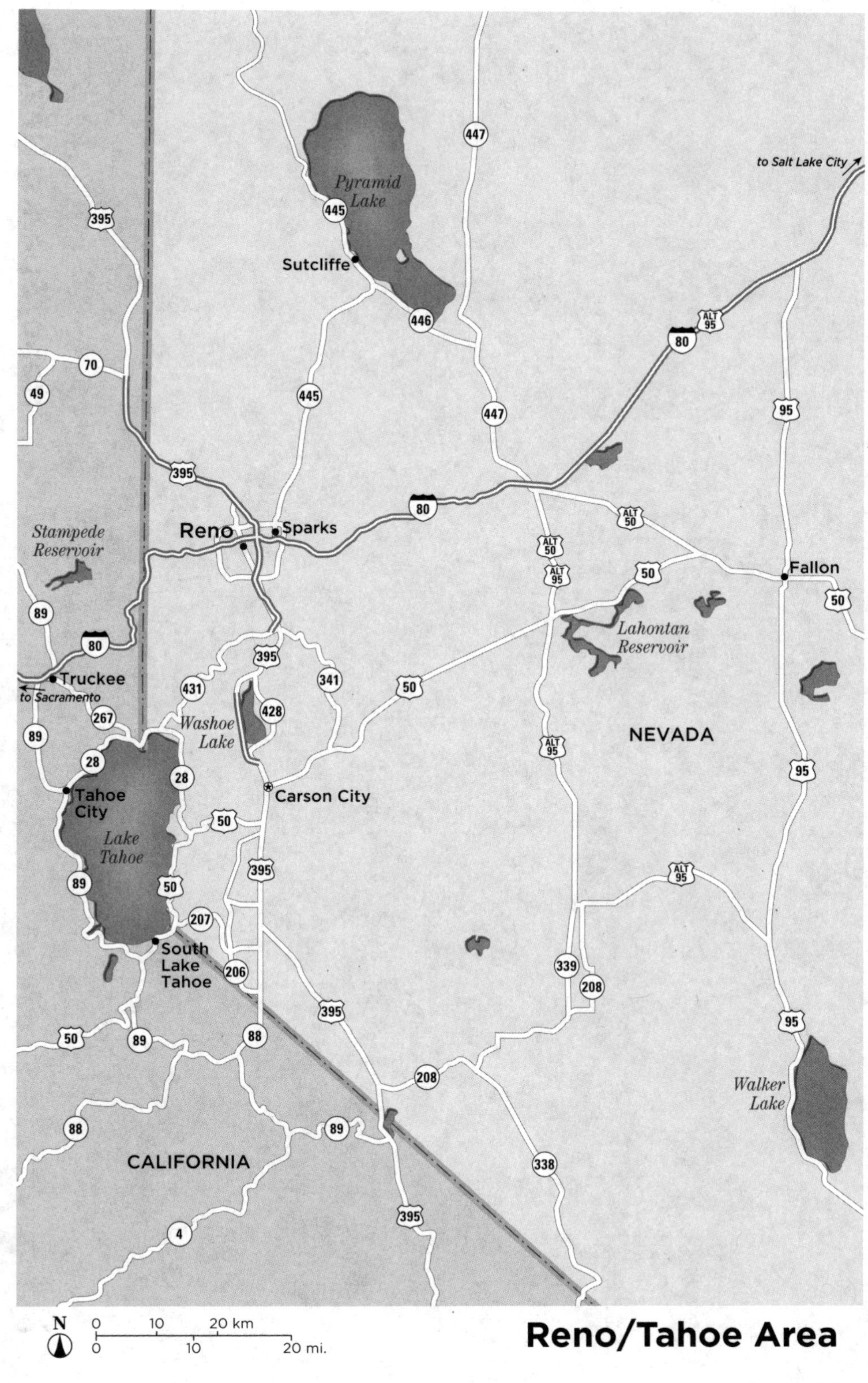

Reno/Tahoe Area

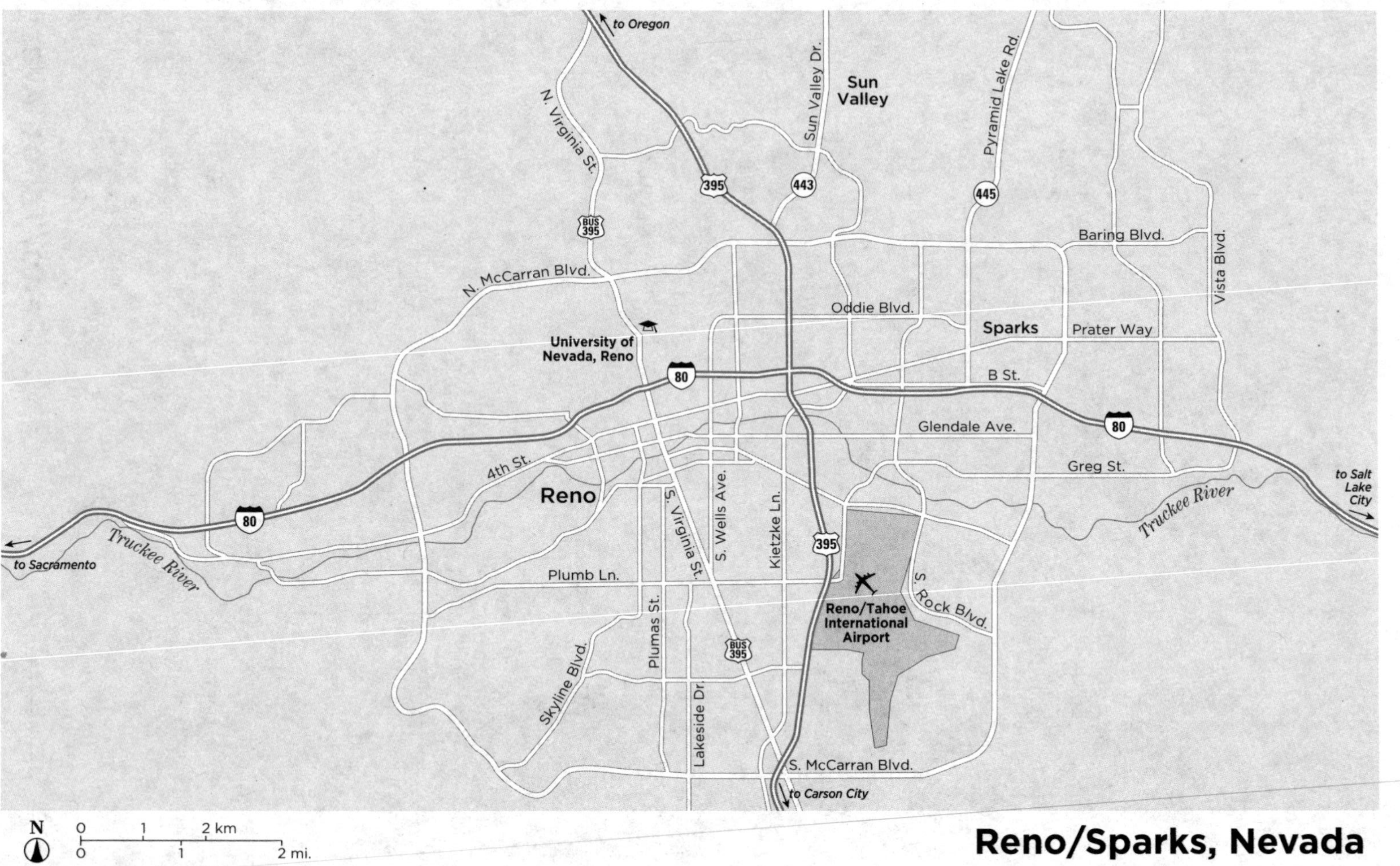

Reno/Sparks, Nevada

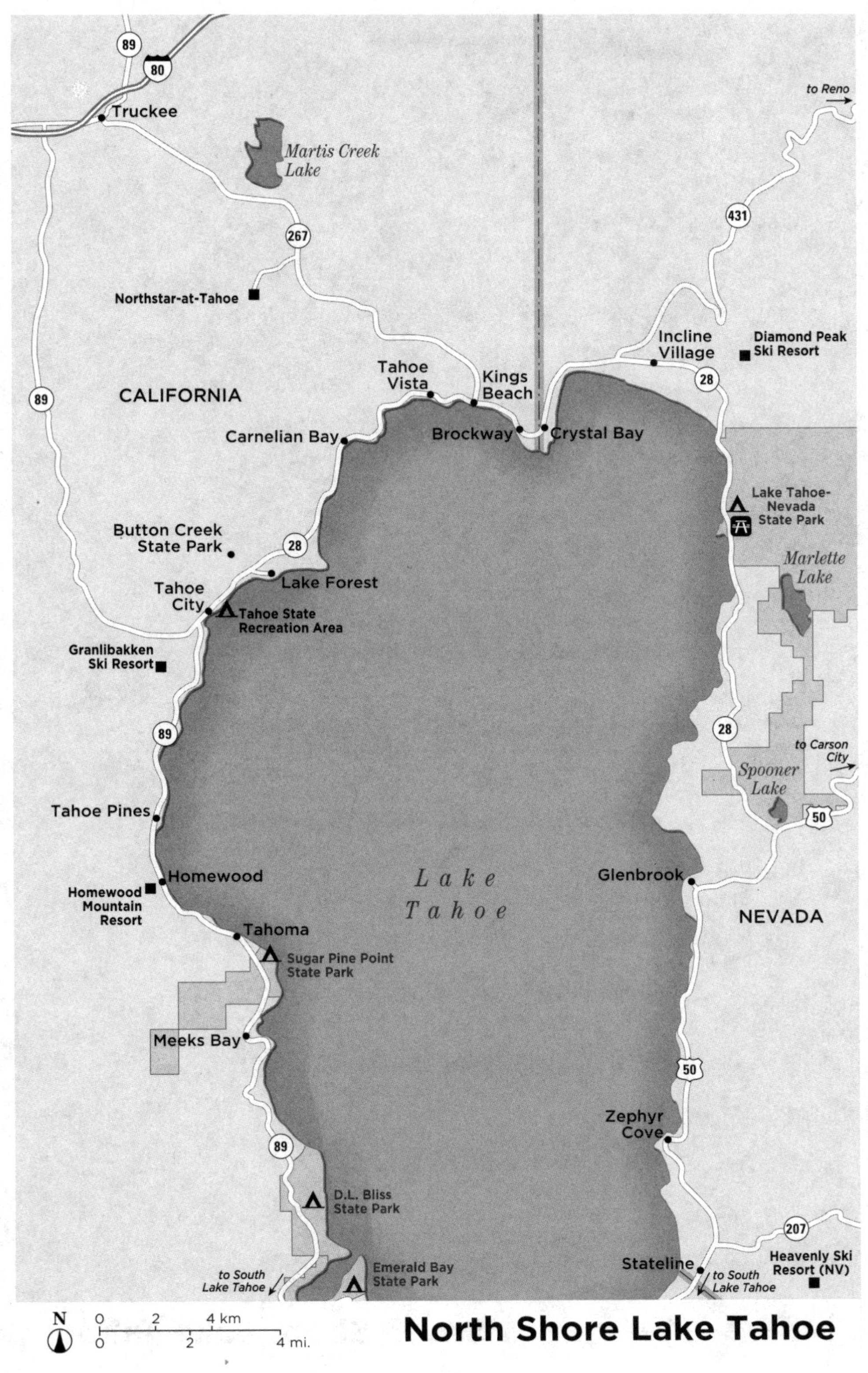

North Shore Lake Tahoe

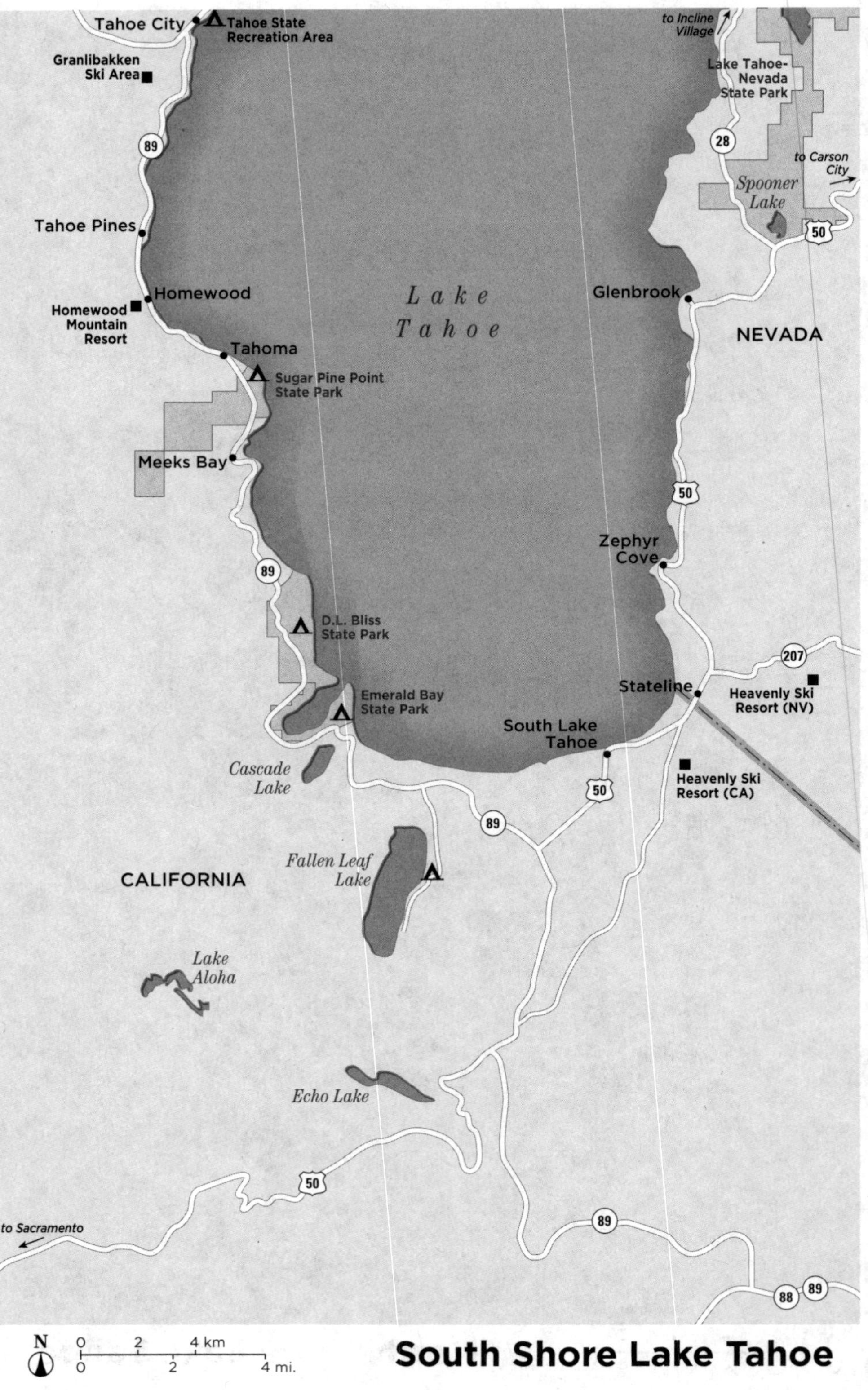

South Shore Lake Tahoe

PREFACE

To a newcomer arriving by air, the Reno/Sparks area might appear arid and uninteresting. But to an Insider it becomes a painter's palette where most of the hues are brown with just a splash of green dotting the banks along the Truckee River, the waterway that snakes from Lake Tahoe through Reno to Pyramid Lake. As all Insiders will tell you when you first arrive, Reno's unique beauty will grow on you. And it does—especially at sunrise when the sun peeking over the eastern mountain range casts purple shadows that seem to stretch forever—or at dusk when you can stand anywhere in the city and have an unobstructed view of an awe-inspiring sunset that bounces golden rays from the tops of the snow-sprinkled mountains.

Visitors soon learn that water is definitely a precious commodity in the Reno area, which has been riddled with droughts over the years, though a short 45-minute drive over the mountains and through the pine trees will bring you to the shores of Lake Tahoe, one of the deepest lakes in the world. In fact, Lake Tahoe is so deep that if you emptied it into California, the lake's water would completely cover the state to a depth of 2 feet. These extremes are just one example of Reno/Tahoe's diversity, a diversity that often makes the area one of the most misunderstood in the United States. Don't fret though. As an Insider I'll help you understand the area's idiosyncrasies, and I'll guide you through the maze of things to see and to do here.

To those who have never visited Reno/Tahoe, the misconception might be that it is an area with acres and acres of slot machines, buckets full of liquor, and rooms so thick with smoke you have to chop your way through them with a machete. Those who have visited the area know that Reno is an uncluttered place with friendly people where we still call our elected officials by their first names and where we still sit down at a neighborhood cafe and share the newspaper. They know that to drive the 72 miles around Lake Tahoe takes the better part of the day, and during that drive they will see multimillion-dollar homes, pristine beaches, and rugged mountains.

Although best known for its gaming and entertainment, Reno/Tahoe is a popular recreation area, too. You name it, we've got it. You can golf, hike, fish, boat, and do just about any other summer activity. And if snow skiing is your pleasure, Lake Tahoe boasts the largest concentration of ski resorts in North America. Because of its plethora of outdoor recreation activities, the Reno/Tahoe area earned Rand McNally's (the road atlas people) highest rating as America's No. 1 place for outdoor fun.

And if it's quality of life you're looking for, the Reno/Tahoe area has been ranked as one of the top 50 places to raise a family, and Reno was recently named the No. 1 literary city by the National Endowment for the Arts.

Varied? Yes. Remote? Maybe. But no one can dispute that the area is packed with excitement. Here, the saying goes that the outdoor fun lasts all day long and so does the nightlife. We don't roll up our sidewalks at sunset. If you have a craving for a steak at 3:00 A.M., you'll have no trouble finding one (and no one here will make you feel guilty for eating it). And, of course, if it's gaming you want, the area has more than enough gaming establishments to entertain you.

Since the choices here are so diverse and so numerous, I figure this *Insiders'*

Guide will come in mighty handy. I hope I've compiled a guide to the area that not only divulges the well-known places but also will lead you to the real Reno/Tahoe, the Insiders' Reno/Tahoe—from the tiny Mexican cafe with zero atmosphere but with the best burritos this side of Mexico City to the best fishing spot on the Truckee River (which I think just happens to be about five minutes from downtown Reno).

I hope you use this guide as a road map to trek off the typical tourist path. I'll offer to you my Insiders' choices of the best restaurants, the prettiest campsites, and the toughest and easiest golf courses. I'll lead you to the best downhill and cross-country ski resorts. I'll give you options for choosing the right health-care facility. I'll discuss the area's newspapers and magazines and radio and television stations. I'll even tell you about the local school districts and the boom in the real estate business. My wish is that you toss this guide into your car's glove compartment along with your area maps and proof of car insurance (required by Nevada law) so you'll be able to whip it out when you continue on your quest for something to do or see in the Reno/Tahoe area.

I'd like to end this preface with a few words from Mark Twain, who, by the way, began his writing career in Virginia City, only 20 miles from downtown Reno:

"Throw away the bowlines, sail away from the safe harbor. Catch the trade winds in your sails. Explore, dream, discover."

Now, come visit us!

ACKNOWLEDGMENTS

Writing this book (now in its fifth edition) is always such fun. Having lived in the Reno/Tahoe area for many years, I take great delight in sharing its very special charms with you. But compiling the vast amount of information needed to make the book as useful and accurate as possible requires the help of many people. So my thanks go to all those who responded to my requests for current data. And because no travel book is truly complete without photographs, I especially thank the photographers who so graciously contributed their work to this project. I am also grateful to Mike Carrigan, my coauthor of the first edition, and to Tracy Salcedo-Chourré and Sandy Weiner, who contributed to the second edition. And last, but by no means least, thanks to James and our dogs, Shelby and Inka, for their patience in missed backcountry outings while I was hunched over my keyboard.

HOW TO USE THIS BOOK

You won't have to flip through many pages of *Insiders' Guide to Reno and Lake Tahoe* to realize I've crammed tons of information into this 350-plus page book. But don't let its length discourage you. Look over the contents page and you'll get a feel for how easy I have made it for you. I have organized the guide so that you don't have to read every chapter; pick and choose only those chapters you find useful. I know that if you're just passing through on a well-earned vacation, the Relocation or Health Care and Wellness chapters might not interest you. But if you are planning to move here, I think these chapters are a must-read.

I do feel that the History chapter is one you should spend an extra few minutes reading. After all, the Reno/Tahoe area is steeped in history. The infamous Donner Party wintered here on its ill-fated journey to California. Two drunken Irishmen discovered millions of dollars worth of silver in a glob of blueish mud in this area. Mark Twain got his literary start here. I've tried to synthesize the history of the area to just a few pages so that you can quickly learn about the origins of one of the best places to vacation or live in the United States.

No other place in America offers the diversity of the Reno/Tahoe area. There is something to do 365 days of the year here, and on the Nevada side of the area, entertainment lasts 24 hours a day.

In this book, I guide you through what I consider the best restaurants, golf courses, ski resorts, vacation rentals, and just about anything else I think would interest visitors and those who are relocating to this paradise.

If you're planning to move here and want to know about local school districts, flip to the Education and Child Care chapter. Then spend some time in the Area Overview chapter; it gives you a feel for the quality of life here, plus a quick look at your new neighbors.

If you're here to enjoy the multitude of sports available, turn to the Winter Sports chapter or the Recreation chapter. Since the Nevada side of the area is known for its casinos, I have included a chapter dedicated to the gambling scene, including information on the basics of the games of chance we play here: Turn to the Casino Nightlife chapter for all of this.

Because the Reno/Lake Tahoe area is so large, I have divided it into four geographical regions: Reno, Sparks, North Shore Lake Tahoe, and South Shore Lake Tahoe.

Reno and Sparks make up the only two incorporated cities in the Truckee Meadows, the area that borders the Truckee River from the California state line to a few miles east of Sparks. Reno and Sparks each has its own infrastructure, but the cities are only separated by a street sign and a zip code.

I define the North Shore of Lake Tahoe as the area from Meeks Bay on the southwestern shore north and east (clockwise) to Spooner Lake on the northeastern shore. The South Shore is the area from Spooner Lake south and west (clockwise) back to Meeks Bay.

Each chapter begins with a short introduction, a quick look at what's to come. Then, I orient you to the various offerings by dividing most chapters into these four standard geographical areas: Reno, Sparks, North Shore Lake Tahoe, and South Shore Lake Tahoe.

If you're a golfer, for instance, and you want to find a recommended course for Sparks, turn to the Golf chapter and thumb through it until you see the subheading of Sparks. In this section, I have listed the courses available for public play in Sparks, including the length of the course, greens fees, and so on.

Exceptions to this standard geographical breakdown occur in the Recreation chapter, which is organized by activity, and the Restaurants chapter, which is first organized by type of food. In several chapters, Reno and Sparks have been combined, and a few chapters, like the Worship chapter, are narrative only.

You'll also notice that throughout the guide, I have listed the area code with every telephone number. In addition, unless a listing appears under a "Reno" or "Sparks" subhead, the address will include the appropriate city and state. I did this because this guide covers a large area that spans two states and five counties. When making phone calls, remember that as of May 1999, the California area code around Lake Tahoe is (530) and that the area code for all of northern Nevada is (775). I've tried to list the toll-free (800, 888, 866, and 877) numbers when possible to help cut down on your long-distance phone bills. I've added Internet addresses when available.

I have scattered Insiders' Tips throughout this guidebook. Insiders' Tips—marked with an i —let you in on local secrets. Some are helpful tips, some are fun facts, and some are interesting area trivia. Whatever they are, I had fun arm-wrestling other Insiders for their well-guarded tips. You'll also find Close-ups throughout the book, which highlight information about unique people, events, and places around the Reno/Tahoe area. Spend a little time with these; they are fun and interesting.

I have tried to include all the information and tips you will need to make your visit or stay in the Reno/Tahoe area enjoyable, but I must include this disclaimer: I probably left something out. After all, even Insiders don't know everything. So, if you discover a restaurant I overlooked or a day trip I failed to mention, let me and the publisher know and maybe we'll include it in the next edition. Write to Insiders' Guides, c/o The Globe Pequot Press, P.O. Box 480, Guilford, CT 06437. The publisher welcomes all criticisms and comments, and the author welcomes all compliments.

My last recommendation is to buy a road map to accompany this guidebook. Together, they will lead you around this spectacular area.

And don't be afraid to dog-ear the pages or write notes in the margins. I expect one of you to doodle in the white spaces while the other is driving the car up the Mt. Rose Highway looking for a ski resort—and I don't expect you to color inside the lines either! This is your guide, so do with it what you want.

I sincerely hope you like the Reno/Tahoe area as much as I do.

AREA OVERVIEW 

Although you'll find dozens of communities touted as the best places to live and retire, simple geography has placed the Reno/Tahoe area at the head of the class. Tucked into the Sierra Nevada Mountains, the area is blessed with some of the most majestic scenery in the country along with unlimited opportunities for year-round outdoor recreation. Hundreds of miles of hiking trails await the outdoor enthusiast, and 26 downhill and backcountry ski resorts are available to skiers. Golfers can tee it up at dozens of golf courses, and water sports lovers can recreate in a plethora of lakes and streams. With all of this recreation just outside the door, it's no wonder that the area is dubbed "America's Adventure Place."

Because of its long history as a gaming destination, the area also offers a rich variety of indoor entertainment. Since gambling was legalized in Nevada in the 1930s, the casinos have offered nonstop gaming and lavish entertainment to locals and visitors alike. As the area has grown in population in recent years, the arts and culture of its communities have flourished. No area of comparable population size has such enormous variety and quality of entertainment as Reno/Tahoe.

The area of coverage for this guide incorporates a large territory, so I have divided it into four locations: Reno, Sparks, North Shore of Lake Tahoe, and South Shore of Lake Tahoe.

Reno and Sparks are sister cities that butt up against each other in the Nevada county of Washoe. This county stretches from the northeastern tip of Lake Tahoe to the Oregon border.

Lake Tahoe, North America's largest alpine lake, straddles the state line with two-thirds of the lake sitting in California and the other third sitting in Nevada. The lake is bordered by Placer and El Dorado Counties in California and Washoe, Carson, and Douglas Counties in Nevada. More than 60 creeks flow into Lake Tahoe, but only the Truckee River flows out of the lake, on its meandering route through Reno and Sparks to eventually empty into Pyramid Lake, north of Reno.

For purposes of this guide, I define the North Shore of Lake Tahoe as that area from Meeks Bay on the southwestern side of the lake clockwise to Spooner Lake, near the intersection of Nevada Highway 28 and U.S. Highway 50. I define the South Shore as the area from Spooner Lake clockwise around Lake Tahoe and back to Meeks Bay.

These four areas are described in a little more detail later in this chapter, but first, some general information on the Reno/Tahoe area as a whole:

POPULATION GROWTH

For more than 20 years Nevada has been the fastest growing state in the country. From a population of 1.6 million in 1995, it grew to more than 2.5 million by 2006. While most of the population is concentrated in Clark County in Las Vegas, Henderson, and North Las Vegas, Washoe County claims around 400,000 residents. The rate of increase from 1990 to 2000 in Washoe was about 33 percent. By 2025 it is estimated that the population of Washoe County will be around 700,000.

The California side of Lake Tahoe boasts a population of about 25,000, with most of the people living in South Lake Tahoe, California. The growth rate around the California side of the lake sits at 2 percent a year, a rate that has remained the same for several years. Because of geographical constraints, the Lake Tahoe Basin is approaching buildout regarding new housing. And even though more people are making the area their year-round residence, the growth rate is kept low simply because there is not enough affordable housing or quality employment to attract and retain large increases in population.

NEW ARRIVALS

New arrivals to the Reno/Tahoe area include singles, young families, executives, and senior citizens. The male-to-female ratio is almost 50/50. And if being an outsider has you worried, it shouldn't. Less than one-fourth of the population on the Nevada side is native-born.

Many folks move here for their retirement. People older than age 55 make up more than 20 percent of our population, and to cater to this large percentage of seniors in the community, dozens of services and facilities are scattered throughout the area. They include services in nutrition, legal matters, volunteer programs, transportation, employment, and educational opportunities (see the Retirement chapter for more information on services and facilities).

RENO AND SPARKS

The cities of Reno and Sparks remain a crossroads for travelers just as they were in the late 1800s, but in addition to the renowned gaming establishments, the two cities are now also prime locations for corporate headquarters and manufacturing and distribution companies. Between 2000 and 2005, more than 100 companies relocated to the area. These communities are definitely pro business. Nevada has no corporate income tax, personal income tax, unitary tax, inventory tax, franchise tax on income, franchise fee, estate tax, or gift tax. Because of their prime location (and with help from these other incentives), Reno and Sparks can truly be called "The Industrial Hub of the West."

Washoe County is named for the Indians who originally inhabited it.

Weather

Reno and Sparks are located in the Truckee Meadows. At an elevation of 4,400 feet above sea level in a high-desert plateau east of the Sierra Nevada, the area borders the Truckee River from the California border to just east of Sparks. Daily temperatures on the whole are mild, with a yearly average of 53 degrees. However, during summer the difference between the high and low temperatures can be as much as 45 degrees. This extreme fluctuation can sometimes cause health problems for people who are not used to such a dramatic temperature range. The humidity is low during the summer (about 25 percent) and moderate during the winter (about 60 percent). The sun shines an average of 300 days a year. Annual rainfall is around 7.5 inches, with the wettest month being January and the driest, July. Annual snowfall runs around 24 inches. The average high temperature in summer is 88 degrees and the low is 34. The average high temperature in winter is 51 degrees and the low is 22.

A real problem for some people, though, is the pollen count. When the sagebrush and the cottonwood trees are in bloom, people who tend to suffer from allergies sometimes have a rough time here. And at times during the winter, when the wind is stagnant, a haze layer will hang over the Truckee Meadows. But as soon as the wind kicks up again, it blows the haze layer away.

Employment

At 3.8 percent, the unemployment rate in the Reno/Sparks area is lower than the national average. But even though it's usually possible to get a job, getting just the right one is a little trickier. As might be

Riding a horse is still a good way of getting around in some parts of the Reno/Lake Tahoe area. LOUIS BASSO

expected in tourist-oriented towns, the want ads are full of service-related positions in the casinos, resorts, and other tourist attractions. Many people have solid full-time employment in these arenas, but other jobs are seasonal and not as secure. Although the gaming industry has historically been the biggest economic factor in Reno and Sparks, in recent years the dependence on gambling has gradually decreased. The burgeoning warehouse industry in Sparks, for example, depends upon a ready supply of not only entry-level, blue-collar employees, but also a fair amount of experienced skilled workers. The area has also thrown out the welcome mat to dot-commers fleeing the high prices and low quality of life in Silicon Valley. The result is the development of a number of high-tech business parks, like Reno Tahoe Tech Center, South Meadows Business Park, and the Damonte Ranch Business Park. The granddaddy of all promises to be Tahoe-Reno Industrial Center, under development just east of Sparks. With 103,000 acres, it will be the largest industrial park in the country when fully built out. The eclectic variety of jobs, from casino dealers to software developers, mirrors the increasing economic diversity of the community. For a closer look at specific jobs, click on www.renohelpwanted.com. To find out about local business trends, pick up a copy of *Northern Nevada Business Weekly,* or read the business section of the *Reno Gazette-Journal.*

Reno

The downtown area of Reno is, without a doubt, the most famous part of town. Reno's nickname, "The Biggest Little City in the World," is recognized around the globe. A stretch of land 3 blocks wide from the Truckee River Bridge on First

Interesting Statistics for the Reno/Sparks Area

Nevada state bird: mountain bluebird
Nevada state animal: desert bighorn sheep
Nevada state flower: sagebrush
Nevada state trees: single-leaf piñon pine, bristlecone pine
Nevada state song: "Home Means Nevada"
Nevada state motto: "All for Our Country"
Nevada state nicknames: Battle-born State, Sagebrush State, Silver State
Nevada state holiday: Nevada Day, celebrated the last Friday of October
Leading newspapers: *Reno Gazette-Journal, Sparks Tribune*
Median home price: $286,200
Percentage of state sales tax charged on purchases in Washoe County: 7.375
Percentage of persons 25 or older with bachelor's degrees or higher: 23.7
Percentage of females: 49.3
Percentage of people who speak a language other than English: 20
Percentage of unemployed: 4
Percentage of annual job growth: 3.8
Number of registered voters in Washoe County: 187,725
Average mean temperature: 53 degrees
Annual days of sunshine: 300
Annual visitors: 11 million

Street north to Interstate 80 is home to the majority of the casinos, but several others are located outside downtown. Although the lion's share of growth in the city of Reno is to the south, where most open land can be found, city planners continue to tweak plans to redevelop the downtown core. They have demolished old buildings (much to the chagrin of historical preservationists) to make way for art galleries, a movie theater, restaurants, and retail shops. The recent conversion of several hotel/casino complexes to condominiums, along with the construction of a number of new condo developments, has breathed new residential life into downtown. And even though the ReTRAC Project (which lowered the railroad tracks at a cost of about $504 million) was highly controversial, it has made the core of the city cleaner and quieter.

The majority of people work in Reno because that's where most of the businesses and commercial complexes in the Truckee Meadows are located. Many strip malls dot its landscape, and many mom-and-pop businesses are scattered around the city. The Truckee Meadows's largest mall, Meadowood, with almost 1 million square feet of retail space, is located in Reno at the intersection of South Virginia Street and South McCarran Boulevard.

Even though the city is growing, the people in Reno still demonstrate that Old Western hospitality that most visitors find charming and refreshing—especially if

they come here from some of the more populated and hurried cities around the United States.

Sparks

In the early days, when Reno was making its mark as the sin capital of the United States because of the legalization of gambling, the old saying went: "Reno is so close to hell you can see Sparks." Today that rivalry still exists between the two cities, but it's all in fun.

About two-thirds of Sparks is residential, with the other third zoned for commercial uses, mostly warehouses. Many people who live in Sparks work in Reno. Sparks has a number of strip malls, and city leaders say they will approve the building of more to help develop a business base for the town.

Because Reno has greater variety in shopping and entertainment, many Sparks residents spend money outside the "Rail City." Attempting to prevent this economic leakage to its neighbor, Sparks has encouraged the proliferation of restaurants. New eateries are particularly obvious along the main arteries such as Vista and Sparks Boulevards. D'Andrea Marketplace, adjacent to D'Andrea Golf Club, is a collection of mostly chain food outlets, which is convenient for new housing developments in the area. The city of Sparks also continues its redevelopment of Victorian Square, a 6-block entertainment complex in the downtown area along Victorian Avenue, where most of Sparks's casinos are located. So far the project has added a 14-screen, state-of-the-art, digital-sound movie complex; a 740-space parking garage; and an interactive fountain adjacent to an 1880s-type central plaza.

An old gravel pit was recently converted into a popular multiuse park. Sparks Marina Park, as it is known now, was once called Helm's Gravel Pit. But during the flood of 1997, the pit filled up with water. With the help of a court settlement, the city began to transform the former eyesore into a complex that features an outdoor amphitheater, 2 miles of trails, a sandy beach area, shops, restaurants, and a trophy trout lake. The city opened the lake to fishing in April 1999 before construction began on any of the structures. The Nevada Department of Wildlife stocks the lake with two- to three-pound trout, and some local anglers have already proclaimed it a good place to fish. The park is also the site of the Legends of Sparks Marina, a large shopping complex scheduled to open in 2008.

i

The Redfield Campus, a satellite of the University of Nevada, Reno, and Truckee Meadows Community College, is totally powered by an adjacent geothermal energy plant.

LAKE TAHOE

The Lake Tahoe area continues to be one of the most popular year-round resort areas in the United States. The crystal waters of the country's largest alpine lake and its location, tucked between mountain ranges high in the Sierra Nevada, make it one of the most beautiful spectacles in the West and one of the most favored vacation destinations for Americans for more than 100 years. No other U.S. lake can boast an average water visibility of 125 feet or a 99.7 percent water purity rate—cleaner than drinking water in most U.S. cities.

Weather

The lake is 22 miles long and 12 miles across, with about 72 miles of shoreline. The 6,200-foot elevation makes its temperature slightly cooler than the Truckee Meadows. During summer, most people opt for casual wear like T-shirts and

Interesting Statistics for the Lake Tahoe Area

California state bird: California quail
California state animal: grizzly bear (although none are found in the state today)
California state flower: California poppy
California state tree: California redwood
California state fish: golden trout
California state insect: California dogface butterfly
California state song: "I Love You, California"
California state nickname: The Golden State
California state dance: West Coast swing dancing
Leading newspapers: *Tahoe World, North Lake Tahoe Bonanza,* the *Sierra Sun, Tahoe Daily Tribune*
Median family income in South Lake Tahoe: $40,572
Median home price: $890,000
Average mean temperature: 43 degrees

shorts, but sweaters and lightweight jackets are usually worn during the cooler evenings. The sun shines an average of 274 days a year here, but the weather can be unpredictable, so a varied wardrobe is advisable when visiting the lake. It's not unusual for snow to fall in every month.

In winter, the 20 feet of average snowpack and annual snowfall of up to 40 feet make it a skiers' paradise (see the Winter Sports chapter for details). Most of the precipitation in the Tahoe Basin arrives as snow, with the annual rainfall clocking in at only around 8 inches. Although you might think the mountains would cause a high proportion of cloudy days, Tahoe is actually a very sunny place throughout the year. On an annual basis, 80 percent of the days have sunshine. Temperatures vary with the four seasons but are not the extremes found in some other mountain areas. The average winter high runs around 38 degrees, while daily summer highs rarely exceed 80.

Starting in the spring when the snow melts away, Lake Tahoe becomes the perfect place to sail, swim, sailboard, fish, and play on the countless white beaches (see the Recreation chapter for more details). The sun shines a lot here and, as the Lake Tahoe Resort Association says, "Lake Tahoe kids smell like summer. It's the combination of fresh mountain air, sunscreen, dirt, sweat, popsicles, and frantic child energy."

The communities along the North Shore and South Shore of Lake Tahoe are varied: small and big, sleepy and bustling. One exists for every mood and every perspective. Now let's take a tour, beginning with the northeast shore.

North Shore

On the California side, the area from Meeks Bay to Tahoe Pines has the Old Tahoe feel to it, with gorgeous mansions tucked away in the woods and expansive white beaches with some of the prettiest scenery along the lake. Old Tahoe-style architecture emerged from the early 20th century when people traveled here by train, men went for groceries in dogsleds, and women carried shotguns to scare away the wild animals. The architecture includes a rustic look with a mix of native wood and stone on the exterior and a touch of 1890s San Francisco-style, plenty of wood on the interior, including the floors, and at least one stone fireplace. This area is home to the Erhman Mansion at Sugar Pine Point State Park, which was the filming location for the movie *Godfather II.*

Lake Tahoe "must surely be the fairest picture the whole earth affords."
—Mark Twain

Traveling clockwise around the North Shore, the next little community is Tahoe City. This town is noted for its dam, Fanny Bridge (see the Attractions and Kidstuff chapters), and as the birthplace of the Truckee River. But when night falls, it transforms itself into a place where everyone seems to go for nightlife action on the California side of Lake Tahoe. Why? Because it has some of the best spots to go dancing on the North Shore where some of the hippest bands around play (see the Nightlife chapter). Some of its smaller nightspots are renowned around the lake for providing some of the most romantic atmospheres, too.

This little hamlet is followed by Carnelian Bay, Tahoe Vista, and Kings Beach. These towns line a flat stretch along the North Shore that is very popular because of its wide, public beaches and easy access to the lake. A variety of small stores can also be found along this stretch of California Highway 28. Carnelian Bay and Tahoe Vista are known for their great restaurants (see the Restaurants chapter) and their unsurpassed views of the lake. Kings Beach, the site of a seven-acre state beach and park of the same name, is the last stop on the California side of the North Shore.

At the extreme northern end of the lake is Crystal Bay, a community of hotels and casinos straddling the Nevada-California border. This is the location of the Cal Neva Resort Hotel and Casino, so called because half of it is in California and half is in Nevada. Onetime owner Frank Sinatra and his "Rat Pack" made this casino-resort famous. Frequent visitors in the old days included the Kennedys and some underworld figures. Crystal Bay is also home to the Tahoe Biltmore, the newly remodeled Crystal Bay Club Casino, Jim Kelley's Tahoe Nugget, and other noted landmarks on the lake.

Continuing in a clockwise direction, you come upon Incline Village, Nevada, an upscale community set on a mountainside. In addition to panoramic views of the lake and great beaches, the village boasts one of the finest championship golf courses at Lake Tahoe (see the Golf chapter) and is also home to Sierra Nevada College (see the Education and Child Care chapter). The cost of housing here is some of the most expensive around the lake (see the Relocation chapter). From Incline Village to the intersection of US 50, NV 28 winds its way around the lake, revealing gorgeous, pristine beaches and sapphire-blue water. Just down the road is Sand Harbor, part of Lake Tahoe–Nevada State Park and home to summer music concerts and a Shakespeare festival in July (see the chapters on Parks, Recreation, Annual Events, and The Arts).

An average of 1.4 million tons of water evaporates from the surface of Lake Tahoe every 24 hours, but this evaporation only drops the lake level about 0.1 inch.

South Shore

Spooner Lake sits near the intersection of US 50 and NV 28 and is the first landmark to define Lake Tahoe's South Shore on our clockwise tour. Down US 50, the next landmark, Cave Rock, is a 25-yard tunnel carved from solid rock.

Zephyr Cove sits along the shoreline and is home to a mile of sandy, white beach. Zephyr Cove Beach is one of the best areas around the lake to bring the family to enjoy tons of water activities, including parasailing, waterskiing, and Jet Skiing (see the Recreation and Kidstuff chapters). It is also the home port of the MS *Dixie II,* a paddle wheeler that cruises the lake.

At Lake Tahoe's extreme south shore, on the Nevada side of the California-Nevada border, sits Stateline, the major casino center on the lake, with quality hotel-resorts featuring great dining, big-time entertainment, and, of course, gambling. MontBleu Resort Casino & Spa, Harrah's Lake Tahoe, Harveys Lake Tahoe Casino & Resort, and the Horizon Casino Resort Lake Tahoe sit snugly along US 50 here, waiting for those of you who feel lucky (see the Resorts and Casino Nightlife chapters for more information). Edgewood Tahoe Golf Course is located here as well (see the Golf chapter).

Traveling over the California state line, you'll come upon Heavenly Ski Resort in the town of South Lake Tahoe. The resort sits high in the mountains, providing panoramic views of the Nevada desert and the entire lake. As part of the Park Avenue Redevelopment Project, a new gondola was put into operation in December 2000, allowing visitors to ride 2.4 miles from the state line to the top of Heavenly Ski Resort at 10,067 feet elevation to enjoy skiing in winter and views year-round. The Park Avenue Redevelopment Project encompasses 34 acres at the California-Nevada state line and has added the new Heavenly gondola, an ice-skating rink, a multiplex cinema, and a shopping village. South Lake Tahoe is the largest town on the lake and has one of the only two small airports serving Lake Tahoe. Many shops, restaurants, bars, and motels line US 50, which cuts through the heart of town.

The Silver State was voted by* Inc. *magazine as one of the best places in the country to start and grow a business. The reasons are its favorable regulatory environment, affordable housing, and pleasing climate.

Continuing around the lake, you come upon Emerald Bay, a sparkling green cove, secluded and framed by mountain peaks. Nestled on its shores is one of the most photographed spots in America—Vikingsholm Castle. The 38-room mansion was built in 1929, and some call it the finest example of Scandinavian architecture in the United States. This spot is also the jumping-off point for hikers burning to explore the high country and the 130 mountain lakes of the Desolation Wilderness, a 63,500-acre nationally designated wilderness area. Hikers have been known to walk the trails of this area for weeks before coming back to "civilization." (A wilderness area is one in which the government has restricted access to only hiking and horseback riding; no motorized vehicles are allowed.)

So take the best in entertainment, gaming, dining, and accommodations, mix them with real, down-home Western hospitality and every outdoor activity you can name, and what do you have? The premier vacation and living location in the United States—if not in the world. Read on to discover why I think the Reno/Tahoe area is the ultimate playground.

GETTING HERE, GETTING AROUND

The Reno/Tahoe area is easy to get to and easy to get around. Because the tourist industry is responsible for about 30 percent of the area's income, a great deal of effort is put into making transportation accessible. So there's a variety of plane, bus, and train services to get you here, and plenty of ground transportation to whisk you around. If you use any commercial mode of transportation to get here, I definitely recommend renting a car or an SUV once you arrive. You'll need to be mobile so you can visit the many fascinating sights waiting for you around the area.

Lake Tahoe sits about 45 minutes to an hour away from Reno/Sparks. It's more convenient to visit the lake if you have your own car; that way, you can stop to smell the pine trees at your leisure. If you don't like to drive, especially during the snowy winter months, don't worry—there's commercial ground transportation to get you around.

RENO/SPARKS

If you're arriving by car, you can get to the Reno/Sparks area via two major highways. If you're leaving the driving to someone else, you can get here via bus, train, or plane. The nice thing you'll discover once you get here is that it's fairly easy to get around. Although Reno/Sparks doesn't suffer the agonizing gridlock found in some other cities, a few areas are congested at certain times of the day. The infamous Spaghetti Bowl (the intersection of Interstate 80 and U.S. Highway 395), the intersection of Moana and Kietzke Lanes, and the intersection of South Virginia Street and South McCarran Boulevard can cause your knuckles to turn white from about 4:00 to 6:00 P.M. during the week. Driving north on US 395 or on Vista Boulevard in Sparks can be an especially nerve-wracking challenge at that time of the day. The streets around Meadowood Mall can cause your blood pressure to rise on Saturday afternoon when shoppers are out in full force. If you're not fond of driving in traffic, it's best to avoid these particular spots at those times of day. Because street construction hasn't kept pace with the rapid growth of the area, government entities are scrambling to catch up. The result is a number of major traffic projects that have lasted several years. One of the most intrusive has been a complete redesign of the Spaghetti Bowl. To keep informed of the latest traffic hassles, read the Street Beat column in the *Reno Gazette-Journal*. Also be aware that the ReTRAC Project, which has lowered the train tracks in downtown Reno, may continue to cause traffic interruptions.

On a happier note, the Reno/Tahoe International Airport is one of the easiest international airports in the United States to get to, park at, and fly out from. Several access routes are available to whisk travelers in and out, and I've never heard of anyone missing a flight because of backed-up traffic. The three-story parking garage, along with the outdoor lot, makes finding a parking spot easy, and local lore holds that hassles are few and far between.

The Regional Transportation Commission (RTC) bus line provides the Reno/Sparks area with public transportation service, and Amtrak provides daily east- and westbound train service.

Highways

The general highway system entering and leaving the Reno/Sparks area hasn't changed much since the 1860s, when the east-west emigrant trail converged with the north-south trail at Lake's Crossing in downtown Reno. Today, the area is situated on two major highway corridors: I-80 and US 395.

Heading westbound, I-80 links the area to California through Donner Pass in the Sierra Nevada. Sacramento is about 160 miles away, and San Francisco lies about 250 miles from downtown Reno. I-80 eastbound transverses the entire northern part of the state, pops you out at Wendover, on the Nevada–Utah border, at about 400 miles, and leads on to Salt Lake City, Utah, some 520 miles from Reno.

US 395 south leads from Reno to southern California, trekking through Nevada's capital, Carson City, 32 miles from Reno, the mountain town of Bishop, California, and eventually to Los Angeles, which is about 475 miles down the highway. Heading north on US 395, you slice through the extreme northeastern part of California and into Oregon; Goose Lake, on the California–Oregon border, is about 240 miles away. Even Las Vegas, the southern metropolis of Nevada, is 445 miles from Reno.

Surface Streets

If Reno is the heart of northern Nevada, then Virginia Street is its major artery. This main drag bisects Reno in a north-south direction and terminates both north and south of the city where it converges with US 395. Virginia Street, where it crosses the Truckee River at the old site of Lake's Crossing, is the zero-zero point for the street-numbering system, which is set up as a grid. For example, Fourth Street west of Virginia Street is called West Fourth Street and switches to East Fourth Street—you guessed it—east of Virginia Street. The north-south roads are similarly split, using the Truckee River as the zero boundary; streets are labeled "north" on the north side of the river and "south" on the south side. The higher the address number, the farther it is from downtown, the Truckee River, and Virginia Street.

Another major thoroughfare that literally encircles Reno/Sparks is McCarran Boulevard. This four-lane road loops metropolitan Reno/Sparks and is about 23 miles in length. Insiders use the boulevard to quickly travel from one part of the area to another, avoiding the many smaller cross streets and traffic signals. The speed limit is 45 to 50 miles per hour. McCarran is called North McCarran north of its intersection with I-80, and South McCarran south of the intersection.

The casinos use a 24-hour, three-shift schedule for employees, but most of the other working folks here are locked into a normal working day. Even though the rush hour is minimal, a prudent driver will stay away from the intersection of I-80 and US 395 during the early-morning and late-afternoon commute times. Insiders call the on- and off-ramps of the two converging highways the Spaghetti Bowl, and even though traffic rarely comes to a halt, it frequently slows to a crawl for 15 or 20 minutes during the commute times. I suggest you use McCarran Boulevard during times of heavy traffic rather than I-80 or US 395, because McCarran will get you where you need to go even if it adds a few miles to your journey.

The driving rules of the road here are not complicated, but there are a few things to be aware of. Pedestrians in the casino area of downtown Reno and in the Victorian Square area of Sparks are notorious for charging in front of vehicles, avoiding crosswalks, and ignoring stop signs and red traffic lights. Special care must be taken when driving around foot traffic in these areas. Be especially alert for pedestrians and pedestrian crossings on all streets.

A big no-no here is failure to observe the speed limit in a school zone. Usually a flashing yellow light and a marked sign will alert drivers to the mandatory 15-mile-per-hour limit. A lapse will cost you about $250.

Speed limits can prove to be a problem for the visitor. On rural highways the limits range from 55 to 65 miles per hour, but on sections of I-80 drivers are allowed to drive at 70 miles per hour, so due care must be observed.

One last note about driving in Reno: Nevada laws on driving under the influence (DUI) of alcohol or drugs are tough. If chemical tests show a motorist has a blood alcohol concentration of .08 or more, or any detectable amount of a controlled substance, the first offense brings with it a revoked driver's license for 90 days, and your vehicle will be impounded. You also will receive a mandatory jail sentence of two days to six months (this can be reduced if you complete a drug or alcohol treatment program), and a fine of $400 to $1,000, plus state fees. The second DUI within seven years yields a revoked driver's license for one year, a mandatory jail sentence or residential confinement for 10 days to six months, and a $500 to $1,000 fine plus fees. If a motorist is convicted of a third DUI in Nevada, regardless of which state the first two were in, he or she is guilty of a felony that carries a mandatory sentence of one to six years in the Nevada State Prison. The third conviction also results in a revoked driver's license for three years and a $2,000 to $5,000 fine. A DUI conviction causing death or serious injuries will result in a prison term of up to 20 years.

Basically the rule here is: One drink, take a taxi. Any way you look at it, a cab ride is much less costly. So listen to the Insiders on this one—the odds are against you if you drink and/or do drugs and drive.

For more information on Nevada's traffic laws, you can contact the Nevada Department of Motor Vehicles & Public Safety at (775) 684-4368. The DMV's Internet address is nevadadmv.state.nv.us/index.htm

Airports

Reno/Tahoe International Airport
2001 East Plumb Lane
Reno, NV
(775) 328-6870
www.renoairport.com

As I said before, Reno/Tahoe International Airport is one of the easiest international airports in the United States to get to, park at, and fly out from. It serves around 5 million passengers a year. The airport provides a full range of aviation services for the Reno/Sparks area, western Nevada, and northeastern California. It is within the Reno city limits and butts up against the city of Sparks. The commute time to the airport from the majority of the hotel/casinos in the area is about 15 minutes, and the drive is less than an hour from Lake Tahoe.

Driving to the airport from anywhere in the Reno/Sparks area is a breeze. The easiest access is to take US 395 (either north or south, depending on your starting location) to the airport exit and follow the signs to the terminal area. If you're in downtown Reno, follow Virginia Street, Wells Avenue, or Kietzke Lane (or any other north-south street) south until you hit Plumb Lane. Go east on Plumb Lane until it ends at the airport, then follow the signs to the terminal.

The airport is classified a medium hub, primary commercial airport by the Federal Aviation Authority (FAA) and is served by Alaska, Aloha, American, Continental, Delta, Frontier, Horizon Air, SkyWest, Southwest, United, and US Airways.

The airport covers some 1,450 acres and is staffed 24 hours per day. The terminal space includes U.S. Customs and Immigration offices and 23 second-level gates on two concourses. It's designated a landing rights and Port of Entry airport.

The airport is also home to the Nevada Air National Guard (NVANG), the

Even when roadways appear clear, be wary. Black ice, which can glaze roads after snowstorms, is a nearly invisible hazard that generally forms after the sun has gone down. Watch for the telltale glare of the taillights of the car in front of you, and proceed with caution.

"High Rollers" who gained fame during the Persian Gulf War flying RF-4 Phantom reconnaissance aircraft. Today the High Rollers fly the C-130 Hercules transport aircraft to provide rapid pickup and airlift duties.

Thanks to a $31 million project to increase parking by 25 percent and improve the roadway in front of the terminal, dropping off and picking up passengers is stress-free and extremely easy. Be aware, however, that you cannot park and leave your car anywhere in front of the terminal because of security concerns. It's pretty easy to drop a passenger off, but when picking somebody up you must stay with your vehicle. I suggest communicating with passengers via cell phone as soon as they land to let them know where you are. If you don't want to join the lineup in front of the terminal, you can park in the short-term area of the parking garage.

The 2,400-space, three-story parking garage takes the hassle out of finding a parking space. The surface lot to the south of the garage provides parking for 1,565 vehicles.

The garage offers long- and short-term parking. The long-term fees are $2.00 for the first hour and $1.00 per hour after the first hour, with a daily maximum of $12.00. The fees for short-term parking are $1.00 for the first 30 minutes and $2.00 for the first hour, with a daily maximum of $20.00. Surface parking is $2.00 for the first hour and then $1.00 an hour, for a maximum of $8.00 a day.

See the "Rental Cars" and other ground transportation sections in this chapter for information on renting cars at the airport and other ways to get to and from the airport.

Reno Stead Airport
4895 Texas Avenue, Reno, NV
(775) 328-6570
www.airnav.com
www.renoairport.com

The Reno Stead Airport is a general aviation airport located 9 miles north of downtown Reno off US 395. The airport has two asphalt runways (8,080 feet and 7,600 feet), lights, hangars, and full services. The airport's tower is not staffed and has a UNICOM frequency of 122.7. Pilots are not charged landing fees.

You can buy Jet A and 100 LL (low-lead) fuel from General Aviation Classics and rent tie-down space. Call (775) 972-5540 for information.

The Nevada Army National Guard has a facility located about 1 mile from the airport out of which military helicopter activities are conducted. Reno Stead Airport is also home to the annual National Championship Air Races in September, closing the airport to all general aviation aircraft (see the Annual Events chapter for details about the Reno Air Races).

Rail Service

The railroads literally put Reno and Sparks on the map, and today the Union Pacific Railroad still provides cargo shipments by rail through the Truckee Meadows. If you wish to experience the old-fashioned, unhurried method of passenger train transportation these days, look to Amtrak.

Amtrak
245 Evans Avenue, Reno, NV
(775) 329-8638
(800) 872-7245/USA-RAIL
www.amtrak.com

Amtrak provides passenger train service through Reno, west to the Bay Area, and east to Chicago. The *California Zephyr* makes one daily stop eastbound and one westbound in the Truckee Meadows. The

westbound *California Zephyr*, train number 5, stops at the downtown Reno station at midmorning on its way to the Bay Area. The eastbound *California Zephyr*, train number 6, stops at the Reno station in the late afternoon on its way to Chicago. Contact Amtrak for exact departure times; weather and track conditions in the mountains may affect schedules. Amtrak also offers bus service to and from the Bay Area and Sacramento to the downtown Reno station.

The one-way coach fare from Reno to Emeryville in the Bay Area runs around $38 depending on the time of year (children ride for half price). The coach fare from Reno to Chicago starts around $120 and goes up to about $200, depending on the time of year.

The *California Zephyr* offers movies, sleeping cars, dining cars, and a sightseeing lounge. The trip to the Bay Area is about six hours. The Chicago run takes about 45 hours. On its way to and from Chicago, the train stops in a number of western towns and cities, including Salt Lake City and Denver.

Buses

The old joke around here is that not a lot of visitors arrive by bus, but after a bad night at the craps tables, a lot return home on one. The fact is that riding a bus may not be the fastest and the most sophisticated method of travel, but it usually is the cheapest.

Amtrak
245 Evans Avenue, Reno, NV
(775) 329-8638
(800) 872-7245/USA-RAIL
www.amtrak.com
In addition to rail service, Amtrak also runs buses from Bay Area cities and Sacramento to the Reno area. Generally, traveling to Reno by bus is less expensive than traveling by rail. Contact Amtrak for schedules and rates.

The Fun Train and the Snow Train are charter services that bring passengers to Reno from the San Francisco Bay Area from January to March. The Fun Train is for young partiers; the Snow Train appeals to families and older travelers. For more information call (800) 783-0783 or click on www.keyholidays.com.

Greyhound Lines
155 Stevenson Street, Reno, NV
(775) 322-2970, (800) 231-2222
www.greyhound.com
Greyhound offers seven westbound, two eastbound, and several north- and southbound departures daily. One-way fares west range from about $20 to Sacramento to $32 to San Francisco. The one-way fare east to Salt Lake City is $60, and if you go south to Las Vegas, the fare jumps to around $74. All fares are subject to change. Tickets may be purchased at the station at the time of departure, but Greyhound offers discounts if tickets are purchased a few days in advance.

Mass Transit

RTC Intercity
Regional Transportation Commission
2050 Villanova Drive, Reno, NV
(866) 687-7433
www.rtcwashoe.com
The commute between Reno and Carson City Monday through Friday can be relatively painless and cheap if you take advantage of RTC Intercity. For just $3.25 per trip you can ride in a comfortable coach that provides individual climate control, reclining seats, and storage space. You can transfer free to RTC Ride or RTC Access in Reno or JAC in Carson City. Rides are paid with cash or passes, which can be purchased for 20 rides at $32.50. For information on routes and schedules, click on the Web site above.

Residents of Washoe County who are at least 60 years old are eligible for the Washoe Senior Ride Program, a taxi subsidy that provides ride vouchers at half price. For more information call (775) 348-0477.

RTC Ride
RTC Ride Administrative Office
2050 Villanova Drive, Reno, NV
(775) 348-0400 (administration)
(775) 348-7433 (customer service)
www.RTCwashoe.com/transportation/citifare

RTC Ride, the public transit service for the area, operates 29 fixed routes in Reno and Sparks. Routes originate at the Citicenter Transit Center in downtown Reno and the Citistation Transit Center in downtown Sparks. Buses travel outbound from these two hubs and go to outlying neighborhoods. The buses run seven days per week from about 4:30 A.M. to midnight, though some routes run 24 hours.

Bus fare is $1.50 for a one-way ticket. Seniors older than age 60, disabled people, and Medicare recipients pay 75 cents. Youths between the ages of 5 and 18 ride the bus for $1.25. Children younger than age 5 ride free. RTC Ride does not charge for transfers, which are valid for one hour after bus ticket purchase.

Frequent passengers may purchase daily, weekly, and monthly passes, which are good for unlimited riding. Fares for a Daily Pass are: adult, $4.00; youth, $3.00; senior/disabled/Medicare, $2.00. For a 7-Day Pass it's adult, $18.00; youth, $15.00; senior/disabled/Medicare, $9.00. For a Monthly Pass, costs are: adult, $60; youth, $50; senior, $30; disabled/Medicare, $22.

RTC Ride also offers RTC Access, a service by which disabled people may be picked up at their homes and taken to their destinations. The lift is $1.25 for a one-way prescheduled trip.

If you need transportation for your pet in the Reno/Sparks area, you can call Pet Taxi at (775) 787-2222.

Sierra Spirit
Regional Transportation Commission
2050 Villanova Drive, Reno, NV
(866) 687-7433
www.rtcwashoe.com

Operating free all day, everyday, Sierra Spirit makes 32 stops between the University of Nevada, Reno, on the north end of downtown and the Nevada Museum of Art on the south end of downtown. Look for the yellow buses that come along about every 10 minutes from 7:00 A.M. to 8:00 P.M. Sunday through Wednesday and from 7:00 A.M. to 10:00 P.M. Thursday through Saturday.

Taxis

On any given day, hundreds of taxis buzz up and down the streets of Reno and Sparks. Riders may hail a cab, but calling ahead is the best way to guarantee a ride when you need one. Most taxis cluster around the big hotel/casinos and the airport.

The three cab companies that serve the Reno-Sparks area are Reno-Sparks Cab, at (775) 333-3333; Whittlesea Taxi, at (775) 322-2222; and Yellow Cab Company, at (775) 355-5555.

In addition, Yellow Cab offers luxury cabs, including Cadillacs and Lincolns, at no extra charge, cars fueled with natural gas, and vans, one of which is outfitted to handle disabled passengers.

None of the companies charge extra for additional passengers, but the maximum per taxi is five. On average, a taxi ride from the airport to downtown Reno or downtown Sparks is $12 to $14.

Limousines

Traveling in the plush comfort of a limousine is the most decadent way to cruise the streets of Reno/Tahoe. Heads turn when you pull up in your Lincoln Town Car with darkened windows, and everyone strains their necks trying to capture a glimpse of who might be riding in such unabashed style.

Most of the stretch limos have a wet bar and a stereo, and some come equipped with a television, cellular phone, and a sliding moon roof. But the biggest asset, as far as I'm concerned, is that someone else drives the vehicle. These chauffeurs are not only the most competent drivers in the area, they are also the most knowledgeable. If a limo chauffeur doesn't know where to find something or how to get someplace, it probably doesn't exist.

The average cost for these luxury automobiles with drivers is $50 to $60 per hour without a wet bar and $75 per hour with a wet bar. Operators include Bell Limo, (775) 786-3700, www.bell-limo.com, and Executive Limousine, (775) 333-3300, (800) 323-3958, www.exlimo.com.

By far the cheapest transportation to and from the airport is on the free courtesy shuttles operated by most hotels and casinos. But the limo companies can also get you there. In addition to their regular limousines, both companies offer service to the airport.

Rental Cars

I really wish I could tell you that a car is not necessary when you visit Reno/Tahoe, but I can't. Sure, you can get along without one if all you want to do is hang around your hotel or casino day and night. But to really enjoy all that the area has to offer, you need to be mobile. You'd miss too much of the fun without a convenient way to get around.

Renting a car is the best way to see the area. Plus, a rental car will allow you to experience some of the day trips we suggest later in this guide.

Rates vary from agency to agency, but the cost for an economy car with unlimited miles is between $16 and $30 per day. The big thing to remember when you rent a car at the airport, though, is that every government agency wants a piece of the rental-car action. So, above and beyond the daily rate, renters have to pay an airport surcharge or concession recoupment fee of 10 to 11.7 percent, depending on the company; a 7.25 percent Nevada sales tax; and a 6 percent Nevada rental fee, or Department of Motor Vehicle license tag fee. This means a whopping 23 to 24 percent is tacked on to the price of your rental car. Most companies also offer a $10 per day collision damage waiver. You'll need a major credit card, a valid driver's license, and a second picture ID. Most companies also require the driver to be at least 21 years old.

You can pick up rental cars at freestanding locations and at major hotels and casinos around town, but it might be more convenient to rent the car at the airport. Here are some of the companies that have offices in the airport:

Advantage
(775) 333-6677, (800) 777-5500
www.arac.com

Alamo
(775) 323-7940, (800) 462-5266
www.goalamo.com

Avis
(775) 785-2727, (800) 831-2847
www.avis.com

Budget
(800) 527-0700
www.budget.com

Enterprise
(775) 329-3773, (800) 325-8007
www.enterprise.com

Hertz
(775) 785-2554, (800) 654-3131
www.hertz.com

National
(775) 785-2768, (800) 227-7368
www.nationalcar.com

Thrifty
(775) 329-0096, (800) 847-4389
www.thrifty.com

LAKE TAHOE

Even though Lake Tahoe rests high in the Sierra Nevada range, tucked in neatly between the borders of California and Nevada, it is quite easy to reach as long as the weather is cooperative. But during the winter months, large amounts of snowfall can make getting here quite a challenge. Be sure to check road conditions before setting out in winter. For California roads call (800) 427-7623 (ROAD) and enter the highway number; for Nevada call (877) 687-6237. The California Web site is www.dot.ca.gov, and the Nevada Web site is www.nevadadot.com.

A four-wheel-drive vehicle is ideal for winter road conditions, and chains may be required on cars during storms. (See the Winter Sports chapter for more about winter driving.)

Be aware that traffic in and out of the Lake Tahoe Basin is very heavy at certain times of the year and hours of the day. On the days immediately before and after holidays and weekends (when everyone seems to arrive and leave all at once), stalled traffic is a distinct possibility. Accidents and snowfall can further complicate driving conditions.

i ***The highways and major roads between Reno and Lake Tahoe are plowed and sanded as necessary in an attempt to ensure the safest driving conditions during snowstorms, but all travelers, regardless of whether they are in a four-wheel-drive vehicle or not, are advised to carry tire chains in winter.***

Traffic out of ski resorts in winter is very heavy from 3:00 to 4:30 P.M., especially from the Alpine Meadows, Squaw Valley USA, and Northstar-at-Tahoe ski resorts. To avoid the congestion you may want to stay away from these areas at that time of day, unless you are skiing. Summer traffic is heavier in the mornings and evenings as visitors and residents alike travel to and from the day's destination.

Avoid traveling to and from Lake Tahoe around the holidays and at peak daily travel times if you want to avoid the masses. Driving around the lake can be particularly busy at certain locations—in South Lake Tahoe and the Emerald Bay areas in summer, for instance—but usually the 72 miles around the lake can be traveled by car with little or no problem. Mass transit can afford you cheap and reliable transportation if you don't care to drive yourself.

Highways

Six highways lead into Lake Tahoe; from the Reno/Sparks area you have the option of using five of the six. The most reliable and easiest way out of the Truckee Meadows to Lake Tahoe is via I-80.

This route follows I-80 west from Reno to the California town of Truckee. From Truckee, California Highway 267 cuts south past Northstar-at-Tahoe to the northern part of the lake. The highway will pop you out at Kings Beach.

If you stay on I-80 through Truckee, you can pick up another scenic route to the lake. Just before Donner Memorial State Park, California Highway 89 heads south to the lake. This highway passes the Squaw Valley and Alpine Meadows ski resorts and brings you out at Tahoe City.

The Reno-to-Tahoe route traveled by most Insiders is over the Mt. Rose summit. To reach this route, you travel out of Reno on US 395 south until the road intersects Nevada Highway 431. The highway climbs southwest over the summit to the lake

and brings you out at Incline Village. A word of warning here: This route is by far the most scenic, but it is also the most dangerous. The highway is loaded with switchbacks and climbs steeply up the mountain from 4,400 feet to more than 8,000 feet at the summit, then rushes down to the lake. In summer, driving the skinny two-lane road can be heart-pounding, and in winter, it can be treacherous. Even though the highway is tight and winding, Insiders will fly up and down it no matter what the road conditions. So if you find yourself with a death grip on the steering wheel and holding up more than three cars, look for a pullout and let the faster traffic pass. I'll also give you odds that four out of five Insiders will not know where NV 431 is located. I know it as the Mt. Rose Highway. (See the Attractions chapter for details about this scenic drive.)

Another route to Lake Tahoe from Reno involves driving south to Carson City via US 395. Outside of Carson City, U.S. Highway 50 heads west over Spooner Summit to the lake. US 50 brings you out just north of Zephyr Cove, a short drive from Stateline.

If you continue south out of Carson City on US 395, you can travel another scenic route to Lake Tahoe. US 395 continues south until it intersects Nevada Highway 88 near Minden. NV 88 intersects Nevada Highway 207, known to Insiders as the Kingsbury Grade. This highway stretches over Daggett Pass to the lake. The highway intersects US 50 just north of Stateline. Once again, this road is scenic but treacherous, especially during winter. Great care should be used when driving this road.

From Sacramento two routes lead to Lake Tahoe: the I-80 route to Truckee and the US 50 route up to the south shore of the lake. The I-80 route is much faster, but US 50 is more scenic. US 50 passes Echo Lake and the Upper Truckee River and brings you out at South Lake Tahoe.

Surface Streets

A single highway encircles the lake, but it changes its designation four times. Beginning just east of Kings Beach and heading clockwise, the highway is Nevada Highway 28 until it intersects US 50 near Spooner Lake. It's US 50 until you leave South Lake Tahoe, where it changes to CA 89 and continues north to Tahoe City. From Tahoe City to Kings Beach, it is California Highway 28. Most of the residential and commercial streets in the little towns that dot the lake are easy to find with the help of a good local map.

Airports

Reno/Tahoe International Airport
(See write-up earlier in the chapter.)

Truckee Tahoe Airport
10356 Truckee Airport Road, Truckee, CA
(530) 587-4119, (800) 359-2875
www.truckeetahoeairport.com

A general aviation airport that is located between Truckee and Kings Beach, Truckee Tahoe Airport offers a full range of airport services for corporate and private aircraft. It has a 24-hour UNICOM year-round on frequency 122.8 and an Automated Weather Observation System (AWOS) on frequency 118.0 or by phone at (530) 587-4599.

The airport has two paved runways (7,000 feet and 4,650 feet) and offers aircraft fueling with octane, 100 LL (low-lead), and Jet A fuel from 6:00 A.M. to 11:00 P.M. It has 210 paved aircraft tie-downs at about $5.00 per night and up, depending on the size of the aircraft. Other services include a deli, scenic flights, summer glider rides, aircraft charters, aircraft rentals, instruction, and aircraft maintenance. Rental cars, including four-wheel-drive vehicles and vans, are available from Hertz at (530) 550-9191. The airport also offers seasonal ground transportation.

Lake Tahoe Airport
1901 Airport Road
South Lake Tahoe, CA
(530) 542-6180
www.laketahoeairport.com
Lake Tahoe Airport is a nonhub airport located just south of the Y intersection of CA 89 and US 50. It's paved runway is 8,544 feet long. The airport does not charge a landing fee for private aircraft but charges $10 per day and up for overnight tie-down fees, depending on the size of the aircraft. Jet A and 100 LL (low-lead) fuel are available from Trajen FBO Network, (530) 541-2110. Charter and sightseeing flights as well as aircraft rentals are offered by High Sierra Helicopters, (530) 544-2211.

Rail Service

Amtrak
Railroad Street and Commercial Row
Truckee, CA
(800) 872-7245/USA-RAIL
www.amtrak.com
The *California Zephyr* makes two daily stops in Truckee, which serves as a jumping-off point for Lake Tahoe. The westbound *California Zephyr,* train number 5, pulls into the unstaffed Truckee station in the late morning on its way to the Bay Area. Passengers have just a few minutes to disembark and board. The eastbound *California Zephyr,* train number 6, arrives in Truckee on its way to Chicago at mid-afternoon. Again, passengers only have a few minutes to board and disembark. Call Amtrak for ticket price information and specific departure and arrival times.

Buses

Greyhound Lines
10065 Donner Pass Road, Truckee, CA
(530) 587-3822, (800) 231-2222
www.greyhound.com
Greyhound Lines offers two eastbound and three westbound departures from its station in Truckee every day. The facility is open from 10:00 A.M. to 6:00 P.M.

No Stress Express
311 South Roop Street
Carson City, NV
(775) 333-6955, (775) 885-7550
www.nostressexpress.com
This bus line runs the Reno Airporter, which provides daily service from the Reno/Tahoe International Airport to both North and South Lake Tahoe. The company uses vans and midsize buses. The one-way fares run $47. Tickets may be purchased at the company's desk in the airport's baggage claim area.

South Tahoe Express
Reno/Tahoe International Airport
Reno, NV
(775) 325-8944, (866) 898-2463
www.southtahoeexpress.com
Formerly Tahoe Casino Express, South Tahoe Express runs 11 departures from Reno/Tahoe International Airport to Lake Tahoe's South Shore hotel/casinos. The cost runs about $40 round-trip. You'll find their office in the airport by carousel five in the baggage claim area.

Mass Transit

Mass transit is not a problem around the lake. About eight different modes of transportation are available to whisk you from one little town to the next and all the beaches and parks in between.

BlueGo
1679 Shop Street
South Lake Tahoe, CA
(530) 541-7149
www.bluego.org
Using the latest technology, BlueGo provides a variety of bus services to the South Shore Lake Tahoe area. Look for computerized kiosks around town for specific information. Services offered include

door-to-door minivans, scheduled bus routes, and the Nifty Fifty Trolley, which operates from 10:00 A.M. to 10:00 P.M. during summer only.

North Tahoe Trolley (TART)
870 Cabin Creek Road, Truckee, CA
(530) 550-1212, (800) 736-6365
www.placer.ca.gov
This trolley service operates between Stateline and Emerald Bay on Tahoe's South Shore, and Tahoe City from late June to Labor Day. The trolley runs a day route from 8:00 A.M. to 5:30 P.M. hourly. Adults ride for $1.50 or can purchase a daily pass for $3.50; seniors, disabled people, and children ages 6 through 12 get an unlimited daily pass for $1.75. Children age 5 and younger ride free.

Tahoe Area Regional Transit (TART)
870 Cabin Creek Road, Truckee, CA
(530) 550-1212, (800) 736-6365
www.placer.ca.gov
This public bus service runs from Incline Village to Sugar Pine Point State Park near Meeks Bay and offers shuttle service from Tahoe City to Truckee. Buses on these routes are equipped with racks for bicycles and snow skis. The one-way adult fare is $1.50. Children age 5 and younger ride free. All-day passes are $3.50 for adults, $1.75 for seniors, and $1.00 for disabled passengers. TART buses operate from 6:30 A.M. to 6:00 P.M. seven days a week.

Full-Service Transportation Companies

Squaw Creek Transportation
400 Squaw Creek Road, Squaw Valley, CA
(866) 909-7433
www.tahoesbest.com (click on transportation link)
This company offers a variety of transportation options, from shuttles to Reno/Tahoe International Airport and other airports, to tours and charter services, along with a complimentary shuttle service in the Squaw Valley area. The fleet includes shuttle buses, a motor coach, luxury SUVs and sedans, vans, and limousines.

Taxis

If you're used to flagging down a cab at a moment's notice, you might find it a little difficult to do so around Lake Tahoe. While a few companies operate here (I list two of them below), taxis aren't the most popular form of transportation here.

North Tahoe Checker Taxi
(866) 420-8294
This company charges a $2.00 step-in fee and $2.40 per mile for five or fewer passengers. For more than five people, the rate increases to $3.00 for step-in and $3.61 per mile. The company operates at North Tahoe and Truckee.

Yellow Cab
(530) 544-5555, (775) 588-1234
This company's standard rate calls for a $2.00 drop with $2.50 per mile in California and $2.64 per mile in Nevada.

Limousines

The following companies offer limousine service around the lake.

Aladdin Limousines
(530) 544-3333, (800) 546-6009
www.aladdinlimo.net
Aladdin's fleet includes a limo and a town coach; the limo rate is $75 per hour and the coach is $95 per hour. There is a two-hour minimum. The company provides service from the South Shore to Reno/Tahoe International Airport for $190 one-way in the limo and $380 in the coach.

All Seasons Tahoe Limousine Service
(530) 577-2727, (800) 334-1826
www.tahoelimo.com
The basic rates for limo service from this company range from $50 to $65 per hour, plus tax and gratuity, with a two-hour minimum. The company services the Reno area as well as Sacramento, San Francisco, Los Angeles, and other destinations.

North Tahoe Limousine
Cal Neva Resort Hotel and Casino
Crystal Bay, NV
(800) 832-8213
www.northtahoelimo.com
The only limo company headquartered at North Shore Lake Tahoe, North Tahoe Limousine offers an eight-passenger stretch limo for $65 per hour and a six-passenger limo for $50. Both cars come with fully stocked bars. A two-hour minimum rental is required. The company will also take you to airports in Sacramento, San Francisco, or Reno, with the one-way run to Reno costing $120. North Tahoe also has a 15-passenger bus for parties and tours and will even throw in complimentary champagne.

Sierra West Limousine
(877) 347-4789
This limo service, which also serves the Reno area, charges $55 per hour for a limo without a wet bar and $66 for a limo with a wet bar.

Rental Cars

North Shore rental agencies include:

Alpine Auto Rental
Incline Village
(775) 833-4424

Hertz
Truckee Tahoe Airport
(530) 550-9191, (800) 654-3131

South Shore rental agencies include:

Avis
Stateline
(530) 544-5289, (800) 331-1212
www.avis.com

Hertz
Stateline
(775) 586-0041, (800) 654-3131
www.hertz.com

Enterprise
Stateline
(775) 586-1077, (800) 736-8222
www.enterprise.com

HISTORY

The cities in northern Nevada aren't like other cities around the United States. Here you can play slot machines in grocery and convenience stores or watch a 60-foot-tall indoor mining rig pump out spendable dollar tokens. Most of the cities are somewhat eccentric with a splash of the fantastic thrown in, and they all have a way of grabbing your attention.

Like the rest of Nevada, the Reno/ Tahoe area is steeped in history, including battles with Native Americans, ill-fated wagon trains, gunfights, gold and silver strikes, and, of course, scandals. These colorful pieces of history are what make the area so fascinating.

Colonel H. B. Maxson, an early Reno/ Tahoe pioneer, wrote in his autobiography the following about his introduction to Reno:

"I was reared in a strict Baptist community in New York and was taught to be respectful to all, but sociable with few without being properly introduced. My first lesson in Western hospitality was received on a train to Reno.

"A very pleasant man passed through the car addressing everyone as 'my son' and extending the greetings of the day. This was contrary to my teachings and I declined to answer him. But later I observed that everybody spoke to him so I asked the conductor who the old gentleman was and he said with a laugh, 'That's the governor of Nevada.' For the first time I realized that the customs of the West were certainly different from the teachings of the East.

"At the first opportunity I apologized and told the governor that I was taught not to talk with strangers and had heard that the trains out West were filled with confidence men who parted innocent eastern travelers from their money. Whereupon, the governor laughed and told everyone on the train that he had been taken for a three-card monte sharp and when we got to Reno he treated the house at the Old Depot Hotel bar and paid for me to stay in the best room in the house."

Many who live here today will tell you that things really haven't changed since then.

THE FIRST NEVADANS

Long before trailblazer John C. Frémont made his expedition through the Truckee Meadows (the area bordering the Truckee River from the California state line to just east of what is now Sparks), Native Americans inhabited the state. Although anthropologists claim that more than 27 tribes roamed the Nevada wilderness, only two—the Washoes and the Northern Paiutes—gathered seeds and other foodstuffs and fished and hunted in the Reno/ Tahoe area. These tribes had to search for food constantly, making survival of the individual family their highest priority. The search for food kept them perpetually on the move, with little time for leisure.

These two tribes were more fortunate than most other Nevada tribes because, for part of the year, they had two abundant lakes to fish. The Washoes fished Lake Tahoe, one of the deepest and highest alpine lakes on the continent, and the Northern Paiutes fished Pyramid Lake, a starkly beautiful watershed 25 miles northeast of present-day Reno. Both tribes also became adept at making decoys from wood and tules (long reedlike plants that grow in the wetlands) to hunt the waterfowl that used Tahoe and Pyramid Lakes as landing zones on their southern migratory trek.

Native American cultures played a large role in the history of the Reno/Lake Tahoe area.
LOUIS BASSO

Native American handicrafts not only included fashioning these elaborate decoys but also basket weaving. These baskets were not for decoration but were essential tools, a means of carrying food and water.

Their decoy- and basket-making became legendary around Nevada. Experts consider the Washoes to be the best basket makers in the United States; Dat-So-La-Lee, a Washoe Indian who died in 1925, was thought to be the best of the best. She was known to spend as long as one year working on a single basket. Some of her work can be seen in the Nevada State Museum in Carson City and at the Nevada Historical Society in Reno (see the Day Trips and Attractions chapters).

These early inhabitants of the Reno/Tahoe area didn't plant crops. They were gatherers, so they used their handcrafted baskets to carry the pine nuts they harvested to supplement their food supply through the sometimes-harsh winters. During late fall, they gathered at the piñon groves for the harvest. The men beat the seed-filled pinecones to the ground with long poles, and the women collected the cones in their baskets. After the nuts were removed from the cones, cleaned, and roasted, they gathered to enjoy a family reunion. Although known for their hard lives, these tribes are also credited with establishing a long-standing Reno/Tahoe tradition—gambling.

That's right, the Washoes and the Northern Paiutes would bet on just about anything, including running games and games of strength and agility. Their wagers sometimes consisted of everything they owned, including their blankets, baskets, jewelry, feathers, and even their prized rabbitskin robes. These gambling games would sometimes go on for days, and while a few families walked away rich with new possessions, others were left with literally just the skins on their backs.

These two tribes remained in the area to greet the first white explorers but soon found them more of a threat to their civilizations than the harshest winter or drought-ridden summer.

TRAILBLAZERS, MAPMAKERS, AND RISK TAKERS

"The beaver are so plentiful a man has no need for traps. The little varmints just jump into your tote-sack."

That's the legend that Jedediah Smith, a trapper with the Rocky Mountain Fur Company, heard in 1827. So he and 15 other trappers blazed a trail into the Reno/Tahoe area to prove the legend of the beaver and to find the mythical San Buenaventura River that supposedly flowed from the Rocky Mountains to the Pacific Ocean. Unfortunately, they found neither.

Smith is credited, however, with being the first white man to cross the present state of Nevada near Reno and the first to encounter and write about the Native American tribes in the area. Because of his early encounter and friendship with the Native Americans, other early Nevada explorers owed Smith a great deal—especially John C. Frémont, a pathfinder for the U.S. Army engineers.

Even though several pioneers, including John Bidwell, John Bartleson, and Joseph Chiles, crossed northern Nevada before him, Frémont is credited with the exploration of the Reno/Tahoe area. In 1844 he led an expedition through northeastern Nevada to Pyramid Lake and finally to the Truckee Meadows. Frémont, along with legendary scout and frontiersman Kit Carson, charted the new territory and, as Smith attempted years before, searched for the San Buenaventura River. When Frémont first saw a river emptying into Pyramid Lake, he thought it might be the Buenaventura, but he realized that it was too small to be the mythical river. He was glad, however, to see his new find teeming with fish. Frémont's band had endured many months in the sparse high desert, living off small game and birds, and the feast of fresh-caught fish was a welcome respite. Frémont's small band filled up on their catch and called the swift river the Salmon-Trout River after the tasty fish. Historians agree that later mapmakers changed the stream's name to the Truckee River in honor of a Paiute chief who served as a guide for other expeditions.

Frémont, Carson, and their group pressed on from the Truckee Meadows and first saw Lake Tahoe from the top of Red Lake Peak, now called Carson Pass. Frémont first named this magnificent body of water Lake Bonpland, for a botanist, but referred to it as Mountain Lake on his maps. The name was later changed to Lake Bigler for a California governor, and finally, in 1945, the California Legislature changed the name to Lake Tahoe, which is derived from a bastardized Native American word meaning "big water."

Frémont's expedition circumnavigated northern Nevada and proved that the San Buenaventura did not exist. But, more importantly for scientists, the expedition also determined that the Great Basin of northern Nevada has no outlet and that all its rivers flowed inward. His wife, Jesse, best sums up Frémont's importance to the area: "From the ashes of my husband's campfires have sprung cities."

Frémont paved the way for other American pioneers to trek through the Truckee Meadows, but without a doubt the most famous emigrants to the Reno/Tahoe area were members of the ill-fated Donner Party. In 1846, George Donner and his brother, Jake, led an 87-member wagon train from Fort Hall, Idaho, on the Oregon Trail to the Truckee Meadows. The two had read a book by Lansford Hastings, who described a shortcut through the Sierra Nevada to the promised land—California. The two Donner brothers persuaded the impatient families in the wagon train that the shortcut was the better route.

After many setbacks suffered during the trek through the treacherous high desert, the Donner Party arrived in the Truckee Meadows in mid-October. After the stark, vast Nevada desert, the plush campsites along the Truckee River were a welcome sight and enticed the party to stay for several days to rest up. This luxury proved fatal.

Fort Hall locals, who knew about the harsh Nevada winters, warned both brothers to cross the Sierra Nevada before the first snowfall, but members of the weary party easily convinced the leaders to stay. After all, they argued, what harm can a few more days make? But by the time they reached the mountain pass (now called the Donner Pass) between Nevada and California, heavy snows forced them to turn around and to head back toward the Truckee Meadows. As fate would have it, deep snow prevented them from reaching the docile meadows. Instead, the party was forced to pitch camp near the present site of Truckee, California, to weather out the winter.

With no game to hunt and a dwindling food supply, the Donner Party struggled to stay alive through the harsh winter by eating their pack animals, their shoes, and their leather harnesses. But their most gruesome act—the one remembered throughout history—was cannibalism. When their supplies ran out and some of the old people and babies starved to death, members of the Donner Party ate their corpses. When rescuers finally reached the lake in April 1847, they found only 47 of the original 87 members alive. (See the Day Trips chapter for more information on Donner Memorial State Park in Truckee.)

The first train robbery in the West occurred 7 miles east of Reno in November 1870. "Smiling Jack" Davis of Virginia pulled the stickup.

Although the Hastings Cutoff garnered a reputation as a death route, pioneers continued to use the shortcut to reach California, even more so when gold was discovered outside Sacramento in 1848. This gold strike soon made the Truckee Meadows a jumping-off point for prospectors heading into California. Wagon train after wagon train poured into the Reno area, and it soon became "an important crossroads where the north-south, east-west emigrant trails met," according to the late local historian Mike Land.

You only have to glance at the variety of names in local telephone books to realize the international flavor of the Reno/Tahoe area. Adding to the melting pot begun with the first Native Americans, early settlers represented such diverse cultures as the Cornish, Irish, Scottish, English, Chinese, French, Mexican, and Basque. They mined silver, built canals, herded sheep, and constructed railroads from the 1850s on. The French and Spanish Basques were especially influential, settling all over northern Nevada and assuming positions of power and leadership in their communities. To indulge in the cuisine of this delightful ethnic mix of peoples, see the Restaurants chapter. For details about the many groups that celebrate their cultures in the area, see The Arts chapter.

LAKE'S CROSSING BECOMES RENO

Myron Lake knew a good deal when he saw one. A capable businessman who was both energetic and visionary, Lake knew when he saw Charles W. Fuller's bridge across the Truckee River in 1861 that Fuller was on to something. After all, travelers on the north-south and east-west trails had to cross the swift little river, and the choices were few—wade, swim, or use the rickety toll bridge.

But Fuller's bridge was flawed—every time the river rose, the bridge washed away. He rebuilt the bridge several times between 1859 and 1861, but Fuller was a Missouri settler, not an architect, so in 1861 he decided to sell out and move on to better business deals, and Lake was ready to buy him out. Just as it has happened so many other times in this area, one man's misfortune turned out to be another man's jackpot.

Lake first rebuilt the bridge (much sturdier this time) and added a trading station, inn, and bar. He also bought up the land 14 miles north and 3 miles south of his bridge. Lake was a veteran of the Mexican War and still kept up on Washington, D.C., politics. He calculated that railroads would soon cross the country, linking the East and West Coasts, and he guessed they would come through the Truckee Meadows. He guessed right.

Lake held all the aces and knew he held a winning hand. The railroad was coming, and the discovery in 1859 of the Comstock Lode in Virginia City sent silver seekers flocking to the Truckee Meadows. The only road to the silver-rich city just happened to be across Lake's new bridge, and he grew richer and richer from the tolls paid by those supplying the miners in Virginia City. And he charged for every single thing crossing his bridge: horses, cattle, wagons, chickens, pigs, sheep, and, of course, the men. If it crossed the bridge, he got money for it.

Lake expanded his holdings, buying more land and constructing more buildings. Besides his river property, he owned a gristmill and a livery stable, and he also continued to buy up rangeland. By 1864, the area that eventually became the city of Reno was known as Lake's Crossing. But Lake's greatest business deal came four years later with Charles Crocker of the Central Pacific Railroad.

The Central Pacific and Union Pacific Railroads raced each other across the west, laying track and acquiring good right-of-way land. The Central Pacific headed east from California, and the

Union Pacific headed west from Nebraska. The Central Pacific reached the Truckee Meadows first, even though the railroad took five years to cross the Sierra Nevada, but the length of time didn't bother Lake. He was waiting for the railroad when it reached Lake's Crossing in March 1868.

Lake had already struck a deal with Crocker of the Central Pacific, asking only that a train depot be built on his property. In return, Lake promised to deed 400 acres to the railroad. Crocker liked the deal, surveyed the land, and divided it into building lots. To thank Lake, Crocker had the railroad deed back 127 lots to Lake. The two then auctioned off the city six weeks later.

The railroaders decided that the new town should be called "Argenta," a poetic term meaning silver. After all, the discovery of the Comstock Lode in Virginia City really put the Truckee Meadows in the annals of history. But Crocker wanted to honor an old family friend, Union general Jesse Lee Reno, who was killed at the Battle of South Mountain, Maryland, in 1862. At first the name met with resistance because Reno had never once stepped foot in Nevada; however, Comstock miners and the new town's citizens admitted that the simple name "Reno" had a good ring to it, and the name stuck.

SILVER PUTS RENO/ TAHOE ON THE MAP

"Can you shoot?"

That's the first question the editor of the *Gold Hill Daily News* on the Comstock asked Wells Drury when he applied for the job of a newspaper reporter in 1874.

"Will you stand without hitching? You can write what you please. Nobody will censor it. But you have to defend yourself if anybody has a kick," the editor said, throwing a shooting-iron down on his desk. "We call this six-shooter the 'family bible.' You may need it. You may not."

Drury got the job and later that day covered "one murder, two fatal mine accidents, and a runaway stage coach." He also gained a reputation as a gunfighter when he pointed the "family bible" at a town bully and blew off the man's left ear. Those were the days when Virginia City and Gold Hill on the Comstock Lode were the "hell-raisingest" mining camps in the world. And a history of Reno/Tahoe would be remiss if it didn't mention the silver find that gave birth to these two towns just 20 miles away from Reno on the slopes of Mount Davidson. The Comstock Lode put Reno on the map and made Lake Tahoe the center of a logging empire that supplied the towns with timber to shore up their mines, build their structures, and lay their railroad tracks.

Brothers Hosea and Ethan Grosh staked their claim in Gold Canyon on the southern slope of Mount Davidson in 1853. Although they didn't find the much sought-after gold, they did identify the "messy blue mud" that got in the other gold prospectors' way. It was silver, and for the next three years the brothers tried desperately to find the financial backing they needed to properly examine the silver deposits. Unfortunately, both brothers died in 1857 before profiting from their discovery. In fact, their find remained a secret.

After the brothers died, a shifty con man named Henry Comstock, for whom the silver find was named, moved into their cabin and announced to the other miners that he had been made the Groshs' partner in exchange for keeping their land free from would-be claim jumpers. According to historian Mike Land, "Comstock had no idea about the silver find. He was just a lucky little man who was in the right place at the right time."

Not far from Comstock's cabin, Patrick McLaughlin and Peter O'Riley discovered more gold flakes surrounded by the blue-black mud. The two men staked a claim and prospected the gold while throwing away the silver-rich earth. Comstock heard about the find and conned McLaughlin and O'Riley into believing that they were trespassing on his land. He offered to make them and an old prospector named James Finney partners for an equal share in their claim. They agreed, and the four formed the Comstock Company and began pulling out gold from a mine they named Ophir, after one of King Solomon's mines. The partners still knew nothing of the silver they were throwing away until some ore wound up in the Truckee Meadows.

The blue-black mud interested two ranchers in the Truckee Meadows, who sent some off to a mining office in California. The sample was assayed and was found to be loaded with silver. But before the two ranchers could act on the welcome news, James Walsh and Joseph Woodward, two insiders who worked in the assay office, scurried to the Ophir Mine to buy out the four prospectors before they could hear about the wealth of silver. Three of the owners sold their shares outright for $2,500 apiece, but Comstock held out for $11,000, thinking he was the better businessman. In reality, the four sold their rights to $310 million worth of silver for $18,500. When Walsh and Woodward returned to California, they spread the word of their find, and the great silver rush on the Comstock Lode began.

Virginia City and Gold Hill grew up from the Ophir Mine; the silver boom helped fatten the coffers of Reno as well. And while Lake Tahoe was pretty much a myth up to this time (known only to Native Americans and a few hardy explorers), the rush to riches beginning in 1860 literally put it on the map. When word of the enormous silver deposit in Nevada reached settlers in nearby California, hordes of aspiring millionaires saddled their horses and hit the hair-raising trail over the Sierras to the mines. Choked daily with hundreds of mule teams, stagecoaches, and riders, the narrow path took travelers right past Lake Tahoe. To accommodate these first travelers to the area, way stations sprang up, including Yank's Station near Echo Summit, and Lake House, Tahoe's first lakeshore hotel, near present-day Al Tahoe in South Lake Tahoe.

In addition to providing the ever-important route to the silver fields, the Lake Tahoe area also offered a resource critical for the development of the mines. The towering virgin forests yielded the massive timbers needed to shore up mine shafts and wood to drive steam engines. The Comstock's insatiable appetite for wood fueled the wholesale plunder of Tahoe's timberlands by lumbermen eager for huge profits. Mills that opened near Glenbrook on the east side of the lake used an innovative flume system to transport the timber over the mountains to the mines.

Lumber was hauled by rail to the top of Spooner Summit and then shot down a V-flume to Carson City, where it was hauled by rail to Virginia City. Near Incline Village, logs were hauled to the top of the mountain via a 4,000-foot tramway and then dumped into a flume that carried them to their pickup point for the railroad. The town of Incline Village derives its name from this tramline. To ensure a steady supply of water to float timbers in the flumes, the lumber companies built dams and created Spooner and Marlette Lakes (see the Recreation and Winter Sports chapters for present-day activities at these lakes).

The Virginia and Truckee (V&T) Railroad began operations in 1869, linking Carson City with the Comstock and later with Reno and the Central Pacific Railroad. The V&T Railroad carried the silver-rich ore down to Carson City and supplied the mines with goods from Reno.

In May 1860, the Pyramid Lake Paiutes met among themselves to discuss the miners who were arriving in the Truckee Meadows. The Native Americans had weathered the explorers, mapmakers, and pioneers who were just passing through, but they could not tolerate the miners who took their land, cut down their piñon trees, and kidnapped their women. On May 12, the Paiutes won the first Battle of Pyramid Lake by luring a scraggly band of volunteers into an ambush. Of the 105 white men who fought in the skirmish, 76 died and 29 were wounded. By June, 1,550 volunteers and four companies of regular Army soldiers marched on Pyramid Lake. The Paiutes, guided by Chief Numaga, didn't engage the white men but retreated to the shores of the lake. The white men were thus the new masters of the Truckee Meadows, and the Native Americans, by treaty, remained at the lake.

The silver extracted from the Comstock Lode also convinced the U.S. Congress to admit Nevada as the 36th state, on October 31, 1864, to help finance the Civil War on the side of the Union.

Thus, from the awful blue-black mud loaded with silver sprang a state, two boomtowns, a Native American war, a railroad, and a host of colorful characters, the most famous being Samuel Clemens, who joined the editorial staff of the *Territorial Enterprise* newspaper in Virginia City in 1862 and in 1863 began using his famous pen name, Mark Twain.

The mines petered out in the late 1880s, and the populations of Virginia City and Gold Hill fell from 10,900 in 1880 to 2,500 in 1900. Gold Hill eventually disappeared, and Virginia City turned into an almost-ghost town. However, Reno and Lake Tahoe thrived. The little town on the Truckee River became the most important city in Nevada, and Lake Tahoe turned to tourism and began building resorts and inns.

RENO/TAHOE OUTGAMBLE TWO DEPRESSIONS

In mining vocabulary inherited from Mexico, the opposite of the *bonanza* (the big strike) is the *borrasca* (the worst of bad luck). Reno/Tahoe learned that Spanish word all too well in the early 1880s. The Comstock mines, which provided the major source of income to most Nevadans, were all but played out by 1881. One by one the mines closed down, and miners left the state in droves, looking for the next "glory hole." From 1880 to 1900 the population of the state dropped from 62,000 to 42,000, and the U.S. Congress even contemplated abolishing Nevada's statehood. Although it had never been done before, Congress was ready to try. It never came to pass, however, and Reno and Lake Tahoe managed to weather a 20-year depression.

The railroads took financial hits from the closing of the Comstock mines, but their Nevada runs continued, this time supplying the growing cattle and sheep ranches. These ranches operated successfully because the railroads were able to transport their stock to California, Nebraska, and other yards around the United States. So Reno continued as the railroad center of Nevada.

Lake Tahoe, meanwhile, diverted its attention from logging to tourism. Although barren mountains remained as the legacy of lumbering and mining (50,000 acres had been cut by the 1890s), the silver rush was responsible for the beginnings of summer tourism in the Lake Tahoe basin. Exposed to thousands of commercial travelers in the 1860s and 1870s, the grandeur of the lake was a secret no more. In spite of the decline of the Comstock mines, travelers continued to arrive in the basin, but now it was for pleasure rather than for business. Way stations, resorts, and hotels flourished all around the lake, introducing wealthy customers to lazy alpine summers in one of the world's loveliest settings.

Resorts such as Tahoe Tavern and the Grand Central Hotel near Tahoe City, the Glenbrook Hotel in Glenbrook, and the Tallac Hotel near South Lake Tahoe pampered guests with extraordinary luxury in a beautifully rustic mountain setting. Not content to reside in resorts, some notables constructed elegant summer residences, such as Vikingsholm Castle, built by Mrs. Lora Knight (see the Attractions and Kidstuff chapters) and the Thunderbird Lodge, constructed later in the 1930s by real estate magnate George Whittell. Less luxurious digs also thrived, including Camp Richardson, which emphasized (as it still does today) a family-oriented experience in the great outdoors.

Because of the absence of roads, the steamers *Tahoe, Meteor, Tod Goodwin,* and others carried passengers and freight from one area of the lake to another. And while the lumber barons pillaged the mountainsides, the first tourists plundered the lake through unbridled overfishing. Because the supply of fish was believed to be inexhaustible, anglers were encouraged to catch as many as they could, with the average running around 20 per person for a four-hour outing. Fortunately, in later years, concern for the environment and natural resources became a priority, with public and private groups working successfully to restore the forests and fish populations.

The second gold rush began in Nevada in 1900, when an old prospector named Jim Butler went looking for his wayward mule near the town of Tonopah, Nevada, and discovered pockets of gold and silver. This time the state grew by 50,000 fortune seekers. During the next 10 years, Reno's population grew from 4,500 to almost 11,000, and Sparks, Reno's sister city, was born.

In 1902, swampland and ranch land made up most of the area 4 miles east of Reno, but by 1904 a new town of 1,000 people sprang up, thanks to the Southern Pacific Railroad. The SP succeeded Central Pacific as the owners of the railroad tracks across northern Nevada, and in order to straighten the rails and snip a few miles from the route, the SP decided to move its maintenance yard and roundhouse closer to Reno from Wadsworth, Nevada. The railroad bought up the ranch land, filled in the swampland with railway carloads of dirt and rock, and moved its employees there. As an incentive, the company gave each family a plot of land on which to build a house. The new town was an instant success and was named for John Sparks, a miner, cattleman, and soon-to-be governor of Nevada.

Reno real estate investors bought up other ranch properties for more housing projects, and the city of Sparks became incorporated in March 1905. In the beginning, Southern Pacific Railroad officials ruled Sparks's politics with an iron hand, making it a company town and giving Sparks the nickname of Rail City, because it relied on the railroad for its existence. Sparks weathered the Great Depression better than other Nevada cities. During the 1930s, Sparks's city government put unemployed men to work on street, sidewalk, and sewer repair and construction projects.

An on-again, off-again romance with gambling exists in Reno and Sparks. Throughout its history, the Truckee Meadows have attracted settlers who like to take risks. Nowhere else in the United States have more fortunes been won and lost. Gambling has always been part of Reno's history, but antigambling factions came to town, too, along with the faro dealers and three-card monte sharks. From the 1860s to the 1930s, Reno's gambling laws were controversial at best.

In 1861, the Territorial Legislature outlawed games of chance, but the law was ignored. In 1879 the state repealed the law and tried to cash in on gambling by requiring a license to operate any gambling establishment. But after heavy betting on the famous Jim Jeffries and Jack Johnson heavyweight prizefight in Reno in 1910, the lid slammed down once again

---

The first woman to practice law in Nevada was Laura M. Tilden, the daughter of the attorney for Virginia City. She was admitted to the bar in 1894.

You know you're an old-time Nevadan if you remember divorcées throwing their wedding rings into the Truckee River in downtown Reno.

on gambling. The *San Francisco Examiner* proclaimed in a headline that "Legalized Gambling Has Drawn Its Last Breath in the United States." It was true—almost. "Legal" gambling did stop, but the betting continued; only now it was moved to the back rooms of saloons and other secret places. Two short knocks and a "Joe sent me" could get a person into a high-stakes game that was usually held at night with full permission of the local police force. The only thing the ban seemed to do was to bring gangsters to Reno.

The two biggest hoods in Reno were "Big Bill" Graham and Jimmy "The Cinch" McKay. These two "gentlemen" owned the infamous Bank Club and had friends from back East who found Reno both a great place to hide from the FBI and to launder stickup money. Gangsters Pretty Boy Floyd, John Dillinger, and Baby Face Nelson visited the Truckee Meadows in the late 1920s and early 1930s. Graham and McKay ruled downtown Reno for years, but eventually they went too far and were sentenced to nine years in prison for mail fraud. Still, illegal gambling went on.

To erase the stigma, Reno mayor E. E. Roberts called for a repeal of the antigambling law during his reelection campaign in 1931. "You cannot legislate morals," he said. "You can't stop gambling, so let's put it out in the open."

The people reelected Roberts, and on March 19, 1931, Nevada repealed its antigambling law. The reaction around the United States, however, was more vicious than expected. The *Los Angeles Times* called Nevada "a new Babylon," and the *Kansas City Star* called Reno a cross between "Sodom, Gomorrah and Hell." Once again, legislators in some states called for the repeal of Nevada's statehood. But Nevada survived the threat, and Reno survived the two depressions because of its legalized gambling and because it cashed in on a new business—divorce.

About the same time Roberts was hoping legal gambling would bring a new bonanza to Nevada, Governor Fred Balzar gave promoter Norman Biltz the green light to try to populate the state with millionaires. Citing the tax advantages offered by the state, Biltz found wealthy people from around the country who managed to survive the stock market crash of 1929 and wined and dined them in elaborate style at Lake Tahoe. Many of them were favorably impressed, including Jim Stack (brother of the late well-known movie star Robert Stack), E. L. Cord, Max Fleischmann, and Cornelius Vanderbilt III. They were the first of many influential people to invest in real estate around the lake.

DIVORCE CITY

No one really paid much attention to Nevada's residence requirements to become a voting citizen: It took only six months because itinerant miners made up most of the state's population, and if stricter requirements existed, not very many citizens would be eligible to vote. No one looked hard at Nevada's liberal divorce laws either, until the 1920s, when a Reno lawyer advertised quickie divorces in New York and California newspapers.

Nevada's short residency requirements and wide range of grounds for divorce soon made Reno the divorce capital of the world. In fact, the business became so lucrative that the Nevada Legislature dropped the required residency period down to three months and later in 1931 dropped it further to only six weeks. Now the rich and famous flocked to Reno to shed their undesirable mates. Some old-timers swore that they found more gold in the Truckee River beneath the Virginia Street Bridge, where new divorcées threw in their wedding bands, than in all the mines on the Comstock.

The new divorce phenomenon also provided another business for Reno—dude ranches. Neil West was the first to recognize that those seeking a divorce needed somewhere to stay during the six-week period. So he built cabins on his cattle ranch near Reno and rented them to the "dudes." Reno also ensured that soon-to-be divorcées waited out their residency requirement in comfort and luxury. The late Hope Roberts, a well-known community activist, pampered the well-heeled women at Roberts House on Forest Street in Reno for many years. Even Lake Tahoe followed suit, and resorts and inns sprang up all over the Nevada side of the lake. Nearly every community around the lake today owes its existence to a resort or a hotel.

The flip side of the divorce coin provided another lucrative business for Reno—weddings. Because Reno had no waiting period to get married—just the time it took to buy a marriage license—wedding chapels popped up around Reno. The business bloomed in the war years of the 1940s, and by 1952 Reno weddings outnumbered divorces.

THE BIGGEST LITTLE CITY IN THE WORLD

In the 1950s and 1960s, the Reno/Tahoe area got down to the business of expanding. After all, Reno's nickname, "The Biggest Little City in the World," had been made world-famous since the summer of 1928 when a Sacramento man won $100 for suggesting it, and the city fathers wanted to live up to the saying. But two families can really be credited with putting Reno on the map—the Smiths and the Harrahs. Raymond "Pappy" Smith and his son Harold started the world-famous Harolds Club, and Bill Harrah began Harrah's.

In 1942, Harolds Club came up with the slogan "Harolds Club or Bust," incorporated it with the drawing of a Conestoga wagon, and plastered the signs along the highways of the United States. More than 2,000 signs adorned the roadways of America, reminding travelers to visit Reno, the "biggest little" gambling spot in the country. At that time, Reno and Harolds Club were the most popular tourist attractions in the United States. Some of the signs reportedly found their way to Australia, Europe, Asia, and even Africa. The club prospered and along with it, Reno.

Harrah began his operation with only a few hundred dollars and no partners, but his willingness to take risks, like so many Reno pioneers before him, enabled his empire to grow. After World War II, he began buying up all the Reno property and clubs he could—and couldn't—afford. He also expanded his holdings to the South Shore of Lake Tahoe. Harrah continued his philosophy of using profits to expand properties and to build newer and bigger casinos. He was one of the first casino owners to feature Hollywood celebrities to attract customers to his showrooms. (For more information on Harrah's, see the Resorts chapter.)

The building boom began again, and more and more entrepreneurs flooded into the area. Lake Tahoe experienced unregulated growth in the 1950s and 1960s with the development of gambling on its South Shore. The Winter Olympics of 1960 in Squaw Valley added to the urbanization of the lake. Developers drained and filled marshland for waterfront homes, and hotels and motels sprang up around the lake.

As the Lake Tahoe Basin experienced

***Reno was ranked third among the nation's best places to live by* Men's Journal.**

---

more and more growth, the influence of the Washoe Tribe almost completely disappeared. By 1870, only about 500 Native Americans were known to still frequent the area. What was once the Indians' ancestral summer home became a playground for the rich, the famous, and almost anybody who could manage to get there. Accessible only in summer because of heavy snow for many years, it became a year-round resort in 1947 when U.S. Highway 50 was opened as an all-season roadway. Today the Washoes are returning to the lake, beginning with their 30-year permit to run Meeks Bay Resort, which was awarded by the USDA Forest Service in 1998.

The casinos continued to bring in visitors by the millions, pumping megadollars into the area's economy, but nonetheless some antigambling activists convinced the Reno City Council to restrict the building of casinos to a small, downtown area. The council literally drew a red line on a map around a 5-square-block area. This, they said, would be the only section of Reno to allow casinos. The area outside the red line would cater to "businesses, homes, churches, banks, schools, and all other entities that represented normal life."

The "red-line district" worked for the first two decades, but in 1955 one of the owners of the Primadonna Casino challenged the restriction. The Reno City Council relented, and casinos expanded past the red-line area—some even sprang up in Sparks. The ordinance was not officially repealed, however, until 1972.

After word spread about how much profit Nevada casinos could provide their owners, corporations poured into the Reno/Tahoe area looking to cash in on the lucrative business. The eccentric Howard Hughes even bought out the Smiths and acquired Harolds Club. Hughes's presence in Reno spurred even more corporations to invest in Reno and Lake Tahoe. Hilton Hotels, MGM, Ramada Inn, Holiday Inn, Circus Circus, Caesars, Sahara, and the Del Webb corporation all own or owned a casino property in the Reno/Tahoe area.

As Reno/Sparks settled into the new millennium, the competition from casinos on riverboats and Indian reservations as well as from state lotteries made inroads into Nevada gaming. While recognizing that gaming will always be part of the local landscape, business movers and shakers began to successfully diversify the economy to include other industries.

With the economic climate and quality of life in neighboring California becoming less attractive, Nevada discovered it was relatively easy to attract new residents because of its business-friendly environment. Hundreds of businesses either relocated or began operation in the area, which resulted in an annual job-growth rate of more than 3 percent beginning in the early 1990s. The population of the Reno area has increased by about 13 percent a year since 2000. Because of its sustained job-growth rate, Reno was selected as the nation's top city for doing business by *Inc.* magazine in 2005.

But not everyone who moves to the Reno/Tahoe area expects or needs to get a job. Many are retirees who are attracted by the high quality of life. Around 18 percent of the total population is age 55 and older.

Meanwhile, as the Lake Tahoe area continues its struggle to protect the environment in the face of increased growth, Reno/Tahoe emphasizes adventure recreation and outdoor activities along with gaming glitz as attractions to visitors.

Branding itself "America's Adventure Place," Reno/Tahoe reaches out to physically active people who are just as eager to explore the outdoor environment as the indoor action. As more and more people "discover" the area, managing the resulting growth continues to be a hot topic. The population of Reno is expected to increase from about 386,000 in 2005 to 443,000 in 2015. The obvious challenge is to be able to keep the welcome mat out to new residents and businesses without destroying the ambience that makes the region so attractive.

RESORTS

Because tourism is the lifeblood of the Reno/Tahoe economy, visitors to the area have a tantalizing array of accommodations to choose from. In the Vacation Rentals chapter I tell you how to rent or lease a home away from home, ranging from cabins and condos to large sumptuous houses. In the Hotels and Motels chapter I describe more conventional lodging, such as luxury hotel/casinos and back-to-basics motels. In this chapter I give you a rundown on gaming and vacation resorts that stretch beyond the essentials to provide everything a guest could wish for, and then some.

GAMING RESORTS

Because gaming's legal in Nevada, Lady Luck plays a prominent role in available accommodations in the Reno/Tahoe area. Restricted gaming in Nevada (slot machines only) is found in a variety of locations, such as grocery stores, drugstores, and bars. You can even pay for your groceries at the checkout and hopefully win your money back at the slots before leaving the store. Unrestricted gaming (table games, sports books, and keno together with slot machines) is limited to casinos. While most small casinos do not offer overnight lodging, the large gaming establishments do. And because of increased competition in recent years, many large casinos have evolved from just hotel/casino properties into themed gaming resorts offering a diverse array of comforts and amusements for their guests.

Although it can be difficult to distinguish between a hotel/casino and a gaming resort, I believe a gaming resort offers more than just the minimum in food, lodging, and unrestricted gambling. Reno/Tahoe gaming resorts provide a comprehensive package to guests, including multiple options in rooms, restaurants, and entertainment. You can bed down in a variety of accommodations, from a standard room to a luxurious penthouse suite, all with full-service hotel amenities. You can satiate your appetite at a lavish buffet, a casual coffee shop, or an elegant gourmet dining room. And you can entertain yourself with nonstop casino action, dazzling stage revues, headliner entertainers, intimate piano bars, swinging discos, and lively video arcades—all without ever leaving the building.

In their quest to satisfy guests' every need, some gaming resorts also provide upscale shopping arcades, theaters, swimming pools, health clubs, and spas. Many provide convention facilities, group rates, and shuttle transportation. And if you finally tire of the on-site recreation, many gaming resorts will arrange for skiing, golfing, and other area activities.

A gaming resort can be a destination in and of itself, a place to stay and play and truly pamper yourself for several days. For details on casino entertainment, see the Casino Nightlife chapter; for detailed descriptions of some dining options, see the Restaurants chapter.

As each gaming resort offers every amenity imaginable, choosing among them can be difficult. But if location and atmosphere are important, then differences do exist. For visitors who prefer elegance and sophistication, the Eldorado Hotel/Casino Reno is a good choice. But for families with children, Circus Circus is probably a better choice.

To help you distinguish between the properties I recommend, in this chapter I describe the general flavor of the resort as well as all its amenities. All gaming resorts accept credit cards and offer nonsmoking accommodations. Children are welcome; in fact, many resorts make special provisions for them. Also, most accommodations are wheelchair accessible, but be sure to confirm this when making reservations.

If you're lucky enough to be flexible in your travel plans, it can be a distinct advantage when booking lodging in a Reno/Tahoe gaming resort. Rates and availability vary a great deal with the time of the year; some resorts go so far as to double rates during peak holidays. Accommodations at all these resorts are more expensive and difficult to obtain if the bookings include Martin Luther King Jr. Day, Presidents Day, Memorial Day, the Fourth of July, Thanksgiving, Christmas, and New Year's. High season at Lake Tahoe resorts also includes January to mid-April and mid-June to mid-September.

Bookings at gaming resorts in the Reno area are also affected by special events that draw large numbers of visitors (see the Annual Events chapter). The most heavily booked week of the year is during Hot August Nights (usually in early August), when rooms in some gaming resorts are sold out a year in advance. Other major events are the Reno Rodeo, mid- to late June; the Nevada State Fair, in August; The Best in the West Nugget Rib Cook-Off, Labor Day weekend; and the National Championship Air Races, The Great Reno Balloon Race, Street Vibrations, and the Virginia City International Camel Races in September. If you're planning to attend any of these events, it's wise to book as far ahead as possible.

In general, high season in the Reno area is July to mid-October, midseason is April to June, and low season is mid-November through December (excluding Christmas and New Year's) and January to March. But because high and low seasons are not always the same at Lake Tahoe as they are in the Reno area, it's possible to find accommodations in one area during its low season and still enjoy the activities of the other during its high season. For example, if you can't find lodging at Lake Tahoe during peak ski season, you may have better luck finding it in Reno; and if you're shut out of a room during Hot August Nights in Reno, you can try finding lodging at Lake Tahoe. With less than an hour separating the two areas, plus shuttle transportation that's available from some gaming resorts, getting from place to place is pretty easy, so this definitely provides an attractive option.

When booking, be sure to inquire about any packages that might result in savings and convenience. Also ask about any special events that might be going on, such as gaming tournaments, which could result in additional perks or benefits for resort guests. You also need to be aware that some resorts have minimum stay requirements during high season.

For reservations at any of the following gaming resorts, you can either call them direct or call the Reno/Tahoe Visitors Information Center, (800) 367-7366.

If you don't want to be told "how important you are" and then be put on interminable hold, however, I strongly recommend that you try booking on the Internet. You can access individual hotel sites or use www.reno-hotels.com. General travel sites, such as www.orbitz.com, www.hoteldiscounts.com, or www.expedia.com, are very efficient. You'll also find deals that are only available to those booking online.

PRICE CODE

Each resort's listing includes a symbol that represents the price range for a standard room for one weekend night during high season. The figure is based upon double occupancy and excludes tax. Be aware that these rates are estimates only and that actual prices may vary based on room availability.

$	**$99 to $148**
$$	**$149 to $209**
$$$	**$210 to $379**

Reno

Atlantis Casino Resort **$**
3800 South Virginia Street
(775) 825-4700, (800) 723-6500
www.atlantiscasino.com

The only thing missing in this lush tropical paradise is Tarzan and Jane swinging from a vine over the 21 tables. With its thatched canopies, floral carpet, and jungle foliage, Atlantis is a touch of Tahiti in southwest Reno. Like many gaming resorts, it started small. In 1972, it was the Golden Road Motor Inn and had one restaurant, the Copper Kettle. But with steady growth and major expansion, today Atlantis offers 1,000 rooms, seven restaurants, and a full array of entertainment options.

If you like the tropics, you'll love Atlantis; the jungle theme seems to envelop you. From the colorful parrots talking at the buffet to the exotic fish swimming in the steak house, this resort is fully themed. Even the names of the restaurants—Purple Parrot and Toucan Charlie's—reflect the tropics. You can't miss the signature landmark, the huge glass Skyway that connects the parking area with the main casino. With twin Grecian columns, the Skyway depicts the Lost City of Atlantis and offers Reno's only gaming with a view.

Guests can choose from rooms or Jacuzzi suites in the hotel towers or from comfortable standard guest rooms in the economy motor lodge. All accommodations feature 24-hour room service, in-room keno, and deluxe amenities. Some tower rooms have mountain or city views. And, for the comfort of all guests, Atlantis has a high-tech environmental control system that creates an almost smoke-free atmosphere.

---

i

For a bird's-eye view of the action along South Virginia Street, try dinner and drinks at the Oyster Bar at Atlantis. Its glass-enclosed skybridge hangs suspended over the busy street below.

In addition to all the excitement of the casino games, nightlife includes free cabaret entertainment in the Center Stage Cabaret and stage productions in the Atlantis Grand Ballroom. For relaxation in the casino area, guests can choose from a variety of lounge areas, including the Oyster Bar on the sky terrace. Other amenities include a swimming pool with large sundeck, a health club and spa, free valet parking, and the Atlantis Family Entertainment Fun Center with the latest in video arcade games.

Atlantis has won many "Best" awards from local newspapers, and we can certainly see why. Toucan Charlie's Buffet & Grille offers the "Best Buffet of the Millennium," a feast sure to please even the most hard-core gastronomes. It's not only the quantity but also the quality that makes this international buffet truly an event in eating around the world. And the Atlantis Seafood Steakhouse, with its exotic undersea decor and exquisite food, is easily one of the top dining spots in Reno. The resort also features six other restaurants: Cafe Alfresco for delicious pasta and salads, the Purple Parrot for American favorites, the Java Coast Espresso Lounge and Pastry Bar for quick snacks, the Oyster Bar for fresh seafood, the Sushi Bar (adjacent to the Oyster Bar), and Monte Vigna Italian Ristorante for delectable Italian specialties.

Atlantis is popular with both locals and visitors because of its frequent slot, blackjack, and keno tournaments. Locals also perceive its nightclub and restaurants as good values and "in" places to be. It's just down the street from the Reno/Sparks Convention Center, so convention attendees find Atlantis a very convenient home base. But before you reserve a room here, be aware that it's about 3 miles from downtown Reno, and the next nearest casino is several blocks away.

If you're a skier, be sure to inquire about ski packages.

Circus Circus Hotel/Casino—Reno $
500 North Sierra Street
(775) 329-0711, (800) 648-5010
www.circusreno.com

Circus Circus Hotel/Casino—Reno opened in 1978 with the same family-oriented entertainment concept as the immensely successful Circus Circus in Las Vegas. From its original 104 hotel rooms, the resort has grown to encompass 4 city blocks, including 1,572 rooms and suites. Connected by skybridges to Silver Legacy Resort Casino and the Eldorado Hotel/Casino Reno, Circus Circus is part of a tri-property complex that offers 20 restaurants and more than 200,000 square feet of gaming space.

Circus Circus has been a family destination for years because of its live circus acts on the Midway Stage and its carnival-style arcade (see the Attractions chapter for details). While recent renovations have toned down the original hot pink decor in favor of a classic turn-of-the-20th-century European motif, it's still a three-ring circus complete with clowns, balloon sculptures, and brightly colored stuffed animals everywhere.

Circus Circus not only has entertainment for the whole family but affordable accommodations and meals, too. It has six restaurants: The Steakhouse, the Courtyard Buffet, the Main Street Deli & Ice Cream Shoppe, the Americana Cafe, Kokopelli's Sushi, and Bonici Brothers Pizzeria. The resort offers free shuttle service to and from Reno/Tahoe International Airport and complimentary garage and valet parking on the property. Although this resort is best known for its family appeal, it's also popular with adults because of its choice VIP and executive suites.

Eldorado Hotel/Casino Reno $
345 North Virginia Street
(775) 786-5700, (800) 879-8879
www.eldoradoreno.com

When it opened in 1973, the Eldorado Hotel/Casino's location north of the world-famous Reno Arch was considered dubious. The heartbeat of downtown Reno gaming was several blocks south, literally on the other side of the railroad tracks. But today the Eldorado is in the center of the action, part of a tri-property complex that also includes the Silver Legacy Resort Casino and Circus Circus Hotel/Casino—Reno gaming resorts.

The Eldorado Hotel/Casino Reno is an upscale resort in the heart of downtown Reno. ELDORADO HOTEL/CASINO RENO

Family-owned and -operated, the Eldorado's success is a testament to hands-on personal management. The attention to detail is everywhere, from the plush linens in the rooms to the elegant interior appointments to the creative culinary delights in its 10 restaurants. Rising 25 stories above North Virginia Street, the Eldorado has 817 rooms and suites that range from deluxe king rooms to luxurious penthouse suites with whirlpool tubs and sitting and dining areas. Every room was completely upgraded during 2006 with new decor and furniture.

The unobstructed view of the Sierra Nevada mountains from many of the rooms is a delightful plus. But with such diverse entertainment available just downstairs, most guests don't spend a lot of time con-

The fountain at the Eldorado Hotel/Casino Reno exemplifies the luxury accoutrements of many resorts. ELDORADO HOTEL/CASINO RENO

templating the luxury of their rooms. After checking in, you can try your luck at one of the more than 1,800 slot machines, table games, and keno in the street-level casino. If you're a sports aficionado, you can place your bet and quench your thirst at the Race & Sportsbook and Stadium Bar, which features a huge selection of beers from all over the world.

Moving up to the mezzanine level, you can stroll along a European-style promenade lined with an eclectic array of shops, restaurants, and bars. The specialty boutiques offer fine collectibles, souvenirs, and apparel for the most ardent shoppers. The restaurants serve cuisine from around the world in everything from a casual buffet setting to an elegant formal atmosphere. You can enjoy fine Italian dining in one of three settings at La Strada: a courtyard terrace, an authentic wine cellar, or a countryside villa. You can sip beer made on-site, watch your favorite sporting event, and dance the night away in the upbeat environment of the Brew Brothers microbrewery.

At the far end of the promenade you can treat yourself to a taste of Paris in Roxy's by the Fountain of Fortune in the Grand Plaza. Although it seems a bit gaudy to some people—five ornate figures spew water toward a colorful painted sky—the fountain helps set the mood of a European sidewalk cafe. Other restaurants at the Eldorado include the Chefs' Buffet, for a sumptuous buffet; Choices Express Cafe, for American snacks and meals; Tivoli Gardens, for international entrees; and Golden Fortune, which features more than 90 Hong Kong–inspired specialties. The quality of food and the choice of wines at the Eldorado are considered some of the best in the Reno area. The owners of this resort are also part-owners of the Ferrari-Carano winery in Napa, California, so their interest in fine cuisine is well documented.

If you've come to Reno/Tahoe to see world-class entertainment, you won't be disappointed at the Eldorado. Broadway shows and headliners are regularly featured in the state-of-the-art Eldorado Showroom. You can also dance the night away in the BuBinga Lounge, one of Reno's hottest nightclubs, featuring live music and on-tap infusion drinks in an elegant atmosphere. See the Casino Nightlife chapter for details. And if this isn't enough, the resort further pampers its guests with a health spa, swimming pool, video arcade, and free valet parking.

When it's finally time to bed down for the night, Insiders know it's very important to remember where you've booked your room. Because the Eldorado is connected to Silver Legacy and Circus Circus via the promenade, it's easy to stroll from one to the other without realizing it, and it's not uncommon to see guests at any of these three resorts wandering around lost because they can't find the particular elevator that delivers them to their room. The Eldorado is decidedly upscale and appeals to guests who want to be downtown where all the action is.

Grand Sierra Resort and Casino **$**
2500 East Second Street
(775) 789-2000, (800) 501-2651
www.grandsierraresort.com

Sprawling over 148 acres inside the city limits of Reno, the Grand Sierra Resort and Casino (formerly the Reno Hilton) is pretty hard to miss. In fact, if you arrive by air at Reno/Tahoe International Airport, you often get a marvelous bird's-eye view of the resort just before touching down. When it roared into town in 1978 as the MGM Grand-Reno (complete with a real lion), it dwarfed everything else around. It had the world's largest casino, with more than 2,000 slot machines. It had the world's largest stage, with a DC-9 jet as a prop in the extravaganza *Hello Hollywood, Hello.* And it had more than 1,000 hotel rooms, which quickly doubled to more than 2,000. It was owned briefly by Bally Manufacturing and renamed Bally's Reno and then became the Reno Hilton in 1992.

As this book went to press, it had been renamed Grand Sierra Resort and Casino and was being completely renovated with luxury amenities that include the largest indoor water park in the country. Although

Station Casinos, Inc. will soon enter the Reno/Tahoe market in a big way with two regional gaming entertainment resorts. One complex will be across from Summit Sierra, the new lifestyle shopping center at the corner of Mount Rose Highway and U.S. Highway 395; the other, at the northwest corner of South Virginia Street and Kietzke Lane in Reno.

it has since been eclipsed in size by other gaming resorts in Nevada, the Grand Sierra still entertains its guests in grand style. Built around a Hollywood theme, it oozes opulence, from its enormous chandeliers to the signed pictures of movie stars lining the walls. The carpets are plush, and the ambience is quiet elegance, quite a contrast to the earsplitting din of many other casinos.

A stay at this resort is entertainment personified. Besides all the usual casino games, sports-book enthusiasts rave about the huge Race & Sports book that has set new standards of technological sophistication not found in other casinos. In addition to a vast array of huge TV screens showing live sporting events from all over the country, it has 400 seats, many with individual color monitors and writing desks.

If you should tire of the nonstop action in the full-service casino, try bowling in the 50-lane bowling alley or shopping in the large upscale shopping mall. You can even practice your golf swing at Nevada's only aquatic golf driving range, Grand Sierra Bay, and win prizes by shooting at the floating greens. Or you can play a round on the golf simulators in The Bunker. The Grand Sierra also has a large swimming pool, health club, and Fun Quest family amusement center. And when the sun goes down, the world-class fun really begins—the Grand Sierra is in the forefront for nightlife (see the Nightlife and Casino Nightlife chapters for specifics). You can let your imagination run free in the lavish stage productions in the Grand Theatre. You can dance the night away with top-name bands in The Garage Nightclub. And during the summer months, you also can see headliners in the resort's outdoor amphitheater.

And speaking of outdoors, the strange-looking contraption in the northwest corner of the parking lot is the Ultimate Rush Thrill Ride. If you can't find enough excitement within the building, you can be hoisted 180 feet to the top and free-fall 60 feet. It might be especially appealing if you've just lost a bundle in the resort's casino. For a tamer thrill you can zip around three different race tracks in a car at Ultimate Go-Karts.

To satisfy your every eating whim, the Grand Sierra has a variety of restaurants. Designed for big appetites, the Lodge Buffet offers breakfast, lunch, and dinner, all for a moderate price. For a more formal dinner setting, the Steak House specializes in gourmet continental and American cuisine. Dolce Enoteca & Ristorante serves luscious Italian entrees in a contemporary neoclassic setting. Chevy's Fresh Mex offers Mexican food in a Southwestern-themed setting, and Johnny Rocket's offers a trip back to the 1940s with its diner motif and great hamburgers and shakes.

When booking a room at the Reno Hilton, it's important to remember it's not within walking distance of other casinos or the downtown area. But with all the amenities the resort offers, maybe that's not important. It's a favorite place for all who enjoy elegance without the hustle and bustle so common to many other resorts.

Harrah's Reno **$**
219 North Center Street
(775) 786-3232, (800) 427-7247
www.harrahs.com

It's hard to speculate what casino gaming would be like without the influence of the late Bill Harrah, founder of Harrah's Casino Hotels. When he arrived in Reno in 1937 at the age of 26, Harrah learned that legalized gambling was a rough business not far removed from the card rooms and saloons of the wild, wild West. But he opened his first club, a one-room bingo parlor with six employees, and began a style of management and growth that would become industry standards over the years. Harrah reasoned that the comfort of his guests was the first priority, so customer service has always been the watchword at Harrah's. Although guests may not be aware of this philosophy, they do know that the attention to the little things makes their stay more enjoyable.

From that inauspicious beginning in 1937, Harrah's Reno has grown and prospered during the years and is now a four-star destination gaming resort. Harrah's Entertainment, Inc., is also a publicly traded corporation that operates more than 40 casino resorts in three different countries, including Harrah's Lake Tahoe and Harveys Lake Tahoe Casino Resort. Always a luxury destination for discriminating guests, the resort has recently completed new renovations of the casino area, hotel rooms, and a buffet restaurant, which was renamed Carvings Buffet. Expansion has added The Plaza at Harrah's, an outdoor entertainment arena, and the High Limit Salon, an elegant private gaming room especially for high rollers. Guests at Harrah's Reno can choose from more than 900 deluxe guest rooms and suites (including about 400 formerly operated as the Hampton Inn), each with a 100 percent satisfaction guarantee and 24-hour room service. Amenities include an extensive health club, a swimming pool, in-house massage services, and a beauty shop.

Harrah's Reno has always been known for its award-winning cuisine, and with seven restaurants to choose from, guests will never go hungry. The Steakhouse, with its impeccable service and outstanding entrees, provides a first-class dining experience for any occasion. It's also popular with locals for power lunches. A variety of fine food is also available at Café Napa, Starbucks, Cafe Andreotti, the Lucky Noodle Bar, and Carvings buffet. Bill Harrah was also a pioneer in using celebrity entertainers to attract casino customers. The Headliner Room in Harrah's Reno has

Harrah's Reno is known for its impeccable hospitality and luxury. HARRAH'S RENO

showcased literally hundreds of top-name entertainers since it first opened in 1966. Until just a few years ago, the dinner shows were legendary events because they afforded guests as well as locals a chance to dress up and "do the town." Although the attire is more casual now and only cocktails are served, the quality of entertainment remains just as high, with either headliners or stage revues playing nightly. The Headliner Room was renamed Sammy's Showroom in 1991 in honor of the late Sammy Davis Jr., who performed there more than 30 times from 1967 to 1989. The resort recently added the snazzy Sapphire Lounge to its entertainment mix, where you can dance to live music and enjoy elegant drinks and appetizers (see the Nightlife chapter for details).

Harrah's downtown locale makes it easy for guests to walk from casino to casino and also to stroll along the Truckee River, which is just a block away. It's also close to the National Automobile Museum, which houses a portion of Bill Harrah's original collection of vintage cars (see the Attractions chapter for details).

Peppermill Hotel Casino Reno **$**
2707 South Virginia Street
(775) 826-2121, (800) 282-2444
www.peppermillcasinos.com

Back in 1971, the Peppermill was a popular coffee shop known for the enormous servings of fresh fruit that accompanied almost all of its menu selections. The fresh fruit is still served today, but the coffee shop is just a small part of the full-service gaming resort that offers a tantalizing choice of first-class accommodations, entertainment, and dining options.

For lodging, guests can choose from 1,100 luxurious rooms featuring 24-hour room service, telephones with voice mail, in-room movies, and minibars. Suites with Jacuzzis and fax machines are also available. Premier dining choices include the original 24-hour coffee shop with an American and Chinese menu; the Island Buffet, with international cuisine served underneath four 26-foot-high waterfalls; the Steak House for American favorites in a casual setting; and the White Orchid, for elegant dining in an intimate, romantic environment. The $65 million expansion completed in 2000 added the Romanza Ristorante Italiano, where you can enjoy the finest cuisine of northern Italy served beneath a domed ceiling that features laser light shows set to music. Oceano is the newest restaurant, serving gourmet seafood in a stunning high-tech setting.

The outdoor pool at the Peppermill is especially beautiful; it's tucked at the base of a waterfall that cascades down a replica of a Sierra Nevada mountain. Other amenities of this first-class resort include a health club, gift shop, beauty salon, full-service concierge desk, and a free shuttle to and from downtown and the airport. Besides the casino with its several thousand slot and video poker machines and wide variety of table games, the Peppermill offers cabaret entertainment as well as celebrity headliners. The casino area of this resort is particularly busy and surrounds you with a dazzling display of flashing lights and clanging bells. If you like glitzy Hollywood-style decor, you'll love the Peppermill. For an island of calm away from this din, try the Fireside Lounge (ask for directions, because it's hidden in the sea of slot machines). With its circular gas fireplace/fountain and plush couches, it's a lovely oasis, one at the top of the list of Insiders' favorite romantic hideaways: The Fireside Lounge is well known as a great place for marriage proposals. However, if the Fireside Lounge is not for you, you're almost guaranteed to be just steps from your favorite drink at any time; a variety of other bars are scattered around the casino for the ultimate convenience of the guests.

When completed by the end of 2006, a $230 million expansion project will add an all-suite hotel tower, additional casino, bar, retail and restaurant space, a new two-story nightclub, and a state-of-the-art parking plaza.

The Peppermill is close to the Reno/Sparks Convention Center and to shopping at Meadowood Mall (see the Shopping chapter). If you're in the mood to walk and commune with nature, Virginia Lake, with its 1-mile walking path, is just a block away.

Silver Legacy Resort Casino **$$**
407 North Virginia Street
(775) 325-7401, (800) 687-8733
www.silverlegacyreno.com

When Silver Legacy Resort Casino opened in 1995, it redefined the Reno skyline. Its 38 floors of gleaming glass and concrete make it a vivid landmark, but it's the massive sphere alongside it that really catches your attention. Initially criticized by local residents as being ugly, tasteless, and ordinary, the big globe is the world's largest composite dome and measures 180 feet in diameter. To find out what happens inside the dome, see the description of the Mining Machine at Silver Legacy in the Attractions chapter.

As part of the tri-property complex that also includes Circus Circus Hotel/Casino—Reno and the Eldorado Hotel/Casino Reno, Silver Legacy's street-level exterior takes you back to the 1800s with turn-of-the-20th-century storefront facades. This same theme is carried out inside the resort, where you'll find rich, dark woods and vibrant furnishings reminiscent of Nevada's silver-mining days.

If you take the time to really look around the public areas of the property, you'll be surprised at the number and quality of antiques and collectibles that are casually displayed everywhere. You'll see an authentic Wells Fargo stagecoach, complete with leather baggage holders and straps; a colorful carousel that was handmade in 1910; and countless smaller items, such as bronze streetlights, old-time model planes, and antique cash registers. But you really can't miss the 43 pieces of the Mackay Silver Collection that are beautifully displayed in the grand hotel lobby. The entire 1,300-piece collection was commissioned in 1876 by the late John W. Mackay, a silver baron, for his wife, Marie Louise. Mackay sent a half ton of silver from a Comstock mine in Virginia City, Nevada, to Tiffany & Company in New York, where it took 200 men two years to craft the service. The dies were later destroyed so the pattern would truly be one of a kind.

Sprawling over 2 blocks of downtown Reno, Silver Legacy has 1,720 guest rooms and suites. Amenities include an outdoor swimming pool and sundeck, a health spa, and a beauty salon. The upscale shops, which feature elegant clothing and jewelry along with fine wines and one-of-a-kind souvenirs, are especially appealing to discriminating shoppers. The resort boasts six restaurants that offer a tempting variety of cuisine, such as the fresh shellfish served at Fairchild's Oyster Bar and the melt-in-your-mouth steaks at Sterling's Seafood Steakhouse. Silver Legacy also has several lounges and a large exhibition hall where headliners perform, plus the Catch a Rising Star comedy club (see the Nightlife chapter). Remember, when you stay at any of the three resorts in this tri-property complex, you can easily wander from one to the other because they're all interconnected with skywalks.

Insiders know this is definitely the liveliest place in Reno—it's noisy, it's crowded, and it's exciting.

Sparks

John Ascuaga's Nugget **$**
1100 Nugget Avenue
(775) 356-3300, (800) 648-1177
www.janugget.com

From a 60-seat coffee shop across the street from its current location, John Ascuaga's Nugget has grown since 1955 into one of the largest gaming resorts and convention centers in the Reno/Tahoe area. Its twin 29-story towers dominate the skyline east of downtown Reno.

While this resort doesn't have an obvious theme, luxury still abounds, from the gorgeous, year-round rooftop spa to the colorful Basque decor of its most recently opened restaurant, Orozko. A family-owned and -managed property, the Nugget prides itself on personalized service. It offers 1,661 deluxe rooms and suites, most of which provide stunning views of the Sierra Nevada mountains or the valley.

The resort is also home to the only golden rooster declared an object of art by a jury in a highly publicized trial against the U.S. Government. Weighing 206 troy ounces and standing more than 9 inches tall, the rooster was crafted to promote a new restaurant in the casino. And even though the resort had obtained permission from the San Francisco Mint to create the bird, the government prosecuted the Nugget, declaring that individuals are not allowed to have more than 50 ounces of gold unless it is an object of art. Anyway, the government lost the case; the jury declared that the rooster is art, and now he is free as a bird and can be seen near the hotel entrance.

Well known for its quality cuisine, the resort can satisfy any taste in food with its

John Ascuaga's Nugget offers property-wide wireless Internet service.

eight restaurants. A longtime Insider favorite is John's Oyster Bar, where you can sit at the bar and watch the seafood (which is flown in fresh daily) being prepared in a variety of mouthwatering ways. The Steakhouse Grill has some of the best steaks in town, and Trader Dick's provides a fully themed Polynesian dining experience, complete with an enormous saltwater aquarium over the bar, loaded with gorgeous fish.

The Nugget is also a hot spot for entertainment. The 900-seat Celebrity Showroom features headliners in a comfortable, intimate environment. Headliners also appear in the larger Rose Ballroom, which seats about 2,000 people. The Cabaret showcases musical lounge acts.

As Victorian Square is right across the street, the Nugget is an especially lively place during special events that take place there, such as the Best in the West Nugget Rib Cook-Off (see Annual Events). Victorian Square also plays host to some events connected with Hot August Nights. (See the Attractions chapter for a description of this 6-block area of Victorian Square, and the Annual Events chapter for more about Hot August Nights.)

If you're a golfer, you might be interested in playing in John Ascuaga's Nugget Amateur Challenge, the only amateur open golf event in the Reno/Tahoe area. Players of all handicaps are flighted with the top 72 competing on the final day at Grizzly Ranch in nearby Portola, California. For details on this July event, call (800) 803-6918 or click on www.renoamateurchallenge.com. (Also see the Annual Events chapter.)

North Shore Lake Tahoe

Cal Neva Resort Hotel and Casino $$
2 Stateline Road, Crystal Bay, NV
(775) 832-4000, (800) 225-6382
www.calnevaresort.com

It was once owned by Frank Sinatra. And Marilyn Monroe and John F. Kennedy were frequent guests. Known as the "Lady of the Lake," the Cal Neva Lodge (now the Cal Neva Resort) was a favorite playground for Hollywood's biggest stars during the 1940s and 1950s. But when the Nevada State Gaming Control Board learned Sinatra was also entertaining people with questionable backgrounds, it rescinded his gaming license. The lodge fell upon hard times until a succession of new owners revived it beginning in the 1980s.

Today the Cal Neva Resort retains the romance, history, and elegance of its past. It has all the touches and amenities of a modern full-service casino resort. Since the California-Nevada state line bisects the property, you can swim from state to state in the lovely outdoor pool overlooking Lake Tahoe or stand with one foot in each state in front of the enormous rock fireplace in the Indian Room. Used for special events, the Indian Room also showcases the history of Lake Tahoe with displays of Washoe Indian artifacts and pictures of early settlers.

The main lodge of the resort has been restored to its original 1937 design, including open-beamed ceilings and hardwood floors. A focal point is the Circle Bar, with its domed ceiling that contains 7,000 pieces of glittering multicolored German crystal. It's hard to beat this favorite watering hole's view of the lake at sunset. But lake views are a given here since all the private rooms as well as public areas of the lodge have large windows facing the water.

You can choose from hotel rooms in the tower or cabins and chalets on the lakeshore, including a variety of accommodations once used by celebrities. Fireplaces and patios are also available. Besides the 24-hour casino (which is the oldest originally operating casino in the country), other amenities include lakeview dining, a bar, tennis courts, a video arcade, and a full-service European health spa and fitness facility.

Romance, however, is still the name of the game for this grand old dame. The Cal Neva is one of the hottest spots for weddings at Lake Tahoe. With four distinct wedding locations and a complete bridal

The best accommodations at Lake Tahoe include beach access. HYATT REGENCY LAKE TAHOE RESORT, SPA & CASINO

and honeymoon service on-site, the resort specializes in personalized weddings performed in exquisite surroundings overlooking the lake.

For a taste of Old Tahoe with all the comforts of today, the Cal Neva is a fun place to stay. It's in the center of Crystal Bay, where you can walk to three other casinos and several more restaurants. During winter we highly recommend stopping by this historic resort to enjoy its dazzling display of half a million lights, snowfall curtains, and fantasy figures, which celebrate the winter wonderland of Lake Tahoe.

As the book went to press, negotiations were under way to convert some units to condominiums.

Hyatt Regency Lake Tahoe
Resort, Spa & Casino $$$
111 Country Club Drive, Incline Village, NV
(775) 832-1234, (800) 233-1234
www.laketahoehyatt.com

If you've stayed in Hyatts anywhere in the world, you know they offer the utmost in luxury. The Hyatt Regency Lake Tahoe Resort, Spa & Casino is a top-of-the-line mountain retreat that appeals to families, couples, and groups. Tucked away in a splendid forest of pine trees on the shore of Lake Tahoe, the resort has a variety of luxurious accommodations, including deluxe alpine guest rooms, suites, and beachfront cottages. Phase one of a $60 million renovation of the property has transformed the Hyatt into a turn-of-the-20th-century grand old lodge complete with all the modern amenities today's discriminating travelers look for. Phase two of the renovation involved complete demolition of the Aspen Terrace wing of the resort along with its pool/jet tub area and health club. A wing with 150 additional guest rooms and suites plus a state-of-the-art spa was completed several years ago.

Decorated with natural pine, distressed

wood, and leather furnishings, the guest rooms reflect the environment of the lake. All rooms have private butler servibars, two phones, in-room safes, and cable TV that includes more than 100 movies to choose from. The suites are larger and offer either a lake or mountain view, plus parlor rooms that separate the bedrooms.

Two-bedroom cottages situated on the resort's private beach are also available and include fireplaces in the parlor rooms, private decks overlooking the lake, and wet bars. Several units also have kitchens.

Like many Hyatts, this resort also has a Regency Club with VIP services and amenities such as morning newspaper delivery, nightly turndown, bathrobes, and access to the Regency Club Lounge.

A stay at this resort can be as relaxed or as fast-paced as you want it to be. With magnificent views of the lake and mountains, many guests are perfectly content to just unwind and enjoy the scenery from a comfortable chair on the beach. But for those looking for more activity, the Hyatt provides enough variety to keep guests entertained around the clock. Besides the casino, the resort offers tennis courts, heated pools and spa, a health club, a video game room, and shops.

If this resort is in your price class, it can be a great choice for families because Camp Hyatt offers a comprehensive, supervised activity program for children of guests (see the Kidstuff chapter for details). The restaurants offer four distinct dining styles—Pacific Rim and Italian food is served in Ciao Mein Trattoria, casual cuisine in the Sierra Café, sports-bar favorites in Cutthroat's Saloon, and hearty American and continental entrees in the Lone Eagle Grille.

A favorite with locals, the Lone Eagle Grille is a must-stop, if only for a drink. With two huge rock fireplaces and a cathedral-like beamed ceiling, it's Old Tahoe personified. The interior is warm and the view of the lake, dazzling. On cold days, it's a special treat to bundle up and sip your favorite drink by the outdoor firepit on the grille's lakeshore deck.

The Hyatt is close to Diamond Peak Ski Resort, golf courses at Incline Village, and a variety of hiking trails.

South Shore Lake Tahoe

Harrah's Lake Tahoe **$$$**
U.S. Highway 50, Stateline, NV
(775) 588-6611, (800) 427-7247
www.harrahs.com

When the late legendary gaming pioneer Bill Harrah first set eyes on the Gateway Club in Stateline, he was amazed that such a small, run-down establishment could be making so much money. But location was the key, as the club sat on the border between California and Nevada at beautiful South Shore Lake Tahoe. Harrah bought it, remodeled it, and reopened it as Harrah's Lake Tahoe in 1955. The rest is history, as the saying goes. With his unique management style, Harrah crafted a five-star resort that has been called the Cadillac of gaming resorts. (See the listing for Harrah's Reno in this chapter for details about Mr. Harrah.)

The hotel is a vision of luxury. Each room includes a baylike window, several telephones, TVs, and two bathrooms. Although it's an 18-story high-rise, the hotel's earthen colors blend perfectly with the surrounding Lake Tahoe landscape. The natural textures of the interior also reflect the mountains, giving guests the feeling they are in a splendid alpine lodge. In its dedication to providing the finest in comfort and luxury, Harrah's is frequently refurbished. Recently the resort completed a $33 million renovation of the 16th and 18th floors and a complete remodel of the casino area.

But the luxury doesn't stop there. In typical Harrah's style, the cuisine in its restaurants is also world-class. At Friday's Station Steak & Seafood Grill on the 18th floor, you can enjoy a moderately priced dinner with a million-dollar view of Lake Tahoe. There is an equally spectacular view from the top floor at the Forest Buffet, where you can enjoy a bountiful buffet. Or, if your idea of a view is a river, you can eat in a grove of aspens with a river running through it in the American River Cafe.

The shining star of all the restaurants, including both a setting and a menu sure to please even the most discriminating gourmet, is The Summit. It's intimate, it's exclusive, and it's difficult to get in, but if you're lucky enough to get a reservation, we guarantee you won't be disappointed. Set in the penthouse suite where Sammy Davis Jr., Frank Sinatra, and Wayne Newton stayed when they appeared in the show room, The Summit provides a dining experience you will not soon forget. For reservations call (775) 588-6611. If you're not up to the fine dining, you can always enjoy the view from Cliché just across the hall. Featuring distinctive wines and 50 brands of cigars, it's one of the most elegant bars in the Lake Tahoe area.

And what would a casino resort be like without live entertainment? The South Shore Room has been a must-stop for celebrity entertainers since it opened in 1959; the roll call of past and present performers reads like a list of "Who's Who in Entertainment." Although it used to include dinner and dressing up, the shows are now more casual and include drinks only. Thursday through Sunday the room is transformed into the VEX nightclub from 10:00 P.M. on. Outside the South Shore Room, the show rocks on as live bands perform nightly at the Casino Center Stage.

Amenities at the hotel include a large, dome-covered swimming pool and spa, a health club, and a variety of shops. Its location in the heart of Stateline makes Harrah's Lake Tahoe appealing to guests who want to be in the center of the action. This resort is first-class in every respect, but be aware that it can be very busy, especially during high season.

Harveys Lake Tahoe Casino & Resort $$$
U.S. Highway 50, Stateline, NV
(775) 588-2411, (800) 427-8397, (800) 427-7247
www.harrahs.com

Founded in 1944 by the late Harvey Gross, Harveys Lake Tahoe Casino & Resort has the distinction of being South Shore Lake Tahoe's original casino property. It was recently acquired by Harrah's Entertainment, Inc. From its humble beginnings as a one-room gambling club, it has grown to a full-service resort with the largest hotel at Lake Tahoe. Its modern glass towers and slick decor present a striking contrast to the woodsy ambience of most other Lake Tahoe resorts.

The contemporary theme is carried through to the 740 rooms and suites, most of which offer a view of the mountains or Lake Tahoe. The rooms are large and luxurious, with all the extras expected of an award-winning property. Resort amenities include a shopping galleria, health club, swimming pool, spa, and video-game arcade.

Harveys casino boasts 52,000 square feet of gaming—with more than 1,100 slot and video gaming machines along with 100 table games. You'll find live revues along with Improv at Harveys Cabaret. The Tahoe Live Casino area also has live entertainment. It's not hard to find great food at this luxury resort; the restaurants offer enough variety to fit any mood and taste. Locals particularly prefer the Sage Room Steak House because of its absolutely mouthwatering steaks served in a casual Western environment. The newest eatery is 19 Kitchen-Bar, which was formerly Llewellyn's Restaurant. More than $1 million in remodeling created an elegant setting for the eclectic, upscale cuisine.

Since Harveys is directly across US 50 from Harrah's Lake Tahoe, guests at either of these resorts can easily walk from one to the other. This area of Stateline is the busiest at South Shore Lake Tahoe, so if you want to be in the center of the action, this is definitely the place.

Horizon Casino Resort Lake Tahoe $$
U.S. Highway 50, Stateline, NV
(775) 588-6211, (800) 648-3322
www.horizoncasino.com

Of the four gaming resorts in MontBleu

Resort Casino & Spa, Harrah's Lake Tahoe, Harveys Lake Tahoe Casino & Resort, and the Horizon Casino Resort Lake Tahoe—the latter is the least expensive and the least lavish. Formerly the Sahara Tahoe, it was refurbished in 2001 with soft pastel colors and light woods.

Accommodations include deluxe and standard rooms and, for that very special occasion, the suite formerly used by Elvis Presley. Amenities at the Horizon include the largest outdoor heated swimming pool at Lake Tahoe, three outdoor hot tubs, a shopping arcade, an amusement center, and a fitness center.

Claiming to have the "friendliest tables in Tahoe" in its 24-hour casino, the Horizon has a casual and laid-back atmosphere.

Dining choices include Josh's, which specializes in fresh seafood, and the Four Seasons, which serves American specialties 24 hours a day. To round out your evening's entertainment, you can catch family-friendly productions in the Golden Cabaret. And for a nightcap before calling it a day, you can drop in at the Aspen Lounge for a turn around the dance floor.

The Horizon appeals to families with its eight-screen movie complex and free summer events, such as Harleys at the Horizon and Hot August Nights. The Horizon is within walking distance of other casinos and shopping, and it's also close to Heavenly Ski Resort.

MontBleu Resort Casino & Spa $$$
55 U.S. Highway 50, Stateline, NV
(775) 588-3515, (888) 829-7630
www.montbleuresort.com

Formerly Caesars Tahoe, this property has recently tossed out the Roman togas in favor of a contemporary French Alp theme. The face-lift includes a new nightclub and bar along with seven restaurants and the area's largest spa. The hotel has 400-plus rooms, many with in-room Jacuzzis, and a variety of themed suites. Amenities include its full-service casino and live entertainment. Directly across from the prestigious Edgewood Tahoe Golf Course, many rooms at MontBleu enjoy gorgeous golf course and lake views. If you want the convenience of walking to other resorts, shopping, and restaurants, this hotel will be attractive to you. As this edition went to press, renovations were still not complete.

VACATION RESORTS

Although Northstar-at-Tahoe and the Resort at Squaw Creek in the North Shore Lake Tahoe area do not have casinos, these resorts offer every other year-round amenity you can think of. For an explanation of high and low seasons and general booking information, refer to the beginning of this chapter.

North Shore Lake Tahoe

Northstar-at-Tahoe $$$
California Highway 267
6 miles north of Lake Tahoe
(530) 562-1010, (800) 466-6784
www.skinorthstar.com

With its impressive array of activities and amenities, Northstar-at-Tahoe has been in a class of its own since it opened in 1972. From the wooded slopes of Mt. Pluto, where you can hike, bike, and ski down a dormant volcano, to the pristine meadows of Martis Valley, where you can golf and hike, Northstar offers a mountain vacation that is hard to beat. Expansion of the Village at Northstar at the base of the ski area has recently added 100 luxury condominiums and an ice-skating rink along with a plethora of new boutiques, restaurants, and galleries.

More than 300 on-site lodging units range from hotel-type rooms to condominiums to spacious mountain homes. Accommodations feature fireplaces, color TVs, VCRs, and telephones. All units, except rooms in the Village Lodge, have fully equipped kitchens.

Winter sports include downhill skiing and snowboarding on 2,420 acres of mountain terrain, cross-country skiing on 50 kilometers of groomed trails, sleigh rides, tubing, and snowmobile and dog-sled tours. Kids especially enjoy the five terrain parks and two pipes. See the Winter Sports chapter for details.

The resort shifts gears in summer, but the fun doesn't stop. Guests can enjoy golf at Northstar's challenging 18-hole course (see the Golf chapter), mountain biking in the park, free tennis on its 10 outdoor courts, horseback riding and guided nature hikes on mountain trails, and fly fishing at Sawmill Lake. Northstar also has two outdoor heated swimming pools, spas, saunas, and a fitness center. It's the perfect place for families because all activities have special provisions for children, including special ski and golf packages, an adventure camp, and the Minors' Camp child-care center.

During winter the resort serves breakfast and lunch at the Big Springs Day Lodge at the top of the gondola and lunch at the top of Mt. Pluto at the Summit Deck & Grille. The clubhouse at the golf course offers casual dining in summer.

Insiders agree that one of the best features of Northstar is the free shuttle that continuously runs throughout the resort. So if you arrive by car, you can just park it and leave it. When you're ready to ski, you simply call the shuttle. You'll be picked up practically at your door and transported to the base of the mountain. No more struggles through crowded parking lots with all your ski equipment. The shuttle will take you anywhere in the resort—to dinner, to the tennis courts, or to the golf course. If you're coming in just for the day to ski, you can hop on the tram that runs through the main parking area and ride it to the base of the ski hill.

When booking lodging at Northstar, be sure to inquire about special packages. There's such a variety, you're bound to find one that will save you money and make your stay more convenient. You can also reserve lodging at Northstar through some of the rental agents listed in the Vacation Rentals chapter. They rent a number of additional privately owned properties at the resort that might not be available through resort reservations. But when using an off-site rental agent, be aware that resort packages might not be available.

i

Northstar-at-Tahoe offers valet parking at the entrance to the village.

I highly recommend this resort at any time of the year for adults and families. Because of the variety of activities available on-site and the range of lodging from moderate to deluxe, it has something for everyone.

Resort at Squaw Creek **$$$**
400 Squaw Creek Road
Olympic Valley, CA
(530) 583-6300, (800) 327-3353
www.squawcreek.com

Everything about the Resort at Squaw Creek is delightfully discriminating—its location in Olympic Valley, surrounded by the magnificent jagged peaks of Squaw Valley USA; its lavishly appointed accommodations, offering the optimum in comfort and luxury; and the endless variety of year-round activities that are conveniently available just outside.

When it opened in 1990, this resort set new standards of elegance for the North Shore Lake Tahoe area. And it has been winning prestigious awards for excellence from publications ever since, including *Condé Nast Traveler, Gourmet,* and *Wine Spectator* magazines.

All guest rooms have gorgeous views of either the snow-dusted peaks or the pristine mountain meadow. They also feature custom furnishings, original artwork, refrigerators, minibars, and spacious windows that open to the fresh mountain air. Of the 403 accommodations, 200 suites are available, some with fireplaces, sitting areas, and complete kitchens.

But the stunning decor is by no means confined to the rooms—the public areas of this resort are simply gorgeous. The tasteful combination of wood, stone, and glass used to construct the buildings blends beautifully with the surrounding mountain terrain. The resort recently remodeled its lobby at a cost of $2.5 million. In summer, the exterior areas are especially enjoyable; the stone terraces and pool area offer lovely views of the landscape, including the cascading waterfall that runs through the property.

Winter activities at this premier resort include downhill skiing, snowboarding, cross-country skiing, ice-skating, sledding, sleigh rides, dogsled rides, and snowshoeing. Squaw Creek also has its own lift that gives skiers access to the lifts at Squaw Valley USA, the site of the 1960 Winter Olympics (for details on winter activities at Squaw Valley, see the Winter Sports chapter).

Summer activities include golf on the 18-hole Robert Trent Jones Jr. golf course (see the Golf chapter for more information), tennis, horseback riding, rafting, boating, hiking, mountain climbing, and biking. The resort also has a three-pool water garden with a 120-foot waterslide and the largest, most elegant spa in the Lake Tahoe area, which was recently renovated at a cost of $3 million. Additional summer activities are available at Squaw Valley USA. A variety of supervised children's programs are also offered summer and winter.

Dining can also be an exceptional experience at Squaw Creek, with four restaurants to tempt your palate. Six Peaks Grille offers family-style comfort food. Ristorante Montagna specializes in California Italian cuisine. Sweet Potatoes Deli serves delectable breakfasts and lunches and will even pack a picnic basket or backpack lunch for you to take along on a hike through the valley. Sandy's Pub serves burgers in a lively microbrew atmosphere.

If you're arriving by air at Reno/Tahoe International Airport, Squaw Creek provides transportation to the resort. It also operates a free shuttle to Squaw Valley USA. And whether you're booking winter or summer, inquire about packages because the resort offers a large assortment.

Although you can easily spend your entire vacation right on the property, Squaw Creek is just 5 miles from Lake Tahoe. If you can afford to stay at the resort, it offers the optimum in elegance. But even if you can't afford the rooms, drop by for a drink or dinner; you can still enjoy the gorgeous views. And don't be surprised if you're rubbing elbows with TV and movie stars, since the Resort at Squaw Creek is a well-known celebrity destination.

The resort recently unveiled plans to convert the guest suites to luxury condominiums, which would be sold. Many of these units would be available for rent as hotel accommodations. For information on the project go to www.squawcreekliving.com or call (800) 905-2753.

HOTELS AND MOTELS 

Because many visitors come to Nevada to gamble, most Nevada hotels in the Reno/Tahoe area have casinos. Casino owners learned years ago that by providing rooms for their patrons, they would have captive players for their gaming tables and slot machines. With the exception of the Quality Inn in Sparks and the Best Western Airport Plaza Hotel in Reno, all the Nevada hotels I recommend in this chapter have gaming. And since casino gambling's not legal in the California area of Reno/Tahoe, the hotels there don't have casinos.

The hotels in this chapter are really scaled-down versions of the gaming and vacation resorts I tell you about in the Resorts chapter. Although the hotels provide a variety of amenities, they don't offer the same level of comprehensive options as the resorts do. But if you don't want all the extras of a full-service resort, why pay for them? And if you're uncomfortable with the endless sprawl of resorts, hotels are a good alternative because usually they are smaller and quieter.

For accommodations that are more back-to-basics, motels are a good choice. While a few motels have restaurants and bars and many have swimming pools and other extras, in general they're in the business of just providing you with a clean, comfortable room for the night and not entertaining you. Notable exceptions to this are the Western Village Inn/Casino in Sparks, Nevada, and the Lakeside Inn and Casino in Stateline, Nevada, which have casinos as well. Many motels are cheaper than hotels or resorts, and their rooms may also be more readily available, especially during high season.

This list of recommended motels is not meant to be exhaustive, but as an Insider I have singled out examples of the kinds of accommodations that are available. You can find out about additional motels in the Reno/Tahoe area by calling the 800 numbers below.

The hotels and motels in this chapter accept credit cards, and most have nonsmoking accommodations and rooms that are wheelchair accessible. Since rates and availability vary with special events as well as the season of the year, check out the Resorts chapter for Insiders' advice about the easiest and most difficult times to book rooms. Be aware that during holidays and sometimes on weekends, some properties may require a minimum stay of more than one night. You can reserve accommodations by calling any of the hotels or motels directly or also by calling the Reno/Tahoe Visitors Information Center, (800) 367-7366, or Lake Tahoe Reservations, (800) 288-2463. Many of the properties listed will also allow you to make reservations online using their Web or e-mail addresses. Be sure to inquire about special rates, such as golf and ski packages. To avoid confusion about the physical addresses of some of the properties at Lake Tahoe, it's important to know that some highways are called by street names within the towns. Along North Shore Lake Tahoe, Nevada Highway 28 is called Tahoe Boulevard in Incline Village, and California Highway 28 is called North Lake Boulevard in Brockway, Kings Beach, and Tahoe City. Along Lake Tahoe's west shore, California Highway 89 is also called West Lake Boulevard. In South Lake Tahoe, California, U.S. Highway 50 is also known as Lake Tahoe Boulevard. Now, with that said, let's take a look at some of the accommodations that are available.

PRICE CODE

Each hotel or motel listing includes a symbol representing a price range for a standard room for one weekend night during high season based upon double occupancy and excluding tax. Keep in mind these rates are estimates only and that specific prices can vary according to room size and availability. I strongly suggest you call ahead to check.

$	**$35 to $60**
$$	**$61 to $90**
$$$	**$91 to $120**
$$$$	**$121 to $210**
$$$$$	**More than $210**

HOTELS

Reno

Best Western Airport Plaza Hotel $$
1981 Terminal Way
(775) 348-6370, (800) 648-3525
www.bestwestern.com/airportplazahotel

Right across the street from Reno/Tahoe International Airport, the Airport Plaza Hotel is very convenient for visitors arriving by air. In fact, if you aren't loaded down with lots of luggage, you can easily walk from the terminal to the front desk. Its 269 rooms are clean and comfortable as indicated by the property's AAA 3 Diamonds rating. The restaurant has a cozy, intimate atmosphere and is a great place for lunch, especially if you like sumptuous salad bars.

The Crosswinds Lounge offers a quiet place to relax after a long day of travel or fun. Other amenities include a putting green, a garden courtyard, an outdoor pool, and a health club. Pets are welcome. A free shuttle is available to the airport, but you'll need other transportation to local attractions.

Boomtown Casino & Hotel Reno $$
Interstate 80, 7 miles west of Reno
(775) 345-6000, (800) 648-3790
(877) 726-6686
www.boomtownreno.com

A last outpost as you head west over the summit on I-80, Boomtown Casino & Hotel Reno has always catered to travelers. Originally a bare-bones truck stop called Bill and Effie's, it has provided truckers and travelers alike a much needed shelter to wait out the winter storms that frequently close I-80.

Boomtown has continued to boom over the years, and today it's a large hotel/casino with a Hollywood western theme. It appeals to families and people traveling on a budget but is still a hangout for truckers—because where else are they treated so special? With private dining digs, accommodations, and perks for truck drivers, no wonder the parking lot is jammed with 18-wheelers, with or without a snowstorm. For more information on amenities for truckers, go to www.thetruckstop.com

Boomtown's 300-plus rooms have been remodeled recently for the added comfort of its guests. The hotel also features 29 suites and minisuites, most with Jacuzzi baths and enclosed balconies. Hotel amenities include a newly refurbished indoor/outdoor swimming pool and patio. Because the management of this resort uses modest food prices to attract both locals and travelers, eating in Cassidy's, Sundance Cantina, or the Silver Screen Buffet can be a bargain.

Boomtown is a great place for families because it has a huge Family Fun Center that kids simply adore. Its focal point is a large antique carousel built by Herschell-Spillman in 1908. But the rest of the amusements are modern and high-tech, such as the latest video games, miniature golf, virtual reality, movies, and a dynamic motion theater (see the Kidstuff chapter for more information).

For adult entertainment, Boomtown has a full-service casino with live entertainment in the Can Can Cabaret Lounge nightly except Monday. RVers have also found that the RV park at this resort is a great base camp because it's in between Reno and Lake Tahoe. I tell you more about it in the Camping and RVing chapter.

When staying at Boomtown, keep in mind it's not within walking distance of other casinos or shopping because it's 7 miles west of Reno, though there is a shuttle to the downtown area and to the airport.

Club Cal Neva **$$**
140 North Virginia Street
(775) 323-1046, (877) 777-7303
www.clubcalneva.com

When Club Cal Neva opened in Reno in 1962, you could buy breakfast in the coffee shop for 65 cents. Since then, the property has grown from a small gaming establishment to a large hotel/casino—but the breakfast is only 99 cents.

In spite of recent renovations that have made it more competitive with glitzy downtown resort casinos, the Club Cal Neva still looks to its past to offer Nevada-style hospitality reminiscent of gaming's earliest days. If you're a comparison shopper, you'll do well here because food and room prices are very reasonable. Amenities include six eateries and a variety of bars along with a casino boasting more than 1,000 slots. One of the biggest selling points of Cal Neva is its downtown location next to theaters, galleries, special events, and the Truckee River.

Fitzgeralds Casino/Hotel Reno **$$**
255 North Virginia Street
(775) 785-3300, (888) 465-4329
www.fitzgeraldsreno.com

If you've always wanted to visit the Emerald Isle but never made it, you can sample Irish hospitality in the Nevada desert at Fitzgeralds Casino/Hotel Reno. The luck of the Irish is alive and well in this Irish-themed hotel that's situated right beside the world-famous Reno Arch in downtown.

Constructed in 1976, the 351 rooms are spacious and comfortable and offer stunning city and mountain views. The Fitz, as Insiders call it, has three restaurants—Molly's Garden Restaurant, Limericks Pub and Grille, and Lord Fitzgerald's Feast and Merriment buffet. You can easily walk to other downtown casinos and restaurants when staying at the Fitz. (See the Nightlife chapter for more information.)

Holiday Inn Reno Downtown **$$$**
1000 East Sixth Street
(775) 786-5151, (888) 465-4329
www.holiday-inn.com

You can get a hot dog and a beer at Club Cal Neva for just $1.50.

It's hard to tell what you'll get at a Holiday Inn these days, as there doesn't seem to be a generic standard for them anymore. But the Holiday Inn Reno Downtown is a cut above most, including 283 comfortable rooms in a high-rise that affords gorgeous mountain views. The hotel also has a restaurant, an outdoor swimming pool, a fitness facility, a game room, and an airport shuttle. It's adjacent to Diamond's Casino. Pets are welcome and are even provided their own outside walking area.

Just down the street from the Reno Livestock Events Center, this hotel is ideally located if you're attending events there, such as the Reno Rodeo or the Nevada State Fair (see the Annual Events chapter for details about these events). But it's a little remote from downtown, so don't expect to walk to other casinos or attractions. The hotel's complimentary shuttle will take you anywhere you want to go within a 1-mile radius, which includes downtown Reno.

Sands Regency Casino and Hotel **$$**
345 North Arlington Avenue
(775) 348-2200, (866) 386-7829
www.sandsregency.com

The Sands Regency advertises itself as "Reno's greatest getaway destination for the value conscious visitor." If you're traveling on a budget and don't need five-star digs, we suggest you check this place out. Its 800 rooms are supposedly the largest standard rooms in downtown Reno; I haven't measured them all but will take the hotel's word on this. Amenities include five restaurants, several bars, a full-service casino, a health club, a beauty salon, airport transportation, and the largest outdoor swimming pool in downtown. The Sands promotes pool parties and volleyball games to attract young singles. Nighttime entertainment includes the Funny Bone Comedy Club along with lounge acts at the Tequila Bar. This hotel is popular with bus tours and groups, so it can be very hectic at times.

Siena Hotel Spa Casino **$$$$**
1 South Lake Street
(775) 327-4362, (877) 743-6233
www.sienareno.com

Hugging the banks of the Truckee River in downtown Reno, the Siena Hotel Spa Casino is a year-round "boutique" hotel dedicated to fine service in the European tradition. Modeled after a Tuscan villa, it offers discriminating travelers luxury amenities in an intimate setting. The 185 rooms and 29 suites range in size from 300 to 1,200 square feet and include such high-tech amenities as interactive Web TV, high-speed Internet access, and two-line speakerphones with dataports. To make your stay even more comfortable, the hotel also supplies robes and slippers, minibars with refrigerators, and European-style linens. Specialty rooms and suites on the top floor offer butler service. on-premise dining options include Lexie's on the River, for fine Italian dining overlooking the river, and the 24-hour Contrada Cafe. Wine lovers especially enjoy Enoteca, a delightful wine bar that offers gourmet appetizers and tastings. Other on-site amenities include a 24-hour casino, live entertainment, and a full-service European health spa. In the location formerly occupied by the Holiday Hotel (which was demolished as part of the construction), this classy new property is in the forefront of downtown renewal. Its location on the river is reason enough to stop by, if only for drinks and dinner.

Sparks

Quality Inn **$$**
55 East Nugget Avenue
(775) 358-6900, (800) 548-5798
(877) 424-6423
www.qualityinn.com
www.choicehotels.com

If you don't want to fight your way through the slot machines to find guest registration, you can find your comfort zone at the Quality Inn. Absent a casino, it's just a regular hotel. But the 220 rooms are clean and modern, and hotel extras include an outdoor swimming pool, spa, game room, bar, and a free 24-hour shuttle to the airport and around Sparks. It's just down the road from Victorian Square, where special events are held (see the Annual Events chapter for a list).

Silver Club Hotel/Casino **$$**
1040 Victorian Avenue
(775) 358-4771, (800) 905-7774
www.silverclub.com

You can't get much closer to the action at Victorian Square in downtown Sparks than the Silver Club Hotel/Casino. It offers 206 moderate rooms, four restaurants, several bars, live entertainment in the casino, and an airport shuttle. If you're in town Labor Day weekend for the Best in the West Nugget Rib Cook-Off, it's right outside the door (see the Annual Events chapter).

North Shore Lake Tahoe

Sunnyside **$$$$**
1850 West Lake Boulevard, Tahoe City, CA
(530) 583-7200, (800) 822-2754
www.sunnysideresort.com

It's warm, it's romantic, and it's cozy. Sunnyside is everything you could hope for in an intimate Old Tahoe lodge. Insiders know it as a favorite watering hole and place to be seen, especially on the large deck overlooking the marina during summer.

If you're lucky enough to book one of the 23 unique rooms here, your stay is bound to be a delightful alpine experience. The ambience of both the public areas and the individual rooms can best be described as one of rustic elegance. While the rock fireplaces and heavy wooden beams give it a snug atmosphere, the overall feeling is light and open because of the large windows that face Lake Tahoe and afford gorgeous views of the water and mountains.

The small lounge on the mezzanine level is especially delightful; you can curl up in a comfortable chair away from the people below and drink in the beauty of the lake.

There's a full-service restaurant and bar, and hotel guests are treated to both a complimentary continental breakfast and afternoon tea.

Reservations are highly recommended for the Sunnyside—to book a room for a weekend in July or August, you'll need to call at least six months in advance. Check the Web site during winter for special ski packages.

Even if you can't book a room here, you should stop by to eat or drink, since it's a great people-watching place. Don't be discouraged by the difficult parking situation, particularly in summer—just be creative, as it's well worth the effort. Sunnyside is 2 miles south of Tahoe City on CA 89.

Tahoe Biltmore **$$**
5 Nevada Highway 28, Crystal Bay, NV
(775) 831-0660, (800) 245-8667
www.tahoebiltmore.com

Built in 1946 as the Tahoe Biltmore, this hotel has had a succession of names through the years, including the Cal-Neva Biltmore and the Nevada Lodge. In 1986 the present owners decided to call it by its original name, and it is again the Tahoe Biltmore.

One of the oldest hotel/casinos at Lake Tahoe, the Biltmore boasts an interesting history of appearances by big-name stars, including Rowan and Martin, Regis Philbin, and Phyllis Diller, who reportedly shocked theatergoers with her vivid green hair. The hotel also claims to have a resident ghost—a showgirl named Mary who was murdered in her room and whose spirit has reportedly been seen by employees and guests throughout the years.

The main casino tower has 47 recently refurbished rooms with room service, bell service, and lake views. The other 45 rooms are motel-style accommodations and are located at the rear of the property.

Besides the full-service casino, amenities include a swimming pool, several restaurants, and a sports bar. The Biltmore is known by Insiders to offer some of the best values in rooms and food at Lake Tahoe. Check the Web site for ski packages and manager's specials. It's also within easy walking distance of several other casinos and restaurants. Be sure to ask about membership in Club Biltmore, a cash-back players club that entitles members to prizes and perks at the hotel.

South Shore Lake Tahoe

Embassy Suites **$$$$$**
4130 Lake Tahoe Boulevard
South Lake Tahoe, CA
(530) 544-5400, (877) 497-8483
www.embassytahoe.com

Perched right on the California-Nevada state line, Embassy Suites has 400 luxurious suites with separate living rooms, minibars, microwave ovens, and coffeemakers. Guests can enjoy a complimentary breakfast each morning, a free cocktail reception each evening, and dinner in Echo Restaurant & Lounge.

On-site recreational facilities include an indoor pool, whirlpool, sauna, fitness center, and outdoor sundeck. The hotel also has heated valet parking and several shops. If it's convenience you want, Embassy Suites is a good choice because it's in the center of all the casino action and just steps from the shops at Heavenly Village, where you can hop on the gondola and be on the ski slopes within minutes. It's a beautiful upscale property sure to please most any visitor to Lake Tahoe.

MOTELS

Reno

Adventure Inn **$$**
3575 South Virginia Street
(775) 828-9000, (800) 937-1436
www.adventureinn.com

If you're in the mood for romance, Adventure Inn can help set the stage. The 45 themed rooms and suites can transport you to a variety of fantasylands such as space, the jungle, a cave, or ancient Rome. Nothing is ordinary here, from the 8-foot round- or heart-shaped beds to the in-room spas and rain-forest showers. There's even stretch-limo service to and from the inn (radius of 10 miles) and free champagne in the rooms. It's not surprising that the inn also has on-site wedding chapels.

Airport Travelodge **$$**
2050 Market Street
(775) 786-2506, (866) 473-6668
www.renotravelodge.com
This newly renovated property offers 118 accommodations that are distinctly bright and cheery. In addition to standard rooms, you can choose from executive units with kitchens or Jacuzzi rooms with cathedral ceilings. Amenities include a heated pool, hot tub, sauna, complimentary breakfast, free casino shuttle, free high-speed Internet access, and complete laundry facilities. Pets are allowed. It's especially convenient to the aiport and the Grand Sierra Resort and Casino.

Bonanza Motor Inn **$**
215 West Fourth Street
(775) 322-8632, (800) 808-3303
With 57 affordable rooms and an outdoor pool, the Bonanza Motor Inn is within walking distance of downtown casinos and attractions. It's also OK to bring your pet along.

Courtyard Reno **$$$**
6855 South Virginia Street
(775) 851-8300, (800) 321-2211
www.marriott.com
If you've stayed in the Marriott Courtyard hotels before, you won't be surprised (or disappointed, either) with this property. One of Reno's newest lodging options, it's the usual cookie-cutter Courtyard with an indoor pool and hot tub, exercise room, on-site breakfast buffet, and rooms designed for the business traveler as well as families. Because of recent commercial growth along South Virginia Street, the Courtyard is surrounded by much of the best shopping in the area, as well as a plethora of good restaurants.

Days Inn **$**
701 East Seventh Street
(775) 786-4070, (800) 448-4555
www.daysinnreno.com
If you're a Reno Rodeo fan, the Days Inn is a good location; it's just a couple of blocks from the Reno Livestock Events Center. On-site amenities for its 137 rooms include an outdoor swimming pool. Pets are OK, but you'll need transportation to casinos and attractions. A 24-hour restaurant is close by.

Extended Stay America **$$$**
9795 Gateway Drive
(775) 852-5611, (800) 804-3724
www.extendedstayamerica.com
If you want all the comforts of home during your stay in the Reno/Sparks area, a good choice of accommodation might be the suites offered by Extended Stay America. Designed like mini-apartments with separate sleeping, working, and living areas, the studio suites come with fully equiped kitchens. These are especially attractive for business travelers and families. The location of this property is close to the business parks in South Reno and many of the newer shopping malls.

La Quinta Inn—Reno **$$$**
4001 Market Street
(775) 348-6100, (866) 725-1661
www.laquinta.com
If you're arriving by air, La Quinta Inn is convenient—it's just across from Reno/Tahoe International Airport. Its 130 rooms are pleasant and modern. The inn has an outdoor swimming pool, and an airport shuttle. Pets are allowed. With free breakfast and no charge for children younger than age 18, this property is especially appealing to families.

Meadow Wood Courtyard **$$**
5851 South Virginia Street
(775) 829-4600, (800) 797-7366
www.meadowwoodcourtyard.com
Directly across the street from Meadowood Mall, the Meadow Wood Courtyard is a great location for shoppers. It's also convenient to restaurants along the busiest section of South Virginia Street. Affiliated with Super 8 Motels, this property has a year-round spa, and outdoor swimming pool, and an airport shuttle. The Sage Creek Grill & Taproom serves typical pub fare along with a selection of microbrews. Its 155 rooms are clean and comfortable, and you can bring your pet along. But it's not close to attractions or casinos, so you'll need your car or other transportation to get around.

Quality Inn South **$$$**
1885 South Virginia Street
(775) 329-1001, (877) 424-6423
www.choicehotels.com
On one of the busiest corners in southwest Reno across from Park Lane Mall, the Quality Inn South has 103 moderate rooms, a restaurant, and a delightful outdoor pool area. Although it's a bit of a hike to the casinos, the Century Park Lane movie complex is just a block away. It's also within easy walking distance of Virginia Lake.

University Inn **$$**
1001 North Virginia Street
(775) 323-0321, (877) 864-8466
www.howler.unr.edu
For economical lodging right at the University of Nevada, Reno campus, the University Inn has 173 rooms and suites that have been recently renovated. It's especially convenient if you're attending sporting or musical events at Lawlor Events Center. Availability is sometimes limited, however, by what's happening at the university. It's easier to book in summer and any time classes are not in session. The on-site restaurant, Cafe Ten-O-One, offers very affordable breakfasts and lunches. The inn is close to downtown casinos and restaurants.

If traveling in a group, it might be far more economical to rent a house or cabin for the weekend, week, or month. Check out the Vacation Rentals chapter.

Vagabond Inn **$$$**
3131 South Virginia Street
(775) 825-7134, (800) 522-1555
www.vagabondinns.com
The Vagabond Inn has 129 basic rooms and provides an airport shuttle, free continental breakfast, and an outdoor swimming pool. It's south of downtown, just a few blocks from the Peppermill Hotel Casino Reno. If you're ambitious and want an interesting outdoor walk, Virginia Lake, with its mile-long path, is close by. Pets are welcome.

Sparks

Fairfield Inn & Suites Reno/Sparks **$$**
2085 Brierly Way
(775) 355-7700, (800) 321-2211
www.marriott.com
Another Marriott property, the Fairfield Inn has 88 deluxe suites and designer rooms that appeal to both families and business travelers. An expanded continental breakfast is included in the price of the room, which is great if you're on the road with a bunch of hungry kids. The property also offers an indoor pool, whirlpool, and exercise room. Located on the easternmost edge of Sparks right off I-80, the inn is close to special events in Victorian Square and Sparks Marina Park.

Inn Cal **$**
255 North McCarran Boulevard
(775) 358-2222, (800) 550-0055
The Inn Cal has 133 modest rooms and is close to John Ascuaga's Nugget and Victorian Square (see the Resorts, Attractions, and Kidstuff chapters for information on these).

Motel 6 Sparks **$**
2405 Victorian Avenue
(775) 358-1080, (800) 466-8356
www.motel6.com
The 95 rooms at this Motel 6 are clean, comfortable, and economical. There's an outdoor hot tub, and pets are welcome.

Western Village Inn/Casino **$$**
815 East Nichols Boulevard
(775) 331-1069, (800) 648-1170
At the east end of Sparks, right off I-80, the Western Village Inn/Casino has 280 economy rooms plus a number of amenities not usually found with basic motels. It offers a casino, a variety of restaurants and lounges, and an outdoor swimming pool in a down-home Western atmosphere. It's close to Victorian Square and right next to Sparks Marina Park (see the Parks chapter). You'll need transportation to downtown Reno and other area attractions.

North Shore Lake Tahoe

The Cottage Inn at Lake Tahoe **$$$$**
1690 West Lake Boulevard, Tahoe City, CA
(530) 581-4073, (800) 581-4073
www.thecottageinn.com
Ideal for a sentimental getaway, the original cottages at The Cottage Inn at Lake Tahoe were built in 1938 in Old Tahoe style, with warm woods and knotty pine throughout. Each unit is unique; there is the Romantic Hideaway, with its two-story fireplace and natural rock Jacuzzi with waterfall, and the Enchanted Cottage, with its life-size indoor tree, as well as rooms decorated with the skier, hunter, and angler in mind. New in 2005, the Bear Lodge offers five individually themed units.

Nestled amid huge pines, The Cottage is just steps from a gorgeous beach, where you can swim, sunbathe, picnic, play volleyball, or just enjoy one of the most glorious views on the planet. Country breakfast is included, and you can enjoy it in the dining room, on the outdoor deck at the main lodge, or in your room. Wine, cookies, and coffee are available in the sitting room of the lodge, and there's also a sauna.

The delightful Cottage Inn exudes country charm with a touch of elegance, all in a natural setting. Two miles south of Tahoe City on CA 89, it's close to restaurants both in Tahoe City and along the west shore of the lake, and to skiing at Homewood, Alpine Meadows, and Squaw Valley USA. The paved bike path that runs along the lake is right outside the door.

Parkside Inn at Incline **$$$**
1003 Tahoe Boulevard, Incline Village, NV
(775) 831-1052, (800) 824-6391
www.innatincline.com
It's pretty hard to find reasonably priced accommodations in upscale Incline Village. But the 38 rooms at the Parkside Inn at Incline are a good value for the area. Tucked into tall pines close to the lake, the inn offers a cozy mountain lodge ambience with the only indoor pool, spa, and sauna facility along the North Shore. Other amenities include access to a private beach, indoor parking, limited room service, complimentary continental breakfast on weekends, a lounge with fireplace, and refrigerators in the units. As the only lodging of its kind in this area, the inn seems to be in high demand. I suggest booking far ahead, especially for high season and holidays.

Pepper Tree Inn **$$$$**
645 North Lake Boulevard, Tahoe City, CA
(530) 583-3711, (800) 624-8590
www.peppertreetahoe.com
Even though the Pepper Tree Inn is not right on Lake Tahoe (it's across the street), many of its rooms have unobstructed lake views. You can also enjoy great views of the lake and all the action in downtown Tahoe City from the swimming-pool deck and the upper-level sundeck. A hot tub is also available.

The inn has 50 rooms, many of which have been newly renovated. The accommodations are pretty basic, but the location is within walking distance of the paved path along the Truckee River, Fanny Bridge, area restaurants, the Tahoe City Marina, and the Tahoe City Golf Course. The nearest ski resorts are Alpine Meadows and Squaw Valley USA.

Sun 'n Sand Lodge **$$**
8308 North Lake Boulevard
Kings Beach, CA
(530) 546-2515, (800) 547-2515
www.sunandsandlodge.com
The accommodations at the Sun 'n Sand Lodge are average, but the location is definitely upscale—it sits right on sandy Kings Beach. A walkway outside the rooms is a great place to sit and enjoy coffee in the morning or cocktails in the evening while taking in a million-dollar view of Lake Tahoe. It's within walking distance of a movie theater, restaurants, shops, and both a miniature and regular golf course in Kings Beach. North Shore casinos are about 1.5 miles from the lodge.

Tahoe Inn **$$**
9937 North Lake Boulevard
Brockway, CA
(530) 546-3341, (800) 648-2324
www.tahoeinn-laketahoe.com
Sitting on the California-Nevada state line across from the Cal Neva Resort, the Tahoe Inn, formerly known as the Cal Neva Inn, has 90 comfortable, casual rooms. It's clean but not exactly luxurious. Some family units, and rooms with decks and patios, are available. It offers an outdoor swimming pool but no access to Lake Tahoe. You can easily walk to casinos and restaurants in Crystal Bay, Nevada.

Woodvista Lodge **$$**
7699 North Lake Boulevard
Tahoe Vista, CA
(530) 546-3839
Set amid the pines, the Woodvista Lodge is humble, but perfect for families. Its 17 rooms ring a common area in which you'll find a year-round hot tub and a play structure that will delight and entertain the kids. In summer you can also enjoy the swimming pool and Ping-Pong table. The rooms are wood-paneled and evoke country cabins; some have kitchenettes. There is no direct beach access, but the lodge is 1 mile from Kings Beach.

South Shore Lake Tahoe

Holiday Inn Express **$$$$**
3961 Lake Tahoe Boulevard
South Lake Tahoe, CA
(530) 544-5900, (800) 544-5288
www.holidayinnexpresstahoe.com
The winner of several awards for its recent upscale renovation, the Holiday Inn Express offers luxury at a reasonable price. Each of the 89 rooms and suites has a refrigerator, coffeemaker, ice, and large remote-control TV. Some suites have fireplaces, fully equipped kitchens, and private spas. Other amenities include a free continental breakfast, an indoor spa and sauna, and an outdoor swimming pool. It's a little removed from the casino action at Stateline, Nevada, but it's right across from Lake Tahoe.

Homewood Marina Lodge **$$**
5180 West Lake Boulevard
Homewood, CA
(530) 525-6728
On the quiet west shore of Lake Tahoe, the Homewood Marina Lodge has cottages and motel rooms; some include kitchens and fireplaces. You'll find an on-site outdoor restaurant and bar, summer only, as well as a private beach with an expansive lawn area.

Inn by the Lake **$$$$**
3300 Lake Tahoe Boulevard
South Lake Tahoe, CA
(530) 542-0330, (800) 877-1466
www.innbythelake.com
Across from sandy El Dorado Beach, all the beautifully appointed rooms and suites at the Inn by the Lake have private balconies. Some units have kitchens, wet bars, and refrigerators. It's a great location

Using the Internet makes it easier to shop around for hotel/motel accommodations. You can comparison shop at www.resplus.com, www.renotravel.com, or www.travelworm.com.

for skiers because Heavenly Ski Resort is just a mile away. A continental breakfast is offered daily, and there's a year-round heated swimming pool with spa and sauna. In summer you'll enjoy the miles of hiking and biking trails that are just outside the door.

Lakeside Inn and Casino $$$$
168 U.S. Highway 50, Stateline, NV
(775) 588-7777, (800) 624-7980
www.lakesideinn.com

The Lakeside Inn and Casino has many of the amenities but not the hubbub or size of larger properties at South Shore Lake Tahoe. It's a little off the beaten path and several blocks from the heart of the action near Harrah's Lake Tahoe in Stateline, Nevada. But don't sell it short; it boasts two restaurants in addition to a casino, several bars, an outdoor swimming pool, a year-round hot tub, and a gift shop.

The 124 rooms are comfortable and spacious but not elegant. Insiders know that the Timber House Restaurant is a great place for prime rib at a reasonable price. Lakeside recently underwent a $1 million renovation and now boasts the Taverna for some hot Mexican food and cool margaritas and a new sportsbook bar with more than 30 televisions.

Lazy S Lodge $$-$$$$
609 Emerald Bay Road
South Lake Tahoe, CA
(530) 541-0230, (800) 862-8881
www.lazyslodge.com

The Lazy S Lodge has cozy, rustic cottages with fireplaces and kitchenettes, and studio units with wet bars or kitchenettes, microwave ovens, and refrigerators. You'll also find a swimming pool, hot tub, and large lawn with barbecues and picnic tables.

Quality Inn & Suites $$$$
3838 Lake Tahoe Boulevard
South Lake Tahoe, CA
(530) 541-5400, (877) 424-6423
www.choicehotels.com

Tucked away in tall pines, Quality Inn & Suites has 121 standard rooms, suites, and condos, with some kitchens available. If you're too tired to drive to a restaurant after a full day's activities at Lake Tahoe, you can have a savory Indian dinner at the on-premises restaurant, the Taj Mahal.

Other amenities include complimentary continental breakfast as well as a year-round hot tub, swimming pool, courtesy shuttle to ski resorts and casinos, and a picnic and barbecue area. This establishment is about a half mile from the casinos at Stateline, Nevada.

Royal Valhalla Motor Lodge $$$
4104 Lake Shore Drive
South Lake Tahoe, CA
(530) 544-2233, (800) 999-4104
www.tahoeroyalvalhalla.com

You can't get much closer to Lake Tahoe than the Royal Valhalla Motor Lodge—it's right on the shore and has its own private beach. The lodge offers accommodations that include kitchenettes and balconies, and you'll also enjoy continental breakfast, a hot tub, and a swimming pool. The ambience of this property is very light and airy, blending the indoors with the outdoors.

Tahoe Chalet Inn $$
3860 Lake Tahoe Boulevard
South Lake Tahoe, CA
(530) 544-3311, (800) 821-2656
www.tahoechaletinn.com

The Tahoe Chalet Inn is a touch of European elegance right in the heart of South Shore Lake Tahoe. From its standard rooms to themed suites to chalets, you are sure to feel pampered and at home. One of the themed suites is the Marie

Antoinette Room (no, it doesn't have a guillotine), featuring lovely antique-style furnishings and a roaring fireplace. The inn also provides complimentary continental breakfast, an indoor spa, a heated seasonal swimming pool, and a fitness room. You also can walk to the casinos, shops, and restaurants in Stateline, Nevada.

Tahoe Tropicana Lodge **$$**
4132 Cedar Avenue
South Lake Tahoe, CA
(530) 541-3911, (800) 447-0246
www.tahoetropicana.com

The Tahoe Tropicana Lodge has great ski packages for Heavenly Ski Resort, Squaw Valley USA, Northstar-at-Tahoe, Kirkwood, Alpine Meadows, and Sierra-at-Tahoe. Just a half block from the casinos at Stateline, Nevada, and 3 blocks from Lake Tahoe, it's convenient to nightlife, restaurants, and shopping. The on-premises Greenhouse Restaurant and Bar has a cozy atmosphere of lush green plants and European stained glass. Amenities include a hot tub and free shuttle service to casinos and ski areas.

VACATION RENTALS 

For accommodations in the Nevada cities of Reno and Sparks, I recommend hotels, motels, and gaming resorts (see related chapters for these). But if you're planning on staying anywhere in the Lake Tahoe Basin, you can choose from a large selection of vacation rentals in addition to hotels, motels, and resorts. Vacation rentals include condominiums, homes, and cabins that typically offer more privacy, space, and amenities not always available in more traditional accommodations. Vacation rentals have particular appeal for visitors planning to stay longer than just a night or two. They are also popular with large groups of people such as families or several couples who are traveling together. While their biggest appeal may be a greater degree of comfort, vacation rentals can also be more economical in certain situations. Some vacationers find it cheaper to rent a home or condo rather than several hotel rooms, especially if the cost is split among several couples.

The variety of properties available is immense. For your home-away-from-home you can rent a cozy cabin tucked away in the forest, a luxurious condominium on the beach, or a private residence with a spectacular view of Lake Tahoe. The choice is yours, depending upon your budget and your expectations. Vacation rentals include fully equipped kitchens, linens, color televisions, and telephones. Many also include fireplaces, VCRs, private decks, hot tubs, saunas, microwave ovens, and washers and dryers. Some have security systems, parking garages, and access to private beaches, tennis courts, spas, and pools. Many accommodations are wheelchair accessible, and some with secure yards allow pets. Ski-in/ski-out properties and nonsmoking accommodations are also available.

The cost of rental usually depends upon the sleeping capacity, the view, the location, the amenities, and the degree of luxury. It also varies with the season. Rates can range from as low as $60 a night to as high as $2,000 or more. Top prices are charged during high season, January to mid-April and mid-June to mid-September, and premium rates also apply for bookings that include Martin Luther King Jr. Day, Presidents Day, Memorial Day, the Fourth of July, Thanksgiving, Christmas, and New Year's. Insiders know you can expect lower rates at Lake Tahoe in fall and late spring.

Most properties also require a minimum stay of two to five nights. The required length depends upon the time of year as well as the particular property requested. For longer stays, some properties can be rented on a weekly rate.

A reservation deposit is usually requested at the time of booking, and full payment plus a security deposit is due before arrival. Since cancellation policies vary, it's wise to inquire when booking. Most properties accept credit cards, but be sure to confirm this when you reserve.

Although size and amenities are considerations in choosing a vacation rental, location can be equally important in the Lake Tahoe Basin. Depending upon the season of the year and the activities you'll be pursuing, you'll want to choose a rental that is most convenient for you. If you're a nonskier, you probably won't want to pay a premium price for a ski-in/ski-out location in winter. But if water sports are your main interest, you may want to pay more to be right on the beach in summer. And if nightlife is important to you, you may want to be close to the casinos in Stateline, Nevada, or the clubs in Tahoe City. But if your idea of a vacation is hiking and cooking dinner in, you may be more comfortable in laid-back communities at the lake such as Homewood or Incline Village. The weather can also dictate your level of comfort. A secluded cabin in the woods may be wonderfully private during summer but extremely challenging to reach in winter, especially without a four-wheel-drive vehicle.

Because vacation rentals are in such demand during holidays and high season, I recommend you plan as far ahead as possible. If you decide the week before Christmas to pack up the family and spend the holidays in a winter wonderland at Lake Tahoe, don't be surprised if there's no room at the inn. Although it's easier to book during low season, I still recommend arranging your accommodations as soon as you can to avoid being disappointed.

The Lake Tahoe Basin is composed of a variety of communities, each offering its own particular personality and appeal. When choosing a vacation rental as your home base, it's a good idea to consider the ambience and amenities of each area.

COMMUNITY OVERVIEWS

North Shore Lake Tahoe

Incline Village and Crystal Bay, Nevada

An exclusive community of about 10,000 year-round residents, Incline Village is home to a growing number of people who can live anywhere—airline personnel, computer experts, and entrepreneurs who work from home offices. The governing arm, the Incline Village General Improvement District (IVGID), owns and manages several parks, golf courses, and a ski resort for residents and visitors to enjoy. The fees and access extended to residents are occasionally available to those staying in vacation rentals as well.

Just 2 miles from Incline Village, Crystal Bay is smaller and offers less shopping and fewer restaurants. But this short stretch of the Lake Tahoe shoreline seems to have it all—sandy beaches, golf, skiing, casino nightlife, and hiking. It is home to the Incline Village championship and executive golf courses and Diamond Peak Ski Resort. It's a great place for exploring the hidden beaches and coves of the lake's undeveloped east shore. Vacation rentals can be anything from posh lakefront homes to condos with a view to modest cabins.

The Reno/Sparks area offers 20,000 guest rooms within 5 miles of Reno/Tahoe International Airport.

Kings Beach and Brockway, California

Kicked back and unpretentious, Kings Beach and Brockway are less ritzy than some other areas along the lake. But if casual is the name of your game, you're bound to feel comfortable here. Skiing, golfing, and nightlife are nearby, and restaurants are decidedly informal. Vacation rentals include quiet condos in the pines, lakeview homes, and secluded chalets.

Tahoe City, California

About the same size as Incline Village, Tahoe City is especially appealing to young singles because of its nightlife, shopping, and close proximity to Squaw Valley USA and Alpine Meadows ski resorts. It's a lively community any season of the year, as visitors and residents alike use it as a jumping-off point for river rafting, biking, and winter sports. While some other communities along the North Shore seem to roll up the sidewalks at night, the night spots in Tahoe City rock on into the wee hours. Rentals include luxury home condos in the Dollar Point area, with its private beach and summer amenities.

For holiday and premium season bookings, it's usually necessary to reserve six months ahead. For specific properties, particularly homes, many visitors reserve a year in advance.

South Shore Lake Tahoe

Stateline, Nevada, and South Lake Tahoe, California

Stateline, Nevada, and South Lake Tahoe, California, may seem like one community, but they're actually two, since the state line runs through the middle of the area. But most visitors don't notice unless they spot the separate visitor centers and law-enforcement agencies. With a combined permanent population of about 35,000, which can triple during holidays, this area of the Lake Tahoe Basin is easily the most densely populated.

Stateline is home to glitzy casinos such as Harrah's Lake Tahoe, Harveys Lake Tahoe Casino Resort, MontBleu Resort Casino & Spa, and the Horizon Casino Resort Lake Tahoe. If it's nightlife you're after, this is the place—the fun goes on 24 hours a day. You'll find both Heavenly Ski Resort, which also straddles the California-Nevada state line, and Kirkwood ski area close by (see the Winter Sports chapter for details). This area of the Lake Tahoe Basin is probably a good choice for visitors looking for a more fast-paced environment. During high season, however, traffic can be a problem and parking can sometimes require creative ingenuity. Vacation rentals run the gamut, from condos on the Nevada side of Heavenly Ski Resort to luxurious executive homes on the lake to less pretentious cabins in the woods.

Old Tahoe Communities

Considered "Old Tahoe" because of their rustic charms, Homewood, Meeks Bay, Rubicon, Sunnyside, and Tahoma are small west shore communities that appeal to outdoor enthusiasts. Nightlife here may consist of a barbecue at the beach while watching the sun go down or dinner in one of the fine restaurants along the lake. The pace is slow as visitors are intent on soaking up the spectacular environment that surrounds them. For skiers, Homewood Mountain Resort, Squaw Valley USA, and Alpine Meadows are close by (see the chapter on Winter Sports). Summer visitors delight in the sandy beaches, numerous hiking trails, and historic sites in this area. A variety of vacation rentals is available, but multiunit complexes have fewer units than those in the Stateline and South Lake Tahoe areas.

Outside Lake Tahoe

Northstar-at-Tahoe
6 miles north of Lake Tahoe on California Highway 267

Although it's not on Lake Tahoe, Northstar-at-Tahoe's lovely mountain setting offers skiing, golfing, horseback riding, tennis, and hiking.

See the detailed description of Northstar in the Resorts and Winter Sports chapters. Vacation rentals at Northstar include cozy ski condos and luxurious golf-course homes.

Squaw Valley USA and Alpine Meadows
6 miles north of Lake Tahoe on California Highway 89

Not just a world-class ski resort, Squaw Valley USA is a year-round playground offering an amazing array of activities for any season. Alpine Meadows ski resort, just over the ridge from Squaw, offers a quieter environment with world-class skiing in the winter and hiking in the summer. Vacation rentals at these resorts can include affordable mountain hideaways, posh condominiums, and large homes. (See the detailed descriptions of these resorts in the Winter Sports chapter.)

INDIVIDUAL PROPERTIES

Because the sheer number and variety of vacation rentals available in the Lake

Tahoe Basin is exhaustive, I can't begin to list them all. But to give you a better idea of the kinds of properties you can rent, I'll take a peek at some of the individual accommodations.

North Shore Lake Tahoe

Chinquapin
3600 North Lake Boulevard
Tahoe City, CA
(530) 583-6991, (800) 732-6721
www.chinquapin.com
Secluded along a mile of lakefront property, Chinquapin offers luxurious condos with one to four bedrooms. Although close to the hustle and bustle of Tahoe City, the complex is a quiet oasis for enjoying the beauty of the lake and the surrounding forest.

Club Tahoe
914 Northwood Boulevard
Incline Village, NV
(775) 831-5750, (800) 527-5154
www.clubtahoe.com
Centrally located in beautiful Incline Village, Club Tahoe provides guests with a vast array of on-site amenities including tennis courts, spas, a swimming pool, a game room, an exercise area, and a lounge. Each fully equipped two-bedroom condo will sleep up to six people. These modestly priced accommodations appeal both to families and couples.

Tahoe Edgelake Beach Club
7680 North Lake Boulevard
Tahoe Vista, CA
(530) 546-5974
www.tahoeedgelake.com
In the laid-back Kings Beach area, Tahoe Edgelake Beach Club has lakefront and lakeview accommodations along its private sandy beach. Amenities include a seasonal swimming pool and an outdoor hot tub. Boat owners can also take advantage of its pier and buoys.

South Shore Lake Tahoe

Camp Richardson Resort
1900 Jameson Beach Road
South Lake Tahoe, CA
(800) 544-1801
www.camprichardson.com
A favorite for families because kids have plenty of room to roam, Camp Richardson has rustic accommodations near historic sites, hiking trails, and beaches. Its corrals offer pack trips into nearby wilderness areas, and it has a complete outdoor sports center for a variety of summer activities.

Inn at Heavenly
1261 Ski Run Boulevard
South Lake Tahoe, CA
(530) 544-4244, (800) 692-2246
www.innatheavenly.com
www.firesidelodge.com
Hidden among two acres of pines, the Inn at Heavenly offers guests country mountain decor with a touch of luxury. Although constructed of logs, the inn is anything but rustic as the fireplaces are meticulously crafted and the woodwork is hand-stenciled. You can enjoy breakfast in your kitchenette or join guests in the nearby lodge for an expanded continental breakfast. A dog-friendly resort, the inn lists doggie activities on its Web site. The owners also operate the Fireside Lodge on Emerald Bay Road.

Lakeland Village Beach & Ski Resort
3535 Lake Tahoe Boulevard
South Lake Tahoe, CA
(530) 544-1685, (800) 822-5969
www.lakeland-village.com
In the heart of the South Shore area, Lakeland Village Beach & Ski Resort has all the amenities for a perfect vacation—a private, sandy beach; tennis courts; swimming pools; and beachside games. The underground parking garage is especially convenient in winter, and the resort runs free shuttles to ski areas and casinos.

Helpful Web Sites

Whether you're looking to book accommodations or just want general information, these Web sites are a good resource:

www.reno-sparkschamber.org
www.gotahoe.com
www.virtualtahoe.com
www.tahoefun.org
www.visitrenotahoe.com
www.skilaketahoe.com
www.sparkschamber.org
www.tahoechamber.org

Pine Cone Resort
601 U.S. Highway 50 East
Zephyr Cove, NV
(775) 588-4811, (800) 568-2463
www.michelsens.com
It's quaint, it's rustic, and it has all the comforts of home. In a lovely forest overlooking Lake Tahoe, Pine Cone Resort is a small complex of just 22 units. While not luxurious, it's a favorite for families, especially in summer.

The Ridge Tahoe
400 Ridge Club Drive, Kingsbury, NV
(775) 588-3131, (800) 334-1600
www.ridge-tahoe.com
Perched high above Lake Tahoe on the Nevada side of Heavenly Ski Resort, The Ridge Tahoe is the ultimate in convenience for skiers. With its own gondola connecting the condo complex to the ski resort lifts, skiers can be on the slopes in a matter of minutes. Although its location on the eastern side of the mountain range blocks a view of Lake Tahoe, many units have panoramic vistas of the Carson Valley to the east. Just 10 minutes from the casinos at Stateline, the two-bedroom units at The Ridge Tahoe are a handy location year-round.

Tahoe Seasons Resort
3901 Saddle Road, South Lake Tahoe, CA
(530) 541-6700, (800) 540-4874
(866) 469-8222
www.tahoeseasons.com
At the base of the tram on the California side of Heavenly Ski Resort, Tahoe Seasons Resort provides easy access to skiing as well as all the activities in the South Shore area. In addition to all the amenities of a condominium, it has a restaurant, room service, a fireside lounge, and a gift shop. And you can choose from a variety of lodging packages tailored to meet your individual needs.

RENTAL AGENCIES

Although you can contact individual properties directly, I recommend using rental agencies because they have large lists of every type of property available. With your budget and specific needs in mind, they can find the accommodation that is exactly right for you. Rental agencies can also assure you that your property is clean and well maintained and that everything included is in good working order. Most agencies have conveniently located offices for check-in and checkout, eliminating a lot of the hassle typically involved in arrival and departure. Some are also full-service real estate offices and are described in more detail in the Relocation chapter.

Space doesn't permit me to list all the rental agencies in the Lake Tahoe area, but here's a few to help you find that perfect vacation hideaway. I recommend clicking onto their Web sites, which will allow you to preview the listings and even book online.

Accommodation Station
2516 Lake Tahoe Boulevard
South Lake Tahoe, CA
(530) 542-5850, (800) 344-9364
www.tahoelodging.com
This agency handles rentals in the South Shore Lake Tahoe area with more than 100 condos and homes priced from $100 to $1,000 per night.

Coldwell Banker
120 Country Club Drive
Incline Village, NV
(775) 831-4800, (800) 572-5009
www.cbvillagerealty.com
Coldwell Banker manages about 65 cabins, condos, and homes in Incline Village that rent for $85 to $650 nightly.

Lake Tahoe Accommodations
2048 Dunlap Drive, Suite 4
South Lake Tahoe, CA

800 Southwood Boulevard, Suite 112
Incline Village, NV
(800) 544-3234
www.tahoeaccommodations.com
One of the largest rental agencies in the Tahoe area, this company has 400 units ranging in size from studio apartments to seven-bedroom homes. The properties are scattered all around the lake, and nightly rates run anywhere from $99 to $1,700.

Lake Tahoe Lodging
212 Elk Point Road, Suite 554
Zephyr Cove, NV
(775) 588-5253, (800) 654-5253
www.laketahoelodging.com
With more than 150 properties ranging from studio apartments to large homes, this company specializes in high-end luxury homes in the South Shore Lake Tahoe area. You can bed down for the night in digs costing anywhere from $75 to $3,000 per night.

Northstar-at-Tahoe
California Highway 267, 6 miles north of Lake Tahoe
(530) 562-1010, (800) 466-6784
www.skinorthstar.com
About 250 rental units are available at Northstar, and they range from hotel-type rooms to condominiums to mountain and golf course homes.

South Lake Tahoe Reservation Bureau
599 Tahoe Keys Boulevard
South Lake Tahoe, CA
(530) 544-5397, (800) 698-2463
www.tahoevacationguide.com
This large reservation bureau has about 200 condos, homes, and cabins in the South Shore Lake Tahoe area, with a price range of $125 to $1,200 a night.

Squaw Valley USA
1960 Squaw Valley Road
Olympic Valley, CA
(530) 583-5585, (800) 403-0206
www.squaw.com
This rental office can find you digs right at Squaw or anywhere else in the Tahoe area.

Tahoe Rental Connection
2241 James Avenue, Suite 3
South Lake Tahoe, CA
(530) 542-2777, (800) 542-2100
www.tahoerentalconnection.com
The Tahoe Rental Connection handles property on the California side of Lake Tahoe only. Its 120 units rent for $85 to $600 nightly.

Tanager Realty Vacation Rentals
570 Lakeshore Boulevard
Incline Village, NV
(775) 832-4646, (800) 948-7311
www.tanager.net
One of the most prominent realty offices in the North Shore Lake Tahoe area, Tanager specializes in properties in Incline Village.

CAMPING AND RVing 

Whether your idea of a night in the outdoors involves throwing a sleeping bag on the ground or settling into a fully equipped motor home complete with a satellite dish, the welcome mat is out at a variety of campgrounds and RV parks in the Reno/Tahoe area. These facilities run the gamut in terms of amenities and luxuries, from sites with just a water spigot to luxury mini-neighborhoods with swimming pools and convenience stores.

Although most of the RV parks in Reno/Sparks are in urban areas, many have trees and attractive landscaping, and some even provide access to the Truckee River. Conveniently located near casinos and major attractions, they offer RVers attractive accommodation options at considerable savings over hotels and motels. If you're looking for more of a bona fide back-to-nature experience (especially if it includes a tent), however, you'd best head to the campgrounds and RV parks in the Lake Tahoe Basin. You will find a few snazzy facilities with all the comforts of home around the lake, but most campgrounds are geared toward enjoying an awesome night sleeping under the stars.

The camping and RV facilities in the Reno/Sparks area are privately owned and are open year-round. Rates vary from season to season, with the highest fees charged in July and August and during special events (see the Annual Events chapter for details). Facilities in the Lake Tahoe area are owned either privately or by government entities. They are open usually from Memorial Day weekend through October, with the exception of General Creek campground at Sugar Pine Point State Park and Tahoe Valley, which are open all year.

This chapter is organized using the usual four geographical areas: Reno, Sparks, North Shore Lake Tahoe, and South Shore Lake Tahoe. You'll find a thumbnail sketch of some of the camping and RVing facilities, listing basic amenities and describing general ambience. Included as well are approximate rates, but keep in mind fees may have changed by the time you book space. The listings aren't meant to be all-inclusive, but rather a sample of the kinds of options you can choose from. For more information on the amenities and terrain surrounding campgrounds located in area parks, such as D. L. Bliss State Park in California, see the Parks chapter.

If you really want to get away from it all, you can strap on a pack and head to the backcountry, where you can make your own camp in an exquisite alpine setting. Find out where and how to do this in the Recreation chapter.

RENO

Boomtown Casino & Hotel Reno
Interstate 80 at exit 4
7 miles west of Reno
(877) 626-6686 (RV park); (775) 345-6000, (800) 648-3790 (casino)
www.boomtownreno.com

In spite of its easy access to I-80, the RV park at Boomtown Casino & Hotel Reno is quiet and almost in a world of its own. Hugging a bluff above the Truckee River, the park offers eye-catching desert and mountain views. The daily rates start at around $20 plus tax, with additional charges on the weekends, special events, and for pull-through slots. Weekly rates, available from October through April, start at around $116. If you're a member of Good Sam or AARP, be sure to show your card for a 10 percent discount. The maximum stay, regardless of time of year, is 28 days.

The park offers the basic services, including sewer, water, electric, wireless

Internet, and cable TV hookups. There are also shower and laundry facilities, a year-round hot tub, and a seasonal swimming pool. Pets are OK (there's a designated pet-walking area), but no tents are allowed. Tent trailers are allowed.

You'll find plenty of entertainment at the neighboring Boomtown Casino (see the description in the Hotels and Motels chapter). Just minutes from downtown Reno and Truckee, California (the gateway to Lake Tahoe), this park is also a convenient jumping-off spot for many other sights in the area.

Keystone RV Park
1455 West Fourth Street
(775) 324-5000, (800) 686-8559
www.keystonervpark.com

The Keystone RV Park has 104 RV sites just across the street from the Truckee River near downtown Reno. Daily rates range from about $20 to $24, depending upon the size of your RV. Weekly rates start at $130 and monthly at $330. Discounts are given for seniors. There's no maximum on the number of days you can stay.

The park provides water, electric, sewer, cable TV, free Internet access, and phone hookups. You'll find all the basics, including propane, at nearby stores. Amenities also include laundry and shower facilities. Pets are accepted upon approval, but no tents are allowed.

Reno KOA
2500 East Second Street
(775) 789-2147, (888) 562-5698
www.koa.com/where/nv/28136.htm

You can take advantage of many of the same amenities hotel guests enjoy, such as a gorgeous swimming pool and health club, when you park your rig at the RV park at the Grand Sierra Resort and Casino (formerly the Reno Hilton). Daily rates run from about $24 to $62, depending on the time of year. The maximum allowable stay is 28 days, and rates are by the day only.

The park provides water, propane, Wi-Fi, sewer, and electric hookups but no cable TV. Other amenities include a mini-mart along with laundry and shower facilities. Pets are welcome, and the cancellation policy is 24 hours. The 230 spaces are for RVs only, with no tent camping allowed. You'll be right in the middle of the action here: The Grand Sierra is a major gaming resort, with all the bells and whistles (see the Resorts and Casino Nightlife chapters for more about this classy resort).

Reno RV Park
735 Mill Street
(775) 323-3381

Reno RV Park offers a tree-shaded park for 46 RVs just a few blocks from all the casino action downtown. Daily rates run $24 to $27, weekly $154, and monthly $540. Discounts are available for Good Sam, AAA, and Golden Age members.

On-site services include sewer, water, Wi-Fi, electric, and extended cable hookups, along with laundry and shower facilities. You can fill your propane tank at the park, and the nearest mini-mart is less than a block away. Each site has its own lawn and tree, and a large, fenced grassy area is provided for the enjoyment of your canine companion. Since the park is in demand in summer, I recommend you call ahead for bookings during that time of year. Be aware the park has a 24-hour cancellation policy. Self-standing tents are allowed on the asphalt but may not be staked down into the grass.

Shamrock RV Park
260 East Parr Boulevard
(775) 329-5222, (800) 322-8248
www.shamrockrv.com

Shamrock RV Park offers 121 sites just off U.S. Highway 395 north of Reno. Rates are competitive, but call for specifics.

You'll find all the basic necessities, including hookups for electricity, sewer, water, telephone, free Internet, and cable TV. There are also shower and laundry facilities, a swimming pool, and propane provided on-site. The park is generally very quiet, even though you can easily walk to

Some campgrounds charge extra fees for pets, and most charge for additional vehicles.

the nearby Bonanza Casino. No tents are allowed. Pets are OK upon approval.

SPARKS

River's Edge RV Park
1405 South Rock Boulevard
(775) 358-8533, (800) 621-4792
It's pretty hard to find such an idyllic setting in an urban area. Nestled along the banks of the Truckee River, River's Edge RV Park provides 164 RV spots in a grassy wooded environment. Daily rates run from $30 to $35, with discounts available for Good Sam and AAA members. Weekly and monthly rates are available from October through April and run $183 and $475, respectively. Permanent sites are $330 a month.

In addition to the standard amenities of sewer, water, telephone, cable, and electric hookups, the park also has shower and laundry facilities. Management is in the process of adding Internet access.

To make the most of your stay in this lovely spot, I recommend a picnic on one of the tables scattered among the trees or a relaxing afternoon around the beautiful, renovated swimming pool. For a more ambitious endeavor, head west toward Reno on the Truckee River Walk, which is just outside your door, and enjoy all the delights the river has in store for you. You can check in with your pet (on approval), but no tents are allowed. The only disadvantage to River's Edge is noise from aircraft using Reno/Tahoe International Airport.

Victorian RV Park
205 Nichols Boulevard
(775) 356-6400, (800) 955-6405

When the campfire has died down, the clear skies above Lake Tahoe are perfect for stargazing.

One of the newest RV parks in the area, Victorian RV Park is a great place to stay if you're attending events such as Hot August Nights at Victorian Square (details are in the Annual Events chapter). Clean and well maintained, the park has 92 sites strictly for RVs. Daily rates are about $28 and monthly $434. Members of Good Sam, AARP, and AAA are offered discounts. The basic essentials, such as sewer, electric, water, and cable TV, are provided, along with shower and laundry facilities. And don't forget Fido—he's welcome, too.

NORTH SHORE LAKE TAHOE

Granite Flat
California Highway 89
1 mile south of Truckee, CA
(530) 587-3558
(877) 444-6777 (reservations)
www.reserveusa.com
You can almost cast your fishing line into the Truckee River right from your campsite at Granite Flat campground: Many of the 75 RV and tent sites sit right on the banks of the rushing water. Granite Flat is also especially wheelchair friendly, with 16 accessible campsites and a wheelchair-accessible river trail. Seven walk-in campsites are also available. Basic services for the $15 fee include piped water and vault toilets. Pets are okay on leashes. Since the campground is just off the highway, it's noisy sometimes and also lacks the seclusion of more isolated sites.

Lake Forest
Lake Forest Road, 2 miles northeast of Tahoe City, CA
(530) 583-3796, ext. 29
www.tahoecitypud.com
With one of the only public boat ramps in the North Shore Lake Tahoe area, the campground at Lake Forest is a great location for boaters. The 20 tent and RV sites rent for $15 a night on a first-come, first-served basis. You can bring Fido along, but be sure he also brings his leash.

Amenities include flush toilets, piped water, picnic tables, and barbecue pits. A public swimming beach, shops, and restaurants are nearby. To get to the campground from Tahoe City, head northeast on California Highway 28 for about a mile, turn right onto Lake Forest Road, and follow it to the lake. The campground is near the U.S. Coast Guard Station.

Martis Creek Lake
California Highway 267
7 miles north of Kings Beach, CA
(530) 587-8113 (April through November) (530) 432-6427 (December through March)
www.spk.usace.army.mil/organizations/cespk-co/lakes/martis.html

Tucked on the edge of Martis Creek Lake in an 850-acre wildlife preserve, Martis Creek Lake campground offers marvelous opportunities to view birds and animals, such as Canada geese, ducks, coyotes, and deer. It's also an angler's dream—the reservoir is well stocked with Lahontan cutthroat and German brown trout. Fishing is catch-and-release only, and other restrictions apply.

With a total of 25 RV and tent sites, the campground offers the basics of piped water, chemical toilets, barbecues, and picnic tables. The daily fee is $12, with discounts for Golden Age and Golden Access Passport holders. No reservations are accepted. Pets are allowed but should be leashed on the campground property. Even though it's just off CA 267, about halfway between Kings Beach and Truckee, the campground is peaceful and quiet, with great views of Martis Peak. There's a wonderful world of outdoor fun all around (see the description of Truckee in the Day Trips chapter for more details), including all the amenities of Northstar-at-Tahoe. Be sure to ask the on-site ranger about tours of the dam; campfire programs are offered on Saturday night. The campground is open seasonally from May 1 to November 15.

Mt. Rose Campground
Nevada Highway 431
20 miles southwest of Reno, NV
(775) 882-2766
(877) 444-6777 (reservations)
www.reserveusa.com

Surrounded by gorgeous alpine hiking terrain, Mt. Rose Campground is nestled in the trees at 8,900 feet in elevation. If it's hot in Reno or at Lake Tahoe, you can always beat the heat up here. Amenities for the 24 RV and tent sites include piped water, flush toilets, picnic tables, and fire pits. Although some sites are first-come, first-served, most are on the reservation system. Because this campground is the only one along the Mt. Rose Highway (NV 431), I recommend that you reserve a spot in advance. The daily rate is $13, but there is a discount for those holding Golden Age and Golden Access Passports. If you intend to use passport membership for the discount, mention it when you book the reservation.

Because snow is often on the ground until late spring, quite often the campground doesn't open until July. Whatever the time of year, be sure to bring along warm clothing—nighttime temperatures can be cold all year. This area is especially great for dogs, since there's plenty of room for them to roam in the surrounding wilderness. When in the campground, however, they must be leashed.

If your idea of camping involves a pristine mountain setting, you won't be disappointed at Mt. Rose. You can wade through knee-high wildflowers in Tahoe Meadows, conquer the summit of windswept Mt. Rose, and hike through stands of tall timber for magnificent views of Lake Tahoe. Or you can just sit around a blazing campfire and listen to coyotes howling at the moon (see more about

---

When camping in the wilderness, practice the Leave No Trace policy by burying human waste and packing out all garbage.

Camping Contacts

For general information on campgrounds in the Lake Tahoe Basin, you can contact:

California State Parks: (530) 525-7232; www.cal-parks.ca.gov

Nevada State Parks: (775) 687-4379 or (775) 831-0494 (Lake Tahoe); www.parks.nv.gov

USDA Forest Service: (530) 543-2600; www.fs.fed.us/r5. Ask for a copy of the *Lake of the Sky Journal* from the Forest Service: It has a grid showing services available at most area campgrounds, plus hiking and backcountry information. The Lake Tahoe Basin Management Unit Web site also provides good basic information on Forest Service campgrounds and private campgrounds in the area.

If you want to make reservations to stay at area campgrounds, use either of these two Web sites:

www.reserveusa.com (Forest Service)

www.reserveamerica.com (California and federal campgrounds)

I strongly recommend that you reserve space as soon as you can, because the demand for campsites is heavy. Also be aware that the central reservation systems used by some campgrounds may be difficult to reach. The number for Forest Service facilities is (877) 444-6777; for California state sites call (800) 444-7275.

Tahoe Meadows and Mt. Rose in the Recreation, Attractions, and Winter Sports chapters).

Tahoe State Recreation Area
California Highway 28
Tahoe City, CA
(530) 583-3074
(800) 444-7275 (reservations)
www.reserveamerica.com

The good news at Tahoe State Recreation Area is that you're right on the lake and close to restaurants and shops. The bad news is the noise from the nearby highway. But if you don't mind the swish of cars, you can enjoy great views of the lake. It's probably a better location for RV campers than tent campers, since the noise is less noticeable if you're inside a vehicle. Amenities at this 26-site campground include piped water, flush toilets, showers, and swimming. The fee ranges from $12 to $20 per day. Sites in the Lakeside Loop may be reserved in advance. You can bring your dog, but keep him or her on a leash.

You can find more information about Tahoe camping at www.tahoebest.com.

William Kent
California Highway 89, 2 miles south of Tahoe City, CA
(530) 583-3642 (summer only)
(877) 444-6777 (reservations)
www.reserveusa.com

You can be in the middle of all the action around Sunnyside Resort but still enjoy seclusion in a deep forest at William Kent campground. Just across the road from William Kent Beach and Sunnyside, the campground gives easy access to Lake Tahoe and all water sports. To get around you can use the extensive system of bike trails or hop on a Tahoe Area Regional Transit (TART) bus nearby.

The daily fee is $16, and amenities for the 91 sites (there is a 40-foot limit on the length of RVs) include piped water, flush toilets, picnic tables, and fire rings. Pets are OK but must be leashed.

SOUTH SHORE LAKE TAHOE

Camp Richardson Resort
1900 Jameson Beach Road
South Lake Tahoe, CA
(530) 541-1801, (800) 544-1801,
www.camprichardson.com

You can enjoy all the amenities of a full-service mountain resort when you set up camp at Camp Richardson Resort. Its fabulous sandy beaches offer endless opportunities for every kind of water sport imaginable. You can also ride horses into the nearby mountains, pedal along the lakeshore bike trail, and hike to neighboring alpine lakes.

Camp Richardson is close to the casino action at Stateline, Nevada, and to Tallac Historic Site, with its enchanting arts programs (see the Attractions and The Arts chapters for details).

The campground has 100 RV sites with hookups and 300 camping sites. All sites have fire rings and picnic tables; showers, piped water, and flush toilets are available. You can buy supplies in the convenience store, launch your boat at the boat ramp, and eat dinner out (complete with live music) in the on-site restaurant. Families of all sizes are welcome, but they must leave their pets at home. Daily rates run $20 to $30.

D. L. Bliss State Park
California Highway 89
9 miles north of South Lake Tahoe, CA
(530) 525-7277 (summer)
(530) 525-9529 (winter)
(800) 444-7275 (reservations)
www.reserveamerica.com

With heavily wooded, secluded sites along the spectacular west shore of Lake Tahoe, D. L. Bliss State Park is pure bliss. Of all the camping options in the Lake Tahoe area, Bliss is premier. You can swim and sunbathe on one of Tahoe's largest white-sand beaches, hike the ruggedly picturesque shoreline to beautiful Emerald Bay, and bike to Tahoe City on the area's longest paved bike path (more information about the park is in the Parks chapter).

Basic services for the 168 sites include piped water (which must be boiled before drinking), showers, group sites, and flush toilets. The daily fee ranges from $12 to $30, and pets are OK on leashes. This campground is mostly for tent campers. There is an 18-foot limit on the length of RVs.

Eagle Point at Emerald Bay State Park
California Highway 89
6 miles north of South Lake Tahoe, CA
(530) 541-3030
(800) 444-7275 (reservations)
www.reserveamerica.com

Hugging the rocky cliffs above Emerald Bay, Eagle Point campground offers gorgeous views of one of the loveliest spots in all of Lake Tahoe. With easy access to the Desolation Wilderness, there's hiking galore. The beach at Emerald Bay is a short quarter-mile walk from camp (see the Parks chapter for more details about Emerald Bay State Park).

Services available for the 100 RV and tent sites include showers, piped water, and flush toilets. Dogs are OK, and daily rates run around $25.

Fallen Leaf
California Highway 89
2 miles south of South Lake Tahoe, CA
(530) 544-0426
(877) 444-6777 (reservations)
www.reserveusa.com

Fallen Leaf campground has 205 sites for tent and RV campers, providing picnic tables, flush toilets, fire rings, and piped water. A convenience store and firewood are also available. Daily fees are $20, and pets are allowed on a leash. The sites are scattered among the tall pines just a short distance from lovely Fallen Leaf Lake. It's also close to trailheads leading into the Desolation Wilderness.

General Creek at Sugar Pine Point State Park
California Highway 89
1 mile south of Tahoma, CA
(530) 525-7982
(800) 444-7275 (reservations)
www.reserveamerica.com

As part of Sugar Pine Point State Park, General Creek campground enjoys a lovely tree-shaded setting along the west shore of Lake Tahoe (see the Parks chapter for more details). Services for the 175 tent and RV sites include piped water, showers (summer only), flush toilets, fire rings, and picnic tables. It is open all year and, because of heavy summer use, I recommend making reservations in advance for stays planned for July and August.

Although the park extends across CA 89, there are no campsites on that side, but you can still enjoy swimming, biking, and hiking in the area. Daily fees are around $25, and pets are OK on leashes.

Nevada Beach
Elks Point Road
1 mile northeast of Stateline, NV
(775) 588-5562, (800) 280-2267
(877) 444-6777 (reservations)
www.reserveusa.com
www.fs.fed.us/r5/ltbmu/

Nevada Beach campground is on a lovely sandy beach but still close to all the casino action at Stateline. Of the 54 sites, 30 are OK for RVs, but there are no dumping facilities. Daily rates are about $24, with services including flush toilets, piped water, picnic tables, and fire rings. Since the campground is located right on the lakeshore, activities are water-oriented, such as swimming and boating. The east beach is wheelchair accessible. Pets are allowed in the campground if they are on a leash but are not allowed on the beach.

Tahoe Valley
1175 Melba Drive
South Lake Tahoe, CA
(530) 541-2222, (877) 717-8737
www.RVonthego.com

The largest year-round camping facility in the Reno/Tahoe area, Tahoe Valley offers just about everything you'd ever want to make your camping/RVing experience enjoyable. You'll find all the basics: piped water, flush toilets, cable TV, barbecues, picnic tables, showers, and complete hookups for recreational vehicles of any size. Amenities also include a swimming pool, convenience store, tennis courts, recreation hall, sports courts, storage facilities, and a tourist information center. Daily fees range from $26 to $46. Pets are OK on leashes.

The 413 sites at Tahoe Valley are sprinkled among the tall pine trees bordering the Upper Truckee River near the Factory Stores at the Y. You'll find biking, hiking, horseback riding, and golf nearby. Look for the campground at the intersection of U.S. Highway 50 and C Street.

Zephyr Cove Resort
760 U.S. Highway 50
Zephyr Cove, NV
(775) 589-4907, (800) 288-2463
www.tahoedixie2.com

This popular family resort, which is open during summer and for portions of spring and fall, is a beehive of activity during the summer months. I strongly recommend making reservations far in advance if you plan on staying during July and August.

A $4 million renovation has added significant improvements to the campground, including larger spaces, underground utilities, cable TV, and telephone service. Sites are available for both tents and RV campers, with full hookups, flush toilets, showers, and piped water. RV sites have a second line dedicated to Internet service. Daily rates range from $15 to $48. Other amenities include a mini-mart, horseback riding, snowmobiles, lake cruises, a swimming beach, and restaurants. Pets are allowed on leashes.

RESTAURANTS 

Nowhere is the Reno/Tahoe area's character and diversity more apparent than in its restaurants. The menus read like the world atlas: Basque, Chinese, Mexican, French, German, Japanese, American, Italian—you'll find it all.

And the ever-changing population expects only the finest in cuisine. Some critics have compared the restaurants here to those in San Francisco. In fact, many Bay Area restaurateurs are reaching out into the Reno/Tahoe market. The significant upside to this highly competitive market is a plethora of fine restaurants.

I'm sure you've heard already that every hotel/casino has its own signature steak house, gourmet dining room, coffee shop, or cafe. I'm confident that you will discover these gastronomical delights on your own, so I've concentrated this chapter on restaurants located away from the bright lights of the casinos. I'll take you on a gourmet tour of restaurants off the beaten path, into the back alleys of towns, into the strip malls, into the Insiders' neighborhoods. I'll take you to the locals' favorite eating establishments. I'll give you a list of restaurants to die for.

Other venues not suggested in this chapter are chain restaurants and fast-food joints. Sure, most of the chains and most of the fast-food places are here, but you're no doubt already familiar with these. I'll concentrate on what's unique to these parts.

This chapter is arranged a little differently than the others. It's divided into two main regions—Reno/Sparks and Lake Tahoe Area—then broken down by type of restaurant (American, Italian, Mexican, etc.), then broken down yet again by the standard geographical areas. So, for instance, if you're in Reno and are hankering for Mexican food, it'll be easy to browse through the Reno/Sparks "Mexican" section until you find the taqueria that strikes your fancy (or the one closest to you). Or if you'll be heading to the Lake Tahoe area and want to plan a special evening with that special someone, you can look through the listings around the lake to find just the right place.

Most of the restaurants have very casual dress requirements, so don't be surprised to see someone dressed up in a coat and tie dining next to someone wearing a pair of shorts and a T-shirt.

Most of the restaurants listed accept major credit cards. Some establishments with Web sites allow diners to make reservations online.

Many of the restaurants serving both lunch and dinner open between 11:00 and 11:30 A.M., then close for a few hours before reopening again for dinner. Also, some of the restaurants around Lake Tahoe have different schedules during high season than during the off-season. And, of course, hours and days of operation change from time to time. If a particular time or day is important to you, I suggest that you call to confirm the restaurant's hours.

While smoking is not permitted in restaurants in California, it is allowed in designated areas in Nevada. Because many nonsmokers are still bothered by smoke drifting from the smoking sections, a push is on to outlaw smoking in eating establishments in Nevada. In the meantime, some restaurants have voluntarily become smoke-free, and I'll indicate which of the recommended eateries have done so.

PRICE CODE

To give you an idea of how much you can expect to pay, the entries in this chapter have been coded using the following system. The price-code rating reflects the average cost of entrees for two, without cocktails, appetizers, wine, dessert, tax, and tip.

$	$25 or less
$$	$26 to $55
$$$	more than $55

With all that out of the way, it's time to loosen your belts a notch and prepare to take a guided tour of the gastronomical haunts of the Reno/Tahoe area.

RENO/SPARKS

American and International

RENO

Amelia's Restaurant and Flightline Bar **$$**
655 South Rock Boulevard
(775) 858-7316
The best thing about this eatery is that its bar overlooks the runways at the Reno/Tahoe International Airport and the Sierra Nevada mountains, so you get a great view of takeoffs and landings and a fantastic view when the sun ducks behind the mountains. The restaurant is open for breakfast, lunch, and dinner Monday through Friday. The food is fine, but the real draws are the view and atmosphere. The sandwiches are the forte, so lunch tends to be better than dinner. And, yes, it's named after Amelia Earhart.

Anthony's Dandelion Deli and Cafe **$**
1700 South Wells Avenue
(775) 322-6100
Although it's not strictly vegetarian, Anthony's offers plenty of choices that are meat-free. For lunch, how about eggplant Parmesan with green salad, or sweet potato and spinach soup? Like many other veggie eateries, Anthony's specializes in hummus, which is used in a variety of creative ways. The decor is decidedly casual, with customers ordering at a counter. Hours are 7:00 A.M. to 4:00 P.M. Monday through Friday and 10:00 A.M. to 4:00 P.M. Saturday.

Archie's Famous Grill **$**
2195 North Virginia Street
(775) 322-9595
If you want just plain, good food, try Archie's. It's located across the street from the University of Nevada, Reno, and is a student hangout, so you know the prices are reasonable. Breakfasts are huge here and include tons of home-style grilled potatoes, and Archie's can whip up a mean sourdough French toast. Its lunch special is a quarter-pound hamburger on a fresh, soft bun. For dinner, most patrons recommend the Jamaican chicken. Archie's has an outdoor patio, which is a great place to be when the balloon races are in town. Archie's sits across the street from Rancho San Rafael Park, where the hot-air balloons take off, and is open daily for breakfast and lunch.

Country Garden **$**
606 West Plumb Lane
(775) 825-0213
The walls of the Country Garden restaurant know more secrets about local residents than any priest sitting in a confessional. For years the No. 1 choice for "ladies who lunch," its smallish tables are crammed with women sharing their lives (or those of their friends) with their luncheon companions. Although it's supposed to resemble a garden, the decor is actually quite pedestrian. But take heart because the food is delicious. In this day of boil-in-the-bag portion control (as ardently practiced by many restaurants), the fresh, homemade menu items at the Country Garden are a pleasant surprise. You'll find a wonderful assortment of fresh salads, soups, sandwiches, and quiches. And, of course, the desserts are simply divine. While the upside is the wonderful food, the downside is the noisy environment. It's a great place to "meet and greet," and you can even bring a male along. The Country Garden is open for lunch Monday through Friday and Saturday for breakfast and lunch. Smoke-free.

Famous Murphys Restaurant Grill & Oyster Bar $$
3127 South Virginia Street
(775) 827-4111, (775) 827-3663 (takeout and delivery)
www.famousmurphys.com
Although the name and decor are decidedly Irish, the cuisine is American, featuring prime rib, steaks, seafood, chicken, and pasta. You can eat in the main dining rooms or, for lighter fare in a more casual environment, you can try the grill and oyster bar. Local sports fans know that the bar at Murphys is a great place to enjoy fresh oysters on the half shell while watching their favorite sporting event. You can become a member of the free wine club and enjoy discounts and wine tastings. The restaurant serves dinner nightly and lunch Monday through Friday.

Moxie's Spirits & Dining $
4792 Caughlin Parkway
(775) 826-2665
The panoramic city view from Moxie's is impressive whether you're grabbing a quick lunch, enjoying a drink with friends, or relaxing over a leisurely dinner. And the best part is that almost any seat in the house will give you a good view. The stunning view is the star in this place: The menu and decor are simple and laid-back. You'll find an interesting selection of soups, salads, and sandwiches for lunch and chicken and pasta entrees for dinner. Live music is offered periodically (call for dates and times), which attracts the older singles crowd around the bar area. Moxie's is open for lunch and dinner daily and also for breakfast Saturday and Sunday.

Peg's Glorified Ham & Eggs $
425 South Sierra Street
(775) 329-2600
Peg's is close to downtown and is a favorite hangout for Reno attorneys. Open daily for breakfast and lunch, Peg's specializes in, of course, egg dishes. The house specialty is huevos rancheros, served in a tortilla, smothered in sauce with plenty of hash browns. The portions are huge here, and the service is very friendly. A great place to go for a quick breakfast or lunch if you're downtown or if you're looking for legal representation. Smoke-free.

PJ & Co. Restaurant Saloon $$
1590 South Wells Avenue
(775) 323-6366
PJs is located kitty-corner from the Rapscallion restaurant (see subsequent entry under "Seafood") and next door to Corrigan's Irish pub (see the Nightlife chapter). PJs, a regular mainstay, is casual, homey, and a favorite local hangout, especially on Friday night. Breakfast is served daily from 7:00 A.M., and locals keep coming back for its eggs Benedict and veggie omelets. PJs features gigantic burgers and homemade fries for lunch and specializes in Tex-Mex cooking for some of its dinner items, but the pork back ribs keep most diners happy. PJs has an outside area for dining and a full bar that offers eight different beers on tap. It also has three TVs, which are always tuned to some sports channel. The restaurant and bar are only separated by a wooden railing, so it can get noisy, especially on Friday night after work.

Skyline Cafe $$
3005 Skyline Boulevard
(775) 825-5611
www.renodining.com
Nestled in an upscale residential area, Skyline Cafe is a popular locals' hangout. You can enjoy delicious seafood and pasta entrees along with panoramic views of the city. Seating on the patio is available when weather permits, and there's a small bar up front where patrons meet and greet friends. The bar opens daily at 4:00 P.M., and dinner is served from 5:00 to 10:00 P.M. Reservations are advised. You'll find the catering, to-go, and delivery menus at the Web site listed above.

Tapestries Restaurant & Wine Bar $
1655 Robb Drive
(775) 336-3333
With its warm Tuscan ambience and

expansive international cuisine, Tapestries can fool you into thinking you're on vacation in Europe. The owners have successfully come up with a menu that offers American cuisine along with Thai, Greek, German, and Mediterranean influences. Dinner entrees include duck breast served with lingonberry demi-glace, vegetable strudel, and Cajun jambalaya. The restaurant also has a weekend brunch menu. The wine list reflects an international flair with wines from South America, Australia, New Zealand, Germany, and South Africa offered along with those from North America. If you're fussy about where you sit in a restaurant, you'll have four choices here: the glassed-in patio, the bar area, the main dining room, and the banquet room. Tapestries is open for lunch and dinner daily.

SPARKS

Anchors Bar & Grill **$$**
325 Harbor Cove Drive
(775) 356-6888

The most distinguishing feature of Anchors is its waterfront location at Sparks Marina. Insiders still marvel at the lake that not too long ago was a gravel pit. Along with the development of Sparks Marina Park in recent years has come attractive condominiums, retail shopping, and restaurants like Anchors. From its second-floor perch above the water, Anchors offers a bird's-eye view of the lake and mountains to the west. Almost any seat in the house, especially those on the expansive outdoor deck, will add an appropriate nautical view to enhance your dining experience.

The menu combines American and international cuisine in a selection of steaks, pasta, and seafood. Casual fish entrees include salmon wraps and trout tucked in prosciutto. I highly recommend the warm vegetable chips, which can be ordered instead of french fries, along with any hamburger that's guaranteed to be well worth the calories and cholesterol.

Because signage is almost nonexistent around the marina, Anchors is a little tricky to find. From North McCarran Boulevard, turn right on Lincoln Way and then right on Harbor Cove Drive. The restaurant is on the second floor of the building to the right. You'll need to go up the stairway on the east side of the building or take the elevator. Anchors is open daily for lunch and dinner.

Cozy's Coffee Shop **$**
2258 Oddie Boulevard
(775) 359-8008

Cozy's serves down-home American food and lots of it—so don't come here expecting finger food and small, dainty portions. Every day, for breakfast, lunch, and dinner, its cooks prepare rich, flavorful food from scratch using only fresh produce and top-quality meats. Its specialties include pot roast, just like Grandma used to make, with a gravy to kill for. But you can't go wrong ordering that old standby T-bone steak with Cozy's special sautéed mushrooms. If you'd rather have breakfast—a big breakfast—try the chicken-fried steak with three eggs and hash browns smothered in country gravy. If you have room for dessert (and I'm betting you won't, but don't let that stop you!), tell your waitress to slice a generous portion of one of Cozy's homemade fruit pies. The atmosphere inside reminds you of being in a friend's kitchen, and the waitresses are some of the nicest and friendliest in town. The restaurant is located in a strip mall between ShopKo and Albertson's market. Open daily. You can't miss the hot pink and violet exterior of this popular eatery.

David's Grill and Sports Bar **$$-$$$**
The Steakhouse at Red Hawk
6590 North Wingfield Parkway
(775) 626-1000
www.wingfieldsprings.com

Formerly named Freddie's Roost, David's has been the hangout for the Wingfield Springs crowd ever since it opened a few years ago. An upscale sports bar with exceptional food and ambience, it seemed to satisfy the needs of most patrons. But recently management took the east wing of the restaurant and converted it to The Steakhouse at Red Hawk, which offers a more intimate environment for fine dining in the evening Wednesday through Sunday. Both restaurants offer comfortable seating along with lovely views of the golf course and surrounding wetlands. Although it's a bit of a drive from Sparks, it's definitely worth it. David's serves standards such as grilled chicken and Reuben sandwiches for lunch daily and is also open for breakfast and dinner.

Great Basin Brewery **$$**
846 Victorian Avenue
(775) 355-7711
www.greatbasinbrewingco.com
This microbrewery not only makes fresh, handcrafted beers right before your eyes in its special, glass-enclosed brewroom, it also serves up a wide variety of excellent food. Yes, most patrons come here and crowd around the L-shaped bar to savor one of their favorite brews, but when you walk in, take a look around and you'll see a packed dining room, too. The brewery's beers are among the best in America and have won numerous awards at the Great American Beer Festival, but some Insiders think this brewery also has the best fish-and-chips in the Reno/Tahoe area. Its secrets are the fish and batter. Instead of frozen fish, it uses hand-cut Alaskan cod and deep fries it in Wild Horse Ale batter (Wild Horse Ale is one of the brewery's signature beers).

Other unique specialties are the garlic fries made with real pieces of garlic scattered throughout the potatoes and its adaptation of an old-world pub-fare favorite, Shepherd's Pie. The pie is made with tender, braised lamb, veggies, and gravy surrounded by mashed garlic potatoes. If pub grub is your preference, try the sausage sampler, which includes all of the brewhouse's four kinds of sausage. Great Basin also has special events, which you'll find posted on their Web site. Located just a few blocks from Victorian Square Plaza, this is a local hangout before and after the movies. During summer, it has an outside sitting area with a stage presenting free entertainment. The wait for a table on Friday and Saturday can be lengthy, especially if Victorian Square is hosting a special event. Great Basin serves lunch and dinner daily.

Landrum's Cafe **$**
415 South Rock Boulevard
(775) 359-8686
The owners of this cafe call it the area's last real diner, and when you walk through the door you may agree. The decor is 1950s, the service is fast and friendly, and the menu is short and without regard for cholesterol or calories. Landrum's has been in the Reno/Sparks area since 1947, and Insiders say it hasn't changed its menu. In fact, most patrons don't even look at the menu when they order, and the cook still prepares everything in plain sight of diners sitting on stools. You can still order its original hearty chili-cheese omelet or its biscuits and home fries smothered in country gravy loaded with hunks of pork sausage.

This is a locals' hangout that serves breakfast and lunch daily except Monday. For a real treat, try the one-third-pound hamburger, cooked the way you want it and topped with a thick slice of grilled Bermuda onion—and don't forget one of its signature milk shakes. An Insiders' favorite is the rich and thick homemade chili. And, yes, rock 'n' roll music is definitely on the jukebox. This diner is packed during Hot August Nights (see the Annual Events chapter), so be prepared.

Asian

RENO

Bangkok Cuisine **$$**
55 Mt. Rose Street
(775) 322-0299
If you love the vibrant flavors of Thailand—lemongrass, peppers, and curries—Bangkok Cuisine should please your palate. Be sure

to ask about how spicy the food is, and order it according to your taste: Many entrees served at this restaurant are very hot. The decor is pleasant, with black lacquered furniture and souvenirs of Thailand lending a slightly Asian feel to the place. The menu is extensive, with chicken, fish, meat, and vegetables prepared in a variety of Thai styles. The restaurant is open for lunch and dinner Monday through Saturday and for dinner only on Sunday. Smoke-free.

Cafe de Thai **$$**
7499 Longley Lane
(775) 829-8424

With an 18-foot waterfall as the centerpiece of its contemporary decor, Cafe de Thai offers an unadorned oasis for your dining pleasure. The concrete floors and simple wood/chrome furnishings may seem overly stark at first, but once you've begun eating they become the appropriate background for the spicy, somewhat complex cuisine. The food here is easily some of the best you'll find in the Reno/Tahoe area. The outdoor patio is very popular in summer, and the separate bar area offers a welcome retreat if you're waiting for a table. The restaurant is open Monday through Saturday for lunch and dinner and for dinner only on Sunday. One note of warning: The restaurant may be tricky to find, especially after dark, because its exterior signage is not obvious. To make it easier, look for a geometric concrete structure with splashes of pumpkin about 1 block east of South Virginia Street. Smoke-free.

Francis' Asian Bistro **$$**
4796 Caughlin Parkway, Suite 101
(775) 827-3111

Offering unique tastes from China and Japan, Francis' Asian Bistro boasts one of the most comprehensive menus in the area. You simply aren't hungry if you can't find something appealing in this tasteful establishment. Mouthwatering selections include teriyaki baby back ribs, clams with black bean sauce, shrimp with lobster sauce, and fresh New Zealand greenlip mussels. The restaurant also has a fresh oyster and sushi bar. In the location formerly known as Cafe Soleil, the bistro maintains the same neighborly feel Soleil cultivated over years of business. It's off the beaten track from downtown and the casinos, but it's easy to find just off McCarran Boulevard. Francis' is open daily for lunch and dinner.

Kyoto Restaurant **$$**
915 West Moana Lane
(775) 825-9686

For mouthwatering Japanese tempura, sushi, teriyaki, and sukiyaki, I highly recommend the authentic cuisine at Kyoto Restaurant. The food is delightful, the prices are reasonable, and the contemporary ambience is relaxing and enjoyable. You'll find all your Japanese favorites on the menu plus a selection of tantalizing daily specials. Kyoto is open for lunch and dinner Monday through Saturday.

Palais de Jade **$$**
960 West Moana Lane
(775) 827-5233

A well-decorated and sophisticated Chinese restaurant that is constantly voted No. 1 by Reno Insiders, Palais de Jade has a wide variety of plates, including noodles and vegetable entrees. Specialties are the Kung-Pao chicken and pan-fried noodles. The menu sports about 100 different entrees. The cooking styles are mostly Cantonese and Mandarin, but a few dishes are cooked in the Szechuan style. The best thing about this restaurant, besides the food and friendly service, is the lazy Susan tables. The spinning shelves make it easier to sample everyone's entrees, and you can enjoy them and the great food daily from 11:00 A.M. to 9:15 P.M. Smoke-free.

i

You'll find Reno/Sparks restaurant reviews at http://news.rgj.com/eatingout.

Pho 777 **$**
201 East Second Street
(775) 323-7777
Pho 777 derives its name from the north Vietnamese broth (pho), a Vietnamese belief that seven is a lucky number, and that three of anything is extremely lucky. The owner will tell you that the three sevens are extraordinarily lucky because when you add them together they equal 21, and if you add the two plus the one, you get three again. We're not sure how lucky the name is for the owner, but diners are lucky to have such a tastefully inexpensive noodle shop for lunch and dinner daily. The restaurant has room inside only for about 20 diners, and it's so popular, you'll often see people waiting outside for a seat. And for good reason: Pho 777 combines warm broth with soft noodles to concoct a low-calorie, extremely tasteful meal that's also very affordable. The restaurant has about 14 different phos listed on its menu, as well as egg rolls, shrimp, and pork flame-broiled over rice; pork slices; and fried rice combinations. And none of the dishes are prepared spicy because each table is equipped with its own condiment tray, so you can add as much of the hot pepper sauce as you wish. But take care when adding the chili sauce from the small jar: It's fire. Pho 777 is open from 10:00 A.M. to 9:00 P.M. daily.

Rickshaw's Fine Asian Bistro **$**
4944 South Virginia Street
(775) 828-2335
Nicknamed "an Asian bistro," Rickshaw's offers a tour of Asian taste treats based upon the legend of Seamus McGillicuddy, an Irishman who collected recipes as he traveled throughout Asia. You can savor the flavors of China, Thailand, Japan, the Philippines, and Malaysia in a variety of luscious dishes, such as curry roast duck, Nasi Goreng, Malaysian chicken, and grilled Mongolian lamb chops. The atmosphere is not the thing here, but the food is to die for. Because it's sometimes crowded during peak meal times, I suggest you try to eat earlier or later than most people. Rickshaw's is open for lunch and dinner daily.

A Taste of Thai **$**
6135 Lakeside Drive
(775) 828-6400
A Taste of Thai prides itself on serving authentic dishes from Thailand. The service is friendly, the wine list is respectable, and the ambience is intimate and quiet. You can savor this increasingly popular cuisine for lunch and dinner Monday through Saturday.

SPARKS

Shanghai Restaurant **$$**
1269 Baring Boulevard
(775) 358-1122
This may be the best Chinese restaurant in Sparks, though it's often overlooked by visitors because it sits tucked away in a remote corner of Baring Village Shopping Center. It has attractive Chinese decor, and the menu is extensive with reasonable prices. The waiters and waitresses are extremely friendly, and it's easy to see why Sparks locals love this place. The food is tasty, especially the General's Chicken and the sesame beef. Shanghai Restaurant is open daily for lunch and dinner.

Barbecue

SPARKS

B.J.'s Bar-B-Q **$**
754 North McCarran Boulevard
(775) 355-1010
This tiny restaurant is located in the Silver State Plaza in Sparks and could just be the best barbecue joint in the area. The interior of the restaurant is spartan, with few tables and chairs. But you won't care about the atmosphere when you sink your teeth into any of the entrees topped with the restaurant's special sauce. This barbecue sauce has won several awards and is a local favorite. The smoked pork barbecue sandwich is worth writing home about.

B.J.'s is open every day but Sunday for lunch and dinner.

Basque

RENO

Louis' Basque Corner **$$**
301 East Fourth Street
(775) 323-7203
Dinner at Louis' is one of the most spectacular dining experiences in the Reno/Tahoe area; it really shouldn't be missed. When you enter this Reno icon, you walk into the Basque country of northern Spain and southern France. Basque sayings line the walls, as well as pictures from the Pyrenees, pottery from Cibourne, and other Basque pieces. But this restaurant's draw is its food cooked in the Basque way—and plenty of it (no one has ever left Louis' hungry). All dinners include soup, salad, French bread, Basque beans, french fries, a first course (shellfish, beef, tongue, oxtails, chicken), a main course (roast pork, steak, lamb chops, rabbit, calamari, paella), a bottle of wine, milk, coffee, tea, and dessert. This restaurant serves dinner family-style at long tables where you may be seated next to strangers if you don't have at least eight in your party. The owners, Louis and Lorraine Erreguible, have been overseeing this restaurant for more than 30 years and often say their diners enter as customers and leave as friends. Before dinner, try one of Louis' Picon Punches. It's an alcoholic concoction where one is plenty and two's too many. Basque Corner is open for lunch Tuesday through Saturday and for dinner every day.

Buffets

Most casinos/hotels in the area have at least one buffet. And why shouldn't they? The concept of the buffet was invented in Nevada in the 1940s. So if you're into lavish productions with carved ice sculptures, all-you-can-eat prime rib and shrimp, and a list of food selections that tops several hundred per meal, from salads to homemade desserts, try one of the following buffets:

RENO

Carvings Buffet
Harrah's Reno
219 North Center Street
(775) 786-3232

Chefs' Buffet Reno
Eldorado Hotel/Casino Reno
345 North Virginia Street
(775) 786-5700

Courtyard Buffet
Circus Circus Hotel/Casino-Reno
500 North Sierra Street
(775) 329-0711

Island Buffet
Peppermill Hotel Casino Reno
2707 South Virginia Street
(775) 826-2121

The Lodge Buffet
Reno Hilton
2500 East Second Street
(775) 789-2000

Lord Fitzgerald's Feast and Merriment
Fitzgeralds Casino/Hotel Reno
255 North Virginia Street
(775) 785-3300

Silver Screen Buffet
Boomtown Casino & Hotel Reno
Interstate 80, 7 miles west of Reno
(775) 345-6000

Toucan Charlie's Buffet and Grille
Atlantis Casino Resort
3800 South Virginia Street
(775) 825-4700

The Victorian Buffet
Silver Legacy Resort Casino
407 North Virginia Street
(775) 329-4777

SPARKS

Fallen Leaf Buffet
Baldini's Sports Casino
865 South Rock Avenue
(775) 358-0116

Rotisserie Buffet
John Ascuaga's Nugget
1100 Nugget Avenue
(775) 356-3300

Victoria's Steak Buffet
Silver Club Hotel/Casino
1040 Victorian Avenue
(775) 358-4771

Coffeehouses

For those of you who are Starbucks purists (and I confess to suffering from this malady as well!), take heart, because a Starbucks is never far away, especially in the Reno/Sparks area. In fact, new ones keep popping up so often that it almost seems like Seattle without the rain. Even though chain operations are not included in this book, I understand the need for a Starbucks fix. Here are a few locations for your java jolt: In Reno: 4809 Kietzke Lane, (775) 827-1192; 10190 North McCarran Boulevard, (775) 624-6464; 18250 Wedge Parkway, (775) 853-2993. In Sparks: 2835 North McCarran Boulevard, (775) 331-8551. In Incline Village: 899 Tahoe Boulevard, (775) 831-6615. In South Lake Tahoe: 1064 Emerald Bay Road, (530) 544-4490.

RENO

Emerald City Espresso & Tea Cafe **$**
3594 West Plumb Lane
(775) 322-1525
Named for Seattle, the city that spawned the current coffee craze, Emerald City is a relaxing spot to enjoy your favorite designer coffees and teas while you chat with friends or read the morning newspaper. On snowy winter days, it's especially inviting to cozy up on the comfy couches around the blazing fireplace. This casual eatery/coffeehouse is a hangout for students as well as residents of the upscale Caughlin Ranch area. You can order homemade soups, salads, sandwiches, quiches, and pastries daily for breakfast, lunch, and snacks. It's open weekdays from 7:00 A.M. to 4:00 P.M. and on Saturday and Sunday from 8:00 A.M. to 3:00 P.M. Smoke-free.

If you prefer dining in with your feet up in front of the TV, call Delivery Diner at (775) 828-3463 for delivery service from more than 40 restaurants in the Reno area.

Walden's Coffeehouse **$**
3940 Mayberry Drive
(775) 787-3307
www.waldenscoffeehouse.com
On one of the busiest corners in southwest Reno (Mayberry Drive and South McCarran Boulevard), Walden's is a comfortable hangout for yuppies living in Caughlin Ranch, students who love studying in a coffeehouse atmosphere, and anybody else who just wants a great cup of coffee and a tasty homemade sandwich. The food is hearty and the ambience unpretentious. It also has occasional entertainment. If you're headed out biking or walking your dogs, stop at Walden's and tuck a lunch to go in your backpack. Smoke-free.

Continental

RENO

Bricks Restaurant & Wine Bar **$$**
1995 South Virginia Street
(775) 786-2277
Named for the Comstock-era bricks used in its construction, Bricks is a classy dining experience even for the most discriminating palates. Each menu selection is almost a work of art, from the colorful design of the food on the plates to the exquisite aromas and tastes each course embodies.

If you happen to be in Reno during the Safari Club International Convention (usually in January), you're in for an exotic taste treat. Area restaurants pull out all the stops to offer such extraordinary menu items as rack of elk, rib eye of yak, and ground alligator cakes.

With entrees including fresh fish, pasta, and meats, you can indulge yourself in such culinary delights as trout stuffed with crab, venison medallions in wine sauce, and pork tenderloin with caramelized apples. Bricks is also well known for its superb choice of wines by the glass and its variety of single-malt Scotches. The ambience is one of old-world elegance, crisp white linens contrasting with dark brown woods. The restaurant is open Tuesday through Friday for lunch and dinner and dinner only on Saturday. Smoke-free.

The Stone House Cafe **$$**
1907 South Arlington Avenue
(775) 284-3895
Oozing a quaint charm all its own, The Stone House Cafe is one of the newest and most delightful additions to the Reno dining scene. Nestled in an old stone house that has been completely renovated, the restaurant offers up a wildly eclectic variety of cuisine for breakfast, lunch, and dinner. Although it's best described as "continental," you'll find something for every taste here—from specialty American breakfasts to Lamb Indini to Guido's Meatball Pasta. Seating during cold weather is limited to several cozy indoor dining areas and the lively bar at the entrance. When weather permits, however, the large garden, with its firepit, fountain, and umbrella-covered tables, makes an especially charming place to eat. When The Stone House first opened, parking was somewhat of a problem. However, staff emphasizes that the situation has been rectified. The restaurant is open everyday, and reservations are advised.

French

RENO

Beaujolais Bistro **$$**
130 West Street
(775) 323-2227
www.beaujolaisbistro.com
If you've loved dining in Paris, the next best thing to it (Reno-style) is Beaujolais Bistro. Not only is the food just what you'd expect from a well-seasoned French chef, but the ambience is perfectly Parisian. The former site of La Vecchia Italian restaurant, the restaurant's brick walls, wood furnishings, and burgundy and blue fabrics give the century-old structure an intimate, cozy feel. You'll find such delights as rabbit with Dijon mustard and frog legs with herb butter on the menu. Just 1 block from the Truckee River in downtown, it's convenient to theaters, galleries, and nightlife. The bistro is open for lunch and dinner Tuesday through Friday and dinner only on Saturday and Sunday.

German

RENO

Bavarian World **$$**
595 Valley Road
(775) 323-7646
A unique restaurant, deli, and bakery rolled into one, Bavarian World specializes in the food and beer of southern Germany. The restaurant is noted for its sauerbraten and its pork roast, and the bakery specializes in crusty German breads and rolls (its rye bread comes highly recommended). The deli offers the largest selection of cold cuts and sausages in the area and features more than 12 different kinds of liverwurst. Bavarian World also has an Alpine Boutique, which sells hats, children's clothes, and dresses. The restaurant section has a huge dance floor and an intimate bar tucked away in the back. A fun restaurant with excellent food, Bavarian World is

open Tuesday through Saturday for breakfast, lunch, and dinner and for breakfast and lunch on Monday.

Indian

RENO

India Garden Restaurant **$$**
1565 South Virginia Street
(775) 337-8002

In the former location of Odette's, India Garden Restaurant offers an extensive menu of curries, tandoori specialities, and vegetarian delights. Although the wine list is nothing to shout about, you'll find a selection of 12 homemade Indian breads. With rich blue goblets adorning the crisp white table linens, the overall ambience is bright and cheery. It's open daily for lunch and dinner and, like most Indian restaurants, serves up a tantalizing lunch buffet from steaming copper chafing dishes. Smoke-free.

Italian

RENO

Johnny's Ristorante Italiano **$$**
4245 West Fourth Street
(775) 747-4511

A longtime local favorite, Johnny's serves up delectable Italian cuisine with a touch of elegance. With classy high-backed chairs and a marble sculpture that dominates the room, the dining area is reminiscent of a lovely old Roman villa. Some menu selections tend to be on the rich side, but low-fat entrees are also included. You'll find a tantalizing variety of fresh seafood, pastas, and meats to choose from. If you're looking for lighter fare, I suggest pizza and salad in the delightful Italian contemporary bar up front. The pizza is low-fat and absolutely delicious. Johnny's is open for dinner Tuesday through Saturday and is closed the first three weeks of January each year.

La Vecchia **$$**
3501 South Virginia Street
(775) 825-1113

Many regulars at La Vecchia lamented the restaurant's recent move from its intimate old-world digs near the Truckee River to a larger, utterly contemporary location south of downtown. Progress for the business apparently dictated more room plus the sleek modern look typical of many Italian restaurants these days (whatever happened to the red-and-white-checked cloths and bottles of Chianti that used to be standard fare on Italian tables?). Although some of the old romance is gone, the new decor is pleasant, with a variety of woods creating a lustrous backdrop for the snappy white tablecloths. The menu remains the same, featuring only foods that are freshly prepared on the premises. Far from the usual spaghetti house, La Vecchia offers a tantalizing selection of food that combines the flavors of several cultures. But be prepared for a rich meal. The restaurant is open for lunch Monday through Friday and for dinner nightly.

Luciano's **$$**
719 South Virginia Street
(775) 322-7373

6135 Lakeside Drive
(775) 828-0400

Luciano Parisi, the owner/chef of these fine Italian restaurants, hails from Bologna, Italy, and has brought with him some excellent family recipes. He offers a great selection of appetizers, soups, salads, and more than a dozen pastas along with meat, chicken, and fish dishes. The porcini mushroom ravioli is the signature dish.

The Virginia Street location is reminiscent of the small family restaurants so prevalent in large cities, such as New York and San Francisco. It offers an intimate bistro ambience in a traditional environment. Because there are so few tables, I strongly recommend calling for a reservation. In the former location of Einstein's Quantum Cafe, the Lakeside Drive restaurant is much larger and features a slick, modern decor. The Virginia Street location is open for dinner Tuesday through Saturday, and the Lakeside Drive site serves lunch Tuesday through Friday and dinner Tuesday through Sunday. Smoke-free.

Viaggio $$
2309 Kietzke Lane
(775) 828-2708
The Reno/Tahoe area has an abundance of Italian restaurants, but this one, located in Franktown Corners, has by far the best selection of wines. Almost half of this place is a wine shop where you can sample about 25 good to excellent wines by the glass. The other half is an intimate restaurant with a modern motif and an open kitchen in the back. Viaggio makes all of its pastas from scratch, including the ravioli. It serves all of the Italian favorites: osso buco, fettuccine Alfredo, saltimbocca—but its forte is its extensive wine list with more than 1,000 selections. Viaggio's is open Monday through Saturday for lunch and dinner and for dinner only on Sunday. Smoke-free.

Zozo's Ristorante $$
3446 Lakeside Drive
(775) 829-9449
www.zozosreno.com
Tucked in the Moana West Shopping Center, Zozo's offers the regional cuisine of Italy in an old-world environment. Its intimate ambience reminds me of many of the small ethnic restaurants sprinkled all over San Francisco. As expected in any Italian eatery, you'll find lots of pasta dishes on the menu along with veal, game hen, seafood, and beef prepared in traditional ways. With personable, friendly service, the staff at Zozo's makes you feel almost like family. Reservations are advised, since the place is quite small. It's open for lunch Monday through Friday and dinner daily.

Mexican and Southwestern

RENO

Bertha Miranda's $
336 Mill Street
(775) 786-9697
Bertha Miranda's is one of the most established Mexican restaurants in the Reno/Sparks area. Long before the recent influx of Hispanics and profusion of Latino restaurants, Bertha was serving some of the best Mexican food I've eaten north of the border. If you like Mexican food but can't handle a lot of grease, you'll love the cuisine here. You'll find all the traditional favorites featured, but prepared with a minimum of vegetable oil rather than a maximum of animal fat. In summer you can enjoy outdoor dining on a tree-shaded patio.

Cantina Los Tres Hombres $
7111 South Virginia Street
(775) 852-0202
www.cantinalth.com
At Cantina Los Tres Hombres, you'll find all your Mexican favorites served in a typical south-of-the-border environment. A child-friendly establishment with good food at reasonable prices, it's a great place to take the whole family. The bar up front, with its big-screen TVs, is a popular meet-and-greet hangout for young singles and sports fans. The cantina is open daily for lunch and dinner.

SPARKS

Cantina Los Tres Hombres $
926 Victorian Avenue
(775) 356-6262
www.cantinalth.com
See Reno listing for more information.

El Sazon $
2290 Oddie Boulevard
(775) 351-2352

This Mexican restaurant started in a five-table space in Greenbrae Shopping Center in Sparks but was so popular it quickly outgrew such modest surroundings. A good sign of a great Mexican restaurant is when you hear Spanish being spoken by a majority of the diners, and it happens a lot at El Sazon. The restaurant is open daily for breakfast, lunch, and dinner, and the waiters and waitresses are friendly and helpful if you don't know what to order. Everything is homemade on the premises: no canned refried beans here. Its specialties include the Carne Asada (marinated, grilled rib-eye steak), the Chuletas de Puerco (marinated pork chops), and the Langosta a La Mexicana (Mexican broiled lobster just like in Baja, California). Even the tortillas are homemade here, so you can't go wrong ordering any of the standby's, like tacos and enchiladas. Don't miss this restaurant if you want authentic Mexican food.

Seafood

RENO

Rapscallion Seafood House & Bar $$
1555 South Wells Avenue
(775) 323-1211
www.rapscallion.com

Known for some years as "Reno's Official Seafood Restaurant," Rapscallion Seafood House & Bar prides itself on its selection of freshly caught fish. With historical memorabilia tastefully displayed on the dark wood walls, the dining and bar areas have the look and feel of turn-of-the-20th-century San Francisco. Weather permitting, you can also enjoy outside seating on the surrounding deck. The bar is a popular meet-and-greet hangout, with live entertainment Wednesday through Saturday. Rapscallion is open daily for dinner, Monday through Friday for lunch, and also serves a special brunch on Sunday.

Steak Houses

RENO

Washoe Steakhouse $$$
4201 West Fourth Street
(775) 786-1323
www.washoesteakhouse.com

If you were a fan of the old Glory Hole (the Nevada-style steak place previously located here), you might be stunned to see the slick new decor of the Washoe Steakhouse. The shiny wood floors and stark white walls are a far cry from the 1960s cowboy ambience of yesteryear, but sit back and relax: The cozy fireplace and mile-long (or so it seems) bar with a view are still in place. And best of all, the food is delicious. The grill is open for lunch Monday through Friday, for breakfast Saturday and Sunday, and for dinner daily.

LAKE TAHOE AREA

American

NORTH SHORE LAKE TAHOE

Austin's $$
Country Club Drive, across from the Hyatt Regency Lake Tahoe Resort, Spa & Casino in the Country Club Center
Incline Village, NV
(775) 832-7778

If you miss your mother's cooking, you just might find it at Austin's: The restaurant is well known to Insiders for serving huge portions of good home-cooked food. The outside is unimpressive, but inside the restaurant resembles a rustic log cabin reminiscent of an old hunting lodge. The hearty food and casual decor suit the mountain environment perfectly. For lunch you can choose from substantial hot entrees, a variety of burgers, and super salad bowls. Dinner offerings include steaks and fish, along with such down-home favorites as liver and onions, meat loaf, and grilled pork chops. With delicious homemade pies displayed prominently up front, Austin's is not a place for dieters. Forget the calories and dive into a meal that tastes like it was made by dear ole Mom—you can always ski or hike it off the next day. Austin's is open for lunch and dinner daily during the summer. The rest of the year dinner is served daily and lunch is served weekdays only.

Big Water Grille **$$**
341 Ski Way Drive
Incline Village, NV
(775) 833-0606
www.bigwatergrille.com

Combining American contemporary with Mediterranean and Pacific Rim influences, the cuisine at the Big Water Grille offers a delightful culinary experience to the most discriminating diners. Throw in spectacular panoramic views of Lake Tahoe and a classy Tahoe decor that incorporates upscale art, and you have a truly memorable evening.

You can celebrate a romantic special occasion here or just stop by after skiing (Diamond Peak Ski Resort is just up the road). The roaring fire in the cozy bar up front is especially inviting on a cold winter's evening—the perfect place to enjoy an appetizer of miso-glazed wild hamachi. Menu selections vary, but could include such delights as cervina venison chops or summer truffle squab breast. Be sure to take a look at the petroglyph designs and etched glass that make the atmosphere unique. The restaurant is open for dinner nightly, with cocktails and appetizers served from 4:30 P.M. and dinner from 5:30 P.M. Be sure to call ahead.

Bridgetender Tavern & Grill **$**
At the "Y" intersection of California Highways 89 and 28 in Tahoe City, CA
(530) 583-3342

If a juicy burger and a pint of beer are your idea of the perfect lunch or dinner, then the Bridgetender is the place to be. This humble restaurant boasts an extensive selection of beers on tap, daily beer specials, and a traditional bar menu that includes burgers of every description. For those who don't want beef, the Bridgetender also offers turkey and veggie burgers with all the trimmings, as well as other menu selections.

This restaurant recently moved across the street, so don't be shocked if you find a vacant lot in the prior location. Although not as campy as its old digs, the new building features an extended patio overlooking the Truckee River.

The Bridgetender is open daily for lunch and dinner.

Frederick's Bistro & Bar **$$**
907 Tahoe Boulevard
Incline Village, NV
(775) 832-3007
www.fredsfusion.com

Almost hidden among small retail establishments along Tahoe Boulevard, Frederick's is easy to miss. If you're an Incline regular, you'll remember another restaurant, Jack Rabbit Moon, that occupied this space a few years ago. The decor is California chic, with an intimate feel. The light plank floors, copper tabletops, veggie paintings, and cheery fireplace exude a welcoming ambience. The cuisine is billed as seasonal California with French-Asian Fusion, which means you'll find such delectable entrees as ricotta-stuffed eggplant and Muscovy duck breast along with an extensive list of sushi items. Reservations are advised during high season because seating is limited. Dinner is served Tuesday through Saturday. Smoke-free.

Gar Woods Grill and Pier **$$**
5000 North Lake Boulevard
Carnelian Bay, CA
(530) 546-3366
www.garwoods.com

Named for the elegant mahogany boats developed in the 1920s by Garfield Wood, Gar Woods Grill and Pier celebrates fine food along with Tahoe's classic wood boating era. Nestled on the lakeshore right next to Sierra Boat Company, and bordering on a public pier and beach, Gar Woods is a beehive of activity during the Concourse de Elegance in August, when the wonderful woodies are on display. The dinner menu at this laid-back eatery features a variety of pasta, fresh seafood, and steaks; appetizers include beer-battered coconut prawns; and the lunch menu includes a pepper and garlic turkey burger. The wine list is good, but the cocktail menu, featuring such provocative names as the "Wet Woody," is great. If you arrive by boat (except in winter), you can take advantage of valet boat parking at the pier. The view of the lake (either from the deck or the indoor dining area) is lovely, and the people-watching can't be beat. It's open for lunch and dinner daily during high season; lunch is served weekends only during low season.

Jake's on the Lake **$$**
760 North Lake Boulevard
Tahoe City, CA
(530) 583-0188
www.jakestahoe.com

A classy but casual eatery, Jake's on the Lake is tucked on the lakeside of the Boatworks Mall and features lovely views of the water. It's especially convenient if you've been browsing the shops in the mall. Woodsy and warm, this place has a laid-back Old Tahoe feeling. I suggest enjoying sundown in the bar over an appetizer and your favorite drink. Outdoor seating is available in summer, and some tables in the indoor dining area offer views of the lake. The dinner menu features steaks, chicken, and seafood; sandwiches and salads are available in the bar. Open for lunch and dinner daily; shortened winter hours.

Lone Eagle Grille **$$$**
Hyatt Regency Lake Tahoe Resort, Spa and Casino
111 Country Club Drive, Incline Village, NV
(775) 832-1234
www.laketahoehyatt.com

If decor alone were the measure of a great meal, the Lone Eagle Grille would rank as one of the most outstanding restaurants in the Reno/Tahoe area. With enormous vaulted ceilings, two-story rock fireplaces, huge wrought-iron chandeliers, and mammoth windows opening out onto Lake Tahoe, its ambience is equal to none. Just being here and soaking up the environment is special. From an Insiders viewpoint, however, it may not give you the best value for your money: It's expensive, and the service is so-so.

If you don't feel like splurging, come here for lunch, or enjoy drinks and appetizers in the bar—the view is the same as in the dining room. You can also take your drink to the firepit on the beach just in front of the restaurant. The dinner menu features grilled beef, veal, lamb, fowl, fresh seafood, and pasta. The restaurant is open daily for lunch and dinner. Although it's part of the Hyatt Regency Lake Tahoe Resort, Spa & Casino, you won't find it in the main hotel building: Look for the elegant vaulted structure right on the lakeshore.

Steamers Beach Side Bar and Oven **$**
8290 North Lake Boulevard
Kings Beach, CA
(530) 546-2218

For a kicked-back, inexpensive lunch or dinner, you can't beat the pizza, oven-baked sandwiches, and calzones served up at Steamers Beach Side Bar and Oven. With an amazing array of ingredients to choose from, you can design your own pizza just the way you like it. For lighter fare choose from a tasty selection of soups and salads, including Steamers' own clam chowder. Nestled on the white sands of Kings Beach, Steamers is a great place to feed the whole family. In summer you can enjoy your meal on the small patio overlooking the lake. It's open daily for lunch and dinner.

Sunnyside **$$**
1850 West Lake Boulevard
Tahoe City, CA
(530) 583-7200
www.sunnysideresort.com

The spacious outdoor deck at Sunnyside is the place to be for drinks, lunch, or dinner in summer. From a sun-splashed table, you can soak up a gorgeous panoramic view while watching the boats come and go from the small dock fronting the restaurant. The cozy indoor dining room and bar, with a roaring fire and arcing timbered ceiling, is just as popular in winter: You can warm up and relax after a hard day on the slopes, enjoying a hot mulled wine followed by a gourmet dinner. The menu is typically American, with steaks, seafood, chicken, and pasta. If you're lucky enough to have booked a room in the lodge here, you can look forward to a delightful Old Tahoe stay indeed (see the Hotels and Motels chapter for more information about lodging). The restaurant serves dinner daily and lunch weekends during summer.

SOUTH SHORE LAKE TAHOE

Edgewood Restaurant $$$
180 Lake Parkway
Stateline, NV
(775) 588-2787
www.edgewood-tahoe.com

If decor is an important element in your dining experience, you won't find anything more majestic than Edgewood Restaurant at the Edgewood Tahoe Golf Course (see the Golf chapter for more information about the course). The restaurant/clubhouse perfectly reflects the grandeur of Lake Tahoe in its customized cathedral-like design. From the dramatic central cupola resting on 20-foot timbers to the wooden window dormers with intricate panes, the structure is a testimony to the beauty of custom woodworking. The blend of cedar, ash, teak, and granite lends power and luxury to the natural ambience of the building. And all this with an awesome view: The turquoise waves are lapping at the white-sand beach right outside, with the snowcapped Sierra Nevada mountains directly across the lake.

But aside from gawking at the surroundings, you're here to eat, right? The dinner menu features such delightful entrees as fresh sea bass, elk chops, rib-eye steak, fresh salmon, and ahi tuna, all served with fresh seasonal vegetables. Edgewood is open for dinner daily during summer. It serves dinner Wednesday through Sunday during winter and is closed the month of November. Reservations are advised.

As it's one of the most spectacular and romantic sites along the lakeshore, I highly recommend your visiting Edgewood, even if it's just for drinks and looks.

Evan's American Gourmet Cafe $$
536 Emerald Bay Road
South Lake Tahoe, CA
(530) 542-1990
www.evanstahoe.com

Tucked in a charming little house surrounded by pines, Evan's American Gourmet Cafe offers gourmet cuisine in an intimate romantic atmosphere. You can enjoy such tasty treats as peppered tenderloin of pork with apple-smoked bacon and veal sweetbreads with mushroom ragout. And speaking of wine, Evan's is an ongoing recipient of the "Award of Excellence" from *Wine Spectator* magazine and is continuously rated three stars in the Mobil Travel Guide and three diamonds in the AAA Guide. It's open daily for dinner, but call to verify during off-season. Reservations are advised.

Nepheles $$
1169 Ski Run Boulevard
South Lake Tahoe, CA
(530) 544-8130
www.nepheles.com

After navigating one last run down Gunbarrel at Heavenly Ski Resort, load up your skis and head down the road to Nepheles. The bar opens at 2:00 P.M., and you can relax over your favorite drink and discuss the best (or worst) runs of the day with your skiing buddies. Or how about popping into a hot tub in one of their private spa rooms, where you can enjoy cocktail service and stereo music while soothing your sore muscles? Then stick around for dinner: You can choose from a variety of creative California cuisine items, such as wild boar chops, grilled portobello mushrooms, and broiled elk. It all sounds like the perfect ending to a perfect day to me. Be sure to call for information and reservations for the spa. Nepheles is open year-round, with dinner served nightly.

Asian

SOUTH SHORE LAKE TAHOE

Hunan Garden **$**
900 Emerald Bay Road
South Lake Tahoe, CA
(530) 544-7268
If you've got a healthy appetite but a small budget, try the luncheon and dinner buffets at Hunan Garden restaurant. You can eat all you want of their distinctive Chinese cuisine at very affordable prices. You can also order from their full menu of selections, including beef, pork, chicken, and seafood entrees; vegetarian dishes; chow mein; and mu shu. If your children like Chinese food, it's an economical place for the whole family to enjoy dinner out. Hunan Garden is open for lunch and dinner daily.

Samurai Restaurant **$$**
2588 U.S. Highway 50
South Lake Tahoe, CA
(530) 542-0300
www.sushitahoe.com
It's hard to diet if you're on vacation, but dining at Samurai Restaurant will help you eat healthy: Most entrees are high in nutrition and low in fat and cholesterol. The traditional Japanese menu includes such favorites as teriyaki, tempura, nabemono, shioyaki, and sashimi. All dinner entrees include miso soup or salad and rice. The restaurant also offers some of the best sushi in the Tahoe area. Dinner is served daily.

Buffets

As mentioned in the Reno/Sparks portion of this chapter, buffets are a mainstay of casinos and gaming resorts. On the South Shore of the lake, try the following buffets:

One of the best places to enjoy lunch is along the Truckee River with a sandwich purchased from a local deli.

Forest Buffet
Harrah's Lake Tahoe
U.S. Highway 50
Stateline, NV
(775) 588-6611

Pacifica Seafood Buffet
Harveys Lake Tahoe Casino & Resort
U.S. Highway 50
Stateline, NV
(775) 588-2411

Town Square Buffet
Horizon Casino Resort Lake Tahoe
U.S. Highway 50
Stateline, NV
(775) 588-6211

Continental

NORTH SHORE LAKE TAHOE

Le Bistro **$$$**
120 Country Club Drive, #29
Incline Village, NV
(775) 831-0800
www.lebistrorestaurant.net
Dinner is always a special event at this very fine restaurant. Where the prix-fix menu includes appetizer, soup, salad, entree, and dessert. With an award-winning French chef preparing your dinner, it makes sense to try as many of his creations as possible. Although the menu varies daily, it could include velouté of fresh green asparagus, wild mushroom ravioli, limestone and baby leek salad, aiguillette of black angus, and rose petal crème brûlée. With its intimate elegance, Le Bistro is best suited to adults rather than families with small children. It's open for dinner Tuesday through Saturday, and reservations are advised. You'll find it on the back side of the Country Club Center,

which is across the street from the Hyatt Regency Lake Tahoe Resort, Spa & Casino. Smoke-free.

The Soule Domain **$$**
9983 Stateline Drive, next to the Tahoe Biltmore, Crystal Bay, CA
(530) 546-7529
www.souledomain.com

Voted "Best Place to Take a Date" for six years by *Action Magazine,* and recipient of numerous rave reviews from both local newspapers and the *San Francisco Chronicle,* The Soule Domain is intimate, romantic, and elegant. Nestled in a historic log cabin surrounded by pines, it specializes in continental/nouveau and creative American cuisine. One word of caution: Be sure to ask your server how "hot" the food is, as it can be very spicy. Tantalizing menu selections include Thai curry scallops, a smoked pheasant sausage salad, a tempting vegan sauté, and venison medallions. In winter you can dine at a cozy fireside table, and in summer limited patio dining is available, weather permitting. It's open for dinner nightly, and I recommend calling for reservations, as seating is limited. Look for The Soule Domain in Crystal Bay, just 10 yards across the state line in California.

SOUTH SHORE LAKE TAHOE

The Greenhouse Restaurant & Bar **$$**
4140 Cedar Avenue
South Lake Tahoe, CA
(530) 541-5800

When they named this place The Greenhouse, they weren't kidding: It's absolutely lush with green foliage. The abundance of flourishing plants along with the European stained glass, warm woods, and copper-topped bar creates a comfortable environment for fine dining. You can enjoy familiar entrees from the continent such as veal piccata and scallops alamor. The restaurant is open daily for dinner, and reservations are recommended. You'll find it conveniently located near Harveys Lake Tahoe Casino & Resort.

The Summit **$$$**
Harrah's Lake Tahoe
U.S. Highway 50
Stateline, NV
(775) 588-6611
www.harrahs.com

When Sammy Davis Jr. was a regular headliner in the South Shore Room of Harrah's Lake Tahoe, he stayed in the posh Star Suite tucked away on the 16th floor of the hotel. Other celebrities who made the suite their home-away-from-home included Frank Sinatra, Neil Sedaka, and Liza Minnelli. It was used as a set in the film *Things Change,* starring Don Ameche, and it was where Paul Anka composed many of his most famous hit tunes.

Affording gorgeous views of the lake, the Star Suite is a vision of loveliness, with an enormous two-story fireplace, an intimate bar, and a cozy mezzanine overlooking the main living space. Wouldn't you love to sit back and relax over a gourmet dinner in this very penthouse? Well, you can, since now it's The Summit, ranked one of the top 10 restaurants in the country by the American Academy of Restaurant Sciences.

Although I don't typically feature casino restaurants in this chapter since you're sure to find them on your own, you might not discover The Summit. Intimate and exclusive, it's not as widely known as many other restaurants in casinos. For an exceptional dining experience (especially that romantic special occasion), I highly recommend this restaurant. If you're lucky enough to get a reservation (be sure to call well ahead), expect a very leisurely and memorable evening. Although you won't need a tux, it's certainly an occasion for nice clothing.

The restaurant is open for dinner Friday through Sunday. You can also enjoy a drink in the adjoining Cliché Lounge.

Swiss Chalet Restaurant **$$**
2544 Lake Tahoe Boulevard
South Lake Tahoe, CA
(530) 544-3304

An institution in the South Shore Lake

Tahoe area for more than 40 years, the Swiss Chalet Restaurant is the next best thing to dining in Switzerland. You'll need to throw your diet out the window to enjoy most of the cuisine here, but it's worth it since everything is absolutely delicious. Specialties of the house include Swiss veal, curry Stroganoff, German sauerbraten, and, of course, that old favorite, Wiener schnitzel. It's open for dinner Tuesday through Sunday throughout the year. The restaurant is closed for three weeks beginning in mid-November.

French

NORTH SHORE LAKE TAHOE

Engadine Cafe at Rainbow Lodge $$
Rainbow Road, exit Interstate 80
west of Truckee, CA
(530) 426-3661
www.royalgorge.com

Although it's a little far afield (unless you're cross-country skiing at Royal Gorge), Rainbow Lodge is worth the drive. Built in the 1920s of hand-hewn timber and granite, the lodge oozes the history of the Sierras. You can step back in time and imagine what winters were like when heavy snow made skiing the only possible mode of transportation. Tucked deep in the pines along the American River, the setting is exquisite any time of the year.

The cuisine in the Engadine Cafe features fine French and California entrees. The menu is subject to change, but you might enjoy such tasty delights as swordfish on rice noodles with hoisin glaze, and salmon on a bed of couscous with a mango salsa. Because the lodge is popular with health-conscious hikers and skiers, you'll also find vegetarian selections.

You can soak up Sierra history along with gourmet food for breakfast Monday through Friday, lunch Monday through Saturday, with brunch on Sunday, and dinner daily during high season, but the lodge and restaurant are closed Tuesday and Wednesday during off-season. Dinner reservations are advised during high season, and I suggest you call to verify hours during off-season. For details about cross-country skiing at Royal Gorge, see the Winter Sports chapter.

To get to the lodge from Kings Beach, take California Highway 267 north to Truckee (about 6 miles), then travel west on I-80 for about 10 minutes to the Rainbow-Big Bend exit.

For a list of some of the smoke-free eating establishments in northern Nevada, go to www.notobacconevada.com

Italian

NORTH SHORE LAKE TAHOE

Azzara's Italian Restaurant $$
930 Tahoe Boulevard
Incline Village, NV
(775) 831-0346

A great favorite with locals, Azzara's will more than satisfy your craving for first-class pasta. Other entrees include steak Toscano, paella, and osso buco. The restaurant has a laid-back, comfortable atmosphere, perfect for enjoying a meal with friends or the whole family. If you have to wait for a table (which is likely, since it's a popular place), just have a seat in the bar area and talk skiing, golf, or hiking with the locals. Conveniently located in Raleys Incline Center, Azzara's is open for dinner Tuesday through Sunday. Smoke-free.

Lanza's $
7739 North Lake Boulevard
Kings Beach, CA
(530) 546-2434

With its casual decor and reasonable prices, Lanza's is a good choice for families with children. You can relax in its family-friendly atmosphere after a hard day skiing or hiking. From its varied selections of pasta, pizza, chicken, and veal, you're sure to find everybody's favorite. If you're just too tired to eat in a restaurant, you can give a call and order from the restaurant's take-out service. Lanza's is open for dinner daily year-round.

SOUTH SHORE LAKE TAHOE

Cafe Fiore **$$**
1169 Ski Run Boulevard, #5
South Lake Tahoe, CA
(530) 541-2908
www.cafefiore.com

If you are looking for a romantic, intimate dinner, Cafe Fiore should be one of your first choices. With only eight tables, the restaurant is extremely cozy and provides an ideal opportunity to be especially pampered. A *Wine Spectator* 2000 "Award of Excellence" winner, the restaurant offers such delights as spaghetti with Italian sausage, prosciutto, fresh tomatoes, spinach, red chiles, and garlic; a host of seafood pastas; chicken sautéed with wild mushrooms, artichoke hearts, and tomatoes in a Chardonnay cream sauce; and saltimbocca. Entrees are served with a salad and fresh vegetable. Open daily for dinner.

Passaretti's **$$**
1181 Emerald Bay Road
South Lake Tahoe, CA
(530) 541-3433
www.passarettis.com

As soon as you walk through the front entranceway and see the walls covered with children's colored-in cartoons, you know that you're in the perfect family restaurant. However, the family-friendly ambience is not the only draw here. Passaretti's serves up generous portions of old-style, home-cooked Italian foods such as linguini in clam sauce, fettuccine Alfredo, manicotti, and lasagna. Entrees, which are also served with a soup or salad bar and choice of pasta or potato, include chicken Marsala, calamari almandine, prawns scampi, and veal Parmigiana. Steak lovers can choose between New York steak and a marinated sirloin. There's nothing really fancy here, just plain, old-fashioned, good cooking. Open for lunch and dinner daily.

i ***If you're on a budget, try eating your main meal at lunch. Many restaurants serve the same entrees as at dinner, but at cheaper prices. Since it's better to not eat heavy meals late in the day, this may be healthier for you, too. Cheaper and healthier—what more could you ask for?***

Scusa! on Ski Run **$$**
1142 Ski Run Boulevard
South Lake Tahoe, CA
(530) 542-0100

One of the most popular Italian restaurants in the South Shore Lake Tahoe area, Scusa! on Ski Run specializes in California Italian fare, with creative pasta, seafood, eggplant, veal, and chicken entrees. The ambience is comfortably casual, with white walls and tablecloths, accented by black furniture and splashes of bright color. It's conveniently located on the road to Heavenly Ski Resort and has plenty of parking. Scusa! serves dinner daily. Reservations are advised.

Latino

NORTH SHORE LAKE TAHOE

Sol y Lago **$$**
760 North Lake Boulevard
Tahoe City, CA
(530) 583-0358
www.solylago.com

In response to the growing Hispanic influence in the Reno/Tahoe area, Sol y Lago (which means "sun and lake" in English) is a new eatery specializing in Sierra Latino Cuisine. Located in the site formerly occupied by Hacienda del Lago, this restaurant is tucked in the back of the Boatworks Mall and offers great views of the lake. The menu showcases foods from Spain, Argentina, Chile, and the Basque country, including cassoulet Basque, butternut squash and queso fresco empanaditas, and churascaria-style pork loin chop. Not only is the food a cosmopolitan delight, but the old-world service makes dining here an especially enjoyable experience. The 30-seat bar offers perfect viewing for sunset over the lake while you enjoy a typical Latin cocktail or wine. Patio dining is available during summer, and live entertainment is offered on the weekends. Sol y Lago is open daily for dinner.

SOUTH SHORE LAKE TAHOE

The Cantina Bar & Grill **$**
765 Emerald Bay Road
South Lake Tahoe, CA
(530) 544-1233
www.cantinatahoe.com

If you're driving by the Cantina on a Friday or Saturday night, you know that this is the spot where everyone goes for great margaritas and hearty Mexican food. Voted the best Mexican restaurant in South Lake Tahoe seven years running, this is a popular hangout for both drinking (more than 30 beers are offered) and dining. The Cantina offers your standard Mexican fare of burritos, fajitas, chili verde, enchiladas, and chili rellenos. But if you're feeling a little more adventurous, be sure to try the calamari relleno, the smoked chicken polenta, or the blue corn salmon. Outside dining is available on the patio. Open daily from 11:30 A.M. on for lunch and dinner.

Seafood

NORTH SHORE LAKE TAHOE

Wild Alaskan Restaurant & Bar **$$**
930 Tahoe Boulevard
Raley's Center
Incline Village, NV
(775) 832-6777

Although you'll find plenty of meat, poultry, and veggie choices in this casual eatery, the main bill of fare is decidedly fish. As the name indicates, the salmon is wild from the Copper River in Alaska and can be found in salad, cakes, tacos, and cooked to perfection with a caper-dill aioli. I also recommend the Raspberry Sunflower Salad, the Wild Thai Seafood Soup, and the Thai curry. If your sweet tooth just must be satisfied, take note of the delectable desserts prominently on display up front. Wild Alaskan is very laid-back, so don't stay away because you're in ski clothes. It's open daily for lunch and dinner.

SOUTH SHORE LAKE TAHOE

The Fresh Ketch **$$**
2435 Venice Drive East
South Lake Tahoe, CA
(530) 541-5683
www.thefreshketch.com

What better place to enjoy scrumptious fresh seafood than right on the water? At The Fresh Ketch you can feast on fish in the upstairs dining room, in the seafood bar, or on the patio, all overlooking lovely Lake Tahoe. Menu items include fresh oysters, steamed New Zealand clams, Alaskan king crab, cioppino, and mixed seafood grill. Live music is offered on Friday nights. The restaurant is easy to find in the Tahoe Keys Marina. It's open daily for lunch and dinner, and reservations are recommended.

Steak Houses

NORTH SHORE LAKE TAHOE

Old Range Steakhouse **$$**
7081 North Lake Boulevard
Tahoe Vista, CA
(530) 546-4800

You know this restaurant has something to brag about: The prime cuts of meat are proudly displayed as you walk in the door. The Old Range Steakhouse is a meat-eater's paradise, with every cut of beef served every way imaginable. It's all delicious, it's all tender, and it's all juicy.

Lighter fare is also available at the Range, where you'll also find vegetarian selections on the menu. What more could you want? Well, try views of Lake Tahoe,

Children are welcome at most restaurants in the Reno/Tahoe area, but bear in mind that not every establishment is well suited for kids. Parents may find little on the menu that will satisfy picky eaters, and prices may be exorbitant for small appetites. Look for child-friendly family restaurants, many of which offer activity menus and meals priced and portioned for children.

just across the road, and a warm, homey, Western ambience you can just sink down into. Do I like this place? You betcha. You can ride the range for dinner every night.

If you want to add an artistic element to your evening out, come a little early and drop into the Vista Gallery upstairs, enjoy the view from the deck, and have a drink before settling into a succulent steak. (See the chapter on The Arts for more information on the gallery.)

SOUTH SHORE LAKE TAHOE

Lake Tahoe Chart House **$$**
392 Kingsbury Grade
Stateline, NV
(775) 588-6276
www.chart-house.com

Boasting a recent million-dollar renovation, the Lake Tahoe Chart House offers diners spectacular lake views from its perch in the pines. Specializing in seafood, steaks, and prime rib, signature dishes include Dynamite Mahimahi and the Crab, Avocado and Mango Stack appetizer. It's convenient to find up Kingsbury Grade on the way to the Nevada side of Heavenly Ski Resort. The Chart House is open daily for dinner; reservations are advised.

Tearooms and Coffeehouses

NORTH SHORE LAKE TAHOE

Syd's Bagelry & Espresso **$**
550 North Lake Boulevard
Tahoe City, CA
(530) 583-2666

On your way to a full day at one of the North Shore's ski resorts? Stop in at Syd's for a quick bite and a cup of piping-hot java before you hit the slopes.

In addition to the traditional coffeehouse fare, this busy coffee shop also whips up exotic bagel sandwiches, from a Reuben to The Taj, featuring a curry "schmear" (cream cheese blend) with smoked turkey, cucumber, and cashews. Vegetarian lunch selections include the Dalai Dog, a tofu hot dog on a whole grain bun. If coffee's not your cup, try a smoothie or chai tea. And the breakfast pastries are universally yummy. Try the Morning Glory muffin, fruitful and moist, or the hearty zucchini bread. Syd's is open daily from 6:00 A.M. to 6:00 P.M.

Tahoe House **$**
625 West Lake Boulevard
Tahoe City, CA
(530) 583-1377
www.tahoe-house.com

You may stop by Tahoe House for just a quick bite, but it's almost impossible to leave without armloads of fresh baked goods and gourmet foods that are made right on the premises. The deli serves up absolutely scrumptious salads, soups, and sandwiches and also serves espresso and to-die-for European pastries. You can eat inside or, weather permitting, watch the bikers go by from the outdoor tables. You can indulge here from 6:00 A.M. to 6:00 P.M. daily.

SOUTH SHORE LAKE TAHOE

Alpina Cafe Lake Tahoe **$**
822 Emerald Bay Road
South Lake Tahoe, CA
(530) 541-7449
www.alpinacafe.com

Looking for a great latte, a scrumptious baked good, and a mellow atmosphere to sit and read a great book? This is your spot. If you need more nourishment than caffeine and sugar, the cafe also offers great sandwiches, pasta, and salads. This spot is a vegetarian's haven. The cafe is open from 6:00 A.M. to 6:00 P.M. daily.

Dining outdoors on a patio or deck? Most restaurants have tables with umbrellas, but just in case, don't forget to put on the sunscreen during the day and have a sweater handy in the evening.

NIGHTLIFE

Insiders say that the nightlife in the Reno/Tahoe area is 24-7-365. It's rocking 24 hours a day, 7 days a week, 365 days a year.

The only city in the world that can outdo the Reno/Tahoe area for nighttime entertainment is its big sister to the south. But being second still puts it way, way ahead of other cities. Reno does an outstanding job of keeping visitors and locals alike hip-hopping to the night scene. In fact, Insiders joke that here, the nightlife lasts all day.

Throughout the year, the area jumps and jives from the sounds of big-time production numbers in the casino showrooms to the local punk band pounding out tunes in its first gig at one of those three-stooled, dimly lit dives. Because of the large Hispanic population in the area, a number of nightspots showcase Latino music and dancing. But if you want a cozy place where you can snuggle next to a fire, we've got that, too. In fact, we've got just about every kind of nightlife scene covered. And remember, most of the casinos have cabarets or lounges where some of the best Insider talent performs just about every hour of every night of the week, and the best thing is, the lounge entertainment is free.

Major performing artists like Jay Leno, Chicago, Bill Maher, Jeff Foxworthy, Carrot Top, Glen Campbell, the 5th Dimension, and Olivia Newton-John constantly pop in and out of the area. We've got comedy stores. We've got pubs and microbreweries. We've got nightclubs. So you can see that you can't whine that there's nothing to do at night here.

i ***To some people the best nightlife is sharing songs around a campfire underneath an umbrella of winking stars.***

That's the magnificent thing about this area: No matter what the season or what the weather, you can play hard all day and party hard all night. In this chapter, I'll toss out my favorite picks of the night scene in the Reno/Tahoe area. I'll point you in the right direction no matter what your tastes happen to be. I'll guide you to the best karaoke bars, nightclubs, brewpubs, country and western dance halls, and other nightlife that the area has to offer. (See the Casino Nightlife chapter for a rundown of the entertainment offerings in the casino showrooms.)

This chapter is divided by type of establishment, then by geographical locations to help you find just the right place that tickles your fancy.

I would, however, like to put in a disclaimer here: The Reno/Tahoe area is dotted with hundreds of bars, but I have listed only the Insiders' choices, most of which have entertainment, both live and recorded. As far as the rest of the bars are concerned, you're on your own.

Just heed these words of warning: On the California side of the area, bars usually open at 6:00 A.M. and close at 2:00 A.M., but on the Nevada side of the area, liquor laws allow 24-hour-a-day drinking if you're 21 or older. So pace yourself and be aware of the driving under the influence law (see the Getting Here, Getting Around chapter for a detailed explanation of the law). The one place guaranteed to be a drag during the night is the county jails, so behave in a responsible manner.

Also remember that the night scene changes constantly. There's no guarantee that by the time you read this book that a specific bar may still offer live entertainment at the time listed. To keep up on what's happening, grab one of the weekly entertainment guides (see the Media and Casino Nightlife chapters for a list). Now, let's party.

COMEDY CLUBS

Reno

Catch a Rising Star
Silver Legacy Resort Casino
407 North Virginia Street
(775) 325-7401, (775) 329-4777
www.silverlegacyreno.com
This national chain of comedy clubs has bolstered the careers of such stars as Robin Williams, Jerry Seinfeld, Brett Butler, and Billy Crystal. This theater has a 200-seat capacity and books established comedians. The format generally calls for shows at 7:30 and 10:00 P.M. Friday and Saturday and at 8:00 P.M. Sunday and Tuesday through Thursday. Tickets run from $15 to $17 and include one beverage. Nevada residents can get two-for-one tickets by showing a Nevada driver's license when they buy tickets at the box office at Silver Legacy.

Funny Bone
Sands Regency Casino Hotel
345 North Arlington Avenue
(775) 348-2200
www.sandsregency.com
Show times are 8:30 P.M. Tuesday through Sunday. Tickets run about $13 during the week and $15 on weekends. Probably the best deal is the dinner and show packages, which start at $20. Two-for-one shows are on Thursday. The room is nonsmoking, and you must be at least 18 years old to be admitted. The format usually includes two comedians per show.

South Shore Lake Tahoe

Improv at Harveys
Harveys Lake Tahoe Casino & Resort
U.S. Highway 50, Stateline, NV
(775) 588-2411, (800) 427-8397
www.harrahs.com
With the marriage of Harveys and Harrah's, the comedy club was moved across the street. Now located in the Cabaret at Harveys, the Improv features established comics Tuesday through Thursday and Sunday for $25 and Friday and Saturday for $30. You must be 21 to attend.

COUNTRY AND WESTERN DANCING

Sparks

Pure Country Dance Hall
1955 Oddie Boulevard
(775) 331-4441
If you like to enjoy your country music in a down-home environment, stop by Pure Country Dance Hall. You'll feel it's your home-away-from-home. New to the local club scene, Pure Country is open from 3:00 P.M. to whenever, with country-western dance lessons offered at 7:00 P.M. Tuesday and Thursday; karaoke from 7:00 P.M. on Wednesday. On Friday and Saturday nights the club features live music. The club limits entrance to 185 people, so I suggest you get here early on weekends—a line at the door is not unusual.

MICROBREWERIES

Reno

Brew Brothers
Eldorado Hotel/Casino Reno
345 North Virginia Street
(775) 786-5700
www.eldoradoreno.com
Located inside the Eldorado Hotel/Casino Reno, the Brew Brothers's clientele is usually about 50 percent visitors and 50 percent locals. This brewpub is always crowded, especially on Friday night. The reason: the beer. Try the Redhead Amber or the Double Down Stout. It has local bands performing during the week and headline bands on the weekend. Ages vary from early 20s up to the late 40s. The pub food here is very good, too.

i ***For complete listings of nightlife options, be sure to pick up a copy of the* Reno News and Review *or the "Calendar" insert in Friday's* Reno Gazette-Journal.**

Silver Peak Restaurant & Brewery
124 Wonder Street
(775) 324-1864
www.silverpeakbrewery.com
Tucked in an older established downtown neighborhood, Silver Peak offers at least eight brews on tap every day. Favorites include Red Roadster, XXX Blonde, and Sierra Amber Ale. Besides serving great beer, the owners of this restaurant take pride in offering food that's decidedly above typical brewpub fare. You can enjoy lunch and dinner here daily in a casual indoor environment or, weather permitting, in comfortable outdoor seating on the upstairs deck. Although the beer is brewed at this location, you can also imbibe at their second restaurant, Silver Peak Grill & Taproom on the River, 135 North Sierra Street. Just steps from the Truckee River and theaters downtown, this location is a popular people-watching hangout. Call (775) 284-3300 for reservations.

Sparks

Great Basin Brewery
846 Victorian Avenue
(775) 355-7711
www.greatbasinbrewingco.com
This is the most popular nightspot in Sparks and is located just off Victorian Square. Besides having great food (try the fish-and-chips or the sausage sampler), Great Basin brews its own beers and, for its effort, has been awarded gold, silver, and bronze medals over the years in the Great American Beer Festival. It has also been voted the Truckee Meadows's best brewpub three years in a row. Besides outstanding beer (Insiders recommend the Jackpot Porter or the Nevada Gold), Great Basin features comedy, jazz, and folk music. Check the Web site and the Restaurants chapter for more information.

South Shore Lake Tahoe

The Brewery at Lake Tahoe
3542 U.S. Highway 50
South Lake Tahoe, CA
(530) 544-2739
A well-established hangout for beer aficionados, the Brewery at Lake Tahoe features great home-brewed beer and an outside deck to enjoy it on. The brewery is open from 11:00 A.M. to 10:00 P.M. during summer and mixed hours during winter. This establishment is for drinking home brews only. Its signature beer is the Bad Ass Ale. Give it a try if you like strong, English-type ale.

NIGHTCLUBS

Reno

Alturas Bar and Nightclub
1044 East Fourth Street
(775) 324-5050
Don't come here unless you like Harley Davidsons and the American flag, and you can sing two bars of Nevada's state song. The Alturas Bar bills itself as "biker friendly with no attitudes." Also claiming to be the oldest working bar in the state of Nevada, Alturas has been in its present location since the 1930s. This is really a great place if you are into the biker scene and love the blues. The club offers live music most weekends and karaoke Monday through Wednesday at 8:00 P.M. Don't worry about hours, since Alturas never closes.

BuBinga Lounge
Eldorado Hotel/Casino Reno
345 North Virginia Street
(775) 786-5700, (800) 777-5325
www.eldoradoreno.com

Easily the classiest nightclub in town, BuBinga Lounge is a must-see, if only for the decor. So feel free to get dressed up (the ambience will complement it) and get set to sink into a posh experience. From the rich West African Bubinga wood (guess where the name of the club came from?) to the lovely inlaid ebony veneers, the environment oozes an intimate elegance reminiscent of nightclubs a la 1920s. Highlighting the room are 12 Polages (polarized light collages), which depict a variety of nightclub images. So now that we've set the scene, how about the drinks and the music? BuBinga is the first nightspot in Reno to serve on-tap infusion cocktails using recipes collected from around the world. If you're not into exotic drinks, you can order fine champagne and wine either by the glass or bottle from an unbelievably extensive list. Dancing begins at 9:00 P.M. Tuesday through Saturday, and the cover is around $10.

Hacienda Restaurant & Bar
10580 North McCarran Boulevard
(775) 746-2228
The Hacienda hops with Latino music Wednesday with Hot Salsa Night and Saturday with Chicks with Salsa Night. The music starts at 10:00 P.M., and the cover is just $5.00. Before hitting the dance floor, I'd recommend dinner from their extensive menu of Hispanic foods.

Harry's Watering Hole
1100 East Plumb Lane
(775) 825-2292
By day it appeals to the blue-collar crowd, but when the sun goes down, Harry's Watering Hole attracts a college-age-and-up group. The owner caters to all tastes in music. The atmosphere is decidedly casual, with record albums adorning the walls. Harry's has the welcome mat out daily from 11:00 A.M. on.

Lone Star Lounge
9275 Lemmon Drive
(775) 677-9129
Tucked in a small shopping center in Lemmon Valley, the Lone Star is a comfortable neighborhood bar. Although this used to be strictly a country-western hangout, new owners have broadened the focus. You'll be able to kick up your heels to rock 'n' roll on the weekends and sharpen your pool skills daily. The owners also plan to continue the horseshoe and volleyball tournaments when the weather permits.

Rapscallion Seafood House & Bar
1555 South Wells Avenue
(775) 323-1211
www.rapscallion.com
If you dig a casual bar scene (minus the dance floor), you'll find a variety of music at Rapscallion Wednesday through Saturday. A word of warning about this popular hangout, however: If you're sensitive to smoke, you may want to pass it by. The clouds can hang heavy all over the room sometimes. Be prepared to stand up, as seating is limited, but this also facilitates getting to know those around you. Rapscallion also has one of the best seafood restaurants in the Reno/Tahoe area.

Sapphire Lounge
Harrah's Reno
219 North Center Street
(775) 788-2953
www.harrahs.com
Like everything else at Harrah's, the Sapphire Lounge is a classy establishment. New to the Reno nightclub scene, it capitalizes on club hoppers' renewed interest in exotic cocktails. The beverage menu also boasts a large selection of cognacs, tequilas, and handcrafted bourbons. If you're toasting a special occasion, you'll find a variety of wines and champagnes to choose from, both by the bottle and by the glass. You can enjoy jazz and blues

Museums all over the world have collected Polages, artworks created by artist Austine Wood Comarow. You'll find 12 of them in the BuBinga Lounge at the Eldorado Hotel/Casino Reno.

Call (800) 825-6156 for information on Harrah's charter flights from various U.S. cities.

Thursday through Saturday, starting at 9:00 P.M. The Sapphire opens at 6:00 P.M. Tuesday through Saturday.

The Zephyr Lounge
1074 South Virginia Street
(775) 324-9853
At the Zephyr Lounge, the owners say the excitement comes from not knowing who you might see here—a banker, a veteran, a pacifist, or a teacher. And its music is as varied as its clientele. Some nights there is jazz, some nights blues, and some nights swing music. You can be entertained here nightly.

Sparks

New Oasis
2100 Victorian Avenue
(775) 359-4020
www.newoasisreno.com
You can forget the soft, easy-listening music: The sound at the New Oasis is big and bold, like the industrial dance music belted out by Ministry. Since groups and times vary, it's best to consult the Web site for the current schedule.

Sidelines Bar
1237 Baring Boulevard
(775) 355-1030
This little bar is tucked away in a shopping center on Baring Boulevard. It's definitely a neighborhood bar that caters to its regular customers. The best thing about this bar is the clientele. They're friendly, respectful, and fun. Sidelines has live music on weekends and open-mic and jam during the week.

North Shore Lake Tahoe

Lone Eagle Grille
Hyatt Regency Lake Tahoe Resort, Spa & Casino
Country Club Drive at Lakeshore Boulevard, Incline Village, NV
(775) 832-3250
www.laketahoehyatt.com
Although it's part of the Hyatt complex, the Lone Eagle Grille is tucked along the lake across Lakeshore Boulevard from the main hotel/casino. A quintessential example of Old Tahoe architecture, the building showcases enormous wooden beams, soaring ceilings, and artistic rockwork. It's quiet and sophisticated, with an absolutely drop-dead-gorgeous view of the lake. You don't need to eat here (although the food is wonderful) to enjoy the ambience and the view from the lounge. It's definitely a favorite of the well-heeled crowd. You can also wander across the road to the hotel and take in live music on weekends in Cutthroat's Saloon.

Naughty Dawg Saloon and Grill
255 North Lake Boulevard, Tahoe City, CA
(530) 581-3294
No matter what the season, the crowd here just seems to always spill out the front door and onto the sidewalk. Decked out in doggie decor, the Naughty Dawg is a fun-filled people-watching paradise. Grab your favorite drink and, weather permitting, hang out on the deck and watch the crowd go by. The Dawg welcomes people and dogs from 11:00 A.M. to 2:00 A.M. daily.

Pierce St. Annex
850 North Lake Boulevard, Tahoe City, CA
(530) 583-5800
Consistently voted the "Best and Busiest Dance Bar" by local newspapers, Pierce St. Annex does its best to entertain locals and tourists alike with music daily. Things start really happening about 9:00 P.M. and con-

tinue on to the wee hours. You'll also find a variety of special events to entertain you throughout the year, such as wet T-shirt and bikini contests and a competition for dogs in spring.

River Ranch Lodge
California Highway 89 and Alpine Meadows Road, 3.5 miles north of Tahoe City, CA
(530) 583-4264, (800) 535-9900
www.riverranchlodge.com
River Ranch Lodge is another reason Insiders call their city the party capital of the lake. You have to go here during summer, because the lodge holds its dances on an outside patio that overlooks the Truckee River. It usually books big-name entertainment, so the music is great. But the atmosphere is so romantic, I guarantee that you wouldn't notice if a musician hits a sour note.

Sierra Vista
700 North Lake Boulevard, Tahoe City, CA
(530) 583-0233
www.sierravistatahoe.com
Tucked along the lakeshore in Tahoe City, Sierra Vista features live music on an occasional basis. Since the schedule is sporadic, call for times and specific bands. Sierra Vista is also a great restaurant offering an expansive international menu. If you've been to Tahoe City before, you might remember Grazie Restaurant & Bar in this same location.

South Shore Lake Tahoe

The Beacon Restaurant
Camp Richardson
1900 Jameson Beach Road
South Lake Tahoe, CA
(530) 541-0630
This restaurant sits beachfront at historic Camp Richardson and not only provides great live music Wednesday through Sunday but also provides a fantastic view of Lake Tahoe. The music varies between blues, folk, and jazz and is performed on the outside deck. There are not enough O's in romantic to describe this place. If you're looking for intimacy, you've got to try the Beacon. Outside service starts the week before Memorial Day and usually extends to the end of September, depending on the weather. (See the Recreation and Vacation Rentals chapters for more information about Camp Richardson.)

blu
MontBleu Resort Casino & Spa
55 U.S. Highway 50, Stateline, NV
(775) 588-3515, (888) 829-7630
www.montbleuresort.com
When this property was Caesars Tahoe, its Club Nero was one of the hottest night spots in the area. As this book goes to print, renovations to change the resort to MontBleu were still in progress. A new state-of-the-art nightclub called blu is part of the redevelopment, so call for details.

Rojo's Tavern
3091 Harrison Street
South Lake Tahoe, CA
(530) 541-4960
Rojo's has that Old Tahoe feel to it with its rustic look. Besides being a very good restaurant, the tavern has music in its downstairs cabaret Thursday through Saturday night and karaoke on Tuesday. If you want to get a feel for the Lake Tahoe of the 1920s and 1930s, give Rojo's a visit.

VEX
Harrah's Lake Tahoe
U.S. Highway 50, Stateline, NV
(775) 586-6705
www.harrahs.com
With great dance music and innovative lighting, the South Shore Room at Harrah's Lake Tahoe becomes the place to be after 10:00 P.M. Thursday through Sunday. There's an eclectic variety of drink specials and events to keep the evening interesting. You can also reserve a VIP booth for just you and your friends.

PUBS

Reno

Corrigan's Bit O'Ireland
1526 South Wells Avenue
(775) 322-1977
To give you a sense of the kind of atmosphere here, Corrigan's has an electric sign counting down the days until St. Patrick's Day and a placard that reads, ENGLAND GET OUT OF IRELAND. The owner is really named Corrigan, and you can get Harp and Guinness on tap. What more do you need know about this Irish pub? This is an Insiders' hangout, though its clientele changes often. One day it might be students from the local university, the next it might be the construction workers from across the street. One thing's for certain, don't come here on St. Patrick's Day unless you like crowds. It's standing room only. But you wouldn't expect less from an Irish pub.

The Flowing Tide Pub
10580 North McCarran Boulevard
(775) 747-7707
A newer pub that caters to both the young and old crowds, this pub has a boatload of beers on tap and supplies live music on the weekend. Needless to say, it's a favorite of the university crowd, but it is also the home of the newspeople from a local television station. The atmosphere is friendly, and so are the bartenders and waitstaff.

Foley's Irish Pub
2780 South Virginia Street
(775) 829-8500
Foley's sits right across the street from the Peppermill Hotel Casino Reno. It has good Irish stout on tap and good Catholic whiskey behind the bar (OK, it also has fairly good Protestant whiskey, too). It also has a kitchen that prepares pub food. This pub has room for a small band and books real Celtic musicians once in a while.

Limericks Pub and Grille
Fitzgeralds Casino/Hotel Reno
255 North Virginia Street
(775) 785-3300
www.fitzgeraldsreno.com
This is a good place to find Guinness on tap and for a reasonable price. The reason I recommend this pub is because during the summer months, Fitzgeralds hires college students from Ireland to work in this bar and its restaurant. It's almost like being in Ireland, and the kids are great conversationalists.

South Shore Lake Tahoe

The Tudor English Pub
1041 Fremont Street
South Lake Tahoe, CA
(530) 541-6603
The Tudor bills itself as a typical English pub complete with draft ales and, of course, darts. Give this place a try if you like your ale.

SPORTS BARS

Reno

Bully's Sports Bar & Grill
2005 Sierra Highlands Drive
(775) 746-8006

Bully's Sports Bar & Grill Too
18156 Wedge Parkway/Mt. Rose Highway
(775) 851-7400
With seven locations, Bully's has been voted the No. 1 sports bar in the Reno/Tahoe area for several years, and with good reason. These bars are the epitome of what sports bars should be—big-screen TVs, friendly employees, and everyone screaming for their favorite team. These sports bars are equipped with scrolling scoreboards to keep patrons up-to-date on all the games. Good luck trying to find a seat on Friday or Saturday night. I've

listed two of the most convenient locations here and one in the Sparks section.

Knucklehead's Sports Bar
405 Vine Street
(775) 323-6500
Enjoy your favorite game on one of this bar's five TV screens. Happy hour runs from 4:00 to 7:00 P.M., and you can enjoy live music Friday and Saturday nights from 9:00 P.M. on.

Sparky's Sports Bar & Grill
Mt. Rose Highway and Wedge Parkway
(775) 851-3999
On any given night of the week, you'd swear that every one of the thousands of league softball area players is in Sparky's. It is rapidly becoming the place to go after that hard-played game. The atmosphere is loud, and if you don't like seeing sweaty people in softball uniforms, stay away. Definitely an Insiders' hangout. Sparky's also has several other Reno-area locations.

Sparks

Bully's Sports Bar & Grill No. 3
2955 North McCarran Boulevard
(775) 352-8400
See Reno listing for more information.

David's Grill & Sports Bar
7755 Spanish Springs Road
(775) 626-1000
www.wingfieldsprings.com
This is an upscale sports bar located at Red Hawk Golf Club in the Wingfield Springs area of Sparks. The clientele is mostly locals who live around the golf course. The prices are elevated, and the bar reflects a country-club atmosphere. (See the Golf chapter for more about the course.)

Luckie's Sports Bar & Deli
608 East Prater Way
(775) 331-3321
Luckie's is open 24 hours a day and has a middle-aged, working-class clientele. TVs are in place for watching your favorite games, and it even has a small dance floor if you get bored with the sports.

Sparky's Sports Bar & Grill
1450 East Prater Way
(775) 356-6969
See Reno listing for more information.

North Shore Lake Tahoe

Rookies
930 Tahoe Boulevard
Incline Village, NV
(775) 831-9008
Billing itself as the place "where everyone plays," Rookies makes good on its claim 24 hours a day, seven days a week. You're never far from your favorite sports action: Twelve satellite TVs are scattered around this casual bar/eatery. If you'd rather participate than watch, you can always try karaoke on Thursday and Sunday nights or dance to DJ-hosted music Thursday through Sunday. Rookies has a full menu featuring typical pub fare along with mouthwatering steaks. The patio is an especially popular spot during summer, where you can watch all the people go by on Tahoe Boulevard while you enjoy a tasty burger in the sun.

Sandy's Pub
Resort at Squaw Creek
400 Squaw Creek Road
Olympic Valley, CA
(530) 583-6300, (800) 327-3353
www.squawcreek.com
After a "hard" day of powder skiing at Squaw Valley, head into Sandy's Pub, where you can relax with your favorite microbrew and watch a little sports action on the big-screen TV. Tucked in the lower level of the Resort at Squaw Creek, the pub's casual lodge ambience provides a fitting background for the lovely mountain

views seen through the floor-to-ceiling windows. The wide-ranging menu covers everything from spicy buffalo wings to crisp salads to juicy filet mignon. The large stone patio just outside is a favorite place for lunch in summer. You can also watch live action on the Resort at Squaw Creek championship golf ccourse, with a man-made waterfall tumbling nearby.

South Shore Lake Tahoe

Goalpost
290 Kingsbury Grade
Stateline, NV
(775) 588-6563
Football is the word of the day at this sports bar. TVs line the walls, and the clientele is as varied as the games on TV. It's a good little bar to watch your favorite sports.

PERFORMING VENUES

Reno

City Center Pavilion
Fourth Street and Virginia Street
(775) 329-4777
www.silverlegacyreno.com
Owned by Silver Legacy Resort Casino, the City Center Pavilion is the site of a variety of eclectic gatherings such as meetings and special events. But it also plays host to live entertainment. Located between the National Bowling Stadium and Silver Legacy, it's in the heart of all the downtown action. Check with Silver Legacy about schedules and tickets.

Reno Events Center
400 North Center Street
(775) 787-8497
www.ticketmaster.com
A new facility in downtown Reno, the 7,000-seat Reno Events Center is a popular venue for concerts and headliners. Korn, Larry the Cable Guy, and Brooks and Dunn are just a few of the acts who've pleased audiences here. You can check schedules and buy tickets online through Ticketmaster or at the box office at Silver Legacy Resort Casino.

GAY-FRIENDLY NIGHTCLUBS

Below are listed the clubs and bars that advertise that they're friendly and accommodating to gay men and lesbians. The kind of entertainment and the clientele range across the spectrum. For more information about gay events, go to www.sierravoice.com.

Reno

Carl's
3310 South Virginia Street
(775) 829-8886

The Five Star Saloon
132 West Street
(775) 329-2878

Neutron
340 Kietzke Lane
(775) 786-2121

The Patio
600 West Fifth Street
(775) 323-6565

The Quest
210 West Commercial Row
(775) 333-2808

1099 Club
1099 South Virginia Street
(775) 329-1099

Tronix
303 Kietzke Lake
(775) 333-9696

South Shore Lake Tahoe

Faces Nightclub
270 Kingsbury Grade
Stateline, NV
(775) 588-2333

KARAOKE BARS

Insiders feel the karaoke scene here is more popular than it is in Japan, so I've listed a few places for those of you who feel the urge to sing in public. Most of the places listed have the same format: sign up, build up courage, and then belt out that song. Because schedules can vary, it's advisable to call before warming up your vocal chords.

Reno

Alturas Bar and Nightclub
1044 East Fourth Street
(775) 324-5050
Monday through Wednesday, 8:00 P.M.

Porky's
3372 South McCarran Boulevard
(775) 825-3777
Saturday, 9:30 P.M. to 2:30 A.M.

Sparky's Sports Bar & Grill
4050 South McCarran Boulevard
(775) 827-1550
Saturday, 10:30 P.M.

West Second Street Bar
118 West Second Street
(775) 348-7976
Nightly at 9:30 P.M.

Sparks

Pure Country Dance Hall
1955 Oddie Boulevard
(775) 331-4441
Wednesday, 7:00 P.M.

Sidelines Bar
1237 Baring Boulevard
(775) 355-1030
Wednesday, 8:00 P.M.

North Shore Lake Tahoe

Rookies
930 Tahoe Boulevard
Incline Village, NV
(775) 831-9008
Thursday and Sunday (call for specific times)

MEN'S CLUBS

Reno didn't acquire the nickname "Sin City" by gambling alone. Its adult entertainment scene, especially the men's clubs, help add to this nefarious handle. These men's clubs are found all over Reno and, unlike those in Las Vegas, can serve alcoholic beverages. Listed below are the more popular and reputable clubs in the Reno/Tahoe area. Always expect to pay a cover charge for admittance or a two-drink minimum instead of a cover charge.

Reno

Diamond Jack's
310 Spokane Street
(775) 786-1299

Fantasy Girls
1095 East Fourth Street
(775) 322-2582

The Men's Club
270 Lake Street
(775) 786-7800

Wild Orchid
515 South Virginia Street
(775) 324-1010

CASINO NIGHTLIFE 

With casinos springing up on riverboats and Indian reservations all over the country, you don't have to come to Nevada to gamble anymore. But because the Silver State has been in the business of legalized gambling longer than any other entity (since 1931), Nevada gaming establishments have refined casino nightlife to an art form designed to dazzle the senses of even the most discriminating casino patrons.

You can literally lose yourself (but hopefully not all your money) in a virtual world of gourmet dining, lavish stage revues, celebrity performances, and lively games 24 hours a day. Aside from running out of money, many visitors complain they don't have time to sleep because the action never stops. If you've come to the Reno/Tahoe area to gamble, you'll find casino gaming only in Nevada. But if you're bedded down in California lodging, don't despair since the Nevada casinos aren't very far away from wherever you might be staying.

While many people hit the casinos with the hope of breaking the bank (the casinos', not their own), the chances of that happening are slim because the odds on the machines and table games are in the casinos' favor. For example, if you expect to hit a MegaJackpot on Megabucks, your chances are only about 200,000 to 1 after putting about $25 in the machine. And though the house or casino advantage on other games is not as daunting as Megabucks, it's still about 5 percent on roulette and 22 percent on keno, for example. Remember that casinos make money when you lose and, in the long run, most players eventually do.

The healthiest way to approach gaming is to think of it as entertainment. Don't expect to win big, but do hope to have a good time. Gamble only the amount of money you can realistically afford to lose, and then know when to quit. The best time to quit is when you've won, and if you don't win before your budgeted amount is gone, walk away. To avoid being stuck without money to get home (it happens more often than you'd think), set aside enough for the trip home, and don't touch it until you leave town.

If you're a novice at gambling, it's a good idea to learn something about it before you plunk down your hard-earned cash. After all, you wouldn't invest in a business without finding out about it first, would you? Most casinos have free lessons to teach you the games, or you can go to the Reno Tahoe Job Training Academy for instruction (see details in the Attractions chapter). If you have questions about slot machines, most casino slot employees can answer them for you. And while some dealers on the table games are happy to answer questions, keep in mind that your fellow players may not appreciate your holding up the game if the action is particularly hot and heavy. To help you get started, I'll give you a few basics of the most popular games found in Reno/Tahoe casinos. Good luck!

IS LADY LUCK WITH YOU?

Blackjack or 21

The object of blackjack or 21 is to draw cards totaling 21 or closer to 21 than the dealer. Each player receives two cards face down, and the dealer receives one card face down and one face up. Cards are counted as their face value, except face cards (which are 10) and aces (which are either 1 or 11). After receiving the first two cards, players can take additional cards or "hits" or choose to "stand" with the first two cards. If you exceed 21, or go "bust," you lose.

Many Reno/Lake Tahoe casinos entertain patrons in grand style. HYATT REGENCY LAKE TAHOE RESORT, SPA & CASINO

The dealer has specific rules for playing his hand, and these are posted on the table. If the dealer's hand exceeds 21 after he takes one or more hits, all players who didn't exceed 21 prior to the dealer hitting will be paid. Otherwise the player must be closer to 21 than the dealer. If the player and the dealer have the same count, it's a "push," and no money is exchanged. Other rules include buying insurance, splitting bets, and doubling down; these are best learned when practicing the game.

Craps

One player throws the dice and is the "shooter," while the other players bet either with or against him. If the shooter throws a 7 or 11 on the first throw or "come out," bets on the "pass line" are paid and bets on the "don't pass line" are collected. If the first throw totals 2, 3, or 12, the dealer collects pass-line bets, and if it totals 3 or 12, he pays don't-pass-line bets. A total of 2 on the don't-pass-line is neither paid nor taken. If the shooter throws a total of 4, 5, 6, 8, 9, or 10, that number becomes the "point."

On each subsequent roll, if the shooter throws the point before a 7 is thrown, pass-line bets are paid and don't-pass-line bets are collected. But if the shooter rolls a 7 before the point is thrown again, the don't-pass-line bets are paid and the pass-line bets are collected. To add excitement to the game, a variety of other bets can be made, including "come," "don't come," "any craps," "hard way," and "field." Because of their complexity, we suggest you learn these finer points while actually playing or observing a game in progress.

Keno

In each keno game, 20 balls are randomly selected from a pool of 80 numbered balls. Players try to pick some of these 20 winning numbers in a variety of combinations. Winnings are determined by the number of balls chosen correctly, or the "catch."

Since payouts and combinations differ from casino to casino, players need to consult the keno brochures at the individual gaming establishments. You can play keno while enjoying dinner or a drink at the bar, because the results are displayed on large boards throughout the clubs. Keno runners will collect your tickets and deliver your winnings.

Gaming Machines

Gaming machines come in a variety of colors, shapes, and sizes, with high-tech sound and visual effects designed specifically to attract your attention and money. You can drop coins in one at a time or up to 20 at a time in some multiple-coin machines.

When playing a multiple-coin machine, be sure to check the payoff table; usually, the more coins you put in, the higher the jackpot. For large jackpots look for progressive machines; The more they're played, the more the jackpots increase. To take advantage of skill as well as luck, try the video poker machines, since they allow for more player interaction than some of the other machines.

If you're a real dyed-in-the-wool slot player, check out the free players clubs offered by most casinos. As with frequent-flier benefits awarded by airlines, you earn perks the more you gamble. A player tracking system monitors your play through the membership card you insert in a machine when you play it. Because there's such a variety of machines, don't be surprised if you don't know how to play all of them. But you'll have more fun (and maybe win more) if you understand the basics, so just ask.

Roulette

The numbers on a roulette wheel are numbered 1 to 36 and alternately colored red and black. There's also a 0 and a 00, which are green. Players can bet on as many numbers as they want and in a variety of combinations. The dealer spins the white ball in the opposite direction of the wheel, which rotates counterclockwise, and bets can be placed until the ball is about ready to drop into the wheel. Pays vary from 35 to 1 for 0 or 00 to 2 to 1 for a column of 12 numbers.

IT'S SHOWTIME!

Casino nightlife is not just about gaming, however. Insiders know you can always be a winner when you see the shows, since the odds are definitely in your favor that you'll have a good time. With such a tantalizing array of choices, it's safe to say there's something to please everybody. You can be amazed by mysterious illusionists and amused by the country's top comics. You can delight in the dazzling energy of fast-paced stage revues and dance to your favorite rock group. And if it's celebrities you want, just choose the venue. You can worship them from afar in a large outdoor arena or up close and personal in a cozy theater.

Whichever shows you decide to take in, it's recommended that you call for reservations. Since the Reno/Tahoe area is a popular convention destination, shows are frequently sold out to visitors attending meetings. Hotel/casinos and gaming

---

i

The original Liberty Bell slot machine was developed by San Franciscan Charlie Fey in 1895.

---

resorts frequently give reservation preferences to their guests, so be sure to ask about this when you check in. Some of the best show deals in town are dinner/show and room/show packages utilizing restaurants and accommodations at various casinos.

Remember, all seats are not equal, so check out where yours will be located if they're assigned when you book. If they're not assigned, arrive early for the show. Sometimes you can get the best seats by tipping the maitre d' $10 or $15.

If you have trouble getting a reservation, ask the hotel concierge to help. Although jackets, ties, and cocktail dresses were the order of the evening some years ago, the attire now is more casual. Almost anything goes, except bathing suits, tank tops, and bare feet. You won't be served dinner as part of the show (unless it's a special event), but drinks can be purchased either at your table or at a nearby self-service bar.

Some performances are not suitable for children, so if you're planning to take the whole family, be sure to ask if there are any age limitations to the show you want to attend.

For current Reno/Tahoe show information, check out *Best Bets,* a weekly entertainment supplement to the *Reno Gazette-Journal.* Entertainment guides are also published in *Showtime* and the *Reno News & Review,* which you can pick up free at casinos, hotels, and restaurants. In the South Shore Lake Tahoe area, look for free copies of *Lake Tahoe Action,* and in the North Shore Lake Tahoe area, for *North Shore Truckee Action.*

All the gaming establishments in this chapter have full-service casinos, with hundreds of gaming machines and dozens of table games. But to round out your Reno/Tahoe experience, I hope to whet your appetite for all the other kinds of live entertainment available. So now, let's hit the town!

Reno

Atlantis Casino Resort
3800 South Virginia Street
(775) 825-4700, (800) 723-6500
www.atlantiscasino.com

Voted "Best Late Night Hangout" by readers of the local daily newspaper, Atlantis Casino Resort books a variety of concerts and reviews in its Grand Ballroom, such as the Thunder from Down Under All-Male Dance Revue, Danny Marona, and the 5th Dimension. The prices at this casino for a typical big show run about $20 to $25. Free entertainment is also offered in the Center Stage Cabaret in the main casino area.

Boomtown Casino & Hotel Reno
Interstate 80
7 miles west of Reno
(775) 345-6000, (800) 648-3790
www.boomtownreno.com

The Boomtown Cabaret features top lounge acts nightly except Monday. You can have a seat in the lounge area, where there's no cover or minimum charges, or watch the show while you play slots or table games.

Eldorado Hotel/Casino Reno
345 North Virginia Street
(775) 786-5700, (800) 648-5966
www.eldoradoreno.com

When the owners of the Eldorado Hotel/Casino Reno decided they needed a new theater, they spared no expense and effort in creating a high-tech showroom equal to none in the Reno/Tahoe area. Decorated in a 1940s art deco style, the 580-seat Eldorado Showroom is warm, elegant, and intimate. Plush, comfortable seats are steeply tiered to permit unobstructed viewing from almost every vantage point. And because the technical components, such as acoustics, lighting, and audio, are state-of-the-art, the quality of production is truly amazing.

The room usually showcases hits such as *Smokey Joe's Cafe, Balagan,* and *Spirit of the Dance*. Tickets run around $29, and shows play Tuesday through Sunday. Call (800) 879-8879 for details on dinner/room show packages. When booking a reservation, try to avoid seats on the sides of the upper level as the view of the stage is not nearly as clear as from middle-section seats.

Also at the Eldorado, the Brew Brothers is one of the most popular dance spots for the younger crowd. Live musical groups, ranging from rock to soul, take to the stage at this casual microbrewery nightly. The BuBinga Lounge attracts partygoers looking for a chic sophisticated nightclub experience (see the Nightlife chapter for more details). And for a quiet change of pace, Bistro Roxy has a romantic piano bar in a French country setting.

Grand Sierra Resort and Casino
2500 East Second Street
(775) 789-2000
(775) 789-2285 (ticket information)
www.grandsierraresort.com

If you're looking for a downright dazzling entertainment experience, the lavish shows at the Grand Theatre at Grand Sierra Resort and Casino (formerly the Reno Hilton) will no doubt fit the bill. Not just the usual flash and dash of pretty costumes and intricate dancing, the performances challenge the imagination as well. "Witness the Impossible: The Imperial Circus" featured hoop diving, high pole acrobatics, and spinning diabolo as performed by Far Eastern acrobats. No theater is better suited to these very big shows than the Grand Sierra's because its cavernous size gives exciting depth to the productions.

But Insiders know there are some very bad seats in this house, with some theatergoers actually facing away from the stage. When making a reservation, it's best to actually view the seating chart at the box office. Since individual seats in the booths are also assigned, be especially careful of those seats in booths toward the outside of the room that cause you to sit with your back to the stage.

For your dancing pleasure stop by The Garage, where you can rock on till the wee hours of the morning. Summer visitors have the added choice of seeing headliners outside the building in the outdoor amphitheater. Concerts here are especially memorable when the full moon presents a backdrop to the action on stage. If you are comfortable in the middle of the crowd, the level seating is okay. But if you want a better vantage point of the stage, ask for seats in the bleachers in the back. Since this is a large amphitheater, it's a good idea to take binoculars if you want to get a good look at your favorite star.

Casino showrooms offer lavish entertainment, such as Balagan Cirque Style Extravaganza *at the Eldorado Hotel/Casino Reno.*
ELDORADO HOTEL/CASINO RENO

Celebrities who have recently performed here include Maroon 5, Keith Urban, Willie Nelson, and Heart.

Harrah's Reno
219 North Center Street
(775) 786-3232, (775) 788-2900
www.harrahs.com

The legendary Bill Harrah, founder of Harrah's Reno and Harrah's Lake Tahoe, believed that first-class live entertainment was a vital part of a successful gaming establishment (I tell you more about Mr. Harrah in the Resorts and History chapters). That tradition continues nightly in Sammy's Showroom at Harrah's Reno with exciting production shows, adult revues, and celebrity performers.

With 440 seats, the room is intimate enough to make you feel close to the performers but large enough to showcase full-size productions. The most comfortable seats in the house are the circular booths, so when you arrive be sure to ask the maitre d' if any are available. You can also enjoy live entertainment at the Plaza. There's also live entertainment in the Sapphire Lounge.

Peppermill Hotel Casino Reno
2707 South Virginia Street
(775) 826-2121
www.peppermillcasinos.com

Surrounded by banks of slot machines in the middle of the casino, the Cabaret in the Peppermill Hotel Casino Reno is hard to miss. It sets the tone for this fast-paced club, since the live entertainment is an integral part of the action. You can enjoy the free show and keep an eye on the casino happenings at the same time. Their lounge acts seem to be the best in Reno, and the employees seem to be the friendliest. For more low-key music, you can catch the singles who play in the Piano Lounge Friday and Saturday nights. As this book went to press, the Peppermill had started a $230 million expansion that will include a two-story nightclub that covers 10,000 square feet.

The Peppermill Hotel Casino Reno was voted one of the top-10 casinos in the country by MSN.

Silver Legacy Resort Casino
407 North Virginia Street
(775) 329-4777, (775) 325-7401
www.silverlegacyreno.com

Some of the hottest entertainers in the country play the Grande Exposition Hall at Silver Legacy Resort Casino. The shows are first-class, but the setting is not. Because it's not a theater but a hall that's used for a variety of events, it's less than ideal in a concert situation. Seating is on one level only, in rows of straight-back chairs with no tables or arm rests for your drinks. If you're sitting any farther than four rows back from the stage, your best view of the performance is on the video screens hung all around the room. But if you're not fussy about the surroundings, you can see some of the best acts offered in the area. Tickets are steep here when compared to the rest of Reno and Sparks. The range usually starts at $25 and goes up to $75 depending upon the talent. You can also book tickets for entertainment at the City Center Pavilion directly across the street or the Reno Events Center on North Center Street.

If you're in the mood for laughs, you can see the country's top upcoming comics perform at Catch A Rising Star comedy club (see the Nightlife chapter). Silver Legacy also has live entertainment at Rum Bullions bar.

Sparks

John Ascuaga's Nugget
1100 Nugget Avenue
(775) 356-3300
www.janugget.com

If only the walls of the Celebrity Showroom at John Ascuaga's Nugget could talk, they could write the history of big-name entertainment with tales of all the celebrities who've performed in the room. Some years back theatergoers enjoyed fine dining and a performing elephant before the headliner took to the stage.

Today you'll still enjoy first-class entertainment, but dinner is no longer included and the elephant unfortunately died. One of the best deals in town, however, is the Nugget's dinner/show packages: You can still enjoy gourmet dining before or after the show in a choice of restaurants on the property. The Celebrity Showroom is one of the most comfortable venues in the area, with a luxurious theater setting that's just intimate enough to give you that up-close-and-personal experience. On a larger scale, the Nugget showcases celebrity performances in the Rose Ballroom. Prices in the ballroom range from $35 to $50. For dancing there are also rock groups in the Casino Cabaret. You can also relax to easy-listening music in Restaurante Orozko.

Silver Club Hotel/Casino
1040 Victorian Avenue
(775) 358-4771
www.silverclub.com

Lounge acts play nightly except Monday in the casino at the Silver Club Hotel/Casino. The general ambience is down-home and decidedly casual: Don't expect the elegance offered by glitzier casinos here.

North Shore Lake Tahoe

Cal Neva Resort Hotel and Casino
2 Stateline Road, Crystal Bay, NV
(775) 832-4000, (800) 225-6385
www.calnevaresort.com

The Cal Neva Resort, owned by Frank Sinatra in the 1960s and frequented by Sinatra's "Rat Pack" and the Kennedys, is teeming with history. Marilyn Monroe was supposed to have had a midnight rendezvous with JFK here in the early 1960s. But now the Cal Neva, named so because it straddles the California and Nevada state line, is relatively quiet. It still manages, from time to time, to book big names in its

Dishonest players are called "crossroaders" by casino people.

Frank Sinatra Room. Most of the time the room is dark, but the likes of Jimmy Cliff have been known to perform here.

Crystal Bay Club Casino
14 Nevada Highway 28
Crystal Bay, NV
(775) 831-0512
www.crystalbaycasino.com

Totally renovated with a warm, woodsy ambience, the Crystal Bay Club Casino has upped the bar on entertainment and dining in Crystal Bay. An eclectic parade of entertainers appear in the Crown Room and lounge Monday through Saturday. With very reasonable prices in the Crown Room and no cover for the lounge acts, it's especially appealing to the younger crowd. For a fine dining experience, I'd strongly recommend dinner in the Crystal Bay Steakhouse, although it's not exactly cheap.

Hyatt Regency Lake Tahoe
Resort, Spa & Casino
111 Country Club Drive at
Lakeshore Boulevard, Incline Village, NV
(775) 832-1234, (800) 233-1234
www.laketahoehyatt.com

Besides all the nonstop entertainment provided by a full-service casino, the Hyatt offers live entertainment Friday and Saturday from 10:00 P.M. to 1:00 A.M. in Cutthroat's Saloon. The Lone Eagle Grill on the lakeshore across the street provides live music Wednesday through Saturday from 7:00 P.M. to 11:00 P.M.

Tahoe Biltmore
5 Nevada Highway 28
Crystal Bay, NV
(775) 831-0660
www.tahoebiltmore.com

The Tahoe Biltmore features live music in its Breeze nightclub and revues in the Nevada Room. Both rooms are dark Monday.

South Shore Lake Tahoe

Harrah's Lake Tahoe
U.S. Highway 50, Stateline, NV
(775) 588-6611, (800) HARRAHS
www.harrahs.com
Harrah's South Shore Room, which opened in 1959, prides itself in providing year-round great entertainment with great song-and-dance revues and headliners. If you're planning on attending a show during high season, be sure to call for reservations as soon as possible, because tickets sell out well in advance.

It's a comfortable theater with high-quality sound and lighting, so any production you see here is first-class in every way. At 10:00 P.M. Thursday through Sunday, this room becomes VEX nightclub. (See the Nightlife chapter.) Live entertainment is also featured at Casino Center Stage.

Harveys Lake Tahoe Casino & Resort
U.S. Highway 50, Stateline, NV
(775) 588-2411, (800) 427-7247
www.harrahs.com
The tradition of adult revues is still alive and well at Harveys Cabaret Theater on Friday and Saturday. You can see lavish costumes and intricate choreography in such shows as *Lipstick*. Cabo Wabo Cantina Lounge offers a variety of late-night live entertainment on weekends, and The Improv at Harveys presents some of the country's funniest comics Tuesday through Sunday. Harveys also has an outdoor venue that is used for headliner acts during summer. Check the Web site for the lineup and dates.

Horizon Casino Resort Lake Tahoe
U.S. Highway 50, Stateline, NV
(775) 588-6211, (800) 648-3322
www.horizoncasino.com
A family-friendly resort, the Horizon has been very successful offering large production shows that are suitable for kids. Showtimes for such hits as *Fusion* are 7:30 P.M. and 9:30 P.M. with a kids free matinee on Sunday. Shows take place in the Golden Cabaret Theater. The resort also has live entertainment on weekends in the Aspen Lounge, a Gameworld arcade, and the Stadium Cinemas for first-run movies.

MontBleu Resort Casino & Spa
55 U.S. Highway 50, Stateline, NV
(775) 588-3515, (800) 648-3353
Formerly Caesars Tahoe, MontBleu is a complete renovation from Roman to French alpine ambience. When this book went to press, construction was still in progress. Plans call for an upscale showroom and bars with live entertainment. Call the resort for details.

And If That's Not Enough . . .

Other Reno casinos that have lounge entertainment include Fitzgeralds Casino/Hotel Reno, 255 North Virginia Street, (775) 785-3300; the Sands Regency Hotel Casino, 345 North Arlington Avenue, (775) 348-2200; and Siena Hotel Spa Casino, 1 South Lake Street, (775) 337-6260. The Rail City Casino at 2121 Victorian Avenue in Sparks, (775) 359-9440, also has live entertainment in the casino area.

SHOPPING

Since the first pioneers arrived in the 1800s, the Reno/Sparks area has been a regional trading center, serving the shopping needs of local residents as well as people living in rural northern Nevada and California. While it will never rival glitzy shopping meccas like San Francisco, Dallas, or New York, the Truckee Meadows is viewed by retail marketers as a lucrative and growing market of about one-half million eager shoppers.

Extraordinary growth over the past several decades has caused a retail explosion, with new shopping centers springing up on many vacant lots. Along South Virginia Street, a concrete/asphalt retail row has replaced the peaceful pastures where cattle once grazed lazily on tall, green grass. North of downtown Sparks, retail development and housing subdivisions blanket the previously unspoiled desert landscape. Many locals lament this rapid urbanization and its inherent loss of the wide-open spaces, but for shoppers it means more stores, bigger stores, and ever-increasing choices of treasures to buy.

While shoppers once flocked to downtown Reno to browse the upscale stores sprinkled among the casinos, they now head to the myriad malls strung along major streets and sprawling between housing developments. As in many other cities and towns, shopping in Reno moved from the downtown to outlying areas when malls came into vogue. The movement began in the late 1960s when Park Lane Mall (scheduled for closure in 2007) opened its doors at the corner of Plumb Lane and South Virginia Street. Meadowood Mall, the area's largest shopping mall, pushed development farther south to the corner of South McCarran Boulevard and South Virginia Street. While Reno has experienced robust growth in all directions, the lion's share of shopping expansion has been to the south, with retail establishments now stretching clear up Nevada Highway 431 (the Mt. Rose Highway).

New shopping malls that have been constructed along South Virginia Street within the past several years include Sierra Town Center, South Towne Crossing, The Commons, and The Summit Sierra. (See descriptions later in this chapter.) Perhaps one of the biggest indicators of the vitality of area shopping is the addition of three of the country's best-known sporting goods superstores. Orvis is located at the Summit Sierra, and Cabela's and Bass Pro Shops have plans to open stores in the area soon.

With the preservation of Victorian Square, Sparks has maintained a small-town shopping ambience in its core downtown (see the Attractions chapter for more about Victorian Square). The square has an interesting collection of specialty shops that are especially appealing to visitors. More shopping is clustered in malls along major streets, such as McCarran, Vista, Sparks, and Oddie Boulevards and Prater Way. You can buy the basics, but if you're looking for glitz or clothing, you won't find much here.

Plans call for an 800,000-square-foot shopping development to be opened in 2008 near the Sparks Marina. The Legends at Sparks Marina will include a Scheels store, which will showcase the world's largest selection of sports equipment, sportswear, and footwear. With a collection of innovative eateries such as T-Rex: A Prehistoric Family Adventure along with a collection of creative shopping options, the development is best described as a shopping experience rather than just a mall.

While you can shop for both the necessities and the niceties in the Reno/Sparks area, shopping in the Lake Tahoe Basin is more tourist-oriented. There are plenty of boutiques that offer tantalizing one-of-a-kind specialty items, but if you're looking for essentials at a reasonable price, your choices are apt to be slim. You can't beat the selection of outdoor clothing and ski equipment, but don't expect to find a huge selection of three-piece suits or other office wear. In contrast to the megamarts and chain stores so prevalent in the Reno/Sparks area, shops in the Lake Tahoe region are mostly mom-and-pop establishments, highly individualized and unique in their merchandise and character. They're easy to spot, clustered in a few mini-malls around the lake or tucked next to restaurants and hotels. Most shopping in the South Shore Lake Tahoe area is found at the "Y" (the junction of U.S. Highway 50 and California Highway 89), at the base of Heavenly Ski Resort's gondola, and around the California-Nevada state line. I also highly recommend a shopping expedition to Truckee, where you'll find a plethora of intriguing shops and restaurants clustered all along the main street. (See the Day Trips chapter for details on this historic town.)

To help you maximize your shopping experience in the Reno/Tahoe area, this chapter has been organized by the regular four geographical regions: Reno, Sparks, North Shore Lake Tahoe, and South Shore Lake Tahoe. Each of these regions starts with an overview of the main malls and a sampling of the shopping centers. (Not all the stores in the main malls are described, because they all have a large variety of shops that will meet most of your shopping needs.) Then individual store descriptions follow in the following categories: antiques, books, casino shopping, consignment, gifts and souvenirs, kidstuff, pawn shops, sporting gear, and women's clothing.

The store listings that follow aren't meant to be all-inclusive. I've merely tried to whet your appetite and hope you discover other shopping delights on your own. For a more complete listing of stores, you should consult local telephone directories. Most malls are open daily, but since store hours can vary, a main number or Internet address (if available) has been included so you can verify hours of operation before heading out.

So put on your walking shoes, grab your credit card, and let's shop 'til we drop.

RENO

Malls and Shopping Centers

Airport Square–Costco Center
East Plumb Lane and Harvard Way

If you're searching for bargains, you've found the promised land in this shopping center. Anchored by Costco (who among us hasn't been the proud purchaser of a 50-year supply of something here?), the center caters largely to discount shoppers who are very price savvy. Pull into the parking lot and you know you've arrived, since it's swarming with people packing bulk quantities into the backs of pickup trucks and trunks of cars. So grab a handtruck and load it up at Costco, Office Depot, or PetSmart, to name a few.

The Commons
South Virginia Street and Sierra Center Parkway

Just across the street from Sierra Town Center and adjacent to the Courtyard by Marriott, The Commons offers an eclectic mix of shopping choices from such stores as Linens-N-Things, Petsmart, David's Bridal, DSW shoes, and It's All About Me. The center also has seven eateries, including Marble Slab Creamery, the Pita Pit, and Mexican Grill.

Fire Creek Crossing Shopping Center
South McCarran Boulevard and Kietzke Lane

It's the era of the megastore, and Fire Creek Crossing exemplifies it. Many stores here are big, big, big—almost overwhelming customers with their available choices. If variety is the name of the game for you, you'll love shopping in such stores as Circuit City, Sports Authority, and TJ Maxx. Directly behind this shopping center you'll find a huge Sam's Club and a Babies R Us. Located in the heart of Reno's retail row, Fire Creek Crossing can be a jumping-off point to neighboring malls, such as Meadowood Mall and Smithridge Plaza.

Franktown Corners
2309 Kietzke Lane

Complete with a quaint clock tower, Franktown Corners exudes the ambience of an intimate village. Although the center is relatively small, the specialty shops and restaurants are intriguing and upscale. It's a great place to kill time while your car is getting decked out at the adjoining Franktown Hand Car Wash & Express Detailing. For wining and dining I recommend Viaggio for Italian cuisine (see the Restaurants chapter).

Mayberry Landing
Corner of Mayberry Drive and West McCarran Boulevard
(775) 322-6145

If you're tired of shopping in chain stores that all seem to carry the same merchandise, browsing the small boutiques at Mayberry Landing is a welcome change. Although the exterior appearance of this small galleria is country casual, the wares are decidedly chic. Tucked on the edge of the upscale Caughlin Ranch neighborhood, it's a favorite hangout for financially secure professionals. For simply delightful women's apparel, try cruising the racks at Athena and Boutique Casablanca. For unique gifts for those special people in your life, pop in to Mayberry Mercantile Gifts. And for that very special bottle of wine for dinner, give Whispering Vine Wine Company a try. Eateries include Backstube Austrian Cafe, Buenos Grill, and Walden's Coffeehouse.

Meadowood Court
Southwest corner of South McCarran Boulevard and South Virginia Street

Barnes & Noble, Best Buy, Petco, and Casual Male Big & Tall go head-to-head with other retailers in their new superstores at Meadowood Court. When you're tired of shopping, you can take a load off in two restaurants: Macaroni Grill and On the Border.

Meadowood Mall
South Virginia Street and South McCarran Boulevard
(775) 827-8450
www.shopmeadowood.com

Anchored by Macy's, JCPenney, and Sears, Meadowood Mall is Reno/Tahoe's largest shopping center. With about 100 stores, eateries, and services, Meadowood stores offer a plethora of shopping choices for home furnishings, apparel, jewelry, and sporting goods. The Palms Food Court offers everything from hot dogs on a stick to sizzling Cajun food to Mrs. Field's cookies.

Amenities available at the mall include strollers, wheelchairs, and an information booth. Bus service is available to Meadowood from the downtown Reno bus depot at Fourth and Center Streets and City Station-Sparks on C Street. Call RTC Ride at (775) 348-7433 for details.

If you're an ardent shopper, you're sure to enjoy Meadowood. It's clean and well maintained, with an interesting mix of stores that provides something for everybody.

Plumgate
West Plumb Lane and Arlington Avenue

With a beautiful waterfall tumbling at the entrance, it's pretty hard not to be drawn into this small neighborhood shopping center. You'll find an interesting mix of shops that include Briarwood Finer Flowers & Gifts, Like a Charm, Lodo Loft, and Bark Avenue. For lunch try The Stone House Cafe, just across the street.

Redfield Promenade
South Virginia Street and Kietzke Lane

In the busiest shopping corridor in the Reno/Tahoe area, the Redfield Promenade boasts a collection of glitzy megastores that includes Bed Bath & Beyond, Borders Books, Cost Plus World Market, and The

When shopping for your pet, I recommend Healthy Tails for Cats and Healthy Tails for Dogs, at 3892 Mayberry Drive in Reno, or Scrap's Dog Bakery at Sparks Marina, at 325 Harbour Cove Drive in Sparks.

Good Guys. If you still have enough money to eat after shopping, stop by the Claim Jumper Restaurant, where its legendary single serving of chocolate cake is the size of an entire cake.

Shopper's Square Mall
East Plumb Lane and South Virginia Street
(775) 323-0430
With about 50 stores and 6 restaurants, you can certainly while away a few hours in this mall. The biggies are Sheplers Western Wear, Ben Franklin Crafts, and Sav-On Drugs along with Marshalls, Radio Shack, the Niche and Murdock's Clothing. A decadent stop here is Cold Stone Creamery, where you can custom-order your favorite ice-cream treat.

Sierra Town Center
South Virginia Street and
Sierra Center Parkway
Sierra Town Center is a typical big-box shopping mall that includes Target, Mervyn's, Sierra Trading Post Outlet, and Famous Footwear. Conveniently located next to Home Depot along the South Virginia Street shopping corridor, it can be included in a jaunt to the Summit Sierra, The Commons, and Southwest Pavilion.

Smithridge Plaza
South McCarran Boulevard and
Smithridge Drive
If you're on your way to Meadowood Mall, you can also comparison-shop at Smithridge Plaza, directly across the street. It offers great deals at such stores as Stein Mart, Pier 1 Imports, and Trader Joe's. There's also a Toys R Us, with a store called Parent Teacher Aids right next door. When it's time for lunch (or dinner), try a tasty Mexican meal at Chili's restaurant, right on the corner.

Southwest Pavilion
8175 South Virginia Street
Southwest Pavilion offers one-stop shopping with an up-to-date Scolari's supermarket surrounded by upscale shops, such as Scandia Down and Pendleton of Reno. The exterior is tastefully constructed of soft pink stucco, a standout among the other businesses along the street.

The Summit Sierra
South Virginia Street and
Nevada Highway 431
(775) 853-7800
www.thesummitonline.com
Designed as an outdoor lifestyle center, the Summit Sierra brought upscale cutting-edge shopping options to the Reno/Tahoe area when it opened in 2006. With fountains, sculptures, and outdoor seating interspersing the brightly colored stores, it offers a comfortable ambience that's sure to make most shoppers feel at home. Anchored by Dillard's department store, the list of 70 other establishments is glitzy and varied enough to satisfy even the most ardent shopoholic's dreams. Shops include Chico's, Coldwater Creek, J. Jill, Banana Republic, Tangerine Aveda, Williams-Sonoma, Coach, Pottery Barn, JoS. A. Bank, and Aeropostale. Restaurants include BJ's Brewhouse, Cortina, and Johnny Carino's. You'll also find a Starbucks and a Nestlé Toll House Cafe along with several other specialty food outlets. Century Theaters is scheduled to open soon. To get to the Summit Sierra from Reno or Sparks, take U.S. Highway 395 South; get off at exit 57 B and enter the center from South Virginia Street. From Incline Village take NV 431 (the Mt. Rose Highway) west toward Reno; turn left onto Herz Boulevard just before intersecting South Virginia Street.

Antiques

All "R" Yesterdays
1215 South Virginia Street
(775) 827-2355
Within easy walking distance of both Atlantis Casino Resort and the Peppermill Hotel Casino Reno, All "R" Yesterdays offers everything from A to Z in collectibles and antiques, including a tantalizing selection of furniture and art glass.

Unique to this store is a collection of 1930s and 1940s vintage clothing, along with its Christmas House, which offers year-round holiday shopping. The store is open daily.

Antique Mall
1251 South Virginia Street
(775) 324-4141
With more than 100 dealers showing their wares, the Antique Mall has an amazing assortment of collectibles, decor items, and furniture just waiting for you to buy. Spread out over three malls, this eclectic assortment of fine and funky treasures varies in price all the way from 50 cents to $10,000. There's no hassle to park: just head into the parking lot on the corner of Arroyo and South Virginia Streets. You can shop here daily.

Reno Antiques
677 South Wells Avenue
(775) 322-5858
If you're driving down Wells Avenue, you can't miss Reno Antiques: The front yard is completely full of the vintage bathtubs so highly prized by antiques collectors. Once inside, you'll encounter an intriguing mix of antiques and collectibles. As one of the oldest antiques stores in the area (since 1974), the business prides itself on always offering merchandise at a fair price. It's a "one-horse" show, according to the owner, since he does all the buying and selling himself. The store is open Thursday through Saturday.

Shanghai To Paris
895 East Patriot Boulevard
(775) 853-6533
www.antiqueorientalfurniture.com
With 30 years' experience in importing antiques, the owners of Shanghai To Paris have wide-ranging contacts to buy design pieces from all around the world. The 16,000-square-foot showroom is loaded with lovely furniture and antique items from both Asia and Europe. If you're looking for just the right accent piece for your home, you might hit it lucky here. Prices on many items are surprisingly reasonable.

Books

Barnes & Noble
5555 South Virginia Street
(775) 826-8882
www.bn.com
Comfortably ensconced in a huge new megabookstore, Barnes & Noble is a major literary presence in the Reno/Tahoe area. Much more than purveyors of books and avant-garde magazines, modern bookstores are cultural centers, selling music, videos, and gourmet coffee in addition to a huge variety of reading materials. And to further whet your intellectual appetite, they also sponsor special events (see the chapter on The Arts for details). If you like to read, you'll simply love this store. It's a browser's delight: Hanging out and perusing the shelves is expected and encouraged.

Borders Books
4995 South Virginia Street
(775) 448-9999
www.borders.com
This Borders Books is a cultural superstore. You'll find a gourmet coffee shop, a great selection of videos and music, and zillions of books. The store is bright and spacious, perfect for a relaxed shopping outing. Like Barnes & Noble, the store also sponsors cultural activities (see the chapter on The Arts for details).

Borders Express
Meadowood Mall
South Virginia Street and
South McCarran Boulevard
(775) 826-5690
www.borders.com
In the location formerly occupied by Waldenbooks, Borders Express offers a back-to-basics bookstore minus the bells and whistles of today's megastores. You won't find a coffee shop, but you will find a decent selection of books in a bright and friendly atmosphere.

Deseret Book
1274 East Plumb Lane
(775) 826-8733
http://deseretbook.com
A locally owned independent bookstore, Deseret Book sells books written by and for members of the Church of Jesus Christ of Latter-Day Saints (LDS). It also offers a large variety of religious gift items. The owners pride themselves on their comfortable personalized service: All the employees are very well read and are familiar with everything that's sold in the store. The store is conveniently located in the Airport Square-Costco Center.

His Word Christian Book Store
7689 South Virginia Street
(775) 853-2665, (800) 726-7940
www.hiswordbooks.com
Conveniently located in the Longley West Plaza, the Reno location of His Word Christian Book Store is a cheerful place to browse for books and gifts. See the description of the Sparks store for more information. Be sure to sample the coffee at His Ground, the coffee nook in the Reno Store.

Paperback Exchange
131 Vesta Street
(775) 322-8822
With more than 70,000 titles to choose from, it's pretty hard to say you can't find anything to read in the Paperback Exchange. As the name suggests, the merchandise is exclusively paperbacks, which the store both sells and trades. It's a little tricky to find (the street is only 1 block long), but look for it behind Rapscallion Seafood House off Wells Avenue.

Sundance Bookstore
1155 West Fourth Street
(775) 786-1188
www.sundancebookstore.com
Tucked in the Keystone Square Shopping Center, Sundance Bookstore is a favorite with longtime residents, since it's owned and managed by locals. You can buy a cup of espresso at the cart up front and then relax in the cozy, intimate atmosphere of this very personal store. If you're looking for books about Nevada and the Sierra or works by local and regional authors, you'll find one of the best selections in the area right here. The store is also able to order obscure titles that large chain bookstores are unable to get. Don't be surprised if the service here is impeccable: It always is, since the owner is likely to wait on you.

Casino Shopping

Eldorado Hotel/Casino Reno
345 North Virginia Street
(775) 786-5700
www.eldoradoreno.com
You can shop for fine jewelry, resortwear, collectibles, specialty gifts, and logo items in the shops that line the European-style mezzanine that connects the Eldorado Hotel/Casino Reno to the Silver Legacy Resort Casino. Overlooking the casino areas and lined with bars and restaurants, the mezzanine is bright, brassy, and a bit noisy, but the upbeat gaming atmosphere makes buying a fun experience for many customers.

Grand Sierra Resort and Casino
2500 East Second Street
(775) 789-2000
www.grandsierraresort.com
From jewelry to upscale clothing to

typical tourist souvenirs, the Grand Sierra shopping arcade offers about 20 classy shops to tempt your wallet. You'll find a few shops on the casino level near the hotel check-in area, but the majority are one level down. With its quiet, deep-carpeted ambience, the Grand Sierra (formerly the Reno Hilton) is an especially fun place for a leisurely browse.

Consignment

Coral Rose Vintage
805 South Virginia Street
(775) 324-1953
www.coralrosevintage.com
You'll find an interesting selection of vintage clothing here along with a sprinkling of antiques, glassware, and accessories. It's open Tuesday through Saturday, but call for hours.

Labels Consignment Boutique
3350 Lakeside Drive
(775) 825-6000
A favorite stop for women who love great clothes at bargain prices, Labels Consignment Boutique sells designer clothes at a fraction of their full retail price. You don't need to worry about damaged goods, because everything on the racks is top quality. The store is beautifully appointed, like an upscale retail establishment in any large city.

Once Upon a Child
4040 Kietzke Lane
(775) 825-4448
With the cost of kids' clothing and accessories out of sight these days, it's nice to find a place to shop for them that's easy on the budget. With a complete selection of clothing, toys, books, equipment, and furniture, this consignment shop is a one-stop shopping mecca for many parents. Best of all, after loading the car with all your newly purchased goodies you'll probably have money left over to take the family out to dinner.

Vogue Echos Consignment Boutique
6135 Lakeside Drive
(775) 827-4227
www.vogueechos.com
Vogue Echos offers lovely women's fashions at exceptional bargains. It's especially popular with professional women because the racks are full of suits and career clothing. The store also carries a big selection of large and extra-large sizes. Tucked in a small mall at the end of Lakeside Drive, it's off the usual shopping path but worth the detour.

Gifts and Souvenirs

Best Wishes
2315 Kietzke Lane
(775) 825-1500
www.bestwishesreno.com
Boasting the most stickers in Nevada, Best Wishes also has a wonderful selection of greeting cards and moderately priced gift items. If you're looking for scrapbook supplies, you'll find everything you need right here. Be sure to browse the other shops here at Franktown Corners and perhaps taste the wines at Viaggio restaurant.

Iguana Imports
197-D Damonte Ranch Parkway
(775) 853-2323
www.iguananv.com
The explosion of growth in the Reno/Tahoe area has given rise to an increasing number of interesting home furnishings and decor stores such as Iguana Imports. Although the shop has a wonderful selection of furniture from around the world, it's also chock-full of one-of-a-kind gift items. You can shop for wall decor, original art, and accessories from Mexico, India, China, Costa Rica, Guatemala, and Ireland. The owners do all the buying themselves, taking care to maintain quality as well as variety in their inventory.

Like a Charm
Arlington Avenue and West Plumb Lane
(775) 284-7766
With a little bit of everything, Like a Charm is a great little store for browsing. You'll find jewelry, soaps, candles, and gift items along with casual clothing and a whimsical assortment of hats. And with a Starbucks right next door, you can't go wrong. Like a Charm is tucked in the new complex of shops at Plumgate.

Lucky 7
229 North Virginia Street
(775) 324-4970
For Reno and Lake Tahoe logo T-shirts at reasonable prices, try the Lucky 7 souvenir shop near the casinos in downtown Reno. Open since 1985, the store stocks a wide variety of typical tourist items.

My Country Home
6275 Sharlands Avenue, Suite B-15
(775) 746-5556
Although there's a noticeable country flavor in My Country Home, it also exudes the warmth of other influences, such as Tuscany. If you enjoy shopping in stores with variety, you'll certainly find it here. Besides the usual cards and gift items, the shop carries such things as reproduction Raggedy and Prim dolls, handmade soaps, pet gifts, kitchen crockery, tapestries, and jewelry. It's located in the Sharon Square Shopping Center next to Scolari's off Robb Drive.

Name Droppers
6990 South McCarran Boulevard
(775) 826-7101
With baskets of bright flowers hanging on the front doors, Name Droppers makes you feel welcome even before you walk in. You can find the perfect gift in the selection of candles, bath accessories, writing materials, and knickknacks. You can also order custom invitations for weddings and special events at this store. Open Monday through Saturday, Name Droppers is located in Magnolia Village, an upscale office complex that also has retail establishments.

i

The Summit Sierra lifestyle shopping center has five fountains imported from France.

Kidstuff

Babies R Us, the Baby Superstore
4869 Kietzke Lane
(775) 825-2229
www.babiesrus.com
With absolutely everything a baby could want or need in stock, this establishment is indeed a superstore. Babies R Us definitely offers one-stop shopping for all your children's needs, from clothing to furniture to playthings. With oodles of parking in front, it's conveniently located near Sam's Club.

Gymboree Store
5180 Meadowood Mall Circle
(775) 829-9724
www.gymboree.com
The windows of Gymboree Store are easily the most colorful and cheerful displays in Meadowood Mall, since the store is full of brightly colored clothing that kids just love. Kids like the look and fit of the clothes, but parents appreciate their durability. The store guarantees that their merchandise is kid-tough, and the tags on all the clothes attest to it. You can also shop for accessories, such as sunglasses especially designed for children, or furniture, like Gym Rockers.

Little Angels Boutique
3590 West Plumb Lane
(775) 323-0555
A favorite stop for grandparents, Little Angels Boutique offers very special items perfect for gift giving. The merchandise is beautifully made and very upscale. Although the shop is small, you're sure

to find just the right gift for those special little ones in your life.

Once Upon a Child
See previous listing under "Consignment."

Pawn Shops

Superpawn
190 North Center Street
(775) 323-2352

350 North Virginia Street
(775) 322-4373

1980 Selmi Drive
(775) 324-2188
www.superpawn.com
A family-owned and -operated business dating from the 1930s, Superpawn began with a single location in downtown Reno and has expanded to 30 stores in Arizona and Nevada. If you need money, you can get instant cash by pawning almost anything of value. But if you're shopping, you can find incredible bargains in such things as jewelry, coins, electronics, musical instruments, tools, and sporting goods. The best selection of tools and musical instruments is found at the South Rock Boulevard store in Sparks (see listing). For high-priced jewelry try the North Virginia Street location.

Sporting Gear

Bobo's Mogul Mouse Ski & Patio
475 East Moana Lane
(775) 826-9096
www.bobosmogulmouse.com
If you need to rent equipment, you can choose from Reno's largest ski and snowboard rental department at Bobo's. Friendly, professional service combined with a large variety of inventory makes shopping here a pleasure. You'll find everything you need to buy for the entire family for fun in the snow. When spring has sprung, the skis disappear and out comes the largest selection of patio and outdoor furniture in the Reno/Tahoe area. It might seem like a strange combination of merchandise, but the owners are savvy businesspeople who are very successful in both seasons.

Eclipse Running
960 West Moana Lane
(775) 827-2279
www.eclipserunning.com
Eclipse Running is a running store run by runners. More than just selling shoes, the owners are committed to helping customers become lifelong runners. They offer personalized service that includes help with training and injuries. The store has been open since 1995 and also offers a selection of snowshoes and swimming apparel and accessories.

Golf Headquarters
4112 Kietzke Lane
(775) 826-2246
www.renotahoeghq.com
Dubbed the "Nordstom's of golf shops," Golf Headquarters (formerly Nevada Bob's) is the area's largest and oldest golf shop. The warm woods and plush carpets in this classy store give an air of elegance not usually found in golf shops. But in spite of the rich decor, you don't have to be rich to shop here. Prices are very competitive, and the store stands behind all its products. You'll find all major brands of golf clothing and equipment, and you can even have your clubs custom-fit by the professionally trained staff.

Harley-Davidson of Reno
2295 Market Street
(775) 329-2913
www.hdreno.com
If you're a Harley kind of person, you've found your Eden. Harley-Davidson of Reno will light your fire with its large selection of riding gear, accessories, and Buell bikes. It's better if you arrive on a Harley, but cars are okay.

If you're shopping for exercise clothes, check out the retail shops at local health clubs such as Sports West Athletic Club at 1575 South Virginia Street, Reno; (775) 348-6666.

Orvis Company Store, Reno
13945 South Virginia Street
Summit Sierra, Suite 640
(775) 852-2799
www.orvis.com
Opened in 2006 in the Summit Sierra mall, the Orvis Company Store epitomizes the Orvis country lifestyle experience. Well known for its high-quality merchandise, the company offers an upscale shopping experience in this homey and comfortable store. Although Orvis is best known for its fly-fishing gear, shoppers will also find a full line of men's and women's clothing, furniture, pet items, and gifts.

REI (Recreation Equipment Inc.)
2225 Harvard Way
(775) 828-9090
www.rei.com
Sooner or later every outdoorsman will shop at REI. With everything from clothing to camping gear to sporting goods, the store offers everything you need to be safe and comfortable while connecting with the natural environment. You can even buy freeze-dried food and maps for your next outdoor adventure. REI also offers trips, classes, and equipment rentals. Be sure to ask about an REI membership card that gives you discounts at all their locations. Besides the outstanding selection of merchandise, this establishment is also a standout because of its friendly and knowledgeable employees.

Reno Fly Shop
294 East Moana Lane
(775) 825-3474
www.renoflyshop.com
There's not much question about the owner of Reno Fly Shop knowing his business: He won the prestigious Jackson One-Fly fishing contest in Jackson Hole, Wyoming, in 1994. The sales force is equally knowledgeable, with several fly-fishing books to their credit. Open since 1978, this store is a full-service fly shop, offering fly-tying, rodbuilding, and fly-fishing lessons; Nevada and California guide service; and a complete line of clothing and equipment. You can buy top-of-the-line Simms Gortex waders to go with your Sage, Scott, Orvis, or Winston fly rod. It's a great specialty store for the ardent fly-fishing enthusiast (and this is no fish story).

Reno Mountain Sports
155 East Moana Lane
(775) 825-2855
www.renomountainsports.com
You can buy all the gear and clothing you'll need for skiing, backpacking, hiking, climbing, and kayaking at Reno Mountain Sports. Since the professional staff is sports-oriented, you can be assured that equipment is suited to your ability and body size. Well stocked with all the best-known sporting goods brands, the store is great fun for browsing. For equipment rentals and service, drive around to the back of the building and use the rear entrance.

Snowind Sports
2500 East Second Street
(775) 323-9463
Tucked away in the lower level of the shopping arcade in the Grand Sierra Resort and Casino, Snowind offers sales and rentals for mountain bikes, in-line skates, skis, and snowboards. If your skis need tuning, you'll get the best tune in town here. The easiest access to the store is from the parking lot adjacent to the driving range by the lake.

Sports Authority
4813 Kietzke Lane
(775) 828-1234
www.sportsauthority.com
A megastore with seemingly unlimited choices, Sports Authority is Reno/Tahoe's largest sporting goods store. You can

completely outfit yourself for any sporting activity in all major brands of equipment and apparel. In spite of its size, the store maintains personalized service. Salespersons are hired because of their knowledge of a particular sport: If you're buying skis, a skier will help you select them. Formerly Gart Sports, the store has oodles of parking and is conveniently located in the Fire Creek Crossing Shopping Center.

Women's Clothing

Boutique Casablanca
3888 Mayberry Drive
(775) 746-2070
The beautiful window displays at this boutique are guaranteed to lure you inside. Although the shop is small, the variety of merchandise is enough to keep you pawing the racks for some time. You'll find chic sportswear alongside classy cocktail ensembles. Geared more to the older woman, it's a great place to shop for cruise and travel clothing.

Concepts By Fine 'N Funky
228 Vassar Street
(775) 853-1400
You know Concepts By Fine 'N Funky is special the minute you see the store. Off the beaten path in a semiresidential neighborhood, this charming green-and-white cottage has a lovely 1800s ambience. The store specializes in top-quality merchandise not sold anywhere else in the area, such as Lucky, Big Star, and Diesel jeans and Kiehls natural hair and skin products. The clothes are classy and range from casual to cocktail. You can also shop for men and children. The store has another location at the Boatworks Mall in Tahoe City, California; (530) 583-1400 (see the description of the mall later in this chapter).

Donna's Fashion Boutique
2303 Kietzke Lane
(775) 827-4911
Far from the hustle of major shopping malls, Donna's Fashion Boutique offers customers a warm, intimate shopping experience. Although the selection is somewhat limited, all the merchandise is thoughtfully chosen and decidedly upscale. When you buy an outfit from Donna's, you don't need to worry about seeing it on everyone else in town. You'll find this charming boutique in the Franktown Corners shopping mall.

It's All About Me
6629 South Virginia Street, Suite A
The Commons
(775) 828-0202
www.itsallaboutmereno.com
Epitomizing the area's growth in classy shopping, It's All About Me seeks to offer retail therapy for discriminating buyers. With the latest in European fashions, the choices are tempting indeed. Brands include Vertigo, Streets Ahead, Nicole Miller, Votre Nom, and Avenue Montaigne. It's a casual-chic boutique whose one-of-a-kind lines are only found here.

Lodo Loft
Arlington Avenue and West Plumb Lane
(775) 284-5636
You'll find a tantalizing array of casual clothes, from jeans to pantsuits, in this boutique. Open daily, Lodo Loft is located in the Plumgate complex, just down from Starbucks and Like a Charm. A second location is at 893 Tahoe Boulevard in Incline Village, NV; (775) 833-9333.

Parasols On The Riverwalk
11 North Sierra Street
(775) 323-0777
Don't let the small size of this boutique fool you: It's chock-full of everything from formal to fun and funky clothing. If you're looking for that one-of-a-kind outfit, you have a good chance of finding it here. Next to the Century Riverside 12 theaters on the Truckee River, it's a great place to browse before or after a movie.

Pendleton of Reno
8175 South Virginia Street
(775) 323-1119
www.pendleton-usa.com
Formerly located in the National Bowling Stadium, Pendleton of Reno has found a new home in the Southwest Pavilion shopping mall. This Oregon-based company has been pleasing customers for years with its high-quality woolen goods. You'll find a wonderful selection of clothing for both women and men at this comfortable store. While at Southwest Pavilion you can also stop by Talbots (see subsequent entry).

Ross Stores Inc.
2950 Northtowne Lane
(775) 673-2900

4825 Kietzke Lane
(775) 826-2000
www.rossstores.com
Ross is a discounter's delight, but be prepared to work for your bargains. Since the real treasures are often well hidden, you've got to paw the racks to ferret out the good stuff. Real shoppers enjoy the challenge of the hunt, however, and just roll up their sleeves and plunge in.

Stein Mart
5069 South McCarran Boulevard
(775) 826-7222
www.steinmart.com
Some of the best clothing values in the area are found at Stein Mart, the mini department store in Smithridge Plaza. The store has a wonderful variety of top-quality, name-brand clothes for 25 to 50 percent off regular retail prices. Stein Mart is a cut above most discount stores, with classy merchandise and upscale decor. In addition to its great selection of women's apparel, the store has fine men's and children's departments.

Talbots
The Summit Sierra
South Virginia Street and
Nevada Highway 431
(775) 851-7777
www.talbots.com
Talbots is a class act, selling classic casual, business, and formal clothing. To help you build your wardrobe, the store offers personal shopping service, wardrobe consulting, and appointment shopping. If you don't find what you want in the store, help is merely a phone call away. Just pick up the Red Line Phone in the shop and order your merchandise directly from Talbots catalog.

William Furs, Leather and Cashmere
3370 Lakeside Court
(775) 828-0995
Although fur and leather can be a sensitive subject these days, if you're going to buy and wear it, you want it to be top quality. William Furs, Leather and Cashmere is Reno/Tahoe's most complete full-service salon. All merchandise is personally selected by William on his frequent trips to the best international sources of merchandise. Like the coats themselves, the shop is luxurious, with deep carpeting and a wine bar tucked cozily in one corner. The store also offers trade-in, layaways, consignments, cold storage, repairs, and cleaning. Service is personalized, with William helping you to select just the right purchase and celebrating it with a glass of champagne.

SPARKS

Malls and Shopping Centers

Baring Village
Sparks and Baring Boulevards
Baring Village is a low-key neighborhood mall with a basic collection of shops and eateries. You'll find such stores as the Playful Potter, Baa Baa Black Sheep country store, Vicks' Cards and Gifts, Motor City Music, and Zoyo Comic Collectibles.

Greenbrae Shopping Center
Greenbrae Drive and Pyramid Way
As one of the oldest shopping centers in

the area, Greenbrae has managed to hold on to its loyal customers in spite of the competition from newer, more glitzy shopping alternatives. The stores include Hancock Fabrics and Ben Franklin Crafts. You can also bowl at Greenbrae Lanes.

Iron Horse Shopping Center
Southwest corner of Prater Way and North McCarran Boulevard
The Iron Horse Shopping Center offers one-stop shopping, with Albertson's Food & Drug, Payless Shoesource, Target, Party America (discount party supplies), and Mother Lode Bicycles. For lunch or dinner at a reasonable price, try Applebee's Neighborhood Grill & Bar.

Marina Marketplace
Sparks Boulevard and Prater Way
In addition to basic services and several restaurants, Marina Marketplace offers Country Clutter and Paradise Flowers and Gifts.

McCarran Plaza
Northwest corner of Prater Way and North McCarran Boulevard
Along with a sprinkling of casual eateries, McCarran Plaza offers Foot Locker and a Longs Drug Store. The plaza is just across the street from the Iron Horse Shopping Center.

Silver State Plaza
680 North McCarran Boulevard
Anchored by Safeway and Sav-On Drugs, Silver State Plaza serves most of the basic needs of nearby residents. Stores include Vicks' Books, Radio Shack, and the General Nutrition Center.

Spanish Springs Center
Vista Boulevard and Disc Drive
Anchored by a Scolari's grocery store, Spanish Springs Center offers Silver Spoon children's store, Home Expressions Decor 'n More, and Twisted Scissors salon and gift shop. It's also home to the Vista Grille restaurant.

Victorian Square
Victorian Avenue
With its quaint turn-of-the-20th-century motif, Victorian Square is a delight to shop. You'll find a fun mix of specialty shops perfect for browsing. It's the center of activity for downtown Sparks, so you can also attend special events, take in a movie at the Century Sparks 14 theaters, or play in the interactive fountain (see the description of the square in the Attractions and Kidstuff chapters).

Antiques

Sandy's Attic Collectibles & More
295 Twentieth Street
(775) 331-3188
With a little bit of everything from soup to nuts, Sandy's Attic Collectibles & More makes the most of its tiny little house. Merchandise changes all the time, so you never know what you'll find in the way of furniture and collectibles. The owner constantly searches estate sales and storage auctions for unusual items.

Victorian Square Antique Emporium
834 Victorian Avenue
(775) 331-2288
Not many antiques stores can boast a collection of authentic gaming memorabilia. The Victorian Square Antique Emporium has original oil artworks, felt gaming layouts, cards, dice, and clothing from area casinos. Antiquers know these items are hard to come by, so be sure to ask about them when you're in the store.

Like the historical goodies inside, the emporium's physical location also has a past. It was built in the early 1900s by the Southern Pacific Railroad and served as a hotel during Sparks's heyday as a railroad stopover. Today it's packed with the treasures displayed by about 40 antiques dealers and crafters. You'll find everything from A to Z, including furniture, antique glassware, jewelry, paintings, and collectibles.

Books

The Book Gallery
1203 North Rock Boulevard
(775) 356-8900
To peruse all the titles at The Book Gallery is a daunting task. With more than 80,000 books in stock, the inventory spills into three buildings. The store buys, sells, and trades used paperbacks and hardbound books of all categories. You'll also find a selection of videos and DVDs.

His Word Christian Book Store
810 Holman Way
(775) 359-7940
www.hiswordbooks.com
Although the mainstay of both locations (here and in Reno) of His Word Christian Book Store is Christian books, the stores are also mini-marts offering a wide selection of other religious items. You can shop for gifts, such as Seraphin angels and Precious Moments figurines. Or you can browse the aisles for pictures, cards, videos, music, and tapes. As in many bookstores, the ambience is comfortable and relaxed.

New Life Christian Book Store
546 Greenbrae Drive
(775) 331-1155
It's probably the only post office in the country that will pray for your mail to arrive on time. Tucked in the back of the New Life Christian Book Store, the postal substation is a full-service post office equipped to handle all of your mailing needs.

Up front, the store has the only large selection of used, out-of-print, and hard-to-find Christian books in the area. You'll be delighted to discover its reasonable prices: Most everything ranges from $1.00 to $3.00. The store also carries new books, gifts, pictures, plaques, T-shirts, hats, and jewelry.

Gifts and Souvenirs

Hippies
1921 Victorian Avenue
(775) 331-8554
Formerly Art Dogs and Grace II, Hippies specializes in hand-dipped incense. If you don't find what you want on the shelf, you can ask the store to customize an order for you. You can also shop for handmade Peruvian jewelry, memorabilia from the Grateful Dead and Haight Ashbury, and smoking products in the tobacco pipe room.

Pawn Shops

Metro Pawn
255 East Glendale Avenue
(775) 359-5151
www.metropawn.com
You can buy watches, jewelry, cameras, VCRs, TVs, and electronics at Metro Pawn. They're never far away, with four locations in the Reno/Tahoe area. You can shop at the Sparks location or at several Reno locations: 800 West Fifth Street, (775) 322-1030; 51 East Grove Street, (775) 828-0770; or 6150 South Virginia Street, (775) 828-5454.

Pacific Pawnbrokers
1246 Victorian Avenue
(775) 359-7761
With three locations in the Reno/Tahoe area, Pacific Pawnbrokers offers a huge selection of jewelry, musical instruments, and electronics.

The largest store is the address above, with smaller stores at 701 Ryland Avenue, Reno, (775) 348-2525; and 920 Victorian Avenue, Sparks, (775) 359-6222. The stores also have Spanish speakers on the staff.

Superpawn
641 South Rock Boulevard
(775) 331-4044
www.superpawn.com
See the Reno listing for more information.

Sporting Gear

The Gilly Fishing Store
1111 North Rock Boulevard
(775) 358-6113

An old-fashioned store with new ideas, The Gilly Fishing Store offers customers personalized service along with the latest merchandise. You'll find the largest selection of fishing tackle in the Reno/Tahoe area, plus clothing, float tubes, rods, and reels. The store also sells custom rods and rents fishing videos. You can also hear your share of fish stories here, since it's the meeting place of the Great Basin Bassers, a local bass-fishing club.

House of Arrows Archery Pro Shop
1121 North Rock Boulevard
(775) 356-6614

The House of Arrows Archery Pro Shop does more than just meet your archery needs: It also offers a unique display of handmade longbows dating from the 1920s. But if the historical equipment isn't your cup of tea, you can buy the latest in new or used, custom fit to your skill level and goals.

Catering to what the owner dubs "the local archery 3-D junkie," the store specializes in upper-end and hard-to-find bows and arrows. It's also an information center for archery meets and competitions held around the country.

RockSport Indoor Climbing Center
1901 Silverada Boulevard
(775) 352-7673
www.rocksportnv.com

If you've ever wondered how mountain climbers learn to inch their way up perpendicular rock walls, you can learn their secrets in a safe environment at RockSport Indoor Climbing Center. In preparation for your own summit attempts, the store will also outfit you with all the appropriate gear and clothing you'll need.

NORTH SHORE LAKE TAHOE

Malls and Shopping Centers

Boatworks Mall
760 North Lake Boulevard
Tahoe City, CA
(530) 583-1488
www.tahoecityshopping.com

With any view of Lake Tahoe at a premium, the Boatworks Mall is special indeed. Hugging the shoreline in Tahoe City, the mall offers a lovely environmental experience along with a fun shopping outing. In a rustic Tahoe atmosphere with periodic glimpses of the lake, you can shop for fine art, food and wine, books, jewelry, games, clothing, and souvenirs. With names like Y.B. Ugleé-Cosmetique and Runes & Jewels by IBA, you can see you're in for a fun time in these stores. When you're through shopping and ready to drop, head into Jake's on the Lake or Sol y Lago for drinks and dinner. You won't be disappointed.

Christmas Tree Village
868 Tahoe Boulevard
Incline Village, NV

It seems like Christmas every day at the Christmas Tree Village shopping mall. The quaint Tyrolean decor makes it festive year-round. You can buy fine art at Art Attack, unique jewelry at Incline Jewelry, collectibles and gifts at The Tahoe Store Emporium, and, last but not least, you can experience the sights, sounds, and smells of Christmas every day in the Christmas Shoppe.

Cobblestone Center
475 North Lake Boulevard
Tahoe City, CA
(530) 583-1580
www.cobblestonetahoe.com

Built in 1966, the Cobblestone Center is Tahoe City's oldest mall. Its charming

Swiss-Bavarian architecture lends a picturesque touch to the lovely alpine setting. Reminiscent of European villages, the clock in the center's tower chimes on the hour and plays carillon music. The center boasts a movie theater and a cafe with outdoor dining, plus an interesting mix of shops selling clothing, gifts, art, home furnishings, and a beauty salon. It's been recently expanded to add additional retail establishments along North Lake Boulevard.

Lighthouse Shopping Center
850 North Lake Boulevard
Tahoe City, CA
(530) 583-3471
Just a hop, skip, and a jump from the Boatworks Mall, the Lighthouse Shopping Center houses a post office, video store, a Safeway supermarket, and a few specialty boutiques. You can easily shop both these malls at the same time, since they're adjacent to each other.

Raley's Incline Center
930 Tahoe Boulevard
Incline Village, NV
Anchored by a large Raley's supermarket, Incline Center is the heart of shopping in Incline Village. You can find basic essentials here as well as tourist items. The stores offer upscale clothing, hardware, video rentals, books, art, and gifts. When hunger strikes, you can choose from fine Italian cuisine at Azzara's Italian Restaurant, gourmet burgers at Rookies Sports Bar & Grill, or fresh bagels at the Sierra Bagel Factory.

Squaw Valley USA
1960 Squaw Valley Road
Olympic Valley, CA
(530) 583-6985
www.squaw.com
If you're not busy skiing, you can browse the small cluster of quaint shops near the base of the lifts at Squaw Valley USA or the upscale boutiques just completed in the village. As you might expect, some of these stores are oriented toward skiing and outdoor activities. Since the business at the ski area is seasonal, some shops are closed during the summer months. While in Olympic Valley, check out the shops at the Resort at Squaw Creek, just off Squaw Valley Road as you enter the valley (see the descriptions of Squaw Valley and the Resort at Squaw Creek in the Winter Sports and Resorts chapters).

The Village at Squaw
Squaw Valley USA
Olympic Valley, CA
(530) 584-1000
www.thevillageatsquaw.com
The newest development at Squaw Valley USA, the Village at Squaw boasts a collection of upscale shops along with its luxurious condominiums. Everything is conveniently located adjacent to the gondola and funicular. Although some old-timers decry the loss of parking and the size of the project, it has brought a new level of luxury to Olympic Valley. Shoppers can browse such stores as Tails by the Lake—A Pet Boutique, Occhiali, Edin Boutique, Gallery Keoki, and PlumpJackSport. You'll also find a nice choice of eateries for either lunch or dinner.

Antiques

Girasole
319 West Lake Boulevard
Tahoe City, CA
(530) 581-4255
At Girasole you'll find a lovely selection of antique country pine furniture imported from England, Ireland, and Mexico. The store also has gift items for the home, including handpainted Italian ceramic dinnerware.

Books

Bookshelf At The Boatworks
760 North Lake Boulevard
Tahoe City, CA
(530) 581-9000, (800) 959-5083
www.bookshelfstores.com

The Bookshelf At The Boatworks has something for everyone, including a children's section. If you want information about local history or Tahoe's great outdoors, you'll find a good collection of books on the region right up front.

Village Hallmark & Books
930 Tahoe Boulevard
Incline Village, NV
(775) 831-3301
In addition to a good selection of books, you can buy cards and logo gifts at the Village Hallmark & Books store. It does not pretend to be a megabookstore, but you can find a generous selection of best-sellers and Lake Tahoe books in the store.

Gifts and Souvenirs

Alpine Heritage
Boatworks Mall
760 North Lake Boulevard
Tahoe City, CA
(530) 581-5202
For a choice of unique gifts, drop in to Alpine Heritage at the Boatworks Mall. As the name hints, the shop specializes in imported collectibles from Austria. The most interesting items are the intricate handmade nativity scenes, which were originally produced in the Steyr Valley in the 1800s. The store also has a wonderful collection of fine glassware from Europe. Even if you're not buying, it's a colorful shop for browsing.

Cabin Fever
551 North Lake Boulevard
Tahoe City, CA
(530) 583-8143
It's easy to get into a Tahoe mood at Cabin Fever, with its lovely displays of mountain and wildlife accessories, and gifts and home furnishings. From the stylish log furniture to the stuffed animals, the merchandise is warm and homey. You can completely decorate your home or just buy gifts for friends in this eclectic shop.

Gundy of Scandinavia
475 North Lake Boulevard
Tahoe City, CA
(530) 583-4533
Festive is the name of the game at Gundy of Scandinavia, where it's Christmas every day. How can you resist buying with all the wonderful sights, smells, and sounds of the holidays enveloping you? Indulge yourself with a great selection of quaint ornaments and collectible gifts imported from all over the world, including gifts styled in Scandinavia. After all, Christmas comes but once a year—except at Gundy.

The Tahoe Store Emporium
868 Tahoe Boulevard
Incline Village, NV
(775) 832-5332
www.thetahoestore.com
This wonderful store does most of its business in candles, but you'll also find Leanin' Tree greeting cards, Beanie Babies, games and toys, and Tahoe T-shirts in The Tahoe Store Emporium. You'll find this shop at Unit 21 in the Christmas Tree Village.

Kidstuff

Lil' Diggs
893 Tahoe Boulevard
Incline Village, NV
(775) 832-5611
With its hip styles, Lil' Diggs appeals to the very fashion conscious parents who want fine clothing for their kids. The store stocks both boys and girls clothes in sizes 0 to 14. Brands include Bloom Love, Cach Cach, Charabia Paris, Jade, and Junk Food. You'll find the store tucked next to Lodo Loft behind Starbucks. A second shop is located in Plumgate in Reno at the corner of Arlington Avenue and Plumb Lane.

Ring Around The Rosie
255 North Lake Boulevard
Tahoe City, CA
(530) 583-8604
This consignment children's shop, located

near the golf course in Tahoe City, is a favorite of locals and also the perfect place to shop if the airline accidentally shipped your child's suitcase to Guam instead of Reno. The selection changes with the season: You'll find snowsuits in winter and bathing suits in summer. In addition to high-end clothing, you'll also find a variety of furniture and accessories like backpacks and toys.

Ruffles & Ruffnecks
475 North Lake Boulevard
Tahoe City, CA
(530) 583-1128
As the name implies, you can buy everything from lacy dresses for little girls to tough jeans for little boys at Ruffles & Ruffnecks. The shop boasts the largest selection of children's clothing in the North Shore Lake Tahoe area, with medium to upscale fashions in such brands as Cach Cach, Mimi, Maggi, Roxy, and Patagonia. You'll also find books, toys, and accessories. The store is easy to find in the Cobblestone Center.

Sporting Gear

Alpenglow Sports
415 North Lake Boulevard
Tahoe City, CA
(530) 583-6917
www.alpenglowsports.com
If you're looking for specialists in all types of mountain adventure, head into Alpenglow Sports. They've been in the business since 1979 and can meet your needs for rock climbing, trail riding, hiking and backpacking, and all forms of backcountry skiing. You can buy clothing and equipment produced by manufacturers including Patagonia, Mountain Hardware, and Black Diamond. The store also features a full-service rental shop.

The Back Country
690 North Lake Boulevard
Tahoe City, CA
(530) 581-5861
www.thebackcountry.net
As the name indicates, The Back Country specializes in all you need to venture off the beaten path. The super-friendly staff is composed of avid backcountry skiers and bikers and is very knowledgeable about the surrounding mountain environment. When you buy or rent equipment here, you can select from the very best and latest merchandise for telemark, cross-country, and randonee skiing, as well as mountain biking. Ski equipment includes Dynafit, Garmont, K2, and Rossignol; mountain bike brands include Marin, GT, and Jamis. A full-service bike shop is open all year.

Olympic Bike Shop
620 North Lake Boulevard
Tahoe City, CA
(530) 581-2500
www.tahoebikerentals.com
According to local cyclists, Olympic Bike Shop is the No. 1 bike shop in the area. You'll find an extensive selection of accessories, parts, and clothing, along with top-of-the-line bikes. Bike brands include Cannondale, Specialized, and Trek. You can also pick up maps and guidebooks of the area to make your biking outings hassle-free. Specializing exclusively in both road and mountain biking, the store is open from the first of May until the end of October.

Porter's Ski & Sport
885 Tahoe Boulevard
Incline Village, NV
(775) 831-3500
www.porterstahoe.com
Porter's Ski & Sport has been a mainstay sportswear shop in the area for more than 40 years. The store sells alpine skis, snowboards, and snowshoes in winter, and water skis and tennis equipment in the

summer. You'll find one of the best selections of sportswear in the area, with great clothing for the entire family from Columbia, Woolrich, and North Face. You can also rent bikes from the store during the summer. The company also has locations in Tahoe City at 501 North Lake Boulevard, (530) 583-2314; and in Truckee at the Crossroads Center, (530) 587-1500.

Village Ski Loft
800 Tahoe Boulevard
Incline Village, NV
(775) 831-3537
www.villageskiloft.com
Voted the No. 1 ski shop in the West by readers of *Snow Country* magazine, the Village Ski Loft can meet all of your family's needs for a great winter in the great outdoors. The shop features a huge inventory of equipment to buy or rent, including all major brands. Even if your skiing or snowboarding skills aren't up to par, you'll look great in the snazzy clothing featured in the loft. During the summer months, the store converts to a mountain bike shop. You'll find a second Village Ski Loft location at Diamond Peak Ski Resort during the winter.

Women's Clothing

Camila's At Tahoe
760 North Lake Boulevard
Tahoe City, CA
(530) 583-0120
From casual clothing to evening dresses, Camila's At Tahoe has just the right clothing for any occasion. Brands change with fashion, but rest assured you'll find the most current styles in this store. With a complete line of scarves, shoes, belts, and handbags to choose from, as well as lovely silver jewelry, you can select the perfect accessories for your new outfits. The store is located in the Boatworks Mall.

Incline Outfitters
930 Tahoe Boulevard
Incline Village, NV
(775) 831-0432
Billing themselves as "logo clothiers for the vacation lifestyle," Incline Outfitters features men's, women's, and some children's clothing from such designers as Brighton, Tommy Bahama, Blue Willi's, and Fresh Produce, as well as high-quality Tahoe logo apparel. It's the Tahoe look personalized—casual, comfortable, and stylish. Look for this store in the Raley's Incline Center.

Jeunesse Better Clothing
930 Tahoe Boulevard
Incline Village, NV
(775) 831-5600
If you're looking for affordable designer wear that's unique and original, you've come to the right place. Jeunesse Better Clothing features relaxed, elegant clothing for the resort lifestyle, selling original designs in denim, gabardine, cashmere, and iridescent wovens, silk, and cotton. The clothing is medium-priced, so you don't have to break the bank to shop here. The shop is easy to find in the Raley's Incline Center.

Lodo Loft
893 Tahoe Boulevard
Incline Village, NV
(775) 833-9333
Specializing in stylish casual clothes, Lodo Loft is next to Lil' Diggs children's store behind Starbucks. For more information, see the listing for the Reno store in this chapter.

SOUTH SHORE LAKE TAHOE

Malls and Shopping Centers

Factory Stores at the "Y"
U.S. Highway 50 and California Highway 89
South Lake Tahoe, CA
(530) 573-5545
www.tahoefactorystores.com
Shop for bargains galore at the Factory Stores at the "Y." Outlets include Bass Shoe Factory, Sierra Shirts, Oneida Factory Store, Sunglass Hut International, Geoffrey Beene, and Van Heusen Factory Store. As the name tells you, the mall is at the "Y," smack in the middle of the busiest shopping area in the South Shore Lake Tahoe area. You can easily use the outlet as a jumping-off point to other nearby stores.

The Shops at Heavenly Village
Heavenly Village Way
South Lake Tahoe, CA
Clustered at the base of Heavenly Ski Resort's gondola, the Shops at Heavenly Village offer an eclectic mix of upscale boutiques and eateries, all in the quaint Old Tahoe style. You can easily combine a gondola ride with shopping and imbibing. There's also a state-of-the-art cinema and ice-skating rink.

Ski Run Marina Village
970 Ski Run Boulevard
South Lake Tahoe, CA
(530) 544-9500
www.skirunmarina.com
You can experience the beauty of Lake Tahoe while you roam the shops at Ski Run Marina Village. Quaint and picturesque, the stores front the lake, affording fabulous views of the water and the mountains beyond. Here you can stroll through Cabin Fever, LJ's Jewelry, Sunglass Time, Wind Chimes by the Lake, and Village Wear & Gifts. You can also enjoy dining with a view at Riva Grill on the Lake or the Marina Village Cafe.

The Village Center
U.S. Highway 50 at Park Avenue
South Lake Tahoe, CA
One of the oldest shopping areas in South Shore Lake Tahoe, The Village Center has an eclectic mix of shops, including Side Street Boutique, Foot Locker, Savvy of Lake Tahoe, and Tahoe Sports LTD.

Books

Mountain Spirit
3045 Harrison Avenue
South Lake Tahoe, CA
(530) 544-2244
Mountain Spirit is a gathering place for spirit, mind, and body, offering a variety of merchandise along with classes and workshops. You can choose from a mind-expanding assortment of books, gifts, jewelry, CDs, and tapes. Escape the hustle and bustle of everyday life and enjoy a quiet interlude in this spiritual oasis.

Neighbors Bookstore
The Village Center
4000 Lake Tahoe Boulevard
South Lake Tahoe, CA
(530) 541-6296
Formerly located at Caesars Tahoe (MontBleu Resort Casino & Spa), Neighbors Bookstore is packed with books on all major subjects. You're sure to find just the right book to settle into on your Tahoe vacation. Or how about a book on tape that you can tuck in your beach bag?

Casino Shopping

Harrah's Lake Tahoe
U.S. Highway 50
Stateline, NV
(775) 588-6611, (800) HARRAHS
www.harrahstahoe.com/galleria.html

You'll find everything you need to make your vacation just perfect at Harrah's Gift Shop and at the Sunrise Sport Shop, with their eclectic selections of clothing, sporting goods, gifts, and collectibles.

Harveys Lake Tahoe Casino & Resort
U.S. Highway 50
Stateline, NV
(775) 588-2411
www.harrahs.com

At Harveys you can have fun buying gifts and souvenirs at Harveys Gift Shoppe and Harveys Flower Shop. For sporting goods and apparel, be sure to stop at Heavenly Sports.

MontBleu Resort Casino & Spa
55 U.S. Highway 50
Stateline, NV
(775) 588-3515

Formerly Caesars Tahoe, MontBleu Resort Casino & Spa offers several boutiques to help you weather any winter storm. For your sporting goods needs, try the Sunrise Sport Shop. Because this property was in transition at press time, it was unclear what the exact mix of stores would be.

Gifts and Souvenirs

Buffalo Trading Post
4039 Lake Tahoe Boulevard
South Lake Tahoe, CA
(530) 541-7676

You can buy everything from Acoma pottery to Zuni jewelry in the Buffalo Trading Post, the oldest trading post in California. Most of the lovely artifacts are made by Native Americans, including masks, dolls, and sand paintings. The colorful merchandise spreads into two stores, offering one of the largest selections of gifts in the South Shore Lake Tahoe area. Don't miss the beauty displayed in this unique shop.

Oneida Factory Store
2014 Lake Tahoe Boulevard
South Lake Tahoe, CA
(530) 541-0826

If it's made of silver, you can find it at the Oneida Factory Store. What's even better, you can buy it for 30 to 40 percent less than regular retail prices. You can find just the perfect wedding or baby gift from the large selection of silver and crystal merchandise. For that very special event, you can have your gifts engraved. The Oneida shop is tucked in the Factory Stores at the "Y" shopping mall.

Tahoe Country
The Shops at Heavenly Village
1001 Heavenly Village Way, Suite 27
South Lake Tahoe, CA
(530) 544-6600
www.tahoecountry.com

There's something for everyone on your gift list at Tahoe Country. You'll find a great selection of books, cards, art, music, videos, Tahoe souvenirs, and household goodies. It's conveniently located in The Shops at Heavenly Village.

Kidstuff

Sidestreet Boutique
The Village Center
4000 South Lake Tahoe Boulevard
South Lake Tahoe, CA
(530) 544-9071
www.sidestreetboutique.com

You'll find an interesting selection of baby and children's clothing at Sidestreet Boutique, including such brands as Baby Biscotti, Hello Kitty, and Charlie Rocket. See the store description under Women's Clothing later in this chapter.

Pawn Shops

Oliver's Fine Jewelry
Round Hill Square, Suite 445
Zephyr Cove, NV
(775) 588-8470

As jewelry brokers, Oliver's Fine Jewelry boasts one of the largest inventories of jewelry in the South Shore Lake Tahoe area. You'll love their prices: Diamonds are 10 percent above their wholesale cost, and most other jewelry is 30 to 50 percent less than retail. The store is easy to find in the lovely Round Hill Square Shopping Center.

Sporting Gear

House of Ski
209 Kingsbury Grade
Stateline, NV
(775) 588-5935, (800) 475-4432
www.houseofski.com

House of Ski is a total ski shop, with retail sales, rentals, and service. The very latest accessories, fashions, and equipment are for sale, with package discounts offered on all equipment. You can also rent equipment and whatever clothing you might need. The shop is easy to find on Kingsbury Grade on the way to the Nevada side of Heavenly Ski Resort.

Rainbow Mountain
1133 Ski Run Boulevard
South Lake Tahoe, CA
(530) 541-7470, (800) 619-7470
www.rainbowwintersports.com

Voted the "Best Ski Shop" by the *Tahoe Tribune,* this full-service shop on the road to Heavenly Ski Resort can meet all of your skiing and snowboarding needs. You can buy new and used top-of-the-line equipment and apparel. If you're a sometime or novice skier or snowboarder, not to worry: You can rent any clothing you might need along with equipment that will meet your skill level. The shop also offers a free van shuttle, but call ahead for the schedule. There's a second location at 3535 Lake Tahoe Boulevard.

Tahoe Bike Shop/Tahoe Boot & Ski Works
2277 Lake Tahoe Boulevard
South Lake Tahoe, CA
(530) 544-8060

Headquartered in a century-old log cabin, Tahoe Bike Shop is South Shore Lake Tahoe's oldest bike shop. Focusing solely on biking during the summer season, the store offers a complete line of BMX, cruiser, mountain, and road bikes. If you're not in a position to buy, you can rent from their large selection of rental bikes. Ardent bikers themselves, the staff is friendly and personal. Don't be surprised if they take you out on a ride to show you the ropes.

Come the snow season, the shop is transformed into a ski shop that sells skis and boots and provides ski tuning and custom fitting for ski boots.

Women's Clothing

Pazazz
1004 Ski Run Boulevard
South Lake Tahoe, CA
(530) 542-4457

Pazazz has a selection of clothing that appeals to all ages, so you'll have a great time trying on everything from classic career suits to smart sports ensembles to smashing cocktail outfits. The shop is appropriately named, so you're guaranteed to have a lot of pazazz when you show off the treasures you purchased here. The owner of this shop also operates Everything Under the Sun at 1013 Ski Run Boulevard, where you'll find Tahoe's most complete selection of swimwear.

Rain Urbana Lifestyle Couture
The Shops at Heavenly Village
Heavenly Village Way
South Lake Tahoe, CA
(530) 544-1700
www.rainurbana.com

Voted the best clothing store in the *Tahoe Daily Tribune's* "Best of Tahoe 2004," Rain Urbana offers fashionable clothing, such as premium denim, for both men and women. While browsing for clothes, you can also shop for candles, gifts, music, and home accessories. It's conveniently located in The Shops at Heavenly Village.

Sidestreet Boutique
The Village Center
4000 Lake Tahoe Boulevard
South Lake Tahoe, CA
(530) 544-9071
www.sidestreetboutique.com

Sidestreet Boutique has high-end clothing for the entire family. You can outfit yourself from casual to cocktail in such brands as Tommy Bahama, Barefoot Dreams, and Blue Willi's. For the perfect head-to-toe look, the sales staff will help you select just the right accessories. For weddings, the shop also has a sales and rental department for bridal wear and tuxedos.

ATTRACTIONS 

When the Nevada State Legislature legalized unlimited gaming in Nevada in 1931, the Reno/Tahoe area became a mecca for people hoping to strike it rich in the casinos. With nonstop entertainment 24 hours a day, the casinos are hard to beat as crowd-pleasing, main attractions. They range in size from giants, like tri-property Circus Circus–Silver Legacy Resort Casino–Eldorado Hotel/Casino complex in downtown Reno, to smaller, locally oriented establishments, such as the Rail City Casino in Sparks.

Some visitors literally never see the light of day during their entire visit to the area, as the dizzying array of casino amusements becomes their main focus. With the exception of the circus acts at the Midway Stage at Circus Circus and the automated mining machine and laser show at Silver Legacy, the amenities of the casinos are explored in the chapters on Hotels and Motels, Resorts, and Casino Nightlife.

But for now let's venture outside and have a look at "the other Reno/Tahoe," a land rich in history, natural beauty, and unlimited opportunities for recreation and personal enrichment. You can reach for the stars at the Fleischmann Planetarium and take a walk down Main Street America circa 1930 at the National Automobile Museum. You can pet a deer at the Sierra Safari Zoo, ogle priceless art at the Wilbur May Center, and ride a paddle wheeler across the pristine waters of Lake Tahoe. Or you can simply drink in the wonder and majesty of one of the most beautiful natural settings on Earth. Once you begin to explore this side of Reno/Tahoe, you can appreciate why it's called "America's Adventure Place."

With Lake Tahoe and the Sierra Nevada mountains just outside, it might seem redundant to list other attractions. A view anywhere can be a breathtaking attraction in itself. Lake Tahoe has been called "America's Treasure" by politicians, travel writers, and nature lovers, and the 72-mile drive along its shoreline has been named "The Most Beautiful Drive in America."

You can pick up information at the local chambers of commerce and visitor bureaus: 969 Tahoe Boulevard in Incline Village, (775) 831-4440; 195 U.S. Highway 50 in Stateline, (775) 588-4591; 380 North Lake Boulevard in Tahoe City, (530) 581-6900; and 3066 Lake Tahoe Boulevard in South Lake Tahoe, (530) 541-5255; or at the Lake Tahoe Visitors Authority at 1156 Ski Run Boulevard, (530) 544-5050. Web sites include www.tahoe.com, www.laketahoechamber.com, www.gotahoe.com, www.tahoefun.org, www.virtualtahoe.com, www.tahoechamber.org, and www.discovertahoe.com.

Lake Tahoe is the largest alpine lake in North America, and its crystal-clear waters reflect an ever-changing kaleidoscope of colors depending upon the weather at that particular moment. In this chapter I'll point out some of the must-see attractions in the Lake Tahoe Basin, other than the scenery. For a description of parks, beaches, and recreational opportunities, see the Winter Sports, Golf, Parks, Camping and RVing, Fishing and Hunting, and Recreation chapters. And for the ultimate mind-blowing Tahoe experience, I wholeheartedly recommend any view of the lake at sunset, preferably with your favorite person and your favorite libation close at hand.

RENO

Animal Ark
1265 Deerlodge Road
(775) 970-3111
www.animalark.org

Animal Ark is a wildlife sanctuary and nature center that shelters animals that don't have the skills to survive on their own. Disabled and orphaned animals such as gray wolves, bobcats, bears, snow leopards, and arctic foxes live in natural surroundings at the Ark. Aside from the animals, the educational displays scattered around the grounds make it an especially appealing learning experience for kids. Founded in 1980, the Ark will be expanded soon due to a $1.6 million capital fund drive. (See the Kidstuff chapter.)

Although most people can't own a wild animal as a pet, you can do the next best thing by adopting one at the Ark. Through their adoption program, you can help pay for the care and feeding of such residents as Effie, the Arctic fox; Shere Khan, the tiger; or Whoopi, the peregrine falcon.

The Ark is open from 10:00 A.M. to 4:30 P.M. from April 1 to October 31. It's closed Mondays except for those that fall on major holidays. Admission is $6.00 for adults, $5.00 for seniors, and $4.00 for children ages 3 through 12. It's a bit of a drive out of Reno, but well worth it. To get to the Ark, take U.S. Highway 395 north to the Red Rock Road exit, turn north onto Red Rock Road, and drive 11.5 miles to Deerlodge Road. Turn right and continue for 1 mile.

Circus Circus Midway Stage
500 North Sierra Street
(800) 648-5010
www.circusreno.com

When Circus Circus Hotel/Casino opened in Reno in 1978, casino patrons were astonished to see trapeze artists and high-wire walkers performing right above their heads as they placed their table bets and pulled the handles of slot machines. The age of the total entertainment concept had been born, complete with an enormous clown as a logo and a pink-and-white-striped circus tent enveloping portions of the building.

Although structural changes during the years have made the circus acts less visible from the casino floor, they can be optimally viewed from the Midway section of the casino. Young and old alike are drawn to the carnival-style arcade at the Midway, where they can win stuffed toy animals and other prizes at the more than 30 games available. The circus acts are free and can be seen daily throughout the year starting in midmorning. See the Kidstuff chapter for more information.

You'll find a dazzling carpet of wildflowers in summer while hiking around High Camp at Squaw Valley USA.

Fleischmann Planetarium
1650 North Virginia Street
(775) 784-4811
www.planetarium.unr.nevada.edu

Perched on a knoll overlooking the campus of the University of Nevada, Reno, Fleischmann Planetarium looks like a saucer-shaped spaceship that has just touched down. Its curious shape is actually a hyperbolic paraboloid canopy that covers the elliptical interior of the building.

Inside you can see such curiosities as all three meteorites ever found within Nevada, find out what your real weight would be on the planet Venus, or see how a black hole acts in space. These and many other exhibits are on display in the Astronomical Museum. But for many visitors the real space experience takes place in the domed theater on the lower level, where you can see spectacular films about nature and the universe. Lean back and relax in the reclining lounge chairs while the show unfolds all around you on the Skydome 8/70 screen.

For unusual space treasures, the gift shop is full of educational games, scientific books, and also Nevada's largest selection of telescopes, spotting scopes, and binoculars. Admission to the museum, gift shop, and observatory is free. Theater prices are $5.00 for ages 13 through 59 and $4.00 for children younger than 13 and persons 60 and older. The building is open Monday through Friday from 11:00 A.M. to 7:00 P.M. and Saturday and Sunday from 11:30 A.M. to 7:00 P.M. except on holidays. As features and show times in the theater vary throughout the year, call ahead for the listings and schedule. See the Kidstuff chapter for more information.

Mining Machine at Silver Legacy Resort Casino
407 North Virginia Street
(775) 329-4777, (800) 687-8733
www.silverlegacyreno.com
Showcasing Nevada's silver-mining heritage, the automated mining machine at Silver Legacy Resort Casino is a working model of how ore might have been processed in the 1800s. Towering 120 feet above the main casino floor, the machine is continuously in motion, with pumping bellows, steam engines, and running ore wagons. Designed so that human hands wouldn't touch the metal throughout the process, the finished product is coins spewing out near the Silver Baron's Bar and Lounge.

Although the resort created a fictitious tale of a miner named Sam Fairchild to explain the development of the machine, it doesn't have to be historically accurate to be appreciated. From an engineering standpoint alone, it's fascinating to see all the parts working together. But if mechanics don't interest you, stick around as this is only part of the action. The machine is encompassed by the world's largest composite dome. The interior of the dome reflects the skies of Reno, showing an entire day from sunrise to sunset.

From noon to 11:00 P.M. daily, the dome is the backdrop for the *Legend of the Legacy Laser Show,* a spectacular but also whimsical production of how the West was won, Reno-style. If you don't plan to be in the building for at least several hours, it's best to call ahead to get show times because the laser show alternates with a light show during the day. Admission is free, and the best vantage point is around the railing on the mezzanine level.

Mt. Rose Highway
Nevada Highway 431
from Reno to Incline Village, NV
For your first-time-ever view of Lake Tahoe, nothing beats the 25-mile drive up the Mt. Rose Highway to Incline Village. In Reno take US 395 south to the junction of NV 431 (Mt. Rose Highway) and follow the signs to North Shore Lake Tahoe.

Beginning at an elevation of 4,498 feet, the road gradually climbs for a few miles through the desert on the eastern side of the Sierra Nevada mountains. But at about 6,000 feet in elevation, the terrain changes dramatically from high desert to alpine forest. Huge conifer and red fir trees dominate the landscape as the road begins to twist and turn toward the summit. As you climb higher, you are treated with magnificent views of Reno and Sparks to the north and Washoe Lake to the south. Near the summit is the Mt. Rose–Ski Tahoe ski resort, with a base elevation of 8,260 feet.

You are rewarded with your first glimpse of Lake Tahoe several miles farther as you pass the sign that reads, MT. ROSE SUMMIT, ELEVATION 8,900, HIGHEST YEAR-ROUND SIERRA PASS. Surrounded by snowcapped peaks, the lake's size and beauty can take your breath away. As the road descends to lake level at 6,225 feet you'll drive through the Tahoe Meadows, an alpine paradise for hikers, skiers, and snowmobilers. See the Winter Sports and Recreation chapters for details of activities here.

The season and weather will have a great deal to do with what you see on this drive. In spring and summer, expect a profusion of wildflowers, such as lupine, paintbrush, and larkspur. In fall you can count on an explosion of color from the aspen trees in several locations, and in winter you may encounter heavy snowfall, with the road appearing to be nothing more than a trail winding through a tunnel of snow. If you are particularly afraid of heights and high mountain roads, however, this drive may not be for you. The road is narrow, and drop-offs on the sides can be very steep.

Since driving in the mountains in winter can be hazardous, it is always wise to call ahead for road conditions. For the most updated information on Nevada roads, call (877) 687-6237, or access the Nevada Department of Transportation Web site at www.nevadadot.com.

National Automobile Museum
10 Lake Street
(775) 333-9300
www.automuseum.org

Nowhere is America's love affair with the automobile more celebrated than at the National Automobile Museum. Housing the most comprehensive public display of cars in the Western Hemisphere, the museum presents a singular history of the automobile and its role in American society.

Four authentic street scenes representing each quarter of the 20th century take visitors back in time to experience vignettes of American history. The real-life scenes are complete with the cars, architecture, and memorabilia of the eras.

On Turn-of-the-Century Street you can see a realistic blacksmith's shop, illustrating the gradual change in transportation from horses to cars. On the 1930s Street you can watch Milton Berle and Ronald Reagan on a vintage television set.

Adjoining galleries contain the remainder of the more than 200 antique, vintage, classic, and special-interest cars in the collection. Of particular interest to many visitors are the cars previously owned by celebrities, such as Elvis Presley's 1973 Cadillac Eldorado Coupe, John Wayne's 1953 Corvette, and James Dean's 1949 Mercury.

The cars in the museum were part of the original Harrah's Automobile Collection, owned by the late William F. Harrah, founder of Harrah's Hotels/Casinos. Following his death in 1978 and the subsequent purchase of the collection by Holiday Corporation, the William F. Harrah Foundation received a gift of 175 cars. The foundation is a public/private partnership that owns and manages the museum. (See the Resorts chapter for more information on Mr. Harrah's ventures.)

Before leaving the building, be sure to stop at the gift shop, where you can buy books and magazines on almost every type of car ever manufactured. The museum is open Monday through Saturday from 9:30 A.M. until 5:30 P.M. and Sunday from 10:00 A.M. until 4:00 P.M. It's closed Thanksgiving and Christmas days. Admission rates are $9.00 for adults, $7.00 for seniors, $3.00 for children ages 6 through 18, and free for children age 5 and younger when accompanied by an adult. (See the Kidstuff chapter.)

On the Lake Street side of the building, be sure to get a look at one of the older Reno Arches with the famous slogan, "The Biggest Little City in the World." A more elaborate version of the arch is on North Virginia Street and Commercial Row. (See the subsequent entry in this chapter for more about the Reno Arch.)

National Bowling Stadium
300 North Center Street
(775) 334-2600
www.visitrenotahoe.com

Described by the American Bowling Congress as the "Taj Mahal of tenpins," the National Bowling Stadium is the world's largest bowling facility. Used primarily for ABC and other tournaments, this ultramodern stadium has 80 Brunswick lanes and state-of-the-art scoring equipment and acoustics.

When the bowlers are in town, you can watch all the action from plush stadium seats. But because tournament schedules vary from year to year, it's wise to check before going to the center expecting to see the country's best bowlers roll it out. For information on booking a tournament, call (800) 304-2695.

Nevada Historical Society
1650 North Virginia Street
(775) 688-1190
http://dmla.clan.lib.nv.us

As Nevada's oldest museum, the Nevada Historical Society provides ongoing support and preservation for the state's fabulous heritage. In its renovated building near the Fleischmann Planetarium, you can take a walk on the historical side through fascinating displays of how such things as mining, gaming, ranching, and various ethnic groups molded the state's unique society. Of special interest is the million-dollar exhibit of rare baskets made by famous Washoe basketmaker Dat-So-La-Lee (see the History chapter). New to the museum with the remodeling is a diorama of a typical general store, complete with all the goods stocking the shelves.

The research library at the museum is a historian's dream come true. Open to the public, it houses the largest collection of materials relating to the history of Nevada and the Great Basin. You can find long-lost relatives plus delve into the minutiae of the past in the library's books, newspaper files, maps, and photographs.

The society also sponsors a provocative variety of ongoing educational events throughout the year, such as lectures, trips, and gala exhibits. If you're looking for volunteer opportunities, it's a great place to investigate: Volunteers are used in many areas, including the expanded gift shop. You can also support the museum by buying an annual membership for about $35.

The museum and gift shop are open Monday through Saturday from 10:00 A.M. to 5:00 P.M., and the library is open Tuesday through Saturday from noon to 4:00 P.M. Admission to the museum is $2.00 for adults. I recommend combining visits to the museum and the Fleischmann Planetarium since they're adjacent to each other (see the earlier entry for details on the planetarium).

Reno Arch
North Virginia Street and Commercial Row

The winner of the 1929 contest that named Reno "The Biggest Little City in the World" walked away with $100 in prize money, even though he copied the slogan from one used for the Jeffries-Johnson boxing match that took place in 1910.

If you're on North Virginia Street in downtown Reno, you simply can't miss the Reno Arch. Blazing with 800 feet of neon tubing and 1,600 lights, it welcomes visitors in grand style to "The Biggest Little City in the World." The slogan was the result of a 1929 contest conducted by the mayor to publicize the city.

The slogan stuck, and the Arch has been the identifying landmark for Reno ever since. It has been redesigned and replaced several times; the present structure was erected in 1987. An older arch constructed mainly of steel and lit with neon is at 10 Lake Street next to the National Automobile Museum.

Reno Tahoe Job Training Academy
130 East Plumb Lane
(775) 329-5665
www.renodealingschool.com

Do you want to play craps, 21, roulette, or poker, but you don't have a clue how to place a bet? Call the Reno Tahoe Job Training Academy for information on learning the basics behind the scenes, where dealers are trained.

Sierra Safari Zoo
10200 North Virginia Street
(775) 677-1101
www.sierrasafarizoo.com

Animal lovers say they have died and gone to animal heaven when visiting this zoo nestled at the base of Peavine Mountain. It offers a rare "up close and personal" opportunity to interact with more than 150 exotic animals. Distinct from the glizty, big-city zoos of concrete cages and prolific souvenir stands, this zoo is just about animals in a natural setting.

Free to roam behind security fences, most of the animals have been born and hand-raised in captivity. Many are exceptionally gentle and tolerant of human touch. Visitors can view 40 different species from around the world, including ringtail lemurs (primates from the Malagasy Republic), audads (sheep from the Middle East), and servals (cats from the African savannas).

Children especially enjoy the petting section of the zoo, where they can wander among the animals to pet and feed them. The signature animal is Hobbs, a 1,100-pound liger. A cross between a lion and a tiger, ligers are unusual because they are born only in captivity and only 40 of them exist anywhere in the world.

Dedicated to the propagation and preservation of animals, the zoo is nonprofit and staffed almost entirely by volunteers. Zoo workers have named all the animals, such as Elvira, the North American alligator who is affectionately known as "the lizard with an attitude," and Baby, an adorable sulfur crested cockatoo who enjoys saying, "I love you."

To reach the zoo, take the Red Rock Road exit off US 395 about 8 miles north of Reno. Turn left and go underneath the underpass to the second road, and then turn left again. Don't be put off by the seemingly unpretentious appearance of the zoo. It's well worth the visit. The zoo is open daily April through October from 10:00 A.M. until 5:00 P.M. If the weather is questionable, you might want to call ahead. (See the Kidstuff chapter for more information.)

Truckee River Walk
Arlington and Island Avenues

On its route from Lake Tahoe to Pyramid Lake, the Truckee River flows through Reno, bringing much-needed water to the desert environment. The river provides a fertile habitat for a wide variety of wildlife as well as a delightful place for residents and visitors to enjoy the outdoors.

One of the easiest ways to enjoy the river is to take the Truckee River Walk in either direction from Wingfield Park on Arlington and Island Avenues. Heading west, the walk meanders past old Victorian homes shaded by huge elms and cottonwoods, and then enters Idlewild Park, with its rose garden, children's playland, and ponds full of waterfowl. From here it continues on for several miles past Oxbow Park to Chrissie Caughlin Park on West McCarran Boulevard.

Going east through the business section of downtown, the path wanders through a variety of other small parks to finally end near Vista Boulevard east of Sparks. The distance from Chrissie Caughlin Park to Vista Boulevard is about 10 miles. As you walk along, keep your eyes peeled for the many birds that live here, such as flycatchers, mallards, belted kingfishers, hawks, and Canada geese. And don't be surprised at the number of anglers trying their luck, as the Truckee is considered a premium fishing stream (see the Fishing and Hunting chapter).

Bikes and in-line skates are welcome on the path, but motorized vehicles are not. Dogs need to be leashed, and owners are expected to clean up after them. See the Parks chapter for more details about Wingfield and Idlewild Parks.

The Wilbur May Center at Rancho San Rafael Park
1595 North Sierra Street
(775) 785-5961
www.maycenter.com

The Wilbur May Center at Rancho San Rafael Park has something for everyone. It's a museum, an arboretum, and an adventure park. The son of David May, founder of the May Department Stores Company, Wilbur D. May lived in Reno from 1936 until his death in 1982. A philanthropist dedicated to the welfare of children, Wilbur D. May's legacy lives on through the foundation that built and maintains the center.

Designed as a comfortable ranch-style home, the Wilbur D. May Museum showcases May's eclectic collection of memorabilia gathered from his more than 40 trips around the world. An avid art and antiques collector, May acquired such treasures as rare T'ang Dynasty pottery, primitive African artwork, and Egyptian scarabs. His life as a rancher is chronicled in the tack room, with its elaborate array of Western artifacts. And his years as a big-game hunter are reflected in the trophy room, with dozens of animals from all over the world. Although the contents are professionally displayed and documented, the museum has the ambience of a home rather than a public building. Visitors almost feel as if May himself had invited them over for a private showing of his residence.

The Wilbur D. May Arboretum and Botanical Garden contains pools, waterfalls, and a xeriscape garden of plants indigenous to the high-desert climate. And designed especially for children ages 2 through 12, the Wilbur D. May Great Basin Adventure has a petting zoo, pony rides, and a log flume ride.

Hours and admission prices of the museum change, so call (775) 785-5961 for current information. The adventure park is open from 10:00 A.M. until 5:00 P.M. Tuesday through Saturday and from noon to 5:00 P.M. Sunday from Memorial Day through Labor Day. Admission costs $5.00 for adults and $3.50 for seniors and children ages 3 though 12. Children younger than age 3 are admitted free. A children's birthday pavilion can be rented for three hours at $30. There is no charge to view the botanical garden. (See the Kidstuff chapter.)

SPARKS

Sparks Heritage Foundation and Museum
820 Victorian Avenue
(775) 355-1144

In 1904 Sparks was the busiest railroad terminal between Ogden, Utah, and Sacramento, California. Its location near the base of the Sierra Nevada mountains was strategic for the large steam engines that pulled trains over the mountain passes to the valleys in California. Much of the city's early history is tied to the railroad, including its nickname, Rail City.

The Sparks Heritage Foundation and Museum allows visitors to step back in time and experience those turn-of-the-20th-century railroad days. Much of the memorabilia is railroad oriented, such as the model train collection that begins with the DeWitt Clinton and ends with the last of the steam-driven engines. Other displays include a barber shop with a collection of 200 razors and a full-size Amish-type carriage, circa 1910. While the displays are not elaborate, history buffs will love the variety and attention to detail.

Hours are 11:00 A.M. until 4:00 P.M. Tuesday through Friday and 1:00 to 4:00 P.M. Saturday. It's closed Sunday and Monday. Although admission to the museum is free, donations are welcomed. (See also the Kidstuff chapter.)

Victorian Square
Victorian Avenue

When the citizens of Sparks decided to revitalize their downtown area some years ago, they selected a colorful turn-of-the-20th-century theme appropriate to the Rail City's history. The result was Victorian Square, a 4-block area featuring a bandstand gazebo, Victorian-style storefronts and streetlights, park benches, a fountain, and a 14-screen movie theater complex.

Also in keeping with the historical theme is the Glendale School at the east end of the square. Constructed in 1864 on a nearby ranch, it is the oldest remaining school building in Nevada. It was relocated to the square in 1993.

Victorian Square is the place to be for special events, such as the Best in the West Nugget Rib Cook-Off, Hot August Nights, and the Sparks Hometowne Christmas. (See the Annual Events chapter for details on these.) On Thursday from June through September, you can buy fresh produce and enjoy cooking demonstrations and musical events at the Sparks Hometowne Farmers' Market. Hours for the market are 4:00 to 9:00 P.M. June through late August.

To get to the square, take Interstate 80 east and exit on Rock Boulevard. Turn left onto Rock, and then right onto Victorian Avenue.

Wild Island Family Adventure Park
250 Wild Island Court
(775) 359-2927
www.wildisland.com

Wild Island Family Adventure Park has more than enough excitement to keep the family entertained all day. With eight exciting water adventures, two miniature golf courses, a 40-foot roller coaster, and a variety of racetracks in the Formula K Raceway, it's hard to decide which adventure to tackle first. (For more details see the write-up in the Kidstuff chapter.)

NORTH SHORE LAKE TAHOE

Cable Car at Squaw Valley USA
California Highway 89
6 miles north of Tahoe City, CA
(530) 583-6955, (800) 545-4350
www.squaw.com

Best known as the site of the 1960 Winter Olympics, Squaw Valley USA is one of America's premier year-round resorts. The Olympic flame still burns brightly as you make the turn into Olympic Valley, but other amenities of the games, such as the ski jump and Olympic ice rink, have been torn down.

Squaw Valley is a veritable paradise of recreation and activities, which are covered in more detail in the chapters on Resorts, Recreation, Golf, and Winter Sports. But whatever your choice of activity, winter or summer, a ride in the tram from the Base Village to High Camp Bath & Tennis Club is a must. From a base elevation of 6,200 feet, the tram rises 2,000 feet to a world-class playground perched high above Lake Tahoe. The unobstructed views are simply awe inspiring.

You can while away an entire day in this alpine Eden. Enjoy hiking, skiing, ice-skating, swimming, bungee jumping, playing tennis, and mountain biking. In the winter it's crowded with skiers, but in the summer it can be a quiet getaway undiscovered by most. If just relaxing in the sun is what you want, you won't find a better place than the decks around the swimming lagoon and spa. And you won't go hungry, as the bars and restaurants at High Camp offer everything from casual fare to fine dining.

During ski season, the tram operates from 9:00 A.M. until 9:00 P.M. weekdays and from 8:30 A.M. until 9:00 P.M. weekends. Daily hours during the summer are 9:40 A.M. to 4:00 P.M. Most services at the resort are unavailable from mid-October to mid-November. Tram-only tickets cost $19.00 for adults and $5.00 for children age 12 and younger. A variety of packages that combine activities such as skating and swimming with the cable-car ticket are also available.

In summer, I strongly suggest bringing along sunscreen and also a jacket, because the temperature is much cooler here than in the valley. If the weather is questionable, call (530) 583-6985 to check the cable-car operation schedule. (See also the Kidstuff chapter.)

Fanny Bridge
Junction of California Highways 89 and 28, Tahoe City, CA

Fanny Bridge spans the Truckee River where it empties from Lake Tahoe on its journey toward Pyramid Lake. Also at this site is the concrete dam with 17 gates used to raise or lower the level of the lake. While this in itself may not be particularly interesting to visitors, the number of enormous rainbow trout living in the waters around the bridge merit your attention.

Although catching fish is not permitted anywhere near the bridge, it's perfectly legal to feed them. Almost any day of the year, groups of people can be seen leaning over the edge of the bridge (fannies sticking out) to feed the fish. (See also the Kidstuff chapter.)

Gatekeeper's Museum
Junction of California Highways 89 and 28, Tahoe City, CA
(530) 583-1762
www.northtahoemuseums.org

The gatekeeper of Lake Tahoe was entrusted with the responsibility of monitoring the level of the lake, using a hand-turned winch system to keep the water at prescribed levels. He lived in the gatekeeper's cabin on the south side of Fanny

CLOSE-UP

Reliving Tahoe's Early Grandeur

To say that George Whittell Jr. was born with a silver spoon in his mouth is a gross understatement. Heir to a legendary San Francisco banking and real estate fortune (which originated in the Comstock Lode in Virginia City, Nevada), Whittell partied hardy long before jet-setting was even heard of. Although much of his life seems frivolous and wasteful, he has the distinction of having preserved an enormous tract of land at Lake Tahoe largely in its natural state.

Owning more than 40,000 acres of land, or the entire Nevada side of the lake at one time, the eccentric land baron selected one of the most spectacular locations along the lake as the site of his summer home. Construction of his Thunderbird Lodge began in 1936 with more than 100 workers toiling for three years to complete the historic stone French chateau. Designed by Frederic DeLongchamps, Nevada's most prominent architect, the lodge and outbuildings blend with the surrounding forest. With expertly crafted stone, iron, and woodwork, the lodge is considered to be a quintessential example of the stunning Tahoe estates built during this era by wealthy San Franciscans.

From the estate's completion to his death in 1969, Whittell entertained here in grand and, more often than not, raucous style. A roster of who's who of the rich and famous soaked up his hospitality in elaborate parties that went on for days. And to further entertain his guests, Whittell also kept exotic animals on the property, including a lion named Bill and an elephant named Mingo.

Although some of his original land holdings have been developed, a large tract of land adjacent to the estate is owned by the USDA Forest Service and open to the public as Lake Tahoe–Nevada State Park. Through a recent land exchange, the Thunderbird Lodge Preservation Society now manages the estate structures along with six acres of surrounding land. The society conducts tours from May through October on Wednesday and Thursday between 9:00 A.M. and 2:00 P.M. and on Friday and Saturday from 9:00 to 11:00 A.M. Parking and shuttle pickup (there's no parking at the estate) is at the Incline Village/Crystal Bay Visitor's Center at 969 Tahoe Boulevard in Incline Village. Reservations are neces-

Bridge. The original cabin, built sometime between 1910 and 1916, was destroyed by fire in 1978. The present cabin was built in 1981 with funds raised by the North Lake Tahoe Historical Society.

Since 1986 the Federal Watermaster's Office in Reno has regulated the level of the lake. Today the gatekeeper's cabin is a museum showcasing Lake Tahoe's past through natural history displays, stories of pioneers, and priceless artifacts. Of particular interest are exhibits showing the effects of growth and pollution on the Tahoe Basin.

The historic Thunderbird Lodge exemplifies a sumptuous lifestyle of a bygone era. TERRY BAADE

sary. The cost is $25 for adults and $10 for children younger than age 12. Since tours are limited to 15 people, call early and be flexible in the times that you can go. Thunderbird Lodge is at 5000 Nevada Highway 28 in Incline Village. For more information call (775) 832-8750 or (800) 468-2463 (for tours), or log onto www.thunderbirdlodge.org. For information on boat tours from South Shore Lake Tahoe, call (888) 867-6394, and from North Shore Lake Tahoe, call (775) 832-1234.

Tucked away in a forest of ancient conifers, the handcarved, lodgepole pine structure is an exemplary specimen of Tahoe-style architecture. Its interior is cozy and warm, almost inviting you to curl up in front of the fire with a good historical novel. Be sure not to miss the Marion Steinbach Indian Basket Museum, a collection of more than 800 baskets from tribes all over the country, that is on display here.

The museum is open Wednesday through Sunday May 1 through June 15 and from Labor Day until October 1, and it's open every day from June 16 through

For information about scheduling a special event on the lakeshore near the Gatekeeper's Museum, call (530) 583-1762 or click on www.northtahoe museums.org.

Labor Day. The hours are 11:00 A.M. until 5:00 P.M. Admission is nominal, and donations are welcome.

Watson Cabin Living Museum
560 North Lake Boulevard
Tahoe City, CA
(530) 583-8717
www.northtahoemuseums.org
Built in 1909, the Watson Cabin Living Museum is the oldest building in Tahoe City. Listed on the National Register of Historic Homes, the cabin contains the first indoor private bathroom in Tahoe City, as well as antiques and collectibles from the turn of the 20th century. Currently the cabin is open Memorial Day to June 30 on weekends and from July 1 through Labor Day Wednesday through Monday. Hours are noon to 4:00 P.M.

SOUTH SHORE LAKE TAHOE

Emerald Bay and Vikingsholm Castle
California Highway 89
5 miles from South Lake Tahoe, CA
(530) 541-3030 (summer only)
(530) 525-7277
www.comspark.com/eldorado
www.parks.ca.gov
If there is a signature view of Lake Tahoe, Emerald Bay with tiny Fannette Island would be the No. 1 choice. This narrow arm on the southwestern shore of the lake is especially picturesque with its emerald green water surrounded by sheer granite cliffs. The scenery alone is worth the drive, but the real jewel of this spot is Vikingsholm Castle.

The castle is not accessible by car; it's a 1-mile walk from the Emerald Bay parking lot. Built by Mrs. Lora Knight in 1929 as her summer residence, the home is one of the finest examples of Scandinavian architecture in the Western Hemisphere. Because the site of the house reminded her of fjords in Norway, Mrs. Knight decided that the house should also be Scandinavian.

Constructed of granite and timber found at the lake, the 38-room mansion is a replica of an 11th-century Viking castle. Although in some ways the interior seems dark and cold, the building can be appreciated for its workmanship and attention to detail. Tours are usually available 10:00 A.M. until 4:00 P.M. daily from mid-June through Labor Day and on weekends after Labor Day until the end of September. The fee is around $3.00 for adults and $2.00 for children ages 6 through 17.

From Vikingsholm the trail continues for about 2.5 miles along the shore of the bay to Emerald Point on the main body of the lake, and from there another 4.5 miles to D. L. Bliss State Park. The real trailblazers can hike another 1.5 miles to Eagle Point, on the newest leg of this trail system.

Another popular hike from this area is the 1-mile walk to Eagle Lake. The trailhead begins across the road from the Emerald Bay parking lot in the Eagle Falls Picnic Area.

Because this is probably the most visited site at Lake Tahoe, parking in the summer is always difficult. I recommend getting there early in the morning to avoid the crowds. This section of CA 89 is often closed in winter because of heavy snowfall, so be sure to call prior to your visit.

Fallen Leaf Lake
Junction of California Highway 89 and Fallen Leaf Road
South Lake Tahoe, CA
The second-largest natural lake in the Lake Tahoe Basin, Fallen Leaf was an appendage of Lake Tahoe many years ago. Three miles long, Fallen Leaf Lake is considered by many scientists to be a microcosm of Lake Tahoe. Because it is

smaller, researchers are studying the effects of pollution on the lake as they believe the same effects will appear in a similar way later in the larger Lake Tahoe.

A variety of easy hikes begin from the Fallen Leaf Campground about a half mile from CA 89. Other longer hikes begin from the parking lot just past the Fallen Leaf Marina at the end of the lake. The drive alone is worth the trip, though, because the lake is very scenic. Keep in mind that the going is slow—the road is one-way with few turnouts.

To reach the lake, take CA 89 northwest at its junction with US 50 in South Lake Tahoe (the "Y"). Look for Fallen Leaf Road about 3 miles on, turn left, and follow it to the lake. Fallen Leaf Lake is frequently not accessible during winter months because of heavy snowfall.

Fannette Island
Emerald Bay
(530) 541-3030
www.comspark.com/eldorado

Fannette Island is the only island in Lake Tahoe. A granite island sparsely covered with timber and brush, it is located in Emerald Bay on the lake's west shore. Fannette Island was not always known by that name. During the past 100 years it has been known as Coquette, Fannette, Baranoff, Dead Man's, Hermit's, and Emerald Isle. Fannette was the name that finally stuck. The only "structure" on the island is the stone shell remains of a miniature castle that was built around the same time that the Vikingsholm Castle was constructed and used as a "teahouse" by Mrs. Lora Knight and her guests when they boated over from the castle.

Visitors are welcome to use the island for day-use activities between 6:00 A.M. and 9:00 P.M. Camping is prohibited, and dogs are not allowed on the island. From February 1 through June 15, the island is closed to all visitors so that the up to 100 geese that come to the island to nest are afforded ample peace and privacy. Access to the island is by private boat only, unless you are a really strong swimmer. Given that the average temperature for Lake Tahoe is 40 degrees, however, I'd recommend you find a boat.

Gondola Ride at Heavenly Ski Resort
Heavenly Ski Resort
Corner of Wildwood and Saddle
South Lake Tahoe, CA
(775) 586-7000
www.skiheavenly.com

For a million-dollar view of Lake Tahoe, it's hard to beat the 2.4-mile gondola ride that climbs over 6,200 feet from Stateline, providing skiers and hikers alike direct access to the ski resort from the downtown area of South Lake Tahoe/Stateline. From the top station at 9,156 feet, skiers can access the new intermediate trails, and hikers can embark on their journey to explore the resort's 4,800 acres. The gondola is California's longest ski gondola and, with 138 cabins, has the most uphill carrying capacity of any gondola in California. Because Heavenly is a world-class ski resort, the winter amenities are covered in the chapter on Winter Sports. Tickets are $24 for adults, $22 for teens, and $15 for kids 5 to 12.

The base of the gondola is just steps from shops and restaurants in The Shops at Heavenly Village.

Tahoe Queen
Marina Village, at the foot of Ski Run Boulevard
South Lake Tahoe, CA
(800) 238-2463
www.laketahoecruises.com

Seeing Lake Tahoe from the deck of an authentic paddle wheeler is an unforgettable experience. *Tahoe Queen* sails from its pier in South Lake Tahoe across the lake and into Emerald Bay daily throughout the year. The cruises last from two to three hours and are available with options that include meals, drinks, and dancing.

Departures are from 11:00 A.M. to 7:00 P.M. in the summer, but they vary in other seasons. Prices for the cruise only are typi-

> **i** ***When Lake Tahoe was formed 3 million years ago, it was initially hundreds of feet higher than it is now.***

cally $29.00 for adults and $9.00 for children ages 4 through 12 (see the Kidstuff chapter for more details). Dinner/dance cruises cost about $57 for adults and $29 for children. Other cruise options are available, so call for specific prices and times.

Tallac Historic Site
California Highway 89
South Lake Tahoe, CA
(530) 544-7383
www.tahoeheritage.org

Following the discovery of silver in Nevada, Lake Tahoe became a popular summer retreat for wealthy people from San Francisco, Virginia City, and Sacramento. In 1880 Elias J. "Lucky" Baldwin built an opulent resort including a casino and two hotels on this site. For more than 30 years it was *the* place to be at Tahoe. But as the area became more accessible through the use of automobiles, those who could afford it were building their own lavish estates all around the lake.

The Tallac Resort was torn down in 1916, but the foundation is still visible. Visitors to the Tallac Historic Site can see several examples of luxurious old private estates. The Baldwin Estate, built in 1921 of handhewn logs, is now the Tallac Museum. The museum is free and is open daily from 10:00 A.M. until 4:00 P.M. from Memorial Day weekend through September. The Pope Estate, the largest and most luxurious at the site, was constructed in 1894 and has art exhibits and a living-history program. The outbuildings have viewing screens that allow visitors to see the opulence of the interior furnishings. The Heller Estate, also known as Valhalla, is a community events center where concerts, art shows, and special events are held during the summer.

Aside from offering a peek into Tahoe's past, Tallac Historic Site is a lovely place to enjoy a beautiful white-sand beach bordered by large pine trees more than 400 years old. Taylor Creek Visitor Center is just a stone's throw away on the Tallac Historic Site Trail.

To reach the site, take CA 89 northwest for 3 miles past its junction with US 50 in South Lake Tahoe (the "Y"). Parking is available at either the Tallac Historic Site or the Taylor Creek Visitor Center.

Taylor Creek Visitor Center
California Highway 89
South Lake Tahoe, CA
(530) 543-2674
www.r5.fs.fed.us

Adjoining the Tallac Historic Site, the area around Taylor Creek Visitor Center, run by the USDA Forest Service, gives the visitor ample opportunities to experience the Taylor Creek ecosystem and to understand its relationship to Lake Tahoe. With Mt. Tallac rising 9,735 feet in the background, you can wander the paths through this meadow to view the native flora and fauna.

In spring and summer tiny wildflowers spring up everywhere, and in the fall much of the vegetation turns crimson and gold. Flowing from Fallen Leaf Lake to Lake Tahoe, Taylor Creek is a premier spawning ground for kokanee salmon in October. The creek becomes a ribbon of red during the spawning season as the fish leave Lake Tahoe to mate and die upstream. Taylor Creek is one of the few places outside Alaska where the salmon spawn can be seen so easily. Visitors can study a diverted section of Taylor Creek through aquarium-like windows at the Lake Tahoe Stream Profile Chamber in the visitor center.

Be sure to pick up brochures and trail maps inside the building; they'll direct you to special events and other hikes in the area. The center is open 8:00 A.M. to 5:30 P.M. June 15 to September 30 and 8:00 A.M. to 4:30 P.M. weekends only in October. Admission to the stream profile is free.

KIDSTUFF

Even though the Reno/Tahoe area is normally thought of as an adult playground, you'll find plenty of things to do here as a family. One thing that Insiders will tell you is that local businesses are definitely kid-friendly.

So what does the area have to offer? A lot of activities, both indoor and outdoor, to keep you and your kids entertained.

You'll notice that most of the activities I recommend are outside—after all, the area is renowned for its scenic beauty, and I feel it imperative that you and your kids get away from your hotel or motel room. Some of my suggestions keep you inside, though, and some even include things to do in and around the casinos.

On the subject of kids and casinos, heed these words of warning: When traveling through the casinos with your children, don't dillydally. Kids are allowed to walk through casinos as long as they don't linger, especially near the slot machines or the table games. Also, parents are not allowed to make bets with their children in tow. The best way to traverse the gambling establishments is with your little ones firmly in hand. The hustle and bustle and the bright lights of the casino floor will mesmerize most kids, causing even the least interested to stop and stare unless parents are firm about moving along.

To help you locate the activities that best fit your interests, I have arranged this chapter by category, then I've further divided the activities by my four geographical areas (Reno, Sparks, North Shore Lake Tahoe, and South Shore Lake Tahoe). Although I do my best to give you up-to-date figures for hours and prices, they can vary somewhat by the time you read this book. It's a good idea to call and verify this information before setting out with the entire family, especially if you have a carload of little ones. For other things to do as a family, check out the Recreation, Winter Sports, Spectator Sports, Annual Events, and Day Trips chapters.

AMUSEMENT PARKS AND RIDES

Reno

Boomtown Family Fun Center
Interstate 80, 7 miles west of Reno
(775) 345-6000, (800) 648-3790
www.boomtownreno.com

Boomtown Casino & Hotel Reno has one of the best fun centers in Reno. The center is jammed with about 200 video and arcade games where kids can win tickets and turn them in for prizes. It also has a nine-hole miniature golf course, a merry-go-round, an indoor Ferris wheel, a vertical bouncing Rodeo Rider, and the only Iwerks 3D Motion Theater in town. The theater has hydraulically activated seats that react with the movie on the screen and special polarized 3D glasses. The center is open Monday through Thursday from 11:00 A.M. to 9:00 P.M. , Friday 11:00 A.M. to midnight, Saturday from 10:00 A.M. to midnight, and Sunday 10:00 A.M. to 10:00 P.M.. Individual rides are $1.25, and the Motion Theater is $4.50 for a regular motion-theater ride. All-day unlimited wristbands for the Fun Center are $15. Instead of juggling tokens and tickets, players use game cards for the video games.

Circus Circus Hotel/Casino—Reno
500 North Sierra Street
(775) 329-0711, (800) 648-5010
www.circusreno.com

Kids love this casino because it has a circus and a carnival on the second floor—a circus complete with clowns, trapeze artists, and tightrope walkers. It also has a large area that houses most carnival games, plus its fair share of video and arcade games. Kids can win standard carnival prizes like stuffed animals.

The circus acts take place daily about every half hour. Hours can vary with the season, so it's best to call and verify the times first before bundling the family in the car.

The Ultimate Rush Thrill Ride
Grand Sierra Resort and Casino
2500 East Second Street
(775) 786-7005
www.grandsierraresort.com

Insider kids say this is the best ride in the Reno/Tahoe area. They also say it's the most exciting. This ride is like hang gliding and skydiving rolled into one.

Riders strap into the same kind of harness hang gliders use; up to three people can ride together. The harness is connected to two long poles by cables. Operators pull riders to the top of a 185-foot launch tower. Once riders are at the top, they are released and free-fall for 50 feet toward the ground, clearing it by 6 feet and accelerating to about 65 miles per hour. Riders then swing back and forth until slowed down.

Riders have to be at least 42 inches tall. Weight and age of the rider are not restricting factors—a 3-year-old has taken the plunge, as has an 87-year-old! Insiders say the best time to ride is at night.

It will set you back $25 per person for one ride. The ride is open year-round from noon to 10:00 P.M. daily, but you should call ahead to see if it's open: Sometimes bad weather can shut the ride down. This property was formerly the Reno Hilton.

Looking for other activities for children in the Reno/Tahoe area? The concierges at any resort will have contacts for area activities, and some resorts have activities of their own for the younger set.

Sparks

Wild Island Family Adventure Park
250 Wild Island Court
(775) 359-2927
www.wildisland.com

Wild Island offers a water park, miniature golf courses, a bowling alley, and a go-kart raceway. The water park is the favorite of most visitors.

This water park is a great place to go in the summer, no matter how old you are. There are five mini-slides in the Little Lagoon for small children, including the Dragon and Frog slides, and small ones also can float around in the Lazy River. Older children and some adults can get their thrills on the bigger slides, like the Sting-ray and Shark Bait, which twists and turns all the way down. But if you're looking for a more adventurous ride, try a drop down the Red Viper or slide through the dark on the Black Widow. If you think these two slides are too much for one person, you can rent a double-person tube and go down in tandem.

Wild Island also has a place called Hurricane Cove, where swimmers can get in water fights at the water gun stations or stand underneath a giant waterfall that dumps 650 gallons of water from a bucket at the top of a tree house. Hurricane Cove also has tube slides and rope climbs.

The best waves in northern Nevada can be found at the Montego Bay wave pool. Swimmers can body surf here or just float around in a tube. This place is fun for most everyone. Kokomo's 21 Club is a spa designed for adults.

The water park usually opens in May and stays open all summer until the weather gets cold again. Entrance fees begin at around $16 for children less than 48 inches tall, and season passes are available.

Wild Island also has two 18-hole miniature golf courses with waterfalls and little rivers running through them, along with a 20-lane bowling alley. It's a fun place for families, and it is open all year. A round of golf is $5.50. Inside they also have a game arcade and a booth to trade in tickets for prizes. Both inside and outside are open day and night. Call for the times, as they vary with the season.

Wild Island has the only miniature racetrack in northern Nevada, too. The Formula K Raceway has two tracks, one for larger children and one for smaller. The big kids get to drive Indy cars, and the little ones get to drive Sprint cars. The Indy cars cost $5.50 for five minutes, and the Sprint cars are $3.25 for five minutes. Adding to the excitement of its year-round activities, Wild Island cut the ribbon on its Wild Cat Roller Coaster several years ago. Two six-passenger trains provide thrills on a 40-foot Myler steel coaster that's available to riders at least 42 inches tall. You can buy two trips for $4.00.

Wild Island can also cater birthday parties. Prices vary, so telephone for details.

South Shore Lake Tahoe

Lake Tahoe Balloons
(530) 544-1221, (800) 872-9294
www.laketahoeballoons.com

This is among the most adventurous things to do at Lake Tahoe—float above the crystal blue water in a hot-air balloon. The company's balloons take off and land on a special launch boat on the lake. The only drawback is that it is expensive, $225 per person, but that's a small price to pay for an adventure not soon forgotten. For more information on ballooning, see the Recreation chapter.

Tahoe Family Zone Amusement Park
2401 Lake Tahoe Boulevard
South Lake Tahoe, CA
(530) 541-1300

This is a good amusement park that has lots of rides and carnival games. You can buy a book of tickets that lets your kids ride on go-karts, a blow-up slide, a merry-go-round, a Tilt-A-Whirl, a variety of kiddie rides, and more. It has a snack bar, and the park is open from May through September from 11:00 A.M. to 7:00 P.M. Family packs of tickets and coupons are available.

ARCADES AND GAMES

Reno

Grand Sierra Resort and Casino Fun Quest
2500 East Second Street
(775) 789-1127
www.grandsierraresort.com

This video arcade is located inside a casino and is a favorite of Insider kids because it has more than 200 video and arcade games. Along with these, it has some of the best interactive games available. Kids can get into a great game of laser tag on the Q-2000 Laser Tag battlefield or, along with six other pilots, fly an X-Wing fighter in the Galaxian Theater. They can also take a virtual ride on the Max Flight Roller Coaster.

Fun Quest also runs the Tumble Town Playground, where tiny tots can jump and climb on playground equipment. The arcade is open 3:00 to 10:00 P.M. Monday through Thursday, 3:00 P.M. to midnight Friday and Saturday, and 10:00 A.M. to 10:00 P.M. Sunday. This property was formerly the Reno Hilton.

Sparks

Nugget Skywalk Arcade
John Ascuaga's Nugget
1100 Nugget Avenue
(775) 356-3300, (800) 648-1177
www.janugget.com

The best arcade in Sparks, the Skywalk Arcade is located on the second floor above the casino and features two different rooms, one with video and arcade games for younger children, and one with up-to-date video and redemption games for older kids. Insider kids say the best thing about this arcade is that the prices are the cheapest around. It's a good place to take the kids in Sparks if the weather is bad.

North Shore Lake Tahoe

Hyatt Regency Lake Tahoe Resort, Spa & Casino
111 Country Club Drive, Incline Village, NV
(775) 832-1234, (800) 233-1234
www.laketahoehyatt.com
Children and teenagers staying at the hotel use this small arcade most of the time. It only has about 30 games, but they are all state-of-the-art video. The games start at 25 cents and go up to $1.00 for more advanced games. The arcade is open 24 hours per day, but the state's curfew does apply (10:00 P.M. for children age 18 and younger).

South Shore Lake Tahoe

Harveys Lake Tahoe Casino & Resort
U.S. Highway 50, Stateline, NV
(775) 588-2411
www.harrahs.com
Harveys has more than 180 games for kids and teenagers in its Virtual Forest Arcade. Half of the games are interactive video, and the rest are redemption games. Games begin at 25 cents and climb to $1.00. The arcade is open 24 hours a day, but children age 16 and younger must be out of the arcade by 10:00 P.M. on weekdays and midnight on weekends. The ticket booth is open from 10:00 A.M. to 10:00 P.M.

BOATING AND WATER SPORTS

North Shore Lake Tahoe

Lake Tahoe Parasailing
700 North Lake Boulevard
Tahoe City, CA
(530) 583-SAIL (Tahoe City)
(530) 546-WAKE (Kings Beach)
If you're not afraid of heights, you can enjoy a spectacular view of Lake Tahoe literally below your feet as you parasail high above the water. Older kids love this adventure, since it's not something they can do every day. The height and length of the flight range from 450 feet of line for an 8-minute jaunt to 1,500 feet for a 15-minute thrill. Because takeoffs and landings are done on a launch pad on the back of a boat, you don't even have to worry about getting dunked in the frigid waters of the lake. Lake Tahoe Parasailing can also outfit the family in other water-sports equipment. Call for rates.

Tahoe Sailing Charters
Tahoe City Marina, Tahoe City, CA
(530) 583-6200
www.tahoesail.com
If you ever wanted to try sailing, this is the place. This company rents sailboats and offers a variety of sailing cruises on the lake. They even give sailing lessons. This is a cool way to relax on Lake Tahoe on a hot day. (See the Recreation chapter for more boat-rental information.)

South Shore Lake Tahoe

Take the family on a cruise of Lake Tahoe, and you'll agree with me that it is the best way to see the lake and its surrounding beauty. Two companies run paddle wheelers on the lake and offer about five different cruises, ranging from a strictly sightseeing cruise to a sunset dinner dance. These paddle wheelers are similar to the ones that used to run up and down the Mississippi River; they provide a stable platform for cruising on the lake. The boats run on different schedules depending on the day of the week, so telephone, write, or check Web sites for details before you come. Fares begin at $9.00 for children and $27.00 for adults for the sightseeing cruise.

MS *Dixie II*
Zephyr Cove, NV
(775) 589-4906
www.tahoedixie2.com

Tahoe Queen
Marina Village
South Lake Tahoe, CA
(530) 541-3364, (800) 238-2463
www.laketahoecruises.com

Lakeview Sports
3131 U.S. Highway 50
South Lake Tahoe, CA
(530) 544-0183
This is the place to go on the South Shore to rent just about any type of recreational toy you might need to have fun in the lake or around it. You can rent in-line skates, Jet Skis, and bikes. If you want to rent a boat, they run a shop nearby called Tahoe Key Boat Rentals, (530) 544-8888. Both of these establishments are kid-friendly. (See also the Recreation chapter.)

Zephyr Cove Resort
U.S. Highway 50
Zephyr Cove, NV
(775) 589-4906
www.tahoedixie2.com
This is one of the best places on the South Shore to take the family because you can do and rent just about everything here. You can swim, fish, sail, rent boats or Jet Skis, or go parasailing during the summer months. In winter you can rent snowmobiles, and you can ride the MS *Dixie II* paddle wheeler around the lake anytime. Or you can just relax on the beach. Prices vary depending upon the activity you plan, and an entrance fee of about $6.00 is charged to park your vehicle. This is a great place to spend the day.

DAY AND SUMMER CAMPS

Lake Tahoe's hotels and resorts have excellent reputations for being both kid-friendly and for taking great care of children. A few even have summer and day camps available to keep the kids occupied while you're off doing grown-up things. Most of these camps require that the children be at least three years old and toilet-trained; some have even stricter age guidelines.

The costs for the sessions vary depending upon the length of stay and time of day, but half-day programs start at about $30, and full-day programs begin at about $70, with meals included. The programs vary but can include supervised hikes, swimming, sledding, snowshoeing, arts and crafts, video arcade visits, games, sports, and beach play—all depending upon the time of year.

Here are a few that I think are tops:

North Shore Lake Tahoe

Camp Hyatt
Hyatt Regency Lake Tahoe Resort, Spa & Casino
111 Country Club Drive, Incline Village, NV
(775) 832-1234, (800) 553-3288
www.laketahoehyatt.com
Camp Hyatt will take meticulous care of your children (if you're staying in the hotel) and provide a challenging variety of activities that even the most well-rounded child will enjoy. During the summer, day sessions run from 9:00 A.M. to 4:00 P.M. and night sessions from 5:00 to 9:00 P.M.

for kids age seven and younger, and from 5:00 P.M. to midnight for those age eight and older. The program operates on weekends only during the winter and is limited to children 3 to 12 years old. Be prepared to dig into your wallet, however, as it costs $10.00 per hour for the first child and $7.00 for each additional child.

Mountain Buddies
Resort at Squaw Creek
400 Squaw Creek Road
Olympic Valley, CA
(530) 581-6624, (530) 583-6300,
(800) 327-3353
www.squawcreek.com
Mountain Buddies is a year-round program for children 4 to 12 years old. Chaperones take the kids on hikes; supervise arts and crafts; take the kids swimming; and, during the winter months, take them sledding and ice-skating. This resort program always receives high praise from both parents and children.

The cost for an all-day stay with lunch is $90, and for a half-day stay, the price is $50. A full day begins at 9:00 A.M. and ends at 5:00 P.M. Half-day programs go from 9:00 A.M. to 12:30 P.M., 1:30 to 5:00 P.M., and 6:30 to 9:30 P.M.

South Shore Lake Tahoe

Kids Camp
Harveys Lake Tahoe Casino & Resort and Harrah's Lake Tahoe
U.S. Highway 50
Stateline, NV
(775) 588-0752, (866) 454-3386
www.harrahs.com or www.tahoekids.com
Kids Camp is the perfect place to leave the children if you want a night out on the town. This camp offers both day and evening sessions, and it's open daily. Kids 6 to 13 years old are welcome, and they don't have to be guests of the hotel. Activities include trips to the movies, the video arcade, bowling, and other activities depending upon the time of year. The cost for the daytime session is $80, and the evening session costs $50. Reservations are required.

FISHING

Reno

The Truckee River
If you or your kids like to fish, you should try the stretch of the Truckee River that runs through Reno. It's a unique place for anglers because there's great trout fishing right downtown. Actually, any place in the river is good for fishing. Some people think that you have to go a long way up or down the river to catch fish, but that's not necessarily true. A lot of fish have been caught from Idlewild Park, Mayberry Park, and Fisherman's Park. The only problem with the Truckee River is that you have to have a fair amount of skill and experience to catch fish. Call the Nevada Division of Wildlife at (775) 688-1500 or log onto www.ndow.org. (See the Fishing and Hunting chapter for more information on these activities.)

Sparks

Sparks Marina Park
East end of Nichols Boulevard
The City of Sparks Parks and Recreation Department
(775) 353-2376
www.ci.sparks.nv.us
The city of Sparks transformed a former gravel pit and community eyesore into one of the best fishing spots in the Reno/Sparks area, and now this lake provides outstanding fishing for both adults and children. The city has spent more than $35,000 stocking the lake with catchable and trophy-size trout. No boats with gas-powered engines are allowed on the water, keeping pollution at a minimum.

Fishing is fun for the whole family. SCOTT LAUF

Bank fishing is excellent, as is fishing from float tubes, and from self-propelled and boats with electric motors. All types of bait except live fish are permitted, including worms, salmon eggs, Power bait, spinners, and flies. There is no charge for fishing at the lake, but a valid Nevada fishing license is required (see the Fishing and Hunting chapter for details).

South Shore Lake Tahoe

Saw Mill Pond
Saw Mill Road
South Lake Tahoe, CA

You'll find lots of places to take kids fishing on and around Lake Tahoe, but as we've said before, you have to be a fairly good angler to catch anything (besides, fishing with kids is not as much fun as *catching fish* with kids!). So, if you're looking for fishing spots that cater to the younger anglers on the South Shore, try Saw Mill Pond. You have to bring your own gear here, and only children younger than age 16 are allowed to fish in the pond. There is no charge. The pond is located about 1 mile south of South Lake Tahoe on US 50.

Tahoe Trout Farm
1023 Blue Lake Avenue
South Lake Tahoe, CA
(530) 541-1491

Tahoe Trout Farm is the other place especially for kids to fish. They loan the young anglers rods and reels and even supply the bait. Prices vary. This farm usually opens in May and closes in September. Questions about other fishing in California can be answered by calling the California Department of Fish and Game at (916) 445-0411, or go to www.dfg.ca.gov.

HORSEBACK RIDING

Reno

Verdi Trails
175 Trelease, Verdi, NV
(775) 345-7600, (888) 345-7603
www.verditrailsranch.com
Verdi Trails is only 10 miles from Reno at the foot of the Sierra Nevada. This stable offers trail rides and hayrides and a full-service equestrian center that is open from 9:00 A.M. until sunset. Call for rates.

North Shore Lake Tahoe

There are many places to go horseback riding around the North Shore of Lake Tahoe. All of these stables offer hourly rides (starting at about $27 per hour) and provide guides. These stables also offer riding lessons. Some also offer hayrides during summer and sleigh rides during winter. Call for the latest information on the stable of your choice.

Alpine Meadows
California Highway 89, between Tahoe City and Truckee, CA
(530) 583-3905

Northstar Stables
Northstar-at-Tahoe exit off California Highway 267, Truckee, CA
(530) 562-2480
www.ranchoredrock.com
www.skinorthstar.com

Squaw Valley Stables
Squaw Valley exit off California Highway 89 between Tahoe City and Truckee, CA
(530) 583-7433
www.squaw.com

Both Nevada and California have 10:00 P.M. curfews for children younger than age 18.

South Shore Lake Tahoe

Like the North Shore, the South Shore also has many outfits that rent horses. At most of them you can have lessons, go riding, and take hayrides in the summer and sleigh rides in the winter. Prices start at around $30 per hour. Call the individual stable for more information.

Camp Richardson
California Highway 89
South Lake Tahoe, CA
(530) 541-3113
www.camprichardson.com

Cascade Stables
California Highway 89
near Cascade Lake, CA
(530) 541-2055

Zephyr Cove Stables
U.S. Highway 50
Zephyr Cove, NV
(775) 588-5664
www.tahoedixie2.com

MINIATURE GOLF

Reno

Magic Carpet Golf
6925 South Virginia Street
(775) 853-8837
This miniature-golf establishment has three different courses that kids find fun to play. The prices start at about $6.00 and go up, depending on how many holes you want to play. After you're finished with the miniature golf, you can try your skills on a special hole: If you score a hole-in-one here, you win a special prize. The course also has a pizza parlor for those hungry golfers.

North Shore Lake Tahoe

Magic Carpet Golf
5167 North Lake Boulevard
Carnelian Bay, CA
(530) 546-4279
This big facility has three recently remodeled miniature golf courses. They're all fun, and prices are reasonable (about $6.00 for a round). But these courses are very popular, and they can be crowded. The courses open when the snow melts in April and close when the snow returns in October. Call for times.

South Shore Lake Tahoe

Magic Carpet Golf
2455 Lake Tahoe Boulevard
South Lake Tahoe, CA
(530) 541-3787
Magic Carpet Golf is the place to play miniature golf on the South Shore. The three big courses are not usually overcrowded and provide great entertainment for kids. The facility is closed during the winter months. The price per round is about $6.00.

MOVIES

No matter how many entertainment choices you have for the family, going to a movie is always a winner. The three Century complexes in Reno/Sparks are relatively new and boast stadium seating, expanded snack bars, video arcades, and the latest sound equipment. At the time this book went to press, a new 16-screen theater was planned by Century at the Sierra Summit Mall on South Virginia Street and the Mt. Rose Highway in Reno. The theaters in the Lake Tahoe area in general are older, smaller, and don't have all the modern bells and whistles, but they all show the same movies, and that's what it's all about, right? The exception is the new state-of-the-art Heavenly Village Cinema. Following is a list of theaters with contact information. You'll also find movie listings in all local newspapers. So grab your popcorn, sit back, and enjoy the show.

Reno

Century Park Lane 16
210 East Plumb Lane
(775) 824-3333
www.centurytheaters.com

Century Riverside 12
11 North Sierra Street
(775) 786-7469
www.centurytheaters.com

Sparks

Century Sparks 14
1250 Victorian Avenue
(775) 353-7469
www.centurytheaters.com

El Rancho Drive-In 4
550 El Rancho Avenue at Oddie Boulevard
(775) 358-6920 (summer only)
www.centurytheaters.com

North Shore Lake Tahoe

Brockway Twin Theater
8707 North Lake Boulevard
Kings Beach, CA
(530) 546-5951

Cobblestone Cinema
465 North Lake Tahoe Boulevard
Tahoe City, CA
(530) 546-5951

Incline Village Cinema
901 Tahoe Boulevard
Incline Village, NV
(530) 546-5951

South Shore Lake Tahoe

Heavenly Village Cinema
1021 Heavenly Village Way
South Lake Tahoe, CA
(530) 544-1100
www.theshopsatheavenlyvillage.com

Horizon Stadium Cinemas/ Wallace Theaters
50 U.S. Highway 50
Stateline, NV
(775) 589-6000
www.horizoncasino.com, www.hollywood.com (for online feature listings)

MUSEUMS

Reno

Fleischmann Planetarium
1650 North Virginia Street
(775) 784-4811
www.planetarium.unr.nevada.edu
This great family outing works on two levels—not only do you get to see a planetarium show with stars and planets, but you also get to see a short movie on an educational subject. In the past the planetarium has shown movies on climbers ascending Mt. Everest and on the Antarctic and penguins in addition to its planetarium shows.

Don't pass up this great place! The planetarium is open all year from 11:00 A.M. to 7:00 P.M. Monday through Friday and from 11:30 A.M. to 7:00 P.M. Saturday and Sunday. Admission is $5.00 for adults and $4.00 for kids age 12 and younger, as well as seniors age 60 and over. (For more information see the Attractions chapter.)

National Automobile Museum
10 Lake Street
(775) 333-9300
www.automuseum.org
If you're a car nut, this is the place for you. The old saying "They don't make cars like this anymore" really fits here. The museum displays a wide variety of vehicles, including the 1949 Mercury James Dean drove in the movie *Rebel Without a Cause* and an Indy 500 race car that most kids really like.

The museum is set with four period street settings. You can also have your picture taken in an old car—the museum even lends you period clothes so the shot looks authentic. (The use of the clothes and the picture are free.) The museum has more than 200 cars in four different galleries, including two galleries with changing exhibits, so there's plenty to see. It is open Monday through Saturday from 9:30 A.M. to 5:30 P.M. and Sunday from 10:00 A.M. to 4:00 P.M. Admission prices are $9.00 for adults, $7.00 for seniors, and $3.00 for children. (See the Attractions chapter for more details.)

Wilbur D. May Great Basin Adventure
Rancho San Rafael Park
(775) 785-5961
www.co.washoe.nv.us/Parks/great.htm
www.maycenter.com
Wilbur May, a department-store mogul, traveled around the world about 40 times, collecting odds and ends. He donated most of his collection to the city of Reno, and now it's housed in a replica of his ranch in Rancho San Rafael Park. Most visitors agree that the most interesting room in this museum is the one with his trophies from big-game hunting. Renovations completed in 2003 include a new gift shop and a gallery for rotating exhibits of local artists.

The best thing about this park is that there is something to do for everyone. The park has a petting zoo, pony rides, an old-fashioned log ride, and a mine where kids can pan for gold. There's also a nature walk and a place where children can climb on one-third-size replicas of dinosaurs. The park also has indoor gardens that have two goldfish ponds, many kinds of flowers and plants, and a waterfall. This is an entire day trip. The park is open from 10:00 A.M. to 5:00 P.M. during summer, except on Sunday, when it is open from noon to 5:00 P.M. The museum entrance fee is around $5.00, but it'll cost you more to take part in the other activities at the park. (See the Attractions chapter for more information.)

Sparks

Sparks Heritage Foundation and Museum
820 Victorian Avenue
(775) 355-1144

Sparks is nicknamed "Rail City" because it used to be a railroad town, so most of the pieces in this museum have to do with trains. There's a collection of old lanterns used by the trains' brakemen, and a stationary train across the street that visitors can walk through. The museum is free, but a donation of $1.00 or more per person is requested for the museum fund. (See the Attractions chapter for more details.)

North Shore Lake Tahoe

Emigrant Trail Museum at Donner Memorial Park, Donner Pass Road
Truckee, CA
(530) 582-7892
www.parks.ca.gov

This park and museum is outside of North Shore Lake Tahoe proper, but it's a great place for the family to visit. The history portrayed in the museum is disturbing: It highlights the pioneers who tried to cross the Sierra Nevada in winter but were snowed in. After they ran out of food, they ate their horses and cows; eventually they had to eat their saddles and leather harnesses. Some of the pioneers also turned to cannibalism to survive.

The museum shows slides of drawings of the Donner Party's wagon train and their encampment. And in summer you can visit two of the original cabin sites. Museum hours are 9:00 A.M. to 4:00 P.M. daily. (See the Day Trips chapter for more to see and do in nearby Truckee.)

South Shore Lake Tahoe

Vikingsholm Castle
Emerald Bay State Park
California Highway 89, 5 miles from South Lake Tahoe, CA
(530) 541-3030 (summer only)
(530) 525-7277
www.parks.ca.gov
www.comspark.com/eldorado

Around here we call it a castle, but it's really an elaborate stone home built at the water's edge. The home was designed with a Scandinavian look and resembles architecture associated with the Vikings, hence its name. The question most visitors ask is how the stones were transported here, since there are only two ways to get to the house: from the lake or down a steep dirt path about a mile long. (When you visit, the rangers will be glad to give you the answer.) Bear in mind that when you visit, you'll have to hike down—and then back up—that same steep trail.

Once at the bottom of the trail, you can swim at the beautiful beach or picnic at one of the many barbecue pits. Don't forget to ask the rangers about the little house the owner built on the island across the water from the main home. They say she had tea there every day. Tours of the main house are offered during the summer months, but call for times as they vary. (See the Attractions and Parks chapters for more information.)

If you're looking for a comprehensive adventure camp for kids in the Tahoe area, call (800) PRO-CAMP or click on www.800procamp.com.

On the Nevada side, children are allowed in establishments that sell liquor as long as the establishments serve food as well. It is always a good idea to check the surroundings to prevent youngsters from being exposed to inappropriate or adult situations.

OUTDOOR FUN

Sparks

Victorian Square
Victorian Avenue
Victorian Square has remained the heart and soul of Sparks in spite of recent growth that has pushed the city north and east. To preserve its historic ambience and past, the city fathers have focused redevelopment efforts along Victorian Avenue. The result is an eclectic variety of shops, restaurants, and businesses that coexist with several casinos and the railroad. Victorian Square is also the site of a number of annual events, such as Hot August Nights, Sparks Hometowne Farmers' Market, and the Best in the West Nugget Rib Cook-Off. You can easily while away a few hours here with the kids by letting them play in the interactive fountain, catch a movie, or grab dinner at Great Basin Brewing Company.

North Shore Lake Tahoe

Fanny Bridge
Junction of California Highways 89 and 28
Tahoe City, CA
This bridge spans the Truckee River as it flows out of Lake Tahoe. The Truckee is the only river that leaves the lake, and this bridge overlooks the charming dam that controls the water. When you lean over the rail, you can see huge trout swimming between the dam and the bridge. It's called Fanny Bridge because so many people lean over it to watch the trout that passersby can only see their rear ends. Drive to the "Y" (the intersection of CA 89 and CA 28) in Tahoe City and look for the fannies—you can't miss them or the bridge. (See the Attractions chapter for more information.)

Children can walk through casinos but can't linger, and they must be accompanied by an adult.

Squaw Valley USA
Squaw Valley, CA
(530) 583-6955
www.squaw.com
Squaw Valley is located just up the road from Lake Tahoe, and it's definitely worth the drive, not only to ride the cable car up the mountain but to try all the other activities in the area, too.

Near the entrance to the cable car, Squaw has a rock-climbing wall that's about 45 feet tall. It's set up for all kinds of climbers, from beginners to experts, so try it out before you hop on the cable-car ride. Once you are at the High Camp (prices vary for the ride), you can visit the Olympic Museum. Squaw Valley was home to the 1960 Winter Olympics. You can also go ice-skating, play tennis or golf, go horseback riding, take the ropes course, go mountain biking, take a swim, or hike. This is definitely an all-day trip. Prices for the different activities vary. For more information see the Attractions, Resorts, and Recreation chapters.

South Shore Lake Tahoe

Gondola Ride at Heavenly Ski Resort
Heavenly Ski Resort
Corner of Wildwood and Saddle
South Lake Tahoe, CA
(775) 586-7000
www.skiheavenly.com

With the right instruction, kids quickly take to skiing. AARONROSEN.COM

The gondola at Heavenly takes you up the mountain for about 3,000 feet, and the views of the Lake Tahoe Basin from the top are spectacular. Up high you'll find a huge deck where you'll be treated to more spectacular views. You can also take a hike from the gondola, basking in the high-altitude sun (don't forget the sunblock). The gondola ride is $24 for adults, $22 for teens, $15 for children ages 5 to 12, and free for those younger than 5. See the Attractions chapter for more details.

Lake Tahoe Adventures
(800) 865-4679
www.laketahoeadventures.com
This company provides what some might call the second most adventurous activity on the South Shore—the first being, arguably, a ride in a hot-air balloon over Lake Tahoe (see the Lake Tahoe Balloons entry in the "Amusement Parks and Rides" section of this chapter).

This company can arrange four-wheeling trips around the lake's rugged trails. You can opt to travel in an ATV, a jeep, or a Hummer to a variety of destinations. The off-road tours last from about one hour to all night—if you want to join one of the company's camping excursions. The trips are classified from "easy" to "difficult." One of the best rides is on Rubicon Trail. Write Lake Tahoe Adventures at P.O. Box 11521, South Lake Tahoe, CA 96115, or visit the Web site for more details. Prices vary, so call for rates.

PARKS AND PLAYGROUNDS

Reno

Idlewild Playground
Idlewild Park
1900 Idlewild Drive
(775) 334-2262
This playground is in a huge park near the Truckee River, which flows through Reno. The playland has a train, a roller coaster, electric cars, and a Tilt-A-Whirl. Most of the rides are for tiny tots, but the bigger kids can play soccer, football, volleyball, softball, and baseball. And, if the kids like to run, the park has a jogging path.

It's a great place to have a picnic or a barbecue, and there is plenty of play equipment. This is one of the best places in Reno to go to spend an inexpensive day with the kids. (For more to do and see in the park, see the Parks chapter.)

Sparks

The City of Sparks Parks and Recreation Department
98 Richard Way
(775) 353-2376
www.ci.sparks.nv.us
The city has more than 30 different parks that have baseball and softball fields, swimming pools, and playgrounds. Plus, the rec department puts on numerous activities for kids throughout the year.

The department has programs in arts and crafts; swimming and other sports like tennis, soccer, and, of course, baseball and softball; gymnastics; dance; poetry; drawing; painting; theater; cheerleading; snowboard lessons; and self-defense classes, just to name a few. The department prints a catalog of activities, which is available at its office on Richard Way. The fees vary by activity and are very reasonable.

North Shore Lake Tahoe

Lake Tahoe-Nevada State Park
2005 Nevada Highway 28
Incline Village, NV
(775) 831-0494
www.parks.nv.gov
This spectacular park offers wonderful recreational opportunities on its 13,000 acres. In fact, there are so many things in the park that a family could spend its

entire vacation here, fishing, swimming, picnicking, hiking, camping, mountain biking, scuba diving, boating, and horseback riding. A telephone call is a must to see what's going on when you arrive. (See also the Parks chapter.)

Sand Harbor
Nevada Highway 28
Incline Village, NV
(775) 831-0494
Although the beaches of Sand Harbor are the best around the lake, don't come here if you're trying to get away from other people. These white-sand beaches are popular, and the water is so clear that you can see the bottom of the lake regardless of the depth. Besides swimming and boating, there are nature trails for hiking. Entrance fees are $6.00 per carload in summer. (See the Parks and Recreation chapters for more details.)

South Shore Lake Tahoe

Taylor Creek Visitor Center
California Highway 89
South Lake Tahoe, CA
(530) 543-2674
www.r5.fs.fed.us/ltbmu
www.tahoeheritage.org
This center is the starting point for a wonderful nature walk called "The Rainbow Trail," where hikers are introduced to the plants and animals that live and grow around the lake. The highlight of this trail is a viewing chamber below the level of the stream where you can see the trout and Kokanee salmon in their natural environment. You can also visit Taylor Creek Marsh, a protected wetlands. The visitor center and trail are great ways for youngsters to learn about the birds, fish, animals, and plants around Lake Tahoe. The rangers are really outstanding, and they love to answer youngsters' questions. (See the Attractions chapter for more information.)

---

i

Interesting day trips from the Reno/Tahoe area can include visits to the Sierra Nevada Childrens Museum in Truckee (11400 Donner Pass Road, 530-587-KIDS) or to the Northern Nevada Children's Museum in Carson City (813 North Carson Street, 775-884-2226, www.cmnn.org).

ROCK HUNTING

Reno Gem & Mineral Society
P.O. Box 2004
Reno, NV 89520
(775) 356-8820
www.renorockclub.com
Around the Reno/Tahoe area are numerous places to hunt for rocks and minerals. If you want to take the kids rock hunting, write to the address above, and the society will be glad to send you a map showing you where to go and what kinds of rocks and minerals you'll find there.

SKATEBOARDING

Reno

Idlewild Park Skateboard Park
Idlewild Park
1900 Idlewild Drive
(775) 334-2270
www.cityofreno.com
This 13,000-square-foot park gets heavy use, and it's free. Skateboards, in-line skates, and bikes can be used at the park. The Reno Parks and Rec Department recommends the use of safety equipment, but it doesn't require its use—if you don't use protective gear, you skate at your own risk. The park is open all year, from sunup until 10:00 P.M. in summer.

Rattlesnake Mountain Skateboard Park at Mira Loma Park
Mira Loma Drive and McCarran Boulevard
(775) 334-2262
www.cityofreno.com

The largest skate park west of the Rocky Mountains, Rattlesnake Mountain offers the latest in challenging terrain. Opened in 2002, the $1.25 million facility provides 38,000 square feet of adventure, with three bowls, ramps, bars, rails, and a mini half-pipe. No bikes are allowed.

North Shore Lake Tahoe

Incline Skate Park
Tahoe and Southwood Boulevards
Incline Village, NV
(775) 832-1300
Incline Village welcomes skateboarders to its park from 8:00 A.M. to dusk daily, weather permitting. Only skateboards and in-line skates are allowed, and adventure seekers must wear helmets, knee pads, and elbow pads.

South Shore Lake Tahoe

South Tahoe Skateboard Park
Bijou Park, Al Tahoe Boulevard
South Lake Tahoe, CA
(530) 542-6055
www.ci.south-lake-tahoe.ca.us
This skateboard park is very well designed and popular. Helmets and pads are required, and you can use skateboards, in-line skates, and bikes. The park is open from sunup to sunset, weather permitting. There is no charge to use the park.

SKATING

Reno

Roller Kingdom
515 East Seventh Street
(775) 329-3472
www.rollerkingdom.org
If your kids like to skate indoors, this is the place to be. It's open all year, and kids can use in-line skates if they prefer.

The rink has special times for certain age groups, so I suggest you call the number above and check the automated messages. You can also schedule birthday parties and other events as roller-skating bashes. Plan to set aside about $7.00 per person for this skating adventure.

ZOOS AND ANIMALS

Reno

Animal Ark
1265 Deerlodge Road
(775) 970-3111
www.animalark.org
A great place to see wild animals, the Animal Ark is a wildlife sanctuary, taking care of animals that can't take care of themselves. The Ark has foxes, mountain lions, bobcats, wolves, bears, tigers, an arctic wolf, and a snow leopard. The best thing about the Ark is that kids can get a close-up look at all the animals. The Ark has animal demonstrations and picnic areas, and during October you can even howl with the wolves at night. Following a serious forest fire that swept through the Ark several years ago, it's back stronger than ever. Recent renovations include educational displays and newly constructed animal exhibits.

The Animal Ark is open from April through October 10:00 A.M. to 4:30 P.M., but it doesn't open if the weather is rainy. It's closed Monday except major holidays. The Ark is slightly off the beaten path; drive north on U.S. Highway 395 to Red Rock Road (exit 78), turn right and drive about 11 miles to Deerlodge Road, then look for the ANIMAL ARK sign. The entrance fees are $6.00 for adults and $4.00 for kids ages 3 through 12. (See the Attractions chapter for more information.)

Sierra Safari Zoo
10200 North Virginia Street
(775) 677-1101
www.sierrasafarizoo.com

With more than 150 animals, Sierra Safari Zoo is Nevada's largest zoo. Besides a liger (half lion and half tiger), the zoo has a zebra, wallaby, buffalo, llamas, camels, and other wild animals. The best thing about this zoo is that children can pet, feed, and play with some of the animals. The people who run it are very hospitable and will try to answer all your questions. This zoo is open daily from April 1 to October 31 from 10:00 A.M. to 5:00 P.M. (See the Attractions chapter for more details.)

ANNUAL EVENTS 

The Reno/Tahoe area is a mecca of entertainment for visitors and locals alike, evident by the thousands of things to do, places to go, and sights to see detailed throughout this book. In this chapter, listed by month, are the events I feel are the biggest crowd-pleasers. But I also touch on the more time-honored events that we Insiders find just plain charming and down-homey.

The more flamboyant and highly visual celebrations that tend to be the norm on the Nevada side of the area are outlined, as well as the less dramatic but equally entertaining and fun festivals and celebrations that touch on the area's historical beginnings and cultural diversity.

Most of the events listed are for visitors, but some are aimed at getting locals involved in the community. No matter which, everyone is welcome.

If you're planning to be in the area for some of the major events, like Hot August Nights, the Great Reno Balloon Race, the Reno National Championship Air Races, or the Reno Rodeo, make sure you reserve your hotel or motel rooms early. And I do mean early: With attendance at Hot August Nights around 800,000, just about every room in the area is booked almost a year in advance.

Specific dates haven't been included because most events are associated with just the month, so the dates are fluid. Therefore it behooves you to call the contact number or check the Web site address to verify the event's actual date and location if you are planning to attend and want to set aside vacation time for the visit. (See the chapter on The Arts for more information on other cultural events.)

I've also included some events that are outside of the geographical area but that I think are definitely worth the time and effort to attend. Along with the major events described in this chapter, nonprofit organizations put on hundreds of cultural and athletic events each year to raise funds and to bring friends, family, and community together. Check local newspapers for specific happenings.

JANUARY

Martin Luther King Jr. Birthday Celebration
(775) 329-8990

The event around the 15th of the month includes free entertainment and culminates with an awards dinner. Past guest speakers have included the Reverend Lewis Anthony. Call for location.

FEBRUARY

American Bowling Congress Championship Bowling Tournament
National Bowling Stadium
300 North Center Street
Reno, NV
(775) 334-2600

You can watch the best professional and amateur bowlers in the country compete when the American Bowling Congress (ABC) Championship Tournament comes to town. The event occurs every three years. Action begins in February and continues through June at the National Bowling Stadium.

North Tahoe Snow Festival
(530) 583-7167
www.tahoesnowfestival.com

This is a 10-day event in North Shore Lake Tahoe and Truckee. Most of the ski areas and businesses on the northern part of the lake participate in the 120 or more events including parades, snow sculpting, ski and snowboard races, fireworks, food events, and a Polar Bear swim. This is truly a family event and includes many spectator-involved activities. The carnival usually begins in late February. Even though some events are free, don't forget to bring money for food and drinks.

MARCH

St. Patrick's Day Celebration
Virginia Street, Reno, NV
(775) 353-5825, (775) 785-3300
www.fitzgeraldsreno.com
March 17 brings a celebration that gives you great Irish music, food, and crafts. The majority of the fun happens in front of Fitzgeralds Casino/Hotel Reno near the famous Reno Arch on Virginia Street. The event kicks off with the lighting of the arch after hundreds of the white bulbs have been replaced with green ones. Virginia Street is blocked off during the event so spectators can enjoy the many food stands and craft booths. Admission is free, but bring money for food and drinks. Almost every bar in Reno with an Irish name is standing room only during this celebration.

World Poker Challenge
Grand Sierra Resort and Casino
2500 East Second Street, Reno, NV
(775) 789-2000
www.grandsierraresort.com
With pots in the thousands and total prize money in the millions, at the World Poker Challenge the best poker players in the world bluff it out for three weeks in the casino of the Grand Sierra (formerly the Reno Hilton). The no-limit games provide plenty of heart-stopping action for players as well as spectators. You can watch it all for free from bleachers set up around the playing arena.

APRIL

Eagle Valley Muzzleloaders' Spring Rendezvous
Carson City, NV
(775) 883-7736
www.visitcarsoncity.com
The Eagle Valley Muzzleloaders are a group of Nevadans trying to preserve America's heritage by reenacting the lives of the rugged mountain men who were among the first white men in the region. In late April these mountain men gather for a weekend at an encampment along Canyon Road in Carson City to participate in a survival hike, black-powder shoot, strongest-man contests, and other antics associated with these rough-and-tumble pioneers. This is a great, free event for the entire family. From Reno take U.S. Highway 395 south for 30 miles to Carson City.

MAY

Cinco de Mayo Reno
Downtown Reno, NV
(775) 826-1818
www.cincodemayoreno.com
www.marathondemayo.com
As the Hispanic population in the Reno/Lake Tahoe area grows (it has tripled in the past decade), Cinco de Mayo Reno just keeps getting bigger and better. A colorful celebration of Hispanic culture, Cinco de Mayo Reno offers food, music, and art for three fun-filled days. Marathon de Mayo combines a first-class running event with Latin music. Be prepared for crowds and weather, because most events are outside.

Reno River Festival
Truckee River Whitewater Park at Wingfield Park
2 North Arlington Avenue, Reno, NV
(800) 367-7366
www.renoriverfestival.com
www.visitrenotahoe.com
The popularity of Nevada's first kayak slalom racing course in downtown Reno has given rise to this action-packed four-day event of white-water racing. Professionals and amateurs paddle it out in

For an expanded list of events, go to www.renosparkschamber.org/calendar.htm.

Crisis Call Center sponsors Run 4 Life each year at Hidden Valley Park. For details call (775) 784-8085 or click on www.crisiscallcenter.org.

open freestyle, boater cross, and invitational freestyle events. The course consists of 11 drop pools over 2,600 feet of Class II and III rapids on a difficulty scale from 1 to 6. With lots of vantage points and picnic spots along the course, the event is especially spectator-friendly. You can also enjoy live music, exhibits, clinics, and a variety of foods for sale.

JUNE

America's Most Beautiful Bike Ride
South Shore Lake Tahoe, NV
(800) 565-2704
www.bikethewest.com
For the conditioned recreational bicyclist, this 72-mile event with plenty of ups and downs is a worthwhile challenge. Beginning at South Shore Lake Tahoe, riders circumnavigate Lake Tahoe with rest stops, food, support, and a plethora of gorgeous scenery along the way. A 35-mile ride is also offered with a cruise on the lake, which can include family and friends. Amenities include an after-ride pool party in South Lake Tahoe. Limited to 3,000 participants, the event attracts riders from all over the country.

Fallon Air Show
Naval Air Station Fallon, Fallon, NV
(775) 426-2880
www.fallontourism.com
The U.S. Navy really rolls out the carpet at this annual event at NAS Fallon. It's such a great event for all ages that it just gets bigger and better every year. While it may seem strange to have such a naval presence in the middle of the desert, the Fallon air station has been a vital part of our nation's defense since the 1940s. (See the Day Trips chapter for more about the base.)

The air show features a variety of precision flying demonstrations, such as those put on by the Thunderbirds and Blue Angels, along with numerous static displays of aircraft and rescue equipment. One of the highlights of the show is the Wall of Fire, a simulated bombing run featuring impressive pyrotechnics. Parking and admission are free. Fallon is 60 miles east of Reno/Sparks. Take Interstate 80 east to Fernley, take the second exit, and look for signs to Alt. U.S. Highway 50 and Fallon. To get to the base, take U.S. Highway 95 south for about 5 miles to Union Lane, and then follow the signs.

Reno Rodeo
Reno Livestock Events Center
1350 North Wells Avenue, Reno, NV
(775) 329-3877
(800) 225-2277 (tickets)
www.renorodeo.com
The Reno Rodeo is considered by some to be the best rodeo in America. World-class cowboys compete for thousands of dollars in prize money in the "wildest, richest rodeo in the West." The nine-day event in late June includes not only rodeo events every night but also a parade, a carnival, and craft booths. This is one of the premier events in the Reno/Tahoe area. Don't miss this one. (See also the Spectator Sports chapter.)

Sparks Hometowne Farmers' Market
Victorian Square, Sparks, NV
(775) 353-2291
www.ci.sparks.nv.us
An old-fashioned farmers' market is held every Thursday from 4:00 to 9:00 P.M. starting in the middle of June and running until late August. More than 120 vendors offer fresh-picked fruits and vegetables, specialty foods, and breads. You can also enjoy cooking demos, a children's play area, homegrown music, and a friendly atmosphere. This farmers' market is a favorite hangout for Insiders. Bring plenty of cash for the great fruits and veggies.

Valhalla Arts and Music Festival
Tallac Historic Site
California Highway 89
South Lake Tahoe, CA
(530) 541-4975 (summer only),
(888) 632-5859
www.valhalla-tallac.com

This is a summer-long program that presents Native American fine arts, reggae, folk, Latin, jazz, and bluegrass concerts, as well as a classic film series, theatrical performances for children and adults, art gallery tours, and a variety of celebrations honoring the Tallac Historic Site. The festival begins in early June and runs through September. The concerts are usually held both on weeknights and weekends. One of the best events held around the lake, it makes money for the historic site from small admission fees. The site is located about 3 miles north of South Lake Tahoe on California Highway 89.

Only the freshest produce is sold at the Sparks Hometowne Farmers' Market. CITY OF SPARKS PARKS AND RECREATION

JULY

American Century Championship Golf Tournament
Edgewood Tahoe Golf Course
180 Lake Parkway, Stateline, NV
(775) 588-3566
www.tahoecelebritygolf.com
www.edgewood-tahoe.com

This early July golf tournament boasts some of the biggest names in entertainment and sports as its participants. This event has featured players the likes of Dan Marino, John Elway, Michael Jordan, James Woods, Kevin Costner, and Randy Quaid. The tournament is open to current and former professional athletes and entertainers. Spectators can buy tickets for one or more days at the gate. Prices vary but usually start at $10.

Artown
Various locations
Downtown Reno, NV
(775) 322-1538
www.renoisartown.com

This monthlong Reno summer arts festival features more than 200 different performers and exhibits at different citywide locations. Highlights include a touring Broadway musical, music concerts, ballet on the banks of the Truckee River, and film and visual arts demonstrations. Children are welcome and even have their own acting and arts workshops. Most of the events are free. (See the chapter on The Arts for more information.)

Fourth of July Celebrations

Many different celebrations are scattered around the area to celebrate our Independence Day (see the Skyfire listing for Reno's celebration). Call the following numbers for locations and starting times:

North Lake Tahoe, (800) 824-6348
South Lake Tahoe, (530) 544-5050
Sparks, (775) 353-2291
Squaw Valley USA, (530) 583-6985

Great Eldorado BBQ, Brews & Blues Festival
Events Plaza
Fourth and North Virginia Streets
Reno, NV
(775) 786-5700, (800) 648-5966
www.eldoradoreno.com

You can wash down some of the hottest barbecue in town with cold microbrews and cool blues at this laid-back summertime event. With booths set up at the busiest corner in downtown Reno (just outside the Eldorado Hotel/Casino Reno), it's also a premier people-watching event.

John Ascuaga's Nugget Amateur Challenge
Various golf courses
Reno and Sparks, NV
(800) 803-6918
www.renoamateurchallenge.com

If you've ever envied the life of a PGA tour participant, playing in this tournament may give you a little idea of what it might be like. No, you don't have to be a zero handicapper, but you do need an established USGA Handicap Index to qualify. The field consists of five divisions: men, women, senior men, senior women, and super senior men (older than age 65). Participants play at a different course each day, each one of which is a gorgeous championship layout. It's a first-class event, with the package including luxury accommodations and transportation to the courses along with many social events.

Lake Tahoe Shakespeare Festival
Sand Harbor Beach
Incline Village, NV
(775) 832-1616, (800) 747-4697
www.laketahoeshakespeare.com

"The Bard Done Lakeside" or "The Bard on the Beach"—that's how Insiders describe this festival. For about five weeks beginning in July, the event features noted classical theater troupes performing some of Shakespeare's greatest plays. The magical backdrop of Lake Tahoe adds to the already perfect atmosphere—you'll see why the event is voted Lake Tahoe's best, year after year. Seating varies from general seats in the sand to assigned reserved seating complete with wait service. You can either bring your own picnic or purchase food at the site. Prices run from about $20 to $65. Don't miss this event. (For more information see the chapter on The Arts.)

Lake Tahoe Summer Music Festival
Various locations
North Shore Lake Tahoe
(530) 583-3101
(530) 581-1184 (tickets)
www.tahoemusic.org

One of the lake's most ambitious undertakings and one of the best organized in the area, this festival consists of a series of outdoor concerts featuring classical, jazz, bluegrass, swing, blues, Broadway, and pops music. The festival begins in mid-July and runs through mid-August. Concert tickets range from $15 for youth up to $35 for preferred seating but are a worthwhile investment. Season tickets are also available. These concerts are always a good way to spend a family outing. (See also the chapter on The Arts.)

MasterCraft Pro Wakeboard Tour Finals
Sparks Marina Park
Sparks, NV
(800) 367-7366
www.visitrenotahoe.com

The world's best wakeboarders compete during this two-day event at Sparks Marina Park. You can bring the whole family and enjoy a picnic and walk around the lake while viewing the acrobatics of the competitors. This area of Sparks has seen a lot of redevelopment in the past couple of years, with upscale condos and restaurants now lining the shore of the lake.

Reno Basque Festival
Wingfield Park
2 North Arlington Avenue, Reno, NV
(775) 787-3039, (800) 367-7366
www.visitrenotahoe.com

A great way to learn about the area's

Basque heritage is to attend this festival. It includes traditional food, dancing, and games. The public is welcome to all of the events, which include a barbecue and a Basque Mass. Don't miss the "Irrinitzi" competition, in which contestants attempt the loudest and longest Basque yell. The events are free, but bring money for food and drinks.

Skyfire
Rancho San Rafael Park
1595 North Sierra Street
Reno, NV
Skyfire is a free Fourth of July fireworks display in the Truckee Meadows. Come and celebrate America's independence with entertainment and food in the park, working up to a spectacular fireworks display. You have to arrive early for this event if you want a parking spot. Insiders flock to the park and the surrounding area for the just-after-dark fireworks show. Admission to the park is free, but bring money for food and drinks.

AUGUST

Burning Man
Black Rock Desert, about 100 miles north of Reno, NV
(415) 863-5263
www.burningman.com
From a tiny Summer Solstice celebration on a beach in San Francisco in 1986, Burning Man has evolved into a one-of-kind event that attracts some 25,000 people from around the globe every year. Attendees become part of an experimental community where they are encouraged to express themselves in some way that depicts the theme of that year. Typical expressions include large-scale artwork, costumes (or lack of clothing), and camps designed with a theme. The climax of the weeklong party is the burning of the statue of man, which rises around 40 feet above the desert. This event is definitely not for everyone. Before considering going, I strongly recommend that you read information provided on the Web site. In general the event has appealed to aging flower children and young laid-back adults. You'll find a fair amount of nudity and typical party behavior. Because no services are provided, other than emergency medical, participants must come equipped to be self-sufficient. Tickets begin at around $200 per person.

Greek Festival
St. Anthony's Greek Orthodox Church
4795 Lakeside Drive
Reno, NV
(775) 825-5365
www.greek-fest.com
Greek-food lovers cannot miss this annual event, usually put on toward the end of August by the parishioners of St. Anthony's. Everything from baklava to gyros is on the menu, plus live Greek music and dances performed by award-winning dance groups. Admission is usually $4.00 and food tickets begin at $10.00. Oh, pah, come on by for a great Greek time.

Hot August Nights
Various locations throughout Reno and Sparks, NV
(775) 356-1956, (800) 367-7366
www.hotaugustnights.net
Hot nights, hot rods, hot times, and a great location to enjoy it—this describes the premier event in the Reno/Tahoe area. It's a celebration of America's love affair with hot cars and rock 'n' roll music. For a week in early August, thousands of pre-1970 autos cruise the streets, accompanied by good food and great live music. This is the largest event in northern Nevada, with 800,00 attendees enjoying the nostalgia of a bygone era. Hotels and motels are usually booked a year in advance, so make sure you plan way ahead for this spectacular event.

CLOSE-UP

Reno Rodeo Cattle Drive

When around 50 guests and 35 volunteers saddle up for the Reno Rodeo Cattle Drive each June, they become part of a tradition that has existed for hundreds of years. Using the same methods and gear that generations of their ancestors employed, Great Basin buckaroos in northern Nevada help keep the culture of the Old West alive by herding cattle on horseback.

Driving a herd of 300 steers across the Nevada desert can go a long way toward fulfilling a city slicker's dream of becoming a cowboy or cowgirl. Each year the aspiring drovers come from all over the world to spend five days in the saddle, helping to drive the cattle 100 miles to the rodeo at the Reno Livestock Events Center. The drive is unique, as it ends by bringing the herd down city streets. The steers are used in the competition, which is the third largest and richest Professional Rodeo Cowboys Association event in the country.

During the drive, guests eat gourmet food around the campfire, sleep under the stars and, depending upon their riding ability, try to maintain their position in driving the herd. But perhaps the most meaningful part of the trip is the singular opportunity to experience firsthand the ranching culture of the American West.

The cost for guests includes the horse, meals, and ground transportation. Riders must be at least 18 years old, but they don't need to be experienced on horseback. For details, cost, and registration, go to www.renorodeo.com or call (775) 329-3877.

Nevada State Fair
Reno Livestock Events Center
1350 North Wells Avenue, Reno, NV
(775) 688-5767
www.nevadastatefair.org

This is a really fun, old-fashioned state fair usually held on the last weekend in August and featuring livestock exhibits, baking and cooking exhibits, special events, entertainment, rides, and midway games. If you ever wanted to visit a down-home country fair, this is the one.

Reno/Tahoe Open
Montreux Golf and Country Club
2500 Spinnaker Drive
Reno, NV
(775) 849-9444, (888) 848-7366
www.renotahoeopen.com

The newest golf tournament on the PGA Tour has quickly become a favorite with many of the world's finest golfers. Hosted by the Jack Nicklaus-designed Montreux Golf and Country Club, the weeklong event is played on one of the toughest but also most scenic courses in the Reno/Tahoe area. Tucked at the base of the Sierras along the meandering Galena Creek, Montreux simply flaunts the

Cattle from the Reno Rodeo Cattle Drive enter the city on their way to the country's richest professional rodeo. LOUIS BASSO

best of high-altitude golf. Because the tournament is still new, spectators have the advantage of watching all the action without the enormous crowds and hassles of many other PGA events. I strongly suggest you stop by before the mobs discover this fun event. A variety of ticket packages is offered, so be sure to call to find out which best suits your needs. Shuttle transportation to the course is provided from various locations in the area.

SEPTEMBER

September is the Reno/Tahoe area's busiest month for annual events. If you're planning an extended trip here, this is the month to do it. Besides a plethora of things to do, the weather is perfect for outdoor activities.

The Best in the West Nugget Rib Cook-Off
Victorian Square, Sparks, NV
(775) 356-3428, (800) 648-1177
www.janugget.com
www.nuggetribcookoff.com
About 300,000 people crowd into Victorian Square in Sparks over the five-day Labor Day weekend each year to munch on some of the best barbecue ribs you'll

find anywhere in the world. And along with consuming about 130,000 pounds of ribs during the event, spectators also enjoy free headliner entertainment and shop at 200 different crafts booths. Even though the cook-off is great fun and has fantastic food for spectators, the participants get down to serious business. About 25 barbecue cookers from all over the United States and the world compete for the title of "Best in the West" and the $7,500 Grand Prize. So for some cookers it's not all fun and games. But for those of us who like barbecue, it's a chance to taste a variety of finger-lickin'-good ribs.

The Great Reno Balloon Race
Rancho San Rafael Park, Reno, NV
(775) 826-1181
www.renoballoon.com

The early-morning Reno sky is alive with color when the nation's top 100 balloonists compete in early September for cash and prizes in the Hare and the Hound and various target drops. The Dawn Patrol, at 5:30 A.M., offers a spectacular light show as the balloonists ascend in their multicolored balloons. Children especially like this event because of the variety of balloons, some in the shapes of champagne bottles, frogs, panda bears, and giant hamburgers. It's a great way to spend an early morning in September, but be sure to dress warmly because temperatures in the desert before dawn are very cold this time of year. Both admission and parking are free. (See the Spectator Sports chapter for more.)

International Camel Races
Virginia City, NV
(775) 847-0311
www.virginiacity-nv.org
www.allcamels.com

This wild and crazy time began in 1960, when Hollywood director John Huston won the first race on a borrowed camel. The yearly event, held in mid-September, turned into an international event when the Australians jumped into the fray in 1987. The races are all in fun and have even included ostriches and water buffalo sprints. Other humorous events include a parade down C Street with the town's legal prostitutes dressed in 1880s fashions. Virginia City comes alive once again during this unforgettable weekend: a fun time for the entire family. An entrance fee, usually $10, is charged for the actual camel races. (See the Day Trips chapter for more on Virginia City and on the origin of the Camel Races.)

National Championship Air Races
Reno Stead Airport, Reno, NV
(775) 972-6663
www.airrace.org

If you like airplanes, you won't want to miss this, the longest-running air race in the world. Hundreds of planes fill the sky during this four-day event, which features six classes of racing.

Besides the air races, military jets are on hand to thrill the crowd, as well as planes doing aerobatics, skywriting, and the ever-popular daredevil wingwalkers. General admission entrance fees vary from $16 to $36 for adults, depending on the day. (See the Spectator Sports chapter for more.)

Street Vibrations
Downtown Reno, NV
(775) 329-7469, (800) 200-4557
www.road-shows.com

Reno is in hog heaven in late September. Reported to be the country's sixth largest motorcycle event, the five-day festivities include arts and crafts, parades, an auction, nightly entertainment, and a motorcycle poker run. These events are free to participants and spectators.

The World Championship Outhouse Races are held in Virginia City in October. Call (775) 847-0311 for information.

OCTOBER

Great Italian Festival
Eldorado Hotel/Casino Reno
Fourth and Virginia Streets
Reno, NV
(775) 786-5700, (800) 648-5966
www.eldoradoreno.com

Celebrated along with Columbus Day, this event includes great Italian food, entertainment, a grape-stomping contest, and a parade. The highlight for most spectators is the spaghetti-eating contest. Admission is free. All you have to do is pay for your food and drinks. Insiders love this festival.

Kokanee Salmon Festival
Taylor Creek
South Lake Tahoe, CA
(530) 543-2600
www.tahoeinfo.com

This event is held when the bright-red kokanee salmon make their annual spawning run up Taylor Creek, usually around mid-October. The salmon can be viewed from windows below water level at the Lake Tahoe Visitor Center's Stream Profile Chamber. Also included in this fun two-day festival are a kokanee cook-off, educational displays and programs, nature walks, and a children's fishing booth. All events are free to the public.

Nevada Day Parade
Carson City, NV
(775) 687-7410
www.nevadaday.com

Nevada joined the Union on October 31—yes, Halloween—in 1864. Nevadans celebrate their heritage the last weekend in October with a parade, live music, an art show, a best beard contest, and a 1860s period fancy ball at the Governor's Mansion (by invitation only). It's definitely an Insiders' event, but visitors also find the day entertaining. All of downtown Carson City is closed off for this celebration.

NOVEMBER

Reno Film Festival
Downtown theaters
Reno, NV
(775) 334-6707, (800) 648-3560 (tickets)
www.reno.com

You can step into the Hollywood of yesterday in a big way during the four-day Reno Film Festival. Highlighted by screenings, workshops, and social events, the festival goes all out to promote the appreciation of classic films. And what film event could possibly be complete without a sprinkling of bona fide celebrities? So get set to rub elbows with the likes of Elliott Gould, Piper Laurie, or Gary Busey.

Spirit of Artown
Various locations
Downtown Reno, NV
(775) 322-1538
www.renoisartown.com

Expanding upon the phenomenal success of Artown, the Spirit of Artown showcases the fall in downtown Reno with more than 100 eclectic cultural events. You can soak up the sights and sounds of autumn by touring galleries, attending concerts, and perhaps just strolling along the river with a cup of hot chocolate in hand.

DECEMBER

Sparks Hometowne Christmas
Victorian Square
Sparks, NV
(775) 353-2291
www.ci.sparks.nv.us

This is the only Christmas event in Nevada that has a parade complete with all the local political figures and Santa Claus. This annual Christmas celebration is sponsored by the city of Sparks and includes a crafts fair, holiday music, and a spectacular tree-lighting ceremony in the evening followed by group caroling. This is a great way to get into the holiday spirit and is a wonderful time for the entire family. It's usually held in early December.

THE ARTS

Most people know the Reno/Tahoe area is absolutely tops for outdoor recreation and nonstop casino action; but they probably don't know that it's also rich in culture, with an appreciation of the arts that's deeply ingrained in its history. Far from a cultural wasteland, Reno has been dubbed "the Paris of Northern Nevada" by *VIA* magazine. And because a national survey of reading habits found Reno to be the most well-read city in the country, it could also be nicknamed "The Biggest Little Literary City in the World."

Since pioneer days, music and drama have been important to people living in this part of the West. The first entertainers wandered from mining camp to mining camp, performing in tents before audiences craving culture and amusement. Banjos, off-color jokes, and fleeting appearances by "real" women were the unsophisticated fare of the day (or night). As the mines prospered, the demand for quality live entertainment increased, ushering in a golden age of theater and music by the second half of the 19th century.

The first real theater in Nevada, The Howard Theater, was built in 1860 in Virginia City. With millions of dollars pouring out of the Comstock mines, the silver barons had plenty of money to indulge their appetites in cosmopolitan pleasures. Other mining towns followed suit (although not in quite so elaborate a fashion), with theaters springing up in such hamlets as Eureka, Gold Hill, and Carson City. While Virginia City was home to a number of theaters and tent shows, the most famous venue is Piper's Opera House, which is listed by the League of Historic Theaters as the most significant vintage theater in the West. This "Grand Dame of the Comstock" is being renovated to its original splendor using a phased-in approach that allows for selected events to take place during the restoration. For details about the theater and upcoming events, call (775) 847-0433 or log onto their Web site at www.pipersoperahouse.org. Be sure to read the Day Trips chapter to find out about other things to see and do in Virginia City.

As frontier entertainment moved to more elegant surroundings, it became more refined, with leading performers from the East eagerly heading to stages in the wild, wild West. Famous players and singers—such as Enrico Caruso, Edwin Booth, Lillie Langtry, and Joe Jefferson—presented Shakespearean drama and popular music to packed houses. A particular favorite was Adah Isaacs Menken, nicknamed "The Menken," who shocked audiences by riding across the stage while lashed to a horse and wearing only flesh-colored provocative tights. During its heyday Virginia City rivaled San Francisco as the cultural center of this part of the West.

But as the fortunes of the mines petered out, so did the ability to pay for top-notch entertainment. The focus of culture shifted to Reno, where its first playhouse, Dyer's Theater, was built in 1871. It was followed by Smith's Academy of Music, Hammond and Wilson's Theater, Wheelman's Theater, the McKissick Opera House, the Wigwam, and the Majestic Theater. By the time the Rialto (later renamed the Granada) opened in 1915, Reno was a major stopover for theater companies en route by train from New York to San Francisco, due to special privileges granted by the railroad. This was somewhat short-lived, however, since World War I put a damper on lavish stage productions and the railroad later rescinded its privileges. By about 1920, Reno's theaters had switched to the latest entertainment craze—movies.

Although films took the place of traveling road shows, art in its various forms

Art lovers browse the booths at an arts festival in Sparks. CITY OF SPARKS PARKS AND RECREATION

continued to develop in the Reno/Tahoe area. The Latimer Art Club was organized in Reno in 1921 and remained the only organization of its kind in the state until other arts groups joined the scene in 1939. The Reno Municipal Band, founded in 1890, continued to perform (as it does today), and the Reno Little Theater opened to enthusiastic performing arts fans in 1935. Beginning in the 1960s the arts blossomed with the arrival of the Nevada Arts Council in 1967, Nevada Opera and the Pioneer Center for the Performing Arts in 1968, the Reno Philharmonic Association in 1969, the Sierra Arts foundation in 1971, the Reno Chamber Orchestra in 1974, the Lake Tahoe Shakespeare Festival in 1978, and the Nevada Motion Picture Division and the Nevada Festival Ballet in 1984. The strong support enjoyed by the arts in the Reno/Tahoe area is the envy of other communities; in fact, Reno boasts more arts organizations per capita than any other city of similar size in the country.

Far from an elitist "arts and furs" scene, the arts reach into every area of the community. Outreach is the name of the game, with a comprehensive variety of programs available to everyone regardless of age or income. The direction of the future is to increase this inclusive appeal, by continuing to cultivate new audiences and to develop more arenas for the celebration of the arts. In Reno the focus is directed in part toward developing an arts corridor downtown encompassing the area along the river between the National Automobile Museum and Oxbow Park. Sprinkled like a string of pearls along the Truckee River, the arts district includes the Lear, Brüka, and Magic Underground Theaters, the Riverside Artist Lofts, the Nevada Museum of Art, the Pioneer Center for the Performing Arts, and the Century Riverside movie theaters, along with a collection of galleries, boutiques, and restaurants. Much like pearls developing from grains of sand, the gems of downtown redevelopment haven't appeared overnight. A lot of work remains to be done as nonprofits join business and government to reenergize the entertainment, business, and arts districts of downtown.

The face of downtown Reno is changing not only because of an expanding arts community but also with increased efforts on the part of business and government leaders to attract residential projects where people will live full-time. The demise of several casinos, such as the Golden Phoenix Hotel Casino, has given rise to condominium conversion projects. Other developments are planned or under construction new from the ground up on previously vacant land. These new upscale addresses include Sierra Vista Towers on West Fourth Street, The Montage on West Second Street, The Waterfront on First and Lake Streets, the Palladio on Sierra and First Streets, and the Village at Idlewild Park on Idlewild Drive. A number of other projects are still on the drawing boards. It is hoped that once these condominiums are fully occupied, residents will support not only the revitalized arts district but also a diverse downtown that is an attractive neighborhood to live in as well as to visit.

As the Reno/Tahoe area continues to grow, support for the arts is anticipated to increase. Many new residents who are transplants from larger cities expect sophisticated cultural choices in their new home and have stepped up to the plate in support of existing as well as future artistic endeavors. For many years artists have been attracted to the area because of its beauty and quality of life. This trend will undoubtedly continue, bringing more residents who embrace the arts as a part of their everyday life.

If you're looking for volunteer activities, there's a wealth of opportunities in myriad events and groups associated with the arts. Virtually every organization welcomes volunteer help with open arms. The entire arts movement in the Reno/Tahoe area owes its success in part to the thousands of devoted arts boosters who give unselfishly of their time, talent, and resources to make the area increasingly artistic and arts-friendly.

In this chapter information about the arts is organized into six categories: support organizations, performing arts (theater, music, dance, and venues), visual arts, literary arts, educational institutions, and galleries. The regular geographical sequence has been used, except Reno and Sparks have been combined into one area because most of the arts offerings aren't restricted to either one community or the other. (Though it's been divided geographically, don't let that limit your options since the regions are close enough for day or afternoon trips. If you're staying in Reno, you might still enjoy some of the offerings in the Tahoe area and vice versa.) Also featured are the some of the ethnic and cultural organizations that celebrate the rich diversity of the area. (For performing arts associated with nightclubs and casinos, see the Casino Nightlife and Nightlife chapters.)

While this treatment of the arts is designed to show the richness and diversity of offerings available, it's not intended to be exhaustive. It's impossible to list everything, but this representative sample should whet your appetite to find out more about your particular interests in the arts. For an all-inclusive listing, you can contact Sierra Arts at (775) 329-ARTS. Ask for a copy of their *Registry of Arts and Cultural Organizations* and also their monthly publication, *Encore*. You can also find updated information about arts events by reading *Artifacts*, a quarterly publication available free in newspaper racks in the Lake Tahoe Basin, and the *Reno News & Review*, a weekly publication distributed free in newspaper racks throughout the Reno/Tahoe area. The *Reno Gazette-Journal* publishes arts news in *Best Bets* on Thursday and *Calendar* on Friday. All of the Reno/Tahoe art galleries aren't listed, but instead examples that illustrate the richness and variety of artistic works available in the area. You'll find additional galleries listed in local telephone directories.

RENO/SPARKS

Support Organizations

Artown
Reno, NV
(775) 322-1538
www.renoisartown.org

Attracting more than 140,000 attendees, Artown celebrates the art and soul of Reno in sizzling style throughout the month of July. Founded in 1996 to bring Renoites back downtown, the phenomenal success of this event has put Reno on the national cultural map. Accolades range from "an awesome festival" by *Good Morning America* to "Reno Is Art Town" by *New York Newsday*.

At a dozen different indoor and outdoor venues in Reno, a smorgasbord of more than 200 performing and visual arts events is offered up to eager arts buffs.

You can learn about history at the Great Basin Chautauqua in San Rafael Park, you can enjoy world-famous art exhibits at the Nevada Museum of Art, and you can experience fine music and dance along the banks of the Truckee River. The festival is unique not only because of the variety of activities but also because most functions are either free or very low-cost. Artown was recently expanded to include the Spirit of Artown, a celebration of more than 100 artistic events held in November and December. (See also the Annual Events chapter.)

City of Reno Arts and Cultural Division
925 Riverside Drive, Reno, NV
(775) 334-2417
www.cityofreno.com

As part of the City of Reno Parks, Recreation and Community Services department, the Arts and Cultural Division promotes a full agenda of artistic events through the auspices of the city. It manages the amphitheater in Wingfield Park, where a large number of outdoor artistic performances are held, as well as the McKinley Arts and Culture Center (see separate listings later in this chapter). The division sponsors the Reno Municipal Band and the Public Art Program. The parks department also offers a variety of arts, crafts, and dance classes for people of all ages. You can pick up a catalog of specific programs at their office at 1301 Valley Road or have one mailed to you.

Nevada Arts Council
716 North Carson Street, Suite A
Carson City, NV
(775) 687-6680
www.dmla.clan.lib.nv.us

Since its creation as a state agency in 1967, the Nevada Arts Council has instituted a number of programs to enrich the cultural life of the people of Nevada. It supports the work of local artists through the Artists' Services Program, promotes art in the schools with its Arts in Education Program, and preserves the traditional arts of Nevada's many cultural groups in the Folklife Program. You can also learn about Nevada's arts scene by reading *neon* and *Nevada Arts News*, the two publications put out by the Nevada Arts Council.

Nevada Film Office
108 East Proctor Street, Carson City, NV
(775) 687-1814, (800) 336-1600
www.nevadafilm.com

The history of Nevada and the movies goes back to 1897, when the state's first film, *The Corbett-Fitzsimmons World Champion Fight*, was filmed in Carson City. From then on, hundreds of movies have been shot in the state, using the picturesque desert/mountain landscapes and the miles of open road as realistic backdrops. The Nevada Film Office, a division of the State Commission on Economic Development, boasts a library of 45,000 photos of location sites in the state. And if producers don't find what they want from that inventory, the film office will customize a search for "locations less known." Favorite locations in Reno include the famous Reno Arch, proclaiming "The Biggest Little City in the World," and the campus at the University of Nevada, Reno, with its wooded Ivy League look. The gorgeous scenery anywhere around Lake Tahoe is a sure winner for any film needing an authentic mountain location. In addition to providing location assistance, the film office also offers production coordination for every aspect of a film project. The list of movies filmed in the Reno/Tahoe area parallels the history of film, and the roster of stars reads almost like a who's who in the industry.

In 1983 the state of Nevada acknowledged what moviemakers had known for years: Nevada is an extremely attractive location for shooting and casting films. To facilitate and attract more film ventures in the state, the Motion Picture Division of the Economic Development Commission was established. With the financial impact from films generating in excess of $70 million each year, movies continue to be big business in the Reno/Tahoe area.

Sierra Arts
17 South Virginia Street, Reno, NV
(775) 329-ARTS
www.sierra-arts.org
If you want to find out about the local arts scene, your first phone call should be to Sierra Arts. Established in 1971 to assist artists and arts organizations, the foundation maintains a complete up-to-date list of all arts groups. It also keeps a master calendar of upcoming performances, exhibitions, and events and publishes a monthly arts magazine titled *Encore*. SA functions in many ways as a large clearinghouse of information for anything that has to do with the arts in the Reno/Tahoe area.

The foundation has an ambitious outreach program that brings the arts and arts appreciation to a wide audience in the community. It places professional artists in school classrooms and helps teach teachers how to use the arts across the curricula. It celebrates cultural diversity in the Sierra Folklife Festival and manages galleries at the Riverside Artist Lofts and the Northwest Reno Library. It also sponsors a variety of special events, such as movie festivals and storytelling presentations. The foundation is headquartered in the renovated Riverside Artist Lofts, in the heart of the arts district in downtown Reno.

The Theater Coalition
528 West First Street, Reno, NV
(775) 786-2278
www.theatercoalition.org
The Theater Coalition was founded in 1994 to meet a growing need for more professional performance facilities for the regional arts community. More than 50 performing arts, educational, and cultural organizations joined the coalition to purchase the First Church of Christ, Scientist, and renovate it into the Lear Theater (see the description of the theater later in this chapter).

Although the coalition has been directly involved in a number of performing projects over the years, the recent focus has been directed at the continuing renovation of the theater, which will hopefully be ready for prime time in 2008. You can still consult the coalition Web site for a listing of events and organizations.

Very Special Arts Nevada
250 Court Street, Reno, NV
(775) 826-6100
www.nv.vsarts.org, www.lakemansion.com
Very Special Arts Nevada brings the arts to children and adults who are underserved because they are disadvantaged, disabled, or at risk. The organization conducts workshops in the visual and theater arts at a variety of events and in conjunction with other community programs. It also brings hands-on arts programs to nursing-home residents, conducts several arts festivals for children each year, and offers visual arts and drama workshops to the general public.

After some years of moving around town, VSA has found a permanent home in the historic Lake Mansion, which was relocated to Court Street in downtown Reno.

Performing Arts

THEATER

Ageless Repertory Theatre
Reno, NV
(775) 345-7323
Ageless Repertory Theatre gathers local actors of all ages together to read plays, perform, and rehearse at local libraries.

Brüka Theatre of the Sierra
99 North Virginia Street, Reno, NV
(775) 323-3221
www.bruka.org
For bare-bones theater (minus high-tech bells and whistles), Brüka Theatre of the Sierra offers children's and avant-garde adult theater at its very best. Stripped of elaborate props, the emphasis is on the quality of acting, which local theater fans know is always top-notch.

Its downtown venue is quintessential casual, with cozy couches tucked casually around the intimate stage. Right next to the Truckee River, it's also convenient to downtown casinos and restaurants. In case you're wondering what "Brüka" means, it was the name of a turn-of-the-20th-century German artistic group.

Magic Underground
Pioneer Center for the Performing Arts
100 South Virginia Street, Reno, NV
(775) 770-2176, (775) 324-6007 (tickets)
www.renomagic.com

The great tradition and illusion of magic is showcased in this intimate 200-seat underground venue at the Pioneer Theater. You can see levitation, transformation, and death-defying escapes. Tickets can be purchased via phone, online, or at the theater box office Monday through Friday from 11:00 A.M. to 6:00 P.M. Performances are at 7:30 P.M. on Friday and Saturday and at 3:00 P.M. Sunday. The theater is also available for special group events.

Reno Little Theater
Hug High School Little Theater
Sutro Street and North McCarren Boulevard
Reno, NV
(775) 329-0661
www.renolittletheater.org

In 1935 the population of Reno was only 19,000, and live entertainment was sparse, to say the least. But a small group of determined theater aficionados joined together to form the Reno Little Theater, which has played to enthusiastic supporters ever since. Call for dates and performance offerings.

MUSIC

Bella Voce
(775) 784-6145

One of the area's premier vocal groups, Bella Voce performs at many musical and special events throughout the year. You must audition to belong to this approximately 20-woman choir. For information about the group, call the University of Nevada, Reno, Music Department at the number above.

MasterWorks Chorale
(775) 333-9224, (775) 324-1940

With an appearance at Carnegie Hall in its résumé, the MasterWorks Chorale is one of the most outstanding performing arts groups in the Reno/Tahoe area. More than 80 trained and auditioned singers make up this volunteer-based choral group. You can enjoy their diverse repertoire, which includes opera, spirituals, Broadway musicals, and classics, in their two annual concerts or in other performances in area communities.

Nevada Opera
(775) 786-4046
www.nevadaopera.com

A nationally recognized regional opera company, Nevada Opera has been called the "grande dame" of Nevada's performing arts groups. It debuted in 1968 in the tiny 260-seat Reno Little Theater (which has since been torn down) with *The Barber of Seville* and *Rigoletto*. In just three years it outgrew this small venue and relocated to the Pioneer Center for the Performing Arts, where it's been performing since 1971.

Far from stuffy and boring, Nevada Opera performances are ambitious, exciting affairs. They are always fully staged with elaborate costumes, sets, and a full orchestra. And even though they are sung in the original language, opera buffs can easily follow the plot because the English translation is projected above the proscenium stage.

The company has performed a provocative variety of works over the years, ranging from the grand *Verdi Requiem* and the familiar classic *Swan Lake* to light operettas, such as *Showboat* and *Mame*. With more than 100 main-stage productions to its credit, the opera usually performs three separate works each season in addition to a variety of concerts and special events. Along with Friday-evening performances, it offers Sunday matinees that appeal to opera fans from out of town and those who prefer not to drive at night.

The company offers emerging artists opportunities to perform with mature talents by showcasing guest performers from other opera companies in Europe and the United States. Many young talents whose careers began with Nevada Opera have gone on to national and world acclaim, including famous mezzo-soprano Dolora Zajick.

As part of the opera's extensive outreach and education program, the Nevada Opera Youth Chorus offers professional training and performing experience to talented school-age youngsters. The Nevada Opera Studio brings shortened versions of standard operas to more than 50,000 area students each year.

Reno Chamber Orchestra
925 Riverside Drive, Suite 5 (office)
Reno, NV
(775) 348-9413
www.renochamberorchestra.org

Known as Reno/Tahoe's "intimate orchestra," the 30-some-member Reno Chamber Orchestra plays music designed specifically for small orchestras. Performances are classy but cozy affairs at the 615-seat Nightingale Concert Hall on the campus of the University of Nevada, Reno. In spite of some ups and downs weathered over the years, the group has enjoyed a growing audience of enthusiastic supporters since its founding in 1974. An impressive roll call of guest soloists and conductors have shared its stage along the way, including Daniel Heifetz, Itzhak Perlman, Scott Yoo, Pepe Romero, Bion Tsang, and Emil de Cou.

Part of the mission of the RCO is to assist the area's young musicians in developing their talents. It sends many promising musicians to summer camps each year and offers opportunities to perform with its Youth String Competition, the Reno Youth Symphony, and the RCO College Concerto Competition. It also reaches outlying areas in northern Nevada and California, where classical music is a rarity, through broadcasts on radio station KUNR-FM.

For your convenience you can order tickets at the Web site listed above.

Reno Municipal Band
(775) 334-2417
www.cityofreno.com

Founded in 1890, the Reno Municipal Band is the oldest performing arts group in the Reno/Tahoe area. It's also one of only three municipal bands in the country that are professional, with funding provided equally by the city and various foundations. With a whopping 150 performances each year, funders don't need to worry about getting their money's worth from this group.

In addition to playing in the principal band, the 50-plus players perform in smaller groups, which include the swing bands, the banjo band, the barbershop group, the country band, the brass quintet, and the String Beings. Most members are professional musicians or music teachers. Although the bands play at special events throughout the year, the best place to catch a performance is during the band's Summer Concert Series in Wingfield Park in downtown Reno.

Reno Philharmonic Association
925 Riverside Drive, Suite 3, Reno, NV
(775) 323-6393
www.renophilharmonic.com

Frequently voted Best Performing Arts Group in the *Reno Gazette-Journal*'s annual "Best of Reno" contest, the Reno Philharmonic Orchestra is a splendid mainstay to the Reno/Tahoe music scene. A professional symphony comprising the area's finest musicians, the Phil (as it's affectionately known by locals) has grown steadily in stature and popularity since its founding in 1969. The prestige of this musical group is further enhanced by its present music director conductor, Barry Jekowsky, who is one of the most innovative young conductors on the American music scene. In a typical year the group performs six MasterClassics subscription concerts and six Young People's Concerts for students plus a variety of special performances. A not-to-be-missed gala is Pops on the River, where music fans feast on gourmet picnics and pops music at festively decorated

With 1 percent of the construction budget of public buildings mandated for art, Reno is enjoying an increase in the number of public art pieces being placed around town.

tables along the banks of the Truckee River. Over the years the Phil has also had the honor of performing with a number of well-known guest artists, including Luciano Pavarotti, Ray Charles, Jose Iturbi, George Shearing, and Jerry Lewis.

In keeping with its commitment to Reno/Tahoe's young people, the Reno Philharmonic Association sponsors the Reno Philharmonic Youth Orchestras, consisting of the brightest up-and-coming school-age musicians in the area. The youth orchestras usually perform about 15 concerts each year in various venues around the region. Through the youth and adult orchestras and the in-school Discover Music program of ensemble performances, more than 40,000 students enjoy first-rate live concerts every year.

The social and fund-raising arms of the association are the Reno Philharmonic Guild for the Reno/Sparks area and the Sierra Philharmonic League for the Carson Valley. Both groups sponsor events during the year that support the Philharmonic's programs while also enhancing the culture of the region.

Reno Pops Orchestra
Reno, NV
(775) 826-3995

The love of music and performing motivates the 40-plus members of the Reno Pops Orchestra. Composed of players from all walks of life, it's truly a community group. With a mission to make music available to everyone, the group offers its six annual concerts free as gifts to the general public. The orchestra also brings its performances to area at-risk schools for no cost.

Although you might think all concerts are just "pops" music, the orchestra's repertoire is much broader. Beyond the basic criteria that selections have instant audience appeal, programs include overtures, well-known symphonies, and concertos.

If you've ever contemplated dusting off your old clarinet from high school band days, now might be the time: The orchestra is always looking for additional players. You can also join in the chorus at the orchestra's annual *Messiah* sing-along during the Christmas season.

Trinity Episcopal Church
200 Island Avenue, Reno, NV
(775) 329-4279
www.trinityreno.org

One of the most glorious sounds in the Reno/Tahoe area is the Casavant pipe organ at Trinity Episcopal Church. Custom built in Quebec, Canada, the organ has 2,000 pipes and took 85 employees about six months to construct. Aside from hearing this magnificent instrument during church services, you can enjoy concerts and other musical events on a regular basis. Guest organists from all over the country are eager to perform because the acoustics and overall musical experience in the church are of such high quality. Call the church for a schedule of events.

Washoe County Concert Association
(775) 786-7300
www.renoconcerts.org

If you're looking for quality entertainment at an affordable price, the events presented by the Washoe County Concert Association will certainly fill the bill. The season consists of five concerts at the Pioneer Center for the Performing Arts. Performances vary from the classics to popular music and include soloists and small groups. The association has sponsored first-rate touring musicians to the Reno/Tahoe area for more than 50 years. Call or check their Web site for specific dates and offerings.

DANCE

AREA-51 Dance Theatre
(775) 322-1999
AREA-51 Dance Theatre enriches the Reno/Tahoe performing arts scene by making modern dance an accessible art form for all audiences.

Public performances are given in a variety of venues in northern Nevada. The group also offers instruction in dance arts with residencies, lecture demonstrations, artistic presentations, and performance tours.

Ballantine's Ballroom and School of Dance
2920 Mill Street, Reno, NV
(775) 324-1000
Learning the basics of all types of ballroom dancing is fun and easy at Ballantine's. A favorite place to meet and greet for many older folks, the school offers lessons at all levels of proficiency along with open dancing. Call for rates and a schedule.

Ballet Nevada Performing Arts School
2920 Mill Street (Ballantine's), Reno, NV
(775) 284-5000
www.balletnevada.com
Boasting an impressive roster of professional performers, Ballet Nevada Performing Arts School offers high-quality training in dancing, acting, and music. Their NPA North facility has four dance studios that comprise the largest studio space in northern Nevada. Dedicated to promoting excellence and diversity in the performing arts, the school teaches the basics, such as microphone technique, as well as advanced performance skills. Classes are open to all ages.

Community Folk Dance Party
First Congregational Church, Reno, NV
(775) 677-2306
You can celebrate diversity with dances from around the world at the First Congregational Church. You don't need a partner to join in the fun of traditional dances from Greece, Israel, and Serbia. A small fee is charged, and beginners are welcome. Dances are scheduled regularly, but call to verify the day and time.

Let's Dance Studio
1151 North Rock Boulevard, Sparks, NV
(775) 351-1400
You can let the experts help you swing into swing dancing at Let's Dance Studio. Classes are offered at all levels and for all ages. Drop-ins are welcome, but call for a schedule.

Sierra Nevada Ballet
(775) 783-3223
www.sierranevadaballet.com
A new professional ballet company in Northern Nevada, Sierra Nevada Ballet incorporates well-known classical creations with New Age contemporary pieces. It features principal dancers as well as apprentices. The company specializes in outreach lectures and performances. Summer intensive workshops are given in Reno at In Motion Studio on Prototype Drive. Call or check the Web site for the performance schedule and more information.

Wing & A Prayer Dance Company
(775) 323-0766
With members ranging in age from 6 to 47, Wing & A Prayer Dance Company is one of the few intergenerational dance companies in the country. It was born in 1992 as a choreography project at the University of Nevada, Reno and now, as a mature company, offers lecture presentations, artist-in-residence programs, dance workshops, and master classes as well as a full schedule of exciting contemporary performances. Its Dance-in-Education Series provides free performances for students; its Master Dance Workshops offer classes taught by nationally acclaimed dancers; its Loneliest Roads Tour brings quality dance to rural communities in Nevada and California.

The name of the group reflects the uplifting nature of its performances. To celebrate the joyful aspects of life and movement, catch this group in action at any of their appearances in the Reno/Tahoe area.

VENUES

Brewery Arts Center
449 West King Street, Carson City, NV
(775) 883-1976
www.breweryarts.org

Even though Carson City is covered as a day trip in this book (see the Day Trips chapter), I'd be remiss by not telling you about the Brewery Arts Center in this chapter. Since its founding more than 20 years ago, it's been a veritable hotbed of artistic activity. The 140-seat black box theater hosts more than 50 dramatic and musical performances every year. Resident companies include the BAC Stage Kids and the Proscenium Players, the second-oldest local theater group in northern Nevada.

The visual arts are equally well represented in the center, with a full-service pottery studio, a full array of classes and workshops, receptions, exhibits, and the Artisans' Store, which features works from more than 70 local artisans.

Just as interesting as the events that take place here is the physical structure itself. Built originally as part of the Carson Brewery in 1864, the building is one of the most historic landmarks in downtown Carson City. It was listed on the National Register of Historic Places in 1977 and is easily identifiable by the mural of 11 pioneers on its front facade.

Because Carson City is within an hour's drive of most parts of the Reno/Tahoe area, it's easy to attend events at the Brewery Arts Center.

Lawlor Events Center
University of Nevada, Reno
North Virginia Street, Reno, NV
(775) 784-4444, (800) 225-2277 (tickets)
www.unr.edu/lawlor

Lawlor Events Center is a multipurpose arena that's the home address for many University of Nevada, Reno, athletic events. But when it's not busy hosting Wolf Pack basketball, it's available for ice shows, concerts, and other special events. With a seating capacity of about 12,000, the center is a large, no-frills venue. When attending events here, don't expect luxury since the ambience is strictly gymnasium. You can buy tickets at the box office or at www.tickets.com.

(I can't give you a physical address for the center because it doesn't have one. Just look for the large circular building perched on North Virginia Street on the north end of the UNR campus.)

Lear Theater
501 Riverside Drive
Reno, NV
(775) 786-2278
www.theatercoalition.org

Designed by internationally acclaimed architect Paul Revere Williams, the First Church of Christ, Scientist, has been a historic landmark in downtown Reno since it was constructed in 1939. Williams achieved fame during the Golden Age of Hollywood with such works as Chasen's and Perino's restaurants, the Fountain Coffee Shop at the Beverly Hills Hotel, and the Los Angeles Airport.

The Theater Coalition purchased the Reno church in 1998 and is in the process of converting the building into a state-of-the-art theater facility named for the late philanthropist Moya Olsen Lear. Renovations will preserve the historical integrity of the building while providing a 450-seat auditorium, a studio theater, a rehearsal hall, and dressing rooms. With its picturesque location on the banks of the Truckee River, the Lear Theater is part of a growing arts presence in the heart of downtown Reno.

McKinley Arts and Culture Center
925 Riverside Drive, Reno, NV
(775) 334-2417
www.cityofreno.com

Nestled in an old historic neighborhood along the banks of the Truckee River, the McKinley Arts and Culture Center was formerly the McKinley Park School. Constructed in 1910 in Spanish Mission style, the facility houses galleries, arts and crafts workshops, classrooms, an auditorium, and offices for nonprofit organizations. Although it was completely renovated recently, the building maintains its quiet integrity as a faithful example of this particular type of architecture. If you're strolling along the Truckee River Walk in downtown Reno, you can't miss it: Look for the circular steel sculpture in the front yard.

Pioneer Center for the Performing Arts
100 South Virginia Street, Reno, NV
(775) 686-6600 (information)
(877) 840-0457 (tickets)
www.pioneercenter.com

The Pioneer Theater Auditorium was constructed in 1968 to meet the need for more convention and meeting facilities in downtown Reno. Later renamed the Pioneer Center for the Performing Arts, it's become the focal point and premier venue for many top-notch cultural events in the Reno/Tahoe area. Some of the groups that call it home include the Reno Philharmonic, the Nevada Opera, the Washoe County Concert Association, and the Sierra Nevada Master Chorale. With about 130 different cultural productions presented annually, the facility is busy with events approximately 240 days of the year. In addition to local and regional groups, it hosts a variety of touring performances. As part of the center's Broadway Comes to Reno series, theatergoers have enjoyed world-class presentations of *Les Miserables, Cats, 42nd Street, Tommy, Stomp,* and *She Loves Me.*

The theater's gold geodesic dome, considered an architectural masterpiece at the time it was constructed, is a standout among the mostly mundane banks and office buildings close by. Its upscale interior is hushed and quiet, almost cathedral-like, which lends an air of expectation to most performances. Since the classy surroundings provide just the right background for formal attire, don't be surprised if you find yourself in a sea of fur coats, especially at the opera or philharmonic concerts.

But even a facility as lovely as this has downsides, mainly its small size and lack of parking. Although its 1,500-seat capacity gives an almost intimate feel to large productions, many shows are sold out early. And with no parking provided by the center, patrons are forced to park on the street or in nearby garages.

I recommend you reserve tickets as early as possible and that you allow plenty of time to park prior to performances. When buying tickets ahead of time, I also recommend that you try to pick them up before coming to the performance. The box office is open weekdays from 11:00 A.M. to 6:00 P.M.

R. Z. Hawkins Cultural Amphitheater
Bartley Ranch Regional Park
6000 Bartley Ranch Road, Reno, NV
(775) 828-6642
www.washoecountyparks.com

Tucked into a natural bowl in Bartley Ranch Regional Park, the R. Z. Hawkins Cultural Amphitheater is a 400-seat outdoor facility for drama and music productions. In keeping with the ranch theme of the park, the stage has a country look, with barn doors and a corrugated tin roof. You can picnic in the park and then attend evening performances under the stars when the weather permits. See the Parks chapter for details about the park.

Riverside Artist Lofts
17 South Virginia Street, Reno, NV
(775) 329-2787

Several years ago it was hard to believe the Riverside Hotel's guest list once read like a who's who in show business. Vacant and crumbling, it entertained migrating flocks of birds and groups of transients instead of glitzy celebrities and powerful politicians. Oozing of history of the early days of gaming in Reno, this historic old structure was designed by noted architect Frederic DeLongchamps and erected on the founding cornerstone of Reno in 1927. But by 1987 it was shut down, its glory days long gone, eclipsed by larger, newer hotel/casinos.

Ten years later it was saved from further decay by an alliance between the

The county library in Incline Village exhibits works by local artists.

city, Sierra Arts, and Artspace Projects, Inc., who completely renovated the building into live/work spaces for artists. In addition to the 35 lofts, the structure also houses retail space, an art gallery, and the offices of Sierra Arts. The outstanding success of the project is indicated by a number of awards it's received, including the 2001 Audrey Nelson Community Development Achievement Award and the 2000 Tourism Development Award.

Wingfield Park Amphitheater
2 North Arlington Avenue, Reno, NV
(775) 334-2262
www.cityofreno.com
In downtown Reno next to the Truckee River Walk, the Wingfield Park Amphitheater is a venue with a view: You can drink in the beauty of the river, with the city lights of downtown Reno as a bedazzling backdrop. It's the outdoor site of numerous concerts and special affairs, and it's a real treat to attend events here when the weather permits (see the description of Wingfield Park in the Parks chapter).

Visual Arts

Great Basin Basketmakers
(775) 626-6767, (775) 825-4397
www.greatbasinbasketmakers.org
Baskets are a magical art form when created by artisans in the Great Basin Basketmakers group. Members gather each month to network, attend workshops, and sponsor exhibits. The yearly dues of $15 entitles these artists to the group newsletter and access to a large library.

Latimer Art Club
(775) 787-5047
Founded in 1921 by acclaimed landscape artist Lorenzo P. Latimer, the Latimer Art Club is the oldest art group in Nevada. It sponsors workshops and brings well-known artists to the Reno/Tahoe area to teach. Besides painting and studying, members travel to neighboring states and cities to view exhibits. Latimer is also known as one of the founders of the Nevada Art Gallery, which later became the Sierra Nevada Museum of Art.

Nevada Casting Group, Inc.
100 Washington Street, Suite 100
Reno, NV
(775) 322-8187
www.nevadacasting.com
So you wanna be a star? Nevada Casting Group, Inc., gives many newcomers a start in the movies and television. You can pick up information about how to sign up at their office on Washington Street. Just look in the box next to the office door for printed materials. Don't be surprised if the staff isn't in, since they're usually out filming somewhere in the area.

Sierra Watercolor Society
P.O. Box 70564, Reno, NV 89570
The Sierra Watercolor Society was organized in 1989 to help promote local artists' love of watercolors. With about 100 member artists from around the area, the group sponsors exhibits of members' works, gives demonstrations in the schools, and presents workshops by visiting artists. Members network through their bimonthly meetings and also keep in touch through a monthly newsletter.

Literary Arts

Barnes & Noble
5555 South Virginia Street
Reno, NV
(775) 826-8882
www.bn.com
The epitome of a super bookstore, Barnes & Noble is a one-stop cultural emporium. More than just a splendid shopping mart for books, music, and videos or a cozy

place to enjoy a steaming cup of espresso, it's a vibrant center for special cultural events. Literary-minded Insiders will tell you it's also a great place for culturally inclined singles to meet and greet.

Borders Books
4995 South Virginia Street
Reno, NV
(775) 448-9999
www.borders.com
It's not enough for megabookstores to simply sell books, videos, and music. They also sponsor special events, such as book signings, poetry readings, and concerts. As a mini cultural center with its own gourmet cafe, Borders is a comfortable hangout for literary fans. Check local newspapers or call the store for its upcoming events.

Nevada Poetry Society
(775) 322-3619
As a member of the National Federation of State Poetry Societies, the Nevada group helps area poets hone their craft. At the monthly meetings, members critique one another's work and study different forms of writing poetry. It's literally a prize-winning group: With the encouragement of their peers, many members have won awards in national and state poetry contests.

Unnamed Writers' Group
www.unnamedwriters.org
Started by three writers in 1995, the Unnamed Writers' Group has about 150 members who are published and unpublished writers. With its mission of "helping writers write better," the group sponsors workshops and seminars on different forms of writing and presents guest speakers at its monthly meetings. Members also critique one another's work and participate in a community writing project that involves charity each year. Meetings are held at the Truckee Meadows Community College campus at 5270 Neil Road.

Washoe County Library System
301 South Center Street, Reno, NV
(775) 327-8300
www.washoe.lib.nv.us
When the Washoe County Library System tells you it "offers more than just books," you'd better believe it. Its 13 physical facilities are focal points for community activities as well as storehouses of information for every interest imaginable. The main branch on Center Street in Reno is a wonderful place for reading and browsing. With loads of leafy green plants and trees, its arboretum atmosphere is a delightful haven from the busy downtown streets outside. The branch on Robb Drive is especially user-friendly, with a latte cart, a drive-up window, and a used bookstore operated by the Friends of Washoe County Library.

Although libraries have been synonymous with the printed word for many years, today most of them are also high-tech, with all the bells and whistles needed for high-speed transmittal of electronic information. The Washoe system is no exception since its Internet Branch provides access to more than 1,000 information sources on the Internet.

Outreach is alive and well in this library system, with about 130 programs for adults and an amazing 1,737 for children and young adults. The variety of specific events is impressive to say the least and much too long to list in this chapter. You can call the library for its calendar of events and watch local newspapers for current happenings.

If you love to buy books (and what avid reader doesn't?), you won't want to miss the "Booksale Bonanza," sponsored by the Friends of Washoe County Library. It's northern Nevada's largest community-wide book sale, with more than 25 tons of books up for grabs.

Educational Institutions

Truckee Meadows Community College
7000 Dandini Boulevard
Reno, NV
(775) 673-7000
www.tmcc.edu

TMCC offers a wide variety of classes in the performing, visual, and literary arts. I can't begin to describe them all: Consult the college catalog for a complete listing. The public frequently shares the work and accomplishments of TMCC's arts students and faculty through their theater productions and visual arts exhibits. The college does more than just teach the arts: it brings them to the community as a way of enriching life in the Truckee Meadows. (For more information on the school, see the Education and Child Care chapter.)

University of Nevada, Reno (UNR)
North Virginia Street
Reno, NV
(775) 784-1110
www.unr.edu

It's possible to estimate the economic impact of the University of Nevada, Reno, on the Reno/Tahoe area, but how do you begin to describe its influence on the local culture and quality of life? Since the answer to that question is quite subjective, I think it's enough to simply understand that a major university permeates every facet of life in a community, injecting intellectual choices and cultural contributions that the area might not have had otherwise.

Because it offers a wide variety of programs and degrees in various artistic disciplines, UNR has been a focal point for the local arts scene for many years. The university sponsors a veritable kaleidoscope of stimulating events throughout the year, presented by students and faculty as well as members of the community, guest artists, and speakers. In the university's Nightingale Concert Hall you can enjoy first-class performances by such talented resident groups as the Argenta Quartet, the UNR Orchestra, the UNR Mastersingers, and the Reno Jazz Orchestra. In the Redfield Proscenium Theatre and the Redfield Studio Theatre you can delight in exquisite dance and lively theater. And in the Lawlor Events Center (when not used for major athletic events), you can attend large productions, such as ice shows and rock concerts, in a typical arena-style venue.

As the only university repertory company in the country, the Nevada Repertory Company gives students, faculty, and community members the opportunity to work in a different show each night. With four distinct productions offered each season, the company provides a well-rounded theater experience to both cast and crew. Selections from previous seasons have included *Into the Woods, Angels in America, A Clockwork Orange,* and *A Grand Night for Singing.* For information call (775) 784-4444 or go to www.unr.edu/nevadarep. Be sure to ask about weekend dinner/theater options. For tickets call (800) 225-2277.

Aside from this tantalizing array of performing arts events, UNR is also a dynamic supporter of the visual and literary arts. You can always count on a top-notch exhibit in the Sheppard Art Gallery plus an interesting display of student literary work outside the Kenneth J. Printing Studio in the Getchell Library. The university's Black Rock Press has been a mainstay for local writers for many years, publishing such well-known authors as Robert Laxalt and Gary Snyder.

Although parking on university campuses is often restrictive and challenging for visitors, UNR's parking garage just north of the Church Fine Arts building provides adequate parking for most events.

For updated information on all UNR arts events, call the University Arts Hotline at (775) 334-9696.

Galleries

Artists Co-op Gallery
627 Mill Street, Reno, NV
(775) 322-8896

Situated in a historic brick building at the

corner of Wells Avenue and Mill Street, the Artists Co-op Gallery was the first art cooperative in Nevada when it opened in 1966. The 20 award-winning artist members offer original art at reasonable prices and with payment schedules. The works include oils, watercolors, pastels, mixed media, photography, and pottery. The gallery is open daily from 11:00 A.M. to 4:00 P.M.

Art Source
Foothill Commerce Center
9748 South Virginia Street, Reno, NV
(775) 828-3525

With 8,000 square feet of display space on two levels, Art Source has an eclectic array of art, prints, and sculpture. They also offer custom framing service. Hours are 10:00 A.M. to 7:00 P.M. Monday through Friday and 11:00 A.M. to 3:00 P.M. Saturday. The Foothill Commerce Center is next to Winco on South Virginia Street.

Boyce Art Images
4900 Charlotte Way, Reno, NV
(775) 857-6136

Award-winning wildlife artist Fred Boyce is one of the best-known outdoor artists in the Reno/Tahoe area. For those who love "nature" art and Nevada landscapes, his gallery is truly a treasure. He has also published two coffee-table books with photos of his work, *The Other Nevada* and *The Other Nevada II*. You can view his originals, limited editions, and lithographs by appointment.

La Bussola
211 West First Street, Reno, NV
(775) 348-8858

La Bussola features original art and refurbished furniture. The focus is on emerging local artists in all types of media. If you're looking for affordable art, I recommend you check this place out, since prices are very reasonable. You can easily combine a jaunt along the Truckee River with a visit to the gallery. Hours are 10:00 A.M. to 6:00 P.M. Wednesday through Saturday and Monday and 10:00 A.M. to 5:00 P.M. Sunday. It's closed on Tuesday.

Nevada Museum of Art
160 West Liberty Street, Reno, NV
(775) 329-3333
www.nevadaart.org

The only accredited fine-arts museum in Nevada, the Nevada Museum of Art is housed in an intriguing structure of black geometric shapes interspersed with glass. Once you've admired the building, I invite you to enjoy the delights inside. You'll find 55,000 square feet of experimental, rotating, and permanent works. The building also boasts a theater, library, classrooms, museum store, and a rooftop sculpture garden. A delightful place for lunch, the Cafe Musee is frequently the site of wine tastings, special events, and concerts. If you're an art lover, this museum is a must-see. Hours are 11:00 A.M. to 6:00 P.M. Tuesday through Sunday and until 8:00 P.M. on Thursday.

Richardson Gallery of Fine Art
3670 South Virginia Street
Reno, NV
(775) 828-0888

Showcasing a delightful variety of inspirational paintings and exquisite sculptures, Richardson Gallery of Fine Art is a great place for both art browsers and serious buyers. Conveniently located between the Peppermill and Atlantis casinos, at Richardson you'll find a large variety of works by today's most talented and well-known artists. The gallery is open 10:30 A.M. to 6:30 P.M. Monday through Saturday and 11:00 A.M. to 5:00 P.M. Sunday.

Sheppard Gallery
Church Fine Arts Building
University of Nevada, Reno, Reno, NV
(775) 784-6658

Sheppard Gallery showcases the wonderfully eclectic works of students and faculty at the University of Nevada, Reno as well as nationally known artists. Exhibits change every month and include all types of media. You can browse or buy from 9:00 A.M. to 5:00 P.M. Monday through Friday. To park at the university, pick up a visitors parking pass from the information booth just off Ninth Street.

Sierra Arts Gallery
17 South Virginia Street, Reno, NV
(775) 329-1324
www.sierra-arts.org
Showcasing the best of new and emerging contemporary artists, Sierra Arts Gallery is always full of surprises. Housed in the Riverside Artist Lofts, the gallery boasts 17-foot ceilings that accommodate large works and major sculptures. This historic building is also home to 35 resident artists, the offices of Sierra Arts, and Dreamer's Cafe (see separate listings in this chapter). Call for hours.

Stremmel Gallery
1400 South Virginia Street, Reno, NV
(775) 786-0558
www.stremmelgallery.com
Founded in 1969, Stremmel Gallery is one of the oldest galleries in the Reno/Tahoe area. Its modern, sleek exterior is a reflection of the contents within, mainly abstract and representative contemporary art. The gallery displays an interesting mix of two- and three-dimensional works, in such media as oils, pastels, bronzes, and marbles. The gallery recently was renovated to double its space. It's open from 9:00 A.M. to 6:00 P.M. Monday through Friday and 10:00 A.M. to 3:00 P.M. Saturday. It's closed on Sunday.

NORTH SHORE LAKE TAHOE

Support Organizations

Arts For The Schools
(530) 546-4602
Arts For The Schools is the only organization that provides year-round artistic multicultural programs in the North Shore Lake Tahoe area. Although it was founded to expand quality arts experiences in the schools, the group's accomplishments reach the entire community. Programs include arts outreach, cultural events, and artistic performances.

Performing Arts

THEATER

Lake Tahoe Shakespeare Festival
Sand Harbor, Incline Village, NV
(775) 832-1616, (800) 747-4697
www.laketahoeshakespeare.com
Shakespeare might be astonished to see his classic works performed on the shore of North America's largest alpine lake, but somehow the richness of productions like *Romeo and Juliet* and *Twelfth Night* is enhanced by the awesome beauty of the outdoor venue. The Lake Tahoe Shakespeare Festival has enjoyed robust success since its founding in 1978 and in 1999 was named one of the "Top 100 Festivals in North America" by *Destinations* magazine. Although the setting is laid-back and natural, a night at the festival offers much of the pageantry found in a traditional theater, from the call of the trumpets signaling the start of the performance to the colorful Shakespearean banners decorating the entrance. The performances are further enhanced by the comprehensive new stage with state-of-the-art sound and lighting systems.

With a first-class setting and a first-rate performance, only fine wining and dining can complete the picture. You can bring your own gourmet picnic or choose from a wide variety of delicacies offered for sale at the park. For maximum comfort bring beach chairs (they must be the low-back, short-legged type) or consider renting them for $3.00. And because the temperature drops rapidly after the sun goes down, be sure to bring a sweater or jacket to avoid getting cold.

Performances begin at 7:30 P.M. Tuesday through Thursday and at 8:00 P.M. Friday through Sunday, but theatergoers begin arriving earlier to enjoy dining with a world-class view. The festival takes place the last five weeks of the summer before

Labor Day. Reserved seating is $65 and guarantees comfortable wood-frame chairs directly in front of the stage. General admission is around $20 and is open seating. If you suspect a performance may be canceled because of rain, be sure to call on the day you plan to attend. (See also the Annual Events chapter.)

The cast for the festival is provided by The Foothill Theatre Company, which also hosts a Shakespeare Camp for children 8 to 16 years old. Students from all over the country learn set and costume design, acting, makeup, and character design at the one- and two-week sessions in August.

MUSIC

Incline Village Chamber Music Society
(775) 298-0100
Although I've often heard "there's no free lunch," the Incline Village Chamber Music Society proves that old aphorism wrong with its Sunday concerts. For six consecutive Sundays in July and August, you can attend live performances by top-quality classical artists—absolutely free. The series is made possible through the generous support of local patrons. Concerts are at 3:00 P.M. at the Donald W. Reynolds Non Profit Community Center at 948 Incline Way in Incline Village. Call for specific dates and program details.

Lake Tahoe Summer Music Festival
(530) 583-3101
(530) 581-1184 (tickets)
www.tahoemusic.org
The Lake Tahoe Summer Music Festival is a magical marriage of fine classical music and nature at its most exquisite. Founded in 1986 by Edgar Braun, the longtime conductor of the San Francisco Chamber Orchestra, the festival offers an exciting feast of concerts from July through mid-August. Venues are at Alpine Meadows, Northstar-at-Tahoe, Donner Lake Beach, Sierra Nevada College, Squaw Valley, and Tahoe Donner.

If you enjoy high-quality music and gorgeous scenery (and who doesn't?), you simply can't go wrong in attending any of these events. Call for specific locations, programs, and times (see the Annual Events chapter for more information).

Visual Arts

Sierra Artists' Network and
North Tahoe Art Center
380 North Lake Boulevard
Tahoe City, CA
(530) 581-2787
Since its founding in 1989, the Sierra Artists' Network has been the heartbeat of the arts scene in the North Shore Lake Tahoe area. With a membership of about 300 enthusiastic artists and art appreciators, the group sponsors art shows, receptions, guest speakers, and fund-raisers. It also publishes a monthly newsletter, *Tahoe ARTour*. SAN's Tahoe ARTour is mid-August. oldest annual open studio tour and sale, which showcases local artists in their own environment.

Since 1994 SAN has been headquartered in the North Tahoe Art Center, one of Tahoe City's historic lakeside buildings. The center serves as a focal point for artists, with its gallery exhibits, gift shop, and meeting rooms for workshops and classes.

Educational Institutions

Sierra Nevada College
999 Tahoe Boulevard
Incline Village, NV
(775) 831-1314
www.sierranevada.edu
Although it's a small school by university standards (see the Education and Child Care chapter for details), Sierra Nevada College offers an interesting variety of classes in the arts, including art history, ceramics, drawing, painting, photography, printmaking, electronic arts, sculpture, music, and theater. It offers bachelor's

Ethnic and Cultural Groups

Balalaika and Domra Association of America, (775) 329-1333, www.bdaa.com
Daughters of Norway, (775) 826-7751
Daughters of Penelope (Greek Orthodox), (775) 825-5365
Hellenic Dancers of St. Anthony, (775) 825-5365
Inter-Tribal Council, (775) 355-0600
NAACP, (775) 322-2992
Nevada Hispanic Services, (775) 826-1818
Nevada Society of Scottish Clans, www.nvssc.org
North American Basque Organization, www.basque.unr.edu
Northern Nevada Black Cultural Awareness Society, (775) 329-8990
Philoptochas Society (Greek Orthodox), (775) 825-5365
Scottish American Military Society, (775) 826-7848
Sierra Nevada Celtic Society, www.sncs-celtic.org
Sons and Daughters of Erin, www.irishnv.org
Sons of Norway, www.sofn-district6.com
Zenbat Gara Basque Folk Dance Ensemble, www.dantzariak.net

degrees in art and music. For lifelong, non-degree learners it also has a continuing-education program that includes creative arts courses. SNC's summer Visiting Arts Workshops present an amazing potpourri of artists that span the spectrum of disciplines, such as high-fire porcelains, wheel-thrown ceramics, raku firing, conceptual sculpture, digital imaging, musical pet therapy, and modern poetry.

You can also enjoy performances and exhibits by SNC students and visiting artists in the Croom Theater and the Tahoe Gallery at the Mountain Campus. Call for schedules and details.

Galleries

Art Attack Gallery
Christmas Tree Village
868 Tahoe Boulevard, Incline Village, NV
(775) 832-7400

Browsing is a delight in this roomy gallery in the Christmas Tree Village shopping mall in Incline Village. (I tell you more about the picturesque mall in the Shopping chapter.) Art Attack Gallery hosts many well-advertised special exhibits throughout the year in addition to its ongoing displays of originals and limited-edition prints. You can visit the gallery daily from 10:00 A.M. to 6:00 P.M.

Artists of Tahoe–Art's Desire
797 Southwood Boulevard #1
Incline Village, NV
(775) 831-3011

Focusing primarily on local artists, Artists of Tahoe–Art's Desire displays innovative works in a variety of media. The gallery also offers vintage photographs and custom framing service. It's open 10:00 A.M. to 5:00 P.M. Monday through Friday and noon to 4:00 P.M. on Saturday. The schedule can vary, so call ahead.

Frames by Ryrie
Cobblestone Center
475 North Lake Boulevard, Tahoe City, CA
(530) 583-3043

In the picturesque Cobblestone Center

Mall across the street from Lake Tahoe, Frames by Ryrie offers unique gifts, posters, and ready-made frames as well as a beautiful collection of ski prints by Cecile Johnson. The mall is great for browsing (see the Shopping chapter for details). The gallery is open 10:00 A.M. to 5:30 P.M. Monday through Saturday and 11:00 A.M. to 5:00 P.M. Sunday.

James Harold Galleries
Boatworks Mall
760 North Lake Boulevard, Tahoe City, CA
(530) 581-5111
www.jamesharoldgalleries.com
When you're browsing the Boatworks Mall in Tahoe City, be sure to stop by James Harold Galleries. It features a diverse collection of original paintings, objets d'art, sculptures, glass art, limited reproductions, and collectibles. The mall offers an interesting mix of stores and restaurants right on the shore of Lake Tahoe (see the Shopping chapter for details). Winter hours for the gallery are 11:00 A.M. to 7:00 P.M. Sunday through Thursday and 10:00 A.M. to 9:00 P.M. Friday and Saturday. Hours are extended to 10:00 P.M. during the summer months. The gallery recently moved from the second floor to the first floor of the mall.

Lakeside Gallery & Gifts
8636 North Lake Boulevard
Kings Beach, CA
(530) 546-3135
www.lakesidegallery.com
Offering art supplies, painting workshops, and framing service, Lakeside Gallery & Gifts is a full-service art store as well as a gallery. One of the oldest galleries at the lake, it exhibits mostly landscapes, impressionism, prints, and watercolors by local artists. Hours are 10:00 A.M. to 5:00 P.M. Monday through Saturday.

North Tahoe Art Center
380 North Lake Boulevard, Tahoe City, CA
(530) 581-2787
You can view a new exhibit and meet the artist who created it the first Friday of every month in the North Tahoe Art Center. The gallery features an intriguing mix of artistic works throughout the year, mostly from artists who live and work in the Lake Tahoe area. You can also buy local artists' work in the gift shop. Hours are 11:00 A.M. to 4:00 P.M. Wednesday through Sunday and 10:00 A.M. to 5:00 P.M. daily during the summer.

Pogan Gallery
6921 North Lake Boulevard
Tahoe Vista, CA
(530) 546-7846
www.pogangallery.com
The only strictly fine-arts gallery in the Lake Tahoe area, Pogan Gallery sells only original work. Inspired by the beauty of the Lake Tahoe Basin, well-known artists come from all over the country to paint at the lake, and the gallery reaps the rewards with its large collection of landscapes of the region. Hours are 10:00 A.M. to 5:00 P.M. daily.

The Potlatch
930 Tahoe Boulevard
Incline Village, NV
(775) 831-2485
Visiting The Potlatch is a visual delight: The variety of textures and hues in this vibrant collection of Native American and Southwestern art is colorful, to say the least. With a large selection of fine crafts and jewelry, it's a great place to purchase gifts at a reasonable price. It's open daily from 10:00 A.M. to 5:30 P.M.

The Potter's Wheel
8331 North Lake Boulevard
Kings Beach, CA
(530) 546-8400
If you're looking for fine pottery, this store is a must-stop. It offers a selection of weavings, watercolors, and woodworking. Hours are 9:30 A.M. to 5:30 P.M. daily in the summer. It's closed Monday through Wednesday in winter.

Tahoe Gallery
800 College Drive
Incline Village, NV
(775) 831-1314

Sierra Nevada College displays students' work as well as the works of visiting and local professional artists in the Tahoe Gallery in Abernathy Hall at the Mountain Campus. Special exhibits with receptions for the artists are also held every few weeks throughout the school year. Regular gallery hours are 8:00 A.M. to 5:00 P.M. Monday through Friday.

Vista Gallery
7081 North Lake Boulevard
Tahoe Vista, CA
(530) 546-7794
www.vistagallery.com
If you're looking for vintage Lake Tahoe photographs, check this gallery out: It has a collection of more than 600. It also features original antique memorabilia and prints of the lake and the Sierras. Other works displayed include wood sculptures, blown glass, paintings, and ceramics by about three dozen different artists. While many galleries don't encourage children to visit (for obvious reasons), this gallery is child-friendly, with a play area set aside especially for them. The gallery is located above the Old Range Steakhouse with a lovely view of the lake, and I recommend feasting on the artwork upstairs and then feasting on a mouthwatering steak downstairs. The gallery is open 10:00 A.M. to 5:30 P.M. Tuesday through Saturday.

SOUTH SHORE LAKE TAHOE

Support Organizations

Tahoe Arts Project (TAP)
(530) 542-3632
Because Lake Tahoe is geographically isolated by mountainous terrain, exposure to performing arts is limited. The Tahoe Arts Project was established in 1987 in South Lake Tahoe, California, to bring fine arts to children in the schools and artistic performances to the general public. Since its founding, TAP has produced more than 700 lectures, master classes, and workshops in the South Shore Lake Tahoe area. TAP helps fill an important void in the educational curriculum, since school budgets are often inadequate to provide quality arts-in-education.

Public events are a mixed bag and have included such offerings as a mystery dinner, Gamelan music from Indonesia, children's theater, An Evening with the Academy Awards, and musical ensembles. Call for the current schedule of events.

Tahoe Tallac Association
(530) 542-4166 (winter)
(530) 541-4975 (summer)
www.valhalla-tallac.com
The Tahoe Tallac Association was formed in 1979 to restore the historic estates in the Tallac Historic Site near South Lake Tahoe, California (see the description of the site in the Attractions chapter). The association also produces the annual Valhalla Arts and Music Festival, a wildly diverse celebration of art, music, and theater that lasts throughout the year.

Some events include the Valhalla Renaissance Festival, Celtic Sunday, the Brews & Blues Festival, Reggae Sunday, and the Classic Film Festival, to name a few. You can also attend plays in the historic Valhalla Boathouse Theatre, view local artists' work in the Dextra Baldwin Art Gallery and the Pope Fine Art Gallery, or test your acting or artistic wings in a theater or art workshop.

The festival is truly a feast of the sights and sounds of many cultures—a feast that can be relished in one of the most gorgeous natural settings in the world. Be sure to check the schedule of events if you're in the South Lake Tahoe area, especially in the summer. At almost any event, I guarantee you'll experience some of the unique magic of this extraordinary historical setting. (See the Annual Events chapter for more information.)

Educational Institutions

Lake Tahoe Community College (LTCC)
1 College Drive, South Lake Tahoe, CA
(530) 541-4660
www.ltcc.cc.ca.us
Colleges and universities bring a wealth of culture to their home communities, and Lake Tahoe Community College is no exception. Besides its generous class offerings in the arts, the campus of LTCC is an artistic beehive of activity, promoting an array of cultural events for both students and the general public. You can enjoy performances and exhibitions by students as well as by guest performers and artists from around the region.

Drama, dance, music, and films are presented by the Performing Arts League in the LTCC New Theatre. Art shows and receptions are free and are held in the Main Art Gallery in the College Commons and the Foyer Art Gallery in the Theatre Foyer of the Fine Arts building. Call for a complete schedule of activities throughout the year. See the Education and Child Care chapter for more information about LTCC.

Galleries

A Frame of Mind Gallery
The Shops at Heavenly Village
Heavenly Village Way
South Lake Tahoe, CA
(530) 541-8885
www.aframeofmind.com
Voted the "Best of Tahoe" gallery by the *Tahoe Tribune* for 1996–1998, A Frame of Mind Gallery showcases all natural landscape photography. You can drink in the beauty of Lake Tahoe and its surrounding environs in this luscious collection of local photos. The gallery is easy to find in Harveys Resort Hotel/Casino, but hours vary. It's open daily from 11:00 A.M. to 7:00 P.M.

Augustine Arts
Near Stateline, NV
(775) 588-3525
www.augustinearts.com
Serious collectors and lovers of art are delighted with the personalized service offered by Augustine Arts. It's not your usual gallery: The owner will guide you through the international art community, providing access to truly distinctive works just right for your home or office. Call for an appointment and directions.

Lake Tahoe Community College (LTCC)
1 College Drive, South Lake Tahoe, CA
(530) 541-4660
www.ltcc.cc.ca.us
You can view student, faculty, local, and visiting artists' works at the periodic exhibits and receptions in LTCC's Foyer Art Gallery and Main Art Gallery. The Foyer Art Gallery is located in the Theatre Foyer of the Fine Arts building, and the Main Art Gallery is in the College Commons. Both galleries are free and open to the public from 7:00 A.M. to 10:00 P.M. Monday through Friday, 8:00 A.M. to 5:00 P.M. Saturday, and noon to 5:00 P.M. Sunday.

Marcus Ashley Galleries
The Village Center
4000 Lake Tahoe Boulevard, #29
South Lake Tahoe, CA
(530) 544-4278
Specializing in original artwork, the gallery showcases a wide variety of oil and acrylic paintings, sculpture, art glass, jewelry, and limited edition prints. They also offer custom framing, private home shows within 60 miles, and worldwide shipping. You'll find this gallery in the Village Center shopping complex near Starbucks. Summer hours are 10:00 A.M. to 7:00 P.M. daily. Call for winter hours.

Because art gallery hours frequently are flexible, call ahead to check.

Wyland Galleries Lake Tahoe
The Shops at Heavenly Village
1001 Park Avenue, Suite 7
South Lake Tahoe, CA
(530) 541-7099

Art lovers can indulge their passion for marine art to their heart's delight in this upscale gallery. Along with the works of Wyland, the gallery features a large collection of pieces by other international and locally acclaimed artists. James Coleman, Steven Power, Walfrado, John Pitre, and Treas Atkinson are just a few of those whose works are on display. The gallery also has a number of showings throughout the year where artists are present to meet potential buyers. Hours are 10:00 A.M. to 7:00 P.M. Sunday through Thursday and until 8:00 P.M. Friday and Saturday.

PARKS

With Mother Nature as the chief architect, the Reno/Tahoe area is blessed with all the natural ingredients for awesome parks. Managed by a variety of governmental agencies, the plethora of area parks goes a long way toward preserving the environment and making the great outdoors more accessible for everyone to enjoy. You can hike in rugged mountain terrain and sunbathe on pristine sandy beaches in Lake Tahoe Basin parks, bike along the Truckee River and attend cultural events in Reno/Sparks parks, and relax with family and friends over a gourmet picnic in any of the dozens of neighborhood parks scattered throughout the Reno/Tahoe area.

Using the four geographical areas, in this chapter I give you a sampling of the kinds of parks just waiting your exploration. Since descriptions aren't meant to be all-inclusive, I also tell you where to get complete lists of parks from the various parks departments and visitors bureaus. You can also let your fingers do the walking through area telephone directories for maps and parks listings. If you're interested in the myriad programs offered by the parks departments, be sure to request their program booklets. You'll be amazed at the variety of activities offered, from every sports adventure you can possibly imagine to a tantalizing array of arts, crafts, and self-improvement courses.

Many parks, especially the neighborhood variety, are free and accessible year-round. For others I tell you about fees, seasons, and hours as of press time. Be aware, however, that these specifics could change. Your visit to most any of the parks will be more enjoyable if you're informed about what's offered there. I strongly recommend getting information from one of the visitor centers or parks departments ahead of time or picking up maps and brochures when they're available at the parks themselves. Although I describe here some of the recreational opportunities you can enjoy in area parks, the Recreation chapter gives more details, such as additional beaches for swimming at Lake Tahoe and specifics of the area's not-to-be-missed hiking trails.

The Incline Village General Improvement District (IVGID) manages a variety of parks and recreational facilities in Incline Village largely for the benefit of local residents. The golf courses and ski resort are open to the public, but the recreation center is not. Access to Ski, Incline, and Burnt Cedar Beaches is restricted to residents during the summer but is available to the public the rest of the year. If you've booked accommodations in Incline Village, be sure to ask if it includes an IVGID recreation pass.

And last, but by no means least, before you head out to bask in nature's glory, take proper precautions to protect yourself against the elements and the environment. Be sure to use sunscreen and to carry food and water if you're planning to hike or cross-country ski for any distance. Be aware of the weather and wear proper clothing for the occasion. If you're planning to swim in Lake Tahoe, you need to know its frigid waters can be dangerous. Although it's extremely inviting, the lake's 60-degree temperature can cause hypothermia in just minutes: Be sure to take precautions. (For more outdoor safety tips, see the Winter Sports chapter.)

RENO/WASHOE COUNTY SOUTH OF RENO

Bartley Ranch Regional Park
6000 Bartley Ranch Road
(775) 828-6612
www.washoecountyparks.com

Park Information Contacts

California State Parks, (530) 525-7232; www.cal-parks.ca.gov

City of Reno Parks & Recreation & Community Services, (775) 334-2262; www.cityofreno.com

City of South Lake Tahoe Parks and Recreation Department, (530) 542-6056; www.ci.south-lake-tahoe.ca.us

City of Sparks Parks & Recreation, (775) 353-2376; www.ci.sparks.nv.us

Incline Village Parks & Recreation Department, (775) 832-1310; www.ivgid.org

Lake Tahoe Visitors Authority (South Shore Lake Tahoe), (530) 544-5050, (800) 371-2620; www.virtualtahoe.com

Nevada State Parks, (775) 687-4379; www.parks.nv.gov

North Lake Tahoe Chamber of Commerce, (530) 581-6900, (888) 434-1262; www.mytahoevacation.com

Tahoe-Douglas Chamber of Commerce, (775) 588-4591; www.tahoechamber.org

Truckee Donner Recreation and Park District, (530) 582-7720; www.tdrpd.com

USDA Forest Service, Lake Tahoe Basin Management Unit, (530) 543-2600; www.fs.fed.us/r5/ltbmu/

Washoe County Parks and Recreation Department, (775) 828-6642; www.co.washoe.nv.us, www.washoecountyparks.com

On the site of a former working ranch, Bartley Ranch Regional Park gives visitors a snapshot of Nevada's ranching heritage. Tucked in a quiet pastoral setting, the picturesque ranch house and surrounding 2-mile walking trail offer a chunk of quiet solitude on the edge of the city. You can spread a gourmet picnic in the shade, ride horses on the trail or in the arena, and attend cultural events in the amphitheater (see the chapter on The Arts for details). If you're curious about the huge white-fenced spread next door, I'll satisfy your curiosity right now: Once the home of Bill Harrah (founder of Harrah's Hotels/Casinos), it's now the residence of John Harrah, Bill's son.

Bowers Mansion Park
U.S. Highway 395
21 miles south of Reno
(775) 849-1825, (775) 828-6642
(775) 849-0644 (swimming pool)
www.washoecountyparks.com

The next best thing to a time machine, Bowers Mansion (in its namesake park) allows visitors to step back into the opulence enjoyed by Nevada's mining barons in the 1860s. Built by L. S. "Sandy" Bowers, the first Comstock Lode millionaire, the 16-room mansion is completely restored and decked out with furnishings from around the world. Call for times of daily tours.

Surrounded by expansive lawns and huge shade trees, the mansion is a delightful playground for picnics and affords a lovely view of Washoe Valley. The park also has a swimming pool along with a children's playground. Daily summer hours usually run from 8:00 A.M. to 9:00 P.M. and winter hours from 8:00 A.M. to 5:00 P.M. No pets are allowed.

Davis Creek Park
U.S. Highway 395
20 miles south of Reno
(775) 849-0684
www.washoecountyparks.com

Tucked in tall Jeffrey pines on the eastern slope of the Sierra Nevada, Davis Creek Park offers hiking, picnicking, and overnight camping. You can take easy self-guided nature strolls around the park or head up the Ophir Creek Trail to Price Lake (about 3 miles) and on to Tahoe Meadows (about 6 miles). The campsites have water and showers but no trailer hookups. The park is open year-round, and camping facilities are on a first-come, first-served basis.

Galena Creek Park
18350 Nevada Highway 431
(775) 849-2511
www.washoecountyparks.com

Nestled in the shadow of Mt. Rose, Galena Creek Park boasts a refreshing alpine environment just 25 minutes from downtown Reno. The recreational day-use area offers lovely picnic spots under immense pine trees, a self-guided nature trail, and evening campfire programs during the summer. The park is also the trailhead for hikes along Galena, Whites, and Jones Creeks. Because it's so close to Reno, it's a favorite with hikers and bikers who want a quick escape from the summer heat. In winter it's often the closest spot for cross-country skiing, sledding, and snowshoeing.

The park and creek are named for the town of Galena, a hamlet founded in 1860 just several miles away. Originally developed as a mining property, the settlement became more important as a lumbering center when the "galena" (lead sulfide in the gold float) made the mining operation unprofitable. The town boasted 11 sawmills, a school, saloons, and dozens of homes at its peak. Fires in 1865 and 1867 destroyed much of the town, and it was eventually abandoned.

Idlewild Park
1900 Idlewild Drive
(775) 334-2262
www.cityofreno.com

Stretching along the Truckee River just minutes from downtown casinos, Idlewild Park is a popular oasis for walkers, in-line skaters, and picnickers. You'll find a paved path right alongside the river, meandering through the 49 acres of lush green grass and tall trees. There's also a large kiddie park with a variety of rides, a swimming pool, skate park, picnic areas, and a first-class rose garden sure to delight any horticulturist. If you're strolling west along the Truckee River Walk from downtown, you're sure to wander through Idlewild Park. The park is also home to dozens of Canada geese, who find the river and nearby ponds especially welcoming. (See also the Kidstuff chapter.)

Oxbow Nature Study Area
3100 Dickerson Road
(775) 334-2262
www.cityofreno.com

Tucked along the Truckee River in west Reno, Oxbow Nature Study Area offers the unhurried visitor a stellar opportunity to commune with nature. Take your time as you wander along the path and the viewing areas; there's a good chance you'll spot quail, falcon, golden eagle, beaver, muskrat, and deer up close and personal. It's a great place for kids to learn about native habitats.

Rancho San Rafael Park
1595 North Sierra Street
(775) 785-4512
www.washoecountyparks.com

Rancho San Rafael Park is best known as the starting point of the Great Reno Balloon Race and the site of the Wilbur May Center (see the Annual Events and Attractions chapters for details). It's popular with picnickers, walkers, bikers, and kite flyers. You'll find lovely expanses of green grass, shaded picnic areas, and a 1.5-mile interpretive nature walk. It's open year-round and easily accessible off Sierra Street near the University of Nevada, Reno campus.

Virginia Lake
1980 Lakeside Drive
(775) 334-2262
www.cityofreno.com

With an inviting running path encircling it, Virginia Lake is one of Reno's most popular jogging/walking areas. Come rain or shine it's always a beehive of activity, with kids in strollers and dogs on leashes joining the pack of in-line skaters, walkers, and joggers. The course isn't long—about a mile—but nothing will prevent you from going round and round until you get enough exercise. If you're into bird-watching or feeding, bring a sack of bread crumbs: Virginia Lake is also a favorite hangout for hundreds of local birds.

Future plans for Virginia Lake include rehabilitation of the park along with new residential and retail development on the north and east sides. The resulting increase in traffic will undoubtedly impact the serene nature of the park.

Wingfield Park
2 North Arlington Avenue
(775) 334-2262
www.cityofreno.com

A small oasis in busy downtown Reno, Wingfield Park is easy to spot if you're strolling along the Truckee River Walk. Just three acres in the middle of the river, it's a lovely spot to sit and watch the water rush by, often carrying kayakers on the white-water course. The amphitheater is the site of many outdoor cultural events (for details see the chapter on The Arts).

SPARKS

Pah Rah Park
1750 Shadow Lane
(775) 353-2376
www.ci.sparks.nv.us

Some years ago the city fathers in Sparks decided that every neighborhood should have a park. As the city has grown, they've kept up with this goal by building parks along with the new housing developments. The landscape of Sparks is splashed with the green of around 30 neighborhood parks that offer inviting spots for play and relaxation. They provide a variety of amenities that include tennis courts, swimming pools, picnic areas, and playgrounds.

Typical of parks in Sparks, Pah Rah Park is a great place to bring the family for an outing right in town. Its huge grassy area provides plenty of room for the kids to run and play games. There's also several playground areas with a variety of equipment, a couple of covered picnic spots, tennis courts, and bathrooms. A big plus is the great view of downtown Reno and the Sierra Nevada to the west.

To get to the park from Sparks, take Interstate 80 east, exit on Vista Boulevard, and go north for about 2 miles. You'll see the sign for the park just after crossing Baring Boulevard.

Sparks Marina Park
East end of Nichols Boulevard
(775) 353-2376
www.ci.sparks.nv.us

Not too long ago, the site of Sparks Marina Park was an ugly eyesore and an embarrassment to the city. As part of an ambitious reclamation project, however, what was once a gaping gravel pit has become an 80-acre lake that's a source of pride and joy for the community. Stocked with trophy-size trout, the sparkling lake is a favorite fishing hole with Insiders. Other amenities include a jogging path that encircles the water, a dog park, a swimming lagoon, and shaded picnic areas.

Recent development has added upscale condominiums and retail establishments on the north and east shores of the lake. (See the Restaurants chapter for more information about Anchors Bar & Grill.) The park is the site of a variety of special events throughout the year, such as the MasterCraft Pro Wakeboard Tour Finals and the Mutt Strut.

To get to the park from Reno or Sparks, head east on I-80, exit on McCarran Boulevard, and go north to the intersection of Nichols Boulevard. The park is about 1 block east, just behind the Western Village Inn/Casino.

Dog-friendly Parks

Parks that have designated play areas for dogs include:

Incline Beach (near boat launch), Lakeshore Boulevard across from Hyatt Regency Lake Tahoe Resort & Casino, Incline Village, NV, (775) 832-1310 (October to April)
Sparks Marina Park, east end of Nichols Boulevard, Sparks, NV, (775) 353-2376
Virginia Lake Park, 1980 Lakeside Drive, Reno, NV, (775) 334-2262
Whitaker Park, 550 University Terrace, Reno, NV, (775) 334-2262

NORTH SHORE LAKE TAHOE

Kings Beach State Recreation Area
North Lake Boulevard, Kings Beach, CA
(530) 546-4212
www.cal-parks.ca.gov

With more than 700 feet of lakeshore and ample shade beneath ponderosa pines, Kings Beach State Recreation Area offers yet another site from which you can bask in the beauty of Lake Tahoe. It's a nice spot for water sports with its pier and picnic tables. A parking fee of about $5.00 is levied.

Lake Tahoe–Nevada State Park
2005 Nevada Highway 28
Incline Village, NV
(775) 831-0494
www.parks.nv.gov

One of the loveliest sections of shoreline and backcountry in the Lake Tahoe Basin is preserved for public use in Lake Tahoe–Nevada State Park. Extending along the east shore of Lake Tahoe south and east of Incline Village, the park encompasses miles of exquisite beach from Sand Harbor to Skunk Harbor, beautiful Spooner Lake at the junction of U.S. Highway 50 and NV 28, Cave Rock Marina about 7 miles north of Stateline, Nevada, and more than 13,000 acres of rugged forest in the Marlette/Hobart Backcountry near Spooner Summit. The variety of terrain offers limitless opportunities for outdoor fun.

The crystal white-sand beach and vivid turquoise water at Sand Harbor (about 3 miles south of Incline Village) make it one of the most popular and picturesque playgrounds at Lake Tahoe. You can swim, sunbathe, picnic, hike, launch your boat, or just sit under a spreading Jeffrey pine and drink in one of the most beautiful views on Earth. The parking lot fills fast in the summer, so if you're planning to spend the day, be sure to arrive early. It's open daily from 8:00 A.M. to 9:00 P.M., and the parking fee is $8.00 during summer and $4.00 the rest of the year. Be sure to stop by park headquarters, where you can pick up information about the park. Sand Harbor is also the site of the Lake Tahoe Shakespeare Festival (see The Arts chapter for details).

About 2 miles north of Sand Harbor, you'll find additional beach access at Hidden Beach, and more beach access at Memorial Point, which is about 1 mile north of Sand Harbor. About 2.5 miles south of Sand Harbor, you can park in the paved parking lot above the lake or along the road and walk into Chimney Beach, Secret Harbor, and Whale Beach. Hidden among huge boulders and enormous trees, numerous tiny coves along this stretch of shoreline offer secluded hideaways perfect for nude sunbathing. Just watch the sun on those least-exposed parts.

About 2.5 miles farther south you can park along the highway and walk into Prey Meadows (ablaze with wildflowers in late

To view a photo gallery along with brief descriptions of some Reno/Sparks parks, go to www.visitreno.com.

spring and early summer) or plunge down to secluded and lovely Skunk Harbor. This unmarked trailhead is tucked off the lake side of the highway, and roadside parking is limited.

Even though several parking lots serve these beaches, parking is usually a challenge along this section of NV 28. There's limited parking along the road, but be sure to pay attention to the stretches with NO PARKING signs to avoid getting a ticket. To beat the crowds, try hitting the beach early in the morning or late in the afternoon.

Cupped beneath heavily forested peaks, Spooner Lake offers hiking, biking, and catch-and-release fishing in summer. You can take a leisurely 2-mile stroll around the lake, strike out into the Marlette/Hobart Backcountry to Marlette Lake, pick up north- or southbound portions of the scenic Tahoe Rim Trail, as well as head off to other wilderness destinations (see the Recreation chapter for hiking and biking details). Parking fees are about $6.00. In winter Spooner Lake is a prime cross-country ski resort, featuring more than 80 kilometers of groomed trails (see the Winter Sports chapter for details).

For more information on activities at Spooner Lake, visit www.spoonerlake.com.

North Tahoe Regional Park
875 National Avenue, Tahoe Vista, CA
(530) 546-5043, (530) 546-4212
www.northlaketahoe.net/parks.html

You can enjoy periodic glimpses of Lake Tahoe from about 5 miles of multiuse trails that loop through the tall pines at North Tahoe Regional Park. In summer it's popular with hikers, bikers, and picnickers (see the Recreation chapter for more information). In winter it's a vision of white, perfect for snowshoeing, cross-country skiing, and snowmobiling (see the Winter Sports chapter for details). You'll also find a softball field, tennis courts, sand volleyball courts, playground, restrooms, and picnic areas.

To get to the park from Incline Village, go west on NV 28 to Tahoe Vista (just west of Kings Beach), turn right onto National Avenue, and follow the signs to the park. It's open from 6:00 A.M. to 10:00 P.M. in summer and from 7:00 A.M. to 7:00 P.M. in winter. Pay the $3.00 parking fee using the self-service box.

SOUTH SHORE LAKE TAHOE

Bijou Community Park
1201 Al Tahoe Boulevard
South Lake Tahoe, CA
(530) 542-6055
www.ci.south-lake-tahoe.ca.us

If you want to escape the crowds at the beaches on Lake Tahoe, you can spread your picnic at Bijou Community Park. You'll find sand volleyball courts, horseshoe pits, basketball courts, a skateboard park, a world-class 27-hole disc golf course, playground equipment, group picnic areas, and picnic shelters. (For more information on disc golf, see the Recreation chapter.) The park is open from sunrise to sunset winter and summer. There are no fees. The park is located about 1 mile southeast of the intersection of Al Tahoe Boulevard and US 50.

D. L. Bliss State Park
California Highway 89, 9 miles north of South Lake Tahoe, CA
(530) 525-7277 (summer)
(530) 525-9529 (winter)
www.cal-parks.ca.gov

Boasting 3.5 miles of shoreline along the west side of Lake Tahoe, D. L. Bliss State Park is paradise for anyone who loves the outdoors. Two sun-drenched beaches beckon sunbathers to warm sands—Calawee Cove Beach, a protected cove ringed by boulders and trees, and Lester

Beach, a wide-open expanse of white sand with maximum exposure to the sun.

When you get tired of catching rays, you can take a hike in the area. I highly recommend the spectacular Rubicon Trail, which takes you south along the lakeshore to Emerald Point, the entrance to Emerald Bay. (Learn more about this splendid hike in the Recreation chapter.) The Balancing Rock Interpretive Trail is another favorite, as is the relatively short trek to the lighthouse overlooking Rubicon Point.

The park also has one of the best campgrounds in the area (see the Camping and RVing chapter for details), but it fills fast, so be sure to reserve ahead. Call for day parking rates. To get a place during the busy summer months, especially during July and August, arrive before 10:00 A.M. You can inquire about parking within the park, as well as other park facilities, at the visitor center. The park is open from 8:00 A.M. to dusk, Memorial Day to mid-September.

Bliss is just a few short miles from Emerald Bay State Park (see next entry), Vikingsholm Castle (see the Attractions and Kidstuff chapters), and Sugar Pine Point State Park (also described in this chapter). Together, Bliss and Emerald Bay State Parks preserve more than 1,800 acres of prime Tahoe scenery. Whether you are visiting or planning to stay in the area, these parks are well worth extensive exploration.

Emerald Bay State Park
California Highway 89, about 8 miles north of South Lake Tahoe, CA
(530) 525-7277 (summer)
(530) 525-9529 (winter)
www.cal-parks.ca.gov

Lake Tahoe's Emerald Bay is easily the most photographed site in the entire Lake Tahoe Basin. Its emerald green waters edge into the feet of the snow-capped granite peaks of the Desolation Wilderness—a spectacular sight by any standard.

Attractions in Emerald Bay State Park include the shoreline around the bay, Vikingsholm Castle, and Eagle Falls, a string of waterfalls that tumble out of the Desolation Wilderness into the bay. Created in 1969 to preserve more than 60,000 acres of unique mountain environment, the wilderness is a wonderland of alpine lakes sprinkled among velvety meadows and rugged peaks.

You'll find lovely spots to picnic, swim, and sunbathe along the stretches of Tahoe's shore within the park. You can take a level 1.5-mile hike to Emerald Point, where there are gorgeous views of the rugged mouth of the bay. From the point you can turn north and follow the Rubicon Trail along the lakeshore toward D. L. Bliss State Park.

If you're feeling very ambitious, I recommend following Eagle Creek up to Eagle Lake in the Desolation Wilderness. Although it's a somewhat steep climb, it's only a mile long and affords luscious panoramic views along the way. Once you've made it to Eagle Lake, the grandeur of the Desolation Wilderness unfolds before you, with more than 100 additional lakes that can be explored. The Eagle Lake trailhead is in Eagle Falls Picnic Area, across CA 89 from the parking lot at Emerald Bay State Park. You'll need a permit to enter the Desolation Wilderness: You can either get a permit at the trailhead or at the Taylor Creek Visitor Center, located 3 miles north of South Lake Tahoe at 870 Emerald Bay Road. More information is also available on the Forest Service's Lake Tahoe Basin Management Unit Web site at www.fs.fed.us/r5.

Because this area of Lake Tahoe is extremely congested during the summer, parking is difficult. My advice is to get there as early in the day as possible during July and August. (For more information about Emerald Bay and Vikingsholm, see the Attractions chapter. For hiking and wilderness outings within and around the park, see the Recreation chapter.)

The Lake Tahoe Basin averages 273 days of sunshine every year, each one an opportunity to enjoy the unlimited outdoor activities available in area parks.

South Lake Tahoe Recreation Area
U.S. Highway 50 and Rufus Allen Boulevard, South Lake Tahoe, CA
(530) 542-6055
www.ci.south-lake-tahoe.ca.us

Close to all the casino action in Stateline, the South Lake Tahoe Recreation Area offers access to several Lake Tahoe beaches, along with picnic areas and facilities for horseshoes, basketball, and volleyball. Other amenities include a children's playground, jogging trails, a swimming pool, fitness center, and boat ramp. The campground by the lake (open in summer only) has 172 sites for tents and RVs and provides piped water, fire rings, and flush toilets.

Sugar Pine Point State Park
California Highway 89
1 mile south of Tahoma, CA
(530) 525-7982
www.parks.ca.gov

You can soak up a chunk of Lake Tahoe's history while enjoying its incredible natural beauty at Sugar Pine Point State Park. With more than 2,000 acres stretching along 1.75 miles of shoreline, the park offers a lovely swimming beach and choice hiking trails, along with the historic Ehrman Mansion, a nature center, and a 19th-century log cabin.

Finished in 1903, the mansion is an elegant example of Queen Anne architecture, with about 12,000 square feet of period extravagance. I suggest taking the tour to learn about the turn-of-the-century heydays of the wealthy who spent their summers at the lake. Tours are held every hour from 11:00 A.M. to 4:00 P.M. from July to Labor Day, and a small fee is charged. Also be sure to see the log cabin that was built in 1860 by Gen. William Phipps, a trapper believed to be the first permanent settler of record in this area of the Lake Tahoe Basin. If you're interested in the wildlife of the area, stop in at the nature center and view its bird and animal exhibits; the admission cost is covered by the park's $5.00 parking fee.

You'll find hiking trails suitable for almost everyone at Sugar Pine Point, from the easy Dolder Nature Trail, which meanders along the lakeshore, to the moderate General Creek Trail, which you can take for a 6.5-mile round-trip hike to Lily Pond. From Lily Pond you can continue on to a large variety of alpine lakes and meadows in the Desolation Wilderness. If a laid-back picnic is more your style, the beautifully manicured lawn in front of the Ehrman Mansion is the perfect place.

Open all year, the park is a favorite place for cross-country skiing and snowshoeing in winter. Be sure to pick up a Sno-Park permit for winter parking at the Lake Tahoe Basin Management Unit of the USDA Forest Service, which is located at 870 Emerald Bay Road in South Lake Tahoe. (For a description of the park's camping opportunities—there are 175 sites for tents and RVs—see the Camping and RVing chapter.)

RECREATION 

Dubbed "America's Adventure Place," the Reno/Tahoe area serves up a mind-blowing menu of activities guaranteed to challenge your wildest expectations. The variety is huge—so huge I devote entire chapters to Winter Sports, Golf, and Fishing and Hunting. I describe other recreation in this chapter, organized alphabetically by activity rather than by geographical area.

With so much recreation to choose from, locals take it seriously. Laden with recreational goodies like bikes, skis, kayaks, or hang gliders, sport utility vehicles reign. You'll see a higher percentage of them here than in most communities. But unlike sparkling showroom models, local SUVs are more likely to be frosted with snow or coated with mud from recent four-wheel-drive treks into the mountains.

If gambling's your game, you can enjoy it to your heart's content here. But don't forget that one of the most magnificent destinations on the planet is just outside. You can best see it, feel it, smell it, and taste it from a hot-air balloon hovering over the tops of tall Jeffrey pines or from a kayak sliding silently through crystal-clear waters, or from a forest trail meandering through a meadow hip-high with wildflowers.

This chapter is chock-full of suggestions to help you make the very most out of your time in the Reno/Tahoe area. But whatever activities you choose, remember the most important thing is to relax and have fun.

AUTO RACING

The Reno/Tahoe area is devoid of auto-racing facilities, but if you're a die-hard enthusiast of the "fastest sport in America," I have listed two oval tracks and a drag strip that are close enough to make the drive worthwhile.

Rattlesnake Raceway
2000 Airport Road
Fallon, NV
(775) 423-7483
http://rattlesnakeraceway.tripod.com

Rattlesnake Raceway, located at Rattlesnake Hill in Fallon, offers mud-slinging action Saturday nights and occasional Sunday afternoons April through November. It's the oldest operating oval dirt track in Nevada. The schedule varies, so call or visit their Web site for specifics. Racing fans can expect to pay about $8.00 for a night of racing that can include street stocks, bombers, and Gen X cars. Track modifications in 2005 increased the length, making the track run faster.

To get to Fallon from Reno, take Interstate 80 east to exit 48 (East Fernley). Continue over the railroad overpass and turn left onto Alternate U.S. Highway 50 and follow the signs to Fallon. (For other activities in Fallon, see the Day Trips chapter.)

Reno-Fernley Raceway
Alternate U.S. Highway 95
Fernley, NV
(775) 575-7217
www.reno-fernleyraceway.com

Reno-Fernley Raceway's oval is called the "Racing Field of Dreams" and is located about 36 miles from Reno. Recent expansion added 2.1 miles to the original ⅜-mile track. This facility has it all: clay oval racing, motocross tracks, off-road racing, sand drags, BMX, and go-kart racing. Oval track racing is presented every Saturday during the summer months, with racing action in IMCA & Outlaw modifieds, street stocks, hobby stocks, modified minis, and pure stock minis. The spectator gates open at 3:00 P.M., and racing action begins at 6:00 P.M. Admission ranges from $5.00 to $15.00. The track also offers a special pit pass for $10 to $20. Telephone the track or access its Web site for the detailed schedule of events. Overnight campers are welcome. To help keep kids amused throughout the race day, Herbie's Paintball Games is open from 10:00 A.M. to 4:00 P.M.

To get to the raceway, take I-80 east from Reno to exit 46 (West Fernley). Follow Main Street until the intersection of Alternate US 95. Take Alternate US 95 about 6 miles until you see the signs for the raceway on the right-hand side of the highway.

Top Gun Raceway
U.S. Highway 95, Fallon, NV
(775) 423-0223, (800) 325-7448
www.topgunraceway.com
This is the only sanctioned NHRA drag strip in northern Nevada. The 0.25-mile drag strip is located just 10 miles south of Fallon on US 95 and features drag racing in several different classes on Saturday and Sunday from March through November. For the daytime drags the gates open at 8:00 A.M., with time trials beginning at 9:30 A.M. and the actual races beginning at 1:30 P.M. For the evening drags the gates open at 10:00 A.M., with time runs from 5:00 to 10:00 P.M. Tickets run from $8.00 to $15.00, depending on the type of drags.

To get to Fallon from Reno, take I-80 east to exit 48 (East Fernley). Continue over the railroad overpass and turn left onto Alternate US 50 and follow the signs to Fallon. Once in Fallon, pick up US 95 south and follow signs to the raceway. (For more things to do in Fallon, see the Day Trips chapter.)

BACKPACKING

If you can't get enough of nature with a simple day hike, rest assured that most area hiking destinations are also suitable for overnight camping. With its huge variety of lakes, the Desolation Wilderness is one of the most popular backpacking areas (see the "Hiking" section later in this chapter). Once in the wilderness, you can spend days backpacking from lake to lake.

You can split up longer hikes to any destination by overnight stays, or you can hike into a single site and stay for a day or two. I suggest stopping at visitor centers (see the Attractions chapter for locations) or the USDA Forest Service office at 870 Emerald Bay Road in South Lake Tahoe (530-573-2674) for more information. Be sure to have maps and proper equipment if you're backpacking, and remember you'll need a permit for the Desolation Wilderness. See the "Hiking" section in this chapter for some suggested destinations.

BALLOONING

Lake Tahoe Balloons
South Lake Tahoe, CA
(530) 544-1221, (800) 872-9294
www.laketahoeballoons.com
When you book a flight with Lake Tahoe Balloons, you can marvel at the majesty of the lake from two vantage points: floating over it in a hot-air balloon and floating on it in a 40-foot catamaran. After flying over verdant mountain meadows and hovering above the crystal-clear waters of the lake, the balloon lands on the boat, where you can indulge in a delicious champagne brunch while cruising back to shore. The cost of the three-hour trip is $225 per person, and reservations are required. The company offers free shuttle transportation within the South Lake Tahoe area and customized wedding services, too. All flights begin at sunrise and are seasonal.

Mountain High Balloons
Truckee, CA
(530) 587-6922, (775) 746-4159
The oldest balloon company in the Reno/Tahoe area, Mountain High Balloons will take you up, up, and away on half-hour and one-hour trips in the Truckee area. The balloons lift off from nearby Prosser

Reservoir and then drift lazily over the Martis Valley south of downtown Truckee. You can see gorgeous views of Lake Tahoe to the south and pick pinecones from the tops of huge trees. Floating through the peace and quiet as the sun rises to the east is an incredibly special way to greet a summer day.

The cost per person is $110 for a half hour and $175 for one hour. Kids younger than 10 years old can fly free when accompanied by an adult (limit of one child per adult). Children 10 to 16 years old are half price. Flights are available at 7:00 A.M. daily from May through November, but reservations are necessary. (For more to do and see in Truckee, see the Day Trips chapter.)

BIKING

Due to the hundreds of miles of dirt roads and paved paths that give ready access to the great outdoors, biking in the Reno/Tahoe area is very popular. You'll see cyclists everywhere, zipping along city streets and huffing up rocky mountain paths. Whether you're an experienced rider or first-time-ever cyclist, you'll find terrain and paths just right for you. You can enjoy biking on paved streets and paths, on dirt roads and trails, and in mountain bike parks complete with chairlifts. It's not possible to list all the opportunities and adventures that await you, since it's simply too exhaustive, but I will tell you about some of the favorite rides around the area to give you an idea of the variety of biking fun that's available.

Be aware that many of the paths and trails I describe in the "Walking/Running" and "Hiking" sections of this chapter are also suitable for biking. For maps and other routes, I suggest you stop at area visitor centers (see the Attractions chapter for locations) and also inquire at local bike shops. Also see the Parks chapter for information about walking/biking paths in local parks.

Before heading out, it's important to be aware of a few basic safety rules for biking in the Reno/Tahoe area. Always plan ahead by knowing where you're going and whether the skills of everyone in the group are suited to the expected terrain. Some strenuous routes are not advisable for children, for example. If you're not familiar with a particular trail, find out from appropriate authorities what it's like. Dress for the weather, and be prepared for the sudden storms that frequently come up in the mountains. Use sunscreen and carry plenty of water and snacks. And last, but not least, know the courteous rules of the trail and practice them. Since many trails are shared with others—walkers, joggers, hunters, anglers, animals, and four-wheel-drive vehicles—be ready to yield the trail and ride under control at all times.

If you're interested in biking clubs in Reno, you can contact the Procrastinating Pedalers at president@pedalers.org and the Reno Wheelmen at (775) 690-7385; president@renowheelmen.org. Web sites are www.pedalers.org and www.renowheelmen.org.

Angora Ridge
Fallen Leaf Campground, 2 miles north of South Lake Tahoe, CA, off California Highway 89

For spectacular views of Fallen Leaf Lake and Mt. Tallac, you can take this moderate 8-mile round-trip jaunt to lovely Angora Lakes. Starting at Fallen Leaf Campground, where you can park your car, pedal along Fallen Leaf Lake Road. Take the first left, continue for about 0.5 mile to Angora Ridge Road, and then turn right. Be prepared for a veritable Kodak moment when you reach the abandoned Angora Lookout—the panoramic view from the saddle of this glacial moraine is stunning, to say the least. Just down the road you'll find a dirt parking lot where you can lock up your bike to follow the last 0.5 mile of the route on foot. Your reward at the end of the trail is two sparkling alpine lakes, with a rustic resort tucked on the shore of the second lake. Be sure to save time for a refreshing swim and lunch.

General Creek Loop Ride
Sugar Pine Point State Park
California Highway 89, 1 mile south of Tahoma, CA
(530) 525-7982
www.parks.ca.gov

You don't have to have legs of steel for the General Creek Loop Ride. In fact, you can be a first-time mountain biker and get along just fine. Snaking through the forest for about 6 miles, the trail is mostly level and easy to navigate. Look for the trailhead in Sugar Pine Point State Park (see the Parks chapter for more about this lovely park).

Hidden Valley Regional Park
4740 Parkway Drive, Reno, NV
(775) 828-6612
www.washoecountyparks.com

With 480 acres, Hidden Valley Regional Park boasts an interesting variety of paved and dirt trails for both hiking and biking. Tucked at the base of mountains on the east side of Reno, it offers great views of the city and the Sierra Nevada mountains to the west. It's one of the few places close to town where outdoor enthusiasts can wander for long distances just exploring the natural landscape. A large herd of wild horses inhabits the range above the park, and the animals are often in view. The park also provides a riding arena, children's playground, restrooms, and a picnic area.

Marlette Lake/Flume Trail
Trailhead at Spooner Lake, junction of U.S. Highway 50 and Nevada Highway 28
(775) 831-0494
www.parks.nv.gov

A heart-stopping ride for intermediate bikers and above, the Flume Trail will thrill you with challenging terrain and awesome views of Lake Tahoe. The trail follows an old water flume line, climbing about 5 miles to Marlette Lake, and then continuing another 7 miles to Tunnel Creek Road. Call the park about shuttle service during the summer months. I don't recommend a round-trip of 24 miles, since the first 12 are rugged enough for most bikers.

The most difficult part of this ride is the 7 miles past Marlette Lake, where the narrow trail hugs a ledge with sheer drop-offs toward Lake Tahoe far below. You should be in good physical shape and not be afraid of heights to ride this trail. It's not for families and not for children. You might want to try a trial run to test your stamina by riding the 10-mile round-trip to Marlette Lake and back first.

North Tahoe Regional Park
875 National Avenue, Tahoe Vista, CA
(530) 546-5043
www.northlaketahoe.net/parks.html

With 5 miles of dirt paths winding through the trees, the trail system at North Tahoe Regional Park offers gentle runs for beginners and steeper terrain for more-advanced riders. Never crowded and close to residential areas, it's a favorite with locals year-round. See the Winter Sports and Parks chapters for more details on this fun-filled spot in Tahoe Vista.

Northstar-at-Tahoe
California Highway 267, 6 miles north of Lake Tahoe
(530) 562-1010
www.skinorthstar.com

With more than 100 miles of forested trails to explore, Northstar-at-Tahoe offers Lake Tahoe's most extensive mountain bike park. You can enjoy everything from gentle leisurely loops to stiff uphill climbs, including jaunts to Watson Lake and Northstar Reservoir. There's something for everyone, and best of all, you can conserve your stamina by taking advantage of Northstar chairlifts. Northstar skiers especially like to bike their favorite ski runs, because the terrain appears so much different when it's devoid of snow. When you're ready for a refreshing lunch break, you can head down to the village at the base of the mountain, where you'll find a variety of restaurants along with special events on weekends. (I tell you more about this first-class resort in the Resorts and Winter Sports chapters.)

Tom Cook Trail
Woodland Avenue, 4 miles west of Reno, NV
(775) 828-6642
You may have to get off and push part of the way, but the Tom Cook Trail gives access to the Steamboat Ditch Trail along with a bona fide maze of other trails to explore west of Reno. Follow West Fourth Street west of town and turn left onto Woodland Avenue at the sign for Mayberry Park. After parking at the park, cross the footbridge over the Truckee River on the west end of the park (near Patagonia's building). The Tom Cook Trail starts here, and your biking adventure can unfold as you see fit. Because this terrain is fragile, it's important to stay on the trails to minimize your impact.

BILLIARD PARLORS

Though you won't be overwhelmed with options for billiards in the Reno/Tahoe area, here are my favorites if eight-ball is your game.

Classic Cue
1965 Lake Tahoe Boulevard
South Lake Tahoe, CA
(530) 541-8704
Classic Cue calls itself the best billiard room and burger joint on the lake. Besides its 10 pool tables, there's also indoor hoops, Foosball, and darts. This pool hall also provides patrons with a satellite TV. Mostly frequented by a younger crowd, Classic Cue also repairs and sells pool cues. The hours of operation are from 11:00 A.M. to midnight weekdays and from noon to midnight weekends.

Diamond Billiards
5890 South Virginia Street
Reno, NV
(775) 828-0616
With 13 4-foot by 9-foot, top-of-the-line Robertson Black Max pool tables, Diamond Billiards is a classy place. The equipment is meticulously maintained, and players appreciate the attention to detail. Formerly Breaktime Billiards, the parlor now sports a separate cigar lounge along with a full bar and poker machines. The action never stops here because it's open 24/7. Rates are around $9.00 per hour, with the second hour free except Friday and Saturday nights.

Keystone Cue & Cushion
935 West Fifth Street
Reno, NV
(775) 323-2828
The younger crowd likes to congregate here, and Keystone Cue does its best to cater to them. It has 11 regulation-size pool tables and one coin-operated, shorter, bar pool table. Keystone serves beer and wine along with some of the best hamburgers in town. It also has a video arcade. This is a favorite hangout of the university pool shooters. It is open from 10:00 A.M. to 2:00 A.M. Monday through Thursday, 10:00 A.M. to 3:00 A.M. Friday and Saturday, and noon to midnight Sunday. Charges are prorated by the minute but work out to be between $4.00 and $6.00 per hour per person for the pool table. There's a second location at 300 North Center Street in Reno, (775) 322-2001.

Q's Billiard Club
3350 South Virginia Street
Reno, NV
(775) 825-2337
This over-21 club likes to call itself the coolest pool hall in Reno. The going rate for shooting a game of pool on any of its 15 tables is around $8.00 per hour. You can rack them up here from 11:00 A.M. to 3:00 A.M. daily.

BOATING

Nowhere is boating more popular than on the sapphire-blue water of Lake Tahoe. Just imagine gliding across the ripple-free water in the morning with the sun's rays glancing off the mirrorlike surface and soaking up some of the most spectacular scenery in the United States. On any given day, especially during the warmer months, you can see every type of watercraft imaginable navigating the lake from before sunrise to well after sunset. Here, I list the ramps available for launching your private boat, as well as facilities that will rent you just about any type of watercraft to fit your fancy: speedboats, fishing boats, sailboats, pontoon boats, paddle-boats, canoes, kayaks, Jet Skis, WaveRunners, sailboards, and float tubes.

Boat Ramps

All the boat ramps listed charge a fee for launching except Kings Beach, which charges a $5.00 parking fee. The launch fees range from $5.00 each way for the little boats to $35.00 each way for the bigger boats. All the launch facilities listed have paved ramps.

Cave Rock
near Zephyr Cove, NV
(775) 831-0494

El Dorado
South Lake Tahoe, CA
(530) 542-6056

Homewood Marina
near Homewood, CA
(530) 525-5966

Kings Beach
North Tahoe Public Utility District
Kings Beach, CA
(530) 546-4212

Lake Forest Beach
between Tahoe City and Carnelian Bay, CA
(530) 583-3796

Meeks Bay Resort
Meeks Bay, CA
(530) 525-6946, (530) 525-5588

North Tahoe Marina
Tahoe Vista, CA
(530) 546-8248

Obexer's
between Meeks Bay and Homewood, CA
(530) 525-7962

Sand Harbor
Incline Village, NV
(775) 831-0494

Sierra Boat Company
Carnelian Bay, CA
(530) 546-2551

Sunnyside Marina
near Tahoe City, CA
(530) 583-7201

Tahoe Keys Marina
South Lake Tahoe, CA
(530) 541-2155

Zephyr Cove Marina
Zephyr Cove, NV
(775) 588-3833

Boat and Watercraft Rentals

You can find all kinds of watercraft on Lake Tahoe. At last count, about 25 water-sports rental businesses encircle the lake, where you can rent just about anything that floats. Although you'll see boats on the lake almost all year, water-sports rentals are seasonal, with most of these establishments operating during summer and early fall only.

Sailing the translucent water of Lake Tahoe has been a longtime recreational activity, and when the wind kicks up in the afternoon, you'll see why. Sailboarding has also become a popular sport on the lake, and every afternoon brave souls can be seen whipping over the waves, seemingly hanging on for their lives. And if power-

One of the best ways to experience Lake Tahoe is from a boat. TERRY BAADE

boats are more to your liking, speedboat rentals are available for the novice to the advanced boater.

Prices for the rentals seem to change every season and are dependent on the size of the watercraft, the time of the year, and the time of day. Generally, hourly rental rates are close to these prices: powerboats, $110 to $200; sailboats, $40 to $60; paddleboats, $20; fishing and pontoon boats, $35 to $60; canoes and kayaks, $20 to $30; Jet Skis and WaveRunners, $100 to $125; and water-ski tows, $40 to $50.

Action Watersports of Tahoe
3411 U.S. Highway 50
South Lake Tahoe, CA
(530) 544-5387

967 Lakeshore Boulevard
Incline Village, NV
(775) 831-4386
www.action-watersports.com

Action Watersports is located at Timber Cove Marina and rents just about anything that floats. From powerboats to floating lounge chairs, this concession rents them out at some of the most reasonable rates around the lake. Hours are 9:00 A.M. to 6:00 P.M. during the summer months only. Other locations are Meeks Bay, Camp Richardson, and the Hyatt Regency Lake Tahoe Resort, Spa & Casino.

Camp Richardson Marina
1900 Jameson Beach Road
South Lake Tahoe, CA
(530) 542-6570
www.camprichardson.com

This marina is open from May through the end of September from 8:00 A.M. to 8:00 P.M. and offers the best selection of powerboats on the lake. It has Four Winns bowriders, two-person WaveRunners, pontoon boats, kayaks, canoes, and paddleboats. Its location at Camp Richardson makes it a popular and sometimes crowded place. This is one of the only rental concessions that accepts reservations.

Captain Kirk's Beach Club
Zephyr Cove, NV
(775) 589-4908
The Captain's is located at Zephyr Cove Marina and offers almost every type of watercraft for rent. It specializes in powerboats and Jet Skis. It also offers parasailing (see the "Parasailing" section in this chapter). It's open during the summer from 8:00 A.M. to 5:00 P.M. You can write to Captain Kirk's at P.O. Box 481, Zephyr Cove, NV 89448.

H2O Sports
Stateline, NV
(775) 588-4155
www.rphbeach.com
This shop guarantees the lowest rental prices at the lake. H2O has a full line of water-sports rental equipment. It's located 2 miles north of Stateline at Round Hill Pines Beach. It also provides a daily tour of Emerald Bay by SeaDoos. Write to them, if you like, at P.O. Box 311, Stateline, NV 89449.

Tahoe City Marina
700 North Lake Boulevard
Tahoe City, CA
(530) 583-1039
www.tahoecitymarina.com
Tahoe City Marina specializes in powerboat rentals but also has a 21-foot sailboat. It's also a full-service marina that offers fuel and docking and is close to two shopping centers. The marina is open from 8:00 A.M. to 6:00 P.M. during the summer.

Tahoe Sailing Center
700 North Lake Boulevard
Tahoe City, CA
(530) 583-6200
www.tahoesail.com
If you'd like to set sail on Lake Tahoe, this center has it all—skippered sailing cruises, yacht charters, sailing lessons, and regatta racing. Here you can enjoy sailing by yourself or sit back and let someone else do all the work while you enjoy the lake's spectacular scenery. The company offers two-hour trips for $40 or $50 per person. Tahoe Sailing Center is the ultimate sailing rental business on the lake.

BOWLING

The Reno/Tahoe area is usually known around the United States because of its outdoor recreation, but if indoor sports are more to your liking, you have to try the bowling alleys scattered around the area. Remember, too, that if watching professionals hit the lanes is your thing, Reno's National Bowling Stadium has top-ranked tournaments (see the Spectator Sports chapter for more details). If you're relocating here and would like to join a league, contact the individual bowling alleys for more details on league play. Most alleys offer open bowling, but because league schedules vary, you should call for availability.

AMF Starlite Bowl
1201 Stardust Street
Reno, NV
(775) 747-3522
www.amf.com/starlitelanes
This bowling alley is the oldest in Reno and a favorite hangout of Insiders. It has 32 lanes, a snack bar, and video poker machines. Hours are 9:00 A.M. to midnight Sunday through Thursday and 9:00 A.M. to 1:00 A.M. Friday and Saturday.

Bowl Incline
920 Southwood Boulevard
Incline Village, NV
(775) 831-1900
This bowling alley bills itself as the North Shore's only complete family recreation center. Bowl Incline has 16 lanes with automatic scoring, bumper bowling, a pool table, a video arcade, video poker machines, darts, a bar, and a full-swing golf simulator. Sundays are designated smoke-free. The alley is open from 11:00 A.M. to midnight every day. Open bowling prices are $3.75 per game.

Grand Sierra Resort and Casino
2500 East Second Street, Reno, NV
(775) 789-2296
www.grandsierraresort.com

The Grand Sierra has a 50-lane bowling alley that is the most popular in the Reno/Tahoe area. Even though it's open 24 hours per day, 7 days a week, bowling is on a first-come, first-served basis. The best times to find an open lane are early afternoon or late evening. Rates depend upon the time of day, topping out at $3.50 per game and $3.50 for shoes. The most expensive time to bowl is between 6:00 P.M. and midnight and on all holidays. Lower rates are available for children and seniors during the week.

Greenbrae Lanes
670 Greenbrae Drive, Sparks, NV
(775) 358-4477

Greenbrae has 24 lanes, video poker machines, a bar, and a pool table. It charges $3.00 a game for bowling plus $2.50 to rent shoes. It's open from noon to midnight during winter and 11:00 A.M. to 9:00 P.M. in summer.

Tahoe Bowl
1030 Fremont Avenue
South Lake Tahoe, CA
(530) 544-3700

This bowling alley has 16 synthetic lanes and features lighted bumper bowling and a video arcade. It's open from 11:00 A.M. to 11:00 P.M. Tuesday through Thursday, 11:00 A.M. to midnight Friday and Saturday, and 2:00 P.M. to midnight Sunday and Monday. It's relatively quiet during the summer months, so open bowling is no problem. During winter, show up before 6:00 P.M. to get a lane. Rates vary but are in line with other bowling facilities.

CANOEING

If canoeing is your aquatic preference, Lake Tahoe is the perfect spot to take to the paddle. The scenery is magnificent and the water is crystal clear, making a trip by canoe a tranquil adventure. Most canoers cruise close to the shoreline because once the wind picks up, often with no warning, staying upright can be a big challenge. You don't see canoes on the Truckee River because of its swift current and because of the many hazardous boulders poking out from beneath the water. The Truckee River is preferred by rafting and kayaking enthusiasts. Canoes can be rented from the many water-sport companies around the lake (see the "Boat and Watercraft Rentals" section under "Boating" earlier in this chapter).

i

AMF Starlite Bowl offers Xtreme Bowling, an adventure with lights and music.

DISC GOLF

With the cost of playing a round of golf going up, up, up, it's refreshing to find a course that's absolutely free. But you won't be teeing off with a Big Bertha driver, and you won't be chipping out of sand traps. Instead you'll be throwing golf discs (similar to Frisbees) into a series of baskets that are laid out in a golf course format. Played in several area parks, disc golf has been growing in popularity by about 15 percent a year since 1996. It's far less structured than traditional golf and offers a great way for families to get out and have fun in the sun together.

You can try your skill at this up-and-coming sport at Bijou Community Park in South Lake Tahoe, where you'll find an interesting 27-hole layout that's been challenging local golfers since 1994. The park is on Al Tahoe Boulevard, about 1 mile southeast of the boulevard's intersection with US 50. For information call (530) 542-6095 (see the Parks chapter for more details about the park).

You can also tee off at Zephyr Cove Park in Zephyr Cove. To reach the park, drive about 6 miles north of Stateline on US 50, turn right onto Warrior Way, and follow the drive in the park to the end. For information call (775) 586-7271.

If you're in the mood for a drive, try the 18-hole Disc-wood course at Kirkwood Mountain Resort, (209-258-6000), about 90 minutes from Reno, or Truckee Regional Park in Truckee, CA (530-582-7720). (See the Winter Sports chapter for details about Kirkwood Mountain.)

DIVING

Although you won't see coral reefs and schools of tropical fish, diving in Lake Tahoe is a spectacular experience because the water is so clear. Due to visibility from 45 to 90 feet in the summer, you'll feel as if you can reach out and touch the native fish swimming by, including rainbow, brown, and cutthroat trout. But remember the temperature of the water is anything but warm: You'll need drysuits to protect yourself against the frigid water. If you're inexperienced in high-altitude diving, I suggest you contact a dive school for proper training.

Sierra Diving Center
104 East Grove Street
Reno, NV
(775) 825-2147
www.sierradive.com
With more than 30 years of experience in Lake Tahoe diving, Sierra Diving Center can certainly claim to be experts on the subject. The company offers a full range of dive services, including PADI-certified classes, instructor certification, technical training, equipment sales and rentals, and tours. If you've ever had a yen to scuba dive, the professionals here will make it easy for you with short evening and weekend sessions.

To dive safely in Lake Tahoe, you can take the one-day Altitude Specialty Course, which includes two open dives in the lake plus training in all the high-altitude changes that affect divers. For up-to-date schedules and prices, call the number above or access their Web page.

Tropical Penguins Scuba & Water Sports
180 West Peckham Lane, Suite 1160
Reno, NV
(775) 828-3483
www.tropicalpenguinscuba.com
Whether you're a first-timer or an experienced diver just needing a refresher course, the professional staff at Tropical Penguins Scuba & Water Sports will help you splash into the underwater world of adventure. Classes at this complete dive facility include basic and advanced open-water certification, rescue diver, divemaster, instructor development, scuba tune-up, and specialty courses such as altitude diving. The shop features all levels of PADI and ANDI certification plus equipment sales and rentals.

Before you decide to explore the hidden treasures of Lake Tahoe (or other dive sites included in their travel packages), I suggest you stop by and assess your readiness to dive with their trained staff. Call for schedules and prices on travel and classes.

FOUR-WHEELING/ OFF-ROAD ADVENTURES

You'll definitely want to bring your camera or camcorder if you decide to strike out on an off-road tour in the Reno/Tahoe area. One visitor called his four-wheeling trip near Lake Tahoe "the best half-day of my life." If off-roading has been something you've always wanted to try, Lake Tahoe has the premier company to hook up with.

Lake Tahoe Adventures
South Lake Tahoe, CA
(530) 577-2940, (800) 865-4679
www.laketahoeadventures.com
This company offers off-road tours ranging from easy to rugged and challenging. Tours include riding the trails in ATVs, Jeeps, and Hummers, for varying amounts of time. A six-hour tour on the Rubicon Trail is $275 per person; a two-hour trip to Genoa Peak is $55 per person.

Other tours are available, such as the historic desert tour and tours by snowmobile in winter. A yacht is available for touring on Lake Tahoe as well. This company also provides custom tours, so if you have something special in mind, just ask. Reservations are required.

GO-KARTS

Wild Island
250 Wild Island Court, Sparks, NV
(775) 359-2927
www.wildisland.com
Wild Island has a wonderful go-kart racing facility. The raceway has two tracks, one for larger children and one for smaller. The big kids get to drive gas-powered Indy cars, and the little ones drive gas-powered Sprint cars. The cost for the Indy cars is $5.50 for five minutes; for the Sprint cars it's $3.25 for five minutes. In addition to the go-karts, Wild Island has a water park, miniature golf courses, and an assortment of other attractions for kids of all ages.

HANG GLIDING

Adventure Sports
3650-22 Research Way, Carson City, NV
(775) 883-7070
www.pyramid.net/advspts/
In summer, hang gliders are a common sight around Mt. Rose and other peaks along the eastern escarpment as they launch from the high peaks and flirt with the warm currents of air rising from the high desert.

If you've ever wanted to "fly," you should consider learning in the Reno/Tahoe area: The Sierra Nevada offers one of the premier soaring sites in the country. You can earn your wings by taking hang-gliding or paragliding lessons with the professionals at Adventure Sports. A 25-hour hang-gliding or paragliding course will teach you about aerodynamics and the basics of flight in both ground school and on-the-hill training. You can book tandem hang gliding over Lake Tahoe for $179.

Whether you choose to soar in a more stable hang glider, with rigid wings spanning about 18 feet, or to use a paraglider—a parachute that can be stowed in a backpack, enabling the flyer to launch from sites inaccessible to hang gliders—Adventure Sports is a good place to begin.

HIKING

Although you can appreciate the beauty of the Reno/Tahoe area driving through it in your car, the very best way to experience this wonderland is to grab your backpack and hit the trail. Fields of wildflowers, rushing mountain streams, and the crunch of pine needles underfoot await explorers of one of the most gorgeous natural habitats in the world. These hikes are not necessarily extreme: The Reno/Tahoe area encompasses treks for hikers of all abilities. You don't have to scale Mt. Tallac to be a hiker. You can take a leisurely stroll in Tahoe Meadows (one of my very favorite outings any time of the year) and still enjoy nature at its very finest.

In this section I describe some of the not-to-be-missed hikes in the area, which I'm sure you'll enjoy. But with hundreds of miles of trails, I can't list all the magical destinations awaiting your discovery. I leave those for you to find with the aid of maps you can pick up at visitor centers (see the Attractions chapter for locations). Be sure to check out the large variety of hikes in area parks and historical sites. You can take easy jaunts at Spooner Lake and Sand Harbor (see the Parks chapter) and also at the Taylor Creek Visitor Center and the Tallac Historic Site (see the Attractions chapter).

Because this lovely mountain environment is so very fragile, it's important that every visitor minimize his or her impact on the area. Hikers should be especially careful to not disturb the surrounding areas of their wilderness destinations. Zero-impact guidelines include:

- Pack it in, pack it out: Don't leave any trash on the trail. Whether it's biodegradable or not, human discards are not part of the natural environment and may prove harmful to both the flora and fauna of the wilderness.
- Use restroom facilities at the trailheads. If you must "go" on the trail, pack out your waste and toilet paper. Even if human waste is buried, animals can dig it up. Carry a plastic zip-locked bag, and add a little baking soda to absorb odor.
- Don't pollute streams or lakes.
- Stay on the trails to reduce damage to the fragile environment. Shortcutting causes erosion.
- Enjoy the wildflowers, but never pick them; similarly, don't remove artifacts from the trails. Leave them for the next hiker to enjoy.

For more information about responsible hiking, you can call Leave No Trace, Inc., at (800) 332-4100.

For your safety and comfort, always dress properly and be prepared for sudden changes in the weather. All trails around Lake Tahoe are at high altitude; familiarize yourself with the symptoms of altitude sickness, and retreat to a lower elevation if you or one of your party should exhibit signs of this serious illness. The sun is more intense at high altitude, so be sure to wear sunscreen and carry a hat and clothing to protect yourself from harmful rays. Carry a map so you know exactly where you're going and about how long it will take to get there; Tom Harrison's Recreation Map of Lake Tahoe is a good one. Be sure to take food, water, and first-aid items in your backpack. Don't drink the water in the wild unless you have water purification tablets or a good portable filter. Many hikers have learned the hard way that even though the water in mountain streams looks crystal clear, it contains *Giardia lamblia,* an organism that can cause severe intestinal disease.

Also be aware that no fires are allowed in the wild. If you're hiking with dogs, keep them under control and don't let them wander too far from you. For more tips about dos and don'ts in the backcountry, see the Winter Sports chapter.

Miles and miles of hiking trails in the Tahoe area are described on the Internet. You can visit generic outdoor sites like www.gorp.com for more information; or log on to your favorite browser, search for hiking in Tahoe, and explore.

Desolation Wilderness
Southwest of South Lake Tahoe, CA
(530) 573-2600
www.fs.fed.us/r5/ltbmu/

Spanning about 100 square miles high above Lake Tahoe, the Desolation Wilderness is a veritable Shangri-la for hikers and backpackers. Tucked into the backcountry are more than 100 shimmering alpine lakes and 20 majestic peaks towering more than 9,000 feet above sea level. Exploring this entire wonderland would take months: I can't possibly describe in detail all of the hikes you'll find here. I suggest you pick up maps from area visitor centers (see the Attractions chapter for directions) or from the USDA Forest Service office at 870 Emerald Bay Road in South Lake Tahoe. You'll also need a free permit to day hike in the wilderness and a backcountry permit to spend the night. Permits can be obtained from the Forest Service or at the trailheads. Since the number of overnight permits is limited, you should call (530) 644-6048 for reservations.

You can access the wilderness from these major trailheads: Eagle Falls, Glen Alpine, and Echo Lakes. Eagle Falls is 5 miles northwest of South Lake Tahoe on CA 89, directly across from the parking lot at Emerald Bay. Glen Alpine is at the southwest end of Fallen Leaf Lake. To reach the lake from South Lake Tahoe, take CA 89 northwest from its junction with US 50 for about 3 miles. Turn left (west) onto Fallen Leaf Road; continue on Fallen Leaf Road for about 5 miles to a junction, then follow the signs to Lily Lake. To reach Lower Echo Lake, take US 50 southwest from South Lake Tahoe past Echo Summit, and turn right onto Johnson Pass Road. Continue through this residential area to the parking lots at the lake.

One of the most popular hikes in the wilderness is to Eagle Lake, a 1-mile jaunt from the Eagle Falls trailhead that climbs through huge stands of trees. Stunning views of Lake Tahoe are behind you; you can enjoy these more easily on the descent. Eagle Lake is a tiny azure jewel, perfect for a cold dip and picnicking. If you continue on this trail another 4 or 5 miles, you'll reach Middle Velma, Upper Velma, and Fontanillis Lakes. Be prepared for a trail that's steep and rocky in places.

Starting from the Glen Alpine trailhead, you can make an uphill climb of about 6 miles, past Grass, Suzie, and Heather Lakes, to Lake Aloha, perched in a glacial area on top of the Sierra Crest. Return as you came, or make any of several long loops back to Fallen Leaf Lake.

An outing perfect for families begins at the marina on Lower Echo Lake. You can take a 15-minute water taxi across the lake and through the channel connecting to Upper Echo Lake. From the dock at the west end of Upper Echo Lake, you can take a leisurely 3-mile stroll back to the marina at Lower Echo Lake or continue west to a variety of lakes in the Desolation Wilderness, including Ralston, Tamarack, Lake of the Woods, and Lake Aloha.

Five Lakes
Trailhead 2.2 miles west of California Highway 89 on Alpine Meadows Road 6 miles north of Tahoe City, CA

Snuggled in alpine country on the back side of Squaw Peak, Five Lakes (none of which are named) is a popular destination for hikers, anglers, and dogwalkers. The round-trip jaunt is only about 5 miles, with an elevation gain of about 1,000 feet. The well-marked trail is rocky in spots but very easy to follow.

From the trailhead on Alpine Meadows Road, the path climbs sharply through forest sprinkled with an eclectic variety of wildflowers (if you're hiking in spring or summer). After about a mile, the trail breaks into the open and you're treated to breathtaking views of the granite peaks around Alpine Meadows ski resort.

Approaching the lakes, you enter the forest again, and if you look up to the north you can see the ski lifts on top of Squaw Peak and KT-22 at Squaw Valley USA. You can wander around from lake to lake and find your own little Eden for swimming and relaxing. Although this area gets heavy use during high season, it's still possible to find a niche of privacy to enjoy the day. But if you're looking for a total wilderness experience, this probably won't fit the bill, unless you hike after Labor Day.

To reach the trailhead from Tahoe City, go north on CA 89 about 6 miles to Alpine Meadows Road and follow it for about 2.2 miles. The trailhead is on the right side of the road in a residential area and is marked by a GRANITE CHIEF WILDERNESS sign. You'll need to park along the road.

Marlette Lake
Trailhead at Spooner Lake, junction of U.S. Highway 50 and Nevada Highway 28

With an elevation gain of 1,157 feet, the 5-mile hike to Marlette Lake is a bit of a challenge but well worth the effort. The dirt path is wide and easy to follow, but it's aerobic for most hikers, given its steady ascent. As you hike through North Canyon to the lake, you'll climb past thick aspen groves, velvety alpine meadows, and tumbling mountain creeks. In spring and summer you'll see wildflowers ablaze with color everywhere, and in fall you can enjoy the reds, golds, and yellows of the mountain landscape.

When you arrive at the lake, be sure to take time to picnic in this special alpine hideaway. Anglers can try their luck at catching the large trout that are usually quite close to shore. But don't expect to have a fish dinner—it's catch-and-release only. You can continue on toward the Flume Trail, a harrowing 7-mile plunge down the ridge to Incline Village. Drink in the great views of Lake Tahoe from the start of the Flume Trail, but don't go farther, since it's mainly for hard-core mountain bikers (see the "Biking" section in this chapter for more details). Be on the lookout for cyclists throughout this hike, particularly those on the downhill run from the lake.

Marlette Lake is not only scenic but historic as well. A system of flumes (including the one along the Flume Trail) used water from the lake to float timber to the silver mines in Virginia City back in its heyday.

Mt. Rose (Peak)
Trailhead 0.5 mile south of summit on Nevada Highway 431

Because so many things have the name "Mt. Rose," I think a brief explanation might head off any confusion you might have. The Mt. Rose Highway (NV 431) connects Reno and Incline Village, passing between the summit of Mt. Rose and Slide Mountain. The highest point of the highway is called the Mt. Rose summit. Mt. Rose–Ski Tahoe ski resort is on Slide Mountain (not on Mt. Rose), and Mt. Rose Peak (the mountain described in this hike) is located northwest of Slide Mountain.

At 10,776 feet, Mt. Rose is the third highest peak in the Reno/Tahoe area and a challenge worth exploring. The view from its barren summit is truly breathtaking, and in spring and summer the trek offers up an explosion of wildflowers that's hard to beat. With an elevation gain of about 2,000 feet, you should be in good shape to take this hike. Proper clothing is also important: Dress in layers to protect yourself from the winds on exposed ridges, and wear comfortable hiking boots suitable for rocky terrain. Be sure to bring plenty of water and snacks, and don't forget your camera to commemorate your summiting the peak.

Hikers have a choice of two routes to the Mt. Rose summit, both from trailheads off NV 431. The first route follows a closed dirt road, which can be accessed from the summit parking lot on the west side of the highway or from the intersection of the road and highway near an old maintenance building southwest of the lot. You can either use the paved parking lot or park along the road near the building. The round-trip to the top using this route is about 12 miles from the building and about 0.5 mile farther from the parking lot.

The first several miles of this route are a steady climb affording views of Lake Tahoe cupped below the peaks of the Desolation Wilderness. The trail passes through radiant fields of wildflowers, including blue lupine, crimson evening primrose, and yellow mule ears. At a small snowmelt pond the path forks: The right-hand path takes you to the top of Mt. Rose and the left to a relay station that also has great views. If you're not up to going to the top, consider hiking to the pond: It's a great 5-mile round-trip outing, with spectacular views and the aforementioned wildflowers. You can also take time to explore the tiny mountain meadow around the pond and see how many wildflowers you can identify.

If you're continuing on to the summit, the path begins a steep rocky ascent from the pond through a series of switchbacks. Breaking through the trees at the top of the mountain, you enter a special environment indeed—an exhilarating alpine habitat awash in the dazzling colors of hardy wildflowers.

A second route to the summit can be accessed from the trailhead sign near the parking lot. Climb up the steps at the sign for a slightly more direct, forested route to the top of the mountain. You won't have views of Lake Tahoe, at least until you begin the final push to the top, but you'll hike through a quiet forest environment with streams and a waterfall.

To reach the trailheads from Reno/Sparks, take U.S. Highway 395 southwest to NV 431. Follow to the parking lot on the right at the summit, or continue just around the corner to the old maintenance building. From Incline Village take NV 431 northeast just past Tahoe Meadows. Look for the building on the left, or keep going to the summit to the parking lot, also on the left.

Mountain trails are a favorite spot for hiking with dogs. JEANNE LAUF WALPOLE

Prey Meadows/Skunk Harbor Trailhead on Nevada Highway 28, 2 miles north of intersection with U.S. Highway 50

You can stroll through a lovely sun-washed meadow brimming with wildflowers and swim and sun in private coves tucked deep in the forest on this hike to the east shore of Lake Tahoe. From NV 28 the trail descends along a sandy road through stands of Jeffrey pine, white fir, and cedar. Along the way you'll see the remains of a railroad grade used in the 1870s as part of a system to supply timber for the mines in Virginia City, Nevada. About 0.5 mile down, the trail forks, with the left branch going to Prey Meadows and the right to Skunk Harbor.

If you choose the left branch in spring and summer, you'll enjoy it all the way down. You'll likely see pink buckwheats, red snowplants, yellow Sierra wallflowers, and purplish-brown spotted mountain bells. Once in the meadow you can wander along the creek and marvel at the tiny flowers clinging to life along its banks. It's a wonderful place to sit back, relax, and enjoy a picnic lunch.

If you choose the right branch of the trail, you'll have a winding descent to the shore of Lake Tahoe, enjoying teasing peeks of the lake as you go. A prominent San Francisco family built the large gray stone structure that sits near the lakeshore in the 1920s as a secluded picnic spot. The tiny beaches along this section of the lake are perfect for private sunbathing and swimming. Just wander along the path and find the perfect spot.

You can visit both Skunk Harbor and Prey Meadows if you allow enough time. The round-trip hike to the harbor is approximately 3 miles, and the hike to Prey Meadows is about the same distance. With an elevation gain of only about 600 feet, the outing is considered moderate and is suitable for most hikers.

To find the trailhead, look for a green

i

Lake Tahoe contains 39 trillion gallons of water.

gate on the west side of NV 28 about 2 miles north of the intersection with US 50. There are several parking pullouts right near the trailhead. See the Parks chapter for more information about the surrounding Lake Tahoe–Nevada State Park.

Rubicon Trail
D. L. Bliss State Park
California Highway 89
9 miles north of South Lake Tahoe, CA
(530) 525-7277
www.cal-parks.ca.gov

Winding along a heavily wooded rocky section of Lake Tahoe shoreline, the Rubicon Trail is a splendid example of the best Tahoe has to offer. With stunning views of deep turquoise water lapping at huge granite boulders, the trail begins in the campground of D. L. Bliss State Park and ends 4.4 miles later at Vikingsholm Castle on Emerald Bay. You can hike the 9-mile round-trip or leave a car in the parking lot above Emerald Bay, about 1 mile up from Vikingsholm.

The only downside to this hike is the difficult parking situation. If you're planning to hike during July or August, it's a good idea to arrive very early in the day. The trailhead is 2.5 miles past the park entrance, and parking near it is very limited. If you're hiking after Labor Day, call ahead to be sure you can drive to the trailhead. Dogs aren't allowed on the trail but are okay in the park if they're leashed. For more information about Bliss and Emerald Bay, see the Parks chapter.

Tahoe Meadows
West of the Mt. Rose summit on Nevada Highway 431

An enchanting carpet spread beneath imposing granite peaks, Tahoe Meadows is an intriguing escape to another world any time of the year (see the Winter Sports chapter for more on fun in the snow at the meadow). But in spring and summer, when the meandering Ophir Creek becomes a series of streams overflowing with snowmelt, the meadow explodes with color as an amazing variety of wildflowers bursts into bloom.

In late spring this alpine paradise becomes a sea of gold with masses of buttercups flowering among the verdant grass. As the season progresses the meadow becomes an ever-changing kaleidoscope of color—the purples of the larkspurs, the oranges and reds of the giant paintbrushes, the whites of the marigolds, and the blues of the alpine veronicas. The colors are stunning and brilliant, almost seeming to shout at you as you stroll along the bubbling streams. But take the time to look closer: Some of the real treasures in this alpine garden are tiny blooms almost hidden from view. Look for delicate alpine shooting stars, clinging in solitary splashes of pinkish-purple along the banks of the streams, or little elephant head flowers, with their miniature pink trunks nodding in the gentle wind.

You can follow the meandering water and variety of paths to the back of the meadow, where the main trail enters the trees and descends to Price Lake and eventually to Davis Creek Park south of Reno on US 395. If you're planning to go all the way to Davis Creek, I suggest you leave a car there, since the round-trip back to NV 431 is about 12 miles.

Tahoe Meadows is really not about long-distance hiking for most locals, however. It's more of a touchstone with nature, a place to sink into the magic of a mountain meadow all year. The real joy is taking the time to smell the flowers (literally) and viewing this special environment as it changes with the seasons. Tahoe Meadows is very dog-friendly (just be careful of the occasional coyote), so be sure to bring Fido along. You'll find the Whole Access section of the trail at the northeast end of the meadow, where a wide, smooth path that is a little more than a mile long is suitable for wheelchairs. Look for the parking lot and trail access just west of the summit.

To reach the meadow from Reno/Sparks, take US 395 southwest to NV 431 (the Mt. Rose Highway) and follow it south to just past the summit. From Incline Village take NV 431 northeast to where it levels out just before the summit. You can park along the road or in the parking lot just west of the summit.

Tahoe Rim Trail
Various access points around Lake Tahoe
Encircling the ridges around Lake Tahoe, the Tahoe Rim Trail offers 150 miles of adventure for hikers, bikers, and equestrians. The terrain varies from flower-strewn meadows to thick forests with spectacular views of the lake sprinkled in between. You can access the trail from six different trailheads: US 50 at Spooner Summit and at Echo Summit; CA 89 at Tahoe City and at Big Meadows near Luther Pass, California; CA 267 at Brockway Summit; and Nevada Highway 207 at Daggett Pass. For more information call (775) 298-0012 or visit www.tahoerimtrail.org.

HORSEBACK RIDING

Verdi Trails
175 Trelease Lane, Verdi, NV
(775) 345-7600, (888) 345-7603
www.verditrailsranch.com
Horseback riding is an old tradition on the east side of the Sierra Nevada, and at Verdi Trails, the wranglers help keep this tradition alive. This outfit caters to families but suggests that the younger riders be at least six years old unless they are experienced. This stable is located at the foot of the mountains, and the rides provide outstanding scenery. Verdi Trails specializes in trail rides, but this is a full-service equestrian center that also offers hayrides, barbecues, and other fun services. The stables open at 9:00 A.M. and close at sunset. The stables are located off I-80 west of Boomtown.

North Shore Riding Stables

There are many places to go horseback riding around the North Shore of Lake Tahoe. All these stables have hourly rides (starting at about $27 per hour) and provide guides. All of these stables also offer riding lessons. Some have hayrides during summer, and some have sleigh rides during winter. Call each stable for the latest info.

Alpine Meadows Stables
California Highway 89, between Tahoe City and Truckee, CA
(530) 583-3905

Northstar Stables
Northstar exit, California Highway 267
Truckee, CA
(530) 562-2480
www.skinorthstar.com
www.ranchoredrock.com

Squaw Valley Stables
Squaw Valley exit, California Highway 89, between Tahoe City and Truckee, CA
(530) 583-7433
www.squaw.com

South Shore Riding Stables

Like the North Shore, the south part of the lake is home to several outfits that rent horses. At most of them, you can take lessons, go on trail rides, go on hayrides, and in winter go on sleigh rides. Prices start at about $30 per hour. Contact each stable for current information.

Camp Richardson Corral
California Highway 89
South Lake Tahoe, CA
(530) 541-3113
www.camprichardson.com

Cascade Stables
California Highway 89, near Cascade Lake, CA
(530) 541-2055

Zephyr Cove Stables
U.S. Highway 50
Zephyr Cove, NV
(775) 588-5664
www.tahoedixie2.com

KAYAKING

Kayaking is wonderful fun and very easy to learn, but if you've never been in a kayak before, I recommend taking a guided tour on which you can learn the basics. Hugging the shoreline of Lake Tahoe, guided tours for first-timers provide a good introduction to the sport without the rough water sometimes found in rivers. If you're an experienced paddler, however, you can rent a kayak and do your own thing, either on the lake or in nearby rivers. It's important to follow safety instructions, whichever way you choose, and to remember that the water of Lake Tahoe is beautiful but can be deadly if you tip over and can't right yourself.

More experienced kayakers should drop their crafts into the Truckee River Whitewater Park in downtown Reno, where river runners can test their skill on its 11 drop pools year-round. See the Annual Events chapter for more information about the Reno River Festival, which showcases slalom racing on this course.

Kayaks Etc.
2505 Sutro Street, Reno, NV
(775) 849-2714
With more than 150 boats in stock, Kayaks Etc. is sure to have the perfect paddle craft just for you. You can choose from expedition, touring, white-water, and recreational kayaks from tried-and-true brands such as Wave Sport, Pyranha, Wilderness Systems, and Prijon Kayaks. Because of the plethora of choices, owner Bob Krause recommends taking advantage of the free personalized demos before investing in a kayak. If you're not in the business of buying, you can rent a craft for $40 to $55 a day, including life preserver and paddle. Krause also offers half-day lessons for $50 and full-day for $100. Summer store hours are 1:00 to 6:00 P.M. weekdays, 10:00 A.M. to 5:00 P.M. Saturday, and 10:00 A.M. to 3:00 P.M. Sunday. Hours are shortened November to May, so call before heading to the store.

Kayak Tahoe
3411 U.S. Highway 50 and Ski Run Boulevard
South Lake Tahoe, CA
(530) 544-2011
www.kayaktahoe.com
For just $30 per person, you can enjoy the splendor of sunset on Lake Tahoe as you take a guided tour along the shore with the experts from Kayak Tahoe. This outfit also offers wildlife tours on the Upper Truckee River for $45 and trips to Emerald Bay for $65. The company rents kayaks for $15 per person (with a 10 percent discount for early birds) and gives lessons. Kayak Tahoe has several locations, including Timber Cove Marina and on Carnelian Bay.

Sierra Adventures
254 West First Street, Reno, NV
(775) 323-8928
www.wildsierra.com
You can't get much closer to the kayak action on the Truckee River than Sierra Adventures. Tucked just steps from the water's edge, the shop is a full-service outfitter with rentals, tours, retail sales, and lessons. You can book a series of six lessons for $199, including gear, or rent a kayak for $19 an hour. Sierra Adventures also rents equipment and provides tours that include other modes of transport, such as bikes, rafts, and ATVs. You'll find the helpful staff on duty from 10:00 A.M. to 6:00 P.M. daily, usually March through November. Winter hours are shortened, with the shop closed on Tuesday and Wednesday.

A kayaker practices back loops in the Truckee River Whitewater Park in downtown Reno.
JAMES PETERSON

Tahoe Paddle & Oar
8299 North Lake Boulevard
Kings Beach, CA
(530) 581-3029
www.tahoepaddle.com

You can explore the picturesque boulder fields and hidden coves of Crystal Bay on a guided tour hosted by Tahoe Paddle & Oar. The cost is $85 per person, with a minimum of two people, and reservations are required. For a longer trip the guides will take you out to Sand Harbor, where you'll paddle your own kayak along the dramatic granite boulders and turquoise waters between Sand Harbor and Secret Harbor. This trip will run you $110, and there is a two-person minimum. If you're a free spirit and want to go it on your own, you can rent a kayak and explore; the cost is $15 per hour.

MARTIAL ARTS

From young children to retired seniors, interest in martial arts is growing in the Reno/Tahoe area. When you check local telephone directories, you'll find a somewhat bewildering array of self-defense classes listed under the umbrella of martial arts. The various types include karate, kodenkan jujitsu, taekwondo, judo, and tai chi.

Academies in the Reno/Sparks area include Bushidokan Martial Arts Temple, 311 Ninth Street, Sparks (775-358-1518); Aikido of Reno, 135 South Wells Avenue, Reno, (775) 337-8030; and Lou Grasso's Universal Taekwondo Federation, (775) 345-2561. In the South Shore Lake Tahoe area, call the School of Tao Martial Arts, (530) 577-4515. For a complete listing of locations and types of classes, I suggest

CLOSE-UP

Truckee River Whitewater Park

With Truckee River kayakers surfing in the shadows of downtown casinos, it's easy to see why the Reno/Lake Tahoe area is dubbed "America's Adventure Place." Opened in 2003, Truckee River Whitewater Park is the only kayak slalom racing course in the United States that is located in the middle of a downtown resort area. The course encircles Wingfield Park, an island in the center of the river that divides the flow of water into north and south channels. The course is about 0.5 mile in length and offers 11 drop pools for such maneuvers as cartwheeling, spoofing, flat spinning, and slalom racing. The pools decrease slightly in elevation from one to the next, providing a constant flow of fresh water. The course is open for free public use year-round, with water temperatures ranging between 50 and 70 degrees. While it takes only a little over two minutes to run the course straight through, most kayakers stay and play in the pools much longer.

You don't have to suit up and hit the water to enjoy this course, however. Wingfield Park and the paths along the river provide comfortable spectator access. With its amphitheater, playground, and picnic area, Wingfield plays host to many special events throughout the year, including the Reno River Festival. (See the Annual Events chapter for details.)

Use of Truckee River Whitewater Park is expected to increase, since kayaking is the third fastest growing sport in the country. More than 40 million Americans enjoy kayaking and canoeing, according to the Outdoor Industry Association.

you let your fingers do the walking through local telephone directories.

MINIATURE GOLF

Magic Carpet Golf
6925 South Virginia Street
Reno, NV
(775) 853-8837

Located on Virginia Street heading out of town toward Carson City, this establishment has two 19-hole courses and one 28-hole course. It's open daily from 10:00 A.M. to 6:00 P.M. during winter, weather permitting, and from 10:00 A.M. to 10:00 P.M. during the warmer months. Prices start at $6.00 for the 19-hole courses; the 28-hole course costs $8.00. The company offers birthday parties and discounts for groups of more than 20. After your round of golf, you can also enjoy the Magic Carpet's pizza parlor and arcade.

Magic Carpet Golf
5167 North Lake Boulevard
Carnelian Bay, CA
(530) 546-4279

Magic Carpet Golf was remodeled in 1998 and again in 2001 and has a 19-hole course and a 28-hole course. It's open from 10:00 A.M. to 10:00 P.M., April through October, weather permitting. It's usually crowded. Prices are around $6.00 for the 19-hole course and $7.50 for the 28-hole course.

Magic Carpet Golf
2455 Lake Tahoe Boulevard
South Lake Tahoe, CA
(530) 541-3787

The South Shore of Lake Tahoe also has a Magic Carpet, also with 19- and 28-hole courses. The 19-hole course costs $6.00 to play, and the 28-hole course costs $7.50. It's open daily from 10:00 A.M. to 11:00 P.M. during summer and 10:00 A.M. to 7:00 P.M. on weekends during spring and fall. It's closed during winter.

Wild Island Family Adventure Park
250 Wild Island Court, Sparks, NV
(775) 359-2927
www.wildisland.com

Part of the Wild Island water park complex, this miniature golf course has two 18-hole courses, which feature piped-in music on all of the holes. It's open all year: Monday through Thursday from 1:00 to 9:00 P.M., Friday from 1:00 to 10:00 P.M., Saturday from 11:00 A.M. to 10:00 P.M., and Sunday from 11:00 A.M. to 9:00 P.M. Prices are $5.50 for 18 holes and $6.50 for 36 holes.

PAINTBALL

Playing paintball is an excellent way to test your mettle as a warrior without the possibility of dying in battle. At worst, you'll end up with paint splattered all over your clothes.

Hansen Precision Airguns
2450 Valley Road, Reno, NV
(775) 324-7486
www.hpasports.com

You can play war games in relative comfort at Reno's new indoor paintball facility. Hansen Precision Airguns welcomes players from noon to 10:00 P.M. Friday, 10:00 A.M. to 10:00 P.M. Saturday, and 10:00 A.M. to 6:00 P.M. Sunday. Fees are $30 to $52, depending upon whether you have your own equipment and how long you'll be playing. You must buy house paint.

Herbie's Paintball Games Inc.
Alternate U.S. Highway 95, about 6 miles outside of Fernley, NV
(775) 575-6946
www.herbiespaintball.com

Herbie's catch phase is "just show up and squeeze the trigger." The outdoor battlefield is open on Saturday from 10:00 A.M. to 4:00 P.M.; Herbie's welcomes walk-ons and single players but suggests calling ahead to see if a game is on. The course can be rented for private wars or parties for half days and full days, and Herbie's hosts tournaments, too. There are themed battlefields, one of which is a simulated ghost town.

Rates depend on the package you purchase. The deluxe Package #1 at $35 per person includes a semiautomatic paintball gun, 200 paintballs, a camo suit, gloves, goggles, and a mask.

To get to Herbie's from Reno, take I-80 east to the West Fernley exit, number 46. Turn right from the interstate and follow Main Street through town to Alternate US 95. Take Alternate US 95 for 6 miles. The battlefield is on the right-hand side of the road near the Reno-Fernley Raceway. The mailing address is P.O. Box 2434, Fernley, NV 89408.

PARASAILING

If you prefer sailing over Lake Tahoe rather than on it, there are several companies that offer parasailing. Imagine flying high over the water under a multicolored parachute, towed behind a fast-moving speedboat skippered by U.S. Coast Guard-approved captains. Flying high above the shoreline lets you check out the fabulous scenery and the gorgeous lakefront estates. You'll really appreciate the phrase "bird's-eye view" after a parasailing adventure.

Flights last anywhere from 8 to 20 minutes and cost between $45 and $180, depending upon number of flyers and height of the parachute over the lake.

Besides renting water-sports equipment (see listings under the "Boating" and "Boat and Watercraft Rentals" sections earlier in this chapter), the following companies also offer parasailing.

Action Watersports of Tahoe
967 Lakeshore Boulevard
Incline Village, NV
(775) 831-4386

3411 U.S. Highway 50
South Lake Tahoe, CA
(530) 544-5387, (530) 541-4386

Captain Kirk's Beach Club
Zephyr Cove, NV
(775) 589-4908

Lake Tahoe Parasailing
700 North Lake Boulevard
Tahoe City, CA
(530) 583-7245

RACQUETBALL

In Reno you'll find racquetball courts at Double Diamond Athletic Club, (775) 851-7171; Sports West Athletic Club, (775) 348-6666; and The Stadium Sport & Fitness Club, (775) 853-4050. Because the cost of club membership and court availability varies, I recommend you call ahead. Reno Court Sports Connection, a 47,000-square-foot complex with 18 courts, is in the planning stages for a site on Old Virginia Road near Damonte Ranch Parkway.

RAFTING

Tahoe Whitewater Tours
Corner of Squaw Road and California Highway 89
Olympic Village, CA
(530) 581-2441, (800) 442-7238
www.gowhitewater.com
Trips with Tahoe Whitewater Tours offer fun and excitement for first-time rafters as well as experienced paddlers. In the immediate Reno/Lake Tahoe area, you can choose from two-hour or full-day runs on the Truckee River and half-day and full-day outings on the East Carson River. Both these rivers provide a fair amount of pristine solitude and placid water coupled with sections of exciting white water. The company also provides several day trips on the South Fork of the American River and overnighters on the Middle and North Forks. The 21-mile white-water section of this river from Chili Bar (near Placerville, California) to Salmon Falls (near Folsom Reservoir) is one of the most popular river runs in the West. Prices range from about $65 to $125, and longer trips include lunch. The company also offers guided kayak tours to the Truckee River Whitewater Park in Reno.

Truckee River Raft Company
Fanny Bridge Raft Rentals
California Highway 89 at Fanny Bridge
Tahoe City, CA
(530) 581-0123, (877) 583-0123
www.truckeeriverraft.com
Due to its location at Fanny Bridge, you won't have any trouble finding this raft company: Just look for their trademark red bus. The first 5 miles of the Truckee River, as it empties out of Lake Tahoe at Fanny Bridge to the River Ranch near Alpine Meadows ski resort, is the most popular rafting run in the Reno/Tahoe area. Meandering lazily through the huge trees along CA 89, this self-guided float takes most rafters two or three hours to complete. The turquoise water found along this route makes it easily one of the most beautiful sections of the Truckee River. After taking your raft out at River Ranch Pond, be sure to head up to the River Ranch deck for drinks and lunch before catching the free shuttle bus back to your car at Tahoe City.

Although this outing is convenient, safe, and scenic, most of the time it's quite crowded. If you're looking for solitude, you probably won't find it here unless you go after Labor Day. Weather and water permitting, the rafts operate daily May through October from 8:30 A.M.

to 3:30 P.M. The last shuttle from the River Ranch back to Tahoe City runs at 6:00 P.M. Rates are $27 for children age 12 and younger and $32 for adults. Group discounts are also available.

ROCK CLIMBING

Insiders who thrive on the excitement of scaling the face of solid rock cliffs will tell you the secret to great rock climbing: Find a place with perfect rocks and perfect weather. I've tried to make it even easier for you by listing some of the Reno/Tahoe area's best indoor and outdoor rock-climbing centers with instructors just waiting to help you take that first step. Today the wall, tomorrow Mt. Everest.

In addition to the locations below, you can also learn to belay in Reno at Sports West Athletic Club, 1575 South Virginia Street, (775) 348-6666; and at REI, 2225 Harvard Way, (775) 828-9090.

Adventure Park
Northstar-at-Tahoe, U.S. Highway 267 (6 miles north of Lake Tahoe), Truckee, CA
(530) 562-1010
Northstar provides climbers of all ages and abilities a 25-foot-high, granitelike, multi-faced outdoor climbing wall to practice on. It's located in the Adventure Park behind Northstar Village. The friendly and talented staff teaches belaying and supervises the climbs. The wall is open for climbs from 10:00 A.M. to 6:00 P.M. Wednesday through Sunday from mid-June until early September. All ages may climb, but belayers must be at least 14 years old or have staff approval. An hour pass runs about $10, but they do offer discounts for three or more climbers in the group. All-day passes are available for around $20. Groups are welcome to schedule events.

Headwall Cafe and Climbing
The Cable Car Building
Squaw Valley, CA
(530) 583-ROPE
www.squaw.com
This climbing center is located in the Cable Car Building at the base of Squaw Valley USA. The wall is 30 feet high and has 25 different routes, ranging in difficulty from beginner to expert. The center supplies harnesses and ropes that must be used when climbing. Unlimited climbing is $12.00, with climbing shoes costing $4.00 extra to rent. It's open from noon to 8:00 P.M. in winter and from 10:00 A.M. to 8:00 P.M. in summer. It's a low-key, fun climbing facility.

RockSport Indoor Climbing Center
1901 Silverado Boulevard, Sparks, NV
(775) 352-7673
www.rocksportnv.com
RockSport's climbing wall is the biggest in the Reno/Tahoe area. It's 32 feet high and spans the entire length of this warehouse's wall. The center offers several workshops during the week, ranging from belaying lessons to kid's climb night. It also offers monthly memberships. If you just want to climb, it's open from 10:00 A.M. to 10:00 P.M. during the week, 10:00 A.M. to 8:00 P.M. on Saturday, and 10:00 A.M. to 6:00 P.M. on Sunday. RockSport offers day passes for $12 and a variety of special pricing throughout the week for activities such as Monday Night Madness, ladies and youth nights, and kids climb time. The center provides all the necessary equipment, which you can rent for $5.00 per day.

SHOOTING

Sage Hill Clay Sports
7370 Desert Way, Reno, NV
(775) 851-1123
Practice makes perfect on the trap fields and skeet ranges at Sage Hill Clay Sports. The club is also home to several leagues and hosts tournaments throughout the year. Tucked in the foothills south of Reno on the way to Virginia City, it's a little tricky to find, so call the number above for recorded directions.

SKATEBOARDING

With the rising popularity of skateboarding, boarders are deserting the sidewalks for sophisticated parks that challenge their abilities. In addition to the parks below, you can also twist and turn at the Incline Skate Park on Tahoe and Southwood Boulevards in Incline Village. See the Kidstuff chapter for more information.

Idlewild Park Skateboard Park
Idlewild Park, 1900 Idlewild Drive
Reno, NV
(775) 334-2270
This is a 13,000-square-foot park located at Idlewild that is open to the public. Although recommended, safety equipment is not required, so it's skate-at-your-own-risk. The park is open year-round, weather permitting, during daylight hours.

Rattlesnake Mountain Skateboard Park at Mira Loma Park
Mira Loma Drive and McCarran Boulevard
Reno, NV
(775) 334-2262
The newest and largest skateboard park in the area, Rattlesnake Mountain has quickly become the place to be for the skateboard crowd. Its 38,000 square feet has enough ramps, bowls, and pipes to satisfy even the most ardent boarders.

South Tahoe Skateboard Park
Bijou Park, Al Tahoe Boulevard
South Lake Tahoe, CA
(530) 542-6055
This city-run park requires helmets and pads. It's located in Bijou Park on Al Tahoe Boulevard, 1 mile from US 50. The park is open from dawn to dusk during the non-snow months.

SOARING

One of the most spectacular and serene ways to view the grandeur of the Reno/Tahoe area is from 10,000 feet in the cockpit of a glider. If you think that the excitement of flying motorless high above the Sierra might be your thing, check out these area companies that provide glider rides and lessons. And don't forget your camera!

Palomino Valley Soaring
15000 Winnemucca Ranch Road
Palomino Valley, NV
(775) 475-2440
www.soar-palomino.com
Located at the Air Sailing Gliderport, 25 miles north of Sparks, this company provides glider rides and lessons. It includes scenic flights by Pyramid Lake and provides first-time flyers with introductory lessons and aerobatic flights. Flight prices start at $70. All flights and lessons are conducted by FAA-certified commercial pilots.

To get to the gliderport from Sparks, go north on the Pyramid Highway (Nevada Highway 445) to Winnemucca Ranch Road (about 17 miles). Turn left at Winnemucca Ranch Road and go about 7 miles to the gliderport.

Soar Minden
Minden-Tahoe Airport, Minden, NV
(775) 782-7627, (800) 345-7627
www.soarminden.com
Soar Minden provides year-round glider flights from the Minden-Tahoe Airport. It charges $105 to $220 for a one-person ride and $170 to $285 for a two-person flight. The cost depends on the time aloft. This company soars over the Carson Valley but high enough to catch a great view of Lake Tahoe. It also provides private pilot lessons. Ardent fliers can take advantage of package rates that include hotel and unlimited flying.

To get to the Minden-Tahoe Airport from Reno, take US 395 south to Airport Road, just south of Carson City. Follow Airport Road for about 1 mile to the large paved parking area. From Lake Tahoe take US 50 to US 395 and go south on US 50 to Airport Road. Turn left onto Airport Road and drive down the road to the airport.

Soar Truckee
Martis Creek Dam Road
near Truckee-Tahoe Airport, Truckee, CA
(530) 587-6702, (866) 762-7875
www.soartruckee.com
Soar Truckee is located at the Truckee-Tahoe Airport, just a few miles north of Lake Tahoe on CA 267 (see the Getting Here, Getting Around chapter for details on the airport). This soaring center has everything to keep you entertained—lessons, scenic rides, towing services, rental gliders, and a campground for pilots and passengers. Flights start at $89 for one passenger. The sightseeing flights are usually flown a little north of the airport, but Lake Tahoe is still visible. (See the Day Trips chapter for more to see and do in Truckee.) Soar Truckee is open mid-May to mid-November.

Tropic Bird Soaring
Minden-Tahoe Airport, Minden, NV
(775) 783-1817
www.tropicbirdsoaring.com
If you're a glider pilot and want to sharpen your skills, Tropic Bird Soaring has a state-of-the-art Schempp-Hirth Duo Discus available for hire and instruction. The daily rental rate of $340 includes all equipment but not the tows. Reservations are required.

SOFTBALL

No one in Nevada or California will dispute the fact that softball is the "King of Sports" in the Reno/Tahoe area. The cities of Reno and Sparks are home to most of the teams because of the cooperative weather, but leagues do exist around the lake as soon as the snow melts. In Sparks alone, parks and recreation figures estimate that about 8,700 people (out of a population of 65,000) play softball. Between Reno, Sparks, and Lake Tahoe, you can hook up with one of hundreds of teams in a number of different leagues depending upon your age, skill level, and gender. The leagues consist of 18 and older fastpitch, modified pitch, church co-ed, adult slow-pitch, senior, 65-plus senior, youth slow-pitch, youth fastpitch, and ponytail. So you can see that there's a league and an ability level for anyone who wants to "chuck that white pill around."

For more information on softball leagues near you, contact the following organizations:

City of Sparks Parks and Recreation, (775) 353-2376; www.ci.sparks.nv.us

Incline Village Parks and Recreation, (775) 832-1322, (775) 832-1310; www.ivgid.org/recreation

Reno Recreation Department, (775) 334-2262; cityofreno.com

South Tahoe Parks and Recreation, (530) 542-6056, www.ci.south-lake-tahoe.ca.us

Tahoe City Park & Recreation Department, Public Utility District, (530) 583-3796; www.tahoecitypud.com

SWIMMING

If your accommodations in the Reno/Tahoe area offer a swimming pool, you won't have far to go to beat the heat or to get some exercise. You can also head to one of the glorious beaches at Lake Tahoe or to one of the area's public swimming pools to swim your laps. Remember, however, to take precautions in the frigid waters of the lake: You might consider wearing a wetsuit if you're a serious swimmer.

I describe several popular swimming beaches here and also tell you where to find some local swimming pools (see the Parks chapter for additional swimming holes). For exotic dips I suggest you try the soothing waters at Steamboat Villa Hot Springs Spa at 16010 South Virginia Street in Reno (775-853-6600; www.steamboatsprings.org) or David Walley's Resort, Hot Springs & Spa in Genoa,

Sparks is one of the largest softball communities per capita in the nation.

Nevada (775-782-8155; www.davidwalleys.com). (See the Day Trips chapter for more about Genoa.) You'll also find swimming pools and spas at area health and fitness clubs. Weather permitting, I highly recommend a leisurely day at the spa and swimming lagoon at High Camp Bath & Tennis Club at Squaw Valley USA (see the description under "Tennis" in this chapter).

Swimming Pools

Alf Sorenson Community Center
1400 Baring Boulevard, Sparks, NV
(775) 353-2385 (indoor)

City of South Lake Tahoe Pool
1180 Rufus Allen Boulevard
South Lake Tahoe, CA
(530) 542-6056 (indoor/outdoor)

Deer Park Pool
1700 Prater Way, Sparks, NV
(775) 353-2385 (outdoor)

Idlewild Pool
1805 Idlewild Drive, Reno, NV
(775) 334-2267 (outdoor)

Moana Pool
240 West Moana Lane, Reno, NV
(775) 689-2964 (indoor)

Northeast Pool
1301 Valley Road, Reno, NV
(775) 324-2262 (outdoor)

Northwest Pool
2925 Apollo Way, Reno, NV
(775) 334-2203 (indoor)

Oppio Park Pool
2355 Eighteenth Street, Sparks, NV
(775) 353-2385 (outdoor)

Traner Pool
1600 Carville Drive, Reno, NV
(775) 334-2269 (outdoor)

Beaches

Baldwin Beach
California Highway 89
4 miles north of the "Y" intersection
South Lake Tahoe, CA
This lovely stretch of white sand is tucked along the lakeshore near the Tallac Historic Site. After swimming and enjoying a picnic near the lake, you can take in the cultural events at Tallac (see the chapters on The Arts and Attractions for details). No dogs are allowed.

Kings Beach State Recreation Area
North Lake Boulevard
Kings Beach, CA
(530) 546-4212
www.cal-parks.ca.gov
If you like lots of activity while you swim and sunbathe, this just might be the spot for you. You'll find all the usual water sports at Kings Beach State Recreation Area, along with a day-use park. It's a very busy place, with easy access to shops and restaurants in Kings Beach. Dogs are not allowed.

Nevada Beach
Elk Point Road near Zephyr Cove, NV
Next to a popular campground, Nevada Beach offers a large expanse of sand along with amenities such as picnic facilities and restrooms. It's close to the action at Stateline but worlds away when you're lazing on the beach. Come early in the day: The parking lot and picnic spots fill up fast during high season. No dogs allowed.

Pope Beach
California Highway 89
2 miles north of the "Y"
South Lake Tahoe, CA
Pope Beach offers a picturesque oasis of sun and sand close to all the action in South Lake Tahoe. The unobstructed access to the water is great for families, but leave the family pets at home, since they're not allowed here. You'll find picnic facilities and restrooms on the beach.

Sand Harbor
Nevada Highway 28, 3 miles south of Incline Village, NV
(775) 831-0494
www.parks.nv.gov
With sparkling turquoise water lapping at a mile of white-sand beach, Sand Harbor is considered by many to be the most beautiful beach at Lake Tahoe. You can take nature walks, launch your boat, swim, or just laze on the sand. In the evening, stick around for culture since Sand Harbor is the site of the Lake Tahoe Shakespeare Festival. (For more information on Sand Harbor, see The Arts chapter and the description of Lake Tahoe-Nevada State Park in the Parks chapter.)

Secret Harbor
Nevada Highway 28, 2.5 miles south of Sand Harbor, NV
Although Secret Harbor is no secret to Insiders, its tiny beaches are completely hidden from sightseers on NV 28. Clothing is optional here, which is known locally as the Nude Beaches. You won't find groups of naked people standing along stretches of sand staring at one another, however. Access to the water is found in a series of coves, each secluded from the next. It's also a great place for dogs. To reach the lake from the parking lot above requires a walk of between a half mile and a mile, but the beauty and seclusion at the end of it is well worth every step. (For more information on Secret Harbor and nearby beaches, see the description of Lake Tahoe-Nevada State Park in the Parks chapter.)

TENNIS

You'll find tennis courts in public parks, on school grounds, and at resorts and hotels in the Reno/Tahoe area. If you're used to playing at or near sea level, don't be surprised if you're gasping in the thin mountain air after just a few games. You can take heart knowing your stamina and game should return to normal after a few days of getting used to the higher elevation, however.

Tahoe swimmers win bragging rights competing in the 200-yard Polar Bear Swim near Garwoods restaurant each winter.

I can't list all of the tennis facilities available in the area; they're just too numerous. As an Insider I suggest several places guaranteed to be winners if tennis is part of your vacation. I also direct you to some public courts sprinkled around the area. For more locations you can call parks departments (see the Parks chapter) or inquire about tennis facilities when booking your accommodations.

Incline Village Tennis Complex
964 Incline Way
Incline Village, NV
(775) 832-1235
www.ivgid.org
In a lovely mountain setting, the Incline Village Tennis Complex is sure to meet all of your tennis needs and expectations. Awarded a National Facility Award by the United States Tennis Association, marking it as one of the top 10 facilities in the country, the facility includes a pro shop, viewing deck, backboard, and 24-hour stringing service, along with seven outdoor courts. You can participate in tournaments, take lessons and clinics, and just play for enjoyment. Fees are lower for Incline Village residents and their guests or for those staying in accommodations that include IVGID recreation passes. Because of heavy demand, I strongly suggest you call ahead to reserve your court. The courts are generally open mid-April through September, depending on snowfall.

Lakeridge Tennis Club
6000 Plumas Street
Reno, NV
(775) 827-3300
A members-only club, Lakeridge Tennis Club has 14 outdoor and 4 indoor courts. Along with playing tennis year-round, you can also enjoy all the amenities of a full-

A day at a Lake Tahoe beach is a family affair. HYATT REGENCY LAKE TAHOE RESORT, SPA & CASINO

service health club. For dedicated players living in the Reno area, it's the best place to immerse yourself in the game.

North Tahoe Regional Park
875 National Avenue, Tahoe Vista, CA
(530) 546-5043
www.northlaketahoe.net/parks.html
You can volley long after the sun goes down on the five lighted tennis courts at North Tahoe Regional Park. It's first-come, first-served, so pack a picnic lunch or enjoy a short hike in the park if you need to wait for a court (see the Parks chapter for more information on the park).

Northstar-at-Tahoe
California Highway 267
6 miles north of Lake Tahoe
(530) 562-1010
www.skinorthstar.com/summer/tennis.html
Northstar-at-Tahoe offers tennis lessons, camps, and leisure play for residents and guests only. If you're looking for an all-inclusive resort experience that includes tennis, Northstar is a great choice. Ask about specific packages when booking accommodations. (See the Winter Sports and Resorts chapters for more details about this fun-filled family resort.)

Reno Tennis Center
2601 Plumas Street
Reno, NV
(775) 689-2975
Owned and managed by the city of Reno, the 16 outdoor courts at the Reno Tennis Center are busy all year. It's a popular site for tournaments and group events, which can be arranged for reasonable fees. The city also sponsors a variety of tennis events here, including junior clinics and lessons.

Squaw Valley USA
California Highway 89, 6 miles north of Tahoe City, CA
(530) 581-7255
www.squaw.com

It might be hard to keep your eye on the ball when playing at Squaw Valley USA: The scenery is absolutely first-rate, even if your game isn't. You can play at an elevation of 6,200 feet at the Resort at Squaw Creek or huff and puff your way through a set at High Camp Bath & Tennis Club at 8,200 feet (obviously, this is summer-only playing). A variety of packages, lessons, clinics, and leisure-play options are available, so I suggest you call to find what suits you best.

Indisputably a world-class resort, Squaw is a winner year-round, with activities galore and a natural setting guaranteed to take your breath away. (I tell you more about this very special resort in the Winter Sports chapter.)

WALKING/RUNNING

You can run and walk almost anywhere, but let's face it, some terrain is more scenic and suitable for outings than others. I assume most walkers and runners prefer fairly level courses that are well defined (even though a few super jocks sprint up steep mountain trails designed for hiking), so keeping in mind this average walker/runner, I tell you about some paved and some dirt paths that are free of obstacles and easy to navigate in running or walking shoes.

Incline Village/Lakeshore Boulevard
Incline Village, NV

For scenic Lake Tahoe views and peeks at luxurious gated estates, you can run, walk, or bike the 2.5-mile paved path along Lakeshore Boulevard in Incline Village. For your first visit to Lake Tahoe, it's a great way to get oriented and to ease into the laid-back tempo of mountain life. The level course parallels the shore of the lake, winding through huge trees and past gorgeous beaches. You can access the path easily all along the way, but it's convenient to park at the Hyatt Regency Lake Tahoe Resort & Casino and begin your outing there. Don't forget the family dog (leashed): The route is a veritable dog show, with every breed imaginable on display by proud owners. At the end of your walk, I suggest enjoying your favorite drink by the firepit on the beach in front of the Hyatt (see the Resorts chapter for details).

Pope-Baldwin Bike Path
California Highway 89, 0.5 mile north of the "Y" to Camp Richardson
South Lake Tahoe, CA

Drinking in the gorgeous South Shore Lake Tahoe landscape from this 3.4-mile paved path is entertainment in itself. But you can also take in cultural events at Tallac Historic Site, enjoy a wide variety of outdoor sports at Camp Richardson, and stop for refreshments at picnic spots and restaurants along the way (see the Attractions and Vacation Rentals chapters for more details).

Steamboat Ditch Trail
Reno, NV

Beginning at the California-Nevada border near Verdi, Steamboat Ditch carries irrigation water for 48 miles through ranches and housing developments to its endpoint near Rhodes Road south of Reno. Although its main purpose for many years has been to water thirsty ranchlands and farmlands, the trail used for maintaining the ditch has become one of the most popular walking, running, and biking routes in Reno.

The ecosystem supported along the banks of the ditch is a kaleidoscope of nature, changing with the seasons to offer up delightful surprises for the unsuspecting outdoor enthusiast. In spring and summer you see an amazing array of flowers bursting with color against the beige desert landscape—the regal purple of hardy thistles, the brilliant pink of dainty wild roses, and the soft gray of fuzzy pussy willows. In fall you enjoy the bright oranges and golds of leaves as they drop lazily into the flowing water, and in winter you see the delicate white patterns of crusty snow and ice as they freeze along the ditch banks and the trail.

You can access the trail from a variety of spots as it wanders through Reno, but I suggest trying Horsemans Park at the corner of Skyline and Pioneer Drives.

The trail is bisected by roads as it courses through Reno, so occasionally you need to cross streets and pick up the trail on the other side. It's also an easement through private land, so remember to respect the property rights and privacy of those living along the trail. The trail is one of the most popular areas for exercising dogs, and dogs can run free if they're well behaved. One last note—don't be surprised if the ditch is dry in winter: The water runs only April through October.

Truckee River Recreation Trail
Along California Highway 89, 1.5 miles north of the River Ranch
Tahoe City, CA

Hugging the banks of the Truckee River as it flows from its source at Fanny Bridge, the Truckee River Recreation Trail is a relatively flat, paved path that meanders for about 4.5 miles next to CA 89. Along the trail you'll meet lots of joggers, walkers, and bikers, and in the river you'll see rafters, tubers, and anglers. It's a strikingly beautiful section of the river, with enormous trees shading the crystal-clear water. You can also stop at the River Ranch for people-watching and refreshments as part of your outing (see the description of the River Ranch in the "Rafting" section of this chapter and in the Winter Sports chapter).

Truckee River Walk
Arlington and Island Avenues
Reno, NV

Strolling along the Truckee River Walk, you can trace the route of the river as it flows from west to east through various neighborhoods in Reno. (For details about what you'll see along this paved path, see the Attractions chapter.) Dogs must be leashed.

Virginia Lake
1980 Lakeside Drive, Reno, NV
(775) 334-2262

In a busy urban neighborhood, Virginia Lake is a mecca for runners and walkers. It's a great people-watching and bird-feeding spot but won't offer much in the way of solitude (see the Parks chapter for more details).

West Shore Bike Path
Along California Highway 89 between Tahoe City, CA, and Sugar Pine Point State Park

The West Shore Bike Path winds for about 9 miles between Tahoe City and Sugar Pine Point State Park, passing beaches, picnic areas, and the small towns of Tahoma and Homewood. You can walk or run any section along the way, stopping for sightseeing and meals. The paved route crosses CA 89 several times, so you need to be alert to traffic. If you're looking for a quiet walk, this popular path may be too busy for you, especially during high season. You can access the path in Tahoe City or farther along the way by parking at Kaspian Campground, about 4 miles south of Tahoe City on CA 89, or at Sugar Pine Point State Park.

WATERCRAFT RENTAL

See "Boat and Watercraft Rentals" under "Boating" earlier in this chapter.

WATERSKIING

Only water-skiers truly understand that special thrill of skimming effortlessly across the surface of a sparkling body of water. With a number of lakes nearby, you can indulge in this sport to your heart's content in the Reno/Tahoe area.

If you have your own boat and equipment, you can launch at a number of sites on Lake Tahoe, such as Cave Rock Marina, about 7 miles north of Stateline on US 50; Sand Harbor, about 4 miles south of Incline Village on NV 28; and Captain Jon's at 7220 North Lake Boulevard in Tahoe Vista. You can also head out to neighboring lakes, such as Pyramid and Lahontan or Donner Lake, on I-80 near

Truckee, California, and Boca Reservoir, about 9 miles east of Truckee on I-80.

If you're looking for lessons or a tow, you can try one of the water-ski schools at Lake Tahoe: They'll furnish everything you need (including the all-important wetsuit) to guarantee a great time on the water.

Action Watersports of Tahoe
3411 U.S. Highway 50
South Lake Tahoe, CA
(530) 544-5387
www.actionwatersports.com

Action Watersports of Tahoe can outfit you with almost any equipment you could want for fun on the water. You can rent Jet Skis, SeaDoos, WaveRunners, and a variety of boats. They also offer water-ski lessons. If all this isn't enough excitement for you, ask them to hook you into a parachute for an aerial view of the shoreline from their parasailing rig. (See also the previous listing under "Boating" in this chapter.)

Goldcrest Water Ski School Inc.
8194 North Lake Boulevard
Kings Beach, CA
(530) 546-7412

With a water-ski school right on the premises, the Gold Crest Resort Motel offers water-ski-in/water-ski-out accommodations. You can learn to ski for about $90 per hour, including all equipment, instructor, and experienced boat driver. After an exhilarating ride on skis, you can relax on the lovely sand beach, complete with hot tub and swimming pool. For information about the accommodations, call (530) 546-3301. Open July and August only.

Lahontan State Recreation Area
Alternate U.S. Highway 95, 50 miles southeast of Reno, NV
(775) 867-3500

If you're looking for smooth, warm water (and what water-skier isn't?), try Lahontan Reservoir in the Lahontan State Recreation Area. Less windy and warmer than Lake Tahoe or Pyramid Lake, Lahontan has been a favorite almost since the first skiers strapped wooden boards onto their feet and yelled "Hit it!" some years ago. The best months to ski here are June and July since algae sometimes causes the lake to turn greenish in August.

You can launch your boat for around $8.00 at the Silver Springs entrance to the park (just past the town of Silver Springs) and at the Churchill Beach boat launch at the North Shore Marina. The lake boasts about 70 miles of predominantly sandy shoreline interspersed with clumps of hardy trees, but for dependable shade I recommend bringing along a tarp or umbrellas. To reach Lahontan from Reno, take I-80 west 33 miles to Fernley and then Alternate US 95 south to Silver Springs. (See the description of Fallon in the Day Trips chapter for more information on the reservoir.)

Lake Tahoe Water-Ski School
Camp Richardson Resort
1900 Jameson Beach Road
South Lake Tahoe, CA
(530) 544-7747

For a great time on water skis, at Camp Richardson Resort all you need is to show up with a camera and a smile. For about $150 an hour Lake Tahoe Water-Ski School provides everything you need—wetsuits and skis, plus a boat with an experienced driver. The company also offers 2-mile tows for around $50. A full-service resort on a gorgeous stretch of Lake Tahoe frontage, Camp Richardson has all the amenities needed to keep you entertained all day long (for details see the chapters on Camping and RVing and Vacation Rentals).

Pyramid Lake
Nevada Highway 445
33 miles northeast of Reno, NV
(775) 476-1155, (775) 574-1000

On a calm sunny day, Pyramid Lake is an absolutely prime choice for waterskiing. Its huge expanse of pristine water and miles of isolated beaches ensure quality fun in the sun without being on top of other outdoor enthusiasts. You need to be mindful of the wind, however: Skiing on this placid playground can quickly become a risky venture when the wind churns the surface into a sea of dangerous whitecaps. (See the Day Trips chapter for a detailed description of this lovely desert oasis.)

YOGA

In their pursuit of good health and fitness, an increasing number of people in the Reno/Tahoe area are looking to the ancient art of yoga for exercise and healing. For some aficionados it offers another health practice in addition to other exercise forms, while for others it becomes a total conditioning program and even a way of life. Space doesn't permit me to discuss all the various forms of yoga, but classes on all levels are available in the area.

First Class at The Yoga Center, 720 Tahoe Street #C in Reno (775-881-7848; www.tycreno.com), is designed to demystify yoga and inform first-timers of the many benefits of this form of discipline. The center also has a full schedule of classes for varying abilities and includes prenatal and children's sessions. Many health and fitness clubs include yoga in their class schedules. You can find classes in Reno at Sports West Athletic Club, 1575 South Virginia Street (775-348-6666), and in the North Shore Lake Tahoe area at Incline Athletic/Racquetball Club, 880 Northwood Boulevard, Incline Village, Nevada (775-831-4212).

GOLF

If golf is your game, you'll be delighted to know that the Reno/Tahoe area has enough luscious layouts to last you your golfing lifetime. With the increase in population over the past decade or so, the demand for more golf courses has been intense. The result has been a plethora of links to keep even the most hard-core players swinging. The variety of terrain can be mind-boggling, from ribbons of green snaking through enormous stands of Jeffrey pines to wide-open fairways laid flat along the desert sands. Whatever best matches your game, you're sure to find it somewhere in the area.

Most courses in the flatlands (Reno, Sparks, and surrounding rural areas) are open year-round, weather depending. So if you've got the stamina, it's possible to ski and golf all in the same day. The mountain courses, however, are seasonal from about April to November. Call or consult Web sites to check if you're in doubt. I'll tell you about the public and semiprivate courses that are open for play, but if you're looking for a private course to join, you can choose from the following: Arrowcreek Country Club, Reno, (775) 850-4471; Hidden Valley Country Club, Reno, (775) 857-4742; Montreux Golf Club Ltd., Reno, (775) 849-1090; the Private Club at Red Hawk, Sparks (775) 626-6000; Somersett Country Club, Reno, (775) 787-1800; and Thunder Canyon Golf & Country Club, Washoe Valley, (775) 884-4597.

Nearby Truckee, California, has become a destination for affluent golfers. Three posh courses have recently opened with all the bells and whistles of luxury living and golfing: Lahontan Golf Club, (530) 550-2400, www.lahontanrealty.com; Old Greenwood, (800) 754-3070, www.oldgreenwood.com; and The Club at Gray's Crossing, www.grayscrossing.com. If you're interested in golf course living, keep in mind that you don't have to be on a private course. Most public courses have homes lining the fairways, and the most recently built courses are still selling lots for new construction.

In acquainting you with the public courses, I've included the kinds of information that'll help you choose the one to fit your game and style: the yardage (from the men's white tees), pars, U.S. Golfing Association (USGA) ratings and slopes, greens fees with cart included (summer rates), reservation policy, and a brief description of each course. Unless stated otherwise, each course has a driving range, putting green, pro shop, and restaurant. Rates are ranges for 18 holes with cart unless noted otherwise.

To help orient you to the location of the courses, the chapter is divided into the four standard geographical areas—Reno, Sparks, North Shore Lake Tahoe, and South Shore Lake Tahoe. Some of the courses I mentioned fall outside these areas, but I think they are close enough and worth the drive to play. Consequently, these courses are designated "Worth the Drive" (big pun intended) and are included at the end of the geographical section closest to the course.

So let's tee it up and get started. But remember one other thing: The views from all of the golf courses in the area are so magnificent that you won't mind hooking the occasional ball into the sagebrush or slicing one into that sapphire-blue lake crowned with Canada geese. Honest.

RENO

Lake Ridge Golf Course
1218 Golf Club Drive
(775) 825-2200, (800) 815-6966
www.lakeridgegolf.com

This Robert Trent Jones Jr.-designed

The tree-lined fairways of mountain courses make it challenging to keep golf balls in play.
NORTHSTAR-AT-TAHOE

course built in 1969 has large greens, large tee boxes, large bunkers, and lots of water. Most visitors know the course because of its signature hole—the 15th, a 230-yard par 3, which features a tee box 360 feet above Lake Stanley, requiring a tee shot to an island green. This is probably the most talked-about and most photographed hole in the Reno/Tahoe area. Access to the green is by a footbridge. During winter you are only allowed to walk on this course. The course is located in a prestigious neighborhood and sports a country-club atmosphere with upscale homes lining the fairways. It's closed for several months during winter. Reservations for a group of 20 or more may be made a year in advance. Tee times can be scheduled online. Lake Ridge has been voted the No. 1 course in the Reno/Sparks area for many years.

Yardage: 6,140
Par: 71
USGA rating: 69.1
Slope: 132
Greens fees: $40 to $100
Reservations: 7 days in advance

Northgate Golf Club
1111 Clubhouse Drive
(775) 747-7577
www.visitrenotahoe.com

Northgate is a desert links-style course with fast, undulating greens surrounded by grass and sand bunkers. Nicknamed the "St. Andrews of the Sierras," the course was rated as one of the best new courses in the country by *Golf* magazine. The fairways are hilly and open—if you manage to hit one. The course is one of the most challenging in the area because of the potential to miss the landing zones and hit into the sagebrush and sand of the high desert. Don't come here unless you are sure of your game: The course has crushed the egos of some good golfers.

Many holes have the desert coming into play, meaning that shots have to be made over this natural hazard. This course will require you to use every club in your bag. Designed by Brad Benz and Mile Poellot and built in 1988, Northgate played host to the Ben Hogan Tour in 1990 and 1991 and the U.S. Open Qualifying Tournament in 1988 and 1989.

Yardage: 5,920
Par: 72
USGA rating: 68
Slope: 126
Greens fees: $40 to $45, excluding cart
Reservations: 14 days in advance

Rosewood Lakes Golf Course
6800 Pembroke Drive
(775) 857-2892
www.rosewoodlakes.com

This is not a long course, but it is difficult because it plays like a links-style course. Rosewood was built around 60 acres of protected wetlands preserve, and if you don't hit the ball straight, it will end up in the tules. Once the ball enters the wetlands, you are not allowed to retrieve it, so it's important to bring plenty of balls when you play this course. The fairways are flat and open, and the greens are medium size and on the slow side. Water comes into play on every hole, making this a challenging course. The greens fees are some of the cheapest in the area, and it's popular with the locals. The signature eighth hole is a treacherous par 4, with a bunker and lake lining the entire right side and a lake lining the left. An accurate drive is a must, making the second shot to the large, elevated green easy. One par 3 is a blind tee shot because the tules have grown so tall that they completely block the view to the green. This course, designed by Brad Benz and built in 1991, is one of the top-conditioned municipal courses in the West because of its easy access to year-round water.

Yardage: 6,104
Par: 72
USGA rating: 68
Slope: 115
Greens fees: $20 to $30
Reservations: 7 days in advance; weekends, the previous Monday

Sierra Sage Golf Course
6355 Silver Lake Boulevard
(775) 972-1564
www.washoecountyparks.com

This course is located in Stead, a bedroom community north of Reno located in the sagebrush of the high desert. The U.S. Air Force built the front nine in 1960, and the back nine was added in 1970. Sagebrush lines almost all of its large, rolling fairways, and big hitters have a tendency to go for the long ball here. Accuracy is a must if you go for it, or you will be off into the sagebrush with the quail and the jackrabbits. Water comes into play on six holes, and four holes are built around a lake. The greens are small and fast, with bunkers protecting most. This course is played heavily by locals because of a discount on the greens fees, but visitors seem to forget it's here, which is a shame because it is fun to play and one of the cheapest around.

Yardage: 6,605
Par: 71
USGA rating: 70.4
Slope: 122
Greens fees: $16 to $22, excluding cart
Reservations: 7 days in advance

Washoe County Golf Course
2601 South Arlington Avenue
(775) 828-6640
www.washoegolf.org

Washoe County is the oldest golf course in Nevada. Built in 1936, this course is well established, close to downtown Reno, and popular among locals, especially the seniors (greens fees are cheap for residents in comparison to other courses around the area). The first hole has a great view from an elevated tee box, overlooking a dogleg left par 4. A good drive here sets you up for an easy shot to the green, but trees lining both sides of the fairway can intimidate the best hitters. In fact, trees line the fairways on the entire front nine. Don't let the flat and wide fairways on the front fool you into thinking the entire course is flat: The back nine is extremely hilly and tight, and you still have to contend with some trees. The course has small bent-grass greens, well protected by sand bunkers. The course is always in good shape. Try to do your best scoring on the relatively easy front nine, because you'll need all the strokes you can get for the back.

Yardage: 6,468
Par: 72
USGA rating: 68.8
Slope: 124
Greens fees: $24 to $31, excluding cart
Reservations: 10 days in advance

You can save money at Rosewood Lakes Golf Course by using the City of Reno Discount Card that comes with membership in the course's men's and women's clubs.

Wolf Run Golf Club
1400 Wolf Run Road
(775) 851-3301
www.wolfrungolfclub.com

The Wolf Run golf course winds its way through rolling desert terrain southwest of Reno and offers great views of the valley, downtown, and Mt. Rose. Named for the University of Nevada, Reno, athletic teams, it's also home to their golf teams. The course was designed by John Fleming, Steve Van Meter, and Lou Eiguren, and the three made sure that the high desert and loads of sagebrush come into play on almost every hole. The signature hole, No. 15, is a long par 5 with a large green surrounded by Thomas Creek, creating an island-green effect and making it a great three-shot hole. The course has a no-kidding 19th hole. This short hole is designed in the shape of a wolf's paw and can be used to settle any carryover bets or can be used as a play-off hole. The course is extremely enjoyable and very playable. You can book reservations online.

Yardage: 6,086
Par: 71
USGA rating: 67.9
Slope: 122
Greens fees: $45 to $75
Reservations: 14 days in advance

SPARKS

D'Andrea Golf Club
2900 South D'Andrea Parkway
(775) 331-6363
www.dandreagolf.com

Designed by renowned golf course architect Keith Foster, D'Andrea was opened to the public in 2000. This is the course for those who love the high desert. The back nine offers especially spectacular views as elevation gains offer ever-expanding vistas. The signature hole here is the 162-yard par 3 No. 6, with a green that is almost completely surrounded by water. A rock wall in front of the hole makes the distances quite deceiving. Even if you're unable to ace the hole, however, you'll be sure to enjoy the breathtaking view of Reno and Sparks and the surrounding mountains.

Because it's on the high plateaus in the desert and has no trees, folks should try to get out in the early morning or late afternoon.

Yardage: 6,501
Par: 71
USGA rating: 68.5
Slope: 121
Greens fees: $45 to $100
Reservations: 7 days in advance

Red Hawk Golf Club
6600 North Wingfield Parkway
(775) 626-6000
www.theresortatredhawk.com

The Lakes Course at Red Hawk Golf Club offers magnificent views of the Truckee Meadows and the surrounding mountains. Robert Trent Jones designed this course around the marshlands and lakes of an old hunting club, so water comes into play on several holes. The fairways are so plush that you almost hate taking a divot, and the bent-grass greens are extremely well manicured and fast. The course is lengthy with wide-open fairways, but beware when the wind kicks up.

This is one of the examples of the scenic backdrop being so magnificent that you really don't mind playing a lousy game of golf. The golf carts are equipped with state-of-the-art measuring devices. Red Hawk features a Golf Learning Center, a program designed to teach every part of the game for every level of play. Red Hawk also has the Hills Course, a private layout designed by Hale Irwin.

Yardage: 6,138
Par: 72
USGA rating: 68.4
Slope: 119
Greens fees: $50 to $100
Reservations: 6 days in advance

Wildcreek Golf Course
3500 Sullivan Lane
(775) 673-3100
www.visitrenotahoe.com

This club has two courses—an 18-hole regulation course and a 9-hole executive par 3 course.

Course One—The 18-hole design features rolling fairways, lots of water, bunkers, and sagebrush. The course was carved from a hillside, making the fairways uneven and leading Insiders to nickname the course "Wild Bounce." Besides the undulating fairways, the course has six lakes and a creek running through it to make your game extremely challenging. The bent-grass greens are big and well protected by lots of sand. Some of the holes feature elevated tees and terraced greens, making the course one of the toughest to play in the area. It hosted three Senior Tour events in the 1980s.

Yardage: 6,244
Par: 72
USGA rating: 69.4
Slope: 127
Greens fees: $35 to $59
Reservations: 14 days in advance

Course Two—The nine-hole executive par 3 features tiny greens and tight fairways. Several water hazards are sprinkled in among the holes, making shot placement a priority. The course is always crowded, but it is an excellent place to come to hone your short-game skills or to teach a new golfer.

Yardage: 1,300
Par: 27
USGA rating: N/A
Slope: N/A
Greens fees: $12 for nine holes
Reservations: Walk-on

Worth the Drive

Crystal Peak Golf Course
444 River Pines Drive, Verdi, NV
(775) 345-1551
www.verdi.us

Just 10 miles west of Reno on Interstate 80, Crystal Peak Golf Course is the newest to join the growing ranks of links in the Reno/Tahoe area. Created by Love Golf Design, it boasts several distinctions: It's the only championship nine-hole course in the Reno/Sparks area and the only course that uses an island in the Truckee River. The island houses the green for the second hole along with the par 3 third hole. Meandering through a spectacular forest of Jeffrey pines, the course takes full advantage of its mile of riverfront property. A nature lover's delight, it also challenges even the best golfers with its demand for accuracy. The interesting array of bunkers and the fairways lined with tall trees and sagebrush demand thoughtful shots in order to score well. It's a family-owned enterprise, so don't expect the glitz of full-service courses with restaurants and pro shops. Playing a round of golf here is also communing with nature.

Yardage: 2,520 to 3,253 for nine holes
Par: 71.2
USGA rating: N/A
Slope: 131
Greens fees: $70 for 18 holes, excluding cart
Reservations: Call anytime

Golf Club at Fernley
4000 Farm District Road, Fernley, NV
(775) 835-6933
www.fernleygolfclub.com

This 18-hole bent-grass course, opened in 1996, is located in Fernley, Nevada, about 35 miles east of Sparks. It was built among the sagebrush of the high desert, but just to add a little more of a challenge, designer Bob Bingham laced 30 lakes around the 18 holes. It plays easily, though, if you can control your shots. It's almost a guarantee that errant shots will find water or the sagebrush. Most greens are moderately fast and protected by white-sand bunkers. The course plays fast and is never crowded during the week. The only drawback is the fact that during summer, temperatures in Fernley can reach or even exceed the 100-degree mark. The course features a 605-yard par 5 that doglegs around the sagebrush and a lake. The signature hole is a short par 3 called "The Hanging Tree," which features water in the front and the back and a 100-year-old cottonwood tree looming next to the green. The course is wide open with only a few trees, so when the wind kicks up, usually during the afternoon, it can wreak havoc with your game.

Yardage: 6,085
Par: 72
USGA rating: 68
Slope: 120
Greens fees: $25 to $40
Reservations: 7 days in advance

NORTH SHORE LAKE TAHOE

Coyote Moon Golf Course
10685 Northwoods Boulevard
Truckee, CA
(530) 587-0886
www.coyotemoongolf.com

If you're torn between hiking through the incredibly beautiful Sierra Nevada and wanting to get in a great game of golf, your dilemma has been solved. Coyote Moon Golf Course offers players unbelievable views and vistas on its 250 acres of rolling fairways through the mountainsides and secluded pines of Tahoe-Donner. Designer Brad Bell took full advantage of the natural setting, incorporating the towering pines, enormous granite outcroppings, and beautiful Trout Creek to add dramatic elements of risk to the course. The signature 13th hole, a 227-yard par 3, is a 100-plus-foot elevation drop over Trout Creek. According to *Golf Today* magazine, "the front 9 is captivating, and the back 9 spectacular."

Yardage: 6,211
Par: 72
USGA rating: 69.1
Slope: 130
Greens fees: $95 to $155
Reservations: 30 days in advance

Incline Village Golf Resort
690 Wilson Way (mountain course)
955 Fairway Boulevard
(championship course)
Incline Village, NV
(775) 832-1303
(866) 925-4653 (reservations only)
www.golfincline.com

Owned and managed by the Incline Village General Improvement District (IVGID), Incline Village Golf Resort boasts both an 18-hole championship course and an 18-hole mountain course. The championship course was closed for two years for renovation but welcomed players back in 2005.

The Championship Course—Consistently rated four Stars by *Golf Digest* magazine, this course has tight, rolling fairways bordered by towering pines. A mountain creek snakes its way through the course and provides for strategically placed water hazards on 13 of the 18 holes. Robert Trent Jones Sr. called this course "an example of an ideal mountain course," and he should know because he designed it. His layout demands accuracy as well as distance. Golfers are faced with heavily bunkered greens on almost every hole (more than 50 sand traps are scattered around the course). The greens are

large, undulating, and fast. Almost every shot here poses a challenge to the most experienced golfer. The signature hole, No. 16, is a 406-yard par 4 with a dogleg-right fairway and a spectacular view of Lake Tahoe in the distance. The second shot on this magnificent hole requires you to hit over a ravine to an isolated green. *Golf Digest* always rates this course as one of the best in the West. It lives up to Jones's philosophy that every hole should be a tough par but an easy bogey.

Yardage: 6,447
Par: 72
USGA rating: 70.2
Slope: 129
Greens fees: $155
Reservations: 14 days in advance

The Mountain Course—This par 58, 3,500-yard course was designed by Robert Trent Jones Jr. and is rated as one of the top five executive courses in the United States. It is also cut out of the gigantic pines and has outstanding views of Lake Tahoe. The course is hilly and has all the hazards of the championship course with the exception of length. The mountain course features 14 par 3 holes, averaging more than 170 yards in length. This course has played host to the National Executive Course Championship.

Yardage: 3,513
Par: 58
USGA rating: 56.6
Slope: 94
Greens fees: $55
Reservations: 14 days in advance

Northstar-at-Tahoe Golf Course
129 Basque Drive at Northstar-at-Tahoe
Truckee, CA
(530) 562-2490
www.skinorthstar.com

Spectacular scenery of the mountains near Lake Tahoe add to this course's appeal. Its 18 holes are intertwined among woods and fields, and golfers like to call this kind of course "two-faced" because the front and back nine are totally different. The front nine is played through a valley with rolling, wide-open fairways, and

---

Technology gives players a big boost at Coyote Moon Golf Course, where carts come equipped with GPS and computer yardage systems.

---

the back nine changes looks as it climbs into the tall pines. These holes have skinny fairways, numerous doglegs, and require tricky, target golf shots. The course has plenty of water and sand bunkers, and its par 3s are gorgeous. The greens are medium size and fast. The course has a habit of eating golf balls, so bring plenty. It's usually open May through October. The course is located in the Northstar-at-Tahoe resort (see the Resorts chapter).

Yardage: 6,015
Par: 72
USGA rating: 67.5
Slope: 125
Greens fees: $45 to $99
Reservations: 14 days in advance

Old Brockway Golf Club
7900 North Lake Boulevard (corner of California Highways 267 and 28)
Kings Beach, CA
(530) 546-9909
www.oldbrockway.com

This nine-hole course is located a block from Lake Tahoe and features rolling hills, a meandering creek, tall pines, and excellent views. Built in 1924 and home of the first Bing Crosby Tournament, Brockway is one of the oldest courses at Lake Tahoe. It was also a favorite of the Rat Pack (Frank Sinatra, Dean Martin, Sammy Davis Jr., and crew). Extremely challenging because of its narrow fairways and wooded roughs, it is usually the first to open and the last to close at the lake. Reminiscent of its colorful history, the clubhouse showcases the Old Tahoe style of architecture, with massive logs and soaring ceilings. I suggest lunch or an after-round drink on the lovely patio that faces the lake. The following information is based on 18 holes of play.

Yardage: 6,054
Par: 72

For news, events, and more detailed information concerning the golf courses in the Reno/Tahoe area, visit www.golfthehighsierra.com.

USGA rating: 67.6
Slope: 125
Greens fees: $50 to $65, excluding cart
Reservations: 7 days in advance

Ponderosa Golf Club
10040 Reynold Way, Truckee, CA
(530) 587-3501
www.ponderosagolfclub.com

This is one of the easiest courses at Lake Tahoe and is ideal for the beginning golfer. The nine-hole course is mostly flat and nestled beneath towering pines, but it is forgiving. The course has no water hazards, and the greens are in excellent condition. Don't play this course unless you like to wait while playing. The course is open from May through October. The following information is based on 18 holes of play.

Yardage: 5,800
Par: 70
USGA rating: 66.6
Slope: 111
Greens fees: $52, excluding cart
Reservations: 10 days in advance

Resort at Squaw Creek
400 Squaw Creek Road
Olympic Valley, CA
(530) 583-6300, (530) 581-6637
(800) 327-3353 (reservations only)
www.squawcreek.com

This Robert Trent Jones Jr.–designed course is everything you would expect from both the prolific designer and a Lake Tahoe resort course: beautiful mountain and meadow views and a challenging course set among existing wetlands and forested hills. The course has been honored by *Golf* magazine as one of the "Top 10 Courses You Can Play," and by *Golf Today* as one of the top resort courses in northern California. It's lush and plays like a links course, with tees, landing areas, and greens strategically placed to take advantage of the natural hazards. The front nine has narrow fairways and rows and rows of towering pines. The back nine has elevated wooden cart paths built over the wetlands and has a propensity for eating golf balls, so bring an extra supply. The signature hole is the par 5 13th, which is 500 yards long and requires at least a 200-yard drive off the tee to carry the wetlands. See the Winter Sports, Recreation, and Resorts chapters for more information on Squaw Valley. The course is usually open from April through October.

Yardage: 6,010
Par: 71
USGA rating: 69.3
Slope: 125
Greens fees: $50 to $125
Reservations: 30 days in advance for nonguests; 3 months in advance for guests

Tahoe City Golf Course
251 North Lake Boulevard, Tahoe City, CA
(530) 583-1516

Located behind a commercial block off the main thoroughfare in Tahoe City and easily spotted from Fanny Bridge, this nine-hole course is hilly, wooded, and well bunkered. Built in 1917 and designed by May "Queenie" Dunn Hupfel, it is the oldest course in the Tahoe Basin and has some spectacular views of Lake Tahoe, which is right across the street. Its claim to fame is that it drew Hollywood stars like Frank Sinatra, Bing Crosby, and Bob Hope regularly during the 1940s and 1950s, and it has remained a locals' hangout to this day. It is the shortest course at the lake and is open from April through October. The following information is based on 18 holes of play.

Yardage: 5,261
Par: 66
USGA rating: 65.1
Slope: 111
Greens fees: $20 to $50, excluding cart
Reservations: 14 days in advance

Tahoe Donner Golf Club
11509 Northwoods Boulevard, Truckee, CA
(530) 587-9440
(530) 587-9443 (pro shop)
www.tahoedonner.com

This course is located in a residential/resort development and features narrow, tight fairways through the pines. Here, accuracy is more important than power. The first hole is an example of the kind of play needed on the entire course. The hole is a straight-ahead, 450-yard par 5 lined with pines requiring straight hitting. A slice or a hook here is real trouble. A creek comes into play on eight holes, and the course is hilly, with many drops from tee to fairway to green. This course is extremely well maintained and difficult to play. But it may be even more difficult to get a tee time, because residents get first pick during the season that lasts from May through October.

Yardage: 6,587
Par: 72
USGA rating: 71.2
Slope: 128
Greens fees: $120
Reservations: 10 days in advance for weekdays; Friday before for weekends

Worth the Drive

The following golf courses are located in and around the Graeagle area of California adjacent to California Highway 89 and California Highway 70. (See the Day Trips chapter for more information about Graeagle.) This section of the Sierra has been dubbed "The Pebble Beach of the North" because of the many excellent and scenic golf courses in the area that are open for seasonal play. The driving time is about 40 minutes from the North Shore of Lake Tahoe and one hour from Reno.

The Dragon
33 Bear Run
Clio, CA
(530) 832-4887, (800) 368-7786
www.dragongolf.com

Designed by Robin Nelson, the Dragon is ranked among the likes of Pebble Beach, Spyglass Hill, and Pasatiempo. With holes given names such as "Revenge," "Hope," and "Dragon's Lookout," and ending with the 18th, "Enlightenment," golfers are given an opportunity to play the full gamut—from your easy par 3s to 500-plus par 5s, with such challenges as 100-plus-foot drop-offs, ravines, gulches, and juniper-nestled greens surrounded by bunkers thrown in for good measure. Golfers will need every club in their bag to master this course. As frustrated as one might get, however, the spectacular views of the Sierra and the Feather River will easily calm one's nerves. Once you've experienced the beauty of this golfer's Sierra "jewel," make sure you take the time to visit the Frank Lloyd Wright–designed clubhouse, Nakoma.

Yardage: 6,380
Par: 72
USGA rating: 70.6
Slope: 136
Greens fees: $129 to $139
Reservations: Accepted throughout the season

Feather River Inn Golf Course and Resort
California Highways 89 and 70
Blairsden, CA
(530) 836-2722, (530) 836-2623
www.featherriverinn.com

This nine-hole course has an extremely challenging layout. Like most of the courses in the Sierra, its fairways are tight and lined with trees, and the greens are fast. One thing that favors golfers here is the terrain: At least it's mostly flat. Here again, like the other mountain courses, accuracy is rewarded over distance. The ninth hole is probably the prettiest hole of all the courses in the area. It is uphill to a green surrounded by the resort, which features a rustic-looking lodge. The lodge

A 240-yard golf shot at sea level would be a 280-yard shot at Tahoe because of the 6,000-foot elevation.

was under renovation at press time and scheduled to reopen in 2007. This course has no driving range. The following information is based on 18 holes of play.

Yardage: 5,758
Par: 70
USGA rating: 64.8
Slope: 104
Greens fees: $42
Reservations: First-come, first-served

Feather River Park Resort
8339 California Highway 89
Blairsden, CA
(530) 836-2328
www.featherriverparkresort.com
Because the holes are short and not intimidating, this course is ideal for senior and junior golfers. Located along the Feather River, this nine-hole course is flat and relatively open. A few pine trees are sprinkled around the course, but they pose little problem and mostly just add to the great scenery. The two par 5 holes on the course are less than 450 yards, making them reachable in two. This course is part of a resort with small cabins and other recreational activities. It has no driving range. The following information is based on 18 holes of play.

Yardage: 5,164
Par: 70
USGA rating: N/A
Slope: N/A
Greens fees: $18 to $20, excluding cart
Reservations: Walk-on

Golf Club at Whitehawk Ranch
768 Whitehawk Drive, Clio, CA
(530) 836-0394, (800) 332-4295
www.golfwhitehawk.com
Resting against the eastern slope of the Sierra in the Mohawk Valley, this championship course is located in the middle of a housing development. But don't panic: The development only has 200 homes, and the developers have maintained the rustic, rural charm of the mountain atmosphere. They hired Dick Bailey to design the course (a first for this architect), and he did such a good job that the California Golf Writers' Association awarded Whitehawk its 1997 Environmental Award for protecting the environment while furthering the game of golf. The course was built in 1996 and includes plenty of pines, water, and 45 acres of native grasses and wildflowers bordering the fairways. Some people think this course is on even par with the prestigious Edgewood at South Shore Lake Tahoe. The course has four signature holes, but the prettiest may be the 10th, which has a magnificent view of the Mohawk Valley. Most of the holes have streamlined fairways and multitiered greens. The course is well maintained, and once again the views will almost make you forget your golf game. Don't come here unless you like a challenge. The Northern California Golf Association added Whitehawk to its championship rotation, which includes such renowned courses as Pebble Beach, Spyglass, and the Olympic Club.

Yardage: 6,422
Par: 71
USGA rating: 70.2
Slope: 122
Greens fees: $95 to $130
Reservations: 6 months in advance

Graeagle Meadows Golf Course
18 California Highway 89
Graeagle, CA
(530) 836-2323
www.playgraeagle.com
Graeagle Meadows weaves its way through the Mohawk Valley, straddles the Feather River, and makes good use of the towering pines. This course is always in excellent shape and, like so many others in the Sierra, has spectacular scenery. The most renowned landmark is Chief Graeagle, a rock formation to the west of the sixth tee. Ask any Insider to point out his headdress and moccasins at either end of the 2-mile-long formation. Great scenes like this can almost make you forget about the flat, narrow fairways and well-protected greens. The most intimidating hole is the short par 3 16th, with a pine tree blocking the center

of the green. The course is usually open from late March through October.

Yardage: 6,345
Par: 72
USGA rating: 70.1
Slope: 128
Greens fees: $30 to $70
Reservations: Anytime during season

Plumas Pines Golf Club
402 Poplar Valley Road
Blairsden, CA
(530) 836-1420
www.plumaspinesgolf.com

This golf resort is open to the public and is one of the most popular around if you are a low-handicap player. Another "two-faced" course (distinctively different front and back nines), it has a front nine that lies in a valley surrounded by lots of water and a narrow, hilly back nine that climbs into the pines. One of the best-manicured courses in the Sierra, it demands a high level of play. Water exists on 11 holes, and it has several blind doglegs. The greens are heavily bunkered, and houses parallel many of the holes, making accuracy your prime objective. The signature hole is the 395-yard par 4 No. 9 with its view across a small lake to the clubhouse, which sits on a hill overlooking the course. The most difficult hole may be the 18th, with a double dogleg, an uphill approach, and a tiered green. Some of the holes on this course are the most difficult of all the courses in the area. This golf club is usually open from May through October.

Yardage: 5,894
Par: 72
USGA rating: 68.5
Slope: 123
Greens fees: $50 to $80
Reservations: No limitations

SOUTH SHORE LAKE TAHOE

Bijou Golf Course
3464 Fairway Boulevard off Johnson Boulevard
South Lake Tahoe, CA
(530) 542-6097
www.ci.south-lake-tahoe.ca.us/

A historic nine-hole executive course built in 1920 in the center of South Lake Tahoe, this course is perfect for all level of players. Bijou Creek winds through the course, providing the water hazards, and of course pine trees add to golfers' frustration. It has a great view of Heavenly Ski Resort and Freal Peak. The course allows only pull carts and doesn't take advance reservations, but it is usually easy to get on. The following information is based on 18 holes of play for a nonresident (pull carts are $3.00).

Yardage: 4,056
Par: 64
USGA rating: N/A
Slope: N/A
Greens fees: $29, excluding cart
Reservations: None taken in advance

Edgewood Tahoe Golf Course
180 Lake Parkway
Stateline, NV
(775) 588-3566
(888) 881-8659 (reservations)
www.edgewood-tahoe.com

This course is *IT—the* premier golfing experience in the Reno/Tahoe area. Built along the lush shoreline of Lake Tahoe, Edgewood features both wide-open fairways and narrow ones laced through the pines with both rolling and flat terrain. It is rated by *Golf Digest* as one of the top 25 courses in the country. Edgewood has more than 80 sand traps, many of which protect the large, undulating, and terraced greens that are pro caliber and super fast. Many strategically placed trees come into play; water is a factor on 11 holes. This course is the most difficult to score well on in Nevada. The Crown Jewel of the Sierra, Edgewood has the distinction of having the only holes on the shore of Lake Tahoe: the signature 17th, a 207-yard par 3, and the 574-yard par 5 18th.

This course is a must-play for the true golf aficionado, but its popularity makes it difficult to get a tee time. The course has played host to many professional events and is currently home to the American Century Championship Golf tournament every July (see the Spectator Sports and Annual Events chapters). Do yourself a big golfing favor, and don't leave the area without playing this George Fazio-designed masterpiece.

Yardage: 6,365
Par: 72
USGA rating: 70.2
Slope: 127
Greens fees: $150 to $200
Reservations: 90 days in advance

Lake Tahoe Golf Course
2500 Emerald Bay Road
South Lake Tahoe, CA
(530) 577-0788
www.laketahoegc.com

This course used to be called the Lake Tahoe Country Club, to give you an idea of the quality of play here. Conveniently located in an alpine meadow surrounded by tall Sierra peaks, the course is just minutes from the glitter of Stateline, Nevada. It's flat to slightly rolling, with the Upper Truckee River and artificial lakes coming into play on 16 holes. The greens are in excellent condition. This layout isn't long, but it is treacherous, making good ball placement a top priority. Over the last decade or so, the course has gone through extensive renovations.

Yardage: 6,160
Par: 71
USGA rating: 68.8
Slope: 120
Greens fees: $74
Reservations: 60 days in advance

Tahoe Paradise Golf Course
3021 U.S. Highway 50
South Lake Tahoe, CA
(530) 577-2121
www.tahoeparadisegc.com

This executive course was South Lake Tahoe's first 18-holer. The course is short but once again has all the nasty quirks of a mountain course—narrow fairways, tree-lined roughs, and small greens. But thankfully, water comes into play on only two holes. The most difficult hole is a 377-yard par 4 that requires a tee shot through a gap only 50 yards across. The signature hole is the fifth, a 110-yard par 3 with a lake in front and a view of the surrounding mountain peaks.

Yardage: 4,034
Par: 66
USGA rating: 60.9
Slope: 103
Greens fees: $57
Reservations: 7 days in advance

Worth the Drive

Carson City, Nevada's capital, and the surrounding Carson Valley sit just over the mountain from Lake Tahoe and are 30 miles down U.S. Highway 395 from Reno. Here, excellent golf courses wait for you to tee one up. All of these courses are definitely worth the drive because they are some of the best maintained in Nevada and are a lot of fun to play.

Carson Valley Golf Course
1027 Riverview Drive, Gardnerville, NV
(775) 265-3181
www.carsonvalleygolf.com

Just by the address, you can guess the biggest hazard on this course: water. The East Fork of the Carson River snakes its way through this 18-hole course, creating a natural water hazard on all but two holes, so bring plenty of extra golf balls. Even though it's not in the mountains, its fairways are still narrow with a lot of rough and out of bounds, but at least you won't have to worry about pine trees—here, it's towering cottonwoods that line the fairways. Although it's a joy to play, it can be quite frustrating if you can't hit a straight shot. Carson Valley has a real rustic feel to it and is located on the outskirts of one of the prettiest small towns in Nevada. (Check out the Day Trips chapter for more to see and do in Gardnerville.)

Yardage: 6,003
Par: 71
USGA rating: 66.8
Slope: 111
Greens fees: $30 to $42
Reservations: 7 days in advance; beyond 7 days, a credit card is required

Dayton Valley Golf Club
51 Palmer Drive, Dayton, NV
(775) 246-7888, (800) 644-3822
www.daytonvalley.com

This is a magnificent Arnold Palmer-designed course located 11 miles east of Carson City in the high desert. The course has been open since 1991, and it ranks among *Golf Today*'s list of top 20 daily-fee courses in northern California and Nevada, which means it is in the same company as Pebble Beach, Spyglass, and Spanish Bay.

Palmer designed a beautiful layout that combines the natural beauty of the high desert with rolling fairways sculpted in a links style. Rolling hills are dotted with sand traps that surround the fairways that must be mastered before reaching the huge, sloping greens. The course has few trees, but strategically placed water hazards come into play on 12 holes. The course is superbly maintained and is known for its plush, velvetlike fairways and immaculate greens. The first par 3 on the front nine is dubbed the "Moon Crater" because the green sits below the tee box in a small glade surrounded by steep hills and sand traps, giving the hole a surreal feel.

The number-one handicapped hole is the par 4 No. 9, which requires you to hit over and around two water hazards. After a good tee shot (more than 230 yards), you still have at least 160 yards, all over water, to carry the green. As with the No. 6, a par on this hole is an accomplishment.

Yardage: 5,897
Par: 72
USGA rating: 68.2
Slope: 128
Greens fees: $40 to $105
Reservations: 2 weeks in advance

Eagle Valley Golf Courses
3999 Centennial Park Drive
Carson City, NV
(775) 887-2380
www.eaglevalleygolf.com

This golf facility has two regulation 18-hole courses—The West and The East—which offer two distinctively different modes of play. The West Course has lots of water, trees, sand bunkers, and sagebrush. The East Course is wide open.

The West Course—This links-style course is hilly and requires you to hit the ball straight, since almost every hole is lined with water or sagebrush. It was designed by Jack Snyder in 1977 to challenge you on every hole, and it does that and more. Playing well requires correct club selection and good course management. This course has great views of Carson City as it winds its way up, down, and around the foothills on the northeastern side of town. The 14th tee offers spectacular views of the eastern side of the Sierra. Changes in course elevation and strategically located water and bunkers add to its challenging layout. A round here isn't for the fainthearted golfer. If your game isn't top drawer, you'll no doubt be frustrated.

Yardage: 5,819
Par: 72
USGA rating: 67.3
Slope: 127
Greens fees: $15 to $35
Reservations: 10 days in advance

The East Course—This 18 is wide open and offers a good game for all styles of play. A great course for couples, seniors, juniors, and beginning to intermediate golfers, it features manicured fairways and quick greens. Rambling throughout the flat valley beneath the foothills, it was made for the big hitters who like to go for broke. A wayward shot will usually find another fairway, so trouble is at a minimum here. The East Course is great for walking a quick 9 or riding a leisurely 18.

Yardage: 6,314

Par: 72
USGA rating: 68
Slope: 117
Greens fees: $25 to $35
Reservations: 10 days in advance

Empire Ranch Golf Course
1875 Fair Way Drive
Carson City, NV
(775) 885-2100, (888) 227-1335
www.empireranchgolf.com
This course opened in 1997 and is set among the wetlands overlooking the Carson River. Its 27 holes are squeezed between high bluffs and include 46 acres of wetlands and six lakes. You can see that water hazards are plentiful, so bring a lot of golf balls. You can start on any nine holes, so you really have a choice of playing three courses here. Once again, several shots must carry the wetlands, but course designer Cary Beckler was thoughtful of the high handicappers. He designed a bailout option on almost every hole for those who need the help.

Yardage: 6,207
Par: 72
USGA rating: 69
Slope: 124
Greens fees: $25 to $40
Reservations: 7 days in advance

Genoa Lakes Golf Club
1 Genoa Lakes Drive
Genoa, NV
(775) 782-4653, (866) 795-2709
www.genoalakes.com
A semiprivate club with the amenities of a private one, Genoa Lakes is located in Nevada's oldest town. This Peter Jacobson/John Harbottle–designed course is spectacular and rests against the slopes of the eastern Sierra with miles and miles of valley and mountain views. Built around a large wetlands, this links-style course is long and extremely challenging. Water comes into play on 13 holes, and its huge sand traps have a propensity for reaching out and grabbing even the best golf shots. Home of the 1998 U.S. Open Qualifying Tournament, this course will definitely test every part of your game—but again, the views are so magnificent you won't mind shooting a mediocre game of golf. The signature hole is the 13th, a 652-yard par 5, the longest in Nevada. The trick to this course is a well-placed tee shot. Any other type of tee shot is trouble with a capital "T." Partnered with Genoa Lakes Golf Resort (formerly Sierra Nevada Golf Ranch), this course is also known as the Lakes Course.

Yardage: 5,969
Par: 72
USGA rating: 67.0
Slope: 122
Greens fees: $60 to $120
Reservations: 7 days in advance

Genoa Lakes Golf Resort
2901 Jacks Valley Road
Genoa, NV
(775) 782-7700, (866) 795-2709
www.genoalakes.com
Formerly Sierra Nevada Golf Ranch, Genoa Lakes Golf Resort (nicknamed the Resort Course) was acquired by Genoa Lakes Golf Club in 2005. Because the two courses are paired, you can schedule tee times for both at the same number and Web site. It was designed in what golf architects call a nonparallel format, meaning holes don't run next to one another. This gives the effect that you and your foursome are the only golfers on the course, because you can't peek over onto the next fairway to see anyone else. The holes are laid out with a sense of solitude in mind.

The front nine begins on the valley floor and climbs 300 feet up the eastern slope of the Sierra. The back nine snakes its way through desert terrain. Water comes into play on four holes, including a spectacular waterfall on No. 17. The course also has 114 sand bunkers and several grass ones lining the greens and fairways. The 10th hole is one of the prettiest, with the entire right side framed by a cascading creek. The signature hole is No. 17, a 165-yard par 3 with a huge island green surrounded on three sides by a lake with a waterfall located in back. The hole with the best view from the tee is the 478-yard sixth. The green on this hole seems to float above the purple-hued valley with the Sierra looming in the background. This is also the number-one-handicapped hole, so don't let the wonderful view distract you.

The facility offers 10 acres of practice area, which the club calls "The Shooting Range" instead of the driving range. It also has the largest clubhouse in Nevada, a 20,000-square-foot wood-and-stone building that used to be a hunting lodge.

Yardage: 6,207
Par: 72
USGA rating: 69.7
Slope: 129
Greens fees: $60 to $120
Reservations: 1 week in advance

Silver Oak Golf Club
1251 Country Club Drive
Carson City, NV
(775) 841-7000
www.silveroakgolf.com

Silver Oak is the newest golf course in Carson City. It opened in the summer of 1999 and provides middle- to high-handicappers a great course that is quite forgiving. It's located behind the Kmart store in northwest Carson City and winds its way through the Silver Oak development and the Sierra foothills. The course is relatively short, even from the tournament tees (6,564 yards long), and it offers five tee boxes on every hole (tournament, championship, regular, silver, and oaks).

Designed by Tom Duncan and Sid Salomon, Silver Oak is a fun but challenging golf experience. The golf pro here won't say what the signature hole is because, according to him, all of them are unique and wonderfully laid out. But most golfers who have tested the course say they like the middle-length par 5s, especially No. 12, except when the wind picks up. The 18-hole course stretches over 150 acres, and it has a beautiful practice facility with a driving range, a bunker, and a putting green.

i

Annika Sorenstam of the LPGA and Scott McCarron, Kirk Triplett, and Dan Forsman have maintained homes in the Reno/Tahoe area.

Yardage: 5,716
Par: 71
USGA rating: 66.6
Slope: 118
Greens fees: $25 to $50
Reservations: 2 weeks in advance

Sunridge Golf Club
1000 Long Drive
Carson City, NV
(775) 267-4448
(775) 884-2110 (toll-free from Reno)
www.sunridgegolfclub.com

Sunridge was carved from the steep hills on the southern edge of Carson City. Its entrance is through a development just off US 395, and after rounding the last corner of the development, you can see the course cut from the hills and nestled on the valley floor. The front nine opens with a tough par 5 that is almost impossible to reach in two. The rest of the holes require good club selection and course management. The uphill No. 7 is a par 3 that will scare the daylights out of you. You have to hit a 150-yard shot over a gully to an elevated green surrounded by sand traps. Once there, you have to contend with a big swale that cuts through the huge green. Sunridge could become one of the most challenging courses in the area.

Yardage: 5,947
Par: 72
USGA rating: 68.1
Slope: 128
Greens fees: $25 to $75
Reservations: 14 days in advance

WINTER SPORTS 

When you ask winter-sports enthusiasts to describe winter in the Reno/Tahoe area, one word comes up over and over again—awesome! In some years the heavy storm fronts begin arriving from the Pacific Ocean as early as October, dumping huge amounts of that wonderful white stuff that turns the Sierra Nevada mountains into a winter wonderland. Snow is often measured in feet, not inches, and a normal winter will see accumulations of 30 to 40 feet in the higher elevations. Winter can last up to six months in the mountains, so there's plenty of time to indulge in your favorite outdoor activity. But in spite of massive amounts of snow, the temperatures stay relatively mild, usually above freezing during the day and dipping into the 20s at night. When it's not snowing, you can count on plenty of sunshine, making most days absolutely glorious for outdoor recreation.

Because Reno and Sparks get much less snow than the Lake Tahoe Basin (usually not more than a total of 2 feet), you can live in the banana belt but be on the ski slope in less than an hour. If you wanted to, you could play a round of golf in Reno or Sparks in the morning and ski in the nearby mountains that afternoon.

During normal snow years, many ski resorts are open by Thanksgiving, but when Mother Nature doesn't cooperate, ski resorts compensate by making snow. Occasional droughts have caused most resorts to install sophisticated snowmaking equipment on a large percentage of their terrain. Often the diehards, like Squaw Valley USA and Alpine Meadows, operate through July 4. As the ski season extends into the summer months, you can combine skiing in the morning with river rafting in the afternoon for an especially invigorating day. The first skiers in the Reno/Tahoe area were gold miners from Scandinavia who introduced the long, wooden boards as a means of transportation in the mid-1800s. With deep snow blocking roads and trails during winter, even the mail was carried on skis in those early pioneer days. Between 1856 and 1876, the legendary Snowshoe Thompson made the trip from Placerville, California, to Genoa, Nevada, twice a month, lugging about 100 pounds of mail. During the winter months, Thompson was able to get through the rugged mountainous terrain by strapping on hefty 10-foot-long skis that weighed about 25 pounds. Although skiing was simply utilitarian in the beginning, it wasn't long before it evolved into a recreational sport with lifts, competitions, and established resorts. To find out more about the history of skiing in the West, you can visit the Western SkiSport Museum at Boreal Mountain Resort near Truckee, California. (See the description of Truckee in the Day Trips chapter.)

Today the Reno/Tahoe area has the largest concentration of ski resorts in North America, with 15 alpine resorts and 11 cross-country resorts. Because these resorts offer such a diverse variety of terrain and amenities, it's a good idea to acquaint yourself with them before you decide where to ski or snowboard. For the ultimate in vertical, you can dive off the heart-stopping chutes at Squaw Valley. For all-out cruising you can burn down the meticulously groomed slopes at Northstar-at-Tahoe. For a fun first time on skis, you can snowplow without fear on the gentle runs at Tahoe Donner. To help you decide where it's best for you to ski or board, I give you vital statistics about area alpine and cross-country ski resorts in this chapter. I also give you Insiders' tips, such as where you can find the deepest ungroomed powder, which resorts have the most exciting snowboard terrain, what mountains offer the greatest views, which trail systems are the most interesting, and much more.

Since the weather influences the quality of your ski experience, you need to consider it when choosing where to go. To avoid the wind on stormy days, one of the best places to go is Northstar, because its tree-lined runs will shield you from the gusts. Resorts with high wind exposure include Mt. Rose, Squaw, Alpine, and Sugar Bowl, where it's not unusual to have upper lifts on wind-hold on windy days. If it's raining and you still want to ski, try resorts at the higher elevations, such as Mt. Rose or Boreal, since it may be snowing rather than raining there. For maximum sun exposure you can ski the open bowls at Squaw and Alpine and the upper runs at Diamond Peak Ski Resort and Heavenly Ski Resort, where you're sure to get a winter tan (or burn) after just a few trips down the mountain.

If you're a first-time or novice skier or snowboarder, I strongly recommend you take lessons at one of the resorts. Although your friends may be well-meaning in volunteering to teach you, learning the basics from a professional instructor is the fastest and best way to go. All the resorts offer packages that include rental equipment, lift tickets, or trail passes along with lessons. You can choose from individual or group instruction. If you plan to be at the resort for a full day, try to get a lesson first thing so you can use the rest of the day to practice your new skills.

If you're unfamiliar with a resort, be sure to carry a trail map. It's very easy to become disoriented on the mountain, especially if the weather turns stormy. Many resorts also have large trail maps at the tops of chairlifts, so you can get your bearings without fumbling for the map you've stashed in the inside pocket of your parka. To avoid injury, it's a good idea to stretch before hopping on the lift and to make your first runs easy warm-ups to get the feel of the snow. Also be sure to follow the Skier Responsibility Code that is printed on most trail maps and lift tickets.

To beat the crowds, Insiders ski the major alpine resorts like Squaw, Alpine, Heavenly, Northstar, Diamond Peak, and Kirkwood during the week rather than on weekends. You can try smaller alpine resorts and cross-country locations on the weekends. To avoid being shut out, consider buying your lift tickets online at the resort Web sites. Many offer that option along with special rates for teens, seniors, and small children.

But winter isn't just about skiing and snowboarding; it's also the jingle of sleigh bells on horse-drawn sleighs, the swoosh of skates skimming on ice, the zooming of snowmobiles zigzagging through the forest, the plopping of snowshoes in deep powder snow, and the barking of dogs pulling fur-laden sleds. In this chapter I tell you where and how you can enjoy these other winter activities as well.

Now let's get back to skiing and boarding and take a look at the eclectic variety of resorts you can choose from. The ski resorts in the Reno/Tahoe area are scattered in and around the Lake Tahoe Basin, so they're listed by the two geographic areas at the lake. Prices are quoted as of press time for all-day adult lift tickets and trail passes, but keep in mind that they could be slightly higher because some resorts raise them each ski season.

ALPINE SKIING AND SNOWBOARDING

North Shore Lake Tahoe

Alpine Meadows
2600 Alpine Meadows Road
Tahoe City, CA
(530) 583-4232, (800) 441-4423
www.alpinemeadows.com
Base elevation: 6,835 feet
Top elevation: 8,637 feet
Vertical drop: 1,802 feet
Number of runs: 100-plus
Capacity: 16,500 skiers per hour

Terrain: 25 percent beginner, 40 percent intermediate, 35 percent advanced
Skiable acres: 2,000
Longest run: 2.5 miles
Number of lifts: 13
Average snowfall: 495 inches
Lift tickets: $41
Terrain parks: 3
Snowphone: (530) 581-8374
Getting there: To get to Alpine Meadows, take California Highway 89 north 6 miles from Tahoe City or CA 89 south 13 miles from Interstate 80 in Truckee to Alpine Meadows Road.

From plunging chutes to gentle trails and from open bowls to tree-lined runs, Alpine Meadows has it all. Because of the diversity of terrain for all levels of skiers and boarders, it's a great favorite with locals. The resort includes both sides of Ward and Scott Peaks, with ungroomed advanced territory sprinkled among the groomed beginner and intermediate runs. Novice skiers can feel comfortable with two chairlifts servicing several gentle runs that are out of the way of more advanced skiing terrain. Fearless young boarders and skiers especially like Alpine's adventure zones, which are similar to backcountry areas, along with its terrain parks that feature jumps, spines, halfpipes, and table tops.

The resort has several restaurants on the mountain as well as the usual bars and cafes in the lodge at the base. For the best après-ski action, be sure to stop at the River Ranch Lodge at the intersection of CA 89 and Alpine Meadows Road. Jutting out over the Truckee River, this old lodge, with its huge rock fireplace, is warm and cozy after an invigorating day on the mountain. Check out the trout swimming by while you enjoy your favorite drink, and then stay for a lovely continental dinner in the inviting dining room. During summer the outdoor patio is a great people-watching hangout since it's the termination point for rafters coming down the Truckee River.

Because it's so popular, Alpine can be very crowded. The parking lot fills up fast, so try to arrive early to minimize your walk from the car to the base of the mountain. Shuttle buses will take you from outlying parking lots to the base once the close-in lots fill up.

Boreal Mountain Resort
Interstate 80, 45 miles west of Reno, NV
(530) 426-3666
www.borealski.com, www.jibassicpark.com
Base elevation: 7,200 feet
Top elevation: 7,800 feet
Vertical drop: 500 feet
Number of runs: 41
Capacity: 8,000 skiers per hour
Terrain: 30 percent beginner, 55 percent intermediate, 15 percent advanced
Skiable acres: 380
Longest run: 1 mile
Number of lifts: 10
Average snowfall: 420 inches
Lift tickets: $38
Terrain park: Jibassic Park
Snowphone: (530) 426-3666
Getting there: Boreal Mountain Resort has easy access from I-80, 45 miles west of Reno off the Castle Peak exit.

With short runs on mostly beginner to intermediate terrain, Boreal appeals to those who are learning to ski. You don't have to spend a fortune to learn at Boreal; lift tickets and lessons are cheaper than at some other resorts. It boasts a variety of children's programs, and because of the resort's small size, it's easy for parents to observe their children's learning progress. New in 2005 is Jibassic Park, a state-of-the-art terrain park featuring a 450-foot superpipe along with 50 rails and 50 fun boxes.

Boreal's high elevation and comprehensive snowmaking allow it to be one of the first resorts to open every year. It offers night skiing until 9:00 P.M. and bar and restaurant service in its base lodge. Rooms are also available in the Boreal Inn, just steps from the lifts. While at Boreal, be sure to visit the Western SkiSport Museum (for more information see the Day Trips chapter).

Diamond Peak Ski Resort
1210 Ski Way Drive
Incline Village, NV
(775) 832-1177
www.diamondpeak.com
Base elevation: 6,700 feet
Top elevation: 8,540 feet
Vertical drop: 1,840
Number of runs: 30
Capacity: 7,700 skiers per hour
Terrain: 18 percent beginner, 46 percent intermediate, 36 percent advanced
Skiable acres: 655
Longest run: 2.5 miles
Number of lifts: 6
Average snowfall: 300 inches
Lift tickets: $46
Terrain park: Snowbomb Terrain Park
Snowphone: (775) 831-3211
Getting there: To reach Diamond Peak from Reno/Sparks, take Nevada Highway 431 to Incline Village, turn left onto Country Club Drive, and then look for Ski Way Drive, and follow it to the top. From Incline Village take Nevada Highway 28 to Country Club Drive, and then turn onto Ski Way Drive and continue to the top. For information on free local ski shuttles, call (775) 832-1177 or check www.laketahoetransit.com or www.diamondpeak.com. The Hyatt Regency Lake Tahoe Resort, Spa & Casino also provides free transportation for its guests.

Not very many communities own and manage their very own ski resorts, but Incline Village isn't your average town. Operated by the Incline Village General Improvement District (IVGID), the governing body of the town, Diamond Peak Ski Resort emphasizes family fun. The resort offers a variety of passes that make family skiing a little more affordable, such as teen tickets and interchangeable parent passes. Skiers between ages 6 and 12 and 60 and 79 can ski for only $17. Residents of Incline Village are also eligible for special discounts. You don't have to worry about keeping track of your children at Diamond Peak; all of the runs funnel into one base area, making it a very secure environment for families.

Along with its intimate atmosphere and short lift lines, Diamond Peak offers some of the most spectacular views of any ski resort in the area. For a stunning panorama of Lake Tahoe, ride the Crystal Quad chair to the top and take a leisurely run down the ridge. With an unobstructed all-around view, it will seem as though the lake engulfs you as you cruise to the base. For lunch with a view, nothing beats a big juicy hamburger at the Snowflake Lodge, perched high above the lake at the top of the Lakeview Quad chair.

Because many of the upper runs here are exposed to the wind and sun, conditions may be icy, especially if no snow has fallen recently. Also, the parking lot at Diamond Peak fills up fast on weekends, so try to arrive early. At the end of your ski day, I highly recommend an après-ski drink at the Big Water Grille, which is just across the lower end of the resort parking lot. The sunset view of Lake Tahoe from this tasteful bar/restaurant is absolutely stunning (see the review in the Restaurants chapter).

Donner Ski Ranch
19320 Donner Pass Road, off Interstate 80
Norden, CA
(530) 426-3635
www.donnerskiranch.com
Base elevation: 7,031 feet
Top elevation: 7,781 feet
Vertical drop: 750 feet
Number of runs: 45
Capacity: 7,200 skiers per hour
Terrain: 25 percent beginner, 50 percent intermediate, 25 percent advanced
Skiable acres: 460
Longest run: 1.5 miles
Number of lifts: 6
Average snowfall: 396 inches
Lift tickets: $16 to $32 depending upon day of week
Snowphone: (530) 426-3635
Getting there: To get to Donner Ski Ranch, take I-80 west about 45 miles from Reno and exit at the Soda Springs/Norden exit onto Donner Pass Road. The resort is 3.5 miles east.

Perched at the top of Donner Summit, Donner Ski Ranch is one of Reno/Tahoe's best-kept ski and snowboard secrets. It's not the Ritz, but it offers a back-to-basics mountain experience for half the price of major resorts. One of the oldest ski resorts in the West, it boasts the distinction of being one of California's last family-owned ski resorts. Its setting is simply spectacular, with gorgeous views of Donner Lake and the surrounding Sierra Nevada. Because the runs are wide open, you can enjoy the panorama all the way from the top to the bottom.

Donner Ski Ranch can provide welcome relief from the hassles found at major ski resorts. If you don't need dozens of watering holes, world-class cornices, and multi-mile runs, you can kick back here and just commune with the unspoiled mountain environment. Insiders know it's a great place for beginners: The small size and uncrowded slopes give novice skiers and snowboarders a feeling of comfort and security. Donner Ski Ranch offers the essential amenities found at most resorts, including a ski school, a base lodge with bar, a cafeteria, and a ski shop. Accommodations are available at the Summit House located on the slopes. Call (530) 426-3622 for information and reservations.

My only word of caution about this resort is that it can get very windy when winter storms are coming into the area.

Granlibakken Ski Resort
725 Granlibakken Road
Tahoe City, CA
(800) 543-3221, (877) 552-6301
www.granlibakken.com
Base elevation: 6,310 feet
Top elevation: 6,610 feet
Vertical drop: 300 feet
Number of runs: 1
Capacity: N/A
Terrain: 25 percent beginner, 75 percent intermediate
Skiable acres: 10
Longest run: N/A
Number of lifts: 2
Average snowfall: 325 inches
Lift tickets: $20
Getting there: Granlibakken is about 0.5 mile south of Tahoe City, just off CA 89.

Tiny Granlibakken is the oldest, the smallest, and one of the least expensive ski resorts at Lake Tahoe. Built in 1927 by Tahoe Tavern Resort and the Southern Pacific Railroad, Granlibakken was founded primarily as a training hill for Olympic ski jumpers. While much of the early history of Lake Tahoe skiing took place here, the resort has been eclipsed for many years by the larger, more comprehensive resorts in the Reno/Tahoe area.

The nearby Granlibakken Resort is an upscale conference center with modern condominium accommodations, seminar rooms, and a restaurant. Resort guests can use the ski hill at half price, and family packages are available.

If you're a total novice skier, Granlibakken (which means "hill sheltered by fir trees" in Norwegian) might provide enough challenge for you. Amenities include equipment rentals, lessons, a snack bar in the warming hut, lodging packages, a snow play area, and children's programs. The resort is open Friday, weekends, and holidays.

Mt. Rose-Ski Tahoe
22222 Mt. Rose Highway (Nevada Highway 431)
Reno, NV
(775) 849-0704, (800) 754-7673 (outside Nevada only)
www.skirose.com
Base elevation: 7,900 feet
Top elevation: 9,700 feet
Vertical drop: 1,800 feet
Number of runs: 60
Capacity: 13,400 skiers per hour
Terrain: 20 percent beginner, 30 percent intermediate, 40 percent advanced, 10 percent expert
Skiable acres: 1,200
Longest run: 2.5 miles
Number of lifts: 8
Average snowfall: 400 inches

Lift tickets: $54
Terrain parks: Badlands, Doubledown
Snowphone: (775) 849-0704
Getting there: To get to Mt. Rose, take NV 431 east for about 11 miles from Incline Village or go west for 22 miles from Reno.

With the highest base in the Reno/Tahoe area, Mt. Rose often enjoys snow while resorts lower in elevation may be drenched with rain. And when spring has sprung at other resorts, Mt. Rose's high altitude keeps the snow longer, blessing the resort with some of the best late-season skiing in the area. Although Mt. Rose is the closest major ski resort to an international airport in the world (25 minutes from Reno/Tahoe International Airport), it's always been a locals' resort rather than a tourist destination. When you ski here, you run into all your neighbors and friends. If your attorney wasn't in his office that morning, don't be surprised if you see him whizzing by you on Northwest Passage.

One lift ticket gives access to both the open bowls on the east, or Slide, side and the tree-lined runs on the Rose side. You can ski either side from the top, but I recommend skiing the Slide side in the morning when it's the sunniest and working your way over to the runs on Mt. Rose in the afternoon. The terrain here is varied enough to challenge skiers and boarders of all abilities. New in 2004, The Chutes offer 200 acres of heart-stopping ungroomed vertical between the Slide and Mt. Rose sides of the resort. And when Mother Nature dumps a foot or so of new snow on this peak, the powderhounds rejoice because it's one of the best spots for ungroomed powder in the area.

Both sides of the mountain have parking, ticket sales, food service, and restrooms, but the Mt. Rose side has a ski school, equipment rentals, and a ski shop. The restaurant on the Mt. Rose side is much larger, with a lovely deck for outdoor eating and a bar that really hops when the lifts close down. For really affordable skiing Mt. Rose offers a variety of weekday specials, such as Two-fer Tuesdays, Student Wednesdays, and Ladies' Day Thursdays.

From the summit of this resort, you can see forever, with Reno and Sparks glinting like tiny toy towns far in the distance. But this mountain catches the wind and the weather in a pretty brutal way, so don't be surprised if the resort is closed due to high winds or if the road is impassable because of heavy snow. If the weather looks dicey at all, call ahead or check current conditions at the resort Web site to avoid having to turn around.

i

Check out the Web site for whichever ski resort you plan to ski—you'll find up-to-date information on snow depths and road conditions, and some areas even have resort cams, which offer timely views of conditions on the mountain.

Northstar-at-Tahoe
California Highway 267 North, 6 miles north of Lake Tahoe
(530) 562-1010, (800) GO-NORTH
www.skinorthstar.com
Base elevation: 6,330 feet
Top elevation: 8,600 feet
Vertical drop: 2,270 feet
Number of runs: 73
Capacity: 19,400 skiers per hour
Terrain: 25 percent beginner, 50 percent intermediate, 25 percent advanced
Skiable acres: 2,420
Longest run: 1.3 miles
Number of lifts: 16
Average snowfall: 350 inches
Lift tickets: $63
Terrain parks: Superpipe, halfpipe, 6 terrain parks, 2 fun parks, adventure park
Snowphone: (530) 562-1330
Getting there: To get to Northstar, take I-80 west from Reno about 30 miles to Truckee, and then CA 267 south for 6 miles. From Kings Beach, California, take CA 267 north about 6 miles. For information about shuttle transportation to Northstar from the Lake Tahoe area, call

Snowboarders fly high out of Northstar-at-Tahoe's 17-foot superpipe. AARONROSEN.COM

(775) 883-2100. For information on ride sharing, call (800) GO-NORTH, and for free shuttle service from Reno, call (877) 274-7366.

Northstar-at-Tahoe calls itself the "Mountain of Fun," and as a major year-round destination resort, it's definitely a toss-up whether it's more fun in winter or in summer. I tell you more about Northstar, including warm-weather activities, in the Vacation Rentals, Resorts, and Recreation chapters, but for now, let's talk skiing, snowboarding, and tubing.

Because Northstar is one of the most comprehensive and best-maintained resorts in the Reno/Tahoe area, you can always have a great time here. The north-facing slope of Mt. Pluto is sheltered and tree-lined, providing ample protection from wintry weather. Many runs on this side of the mountain are long intermediate cruisers, impeccably groomed for maximum running speed. But powder seekers and extreme skiers can find chutes and short shots of ungroomed tree skiing scattered among the more gentle slopes.

The back side of Pluto is for more advanced skiers, with 1,860 vertical feet of groomed, ungroomed, and mogul skiing and boarding. Because this side of the mountain faces west (you get a gorgeous view of nearby Squaw Valley when riding the lift), it catches the brunt of storms as they approach from that direction. If the wind kicks up when you're skiing back here, you can find plenty of protected runs on the other side of the hill. Northstar also offers 200 acres of steep and deep on Lookout Mountain. Serviced by a high-speed quad, the five black-diamond runs are named for reservoirs that can be seen from the mountain: Boca, Gooseneck, Martis, Prosser, and Stampede. When it's time for the last run of the day, I recommend a leisurely looping run of about 3 miles starting at the top of Mt. Pluto and heading down East Ridge, Loggers Loop, and The Woods. As you glide on down to the village below, enjoy the spectacular view as the sinking sun paints the surrounding mountains and Martis Valley an intense golden hue. For a meaningful experience with the great outdoors, nothing beats this run for the gold.

As a major destination resort, Northstar is lacking in nothing when it comes to services that enhance your overall mountain experience. The charming Village Mall has a wide variety of shops, restaurants, and bars surrounding a picturesque ice-skating facility. Skating is complimentary, and rentals are available. Expansion of the mall started in 2004 and will continue to add upscale amenities over the next few years. When hunger pangs hit, you can head into the Lodge at Big Springs, which is midmountain, and enjoy hearty skier food while you people-watch from the expansive outdoor deck. Or if you'd rather have lunch with a gorgeous Lake Tahoe view, you can indulge your appetite at the Summit Deck & Grille perched at the very top of Mt. Pluto.

To minimize hassles and maximize the time skiers and boarders have on the snow, Northstar has a large electronic board at the top of Mt. Pluto showing the exact wait times for all lifts and restaurants on the mountain. It also runs a trolley from the parking lot and a free shuttle from all its resort accommodations to get you to the base of the mountain quicker and easier. (For details on accommodations see the Vacation Rentals and Resorts chapters.)

Frequent skiers and boarders at Northstar can save money plus keep track of the number of vertical feet they rack up by joining the Vertical Plus program. You can buy a personal electronic bracelet that logs in your vertical feet each time you board a lift. Vertical Plus members have their own lift access, plus they can receive discounts and rewards based upon the number of vertical feet they ski. For additional details call (530) 562-2267 or (530) 659-7453, ext. 208. The program is interchangeable with Sierra-at-Tahoe Snowsport Resort.

You simply can't go wrong spending a day (or days) at Northstar, since this resort has been delivering quality mountain adventures to outdoor enthusiasts for years. Because the number of skiers and boarders allowed on the mountain is cut off once the parking facilities are full, be sure to arrive early on weekends and holidays.

i

Northstar-at-Tahoe and Sierra-at-Tahoe sell a Double Whammy Pass, which is good for skiing at both resorts. For details call (530) 562-2267.

Soda Springs
Interstate 80 at Donner Summit
Norden, CA
(530) 426-3901
www.skisodasprings.com
Base elevation: 6,700 feet
Top elevation: 7,352 feet
Vertical drop: 652 feet
Number of runs: 16
Capacity: N/A
Terrain: 30 percent beginner, 50 percent intermediate, 20 percent advanced
Skiable acres: 200
Longest run: 1 mile
Number of lifts: 4
Average snowfall: 420 inches
Lift tickets: $25
Terrain parks: Kids X Park, Triple T Park
Snowphone: (530) 426-3901
Getting there: To get to Soda Springs, take I-80 west from Reno for about 45 miles to the Soda Springs/Norden exit, and follow the signs to Soda (about 1 mile). From Tahoe City take CA 89 north to Truckee, and then I-80 west to the Soda Springs/Norden exit.

One of the oldest ski resorts in the Lake Tahoe area, Soda Springs is a great beginner hill. You can count on uncrowded runs, even on weekends and holidays, and the prices can't be beat. It's easy for novice skiers to feel comfortable here, since the runs are comparatively gentle and wide open. Soda's location at the top of Donner Summit affords breathtaking views of the surrounding mountains on clear days. Amenities include a full-service rental shop, snowtubing, sledding, snowshoeing, ski lessons, and a cafeteria.

With an emphasis on family fun, Soda offers a variety of affordable lesson packages plus a moving carpet for first-time skiers and boarders age 8 and under. Kids ages 6 through 12 can also try out mini-snowmobiles on weekends and holidays.

Squaw Valley USA
1960 Squaw Valley Road
Olympic Valley, CA
(530) 583-6985, (800) 545-4350
(800) 403-0206
www.squaw.com
Base elevation: 6,200 feet
Top elevation: 9,050 feet
Vertical drop: 2,850 feet
Number of runs: 150
Capacity: 50,000 skiers per hour
Terrain: 25 percent beginner, 45 percent intermediate, 30 percent advanced
Skiable acres: 4,200
Longest run: 3.2 miles
Number of lifts: 32
Average snowfall: 450 inches
Lift tickets: $65
Terrain parks: Belmont, Riviera/Central Park, Ford Freestyle Superpipe
Snowphone: (530) 583-6955
Getting there: To get to Squaw Valley USA, take CA 89 north for 6 miles from Tahoe City. From Reno head west on I-80 for about 30 miles to Truckee, and then go south for about 13 miles on CA 89. For information on shuttle service from South Shore or North Shore Lake Tahoe and Reno, call (866) 769-4653; from North Shore or West Shore Lake Tahoe, contact (530) 581-7181; from Truckee and Tahoe City, call (530) 550-1212.

In February 1960 the greatest winter athletes in the world, representing 34 different nations, gathered in Squaw Valley to compete in the VIII Winter Olympics. A relatively unknown ski resort with four double chairlifts and one rope tow, Squaw Valley USA was catapulted into the world limelight by the resulting media coverage. Since that time Squaw has blossomed expansively, along with the growing popularity of winter sports in general. Big, bold, and beautiful, today it's a world-class resort in every way. The aura of the Olympics still abounds at Squaw, with the Olympic Flame still burning brightly in front of The Tower of Nations at the entrance to the resort. Sporting the five Olympic rings that represent the continents that compete (the Americas get one ring), the tower stands 79 feet high and 29 feet wide.

Spread out over six spectacular peaks, the amount of skiable terrain is absolutely daunting. It's divided into three sections: the base level at 6,200 feet, the upper level at 8,200 feet, and the Snow King area on the resort's eastern side. Some of the best beginner runs are on the upper elevation, which gives novices the same full mountain experience as more advanced skiers and snowboarders. Intermediates find comfortable runs in all sections, and advanced skiers are challenged by the spine-tingling chutes off Squaw Peak and KT-22, so named for the 22 kick-turns needed by most skiers to get to the bottom. Snowboarders are not forgotten: Squaw also has a variety of terrain parks with a challenging array of jumps, boxes, rails, and pipes designed especially for them. Squaw especially caters to new skiers at the Papoose Learning Area at the base. Dedicated to beginners, this expansive terrain allows novices to learn without worrying about being hit by or running into more advanced skiers and riders.

Because Squaw is so large, it's important to study the trail map to find your way around. Most of the skiable terrain is open and treeless, a disadvantage during windy weather. The state-of-the-art funitel transport system reduces upper mountain wind closures during high winds, but it doesn't diminish the wind on you once you get up to the higher elevation. But even if you decide to confine your skiing and boarding to the lower elevations, be sure to go to the top to enjoy the view. You can literally see for miles in every direction, with gorgeous Lake Tahoe shimmering to the south and magnificent snowcapped mountains all around you.

Because Squaw is a major destination resort by anyone's standards, the list of its amenities goes on and on. (See the Resorts, Vacation Rentals, and Recreation chapters for information about accommodations and warm-weather activities.) You can find dining and entertainment mid-mountain at High Camp and Gold Coast, with a plethora of eating and watering holes to choose from. In the base village you'll find an eclectic variety of more than 20 pubs and restaurants sprinkled among the upscale boutiques and sports shops. You can learn about the 1960 Winter Olympics at the Olympic Winter Games Museum or just continue skiing and boarding until 9:00 P.M., since Squaw also offers night skiing.

For a total mountain experience with all the glitz and glamor you read about in ski magazines, you can't go wrong at Squaw. It has everything any skier or snowboarder could conceivably imagine. But because it has so much to offer, it's usually extremely crowded. Even though its highly sophisticated lift system has been successful in eliminating long lift lines, you still have to contend with crowds at the base. The word to the wise is to arrive early to find a place to park your car in the free lots. Then with so many restaurants to choose from mid-mountain, consider having breakfast with a view before you start your skiing day. Squaw offers a season parking pass in the structure adjacent to Squaw Kids Children's Center. For information call (530) 581-7123. You can also use valet paid parking across from the entrance to the cable car.

Sugar Bowl
Interstate 80 at Donner Summit
Norden, CA
(530) 426-9000
www.sugarbowl.com

Base elevation: 6,883 feet
Top elevation: 8,383 feet
Vertical drop: 1,500 feet
Number of runs: 84
Capacity: 11,300 skiers per hour
Terrain: 17 percent beginner, 45 percent intermediate, 38 percent advanced
Skiable acres: 1,500
Longest run: 3 miles
Number of lifts: 12
Average snowfall: 500 inches
Lift tickets: $46
Terrain parks: Superpipe, Golden Gate, Nob Hill
Snowphone: (530) 426-1111
Getting there: To get to Sugar Bowl, take I-80 west about 45 miles from Reno and exit at the Soda Springs/Norden exit onto Donner Pass Road. The resort is about 3 miles east. From Tahoe City take CA 89 north to Truckee, and then I-80 west about 10 miles to the Soda Springs/Norden exit.

If you've always wanted to ski in Europe but never quite made it, come to Sugar Bowl, where the ambience is decidedly old-world Austrian. Built in 1939 by wealthy families from San Francisco (who continue to own and operate it), Sugar Bowl has a colorful history that includes the rich and famous. It was the winter playground for celebrities like Walt Disney (he even had a mountain named for him), Errol Flynn, and Janet Leigh, who would arrive on the train and cozy up in the charming Sugar Bowl Lodge or in one of the picturesque cabins scattered among the pine trees. Home to the first chairlift in northern California and the first gondola in the country, Sugar Bowl offers a peek into the past with a dash of high-tech. Today it maintains its quintessential classic flavor amid the sophisticated technology of a modern-day ski resort.

Skiing here is on four mountains: Mt. Judah, Mt. Lincoln, Mt. Disney, and Crows Peak. Beginner terrain may be found at both entrances, and intermediate terrain is found on the west side of Disney, the east side of Lincoln, and also on Judah. Because Sugar Bowl is often the snowiest of all Reno/Tahoe resorts, expert skiers

With more than 350 inches of snow each year, skiers frequently enjoy powder days.
AARONROSEN.COM

absolutely revel in its deep ungroomed powder. Insider shredheads (ardent snowboarders) know that Sugar Bowl is one of the best boarding resorts in the area: It offers an abundance of natural chutes along with three terrain parks with pipes, jumps, and rails. With magnificent views from almost any run, Sugar Bowl delivers a quality mountain high for skiers and boarders of all abilities.

Parking is somewhat limited at the Magic Carpet gondola, which you reach first on Donner Pass Road, but if you arrive early enough, I recommend taking the gondola for a picturesque ride to the base of the mountain. Other parking and base facilities are found just a short way down the road at Mt. Judah. Amenities include bars and restaurants midmountain and at both bases, but the most colorful is the original Sugar Bowl Lodge near the gondola. For a truly romantic ski getaway, the lodge offers a classic alpine experience, with comfortable rooms and gourmet dining. New in 2005, a 14,000-square-foot addition to Mount Judah Day Lodge includes a new bar and restaurant.

Tahoe Donner
11509 Northwoods Boulevard
Truckee, CA
(530) 587-9444
www.tahoedonner.com
Base elevation: 6,750 feet
Top elevation: 7,350 feet
Vertical drop: 600 feet
Number of runs: 14
Capacity: 1,000 skiers per hour
Terrain: 40 percent beginner, 60 percent intermediate
Skiable acres: 120
Longest run: 1 mile
Number of lifts: 4
Average snowfall: 300 inches
Lift tickets: $34
Snowphone: (530) 587-9444
Getting there: To get to Tahoe Donner from Reno, take I-80 west about 30 miles to Truckee and exit at the Central Truckee exit, which puts you on Donner Pass Road. About 0.5 mile down the road, turn right onto Northwoods Boulevard and follow the signs for about 5 miles to the ski area. From Tahoe City head north on CA 89 to Truckee and turn left onto Donner Pass Road. Several blocks farther on, turn right onto Northwoods Boulevard and follow the signs to Tahoe Donner.

Tucked away in the Tahoe Donner residential area in Truckee, this resort is a great learn-to-ski hill, especially for children. The terrain is a relatively gentle open bowl with few obstacles for beginners to worry about. Meticulous grooming makes the snow very forgiving, even for the very novice skiers and snowboarders. And since there are no crowds and no lift lines, you can ski till you drop. Amenities include a full-service ski shop and a comfortable alpine ski lodge at the base of the hill. Strong intermediates and expert skiers and boarders won't be challenged here, but I recommend that beginners give it a try—the price is right, and it offers a quality mountain experience with none of the hassles encountered at larger resorts. There's a children's snowplay area next to the Trout Creek Recreation Center at 12790 Northwoods Boulevard.

After a fun day on the snow, try dinner or drinks at the new Lodge, an upscale restaurant at 12850 Northwoods Boulevard.

South Shore Lake Tahoe

Heavenly Ski Resort
End of Ski Run Boulevard, off U.S. Highway 50, South Lake Tahoe, CA
(530) 541-1330, (775) 586-7000, (800) 243-2836
www.skiheavenly.com
Base elevation: 6,540 feet
Top elevation: 10, 067 feet
Vertical drop: 3,500 feet
Number of runs: 85
Capacity: 52,000 skiers per hour
Terrain: 20 percent beginner, 45 percent

intermediate, 35 percent advanced
Skiable acres: 4,800
Longest run: 5.5 miles
Number of lifts: 30
Average snowfall: 360 inches
Lift tickets: $70
Terrain parks: 5 high roller parks
Snowphone: (775) 586-7000
Getting there: Because this resort is often very congested at the base, it's a good idea to take advantage of the free shuttle transportation that's available on both sides of the mountain. For shuttle information call (530) 541-7548. To reach the California side of Heavenly from the Reno/Sparks area, head south on U.S. Highway 395 through Carson City, and then take US 50 west to South Lake Tahoe. The base of the mountain is at the east end of Ski Run Boulevard. To get to the Nevada side from Reno/Sparks, continue south on US 395 past Carson City to Jacks Valley Road, where you turn west and then south through the tiny town of Genoa. Just past Genoa, turn west onto Nevada Highway 207 (Kingsbury Grade) and follow the signs for the resort at the top of the summit.

From Incline Village take NV 28 south to the intersection with US 50. Continue south on US 50 to NV 207, turn east, and follow the signs at the summit to the Nevada side of the resort. To reach the California side, continue south on US 50 to Ski Run Boulevard in South Lake Tahoe, and follow the signs to the east end.

With a name like "Heavenly," how can your ski experience here be anything but out of this world? Sprawling across the California-Nevada border, Heavenly Ski Resort has more skiable acres than any other Reno/Tahoe ski resort. The variety of terrain is awesome to say the least, from the hip-high, knee-burning moguls on Gunbarrel, to the immaculately groomed cruiser snow on Orion, to the deep and steep untracked powder in Mott Canyon. Although there's a smattering of beginner runs sprinkled around the mountain, Heavenly appeals largely to intermediate and expert skiers and snowboarders. Because of its daunting size, it's hard to sample it all in one day. For snowboarders, Heavenly offers five terrain parks, including the area's largest superpipe and the High Roller Night Life Park, which is open all night. With the highest elevation at Lake Tahoe and the most comprehensive snowmaking capacity, Heavenly is usually able to open early in the season and to maintain quality snow until its late closure.

Along with the mind-boggling variety of runs to choose from, Heavenly offers spectacular views of Lake Tahoe to the west and the Carson Valley to the east. True to its name, the mountain experience here is divine, giving you a feeling you are skiing at the top of the world. Amenities include on-mountain lodges, perched on the edge of the mountain on the California side, tubing at the top of the gondola (see the Attractions chapter for more information about the gondola), and licensed daycare facilities for children ages six weeks through six years old. The opening of the The Shops at Heavenly Village added upscale boutiques, lodging, and dining to the California side of the resort. You can start your skiing day from the two lifts on the Nevada side of the resort or at the base on the California side. Because the Nevada side of the mountain is usually less crowded than the California side, I suggest you try to escape the crowds by parking there if you're driving.

Heavenly is the closest ski resort to all the casino nightlife at South Lake Tahoe. You can book packages that include lodging, skiing, shows, meals, and tours to local sights by calling (800) 243-2836.

Homewood Mountain Resort
California Highway 89
Homewood, CA
(530) 525-2992
www.skihomewood.com
Base elevation: 6,320 feet
Top elevation: 7,880 feet
Vertical drop: 1,650 feet
Number of runs: 59

Capacity: 8,500 skiers per hour
Terrain: 15 percent beginner, 50 percent intermediate, 35 percent advanced
Skiable acres: 1,260
Longest run: 2 miles
Number of lifts: 8
Average snowfall: 350 inches
Lift tickets: $27 Monday through Thursday, $45 Friday through Sunday
Snowphone: (530) 525-2900
Getting there: To reach Homewood from the Reno/Sparks area, take I-80 west about 30 miles to Truckee, and then CA 89 south for about 6 miles past Tahoe City. From South Lake Tahoe it's about 19 miles west on CA 89. You can also ride Tahoe Area Regional Transit (TART) in the North Shore Lake Tahoe region. For the schedule and fares, call (530) 550-1212 or (800) 736-6365, or access www.truckee.com.

Far from the crowds but with magnificent lake views, Homewood is very popular with locals. Spread over two slopes, the terrain is diverse and challenging enough to keep skiers and boarders of all abilities busy for the entire day. Since the resort has two separate bases, skiers can start their day at either the South Lodge or the North Lodge. Parking is readily available on both sides. On windy days Homewood is especially attractive because many of its runs are protected; but be careful during spring skiing as its relatively low elevation causes the snow to melt early. If you're looking for glitz, this probably isn't the place for you. This resort offers just the essential amenities in a back-to-basics style. But if maximum time on the snow, spectacular views, and hassle-free skiing and boarding interest you at all, give Homewood a try. It's a great place to kick back and sink into a quality mountain experience.

Kirkwood Mountain Resort
Off California Highway 88 at Carson Pass
Kirkwood, CA
(209) 258-6000
www.kirkwood.com
Base elevation: 7,800 feet

---

i

You can start your ski day on the water by taking the* Tahoe Queen *winter ski shuttle, a paddle wheeler that will pick you up at Ski Run Marina at South Shore and drop you off in Tahoe City at the north end of the lake. A quick shuttle ride will deliver you to the lifts at Squaw Valley USA. For details call (800) 238-2463.

Top elevation: 9,800 feet
Vertical drop: 2,000 feet
Number of runs: 65
Capacity: 17,905 skiers per hour
Terrain: 15 percent beginner, 50 percent intermediate, and 35 percent advanced
Skiable acres: 2,300
Longest run: 2.5 miles
Number of lifts: 12
Average snowfall: 500 inches
Lift tickets: $62
Snowphone: (209) 258-3000, (877) 547-5966
Getting there: To reach Kirkwood from the Reno/Sparks area, take US 395 south to Minden, and then CA 88 west. It's about a 90-minute drive when the roads are clear. From South Shore Lake Tahoe, take US 50 southwest to Myers, and then turn left onto CA 89. Go south for about 12 miles, then turn onto CA 88 west for another 14 miles. For shuttle information call (530) 541-7548 or (530) 587-6128.

Nestled in a box canyon ringed by jagged pinnacles at the end of gorgeous Hope Valley, Kirkwood is an impressive sight, even for the nonskier. Although it's tricky to get to (over winding hairpin mountain passes), it's well worth the effort. This resort is a skier's and snowboarder's joy. The diverse terrain presents challenges for all abilities, with heart-stopping chutes and cornices for advanced skiers and boarders, wide sweeping bowls for intermediates, and easy, gentle slopes for beginners. Kirkwood frequently has the distinction of having America's deepest snow. During the 2004-05 season it

CLOSE-UP

Winter Safety

In winter the Sierra Nevada mountains offer a glorious playground with unlimited opportunities to enjoy the great outdoors. But without proper precautions, this winter wonderland can be unpleasant, and sometimes it can be downright deadly. Extreme weather conditions and high altitude present challenges and dangers if you're not adequately prepared. Being "winter aware" and following recommended mountain safety practices will make your outings safer and more enjoyable.

Anyone who spends time outside in these high altitudes should know about altitude sickness, frostbite, hypothermia, and sunburn. But with proper precautions these mountain health hazards shouldn't present problems for most people. If you have health conditions that could be more hazardous in the mountains, especially heart disease or high blood pressure, you should check with your doctor before planning trips to high elevations.

Because most winter sports in the Reno/Tahoe area are enjoyed at altitudes between 6,000 and 9,000 feet, you are breathing air with less oxygen in it than the air at sea level. This lack of oxygen causes what's known as altitude sickness—chemical changes in the bloodstream that can cause headaches, fatigue, decreased appetite, nausea, shortness of breath, and restless sleep in some people. Although the body will usually adjust within a couple of days, you should avoid overexertion, get plenty of rest, drink lots of fluids, eat lightly, and avoid alcohol, particularly if you experience any of these symptoms.

Frostbite occurs when the water in cells freezes and is indicated by a burning, tingling, numbness, or whitish discoloration of the skin. Fingertips, toes, ears, cheeks, and the nose are especially vulnerable. To prevent frostbite, it's important to cover all areas of your body, especially on cold, windy days. Hats and masks are essential for warmth because a large percentage of body heat is lost through the head. You should dress in layers and even overdress. You can always peel off a jacket or vest if you get too warm. If your toes or fingers start to get cold, keep wiggling them until you can get out of the cold. If you start to feel chilled, keep moving and get inside as soon as possible.

When your body is not able to generate enough heat to keep its core temperature at its normal 98.6 degrees, hypothermia can occur. Your organs can malfunction with this loss of heat, causing shivering, fatigue, distorted thinking, impaired motor skills, and changes in mood. One of the most dangerous aspects of hypothermia is that often those affected don't realize they have it because they are unable to think clearly. It's important that everyone on an outing together monitor each other for any symptoms and help any affected persons get dry and out of the cold right away. To protect yourself against hypothermia, you should wear warm, layered clothing; take periodic indoor breaks on cold days; stay dry; and refrain from drinking alcoholic beverages.

Sunburn is a risk anytime you're outdoors, but in the mountains it's an even greater risk because at high elevations you receive five times the amount of ultraviolet rays that you would receive at sea level. It's pretty easy to protect yourself by using a sunscreen with a minimum of SPF 15 on any exposed areas of your body. Also, because ultraviolet rays are very harmful to your eyes, it's important to wear sunglasses or goggles to protect them. Eyewear also protects your eyes from tree branches when you're skiing or snowshoeing in wooded terrain.

While you should follow these health tips wherever you are in the mountains, I recommend additional safety precautions for venturing into the backcountry: Don't even pack the car until you've checked the weather forecast. If it's snowing or if a storm is on the way, it's wise to play it safe and wait for clear weather. Because blowing snow can greatly reduce your visibility, it's easy to become disoriented in a storm, even in terrain with which you are familiar. If you decide it's okay to go, check your equipment to make sure everything is in working order. If you have a problem with your skis or snowmobile, it's better to fix it before you go when you're in a safe environment. Besides your sporting gear, you should also bring along a backpack or fanny pack containing basic survival items, including waterproof matches, water, dried fruit or granola bars, a whistle, a candle, a metal cup for melting snow, a cellular phone or change for emergency phone calls, two large plastic bags for emergency shelter, a map, a compass, and a first-aid kit. Make sure you're well fed and watered and not overly tired before setting out. And also practice the buddy system by going with at least one other person. It's not only safer but also more fun to share your outdoor experience with a friend. Last but not least, tell a friend or family member where you're going and when you expect to be back.

When you get to your destination, leave a note on the dashboard in your car detailing where you're going, when you'll return, and who is in the group. As you strike out into the backcountry, pay attention to weather and snow conditions, especially in areas that may be avalanche prone. Because these deadly slides are more likely to be triggered on slopes 30 degrees or steeper, stay away from steep-sided ravines and the bottoms of narrow gullies, particularly just after a heavy snowfall. Also avoid terrain where vegetation has obviously been cleared away by avalanches in the past. For updated information about local avalanche danger, you can call the Tahoe National Forest Avalanche Hotline at (530) 587–2158 or access their Web site at www.avalanche.org.

Be sure to drink water often to remain hydrated and eat snacks to keep your energy level up. If you're a newcomer to the backcountry, it's wise to experience it at a leisurely pace that won't exhaust anyone in your group. Leave the macho spirit at home and be willing to finish the outing when others are ready to.

But you won't need these winter-awareness tips unless you can first get to

Proper attire is crucial for safe enjoyment of the outdoors in winter. CHRIS CARNEL

your mountain destination. Winter driving in the mountains can be a fun-filled adventure or a frustrating and hazardous challenge, depending upon how well prepared you are. Before heading into snow country, make sure your car is in good running condition and that you have the proper-size chains. You should also start with a full tank of gas and carry basic survival items, such as a windshield scraper or deicer, a broom, a shovel, sand, food, water, blankets, and warm clothing. Because traffic delays are not uncommon, allow plenty of time to get to where you're going. If you encounter ice or snow on the road, slow down and give other cars around you plenty of room. Because your car needs at least three times more distance to stop on slick roads, remember to maintain a minimum distance of four to eight seconds between your vehicle and the one in front of you. If you need to pull off the road to brush off the windshield or put on chains, be sure to get completely off the pavement and to turn on your hazard lights. When you see the CHAINS REQUIRED signs, you'll have about a mile to install them before the checkpoint. Be sure to comply, because you can be cited and fined if you don't. If you have a four-wheel-drive vehicle, you can usually proceed right to the checkpoint because chains are usually not required for them.

If you're properly prepared for your mountain experience, it will be safer and more comfortable. Although you can't anticipate everything that may happen, you can reduce the potential danger by using common sense and being "winter aware."

boasted 804 inches. With such awesome snow and scenery, you can't go wrong at Kirkwood.

One of the most appealing aspects of this resort is its isolation from crowds and traffic. Tucked away in a world of its own, it offers a total mountain experience, remote from the hustle and bustle of everyday life. Even though the après-ski activities are sedate compared to some other resorts, the recently renovated Kirkwood Village has an interesting mix of watering holes, eateries, shops, and accommodations. Its picturesque alpine style is absolutely perfect in this pristine mountain setting. If you're planning to settle down and stay for a few days in one resort, I highly recommend Kirkwood as an ideal escape for any skier or snowboarder.

Sierra-at-Tahoe Snowsport Resort
1111 Sierra-at-Tahoe Road
Twin Bridges, CA
(530) 659-7453
www.sierratahoe.com
Base elevation: 6,640 feet
Top elevation: 8,852 feet
Vertical drop: 2,212 feet
Number of runs: 46
Capacity: 14,870 skiers per hour
Terrain: 25 percent beginner, 50 percent intermediate, 25 percent advanced
Skiable acres: 2,000
Longest run: 2.5 miles
Number of lifts: 12
Average snowfall: 420 inches
Lift tickets: $59
Terrain parks: The Circuit, Broadway, Upper Main, The Alley, Bashful, Smokey Bordercross
Snowphone: (530) 659-7475
Getting there: To reach Sierra-at-Tahoe from South Shore Lake Tahoe, take US 50 southwest for about 12 miles and turn onto Sierra-at-Tahoe Road. From North Shore Lake Tahoe, take CA 89 south from Tahoe City to US 50 and continue southwest for about 12 miles. From the Reno/Sparks area, take US 395 south to Carson City, and then follow US 50 through South Lake Tahoe to Sierra-at-Tahoe Road, about 12 miles farther. For information on the free shuttle from South Shore Lake Tahoe, call (530) 541-7548.

Although Sierra-at-Tahoe provides great terrain for skiers and boarders of all abilities, beginners especially love it because it has such a wide variety of slopes they can feel perfectly comfortable on. You won't find sharp cornices and steep chutes here, but there's plenty of thrilling cruiser runs cutting through the tall timber. Boarders can choose from six award-winning terrain parks, which are impeccably groomed for the latest thrills.

A sister resort to Northstar-at-Tahoe, Sierra offers the Vertical Plus frequent skier program also available at Northstar (see the previous description of Northstar for details). Listed in *Snow Country* magazine as the best resort in the far West for on-mountain food, the eight eateries at this resort are certainly a cut above the average. For a tasty lunch with a world-class view of Lake Tahoe, drop into the Grandview Bar & Grill at the top of the mountain.

CROSS-COUNTRY SKIING

North Shore Lake Tahoe

Clair Tappaan Lodge
Donner Pass Road, off Interstate 80
Norden, CA
(530) 426-3632, (800) 679-6775
www.sierraclub.org
Tucked deep into the forest on top of Donner Summit, this rustic old lodge is owned by the Sierra Club. It operates its own track system consisting of 13 kilometers of machine-groomed trails, with about 60 percent beginner and 40 percent intermediate terrain. Wandering through stands of magnificent pines, the striding and skating lanes provide a great workout and spectacular scenery. Instruction and rental

equipment are available. Trail passes are $7.00. Accommodations in the lodge are open to both members and nonmembers of the Sierra Club, but because it's a very popular place, I recommend you reserve as far in advance as possible.

To reach Clair Tappaan from the Reno/Sparks area, take I-80 west about 45 miles to the Norden/Soda Springs exit, and then travel east for 2.4 miles on Donner Pass Road. From Tahoe City take CA 89 north to Truckee, and then I-80 west about 10 miles to the Soda Springs/Norden exit. The lodge is on the left, partially hidden in the trees above the road; you need to look carefully so as not to miss it.

Granlibakken Ski Resort
725 Granlibakken Road
Tahoe City, CA
(800) 543-3221
www.granlibakken.com

You can ski free here, but you're pretty much on your own as most of the 7-kilometer trail is not maintained or machine set. For a lovely view of Lake Tahoe, ride the poma lift up and then follow the road to Lookout Point. If you're really ambitious, keep going for about 2 miles and you'll reach Page Meadows. Rental equipment is available, but there are no other amenities.

To get to Granlibakken from the Reno area, head west on I-80 about 30 miles to Truckee, and then south on CA 89 to Tahoe City. The resort is about 0.5 mile south of Tahoe City on CA 89.

Be sure to ask about special deals when buying your lift ticket or trail pass. Every resort has packages that may save you significant amounts of money. If you're also booking accommodations, find out if tickets and passes are included in your rental rate.

Northstar-at-Tahoe
California Highway 267 North
6 miles north of Lake Tahoe
(530) 562-2475, (530) 562-1010
www.skinorthstar.com

Because the 50 kilometers of machine-groomed track at this major destination resort are near the alpine ski runs, you can enjoy many of the amenities offered to alpine skiers and snowboarders. Scenic trails that wind through the trees are groomed for striding and skating. Northstar is also a great telemark and snowshoe area. Rental equipment and lessons are available, and warming huts and picnic tables are scattered throughout the trail system. You can purchase trail passes at the cross-country ticket booth in the village, and then ride the gondola to the Cross-Country Center midmountain for equipment and lessons. Trail passes are $25 for skiers and $20 for snowshoers.

If you cross-country ski to escape the hassles found at many alpine resorts, this may not be the place for you. Although the trail system provides the quiet solitude of a backcountry outing, you're integrated with the alpine skiers in the base area and on the gondola. For more details about Northstar, see the previous description under "Alpine Skiing and Snowboarding" and read the Resorts chapter listing.

To get to Northstar, take I-80 west from Reno for about 30 miles to Truckee, and then take CA 267 south for 6 miles. From Kings Beach, California, take CA 267 north for about 6 miles. For information about shuttle transportation to Northstar from the Lake Tahoe area, call (775) 883-2100, (800) GO-NORTH, or (877) 274-7366.

Resort at Squaw Creek
Cross-Country Ski Center
400 Squaw Creek Road
Olympic Valley, CA
(530) 583-6300, (800) 327-3353
www.squawcreek.com

Tucked in gorgeous Olympic Valley with

the towering peaks of Squaw Valley as a backdrop, the 18 kilometers of trail at the Resort at Squaw Creek are scenic to say the very least. Although it's one of the smaller cross-country resorts in the area, it gives you a chance to soak in the awesome beauty of this very special place without the hassles of alpine skiing at Squaw Valley USA. The trails are groomed for striding and skating, and you can also try snowshoeing. Because much of the terrain is open and relatively level, it's perfect for novices. More-advanced skiers can also find some ups and downs, including several trails that wind up the mountain behind the hotel. Amenities include rentals, instruction, a ski shop, and twilight skiing. The trail pass is around $14. Since the Resort at Squaw Creek is easily one of the most exquisite resorts in the Reno/Tahoe area, I suggest you have dinner or an après-ski drink in the hotel after your day on the snow. (For more details about this resort, see the Resorts chapter. For more information on Squaw Valley, see the description of Squaw Valley USA in this chapter.)

To reach the resort from Reno/Sparks, take I-80 west for about 30 miles to Truckee, and then CA 89 south about 10 miles. After turning into Squaw Valley at the main entrance, look for Squaw Creek Road and turn left. You can either have valets park your car at the resort or use the parking lot. From Tahoe City take CA 89 north about 6 miles. For information on shuttle service to Squaw Valley USA, call (800) 327-3353, (866) 769-4653, (530) 581-7181, or (530) 550-1212.

Royal Gorge
Interstate 80 at Donner Pass
Soda Springs, CA
(800) 500-3871, (800) 666-3871 (from northern California)
www.royalgorge.com

Ranked the number-one cross-country ski resort in North America by *Snow Country* magazine, Royal Gorge has absolutely everything you could want for a perfect Nordic ski vacation. With 330 kilometers of groomed track and more than 9,000 acres of skiing terrain, it's also the largest cross-country ski resort in North America. The 90 trails range in elevation from 5,800 feet to 7,538 feet and are ranked 28 for beginners, 44 for intermediates, and 16 for experts. The resort also has four surface lifts for telemark skiing. Because of its immense size and diversity, Royal Gorge is a world unto itself. You could ski here for a week and still not explore it all. Beginners especially enjoy the Van Norden Track System, a large open meadow ringed by magnificent jagged peaks. Intermediates have a mind-boggling array of trails to choose from, including the Palisade Peak and Devil's Peak systems for awesome views of the surrounding country. Experts have more than their share of challenging terrain, including the 22.6-kilometer track to the edge of the Royal Gorge of the American River.

The resort has warming huts, trailside cafes, and several overnight lodges. For a total mountain experience, I highly recommend the package that includes a stay at the Wilderness Lodge along with lessons and equipment rental. Imagine wrapping yourself in fur robes and snuggling down in a sleigh that carries you to this century-old lodge hidden deep in the wilderness. The rooms are rustic and not very private, but the food is gourmet and the scenery out of this world. For a more traditionally elegant stay, you can choose Rainbow Lodge, which is also owned by Royal Gorge. At this old stagecoach stop along the Mormon-Emigrant Trail, Western history seems to ooze from its heavy rock walls. Insiders have long known that a continental dinner at the lodge's Engadine Cafe, served with just the right wine, is the ideal ending to a day of skiing at Royal Gorge.

With trail pass fees of $28 on weekends and holidays and $24 during the week, Royal Gorge is more expensive than other cross-country ski resorts, but you get what you pay for here since Royal Gorge offers the ultimate cross-country ski experience.

To reach Royal Gorge from Reno/Sparks, head west on I-80 about 45 miles to the Norden/Soda Springs exit and follow the signs to Summit Station. From Tahoe City take CA 89 north to Truckee, and then I-80 west about 10 miles to the Soda Springs/Norden exit.

Spooner Lake Cross-Country Ski Area
Nevada Highway 28, near the junction with U.S. Highway 50
(775) 749-5349, (775) 887-8844
(888) 858-8844
www.spoonerlake.com

With 80 kilometers of groomed track, Spooner Lake is best known for the marvelous lake and mountain views skiers can enjoy from the intermediate and expert trails. The terrain is divided between the high-country trails and the meadow trails, with beginners enjoying scenic loops around frozen Spooner Lake and Spooner Meadow and more-advanced skiers climbing the surrounding slopes toward Marlette Lake, Snow Valley Peak, and Hobart Reservoir. For the ultimate backcountry experience, you can rent a beautiful hand-hewn wilderness cabin right at Spooner. Nothing beats being the first skier to hit the trails in the morning, For reservations call (775) 749-5349. Amenities include lessons, equipment rental, a day lodge, and a warming hut. The carefully groomed tracks have both striding and skating lanes, and snowshoeing is also allowed. In summer Spooner is a popular hiking/biking area and is the access point for the renowned Flume Trail mountain bike ride. Spooner has recently changed its policy about allowing dogs on its trails. If you want to bring Fido along, call to ask when dogs are allowed. The trail pass is $21.

To get to Spooner Lake from the Reno/Sparks area, head south on US 395 through Carson City, and then take US 50 west for about 15 miles toward South Lake Tahoe. The parking lot is just north of the intersection of US 50 and NV 28 on NV 28. From South Shore Lake Tahoe, take US 50 east for about 15 miles toward Carson City. From Incline Village take NV 28 south for about 12 miles. Shuttle services are available from the major casinos and hotels in Reno and from the Hyatt in Incline Village. Call (775) 749-5349 for information.

Tahoe Cross-Country Ski Area
Country Club Drive, Tahoe City, CA
(530) 583-5475
www.tahoexc.org

With 65 kilometers of set skating and striding track, Tahoe Cross-Country (Tahoe XC) has something for every skier. Beginners can enjoy the lower trails that wander through the pristine forest, intermediates can climb higher for peeks at Lake Tahoe, and experts can test their stamina by skiing all the way to Truckee if they wish. Even dogs especially enjoy this resort, since they can cavort off-leash (except in the parking lot and around the lodge) Monday through Friday all day and from 3:00 to 5:00 P.M. on weekends and holidays. The facility is meticulously maintained and offers instruction, equipment rental, moonlight tours, and two restaurants. Trail passes are $20.

To reach Tahoe XC from Tahoe City, head northeast on California Highway 28 for about 2 miles to the Shell service station at Dollar Hill. Turn left onto Fabian Way, then right onto Village Drive. Go up and around the corner to Country Club Drive and turn left. From the Reno/Sparks area, take I-80 west about 30 miles to Truckee, head south on CA 89 to Tahoe City, and then follow the directions above.

Tahoe Donner Cross-Country Ski Area
Alder Creek Road, Truckee, CA
(530) 587-9484
www.tahoedonner.com

Stretching over 4,800 acres of terrain, Tahoe Donner Cross-Country Ski Area offers 115 kilometers of machine-groomed trails over three scenic track systems. Of the total trails, 16 are rated beginner, 24 intermediate, 5 advanced, and 1 expert. There are two wilderness trails and two for snowshoers only. The diversity of terrain includes open meadows, gentle bowls, and tree-lined trails. One of the most pristine track systems in the Reno/Tahoe area, delightful Euer Valley offers trails that meander along picturesque Prosser Creek. Just 4 kilometers from the day lodge, much of this track system is rated for beginners. You can spend the whole day here, stopping just to enjoy the views, and to refuel in the Euer Valley Cookhouse.

Amenities at this resort include snowshoeing, equipment rental, instruction, a retail shop, and four warming huts. Tahoe Donner is also the only cross-country ski area to offer night skiing (Wednesday from 5:00 to 7:00 P.M.). The trail pass is $21.

To reach Tahoe Donner from Reno/Sparks, take I-80 west for 30 miles to Truckee, and then CA 89 north for 2.2 miles. Turn left onto Alder Creek Road and travel about another 7 miles. Coming from Tahoe City, take CA 89 north to Truckee, turn left onto Donner Pass Road, and then right onto Northwoods Boulevard. Follow the signs to the ski area, about 5 miles farther on.

South Shore Lake Tahoe

Camp Richardson Cross-Country Ski Center
1900 Jameson Beach Road
South Lake Tahoe, CA
(530) 542-6584, (800) 544-1801
www.camprichardson.com

For skiing with drop-dead-gorgeous views along the shore of Lake Tahoe, head to Camp Richardson, which offers 18 kilometers of groomed track and 20 kilometers of skier-packed track, with routes to nearby Fallen Leaf Lake and Taylor Creek. Amenities include lodging, rentals, and a restaurant. Most of the groomed trail is geared to beginners since it's fairly level, but skiers of all abilities can certainly appreciate the gorgeous environment. Since most of the skiing is at lake level, the snowpack is less than at higher elevations. It's wise to call ahead to make sure there's enough snow for skiing. The trail pass costs $12.

To get to the resort from South Lake Tahoe, take US 50 west to the "Y" (the intersection of US 50 and CA 89 in South Lake Tahoe), and then turn right and follow CA 89 north for about 2.5 miles. (For more information about Camp Richardson, see the Vacation Rentals chapter.)

Hope Valley Cross-Country
14255 California Highway 88
Hope Valley, CA
(530) 694-2266, (800) 423-9949
www.sorensensresort.com
www.hopevalleyoutdoors.com

Nestled in exquisite Hope Valley, this ski area offers an unspoiled mountain experience that's hard to beat. Environmentalists, including the folks at Sorensen's Resort just down the road, have worked successfully for years to preserve the pristine nature of this valley. It's also blessedly tranquil since snowmobiles and other vehicles are prohibited. There's very little set track, but that's part of the charm, since you can just head out on your own to explore the marked terrain. Amenities include rental equipment, instruction, and guided tours, including one that traces part of Snowshoe Thompson's famous route delivering mail to snowbound residents in the 1800s.

Sorensen's offers cozy overnight lodging in unique alpine cabins with names like Dancehall, Tanglewood, and Saint Nick's. You can even bring the family dog along—pets are welcome in some of the units. A hearty meal near the fire in the country cafe here is a delight after an invigorating day on skis or snowshoes. The resort also sponsors periodic cultural events that showcase the history and natural beauty of the area. Kirkwood ski center is just 20 minutes away, so you can also take advantage of all the amenities offered there.

To reach Hope Valley Cross-Country from the Reno/Sparks area, take US 395 south to Minden, and then CA 88 west. It's about a 90-minute drive when the roads are clear. From South Shore Lake Tahoe, take US 50 west to Myers, and then turn left onto CA 89. Go south for about 12 miles, and turn left again onto CA 88. The cross-country facility is about 0.25 mile past Sorensen's Resort.

Kirkwood Cross-Country & Snowshoe Center
California Highway 88, Kirkwood, CA
(209) 258-7248
www.kirkwood.com

Kirkwood Cross-Country is the largest, most-comprehensive cross-country ski area in the South Shore Lake Tahoe area, with more than 4,000 acres of exceptional terrain. The 80 kilometers of groomed track are rated 20 percent beginner, 60 percent intermediate, and 20 percent advanced. The center welcomes dogs on the High Trail behind Kirkwood Inn and the Inner Loop in the meadow. Kirkwood is easily one of the most picturesque regions outside the Lake Tahoe Basin, where you can ski through lovely meadows and along scenic ridgelines in the shadow of jagged volcanic peaks. Because Kirkwood is higher in elevation than many other cross-country ski areas, the snow here is deeper and drier, and the season is longer. A trail pass costs $21.

The resort offers a full array of amenities, including equipment rental, lessons, a retail shop, three warming huts, a restaurant, and trackside lodging. Kirkwood's ski resort is just down the road, so you can also take advantage of all the activities in Kirkwood Village at the base of the ski mountain. (See the description under "Alpine Skiing and Snowboarding" in this chapter.)

To reach Kirkwood from the Reno/Sparks area, take US 395 south to Minden, and then CA 88 west. It's about a 90-minute drive when the roads are clear. From South Shore Lake Tahoe, take US 50 southwest to Myers, and then turn left onto CA 89. Go south for about 12 miles, then turn right onto CA 88, and go west for another 14 miles.

BACKCOUNTRY AND PUBLIC CROSS-COUNTRY SKI AREAS

You don't have to go to a ski resort to enjoy the great outdoors: There's a large variety of backcountry and public areas where you can play in the snow. You're pretty much on your own at these areas, however, since most don't have any facilities. But if you're on a budget, the price is right—many are free, and some require only a few dollars for a Sno-Park permit. If there's no set track for skiers, it's usually okay to bring your dog, but consider the depth of the snow before you do; smaller animals have a difficult time in very deep snow. When snowmobilers are in the area, it's also necessary to keep a close watch on your pets. In any of these areas you'll find people enjoying the great outdoors in a variety of ways—tubing, sledding, snowshoeing, skiing, and snowmobiling. However you choose to play in the snow, the main thing is to have a good time.

I describe a few of my favorite spots below, but you can find out about others by picking up information at the Tahoe-Douglas Visitor Center at 195 US 50 in Stateline, Nevada. Trail maps and Sno-Park permits are available during business hours at the Lake Tahoe Basin Management Unit of the USDA Forest Service at 870 Emerald Bay Road in South Lake Tahoe. You can call for information at (916) 324-1222. On weekends and evenings, permits can be purchased at the Shell station at the "Y" in South Lake Tahoe (the intersection of US 50 and CA 89), and the Shell station in Myers, California. Many retail businesses near Sno-Parks sell permits, including Alpenglow Sports in Tahoe City, California; Mountain Hardware in Truckee, California; Longs Drug Store in South Lake Tahoe, California; and Homewood Hardware in Homewood, California. You can also buy permits online at www.ohv.parks.ca.gov.

Donner Memorial State Park
Donner Pass Road, Truckee, CA
(530) 582-7892

Operated by the California Department of Parks and Recreation, Donner Memorial State Park has a very scenic 2.5-mile set track that meanders through the trees and along the shore of Donner Lake. The terrain is relatively level and perfect for beginning skiers. It's a great area for skiing and snowshoeing, but snowmobiling and sledding are not allowed.

To get there from Reno/Sparks, take I-80 west for about 30 miles to Truckee, take the Squaw Valley exit, and turn right. At the stoplight, turn left at Donner Pass Road and follow it for 0.5 mile. From Tahoe City take CA 89 north to Truckee, and turn left onto Donner Pass Road at the second stoplight.

Martis Lookout Trail
Martis Lookout Road just north of Brockway Summit, California
Highway 267

Like many Forest Service roads that aren't plowed in winter, Martis Lookout Road becomes a popular access route to the backcountry when it's covered with snow. If you're really ambitious, you can follow the 8-mile loop that climbs about 1,400 feet to the top of Martis Peak. Once on the summit, you're rewarded with top-of-the-world vistas—both Lake Tahoe and the Martis Valley spread out in all their splendor directly below. The trek up is something of a challenge, but the exciting run back down makes it all worthwhile. You'll find cross-country skiers, snowshoers, and snowmobilers, with pets, kids, and the rest of the family enjoying the area. Parking is limited to a small area at the turnoff and along the road, so it's best to go early or late in the day to find a spot. When snowplows are working to clear CA 267, access may be limited even further.

To get to Martis Lookout Road from Kings Beach, take CA 267 north to the turnoff, which is about 0.25 mile past Brockway Summit and on the right. From the Reno/Sparks area, head west on I-80 about 30 miles to Truckee, and then south for about 10 miles on CA 267.

Mt. Watson Road
Brockway Summit, California
Highway 267

At more than 7,000 feet in elevation, Mt. Watson Road is often covered with snow when areas lower down are completely bare. The road winds through deep forest for more than 20 miles, giving periodic peeks at Lake Tahoe along the way. If you keep to the right when the road forks, the climb is gradual and suitable for most levels of skiers. Going to the left puts you on a narrower, steeper path more appropriate for intermediate skiers. This is also a wonderful area for snowshoeing because you can stick to the beaten path or head off into the trees for a first-rate day in the forest. You need to watch out for snowmobiles, however, since snowmobile tour operators frequently bring groups into the area.

To get to Mt. Watson Road from Kings Beach, take CA 267 north to Brockway Summit and either park along the road or use the parking lot at the top. From the Reno/Sparks area, take I-80 west about 30 miles to Truckee, and then CA 267 south for about 10 miles to Brockway Summit.

Nevada Highway 431
Across from Mt. Rose-Ski Tahoe

You can ski, snowshoe, sled, and tube on a little-used tract of heavily wooded land along the northwest side of NV 431 just past the entrance to Mt. Rose-Ski Tahoe ski resort. A Forest Service road winds through the trees, providing a packed surface with a gentle incline. For more ups

If you plan to go backcountry skiing, make sure you are prepared for emergencies. Though the wet "maritime" snowpack of the Sierra doesn't slide as often as drier snows in the Rocky Mountains, you should still carry avalanche beacons, probe poles, and snow shovels. Other important items for any backcountry skier's pack include additional layers of clothing, food, water, a first-aid kit, flashlight, waterproof matches, and a utility knife.

and downs, especially for tubes and sleds, try the slopes alongside the more level surface of the road. You'll find parking at a pullout on the right side of the road as you're traveling from Reno to Incline Village, about a mile from the ski resort. I don't recommend snowmobiling here, however.

To reach the area, take NV 431 east for about 11 miles from Incline Village, or west for 22 miles from Reno.

North Tahoe Regional Park
875 National Avenue, Tahoe Vista, CA
(530) 546-5043, (530) 546-4212
www.northlaketahoe.net/parks.html

Insiders know if the wind is gusting over the upper mountain elevations, you can still have a great day in the snow sheltered by the dense forest at North Tahoe Regional Park. With approximately 5 miles of meandering trails, the park offers enough variety to entertain beginning as well as more-advanced skiers. But don't expect impeccable tracks, since grooming is best described as sporadic. You can rent sleds and snowmobiles, but you're on your own for any other sporting equipment. It's a great place to bring dogs and also a bargain—a trail pass is only $3.00 and is available at the self-pay system near the restrooms at the entrance to the park. Be aware, however, that the park is at relatively low elevation (around 6,000 feet), so check on snow coverage before heading out to ski here.

To get to the park from Incline Village, go west on NV 28, just past Kings Beach, to Tahoe Vista, and turn right onto National Avenue and follow the signs to the park.

Tahoe Meadows
West of the Mt. Rose summit on Nevada Highway 431

An exquisite alpine meadow cupped below Mt. Rose and Slide Mountain, Tahoe Meadows is one of the most popular backcountry playgrounds in the Reno/Tahoe area. You can stick to the flats by staying in the meadow proper, or you can find plenty of up-and-down by venturing through the trees on the surrounding mountains. Climbing up the ridges on the southwest side of the meadow affords gorgeous views of Lake Tahoe and lovely spots to stop for a snowy picnic. If you venture to the end of the main meadow, you also get views of Washoe Lake and Washoe Valley. NV 431 bisects the meadow, with the largest part on the left as you approach from Reno. The smaller area on the other side of the road has less level terrain, providing open slopes popular with sledders. Snowmobilers are also restricted to this side.

Tahoe Meadows is great for family outings (including the family dog), and you'll find people doing just about everything you can do on the snow—skiing, snowmobiling, snowshoeing, tubing, and sledding. There are no facilities, so you need to bring your own food and drinks. Because of its high elevation, the meadow gets snow early in the year and keeps it well into late spring. When other mountain areas are devoid of the white stuff, you can usually find enough to ski on here. But the high elevation means that the weather can get pretty wild, so check on the forecast before you head up the mountain. The snow really piles up here, so don't be surprised if it's over the top of your car when you park along the road. Look for cuts in the snowbanks that you can use to get access to the meadow. Those tall poles with reflectors you see along the road will give you an idea of how high the snow gets; they're used as guides for the snowplows that clear the road.

For a convenient place to get on the snow (it's just minutes from either Reno or North Shore Lake Tahoe), I highly recommend Tahoe Meadows. If you're there at sundown, listening to the swish of your skis on the snow as it turns golden, you'll agree that it's a very special place to be.

To reach the meadow from Reno/Sparks, take US 395 south to NV 431 (the Mt. Rose Highway) and follow it to just past the summit. From Incline Village take NV 431 to where it levels out just before the summit.

Tallac Historic Site Trail
California Highway 89
South Lake Tahoe, CA
When the snow level drops to the shores of Lake Tahoe, the 2-mile loop that winds through the Tallac Historic Site is perfect for novice cross-country skiers. You're treated to scenic views of Lake Tahoe, Mt. Tallac, and some grand old estates dating from the 1800s. (See the Attractions chapter for a complete description of this area.)

The site is about 3 miles north of the "Y" (the intersection of US 50 and CA 89 in South Lake Tahoe) on CA 89. Be sure to pick up a Sno-Park permit before you go. Snowmobiles are not allowed here.

ICE SKATING

City of South Lake Tahoe Ice Arena
1176 Rufus Allen Boulevard
South Lake Tahoe, CA
(530) 542-6262
Operated by the city, the ice arena in South Lake Tahoe offers relatively inexpensive skate sessions from about 11:00 A.M. to 9:00 P.M. during the season. Call for exact schedule. Residents can skate for $6.50, and nonresidents can hit the ice for just a few dollars more. Skates are available for rental for just $2.00.

Heavenly Village Ice Rink
Heavenly Village Way
South Lake Tahoe, CA
(530) 543-1423
Adding to the fun and excitement of the Shops at Heavenly Village, the outdoor ice rink offers skating for just $10 for children under age 12 and $15 for everyone else. The admission price includes skate rental. The rink is open Monday through Thursday from 1:00 to 8:00 P.M., Friday and Saturday 10:00 A.M. to 11:00 P.M., and on Sunday 10:00 A.M. to 8:00 P.M. during winter months.

Northstar-at-Tahoe
California Highway 267 North
6 miles north of Lake Tahoe
(530) 562-1010
Tucked among the quaint shops at the expanded village at Northstar, the ice rink offers complimentary skating and rentals. Call for hours.

Resort at Squaw Creek
400 Squaw Creek Road
Olympic Valley, CA
(530) 581-6624, (800) 327-3353
www.squawcreek.com
The outdoor skating rink at this elegant luxury resort has a classic Christmas-card view of Olympic Valley and the surrounding snowclad peaks. You don't have to be a guest to enjoy all the top-of-the-line amenities here, so lace up those skates and luxuriate in the ambience of one of the country's top winter resorts. (For a detailed description of Squaw Valley USA and the Resort at Squaw Creek, see previous sections of this chapter, along with the Resorts chapter.) The skating rink is open from noon to 8:00 P.M. Sunday through Thursday and from noon to 10:00 P.M. Friday and Saturday. The cost per session is $10.00 for adults, including skate rental ($5.00 if you bring your own skates). The rate for children ages 6 through 15 is $5.00 if they rent skates and free if they bring their own. Instruction is available if you make reservations in advance.

Efforts are under way to attract the 2014 Winter Olympic Games to the Reno/Tahoe area.

To reach the resort from Reno/Sparks, take I-80 west for about 30 miles to Truckee, and then CA 89 south for about 13 miles. From Tahoe City take CA 89 north about 6 miles. After turning into Squaw Valley at the main entrance, look for Squaw Creek Road, and turn left. You can either take advantage of valet parking at the resort or use the parking lot.

Rink on the River
10 North Virginia Street, Reno, NV
(775) 334-2262
www.cityofreno.com/res/com_service/icerink/

Almost resembling a progressive dinner, the skating rink in downtown Reno has been moved from location to location over the past several years. It seems finally to have found a permanent home, however, on the site of where the historic Mapes Hotel once stood in downtown Reno. As an entertainment option, it's relatively cheap, with admission of $5.00 for skaters age 13 and older and $3.00 for those ages 3 through 12 and 55 and older. Skate rental is $2.00. The rink also offers season passes, groups rates, and lessons. If you're into skating, it's worth checking out. After all, where else can you do triple lutzes under the glare of all that casino neon?

Squaw Valley USA Olympic Ice Pavilion
1960 Squaw Valley Road
Olympic Valley, CA
(530) 583-6985
www.squaw.com

When surfing the Web for Tahoe ski information, try these Web sites: www.virtualtahoe.com, www.tahoe.com, and www.tahoeinfo.com.

Perched midmountain, high above exquisite Olympic Valley, the outdoor Olympic Ice Pavilion at Squaw Valley USA gives you a one-of-a-kind skating experience with a breathtaking view. You can buy a transport/skate ticket year-round (which includes two hours of skate rental) for $24 beginning at 11:00 A.M. and for $15 beginning at 4:00 P.M. Children age 12 and younger skate for $10. Termination hours vary with the season. Once on the mountain you can enjoy all the restaurants, shops, and watering holes provided at High Camp. (For more details about all the amenities offered at this world-class resort, see the description earlier in this chapter under "Alpine Skiing and Snowboarding.") Because this part of Squaw Valley can get very windy at times, it's wise to call ahead and get a weather report for the mountain. Also be sure to dress warmly, since you'll be skating outside at 8,200 feet in elevation.

To get to Squaw Valley USA, take CA 89 north from Tahoe City for about 6 miles. From Reno head west on I-80 about 30 miles to Truckee, and then go south for about 13 miles on CA 89.

Truckee River Regional Park
California Highway 267, south of Truckee, CA
(530) 587-6172
www.tdrpd.com

A new ice rink with all the comforts and ambience of a first-class skating experience has outclassed the natural pond that residents of Truckee skated on for years. Set among the pines along the Truckee River, the rink has an ice chilling system to create ice that even Dorothy Hamill would approve of. You can skate daily for just $6.00 a day (all day), in addition to $2.00 for skate rental. Call (530) 587-6172 to find out when it opens for the season and for hours of operation.

Village Ice Rink at Kirkwood
Kirkwood Mountain Resort
Off California Highway 88 at Carson Pass
Kirkwood, CA
(209) 258-6000
www.kirkwood.com

You can skate among the shops and eateries in the Village Plaza at Kirkwood on weekends during winter. Hours are 2:00 to 8:00 P.M. on Friday, 10:00 A.M. to 8:00 P.M. on Saturday, and 10:00 A.M. to 4:00 P.M. on Sunday. Admission is just $9.00 for adults and $6.00 for children age 12 and under, including skate rental.

DOGSLED RIDES

Sierra Ski Touring
Gardnerville, NV
(775) 782-3047
www.highsierra.com/sst

It's the only way to get around in a few corners in the world, but in Hope Valley, just 30 minutes from South Shore Lake Tahoe, riding in a dogsled is a winter experience that's uniquely entertaining. You can drive through this beautiful valley, and you can also cross-country ski and snowshoe in it, but skimming across the snow, bundled in blankets, behind eight highly trained dogs, offers a different perspective altogether. A one-hour ride is $100 for adults and $50 for children, with a minimum charge of $185. The sled can accommodate up to 375 pounds. Moonlight, picnic, and special-event rides are also offered, but you need to reserve in advance.

Other companies offering a comparable service include Husky Express (775-782-3047) and Wilderness Adventures (530-550-8133). To check out other dogsled companies, log onto www.highsierra.com.

SLEIGH RIDES

What's more in keeping with a winter wonderland vacation than dashing through the snow in a one-horse open sleigh? For details and reservations in the South Shore Lake Tahoe area, call Borges Sleigh Rides Stateline at (775) 588-2953 or (800) 726-7433, or click on www.sleighride.com; or Camp Richardson Corral at (530) 541-3113. In the North Shore Lake Tahoe area, call Borges Sleigh Rides at (800) 726-7433.

SNOWMOBILE TOURS

When the mountains and backcountry roads around Lake Tahoe are covered with a deep blanket of snow, one of the most thrilling ways to experience the great outdoors is on a snowmobile. Don't worry if you've never ridden or driven one before—it's easy to learn, and the tour operators make sure you know the basics before heading out.

You can take guided tours out to wild areas for gorgeous views, or you can race around groomed tracks in open meadows and on golf courses. Eagle Ridge Snowmobile Outfitters also offers all-day outings and overnight trips, which include stays in cozy mountain lodges. If you don't have proper clothing, don't spend a fortune buying it, because most operators will also rent you whatever gear you might need.

For details and reservations in the North Shore Lake Tahoe area, call Eagle Ridge Snowmobile Outfitters at (530) 546-8667, TC Sno Mo's at (530) 581-3906, Northstar-at-Tahoe at (530) 562-1010, Lake Tahoe Snowmobile Tours at (530) 583-7192, or High Sierra Snowmobiling at (530) 546-9909. In the South Shore Lake Tahoe area, call Lake Tahoe Winter Sports Center at (530) 577-2940 or Zephyr Cove Snowmobile Center at (775) 589-4908.

FISHING AND HUNTING

Fishing and hunting inspire almost religious devotion among Insiders here in the Reno/Tahoe area. Hang around any of the sports bars, and you can't help but overhear folks talking about the four-pound trout that got away or the huge mule deer that bounded into the shelter of the woods before they could fire a shot.

In this chapter, I'll give you a quick overview of the fishing and hunting scenes in the Reno/Tahoe area. I'm not going to make you experts, but I will give you a few tips and hints to get you started and help you have an enjoyable time. In addition to everything else the area offers, it is a rare paradise that includes many opportunities for anglers and hunters.

FISHING

The Reno/Tahoe area is renowned for its trout fishing—unsurpassed by many other spots in the contiguous 48 states. Within 60 miles of Lake Tahoe, anglers have more than 400 lakes, reservoirs, rivers, creeks, and streams to fish, all set in spectacular, scenic country. Whether you're fly fishing on the cool, swift waters of the Truckee River, have a hankering to land a big Mackinaw from Lake Tahoe, or are out for a day trip to Pyramid Lake, you'll find fishing in the area thrilling and challenging.

Both the Nevada Division of Wildlife and the California Department of Fish and Game operate stocking programs in the Reno/Tahoe area, but which species of fish they plant, where the fish are planted, and when they are planted are subject to change annually, depending on the recommendations of wildlife biologists, angler surveys, and stocking and management plans for specific fisheries. You can find out which fish have been planted where by accessing the weekly reports given on these agencies' Web sites. Also, because water levels in streams and lakes can vary considerably depending upon the amount of snow that fell the previous winter, I recommend checking on the status of your fishing hole before heading out to catch the big one. In addition to fish and game Web sites, some of the best information can be found at local tackle stores. For California click on www.dfg.ca.gov, and for Nevada www.ndow.org.

In Lake Tahoe you can fish year-round because the lake never freezes over. In addition to the game fish that naturally inhabit the lake, the California Department of Fish and Game has, over the past few years, stocked anywhere from 140,000 to more than 300,000 fingerling kokanee salmon in Taylor Creek, hoping to boost the stocks of these popular game fish in the lake.

In the Desolation Wilderness (see the Area Overview and Recreation chapters for a description), some 130 lakes await the trout angler, and all of these lakes teem with fish, including the elusive and scarce golden trout, found only in the highest lakes in the wilderness. Though Desolation Wilderness is among the most used wilderness areas in the United States, most hikers don't head into the high country expressly to fish, leaving an abundance of opportunity for the avid angler.

Pyramid Lake, a high-desert lake just 35 miles north of Reno, is home to the legendary cutthroat trout, which fascinated John Frémont and his group (see the History section for a brief description of Frémont's expedition, and the Day Trips chapter for more about Pyramid Lake). The record size of a cutthroat trout (caught in 1977) was 38 inches and weighed 23.8 pounds. This lake sits on an Indian reservation, so you don't need a Nevada fishing license to cast your line here, but you will have to purchase a permit on the reservation.

The fishing in Lake Tahoe and Pyramid Lake alone is good enough to qualify the area as a trout angler's mecca. There are more opportunities in other lakes and streams, but the limitations of this guide make it impossible to cover every creek, stream, and lake within the 60-mile radius. Instead I'm going to concentrate on the Lake Tahoe–Truckee River–Pyramid Lake water system—the major system in the Reno/Tahoe area. It's easily accessible and will provide more fishing action than the average visitor to the area can handle, as well as plenty of opportunities for the resident angler. (If you're itching for more, you might also want to check out *Dave Stanley's No Nonsense Guide to Fly Fishing in Nevada,* by Dave Stanley, and *The Nevada Angler's Guide,* by Richard Dickerson.)

The Truckee River connects Lake Tahoe and Pyramid Lake, and together they make up what's known as a closed water system—in other words, their waters never reach the ocean. At one time, fish could swim from one lake to the other by way of the Truckee River. Today that's not so, and the system is treated as three different fisheries, each requiring different fishing techniques.

This chapter provides basic information about these three exceptional fisheries, which should enable you to catch more trout and have more fun doing it. Remember that trout fishing, especially in the Reno/Tahoe area, is both a recreational sport and an art. Trout grow big and wily because anglers underestimate them. They're smart, but I hope to make you smarter by giving you a few Insiders' tricks to help you fill your creel. If that creel, by chance or plan, remains empty, keep in mind that you don't have to catch fish to have fun, especially in this area. You will be out in the fresh air, enjoying the scenery, far from the worries and cares of crowded city life, and that is reward enough. Go fishing, and give your mind a chance to relax.

Lake Tahoe

When anglers first get a look at Lake Tahoe, they usually scratch their heads and ask, "Where do I begin?" After all, the lake is 22 miles long and 12 miles wide, and most experienced Lake Tahoe guides will tell you that successfully fishing this lake takes more skill and finesse than many other American lakes. It ranks 5th in the world in mean depth (1,027 feet), and 10th in the world in maximum depth (1,636 feet), and its mirrorlike conditions make for some real spooky trout.

Most first-time anglers have a difficult time landing game fish in Lake Tahoe. In fact, I know one experienced angler who fished the lake for five years and only netted two lake, or Mackinaw, trout. But then, he was a stubborn fellow who wouldn't ask the experts for help; thus my first bit of advice for new anglers on Lake Tahoe is to hire a guide. I understand that to some this is akin to stopping your car at a gas station to ask for directions, but you'll have more fun if you heed this advice.

More than 25 guides make a living on Lake Tahoe (see the end of this chapter for an abbreviated listing), and hiring one to show you the ins and outs of Tahoe's fishing scene is money well spent. A guide can show you the techniques needed to land the "big one"; once you've learned from a professional, catching fish on your own should be a lot easier.

Because Lake Tahoe is located both in California and Nevada, the states have agreed to honor a fishing license from either state when fishing the lake. Any person 16 years of age or older must have a license to fish. Limits are five game fish, of which no more than two may be Mackinaw.

Lake Tahoe is open year-round, and fishing is permitted on a daily basis beginning one hour before sunrise and ending two hours after sunset. Fishing is not permitted in the following areas:

- Within 300 feet of Tahoe's tributaries and upstream to the first lake from October 1 to June 30 on the California side
- Within a 200-yard radius of the mouths of Third, Incline, and Wood Creeks on the Nevada side
- Within a 500-yard radius of Sand Harbor boat ramp
- Within the boat-launch area in the jetty at Cave Rock

BOAT FISHING

The first thing to remember about fishing Lake Tahoe is that a boat with a fish-finder is mandatory if you expect to catch "the big one." Lake Tahoe has a lot of water and several species of game fish (kokanee salmon; brook, brown, rainbow, and Mackinaw trout; and the native, endangered, and extremely rare cutthroat trout), making trolling the most popular method used by anglers on this lake.

The theory behind trolling is that you can cover a lot of territory in a short amount of time, and you can bring the bait to the fish rather than waiting for the fish to come to the bait. On Lake Tahoe, anglers usually use two trolling methods for the prized Mackinaw—downrigging and lead lining.

Downriggers are fishing devices fixed to the boat that enable you to use heavy weights on a separate reel. These weights are attached to your fishing line by clips. Once a fish strikes, the weights are released and reeled in, and it's just you and the monster Mackinaw on the other end of the line. The weights help you troll with lures and live bait at varying depths, depending on where the fish are. The fish-finders help determine the depth of the fish, too.

Lead lining is a technique used to go deep—sometimes as much as 200 feet—for the big Macks. The technique is to use flashy lures like wobbling spoons, Rebels,

i

Disabled anglers delight in the barrier-free fishing platforms on the West Fork of the Carson River. You'll find them in Hope Valley, one of the most beautiful sections of the river, at the intersection of California Highways 88 and 89, 15 miles south of South Lake Tahoe.

and Rapalas behind a lead-core nylon line or metal line. You run the line out—sometimes as far as 300 yards, depending on how deep the fish are—and wait for a strike.

Jigging is another method anglers use to catch Mackinaws in Lake Tahoe. Jigging usually consists of using a live minnow on a treble hook combined with a jig. Jigging lures resemble wounded fish. The idea is to work the rod with small tugs to give the impression that the minnow is wounded, with the hope of drawing the Mack in for the strike.

To go for the feisty rainbows in Lake Tahoe, the preferred method is to top line, trolling a lure just below the surface near the lake's shore. Some anglers find fighting a rainbow on light line a lot more fun than dragging in a half-drowned Mackinaw and 300 yards of lead line. The rainbows fight like crazy, leaping out of the water and making long runs trying to spit the hook. The best place to top-line troll for rainbows is along the rocky shoal areas using Flatfish and Hot Shot plugs, or Rebel and Rapala lures.

During summer and early fall, fishing for kokanee salmon is extremely popular. The salmon spawn up Taylor Creek, and during the migrating run, thousands head to the spawning grounds. They can be caught by trolling with downriggers and, according to one local guide, make a tasty meal.

PIER AND SHORE FISHING

Don't fret if you don't have access to a boat, because pier and shore fishing around Lake Tahoe can be fun and productive, too. You just have to remember a few things—avoid fishing when the lake is mirrorlike calm, and try to make long casts from both pier and the shore so the fish don't see you. Remember, the fish in this lake are already spooky.

The best time to fish from a pier or the shore is when a healthy breeze blows waves on the water. Large trout will cruise into shore looking for minnows, crawfish, or any other food kicked up by the rough water. Spinners and lures work best, but bait anglers using worms, salmon eggs, and Power Bait have been known to pull in a few lunkers. Always use light monofilament line to hide the leaders. You can find trout close to shore at Rubicon Point, Dollar Point, Crystal Bay Point, Sand Harbor, Cave Rock, and south of Tahoe City, but don't restrict your fishing to these points, as trout can be found everywhere around the lake.

The Truckee River

The Truckee River, Lake Tahoe's only outlet, begins its trek from the dam at Tahoe City, California, and continues along California Highway 89 through the town of Truckee, California, then along Interstate 80 through Reno and Sparks, eventually emptying into Pyramid Lake. The 115 miles of river used to be the breeding ground of the monstrous Lahontan cutthroat trout. In autumns long gone, these fish would make spawning runs from Pyramid Lake back toward Lake Tahoe. The days of seeing so many fish you could almost walk on the Truckee River are gone, but thanks to several consecutive wet years, trout fishing in the river is amply rewarding, and attempts are being made to bring back the native Lahontan cutthroat.

The Truckee River is split into three separate lengths for purposes of fishing. The upper section runs from Lake Tahoe to the town of Truckee, California, the middle section from Truckee to the Nevada state line, and the lower section from the Nevada state line to Pyramid Lake.

The upper section is heavily fished because CA 89 runs parallel to the river, and several public campgrounds sit on its banks, making access to great fishing easy. The floods of 1997 and 2006 altered some of the characteristics of this upper section, but big pools of slow-moving water still exist, hiding some monstrous trout. During the summer, many people enjoy rafting and tubing this section of the river, so the best times to fish are usually early morning or late evening. Normally, the river has slowed from late June to early September, making these the best months to fish.

The season lasts from the last Saturday in April to November 15, but fishing is prohibited from Fanny Bridge at Lake Tahoe to 1,000 feet downstream. Just about any trout-fishing technique will work on the upper section of the river—lures, especially Mepps and Panther Martins; salmon eggs and worms bounced along the bottom; and for the fly-fishing enthusiast, caddis flies, streamers, and nymphs presented just before dark. The limit is five trout per day, but a local guide suggests you catch and release all fish along this stretch.

The middle section of the Truckee River is wild trout country, and legal restrictions vary depending on where you fish. A copy of the California Department of Fish and Game regulations is mandatory to stay out of legal trouble with the game wardens and to enjoy fishing this section; you can acquire this guide at any sporting-goods store that sells fishing licenses. From Trout Creek to Glenshire Bridge and from Prosser Creek to Boca Bridge, only artificial lures with barbless hooks are allowed. From Glenshire Bridge to Prosser Creek, only artificial flies with barbless hooks are allowed. From Boca Bridge to the state line, any type of fishing gear is permissible. A 2-mile stretch of the river, from the Glenshire Bridge to the first I-80 bridge downstream, is private property and off-limits. Obviously, close attention to the regulations is mandatory—but the rewards are sweet here.

The middle section is inhabited by rainbows, browns, and possibly some cutthroat. You'll find some of the most challenging fishing on the river in this section. But watch out near the state line: If you fish on it or cross it, you will need a license from both California and Nevada.

The season for this section is open from the last Saturday in April to November 15. The catch limit varies on this stretch, so consult the regulations.

The lower section of the Truckee River, which is entirely in Nevada, may offer opportunities for some trophy trout. And for the first time in many, many years, Lahontan cutthroat trout comprise 50 percent of the catchable trout on this section of the Truckee. The best fishing here will be associated with lower-flow conditions following the winter runoff—usually July through October.

The trophy section of the river, where trout grow big and smart, runs from the California border downstream to the I-80 bridge near Crystal Peak Park in Verdi. Only artificial lures with single, barbless hooks may be used, and the limit is 2 trout and 10 mountain whitefish, with the minimum size for the trout set at 14 inches. The remaining 75 miles of the river in Nevada have no gear limitations. The river in this section is easily accessed from Crystal Peak Park, Dog Valley Road bridge, and both bridges on Third Street.

This section of river often boggles experienced anglers' minds because they can enjoy some of the best trout fishing in the state only a few hundred yards from the glitter of Reno's downtown casinos. And fly fishing on this little river rivals many of the rivers in neighboring states, because the Truckee is home to most of the insects fly anglers like to imitate—stone flies, mayflies, caddis flies, and others. The trout fishing is simply great all along this section.

Bouncing salmon eggs and worms along the bottom is always a good technique in this section of the river, and using lures like Mepps, Panther Martins, Rapalas, and Rebels always works, too. Some of the more popular areas in Reno to fish the Truckee are Mayberry Park, Idlewild Park, and any of the three Fisherman's parks.

You can fish this section year-round, any hour of the day or night, except for the portion 1,000 feet downstream of Derby Dam, which is closed to all fishing. The limit is 5 trout and 10 mountain whitefish.

Pyramid Lake

Pyramid Lake is located 35 miles north of Reno by way of Nevada Highway 445 (the Pyramid Highway). It is located on the Pyramid Lake Paiute Indian Reservation. While a Nevada fishing license is not required, you must purchase a permit to fish on the reservation. Permits are available at the reservation store, at the lake's ranger station, and from most bait and tackle shops in Reno and Sparks.

The lake received its name from a pyramid-shaped tufa mound (calcium deposit) rising out of the water. It is a starkly beautiful lake, flanked by rugged mountains on the east and west. No trees grow here, but the lake is home to monstrous cutthroat trout. The average trout pulled is about 2 feet long and weighs around five pounds.

Fishing Pyramid Lake is great either from shore or from a boat. The cutthroat trout is very active in its search for food and often swims into shallow water. Trolling is the preferred method of catching fish at Pyramid, using lures that imitate minnows, and downriggers to get the lures to the correct depth. Boat anglers use Tor-p-Dos, Apex lures, U20 Flatfish, Pink Ladies, and flashers. Shore anglers stick to using Tor-p-Dos, Rapalas, Daredevils, and Maribu jigs.

Fly fishing is also popular at Pyramid Lake and probably the most exciting method of catching fish here. Cutthroats strike flies with a vengeance. Fly anglers use six- to nine-pound leaders with fast-sinking fly line (shooting heads) when fishing the drop-offs and a slow-sinking line at the shallow beaches. Black and purple Woolly Worms and Woolly Buggers are their favorite flies. And anglers will usually use two sizes of flies, one as a dropper, to find out what the fish are biting on. One of the most peculiar things that you'll see at the lake are anglers standing on small stepladders in the waist-deep water while casting. The added height can help increase an angler's casting distance but also makes for an unusual picture.

The fishing season at Pyramid Lake runs from October 1 through June 30. The keeper size for the cutthroat is 16 to 19 inches and any cutthroat more than 24 inches. The daily limit is two, with only one that is more than 24 inches. One rod and two hooks per angler are allowed, and fishing is permitted with artificial lures only. For more information about the lake, visit www.pyramidlakefisheries.org.

Fishing Licenses

All license fees are subject to change. These annual rates were current for the 2006 season. More details are available on the state wildlife services' Web sites: For Nevada: www.ndow.org; for California: www.dfg.ca.gov.

CALIFORNIA

Everyone 16 years of age and older must have a valid fishing license. These rates were current at press time.

Annual resident: $34.90
Annual nonresident: $94.00
One-day resident or nonresident: $11.30
Ten-day nonresident: $34.90

NEVADA

Everyone 12 years of age and older must have a valid fishing license.

Resident:
16 years of age and older: $29.00
12 to 15 years of age: $13.00
Younger than 12 years old: Free

Nonresident:
16 years of age and older: $69.00
12 to 15 years of age: $21.00
One-day license: $18.00

PYRAMID LAKE

Everyone must have a valid fishing permit to fish Pyramid Lake.

One-day permit: $6.00
Season permit: $40.00

Fishing Guides

LAKE TAHOE

First Strike
Tahoe Keys Marina
South Lake Tahoe, CA
(530) 577-5065
First Strike specializes in year-round charters for trout and salmon using the latest in electronic equipment and lightweight tackle. They have a morning and afternoon charter that includes bait, tackle, and snacks—and they'll even clean your fish. Write P.O. Box 13107, South Lake Tahoe, CA 96157 for more information.

Kingfish Guide Service
5110 West Lake Boulevard
Homewood, CA
(530) 525-5360
www.kingfishtahoe.com
This outfit runs charters year-round on the lake from a 43-foot boat named the *Kingfish.* All equipment—tackle, rods, and reels—is included. Trips leave early in the morning from the pier across from Homewood Mountain Resort. The mailing address is P.O. Box 5955, Tahoe City, CA 96145. The cost is about $80 per person.

Mickey's Big Mack Charters
Carnelian Bay, CA
(530) 546-4444, (800) 877-1462
www.mickeysbigmack.com
Fish year-round with master guide Mickey Daniels. He has been fishing Lake Tahoe for more than 30 years and guarantees he

will find you fish. Call the number above or write for more information: P.O. Box 488, Carnelian Bay, CA 96140.

Tahoe Sportsfishing
900 Ski Run Boulevard, Suite 102
South Lake Tahoe, CA
(530) 541-5448, (800) 696-7797

Zephyr Cove Marina
Zephyr Cove, NV
(775) 586-9338
www.tahoesportfishing.com
Fishing the lake since 1953, Tahoe Sportsfishing trips include all gear, tackle, and bait. A four-hour trip runs $85 per person, five-hour trips cost $95 per person, and a seven-hour trip is offered for $135 per person. Boats leave in the morning and the afternoon. These guides also clean and wrap your catch. Fishing licenses are available here as well.

PYRAMID LAKE

Cutthroat Charters
29555 Pyramid Highway, Sutcliff, NV
(775) 476-0555
www.fishpyramid.com
This family-owned and -operated business, which runs out of the Pyramid Lake Store, guarantees anglers will catch cutthroat trout. Cutthroat Charters is only 30 minutes from Reno and Sparks, and it operates seven days a week during the season. A four-hour trip is $85 per person; a seven-hour outing is $135 per person.

Fly Fishing

The following establishments will supply you with all your fly-fishing needs, including licenses, lessons, fly-tying classes, equipment, and local knowledge.

The Gilly
1111 North Rock Boulevard, Sparks, NV
(775) 358-6113

Mark Fore and Strike Sporting Goods
490 Kietzke Lane, Reno, NV
(775) 322-9559

Reno Fly Shop
294 East Moana Lane #14, Reno, NV
(775) 825-3474
www.renoflyshop.com
The Reno Fly Shop has a sister store, Truckee River Outfitters, that is open from late April through September and offers all the services mentioned above, as well as guide services. The address is 10200 Donner Pass Road, Truckee, CA 96161; (530) 582-0900.

These companies offer fly-fishing guide services in the Tahoe area:

Johnson Tackle & Guide Service
P.O. Box 26, Tahoma, CA 96142
(530) 525-6575 (summer)
(415) 453-9831 (winter)
Randy Johnson is not only a master guide but also a well-known fly-tier with more than 150 designs to his credit.

Tahoe Fly Fishing Outfitters
2705 Lake Tahoe Boulevard
South Lake Tahoe, CA
(530) 541-8208
www.tahoeflyfishing.com
In addition to retail services including fly-fishing equipment, bait and tackle, and fishing licenses, this company offers expert guide service for the entire length of the Truckee River, as well as the Carson Valley, Tahoe, and Truckee areas.

HUNTING

Everything you've heard about the top quality of hunting in California and Nevada is true. Game abounds in these two states. Big animals like deer, bear, mountain lion, bighorn sheep, elk, antelope, and mountain goat roam open coun-

A great source of hunting and fishing information is Dave Rice's Wednesday column in the **Reno Gazette-Journal.**

try in both states, along with migratory fowl, quail, grouse, dove, turkey, chukar, pheasant, rabbit, squirrel, and furbearing animals. Most species have specific hunting seasons, which vary from year to year, and differ depending on whether you are hunting with a conventional weapon, muzzleloader, or longbow.

While you can hunt for game birds, mule deer, and antelope near Reno and Lake Tahoe, the sport is relatively limited in the area. According to one local guide, development in the region has resulted in a reduction of the habitat necessary to support a large population of big game. Because of the relatively limited opportunities, I have limited the hunting section of this guide to just a few paragraphs, which will let you know where to find more detailed information.

In the Reno/Tahoe area, places to hunt small game and birds can be found outside of the cities of Reno and Sparks; for more abundant opportunities and bigger game, you might want to head north toward the Black Rock Desert. Prime hunting for ducks and geese is found around Fallon, about 60 miles east of Reno (see the Day Trips chapter). For information contact Greenhead Hunting Club at 9165 Pasture Road, Fallon; (775) 423-9165. For upland game birds Insiders head to the mountain ranges around Lovelock and Winnemucca, north of Reno, or to central Nevada near the tiny town of Austin. On the California side of Lake Tahoe, hunting for deer, quail, and bear is allowed in some parts of the El Dorado National Forest and in the Desolation Wilderness.

The Reno/Tahoe area is set to welcome three major outdoor retailers: Bass Pro Shops, Cabela's, and Orvis.

Hunting regulations are stringent and detailed—the regulations for Nevada alone fill a large booklet and cover everything from use or possession of a firearm by a child to sunrise and sunset tables, application and tag regulations, and hunting season dates and quotas. The best way to educate yourself is to acquire the regulations for the state you plan to hunt in. Both states require a hunting license and have an established application process for obtaining big-game hunting tags. To hunt in the Reno/Tahoe area, you must apply for a tag specific to that area well in advance of the first day of the season.

NEVADA

For detailed information on hunting regulations in Nevada, you should read the *Nevada Hunt Book,* which is updated annually and available in spring. This will provide you with everything you need to know, including information about regulations and fees and how to obtain the license and tag necessary to hunt the game of your choice. You can access it online or obtain a hard copy by calling or writing:

Nevada Division of Wildlife
1100 Valley Road
Reno, NV 89512
(775) 688-1500
www.ndow.org

CALIFORNIA

The California Department of Fish and Game publishes the *California Hunting Regulations for Mammals and Furbearers* and *Resident and Migratory Upland Game Bird Hunting Regulations* on an annual basis. The fees and regulations are in effect from each July to June of the following year. You can obtain this information online or by calling or writing:

California Department of Fish and Game
P.O. Box 944209
Sacramento, CA 94244-2090
(916) 653-4899
www.dfg.ca.gov

Hunting Guides

Sometimes the best plan of action is to hire a hunting guide, an Insider who knows the regulations, the game, and the lay of the land.

Black Rock Outfitters
P.O. Box 1192, Winnemucca, NV 89446
(775) 623-5926
A lifelong resident of Winnemucca and a guide since 1985, Michael Hornbarger of Black Rock Outfitters knows the backcountry of northern Nevada intimately. Since learning to trap as a child, he's explored every inch of this wild land, guiding friends and clients on hunting and photo trips for years. He'll personalize a tour or hunt just for you, whether you're out to bag a mountain lion, want to go fishing, take a tour of the Black Rock Desert, or capture the wonders of the backcountry in the lens of your camera.

Nevada Trophy Hunts
P.O. Box 10, Gerlach, NV 89412
(775) 557-2238
A former wildlife photographer whose work has appeared in *National Geographic* magazine, Tony Diebold of Nevada Trophy Hunts is the consummate outdoorsman. His personalized trophy hunts for mule deer, desert sheep, antelope, and elk are well known throughout Nevada, and he also leads guided fishing and sightseeing trips. If you shoot with a camera and not a gun, you can take wildlife photo trips with him to some of the most unspoiled animal habitats in the area.

Tahoe Fly Fishing Outfitters
2705 Lake Tahoe Boulevard
South Lake Tahoe, CA
(530) 541-8208
www.tahoeflyfishing.com
Mentioned in the fishing section, this outfit also offers guided hunts for migratory waterfowl in Nevada. The season varies but generally runs from October through January, depending on the type of game.

Hunting Licenses

NEVADA

As with fishing licenses, fees are subject to change annually. Consult the *Nevada Hunt Book* or the Nevada Division of Wildlife for current rates.

Resident:
- 16 years and older: $33.00
- 12 to 15 years old: $13.00

Nonresident:
- General: $142.00

CALIFORNIA

Fees are subject to change annually. Refer to the California Department of Fish and Game, the *California Hunting Regulations for Mammals and Furbearers,* or the *Resident and Migratory Upland Game Bird Hunting Regulations* for the most current rates.

Resident:
- General: $33.35
- Junior, 16 years or younger: $8.65
- Lifetime licenses are available.

Nonresident:
- General: $115.75

SPECTATOR SPORTS 

Over the years, the Reno/Sparks area has seen a succession of professional sports teams come and go. After an absence of such teams for a few years, the Silver Sox came to town in 2006. A professional baseball team affiliated with the Golden Baseball League, the Sox play their games at William Peccole Park on the University of Nevada, Reno, campus. Efforts are still under way to attract a triple-A baseball team to a stadium that would be built in Sparks. But even with a minor professional presence, it's obvious that residents of the Reno/Tahoe area like spectator sports. All you have to do is visit the sports book at any casino on any weekend, and you'll be standing elbow to elbow with sports fans trying to catch a glimpse of their favorite teams on one of the many big-screen TVs lining the walls. You'll also notice that community sports programs are well supported, with large numbers of participants and fans making good use of both indoor and outdoor sports venues throughout the year.

The Wolf Pack sports program at UNR does a fine job in providing high quality and variety for spectators. Fans can choose from baseball, football, basketball, soccer, and volleyball. Once a very winning member of the Big West Conference, the university was moved to a higher level of competition in the Western Athletic Conference several years ago. Support for university sports is strong, with the fund-raising organization hosting a variety of lucrative events throughout the year. To find out how to become an active Wolf Pack booster, call (775) 784-6900. The Reno/Tahoe area is also home to two unique sporting events that attract spectators from all over the country—the annual National Championship Air Races and The Great Reno Balloon Race.

Furthermore, Reno's National Bowling Stadium is one of the largest and best in the country and is host to numerous bowling tournaments throughout the year. And there's always that favorite Western sports event, the rodeo, along with ski and snowboard events around Lake Tahoe.

Read on to see what the Reno/Tahoe area has to offer for those of you who like to be knee-deep in the sports action. I haven't used the usual geographical organization in this chapter, since most of the sports action happens in the Truckee Meadows—but don't let the drive from Lake Tahoe deter you from enjoying some great sports options.

AIR RACES

National Championship Air Races
Reno Stead Airport
4895 Texas Avenue
Reno, NV
(775) 972-6663
www.airrace.org

Bill Stead was a World War II ace, a Nevada rancher, and a dreamer. In 1964 he realized his biggest dream when he convinced local businessmen to bring Midwestern-style air racing to the Reno/Tahoe area. Today the National Championship Air Races are the biggest in the United States, with around 200,000 spectators watching six different classes of racing during the four-day event.

Every September, racers gather from all corners of the United States to participate in the fastest motor sport in the world. In addition to the on-hand, modern military aircraft, unlimiteds, AT-6s, biplanes, Formula Ones, jets, and sport-class kit aircraft swarm to the Stead Airport to race against the forces of nature, gravity, and one another. This spectacle is so amazing and so unbelievable, Insiders say that "the show needs the heavens as its stage." (See also the Annual Events chapter.)

General admission tickets for the Thursday through Sunday event range around $16 to $36 and may be purchased over the phone by calling Ticketmaster at (775) 787-8497 or accessing www.ticketmaster.com.

BALLOON RACES

The Great Reno Balloon Race
Rancho San Rafael Park
330 East Liberty Street, #200 (office)
Reno, NV
(775) 826-1181
www.renoballoon.com

More than 100 hot-air balloons in all shapes and sizes, including panda bears, whiskey bottles, D-cell batteries, and Burger King Whoppers, fill the predawn skies over Reno's Rancho San Rafael Park during The Great Reno Balloon Race. The event, usually held in September, draws a crowd of more than 130,000 over its four days. This free (both admission and parking) spectacular includes two types of balloon flying competition—a Hare and Hound race and various target drops.

In the Hare and Hound race, one balloon launches early (the hare), and the other balloons (the hounds) try to follow the path of the first balloon. The hare lands in a safe area and plants a target. The hounds try to drop a marker closest to the center of the target from the air.

The target drop-style of race has the pilots launching their balloons from a 1-mile radius outside the park. The balloonists navigate into the park where a target has been placed on the ground and attempt to place their markers closest to the center of the target from the air.

On Saturday and Sunday of the event, balloonists launch the Dawn Patrol, a presunrise liftoff. The balloons' ascensions are usually choreographed to music, and it is a spectacular sight, with the balloons lighting up the dark sky. Only a few pilots worldwide are qualified to fly a Dawn Patrol, making the feat extra-special for spectators.

During the events, spectators are welcome to walk through the park and to talk with flight crews and pilots as they fill their balloons with air. Most spectators bring picnic breakfasts, but an extensive concession area is always set up ready to cater to everyone's needs.

BASEBALL

Reno Astros
Moana Stadium, 300 West Moana Lane
Reno, NV
(775) 851-0937

Although the Reno Astros are a semiprofessional team, many of the players have paid their dues playing professional ball. You can see all the action several days a week during the season, which runs from April through October. And, unlike the pros, the admission prices are very affordable for the whole family.

Reno Silver Sox
William Peccole Park
University of Nevada, Reno
Reno, NV
(775) 348-7769 (team phone)
(866) 342-5425 (league phone)
www.goldenbaseball.com/reno

When the Blackjacks left town in 1999, the Reno/Tahoe area was left without a professional baseball team until the Reno Silver Sox arrived in 2006. The team plays its 40 home games at William Peccole Park on the UNR campus. Affiliated with the Golden Baseball League, the team plays such clubs as Long Beach, CA; Mesa, AZ; and San Diego and Chico, CA. Season tickets range from $215 for general admission to $395 for box seats.

UNR Baseball
William Peccole Park
University of Nevada, Reno
Reno, NV
(775) 784-6900
(775) 348-PACK (tickets)
www.nevadawolfpack.com

The Wolf Pack's baseball schedule begins

You can show your support for University of Nevada, Reno, sports by purchasing Wolf Pack logo merchandise at www.nevadawolfpack.com.

in late January and ends in May. A perennial NCAA regional qualifier, the team has a very loyal following. The quality of the program over the years is shown by the number of players that move on to pro teams. Since 1990 more than 40 UNR players have signed professional baseball contracts. As with most college baseball venues, William Peccole Park is outdoors, so check the weather and be prepared to bundle up at the beginning of the season.

BASKETBALL

UNR Basketball
Lawlor Events Center
University of Nevada, Reno
Reno, NV
(775) 348-PACK (tickets)
www.nevadawolfpack.com

Both men's and women's basketball programs at UNR provide exciting action for hoops fans each season. The men play about 15 home games, which attract an average of 6,000 spectators each. The men played in the Sweet Sixteen in 2005 and won the WAC championship in 2006.

Average attendance for the women is around 1,000 per game. Both teams play at Lawlor Events Center, a typical college arena with about 11,500 seats.

BOWLING

National Bowling Stadium
300 North Center Street, Reno, NV
(775) 334-2600, (800) 304-2695
www.visitrenotahoe.com

This bowling stadium is the world's largest and most advanced. Built in 1995, this block-long masterpiece has 80 championship lanes, a circular theater, and a 450-foot-long video scoring system. The facility cost the Reno-Sparks Convention and Visitor's Authority (RSCVA) about $45 million to complete.

Although only professional tournaments were held in the stadium for the first years of its operation, the stadium hosts amateur tournaments and events of all kinds. When the pros are in town (which happens every year or so), visitors are welcome to watch all the action from the 1,200 spectator seats. Because dates of the tournaments vary, contact the stadium for specific days and times. (See the Attractions and Annual Events chapters for more information.)

FOOTBALL

UNR Football
Mackay Stadium
University of Nevada, Reno
Reno, NV
(775) 348-PACK (tickets)
www.nevadawolfpack.com

To die-hard football fans, autumn leaves mean one thing—Wolf Pack action at Mackay Stadium. Although most spectators come for the activity inside the stadium, some come for the events outside, where you'll find elaborate tailgate parties sprinkled around the asphalt parking lot. The six home games are well supported, with an average attendance of around 20,000 per game. The season lasts from September through November.

GOLF

American Century Championship Golf Tournament
Edgewood Tahoe Golf Course
180 Lake Parkway, Stateline, NV
(775) 588-3566
www.edgewood-tahoe.com
www.tahoecelebritygolf.com

See more than 70 sports and entertainment stars including the likes of Michael Jordan, Charles Barkley, Dan Marino,

Jerry Rice, John Elway, Oscar De La Hoya, and many, many more compete for a $500,000 purse. Not only do these sports legends and movie stars provide a fun-filled week for spectators, they actually play three rounds of some intense golf.

The six-day event includes two days of practice rounds, a one-day celebrity/amateur tournament where Insiders get to play alongside their favorite stars, and the 72-hole tournament. The weeklong event has plenty of opportunities built in for spectators to hobnob with the stars at one of the most beautiful golf courses in the United States (see the Golf chapter for details on the Edgewood Tahoe Golf Course). The event is usually scheduled in early July, with tickets costing between $10 and $20, depending on the day.

Reno/Tahoe Open
Montreux Golf and Country Club
2500 Spinnaker Drive, Reno, NV
(775) 849-9444, (888) 848-7366
www.renotahoeopen.com

The newest tournament on the PGA Tour, the Reno/Tahoe Open drew rave reviews from players and spectators alike at its debut in 1999. Now, as a more seasoned event, it draws a large percentage of the top money winners on the tour and offers an attractive $3 million purse. Following the usual tour format, the tournament consists of a Pro/Am on Wednesday, followed by four days of golf for the pros only.

Along with the warm hospitality the tournament extends, the event provides a memorable outdoor experience for anyone who attends. Meandering through huge stands of ponderosa pines at the base of Slide Mountain, the course at Montreux Golf and Country Club is vintage Jack Nicklaus—bad but oh so beautiful. Because it's also very private, the tournament offers nonmembers a rare opportunity to see the layout up close and personal. And since the event is still relatively new to the PGA schedule, it's not as packed with spectators as some other more established tournaments. The Reno/Tahoe Open is a marvelous opportunity to not only see some of the best golf in the world but also to enjoy a hassle-free day in a beautiful mountain setting.

MOTOR SPORTS

Reno Historic Races
Reno-Fernley Raceway
Fernley, NV, 35 miles east of Sparks, NV
(775) 575-7217
www.automuseum.com
www.hmsausa.com
www.reno-fernleyraceway.com

Vintage cars such as Ferraris, Jaguars, and Porches race on Fernley's 4.3-mile course, one of the nation's longest. Sponsored by the National Automobile Museum and the Historic Motor Sports Association, the event also features guided tours of the staging area. About 150 participants enter the race. The raceway is a quick 25-minute drive east of Sparks on Interstate 80 and then 5 miles south on Alternate U.S. Highway 95.

RODEO

Reno Rodeo
Reno Livestock Events Center
1350 North Wells Avenue, Reno, NV
(775) 329-3877
(800) 225-2277 (tickets)
www.renorodeo.com

This rodeo is billed as "The Wildest, Richest Rodeo in the West," and it's not hard to see why. The nine-day event has more than $41 million in prize money waiting for the top cowboys and cowgirls. The event usually kicks off on a Friday in mid-June with a party and a concert featuring a big name in country and western music. From Saturday through the next Sunday, cowboys and cowgirls compete for the prize

Children with special needs are paired with rodeo cowboys to perform in the Special Kids Rodeo on Sunday during the Reno Rodeo.

i

The winner of the annual University of Nevada, Reno, and University of Nevada, Las Vegas, football game takes home the Fremont Cannon, a replica of the mountain howitzer that accompanied Lt. John C. Frémont on his expedition through Nevada in 1843-1844.

money by team roping, barrel racing, bareback riding, bull riding, steer wrestling, saddle bronc riding, and calf roping. The event culminates at 1:00 P.M. Sunday with the championship rodeo performance.

Other attractions at the rodeo include a carnival, cowboy country shops and a Western exhibit hall, and a behind-the-scenes chute tour. Ticket prices range from $8.00 to $17.00 depending on performance, day, and seating.

Snaffle Bit Futurity
Reno Livestock Events Center
1350 North Wells Avenue, Reno, NV
(775) 688-5750
(775) 787-8497 (tickets)
www.nrcha.com
www.ticketmaster.com (tickets)
Though not exactly a rodeo in the classic sense, the National Reined Cow Horse Association's Snaffle Bit Futurity matches three-year-old horses from around the world against one another in contests of steer cutting. Riders and horses are judged on how well they can cut a steer from a herd, and control the steer's movement along the fence and then into the center of the arena. Points are awarded for how well the horses respond to commands to turn and maneuver. The event is held in Reno during the last week in September and brings more than 700 horses and 750 riders to the area. The participants compete for more than $900,000 in prize money.

SOCCER

UNR Soccer
Mackay Stadium
University of Nevada, Reno
Reno, NV
(775) 348-PACK (tickets)
www.nevadawolfpack.com
A relatively new sport to the University of Nevada, Reno, women's soccer pioneered in 2000. Although the win-loss record has not been impressive so far, the team is winning a few more games each year. Players have an extensive travel schedule but play eight games on their home turf each season.

VOLLEYBALL

UNR Volleyball
The Old Gym
University of Nevada, Reno
Reno, NV
(775) 348-PACK (tickets)
www.nevadawolfpack.com
With a history of more than 30 years behind it, the women's volleyball program at the University of Nevada, Reno, is one of the more established ladies' sports programs at the school. As the popularity of female sports has increased over the years, the level of competition has also risen. The action at the 15 home games in The Old Gym is fast paced and intense. Tickets are available at the door and are reasonably priced.

DAY TRIPS

When you're surrounded by majestic mountains, dramatic deserts, and verdant valleys, it's impossible not to wonder what's just down the road or over the next hill. Although the Reno/Tahoe area itself is certainly captivating enough for even the most discriminating visitor, when it comes to nearby day trips, the immediate area is most assuredly not "all she wrote."

In this chapter we'll venture out to explore the wonder and magic that lie just two or three hours' drive away. We'll drift lazily in a hot-air balloon over cattle standing knee-deep in the Carson Valley's velvety green grass. We'll sink blissfully into the same soothing hot springs once enjoyed by Clark Gable and Mark Twain at David Walley's Resort, Hot Springs & Spa. In the historic town of Truckee, we'll visit the site of the most highly publicized acts of cannibalism in America. We'll immerse ourselves in the rowdiness of a Victorian-era mining settlement in colorful Virginia City. And we'll drink in the primal beauty of an enormous mosaic of moving sand at Churchill County's Sand Mountain. These experiences and more are guaranteed to pique your intellectual curiosity, overwhelm your physical senses, and, at the very least, keep you fully entertained for the better part of a day.

But before we head down the road, a word to the wise about the weather in this part of the world. If you're traveling into the desert during the summer months, you should be aware that temperatures during daylight hours often exceed 100 degrees. To beat the heat once you get where you're going, you can't always count on cooling off in the shade of a tree, since some desert regions are completely devoid of large vegetation. If you're expecting to picnic or to set up a day camp, you'll need an umbrella or tarp to provide shade. To be on the safe side, carry plenty of water and be sure to drink frequently to avoid dehydration, even if you're in the car. If you're tramping around in the desert, you should wear comfortable shoes, loose clothing, a sun hat, and sunscreen. Since temperatures can plummet 60 or more degrees in the desert when the sun goes down, it's also a good idea to have a jacket or light sweater handy if you're out after dark.

In the winter months, the enemy is not the sun but winter storms that can create blizzard conditions and make driving hazardous, especially in mountain areas. Insiders know the best rig for winter driving is a four-wheel-drive car, sport utility vehicle, or truck. In the absence of these, you can usually get around pretty well with chains or snow tires when conditions demand them. It's a good idea to keep some warm clothing, water, dehydrated food, and other emergency supplies in the car during winter months, since it's not unusual to get delayed, even on heavily trafficked roads, during winter storms. I don't want to discourage you from venturing out, but you should know that sometimes hazardous conditions do exist. If you're enamored with TV ads showing Hummers racing through deep snow and fording deep rivers, don't rent an SUV as a novice four-wheel driver and expect to do the same. Life-threatening conditions that even Hummers won't get you out of do exist. Be prudent and be safe. The best advice I can give you is to make sure you check the weather report and fill your tank with gas before heading into the mountains or out into the desert. For updated road information in Nevada, call (877) 687-6237 or go to www.nevadadot.com. In California call (800) 427-ROAD (7623) or click on www.dot.ca.gov.

THE BLACK ROCK DESERT AND GERLACH, NEVADA

The magnificent, barren playa called the Black Rock Desert lies about 105 miles northeast of the Truckee Meadows. Once the bed of ancient Lake Lahontan, it rested some 500 feet underwater. The desert now stretches more than 100 miles through three counties (Washoe, Pershing, and Humboldt) surrounded by jagged peaks of rugged mountains. A dark rock about 400 feet tall, which served as a landmark for pioneers and rises above the paler background of the mountains, gave the desert its name. It sits almost in the middle of the stark plain.

Thousands of pioneers passed through this desert on their way to California via the Lassen-Applegate Trail, which branched off the California Emigrant Trail at Lassen Meadows in Nevada. The Lassen-Applegate Trail cut through the heart of the Black Rock Desert, followed High Rock Canyon, and popped the travelers out into northern California. This section of the trail became known as "The Death Route" for obvious reasons. John Frémont and Kit Carson (see the History chapter for more about these trailblazers) navigated straight down the desert on their expedition through Nevada, eventually running into Pyramid Lake and the Truckee Meadows. Not much has changed in the desert since then, and today a trip to the gateway of this historic locale, one of the major deserts in the world, is well worth the drive.

The day trip should begin in Sparks, where you pick up Nevada Highway 445, called the Pyramid Highway by Insiders. Drive north about 30 miles to its intersection with Nevada Highway 446 near Nixon on the Paiute Indian Reservation at Pyramid Lake (see the day trip to Pyramid Lake later in this chapter). Follow NV 446 to its intersection with Nevada Highway 447, then turn left and head north on NV 447 to the town of Gerlach. Between Pyramid Lake and Gerlach, you will see some of the most beautiful desert scenery in Nevada, but you will not find any place to get gas or pick up food or cold drinks except in the little town of Empire, which is about 5 miles from Gerlach. Stock up and fill up before you leave the Truckee Meadows.

The drive between Nixon and Gerlach is about 60 miles, and for 30 miles you will be traveling through the Indian reservation. On the way you will pass through the little town of Empire, noted for its garlic fields and owned by United States Gypsum Co., a mining company. One of the most interesting sights in Empire is the Burning Sands Golf Course. The mining company employees built this nine-hole course over the years, winding it through town and across several streets. It's free to play, but a donation is requested. No one takes credit for designing the course; locals just say it happened. If you're dying to play this unique golf course, the town's post office has score cards. Call (775) 557-2341, ext. 224, for more information.

Gerlach, a little town of 700 people 5 miles north of Empire, is considered the gateway to the Black Rock Desert. The town originally served as a depot stop for the Western Pacific Railroad; now it provides a jumping-off point to the desert and to northern California. While in Gerlach, stop by Bruno's Country Club (775-557-2220), which is really a coffee shop, for lunch or dinner. The house specialty is the overstuffed ravioli, which are renowned throughout northern Nevada.

A word of warning about the Black Rock Desert: If you get the urge to take a drive out into the desert, don't. It is an extremely hazardous place unless you know what you are doing and where you

---

i ***You can rope and ride with real cowboys on the edge of the Black Rock Desert at Soldier Meadows Guest Ranch & Lodge. For information contact them at 16912 Mt. Rose Highway, Reno; (775) 849-2219.***

---

are going, have the correct mode of transportation and the right gear, or ride with an Insider who does. So please heed this warning.

Besides its obvious historical and natural wonders, the Black Rock Desert has several other claims to fame. In 1992 scientists uncovered America's largest complete skeleton of an Imperial mammoth in this desert. The skeleton is on display in the Nevada State Museum in Carson City (see the day trip to Carson City later in this chapter).

On October 15, 1997, Royal Air Force fighter pilot Andy Green made the record books as the first person to drive a car past the speed of sound. He did it in the supersonic *Thrust SSC* on the Black Rock Desert; his speed: 763 mph.

But recently the Black Rock Desert's number-one attraction has been the free-spirited romp called the Burning Man. Some people call it naked fun in the sun. Others call it an abomination. Whatever it may be, the event draws more than 25,000 participants who flock to the desert for this weeklong party over the Labor Day weekend and momentarily convert the barren place into a small town dubbed Black Rock City. If you're not planning to attend Burning Man, I advise avoiding the area while it's going on (around Labor Day every year). See the Annual Events chapter for more information.

Whatever your motivation, the Black Rock Desert and Gerlach make a magnificent day trip. Buck Wheeler described it best in his book *The Black Rock Desert* when he wrote:

"It is a land of mystery where ancient man left evidence of his visits thousands of years ago. It is a place of history where Indian warriors fought for their way of life and where legends of the Old West were born."

For a faster return trip to the Truckee Meadows, once you leave Gerlach, head south on NV 447. Take the highway all the way to Wadsworth, pick up Interstate 80 West, and follow the signs to Reno/Sparks. The total trip length is about 210 miles.

For more information on the desert, contact the Bureau of Land Management at (775) 623-1500 or log on to www.nv.blm.gov/winnemucca.

CARSON CITY, NEVADA

A day trip to Carson City, Nevada's historic state capital, should have history buffs tingling with anticipation: Visiting is like sliding back in time. The city sits just 30 minutes down U.S. Highway 395 from Reno and 14 miles from Lake Tahoe via U.S. Highway 50.

The Carson City Freeway, which branches off US 395 between South Reno and Carson City, provides faster and more comfortable access to the capital city. Routing traffic away from congested streets and the heart of downtown, the freeway allows drivers to avoid much of the stop-and-go traffic that has frustrated them for years. Residents are delighted that, with less traffic, much of the historic downtown will be quieter and more attractive. The first phase of the freeway opened in 2006, and the project is scheduled for completion in 2010.

Settled as a trading post in 1851 on Indian land, Carson City came to life after silver was discovered on the Comstock. This quaint city became the capital of the Nevada Territory in 1861 and remained the state capital when Nevada entered the Union in 1864. Most people think the city was named for legendary frontiersman Kit Carson, who accompanied John Frémont on his expedition through Nevada (see the History chapter), and in a roundabout way, they're right. The city was actually named for the Carson River, which Frémont

The Pony Express route, which traced the route of present-day US 50 and included a stop in Carson City, was in existence for a brief 18 months. One of the best preserved Pony Express sites is in Sand Springs, 25 miles east of Fallon.

Since 1964, eight Winter Olympians have hailed from Truckee.

named in honor of his good friend and scout—so indirectly, the town is a tribute to Kit Carson.

Carson City gained fame around the United States as a town built by the silver barons of the Comstock mines. Among their many accomplishments, these men built the Virginia & Truckee Railroad, one of the most productive small railroads in the United States, to supply their mines with goods from Carson City. These entrepreneurs also constructed mills along the Carson River to process the silver ore, and they convinced the federal government to erect a U.S. Mint in Carson City to pound out silver coins right in their own backyards. They also erected some of the most magnificent mansions west of the Mississippi; and the residential area west of the State Capitol on North Carson Street is one of the largest historical districts in the state and one of the best self-guided tours in Nevada.

If you visit Carson City, whether you are a history buff or not, you must explore this residential district. The best way to do that is to walk the blue-lined Kit Carson Trail. The trail, with blue lines painted on the sidewalks to point the way, is a 2.5-mile walking tour of Carson City that encompasses some 60 points of interest. Maps for the tour are available at the visitor center at 1900 South Carson Street (775-687-7410, (800) 638-2321; www.carson-city.org); the center is open weekdays from 8:00 A.M. to 5:00 P.M. The tour starts at the Nevada State Museum, formerly the U.S. Mint, at 600 North Carson Street (775-687-4810; www.dmla.clan.lib.nv.us/docs/museums/cc/carson.htm). The museum is open year-round from 8:30 A.M. to 4:30 P.M. and features Nevada's silver-rich history. Considered by some visitors and historians to be one of the best museums in the West, the Nevada State Museum houses a full-scale model of a silver mine and a reconstructed ghost town, along with numerous other displays. A visit here costs $5.00 for adults and $3.00 for seniors; children younger than age 18 are free.

On the blue-lined trail, you will also find 24 "talking" homes that broadcast their histories on special radio frequencies. Their locations are listed in a booklet with a map for two self-guided tours. This booklet can be picked up at the visitor center. Included on the tour is the Krebs-Peterson House, featured in John Wayne's last movie, *The Shootist.* For more information on this walking tour, telephone (800) NEVADA-1 or visit www.carson-city.org.

Other points of interest to while away the day in this charming city include the State Capitol at 101 North Carson Street. It's the second-oldest capitol building west of the Mississippi, and its Alaskan marble and polished wood hallways are magnificent. The Governor's Mansion at 606 Mountain Street is another must-stop on the tour. This colonial-style home was built in 1908 and is still used by Nevada's top government official.

Another must-see exhibit is the Carson Nugget Casino's gold display. Located at 507 North Carson Street, this collection is valued at $1 million and contains examples of raw gold in leaf, ribbon, wire, thread, and crystallized forms—just as they were taken from the ground. Call the Carson Nugget Casino at (800) 426-5239, or visit www.ccnugget.com.

For train aficionados, Carson City has a wonderful railroad museum located south of town on US 395. The Nevada State Railroad Museum (775-687-6953; www.nsrm-friends.org) is home to tons of railroad equipment mostly acquired from the Virginia & Truckee Railroad, one of the most famous short lines in the United States. Volunteers offer guided tours of the various pieces of equipment, including steam engines, coaches, and freight cars. Don't forget to ask for a look at the storage warehouse in back, where you'll find more equipment waiting to be refurbished. The museum is open daily from

8:30 A.M. to 4:30 P.M. The admission is $4.00 for adults; free for children 18 years old and younger.

Other points of interest, depending on your tastes, include: the Brewery Arts Center at 449 West King Street (775-883-1976; www.breweryarts.org), an old brewery that features art exhibits and concerts and offers arts and crafts classes; and the Roberts House at 1207 Carson Street, the oldest Victorian home in Carson City, with tours offered May through October. For more information call (775) 887-2174.

Carson City's main drag is also crammed with restaurants, bars, markets, and shopping centers, as well as the state's Supreme Court and Legislature buildings. Ask for a Calendar of Events at the visitor center. If you can, visit during some of the more popular events, like the old-fashioned Nevada Day Parade at the end of October or the Fourth of July picnic and fireworks display. Allow at least a full day to explore this historic city and enjoy a leisurely lunch or dinner at one of the many excellent restaurants around town. I suggest you try Glen Eagles Restaurant, 3700 North Carson Street (775-884-4414) or Adele's in Carson City, at 1112 North Carson Street (775-882-3353).

Carson City, along with many other northern Nevada communities, has become a retirement haven in recent years. With nine golf courses nearby, the new high-tech Carson-Tahoe Medical Center, and a burgeoning variety of shopping options, the capital city is an attractive place to live for many retirees.

CARSON VALLEY, NEVADA

Tucked between the Sierra Nevada to the west and the Pine Nut Mountains to the east, the Carson Valley spreads out like a giant carpet of fertile farms and rich ranchlands surrounding the small towns of Genoa, Minden, and Gardnerville. In spring and summer the valley boasts verdant fields of thick alfalfa bisected by the meandering Carson River. In fall it's a profusion of color as poplars and aspens dress in their vivid autumn hues. In winter it's a vintage Christmas-card scene, with snow sometimes reaching from the nearby jagged peaks down to the valley floor.

You can get to the valley from Reno by taking US 395 south about 14 miles beyond Carson City. I recommend starting your tour of the valley in Genoa, so turn right onto Jacks Valley Road just after you enter the valley.

To reach the valley from Lake Tahoe, you can take Nevada Highway 207 (Kingsbury Grade) east from Stateline to Foothill Road, which is just south of Genoa. NV 207 was part of the historic Pony Express and Overland Stage routes during pioneer days. Turn left, and go north on Foothill Road. You'll reach David Walley's Resort, Hot Springs & Spa just before getting to Genoa.

Built as an elegant spa in 1862, Walley's has been a welcome retreat for the rich and famous for many years. (Coming from Reno, you can visit the resort after touring downtown Genoa.) Historic personalities such as General Grant, Clark Gable, Mark Twain, and Ida Lupino have soothed their souls and bodies in these hot mineral baths. Renovated periodically to keep up with the times, the resort is now a sparkling oasis with a swimming pool, fitness center, and tennis facility in addition to the mineral spas. Much to the chagrin of some locals, recent expansion added a multistory hotel complex to the resort. Although the additional services were welcomed by some, others believe that high-rise modern development is not in keeping with the image of the oldest town in Nevada. The resort is open daily from 7:00 A.M. to 10:00 P.M., and you can bask in its pleasures all day for $20. The optimum time to sink into Walley's might be after an invigorating day of sightseeing, golfing, or skiing in the Carson Valley

Genoa is well known for the large herd of deer that roams freely around town.

and its nearby mountains. For more information on Walley's, call (775) 782-8155 or visit www.davidwalleys.com.

Settled by Mormons in 1851 as a trading station for early pioneers, Genoa was known first as Mormon Station and later renamed Genoa for the Italian birthplace of Christopher Columbus. If you like history, you'll love Genoa, since this tiny town still has the look and feel of early frontier days. The best way to experience it is to park your car and just wander through the many well-preserved historic buildings.

For an introduction to the area, stop at the Genoa Courthouse Museum on Main Street, where eclectic exhibits showcase every facet of pioneer life. The museum is open daily May through October from 10:00 A.M. to 4:30 P.M. For details call (775) 782-4325. Just across the road you can visit another museum at Mormon Station State Historic Park and also view a replica of an early stockade used by pioneers to enclose their livestock. This museum is open daily May through October from 9:00 A.M. to 4:30 P.M. For details call (775) 782-2590 or go to www.parks.nv.gov.

Continuing down Main Street, you can quench your thirst at the same saloon frequented by early settlers, the Genoa Bar, well known as Nevada's Oldest Thirst Parlor. Other historic buildings along the street include the Masonic Hall, built in 1862; the Genoa Country Store, dating from 1879; and the Genoa Town Hall, dedicated in 1886.

The most famous event in Genoa is the annual Candy Dance, held the last full weekend of September. Started in 1919 to raise funds for downtown streetlights, the fair has been so successful that today it raises enough money to pay for all the town's basic services. It's a candy lover's dream, since local residents sell pounds and pounds of their prized homemade fudge, divinity, almond roca, and turtles to eager buyers every year. More than 75,000 people pack the town during the two-day event, enjoying the dinner dance, arts and crafts show, and musical events that are part of the festivities. If you'd like to try the prize-winning recipes yourself, you can buy a copy of the *Genoa Candy Book* at the fair.

If you're in town around dinnertime, I highly recommend dining at La Ferme. Tucked in a historic building across the street from the Genoa Bar, this elegant eatery seems totally out of place in laid-back Genoa. The ambience is Victorian/French Country, and the cuisine is French. For reservations call (775) 783-1004.

From Genoa you can continue your tour of the Carson Valley by heading east on Genoa Lane to US 395, where a right (south) turn will bring you to Minden. When the Virginia & Truckee Railroad extended its service to the Carson Valley in 1905, the town of Minden was founded around the train depot. Named for the Prussian birthplace of early pioneer Henry Fredrick Dangberg, Minden is an orderly little town of quiet streets and historic brick buildings. As you enter town, you pass the Carson Valley Inn, a full-service casino where you can enjoy fine dining and Nevada-style entertainment 24 hours a day. Farther down the street, you can see the old Minden Creamery buildings, and then on Esmeralda Street is the C.O.D. Garage, the oldest continually operating car dealership in the state, founded in 1910 to sell Model Ts. Minden Park and the courthouse lie farther north along this street.

Back on US 395, continue south to Gardnerville, which blends almost unnoticed into Minden. While Minden's roots are traced to the railroad, Gardnerville's beginnings are linked with agriculture. Founded in the 1860s as a convenient settlement for valley farmers, Gardnerville has been a ranching center since Basque sheepherders from Europe's Pyrenees Mountains arrived in the 1890s. Because of its high quality of life and business-friendly environment, the Carson Valley has become a burgeoning tech center and retirement community during the past decade. To get a taste of valley history and a sample of its art, stop off at the Carson Valley Museum and Cultural Center, which is right on US 395 as you go through town. Located in the old renovated high school that dates from 1915, the museum is open Tuesday through Saturday from 10:00 A.M. to 4:00 P.M. January through March and from 10:00 A.M. to 5:00 P.M. April through December. For more information call (775) 782-2555.

If you continue on US 395 south of Gardnerville for about 5 miles, you can visit the Lahontan National Fish Hatchery, which raises Lahontan cutthroat trout for stocking Pyramid Lake. Visiting hours are daily from 7:30 A.M. to 3:00 P.M. Call (775) 265-2425 for more information.

About 13 miles beyond the fishery, you come to lovely Topaz Lake. Like Lake Tahoe, it's ringed by mountains and bisected by the California-Nevada state line. But unlike Tahoe, it's an artificial lake created by storage from the West Walker River. Although Topaz is much smaller and less dramatic than Tahoe, its appeal lies in its natural beauty, relatively uncluttered by homes and businesses. It's a pleasant place to fish, swim, and go boating away from the crowds. For picnicking and camping try Topaz Lake Park, which has a mile of beachfront with 140 campsites and picnic spots. To reach the park, look for its sign on US 395 and follow the access road about a mile down to the park on the lake. For information call (775) 266-3343. Topaz Lake Lodge and RV Park, located on the north end of the lake, also has camping facilities, plus lodge accommodations, a 24-hour casino, and a restaurant with a beautiful view of the lake. For details call (775) 266-3338 or visit www.topazlake.com.

While visiting the Carson Valley, you may want to try a round of golf at the Carson Valley Golf Course, which is just off US 395 in Gardnerville (775-265-3181; www.carsonvalleygolf.com) or at either of the courses at Genoa Lakes Golf on Jacks Valley Road (775-782-7700). With the Carson River carving a picturesque ribbon through many fairways, these courses are extremely scenic as well as challenging. (For details see the Golf chapter.)

If you want a bird's-eye perspective of the valley, nothing beats a glider ride. Soar Minden (775-782-7627) will give you a breathtaking, memorable vista from a glider soaring high above the valley floor. (See the Recreation chapter for more information on these activities.)

When it's time to eat, try sampling Basque cuisine at the Overland Hotel at 691 Main Street in Gardnerville (775-782-2138); the J&T Bar and Restaurant at 1426 US 395 in Gardnerville (775-782-2074); or the restaurant at the Carson Valley Golf Course, 2 miles south of Gardnerville on US 395 (775-265-3181). For steaks and seafood, Fiona's, next to the Carson Valley Inn in Minden (775-783-6650), is a good choice. At Topaz Lake, the Lakeview Restaurant in the Topaz Lake Lodge and RV Park has reasonable prices plus a great view of the water. Weather permitting, you might want to picnic at Topaz Lake or Mormon Station State Historic Park.

For more information about the Carson Valley, you can stop by the Carson Valley Chamber of Commerce and Visitors Authority at 1477 US 395, Suite A, in Gardnerville. Call them at (800) 727-7677 or visit www.carsonvalleynv.org.

FALLON, NEVADA

If you spend any time at all in the Reno/Tahoe area, you're sure to hear about "the other side of Nevada." An expression coined by the Nevada Commission on Tourism some years ago to increase overall knowledge about the state, "the other side" encompasses almost everything not directly related to gaming. Most visitors know you can drink, gamble, and enjoy live entertainment 24 hours a day in Nevada, but few are acquainted with the state's colorful Wild West history, the laid-back lifestyle of its rural ranch communities, or the breathtaking beauty of its unspoiled landscape. If you're curious about what Nevada is like—outside the bright lights of the casinos—head east from Reno on I-80 to Fallon, the seat of Churchill County, just an hour's drive away.

Leaving Reno, you follow the Truckee River as it meanders through the scenic Truckee River Canyon, bordering ranches and farms, to the small town of Fernley. Follow the signs to Fallon, taking exit 48 to connect with Alternate US 50, where you will continue southeast. For an affordable game of golf along the way, you can stop at the Golf Club at Fernley. Winding through the sand and sagebrush, the emerald-green fairways are almost startling to the eye, like an artist's brilliant brush strokes splashed on an enormous beige canvas. The course is open year-round, and greens fees range from about $25 to $40 for 18 holes, including cart. For tee times call (775) 835-6933. (See the Golf chapter for more information about the course.)

From the golf course you continue down Alternate US 50 to Leeteville Junction, where the road joins US 50 about 8 miles from Fallon. The junction was known to early pioneers as Ragtown, where they would wash and hang their clothes to dry after crossing the desert and before the trek over the Sierra Nevada. From Leeteville you travel on US 50, dubbed by *Life* magazine "The Loneliest Road in America," as it crosses the state of Nevada. Far from being just lonely, this ribbon of road bisects a fascinating land of awesome scenery and intriguing history.

With the pinkish Stillwater Mountains as a backdrop, you pass through lush fields of alfalfa as you approach Fallon, which you can see is aptly nicknamed "The Oasis of Nevada." The overused term "family values" is what makes the world go round in this rural farming town. Spectator sports include Little League baseball and watching the high school's "Greenwave" (so called for the fields of green alfalfa that wave in the desert winds) take on other football teams. The social events of the year are fund-raisers for the Churchill Arts Council or the Ducks Unlimited waterfowl habitats in the Pacific Flyway. Small businesses are passed down from parent to child, and local politicians know everyone by their first names. Boring and mundane? Not at all: Churchill County is an interesting mixture of past and present, where supersonic Navy jets zoom over remnants of the Pony Express route, and a state-of-the-art electronic warfare range shares the desert with ancient petroglyphs.

As an introduction to the rich history of the area, you must stop at the Churchill County Museum at 1050 South Maine Street. Bursting with artfully designed exhibits and displays, this free facility immerses you in the heritage of the area from the prehistoric to the pioneer days. It's open daily all year: March through November, Monday through Saturday from 10:00 A.M. to 5:00 P.M. and Sunday from noon to 5:00 P.M.; December through February, Monday through Saturday from 10:00 A.M. to 4:00 P.M. and Sunday from noon to 4:00 P.M. Call (775) 423-3677 for more information, or visit www.ccmuseum.org. At the museum be sure to look for information about Hidden Cave, an archaeological dig east of town, where ancient civilizations lived more than 8,000 years ago. Although you can find the cave on your own by continuing east on US 50 for about 10 miles, the best way to see it is with a group from the museum. Guided tours leave the museum the second and fourth Saturdays of the month at 9:30 A.M. Close to the cave is Grimes Point, where you can stroll along the mile-long path among petroglyphs considered to be thousands of years old.

About 15 miles farther down the road is Sand Mountain, a 600-foot-high sand dune more than 2 miles long. Formed by windblown sand from an ancient prehistoric sea, the mountain booms and moans as the ever-present wind continues to move the fine particles. If you want to enjoy this geological phenomenon in quiet solitude, it's best to visit during the week, since it becomes a lively playground for dune buggies and sand skiers on weekends and holidays. The trek to the top can be treacherous, especially in the summer since the surface is hot, and the deep sand makes the going very difficult. At the base of the mountain, you can learn about the geology and history of the area by walking the short trail through the Sand Springs Desert Study Area. And at the nearby Sand Springs Station you can visit a well-preserved Pony Express station that formed part of the legendary route that passed through the area in 1860. For more information call the Fallon Convention and Tourism Authority at (866) 432-5566 or the Bureau of Land Management at (775) 885-6000. The Web site is www.nv.blm.gov/carson. You can also visit www.fallontourism.com.

Other sights around Fallon include the Stillwater National Wildlife Refuge. In wet years as many as 700,000 ducks, ibises, snow plovers, and herons—along with other shorebirds and raptors—come to visit or nest in this refuge. To view this relatively unspoiled natural habitat, follow US 50 east of town for several miles and turn left onto Stillwater Road. Continue on Stillwater Road until you reach the large serene marsh stretching toward the Stillwater Mountains. Be sure to take insect repellent, since it's a rich breeding ground for bugs as well as birds. For more information on the refuge, you can call (775) 428-6452, visit stillwater.fws.gov, or visit the office at 1000 Auction Road in Fallon.

Heading west out of Fallon, you can visit the Lahontan State Recreation Area, a popular playground for camping, fishing, boating, and waterskiing. Lahontan Reservoir is a 17-mile-long lake completed in 1915 as part of the Newlands Irrigation Project. Water from the Truckee and Carson Rivers is held in the lake behind Lahontan Dam and then used to irrigate the fields of alfalfa, corn, sugar beets, and Heart O' Gold cantaloupes around Fallon. To reach Lahontan, go west on US 50 from Fallon for about 16 miles.

With more than 300 days of clear flying weather each year, the U.S. Navy hasn't found a more suitable training ground for its pilots than Naval Air Station (NAS) Fallon. Home of the Naval Strike and Air Warfare Center (NSAWC), with its prestigious TOPGUN division (remember the movie *Top Gun* with Tom Cruise?), NAS Fallon is the only naval facility that can train an entire carrier air wing in the strike tactics used in combat. The F-18 Hornets and F-14 Tomcats scream off the Navy's longest runway (14,000 feet) and engage in mock dogfights and electronic warfare over the training area east of the Stillwater Mountains. If you want an up-close and personal view of these supersonic flying machines, you can watch them land and take off through a security fence at the base. To get to the base, take U.S. Highway 95 south for about 5 miles until you see the sign for the facility at Union Lane. Follow Union Lane to Pasture Road, where a left turn will give you a view of the runway. The Navy opens its gates to thousands of visitors each spring during the Fallon Air Show, when you can see free flying demonstrations and static displays of aircraft (see the Annual Events chapter for details). For more information call (775) 426-2880 or visit www.fallontourism.com.

If you visit Fallon between August and October, you can challenge your navigational skills at the five-acre living corn maze at Lattin Farms, 1955 McLean Road. For more information call (775) 867-3750 or (866) 638-6293, or go to www.lattinfarms.com.

Aside from the naval air show, Fallon plays host to a large variety of special events and ongoing entertainment throughout the year. You can see professional and amateur race car drivers speed around the track at the state-of-the-art Top Gun Raceway, about 15 miles south of town on US 95. See the Recreation chapter for more information. Call (775) 423-0223 or (800) 325-7448 for race times and dates, or access www.topgunraceway.com. You can watch barrel racers and bull riders from all over the country compete in Wild West action at the Silver State International Rodeo. You can enjoy the sweet, juicy taste of local Heart O'

Gold cantaloupes at the Heart O' Gold Cantaloupe Festival. You can experience local Native American culture at the Nevada Indian Days All Indian Rodeo & Powwow for a taste of the arts and music, you can choose from a large variety of events sponsored by the Churchill Arts Council all during the year; for details call (775) 423-1440 or visit www.churchill arts.org. The Fallon Convention and Tourism Authority at 100 Campus Way (just off US 50 as you enter town from the west) is a good source of information about events in Churchill County. You can call them at (775) 423-4556 or (866) 432-5566; the Web site is www.fallon tourism.com.

If all this activity gives you an appetite, you don't need to leave town on an empty stomach. For good food at reasonable prices, try the Bonanza Inn (775-423-0558), Stockman's Casino (775-423-2117), or the Depot Diner (775-423-3233) on US 50 on the west side of town.

GHOST TOWNS, NEVADA

Old-timers here will tell you that 10 ghost towns exist for every living town in Nevada. Most of the ruins are difficult to find, however, because they are hidden in the hills and tucked away in the gullies overgrown with sagebrush and tumbleweed. Their only inhabitants now are desert creatures and the memories of past glory days. But they're out there, ready for those who wish to explore them. Rummaging through these ruins is more exciting than reading about them in dusty old history books, and they make for a worthwhile day trip if you wish to step way off the beaten path of the Reno/Tahoe area.

Most of these towns sprang up during Nevada's two great mining periods before World War I, and most lasted only as long as the silver and gold in their mines. These towns are sprinkled all over the state, but my suggestion is to explore the ghost towns nestled near the foot of the Shoshone Mountain Range in the Toiyabe National Forest just east of Gabbs, Nevada, a two-and-a-half-hour drive from Reno. To get to Gabbs from Reno, take I-80 east to the east Fernley exit. Pick up Alternate US 50 to Fallon. After Fallon, follow US 50, The Loneliest Road in America, to Middlegate, about 47 miles. Turn right (south) onto Nevada Highway 361 to Gabbs. Most of the ghost towns suggested here are located off Nevada Highway 844, 2 miles north of Gabbs.

The ghost town of Ione sits 24 miles east of Gabbs at the end of State Route 91. This town prospered in 1863 after the discovery of a vein of silver. Ione became the seat of Nye County in 1864, but by 1880 only a few hard-core prospectors remained. Several collapsed and dilapidated buildings can be found at the site.

Ellsworth rests about 10 miles west of Ione via an unmarked graded road. In 1871, at its peak, this town pumped silver out from its mines and boasted about 200 citizens, and several businesses and homes were made from rocks. Some rock walls and a cemetery remain.

Berlin, perhaps the most renowned ghost town in Nevada, owes much of its fame to dinosaurs and the Berlin-Ichthyosaur State Park. This park is home to significant fossil finds of gigantic ichthyosaurs, marine reptiles that inhabited the state more than 200 million years ago. The word *ichthyosaur* means "lizard fish," but these dinosaurs are more closely related to the modern-day whale. The tumbled-down mining town sits close to the park and was abandoned about 100 years ago. Several buildings still stand in what preservationists call "arrested decay." In other words, the buildings aren't restored, but they are not allowed to decay any further, either. Berlin and the state park are located 19 miles east of Gabbs, about 2 miles south of SR 91. Visit the Web site at www.state.nv.us/stparks/bi.htm or call (775) 964-2440 for information.

The ghost town of Union is about 1.25 miles southeast of Berlin. This town sprang up in 1863, about the same time as

Ione. Several stone buildings remain in Union. In Grantsville (located about 5 miles southeast of SR 91, 18 miles east of Gabbs), you can see a few building foundations, as well as a small cemetery. But the high points of a visit to Grantsville are its incredible views and its magnificent setting in the mountains. This town was also established in 1863.

On the way back to Reno, stop by Quartz Mountain, about 13 miles north of Gabbs just off NV 361. This town sprang up in 1920 and withered by 1926. The remains of several wooden buildings still lie scattered about.

I suggest a picnic lunch for this day trip. Be aware that beyond Fallon, gas stations and restaurants are scarce, so it's a good idea to fill up your gas tank and cooler before you leave Fallon.

If you wish to learn more about Nevada ghost towns, find a copy of *Nevada Ghost Town* by Lambert Florin or *Nevada Ghost Towns and Mining Camps* by Stanley W. Paher.

GRAEAGLE, CALIFORNIA

If you already live in a mountain paradise, where do you go to "get away from it all"? Insiders escape to the tiny hamlet of Graeagle (pronounced *gray eagle*), the ultimate getaway, tucked deep in the towering pines of the Plumas National Forest about 60 miles northwest of Reno. Named for Gray Eagle Creek, which runs nearby, this quaint little community began as a lumber town in 1916. The historic red and white frame buildings that line the main drag were brought in by rail and used as housing for workers in the mill. Today these structures are retail establishments that form the picturesque core of the downtown area. After the mill shut down in 1956, Graeagle was purchased in 1958 for $450,000 by a developer who saw its potential as a planned vacation community. Since then it has thrived primarily as a summer/fall retreat for hikers, golfers, and anglers. But in spite of modern development, it retains its historic charm. Quiet and peaceful, Graeagle is worlds apart from the hustle and bustle of many resort communities. And best of all, it's smack in the middle of some of the most gorgeous mountain scenery on the planet.

To get to Graeagle from Reno, take US 395 north about 24 miles to Hallelujah Junction, and then take California Highway 70 west to Blairsden. Finally, turn south on California Highway 89. About 8 miles before Graeagle on CA 70, you'll go through the lumber town of Portola, where you can climb on train cars and locomotives at the Portola Railroad Museum. Follow the signs through Old Town Portola to the museum, which is at 700 Western Pacific Way. It's open daily March through November from 11:00 A.M. to 4:00 P.M. For details call (530) 832-4131 or visit www.wplives.org.

Coming from Lake Tahoe to Graeagle, take California Highway 267 north from Kings Beach or CA 89 north from Tahoe City to Truckee, and then continue north on CA 89 for about 50 miles. This route takes you through some of the loveliest, most unspoiled forest in the Reno/Tahoe area.

With six golf courses in the area, Graeagle has been called the "Pebble Beach of the Sierra." But even if your game isn't up to par, you can't go wrong on any of these layouts, since just enjoying the magnificent scenery can make your round worthwhile. About 5 miles south of Graeagle on CA 89, you can test your skills at the Golf Club at Whitehawk Ranch; call (800) 332-4295 or click on www.golfwhitehawk.com to book tee times. About 7 miles east of Graeagle on California Highway A-15 you can play The Dragon course at Gold Mountain, the newest course in the area. Call (800) 368-7768 or go to www.dragongolf.com for details. Other championship 18-hole courses include Graeagle Meadows, which is right downtown off CA 89 (530-836-2323; www.playgraeagle.com), and Plumas Pines Golf Resort, at 402 Poplar Valley Road in Blairsden (530-836-1420; www

Any good road trip requires preparation. Before setting off, make sure your vehicle is in good working order. Carry emergency equipment, including a flare, blankets, water and some food, and a first-aid kit. A cellular telephone is a nice addition to any road trip, but be aware that you may not have coverage in some locations.

.plumaspinesgolf.com). The Feather River Park Resort on CA 89 (530-836-2328; www.featherriverparkresort.com) and the Feather River Inn on CA 70 in Blairsden (530-836-2722) both offer challenging rounds on beautiful nine-hole layouts. For a more detailed description of these courses, see the Golf chapter.

Bisected by the pristine Middle Fork of the Feather River and dotted with a multitude of crystal-clear alpine lakes, the mountainous terrain around Graeagle is a hiker's dream come true. With literally hundreds of trails to choose from, you'll probably want to get a map by calling the Plumas County Visitors Bureau at (800) 326-2247 (www.plumascounty.org) or the Plumas National Forest at (530) 283-2050 (www.fs.fed.us./r5/plumas). Another good Web resource is www.graeagle.com.

My favorite hike, which takes you to six different lakes, is the Round Lake Loop Trail in the Lakes Basin Recreation Area. With spectacular views and a modest elevation gain, this approximately 4-mile outing offers a fantastic diversity of scenery compressed in a relatively small geographic area. It's best done at a leisurely pace so you can enjoy the landscape as it spreads out before you. You can swim, fish, and picnic along the way—just pick your favorite lake. To get to the trailhead, look for the sign directing you to the Lakes Basin Recreation Area on the Gold Lake Highway just south of Graeagle and travel west for about 7 miles. Then look for the sign for Gold Lake Lodge and the Round Lake Trail at the crest of a hill and park in the lodge parking lot. The Round Lake Loop Trail begins at the end of this lot.

About 0.25 mile down the trail, it forks, with the trail to the right reaching Big Bear Lake in about 0.5 mile and taking you counterclockwise around the loop. I recommend going in this direction, since you arrive at the first lake sooner and because the overall climb is gentler. As the trail meanders through granite boulders and stately pines, it takes you from Big Bear Lake to Little Bear, Cub, Silver, Long, and Round Lakes. In the shadow of rocky Mt. Elwell, the hike is verdant green with splotches of wildflower color in summer, and in fall an explosion of reds, oranges, and golds. At Round Lake be sure to take a look at the abandoned gold mine at the southern end where miners hoped to strike it rich more than 100 years ago. This hike is an absolute jewel, not to be missed by anyone who enjoys the solitude and beauty of the mountains.

If you're curious what life was like for early gold seekers, you can find out at the mining museum in Plumas Eureka State Park. Steeped in history and surrounded by gorgeous scenery, this 6,700-acre park encompasses the old mining settlement of Johnsville, just 5 miles west of Graeagle on Johnsville Road (Plumas County Road A14). The indoor-outdoor museum features a restored miner's home, a blacksmith shop, and exhibits of early mining equipment. On Living History Day, once a month during the summer, costumed docents recreate the daily life of a miner searching for the big bonanza. For details call (530) 836-2380. You can also try your own luck at gold panning in nearby Jamison Creek. Crisscrossed by myriad trails leading to a number of lakes, Plumas Eureka State Park is also popular with hikers.

The more than 100 lakes of the Feather River watershed offer a large variety of fishing spots for anglers. In addition, dozens of small streams and the Middle Fork of the Feather River provide rich habitats for rainbow, brown, and brook trout. For details on seasons and regulations, contact the Plumas National

Forest at (530) 283-2050.

For a picture-perfect ending to your day in the mountains, I suggest stopping at the Long Boards restaurant at Plumas Pines Golf Club for a drink or dinner. You can sit on the deck, high above the 18th fairway, and watch the last golfers play in as the sun sinks golden behind the emerald-green mountains. Other good dinner spots include the Grizzly Grill at 250 Banta Street in Blairsden (530-836-1300), and Olsen's Cabin on Johnsville Road (530-836-2801). For a special treat, try dinner or lunch at the Frank Lloyd Wright-designed Clubhouse at Nakoma Resort & Spa. Call (877) 418-0880 for reservations and directions.

PYRAMID LAKE, NEVADA

In 1844 explorer John C. Frémont was searching for a legendary river that supposedly emptied into the San Francisco Bay. Instead he was astonished to discover one of the most beautiful desert lakes in the world. Shimmering turquoise green against a pinkish-beige desert background, the lake seemed out of place, like a magical mirage in a harsh, barren environment. Frémont named this large landlocked body of water Pyramid Lake for the giant pyramid-shaped rock that juts 475 feet from the surface of the lake near its southern end. (See the History chapter for more about Frémont's explorations.)

The Paiute Indians and their ancestors have made their home at Pyramid Lake for more than 4,000 years, well before Frémont arrived in the area. The oldest anthropological site in the area dates back 9,200 years, according to one local expert. Because fish from the lake was an important staple in their diet, the tribe became known as "Cui-ui Ticutta" or Cui-ui Eaters. Since 1874 the lake and its environs have been owned and managed by the tribe as the Pyramid Lake Paiute Indian Reservation.

As a remnant of a large inland sea that used to cover most of northwestern Nevada, the lake is the terminal point for the Truckee River's 105-mile journey from Lake Tahoe. Stretching for 27 miles against the changing desert hues of the nearby mountains, the lake has a unique beauty and mystery. Adding an intriguing contrast to the sparkling water and naked rocks are the odd-shaped tufa formations, which are white calcium carbonate deposits piled up all along the shoreline. Next to the signature pyramid is one of the most prominent tufas, which is aptly named "Stone Mother and her Basket." But aside from its beauty, the history and geology of Pyramid Lake provide a fascinating lesson about the relationship between humans and their environment.

Two roads lead to Pyramid Lake from I-80: NV 445 from Sparks to Sutcliffe, and NV 447 from Wadsworth (about 30 miles east of Reno) to Nixon. NV 446 runs between these two roads along the south shore of the lake. You can make a loop of this route going either way, but I recommend starting on NV 445, since it's a quicker route to the lake and you will need to stop at the ranger station in Sutcliffe to buy a $5.00 day-use permit.

Traveling east on I-80 in Reno, exit onto Pyramid Way in Sparks, which becomes NV 445. Travel north about 33 miles to the lake. About 20 miles north of Sparks, you'll pass the Wild Horse and Burro Placement Center, which is operated by the Bureau of Land Management. The animals are captured from large herds that roam free in Nevada, cared for in this facility, and then adopted out to qualified people all over the country. For more information on the wild horse program, visit www.wildhorseandburro.blm.gov.

After continuing north to the lake, you can keep to the left on NV 445 or turn right onto NV 446. If you stay on NV 445, you'll travel past several beaches on the way to Sutcliffe; the paved road turns to gravel a few miles farther on. Turning right onto NV 446, you will round the southern end of the lake to the intersection with NV 447, which travels north to Nixon and the tribal headquarters. The Truckee River

A kayaker enjoys the solitude of Pyramid Lake. ROBERT KRAUSE, KAYAKS ETC.

empties into the lake here. To get a better idea of the lay of the land around the lake, pick up a map, preferably in Sutcliffe when you first arrive at the lake.

The waters of the lake provide a rich habitat for Lahontan cutthroat trout and the endangered cui-ui fish. The lake is one of the best trophy-trout fisheries in the world, with the average keeper weighing between 5 and 16 pounds. The prime time to fish is between October and May, when cooler surface temperatures lure the fish up from the 300-foot depths of the lake. (See also the Fishing and Hunting chapter.)

The lake also provides one of only eight nesting grounds for white pelicans in North America. Each spring rocky Anaho Island, just southwest of the pyramid, swarms with thousands of pelicans, double-crested cormorants, California gulls, great blue herons, and Caspian terns as they set up housekeeping and raise their young. And while the surrounding landscape may seem harsh and sterile, it's anything but, in terms of the wildlife it supports. It's not unusual to see herds of deer, antelope, and bighorn sheep quietly grazing on the steep hillsides around the water.

When you visit the lake, you'll find ample opportunities to learn about the area's culture and heritage by visiting its museums and visitor centers. Just off NV 447 between the towns of Wadsworth and Nixon, there's the Numana Hatchery and Visitors Center (775-574-0290), with its wetlands nature trail. On NV 446 near Nixon you can visit the Scenic Byway Visitors Center and Tribal Museum (775-574-1088), which offers tribal history and cultural exhibits as well as permits for fishing, boating, and camping. And in Sutcliffe, on NV 445, you can stop by the visitor center and museum near the Pyramid Lake Marina.

For a fascinating look at one of the most efficient and innovative fishery restoration programs in the country, be sure to stop in at the Dunn Hatchery (775-476-0510), which is just south of the marina in Sutcliffe. Since its establishment in 1974, the program has planted about 2.8 million cutthroat and 10 to 18 million cui-ui fish every year. Overcoming the problem of raising cold-water fish in a desert lake, the hatchery program has helped guarantee the continued propagation of these species of fish. For hours and more information on these points of interest, call the Pyramid Lake Fisheries at (775) 476-0500, the Pyramid Lake Marina at (775) 476-1156, or the Pyramid Lake Paiute Tribal Offices at (775) 574-1000.

Pyramid Lake is a prime spot to enjoy everything the great outdoors has to offer without the crowds found at some other area lakes. As you drive along the shore of the lake, you can choose from a large variety of sandy beaches for swimming and picnicking. You'll need an umbrella or tarp for shade, however, since the shoreline doesn't have trees or shrubs.

On windless summer days, the tepid waters of the lake are a water-skier's dream come true, silky smooth and free of crowds. For the optimum skiing experience, try it at sundown, when you can skim across the glassy surface as the sinking sun turns the water a gorgeous pink and gold underneath your skis. You can launch your own boat or rent one for the day at the Pyramid Lake Marina in Sutcliffe. But if you're out on the lake when the wind comes up, be sure to head for shore right away, since dangerous whitecaps can appear in minutes.

Because the facilities all around the lake are pretty sparse, I don't have a list of recommended restaurants and watering holes. The best dining experience in this natural wonderland is the picnic lunch or barbecue you bring yourself. Head down to one of the beaches and enjoy your own gourmet cuisine along with an unobstructed view of this prehistoric phenomenon.

SACRAMENTO, CALIFORNIA

Sacramento is the first "big city" you come to as you go west over the Sierra Nevada from the Reno/Tahoe area. Most visitors know it as the birthplace of the greatest gold rush in American history. Not many know that it was also the last stop on the Pony Express route and the nation's telegraph system, and the western terminus of the Transcontinental Railroad. About two hours from Reno along I-80, California's state capital sits in a broad valley on the banks of two of the state's biggest rivers and is often described as the "Historic Capital of the West."

John Sutter, a German-Swiss immigrant, founded the first white settlement in Sacramento in 1839 after the Mexican government granted him 50,000 acres of land. He built an outpost known as Sutter's Fort and began ranching. His ranch prospered until an employee discovered gold at Sutter's Mill in Coloma, California, east of the outpost. The find put Sacramento on the map and decimated Sutter's ranch: Within the next five years, 500,000 people flooded into the Sacramento area.

The city became California's capital in 1854 and over the years grew in importance as an agricultural center. During World War II it grew as a military support center when the federal government built several defense plants and two airbases here (these bases are now closed). Today, Sacramento is crammed with attractions like the State Capitol Building, Old Sacramento, Sutter's Fort, the California State Railroad Museum, and the Governor's Mansion. It also has its share of historic buildings, art galleries, serene parks, rivers, and the 23-mile-long American River Parkway.

Like the entire town of Virginia City, Nevada (see the description of the day trip to Virginia City later in this chapter), Old Sacramento is designated a state historic park and national landmark. Located off Interstate 5 and bordering the Sacramento River, the old part of the city was the main riverboat landing for Sutter's Fort. Today, the 28-acre area has more than 60 buildings that have been restored to the 1850–1870 period. Specialty shops, restaurants, bars, and other businesses now partake of the 19th-century feel of this part of the city by operating out of the historical buildings. Don't miss the California State Railroad Museum, 125 I Street (916-445-6645; www.californiastaterail roadmuseum.org), which includes the Central Pacific Depot and the Eagle Theater. This museum houses one of the world's largest railroad locomotive and relics collections. Admission is $8.00 for adults, $3.00 for youths ages 6 to 17, and free for children 5 and younger.

The railroad museum isn't the only bastion of history and culture awaiting you in Sacramento. You can also visit the Discovery Museum, featuring history, science, and technology, at 101 I Street (www.thediscovery.org), the Crocker Art Museum at 216 O Street (www.crockerart museum.org), and a plethora of others. The Web site at www.sacmuseums.org is a good source for more information.

Sutter's Fort State Historic Park (916-445-4422) shares space with the California State Indian Museum (916-324-0971) on 27th and L Streets. Sutter's Fort provides visitors a living history of the gold rush era, presented by volunteers dressed in period costumes demonstrating examples of pioneer and Indian living and skills. Self-guided audio tours of Sutter's Fort are available and explain the exhibits, which include a blacksmith shop, bakery, prison, living quarters, and a livestock area. The fort is open daily from 10:00 A.M. to 5:00 P.M.; closed Christmas, Thanksgiving, and New Year's Day. There is a nominal entrance fee for adults. The Indian Museum, located behind the fort, displays arts and crafts made by California Indians. It's open from 10:00 A.M. to 5:00 P.M. and charges a nominal admission fee for adults. Visit www.parks.ca.gov for more information.

While exploring this section of the city, don't forget to jump onboard one of the sightseeing boats and cruise the Sacramento River alongside Old Sacramento. Contact the Visitors Information Center, 1608 I Street (916-808-7777), or click on www.oldsacramento.com.

Capitol Park sits about 1 mile east of Old Sacramento. This park contains more than 40,000 trees and flowers in an area stretching from L to N Streets and 9th to 15th Streets. The California State Capitol building (916-324-0333) is the main attraction in this park, with its golden dome providing an unforgettable landmark. Construction of the capitol began in 1860 and continued for more than 14 years before finally being completed in 1874. The California Legislature voted to renovate the building in 1972 at the cost of $70 million, and the tour of this well-preserved building is well worth the time. Guided tours run from 9:00 A.M. to 4:00 P.M. daily except Christmas, Thanksgiving, and New Year's Day. There is no admission fee. Visit www.parks.ca.gov for more information.

The Vietnam Veteran's Memorial, located at the east end of the park, provides a sober reminder of California's military personnel who sacrificed their lives during the war. This memorial is one of the finest examples of bronze statuary in the West and contains the names of the war dead etched on granite panels arranged by hometown.

The 1877 Governor's Mansion at 16th and H Streets (916-323-3047) sits close to the park and provides another enjoyable guided tour. The cost of tours is nominal, with children younger than age 16 admitted free, and run daily from 10:00 A.M. to 4:00 P.M.

Located just south of downtown on South Land Park Drive between 13th Avenue and Sutterville Road, William Land Park spreads out over 161 acres. The park has more than 3,000 trees of 50 different varieties, but its main attraction is the Sacramento Zoo (916-264-5888; www.sac zoo.com). This enclosure is considered to be one of the best small zoos in the country, with more than 400 animals representing 130 species, including some rare and endangered species. The park also features a children's theme park, a fishing pond, a wading pool, amusement rides, and a nine-hole golf course. A family can make a day of visiting this park and enjoying its amenities: You'll find baseball, softball, soccer, and basketball facilities; picnic tables; barbecues; and an amphitheater. The park also has a 2-mile jogging and walking path with sit-up and push-up stands. For more information about this park, call (916) 808-6060 or visit www.cityofsacramento.org/parksandrecreation/parks/landpark.htm.

If real outdoor fun is your family's wish, the 5,000-acre American River Parkway should be your destination when visiting Sacramento. This magnificent park winds its way about 23 miles through the center of the city from the confluence of the Sacramento and American Rivers at Discovery Park to just below Folsom Lake. It has more than 20 major recreation areas, including a scenic, two-lane bike path; miles of equestrian trails; hundreds of fishing spots along the river; and several put-in spots to launch a craft for some exciting white-water rafting. For more information and maps, contact the County of Sacramento Parks and Recreation Department at (916) 875-6961 or visit www.sacparks.net.

Sacramento has plenty to do and to see. The difficult task is deciding your game plan. I recommend that you spend the night in the city to break up the excursion into two leisurely days instead of a hectic one. The Visitors Bureau, 1608 I Street (916-808-7777; www.sacramentocvb.org), publishes brochures listing many of the attractions, restaurants, accommodations, and tour information. Such a brochure is a handy guide for planning your trip.

TRUCKEE, CALIFORNIA

Sitting astride the original trail used by pioneers who traveled overland from Missouri to California in the 1840s, the bustling tourist town of Truckee, about 30 miles west of Reno, stands as a modern-day reminder of just how formidable those trips were. After crossing thousands of miles of blistering deserts and tortuous mountains, the final test for early emigrants came just west of Truckee, where the rugged pass through the Sierra Nevada presented a formidable obstacle to the fertile valleys of California on the other side. Because heavy snow made the route impassable once winter set in, travelers had to cross before the storms arrived, and cutting it close sometimes meant getting trapped in the high country or on the eastern side of the mountains. Even today, the section of I-80 that crosses the pass is frequently closed during winter months because of blizzard conditions.

In the winter of 1846-1847, the dreaded storms not only showed up early—they blew in with a vengeance, dumping record amounts of heavy snow on a group of 91 emigrants who attempted to cross the pass late in October. Named the Donner Party for their leader, George Donner, this group of families became stranded at a small lake near present-day Truckee. As the winter progressed and the snow piled up to more than 20 feet, the party's food supplies dwindled, then disappeared. The 49 who survived were forced to subsist off the bodies of those who died of starvation during the long, arduous winter. The lake and mountain pass were later named Donner Lake and Donner Pass for these ill-fated settlers. You can visit the site of the Donner Party's ordeal at Donner Memorial State Park, on the east end of Donner Lake, just west of downtown Truckee.

To get to Truckee from Reno, follow I-80 west and exit at any of the three Truckee exits. Coming from Lake Tahoe, you can take CA 267 north from Kings Beach, passing Northstar-at-Tahoe along the way. If you take CA 89 north from Tahoe City, you'll pass Alpine Meadows ski resort and Squaw Valley USA before reaching Truckee at the 12-mile mark. For a description of activities at these resorts, see the Winter Sports, Resorts, and Vacation Resorts chapters.

Donner Memorial State Park is at the west end of Truckee, just off I–80 on Donner Pass Road. To learn more about the Donner tragedy and the area's natural history, you can visit the Emigrant Trail Museum in the park. The large bronze Pioneer Monument behind the museum depicts a typical emigrant family and honors all those who made the difficult trek to the West. On the lighter side of things, the park has several miles of hiking trails, sites for camping and picnicking, and lovely beaches for swimming. It's also a popular area for cross-country skiing in the winter. For more information call (530) 582-7892 or visit www.parks.ca.gov.

Just as it was in the 1800s, Truckee's geographical location continues to be the root of its prosperity. Nestled along the banks of the Truckee River in the heavily wooded mountains, it profits from the many tourists who arrive on I–80 or on Amtrak. Its historic downtown is crowded with colorful shops and funky restaurants, most within easy walking distance of each other along Commercial Row. You can browse the boutiques for several hours, then enjoy gourmet dining at a variety of eateries right downtown. You can sample Pan-Asian cooking with a view of the main drag at Dragonfly (530–587–0557). For a panoramic view of the river and the downtown area, try the Cottonwood on the edge of town on CA 267 (530–587–5711). While wandering around downtown, be sure to take a look at the historic bronze eagle in front of the train station. Mounted on a granite base and with a 7-foot wingspan, the Victory Monument commemorates U.S. soldiers killed in World War I.

At 6,000-plus feet in elevation, the golf courses around Truckee are a great place to find out if your drive really does go farther at high altitude. You can tee it up at Tahoe Donner, with its daunting array of undulating fairways carved out of rugged mountain terrain. The course is located north of town at 12850 Northwoods Boulevard. Call (530) 587-9440 for rates and tee times, or visit www.tahoedonner.com. Just down the road from Tahoe Donner is Coyote Moon Golf Course, an equally challenging course (530–587–0886; www.coyotemoongolf.com). Located 6 miles south of town, just off CA 267, the narrow fairways and winding creek at Northstar-at-Tahoe will challenge even the best players' games. Call (530) 562–2490 for details, or visit www.skinorthstar.com. And for a quick nine holes right in town, the Ponderosa Golf Course, just off CA 267, is an absolute delight at a reasonable price. Call (530) 587-3501 for information, or visit www.ponderosagolfclub.com. If you've just hit Megabucks in Reno, however, you might want to try a round at Lahontan Golf Club. It will cost you the price of a membership and a multimillion-dollar home, however. As the most recent display of Truckee's growing affluence, Lahontan is a private 27-hole layout tucked deep in the pines south of town. For information call (530) 550–2400. (See the Golf chapter for more details on area courses.)

If you visit Truckee during the summer, you can enjoy watching the gliders that soar and swoop like enormous birds high over the mountainous terrain. If you want to do more than watch, hang onto your hat (and your stomach): Soar Truckee will give you the ride and the view of your life. The natural geography of the area creates the thermal lifts that are absolutely ideal for soaring. Needless to say, the aerial view of Lake Tahoe and the surrounding Sierra Nevada from one of these big birds is simply breathtaking. Rides can be booked daily May through October from 9:00 A.M. to 5:00 P.M. by calling (530) 587-6702. The Web site is www.soartruckee.com. The Truckee Tahoe Airport, where glider flights originate, is just several miles south of town off CA 267. (See the Recreation chapter for more information.)

The lakes and streams around Truckee are especially inviting to those who like to fish, since they provide a variety of natural conditions along with wonderfully challenging species of fish. Martis Creek Lake, just south of town off CA 267, is a premier habitat for brown and rainbow trout. Don't bring your frying pan, however: It's catch-and-release only with barbless hooks. You can also try your luck in Donner Lake, known for its large Mackinaws, or the Truckee River on either side of town.

If your idea of a mountain experience is hiking through the natural beauty of a pristine forest, a trek along a stretch of the Pacific Crest Trail (PCT) will more than satisfy this need. To get to the trailhead, go west on I-80 from Truckee for about 8 miles to the rest stops at the summit, where you'll find a sign directing you to the trailhead. Hiking north on the PCT will take you through dense forest toward Castle Peak, where you can enjoy splendid views of Donner Lake and the surrounding mountains. Heading south will also give you marvelous views of the lake, but from a closer perspective.

For a unique view of area history from the perspective of snow skiing, the Western SkiSport Museum is a must-stop for both skiers and nonskiers. Take I-80 west from Truckee about 8 miles and exit on the Castle Peak exit at Boreal Mountain Resort. A visit to this one-of-a-kind showcase of the area's most popular sport is well worth the drive out of Truckee. While we think of skiing as merely a recreational activity today, it was introduced to the area as a far more utilitarian occupation: For the early gold seekers, skiing was the only way to get around in heavy winter snow. The fascinating exhibits show early, antiquated equipment, such as the 10-foot-long, 25-pound skis used by the legendary Snowshoe Thompson when he delivered mail to snowbound settlers from 1856 to 1876. You can also see the Western Ski Hall of Fame, which honors individuals who contributed to the development of the sport in the West, along with numerous displays of Olympic medals, clothing, and vintage pictures. The museum is free and open from 10:00 A.M. to 4:00 P.M. Wednesday through Sunday during the ski season. The museum generally closes for a few months once the Boreal Mountain Resort closes, then reopens during the summer months on weekends only. For more information call the Auburn Ski Club at (530) 426-3313, ext. 113, or go to www.auburnskiclub.org.

If you arrived in Reno by air and don't have a car, you can easily get to Truckee by bus or train. Greyhound has a number of departures daily; call (800) 231-2222 for exact times or visit www.greyhound.com. For details about Amtrak trains, which will drop you right downtown at the restored railroad depot, call (800) 872-7245 or visit www.amtrak.com (see also the Getting Here, Getting Around chapter). You can pick up a walking tour brochure and other information about Truckee at the visitor center at 10065 Donner Pass Road in the historic railroad station downtown, or call (530) 587-2757. The Web site is www.truckee.com.

VIRGINIA CITY, NEVADA

At the height of its glory, Virginia City, the "Queen of the Comstock," was the hell-raisingest town in the United States. Touring actors put on Shakespearean plays, prostitutes plied their trade in a thriving red-light district, and the town boasted gunfights, murders, opium dens, rival newspapers, and competing fire companies. All of this activity was born of two drunken Irish prospectors and a con man named Henry Comstock (see the History chapter). Today, most people remember Virginia City as the place that Ben, Adam, Hoss, and Little Joe Cartwright visited when they needed supplies or a night on the town in the old hit TV show *Bonanza*.

Miners squeezed more than $300 million in silver from the surrounding lode during Virginia City's heyday, which ended in 1898 with the virtual abandonment of the mines. Today the entire city stands as a national landmark and the largest federally designated historical district in America maintained in its original condition. Boardwalks line the streets, and the shops

Virginia City becomes a real ghost town during its Ghost Town Halloween Spectacular.

and museums are located in original buildings dating from the 1860s and 1870s. The city, once called the "Richest Place on Earth," offers you a great day trip and a glimpse at the town's glorious past.

Even though Virginia City is only 20 minutes from Reno via US 395 and Nevada Highway 341, and 40 minutes from Lake Tahoe via Nevada Highways 431 and 341, you should set aside an entire day for your visit. After all, this is the city that's been "Live & Kickin' Since 1859."

Virginia City offers visitors a rare peek into American history—indeed, its third motto, "Adventure Back In Time," harkens to this theme. Most of us learn about our past through books. In Virginia City, you can relive it. The city features underground tours of mines, as well as tours of churches and cemeteries, plus tours of some of the most opulent mansions in the West. It still has bawdy saloons where you can get "two fingers of redeye," and you can buy keepsakes and souvenirs from the gift and specialty shops that dot every block. You can take a walking tour of the liveliest ghost town in the West or ride the trolley with a guide narrating the history of the buildings it passes.

Not much has changed since the bonanza days of the silver mines except that now, instead of catering to miners, the city takes care of tourists. The city is open all year with several events, celebrations, and attractions for your enjoyment. A few of the attractions include: the Castle Mansion tour, 10:00 A.M. to 5:00 P.M., which gives you an opportunity to visit a mansion built in 1868 still in its original state and not restored; the Chollar Mine tour, open 10:00 A.M. to 5:00 P.M. in summer, which gives you a glimpse of original square-set lumbering, tools, and equipment from the fifth largest producing mine on the Comstock; the Julia Bulette Red Light Museum (775-847-9394), open 10:00 A.M. to 9:00 P.M., which includes displays of contraceptives, medical instruments, and medical cure-alls (Julia Bulette, most famous of the Virginia City prostitutes, was murdered by one of her customers); and the Mackay Mansion (775-847-0173), open daily from 11:00 A.M. to 6:00 P.M., which was built in 1860 as the mining office and superintendent's residence by the Gould & Curry Mining Company and is completely furnished with period pieces. And don't forget to pop in and look around the *Territorial Enterprise,* the original 1876 building where Mark Twain began his literary career.

From May through November there is a narrated, 35-minute ride from Virginia City to Gold Hill on the historic Virginia & Truckee Railroad. This ride lets you view the mining district from the original 128-year-old train. Tickets can be purchased at the train depot in the middle of Virginia City near the train tracks. The trains operate daily from Memorial Day to Halloween, with the first train departing Virginia City at 10:30 A.M., and the last train leaving Gold Hill at 6:20 P.M. The trains run on weekends only during the rest of the year.

Also, don't forget to visit the Comstock Fireman's Museum, Piper's Opera House, the Fourth Ward School, the First Presbyterian Church, St. Mary's in the Mountains Catholic Church, the Bucket of Blood and The Delta saloons, the Marshall Mint and Museum, and ask where you can view the 100-mile canyon. Come to think about it, you may need two days to totally enjoy Virginia City. If you wish to stay overnight in Virginia City, I suggest The Gold Hill Hotel (775-847-0111), which has been operating since 1859. It is located 1 mile south of Virginia City on Nevada Highway 342. Virginia City has numerous cafes and restaurants, and all are about equal in price and value.

For more information about Virginia City, you can contact its chamber of commerce at (775) 847-0311. The official Web site is www.virginiacity-nv.com. You can also contact the Virginia City Convention and Tourism Bureau at (775) 847-7500 or www.virginiacity-nv.org.

The International Camel Races

If we Insiders had to suggest a time of year to visit Virginia City, it would be in September, when the hilarious and raucous International Camel Races are held. Traditionally run on the weekend following Labor Day, these races were the brainchild of a *Territorial Enterprise* editor with a slow news week and a sense of humor.

Originally, the U.S. Army introduced camels into the West in 1856, reasoning that the animals would fare well in the desert here. In 1861 camel-train operators used the animals to carry salt from Nevada's marshes to miners on the Comstock. Prospectors used salt in a process called amalgamation, which reclaims gold and silver ore. These pack camels also hauled supplies and firewood to Virginia City residents. But in the mid-1870s, with mining declining, most camel-train operators went bankrupt and released their animals to roam the high desert. The last wild camel in Nevada was spotted in 1936.

In 1957, in order to fill space in his newspaper, the editor of the *Territorial Enterprise* invented the fictitious camel race. The race never occurred—supposedly the camels became ill. For the next two years, the editor made up more phony excuses to postpone the nonexistent races. In 1960, however, Clark Gable, Marilyn Monroe, and director John Huston were in Virginia City filming *The Misfits* during camel race time. John Huston had heard about the fictitious event and decided to make it a reality. Riding camels that came to town with the *San Francisco Chronicle,* he and other Hollywood celebrities made the yearly tradition real.

These days, the camel races are the most popular event in Virginia City—and since 1962 they also include ostrich races. City fathers added "International" to the title in 1987 when they challenged officials from Virginia City's sister city, Alice Springs, Australia, to come over and join in the races. (Australia also used camels as pack animals during its expansion and exploration.)

For a schedule of Virginia City's International Camel Races events, contact the Virginia City and Gold Hill Chamber of Commerce at (775) 847-0311; www.virginiacity-nv.org.

RELOCATION 

If you're thinking about relocating to the Reno/Tahoe area, it's not surprising. The quality of life here is enough to make many people consider pulling up stakes wherever they are. Nevada has boasted (or suffered from) the highest growth rate in the country for a number of years now, so it goes without saying that there must be something attractive about living here. As far as Reno/Tahoe goes, how about unlimited outdoor recreation with four mild seasons to enjoy it in? Or a tax-friendly environment that's more affordable than many comparable communities? Or nonstop nightlife along with a plethora of arts and cultural activities? But before you schedule the moving van, I suggest you read a little more about what life is like in this area. In addition to this chapter, I suggest reading the Health Care and Wellness, Retirement, Education and Child Care, Media, and Worship chapters, which also have information relevant to relocation.

Since choosing where to live is one of the major decisions you'll have to make when relocating, in this chapter I help you walk that minefield with a discussion of neighborhoods, real estate companies, and information about the housing market in general. But along with that I also tell you where you can register your car, enroll your children in school, and get a free relocation packet. Because not all neighborhoods are the same, let's begin this adventure in moving with a whirlwind look at them, broken down by the four geographic areas: Reno, Sparks, North Shore Lake Tahoe, and South Shore Lake Tahoe.

When relocating it's a good idea to consider renting for a while first. After you are familiar with the new area, you can make better-informed decisions about where to buy property.

NEIGHBORHOODS

Reno

I have divided the Reno area into five neighborhoods: North Reno, Verdi/Mogul, the North Valleys, Southwest Reno, and Southeast Reno. Some of the neighborhoods are part of the incorporated city of Reno and some are in unincorporated Washoe County, but because the services and atmosphere are generally the same, this chapter does not separate the two.

NORTH RENO

I have dubbed the area north of the Truckee River within the city limits "North Reno." This part of town contains just about everything that makes a city like Reno tick. Here you have hospitals, casinos, churches, stores, businesses, condos, apartments, and houses dating from the 1940s to the 1990s. There are three basic sections to this area: the Northeastern, the Northwestern, and the Northwest Suburban.

The Northeastern section contains the University of Nevada, Reno; Truckee Meadows Community College; and a plethora of housing ranging from low-income to upper middle class. Most of the older homes border Interstate 80, with the newer models built farther north.

The Northwestern section of this neighborhood stretches from the university (North Virginia Street) to North McCarran Boulevard. This area is crowded with private homes, apartments, duplexes, and multifamily complexes, and it contains most of the university's fraternity and sorority houses. This section is about 60 years old, with most of the dwellings rented out to students and university personnel. Some of the old homes are in fantastic shape, while others show the wear of being rentals.

The Northwest Suburban section of this neighborhood begins at North McCarran Boulevard and continues west to Northgate Golf Club. This area is mostly residential, with established commercial properties along North McCarran Boulevard. Realtors warn new buyers in this area, which sits on the slopes of Peavine Peak, that mature trees are a rare commodity and the area is extremely windy. From east to west the different developments represent the decades of growth in the northwest. The older homes, circa 1940, are closer in toward the university, and the newer 1990s models border the golf course. From east to west you will pass through developments built in the '60s, '70s, '80s, and '90s.

Realtors call North Reno an "area in transition" where first-time buyers can find older affordable homes and more affluent buyers can find new, upscale developments to trade up to.

VERDI/MOGUL

These two rural areas sit just northwest of Reno along I-80. The Truckee River winds its way through them, and the Toiyabe National Forest butts up against their southern borders.

The splendor of the wide-open spaces dotted with trees and the rural feel make up Verdi's personality. Residents say they like the country atmosphere of the area and also like the idea that Reno and its amenities are only 10 miles away.

Some of the bigger, one-of-a-kind houses are situated in the west Verdi area in neighborhoods surrounding Crystal Peak Park and Dog Valley Road. The most popular areas to live include Lakeview Estates, Belli Ranch subdivision, and Donner Trail Ranch. Most of the homes are custom-built, and you'll find houses that are modestly priced as well as those that cost several million dollars.

Mogul, although rural like Verdi but without the trees, sports a different feel. Closer in toward Reno (only about 5 miles out), Mogul is a large development with similar-looking houses. The area remains popular because, like Verdi, it appears remote but is close enough to Reno to enjoy all the big city has to offer. Because many people live here to enjoy the rural environment, proposed annexation of some land by the city of Reno is a hotbed of controversy. The city's less-restrictive growth guidelines could open the floodgates to more growth and dense housing. This neighborhood also boasts Somersett, a master-planned golf community adjacent to Mogul and Verdi. Amenities are strictly private, and homes range from the $300,000s to $800,000s.

THE NORTH VALLEYS

The North Valley communities include Stead, Lemmon Valley, Silver Knolls, Panther Valley, Raleigh Heights, Golden Valley, and Sun Valley. They are located just north of Reno along U.S. Highway 395. Generally these communities are perfect for people who like the wide-open spaces and want to live away from the busy city but close enough to commute.

Stead evolved during World War II when the government built a training base for the U.S. Army/Air Force. Now it is considered a bedroom community of Reno with an ever-expanding manufacturing and warehouse sector. Most people come here to work in the warehouses or industrial centers and to live close to work. Stead remains a manufacturing community, and its airport is home to the annual National Championship Air Races (see the Annual Events chapter).

Lemmon Valley and Golden Valley are ideal for people who want a large block of land but who also want to live close to Reno. Like Stead, these neighborhoods are north of Reno and border US 395. Lemmon Valley is the farthest out and offers the cheapest, easily accessible property. Golden Valley is closer in, is a little more expensive, and affords easy access to Reno and Sparks. Both of these neighborhoods offer large horse properties. Closer in toward US 395, mobile (manufactured) homes and older houses dominate the landscape. These valleys have a rural flavor but are only 10 to 20 minutes from downtown Reno.

Sun Valley sits on top of the northern border between Reno and Sparks, with mobile homes making up most of this neighborhood. Even though a few single-family homes dot the area and one new housing development sits in the northeastern corner, the neighborhood is still considered to be a manufactured-home haven. Citizen volunteers have been trying to combat the underdeveloped stigma attached to the neighborhood, but it still lacks the amenities of other Reno locations. Sun Valley has few streetlights and even fewer sidewalks, and a large portion of the streets remain unpaved dirt and gravel.

SOUTHWEST RENO

The Southwest area of Reno has it all—businesses, older neighborhoods, newer housing developments, several upper-class custom home sites, and large country plots of land. As growth continues its steady march south, this area of town has experienced a large percentage of the upscale retail and business expansion. Dozens of new office complexes have sprung up interspersed with big box and boutique shopping. The area also boasts the new lifestyle shopping center, the Summit Sierra, along with the highest concentration of restaurants in the Reno/Tahoe area.

This neighborhood gives any buyer a wide variety of locations and home styles from sprawling country living to downtown togetherness. Realtors break the expansive Southwest down into three real estate sections: the Old Southwest, the Southwest, and Southwest Suburban.

The Old Southwest is bordered by the Truckee River to the north, Plumb Lane to the south, South Virginia Street to the east, and South McCarran Boulevard to the west. This section is smack in the middle of downtown Reno and contains several city-maintained parks. The architecture here is the oldest in Reno, and brick is the dominant building material. Mature trees envelop the area, which has housing ranging from modest single-story homes to gigantic mansions.

The Southwest section of Reno sits directly underneath the Old Southwest, bordered by Plumb Lane to the north, South McCarran Boulevard to the south and west, and South Virginia Street to the east. This area has dozens of housing developments both old and new, four city parks, two golf courses, and a lake. Some of the more grandiose and older homes are situated around Washoe County Golf Course in the middle of the Southwest section, and many lower-priced homes and apartments sit south of Virginia Lake just 3 blocks east of the golf course. This area began its growth spurt in the 1980s when Reno expanded southward.

Lakeridge, one of the most upscale developments in Reno, sits in this Southwest section. Lakeridge community is on the golf course, with a montage of houses, condos, and apartments built around it and a tennis center. Insiders recognize the area as one of the most highbrow in the city.

But perhaps the most popular and luxurious development in the Southwest is Caughlin Ranch (pronounced *Collin,* without the "gh" sound). This development is one of the first planned communities in Reno; it contains luxury houses and condos but no apartments. The first development began in 1984, and, according to Realtors, it has added a development a year since then. The developments all use a wide-open-space design, with plenty of winding trails for jogging and hiking.

The Southwest Suburban section is the largest area of any real estate section in Reno and Sparks. This area stretches from South McCarran Boulevard south along US 395 to Nevada Highway 431 (the Mt. Rose

i

Property taxes in Nevada are assessed at 35 percent of the appraised or market value.

Highway), up the highway to the Mt. Rose-Ski Tahoe ski resort. Most of this section is in unincorporated Washoe County, and, like Verdi and Mogul, the expansive space gives the feel of country living.

Huffaker development sits at the extreme north of this section and includes a subdivision of larger, upscale houses with its own park, lake, and tennis courts. Working southward, most of the developments in the area feature the more expensive custom-built homes, but the dedicated buyer can find a subdivision to fit any lifestyle with varied price ranges. This area has four new golf courses and plenty of wide-open spaces.

Among the most popular of the newer subdivisions is Saddlehorn, just northwest of the Mt. Rose Highway. People buying here like the idea that their homes are unique and are located on the edge of Reno as well as close to Lake Tahoe.

Along the Mt. Rose Highway, subdivisions are gobbling up every inch of available vacant land. New buyers looking here have several price ranges and styles to choose from. For the more discriminating buyer, two new gated communities have sprung up around the area's three newest golf courses. Old European-style houses surround the Jack Nicklaus-designed Montreux Golf Course. Realtors like to say that these houses give homeowners a feeling of "private country-club living in an alpine setting."

Arrowcreek's two golf courses, designed by Arnold Palmer and Fuzzy Zoeller, are neighbors to Montreux. The gated community surrounding these two golf courses provides 1,500 acres of open land, large custom homes, semicustom homes, and a 12-acre swim and tennis center. A little farther up the highway, Galena Forest Estates and St. James's Village offer luxurious custom homes tucked deep into the forest.

SOUTHEAST RENO

For this guide I include the neighborhoods of Hidden Valley, Donner Springs, Damonte Ranch, Virginia Foothills, Steamboat, and the Virginia City Highlands in the area I call Reno's Southeast. This section stretches from the Truckee River southeast along US 395 to Tahoe Junction (the intersection of US 395 and the Mt. Rose Highway). This large area contains the Reno/Tahoe International Airport, Meadowood Mall and an extensive commercial sector along US 395.

Hidden Valley and Donner Springs housing developments lie to the east and southeast of the airport and provide quality homes for the more-upscale buyer. Homes in the older, more established Hidden Valley are sprinkled in and around the Hidden Valley Country Club. This neighborhood also has a large county park and includes Rosewood Lakes Golf Course, just east of the country club.

The newer Donner Springs neighborhood southeast of South McCarran Boulevard has more moderately priced homes in the neighborhoods east of Longley Lane. Modestly priced homes also can be found in Huffaker Hills on East Huffaker Lane and Double Diamond Ranch along South Meadows Parkway off US 395.

Just east of Tahoe Junction on either side of Nevada Highway 341 (the Comstock Highway), which winds its way up to Virginia City, sit the communities of Virginia Foothills (north of NV 341) and Steamboat (south of NV 341). Some of the older homes were built in the 1960s, but full-scale development here began in the 1970s. This area is more rural than the rest of the Southeast.

The last neighborhood in the Southeast is the Virginia City Highlands, located up the Comstock Highway just off Geiger Grade, which snakes its way to Virginia City. Houses here are scattered along the mountainside and have an outdoorsy feel and spectacular valley and mountain views. A big problem in this neighborhood is the fact that the Comstock Highway is a two-lane road that gets lots of snow during the winter months.

One of the drawbacks to living in the Southeast is that during the floods of 1997 and in 2006, parts of this area found themselves underwater, including the airport, and the city is still struggling with a comprehensive flood plan. Other drawbacks include the airport's plan to expand to the west, which could entail some homes being demolished or moved to make room for the expansion. One area to be wary of is the neighborhood surrounding Neil Road just north of Meadowood Mall. This neighborhood has a high crime rate.

Sparks

I have divided Sparks into four neighborhoods: Old Sparks, East Sparks, Sparks Suburban, and Spanish Springs. Once again, some of the neighborhoods fall within the city limits and some are within the unincorporated confines of Washoe County. I do not make a distinction between the two.

Generally, Sparks is considered by most residents to be a family-friendly area with a high concentration of single-family homes. Residents of Sparks say they feel that life is laid-back, and the Sparks City Council has made sure that the warehouse areas of the city stay separated from the residential neighborhoods.

OLD SPARKS

This is the oldest section of the city, and it lies north of I-80 between El Rancho Drive and North McCarran Boulevard. This is the original railroad settlement and contains City Hall, the casino area, and Victorian Square, Sparks's redevelopment project (see the Area Overview and Attractions chapters). The area is clustered with older, single-family homes that are very modestly priced. The housing has the late 1940s, early 1950s look and feel, with small, crackerbox designs and mostly single-story homes. Even though this section is old, the Sparks Police Department says the neighborhoods are safe.

EAST SPARKS

East Sparks is bordered by I-80 to the south, Pah Rah Park to the north, North McCarran Boulevard to the west, and Vista Boulevard to the east. Most of Sparks's industrial sector is south of I-80 and along the first few miles of Vista Boulevard. The rest of East Sparks is made up of newer housing developments, such as the D'Andrea Golf Club complex. This area of Sparks houses the largest concentration of single-family residences in the city. The development began in the 1970s and continues today. East Sparks is also the home to Sparks Marina Park, a recreational area built around an artificial lake that was once a gravel pit (see the Parks chapter). As the core of Sparks is built out, the land to the east is destined for increased development.

SPARKS SUBURBAN

The Sparks Suburban area is bordered by Nevada Highway 445 (the Pyramid Highway) to the west, Red Hawk Golf Club to the north, and Pah Rah Park to the south. The east is wide-open, hilly space with tons of room for growth. This area is home to the newest housing developments, including Wingfield Springs, a community surrounding Red Hawk Golf Club. The enormous growth in this area required developers to construct a shopping center at the intersection of Disc Drive and Vista Boulevard to accommodate the suburban residents. Depending upon which development you're looking in, you'll find homes that are modestly priced along with much more expensive property. Wingfield Springs, for example, is a very upscale housing development.

SPANISH SPRINGS

This area stretches north along the eastern side of the Pyramid Highway and is an area where most of the new construction is happening. The feel in this section is definitely rural, with houses built among the sagebrush of northern Nevada's high desert. Most of the residents here say they like the country feel and the fact that the city is only 8 to 10 miles away. As development continues to push north of Sparks, however, increased traffic will be a problem. The challenge is to maintain the quality of life, including the rural flavor, while welcoming new development. When considering relocation here or in Sparks Suburban, it would be wise to picture how future growth will affect the area.

Lake Tahoe

The 72 miles around Lake Tahoe take you on an inspirational tour of some of the most magnificent homes in the United States, from those resting on the shore of this pristine lake to those tucked away in the pine trees. Less expensive homes are available for the motivated buyer, but let's face the facts: Property around Lake Tahoe is expensive. The overall real estate picture in the Lake Tahoe basin is actually somewhat schizophrenic. You'll find a significant number of properties, owned by very wealthy people, that are priced in the millions. But you'll also occasionally find run-down ski cabins that are very overvalued because of their location. As time goes on, more and more of these cheaper properties will become teardowns. Because so little vacant buildable land is left in the basin, new construction relies on demolishing existing buildings.

Here I give a brief description of various areas around the lake; for more details read the Area Overview chapter.

NORTH SHORE LAKE TAHOE

From Meeks Bay, California, on the western side of North Shore, to Incline Village, Nevada, on the eastern border of the area, many of the houses and condos are upscale residences. The notable exception is Kings Beach, which has more run-down real estate than any other area at the lake.

The architecture of most of the homes fits into the Old Tahoe look—wood exteriors and interiors, rock fireplaces, some houses tucked away beneath majestic Jeffrey pine trees and some with lake frontage amid natural boulders and glistening white sand. Property values are based not only upon the physical structure itself but also on its all-important view and proximity to the lake. So a house that may seem like nothing more than a fixer-upper in most markets may actually have a hefty price tag if it has any kind of a view (but watch out for the Realtor's phrase "filtered view of the lake," which could mean a peek from a window in the upstairs closet). Any property actually on the lakeshore is obviously worth millions, regardless of what kind of structure is on it. In fact, older homes with views or lake frontage are considered teardowns and are frequently bulldozed to make way for new spectacular estates.

No fewer than 50 neighborhoods line the lake on the North Shore where prospective buyers can search for their one-of-a-kind homes, but one of the most populated is Incline Village. This unique village once attracted retired people and those looking for second homes. Now, more than 70 percent of the 9,000 citizens are permanent residents less than 50 years old. Lakeshore Boulevard and the steep slopes overlooking the lake showcase the luxurious estates of many of the country's rich and famous. Incline Village is also home to Sierra Nevada College, a four-year liberal-arts school.

SOUTH SHORE LAKE TAHOE

Real estate doesn't get any cheaper as you travel south around the lake from Incline Village. The first community in the northeastern corner of the area I call South Shore is Glenbrook, an upscale gated neighborhood nestled in and around Glenbrook Golf Course, a private layout.

Between Glenbrook and Stateline, Nevada, about 12 residential areas line the lake. From Uppaway, Logan Creek, and Lakeridge in the northern part to Zephyr

Residents who move away from Incline Village are known as "Decliners."

Heights, Roundhill and Lake Village in the southern part of the area, buyers can find a variety of unique mountain and lake homes.

Perhaps the best buys around the lake are located in South Lake Tahoe, California. This city is the most populated around Lake Tahoe and contains amenities expected of a larger community—shopping, fast-food restaurants, an airport, and three golf courses. Here a buyer can find almost any type of residential property, some offered at prices lower than other locales around the lake. South Lake Tahoe has single-family residences, condos, townhomes, and apartments, with some properties, in neighborhoods away from the lake, actually modestly priced. Keep in mind that there's an enormous discrepancy among properties and in the prices listed for them.

REAL ESTATE

You'll find a tantalizing variety of homes awaiting you in the Reno/Sparks area, from ranchettes with plenty of room for horses and dogs to starter homes perfect for newlyweds or small families to apartments and condos with hassle-free maintenance. Although many real estate listings are of older properties, growth in the last decade has caused an explosion of new housing developments that fan out in every direction from the urban core. Because of lower interest rates and large numbers of people moving to Nevada from California, the demand for housing has been unprecedented in the past several years. Consequently, prices have soared, with median sales prices increasing as much as 40 percent in some neighborhoods during the past year. Although that may seem frightening to a house hunter, rest assured that there are still some properties available in a large variety of price ranges. Median home prices range from $206,000 in North Reno and downtown to $634,000 in Suburban Southwest Reno. The median price in Old Sparks and East Sparks is $265,000; in Sparks Suburban and Spanish Springs it jumps to $348,000. The overall median price at Lake Tahoe is $890,000, but in Incline Village alone it's $1,250,000.

While there's certainly enough gorgeous homes at Lake Tahoe that most people would love to own, the big question has always been affordability. You will definitely not get the same bang for your buck at the lake as you will in the Reno/Sparks area. Stringent building restrictions coupled with high demand have caused prices at the lake to skyrocket. Sales of houses in the millions of dollars is the norm, with fixer-uppers selling for hundreds of thousands. If the price of a home is out of your league, consider buying a condo, which could be less expensive. And if you find that you just can't afford anything at all at the lake, take heart: Many people are surprised to learn that they don't have to live there to enjoy all its amenities. Keep in mind it's just a short drive away from Reno/Sparks and surrounding communities.

REAL ESTATE COMPANIES

The following associations of Realtors in the Reno/Tahoe area maintain lists of more than 350 real estate firms with more than 2,500 registered Realtors. The lists are free and can be obtained by contacting one of these five associations:

Reno/Sparks Association of Realtors
(775) 823-8800
www.rgj.com

Incline Village Association of Realtors
(775) 831-3777
www.inclinerealtors.com

Tahoe Sierra Board of Realtors
(530) 583-0275
www.tahoemls.com

South Tahoe Association of Realtors
(530) 541-7007
www.staor.org

Sierra Nevada Association of Realtors
(775) 885-7200
www.sierranvar.com

These associations will answer most of your questions about the real estate market in their particular areas, but they will not specifically recommend one of their member Realtors over another. One way to obtain a Realtor is to choose the area you would most like to live in and see which realty firm is most active there; another is to solicit referrals from friends or coworkers.

My list of Realtors, broken down into two general areas (Reno/Sparks and Lake Tahoe), just touches on a cross-section of the many real estate firms in the Reno/Tahoe area. All of my choices have access to the MLS (Multiple Listing Service). Some of the firms are affiliated with nationwide chains, and some are smaller firms with good local references and reputations. The following list is by no means exhaustive.

Reno/Sparks

Coldwell Banker-Plummer & Associates
290 East Moana Lane, Reno, NV
(775) 689-8228

16500 Wedge Parkway, Reno, NV
(775) 336-6100
www.coldwellbankerreno.com
One of the largest real estate firms in the area, with more than 100 Realtors, this locally owned franchise specializes in relocation. It has a team of Realtors who specialize in making moving into the area easy. Realtors for this firm work in all aspects of real estate, from residential to commercial, including land and lot sales. In business since 1978, this firm also offers concierge service.

Dickson Realty
1030 Caughlin Crossing, Reno, NV
(775) 746-7000

500 Damonte Ranch Parkway, Suite 625
Reno, NV
(775) 850-7001

4870 Vista Boulevard, Sparks, NV
(775) 685-8800
www.dicksonrealty.com
Founded in 1973, this firm is a member of RELO, the largest network of independent brokers in the world. It's also the largest independently owned real estate firm in Reno, with more than 350 Realtors and 12 offices. The company only hires Realtors with proven track records.

Ferrari-Lund Real Estate
3700 Lakeside Drive, Suite 100
Reno, NV

690 Queen Way, Sparks, NV
(775) 688-4000, (800) 622-1777

500 Damonte Ranch Parkway, Suite 804
Reno, NV
(775) 850-7033
www.ferrari-lund.com
The Ferrari-Lund Real Estate firm has been operating in Reno since 1988 and specializes in relocation. It handles mostly residential listings but also has a good supply of commercial properties. The firm is one of the 50 top producers in the United States and hires only veteran Realtors. The firm has a relocation division and has more than 140 Realtors to attend to your needs.

Help-U-Sell Drakulich Realty
2205 North McCarran Boulevard
Sparks, NV
(775) 685-8585
www.helpusellnevada.com

Drakulich Realty specializes in residential properties and charges a flat fee instead of the normal 6 percent of the sale price. The firm has about 20 Realtors. It offers a free, weekly list of properties complete with prices, descriptions, and addresses. Drakulich is a full-service firm that shows both its own listings and listings of other brokers.

Landfinder Country Properties
1010 12th Street, Sparks, NV
(775) 358-0555
A small firm that specializes in out-of-town properties, this office concentrates on horse properties, ranches, and land away from the hustle and bustle of city life. Landfinder has been selling ranches for a number of years and has a good selection of rural properties for sale. Its Realtors are licensed in both Nevada and California. The owner says she is not a "city girl" and points out that she lives on a ranch 20 miles north of Reno.

Prudential Nevada Realty, Inc.
5370 Kietzke Lane, Reno, NV
(775) 829-3131
www.prurealty.com
Prudential Nevada Realty is associated with more than 3,500 Realtors in 150 offices in Nevada and northern California for relocation services. That's one of the reasons its owner says, "Relocating is our forte." Residential property sales make up the majority of the firm's business, and it boasts about its 88 percent success rate in sales of all its listings. The firm also provides each of its Realtors with 12 weeks of intensive training. The office has been around for more than 20 years and has more than 170 Realtors working for it.

For a guide on how to avoid paying too much for a home in the Reno/Tahoe area, call (800) 728-6864 or click on www.renohomeseller.com.

RE/MAX Realty Professionals
6121 Lakeside Drive, Reno, NV
(775) 828-3200
www.remax-renonv.com
This office of RE/MAX has been in business since 1990. It recently changed hands but has maintained a staff of about 70 Realtors. The firm handles both residential and commercial properties and uses a worldwide network for relocating.

Lake Tahoe

Ann Nichols and Company
201 Stateline Road, Crystal Bay, NV
(775) 831-0625
www.annnichols.com
This small, independently owned office specializes in luxury second homes on the North Shore of Lake Tahoe. Its six Realtors are licensed in both California and Nevada, and they handle properties from Tahoma, California, to Incline Village, Nevada. The firm likes to boast that it has Realtors who specialize in personalized service and who really know the area. The office has been selling property since 1956.

Better Homes Realty
3000 North Lake Boulevard
Tahoe City, CA
(530) 583-0199
www.betterhomestahoe.com
Better Homes is a small office with a great reputation around Lake Tahoe. This firm handles single-family homes, condos, and townhomes all over the California side of the North Shore. It has Realtors spread out in Tahoe City, Soda Springs, Truckee, and North Lake Tahoe.

Chase International
190 U.S. Highway 50, Zephyr Cove, NV
(775) 588-6130, (866) 233-7111

Glenbrook, NV
(775) 749-5663

Incline Village, NV
(775) 831-7300

Tahoe City, CA
(530) 581-0722

Reno, NV
(877) 922-5900
www.chaseinternational.com
With an office in London, England, Chase isn't kidding about having an international reputation. The firm's global presence speaks to the worldwide appeal of real estate in the Reno/Tahoe area. Founded at Lake Tahoe in 1986 by CEO Shari Chase, the firm specializes in high-end properties. The real estate boom in this area is reflected in the growth of this company to five offices in the area.

Coldwell Banker Northern California
475 North Lake Boulevard
Tahoe City, CA
(530) 546-5924
Formerly Hauserman Real Estate, this firm has been dealing with buyers and sellers on the North Shore of Lake Tahoe since 1966. The 80-plus Realtors specialize in residential sales from Tahoe City to Incline Village and operate out of four offices in Tahoe City and Truckee, California.

RE/MAX Scenic Properties
8611 North Lake Tahoe Boulevard
Kings Beach, CA
(530) 546-3356
www.scenicproperties.net
This RE/MAX location handles residential properties, condos, and lots on the extreme northern shore of Lake Tahoe. It has a solid reputation among Insiders and offers very specialized services.

Windermere Distinctive Homes International
212 Elks Point Road, Zephyr Cove, NV
(775) 588-7710, (800) 878-1066

Incline Village, NV
(775) 832-5111
www.windermeretahoe.com
Although you'll find a wide range of listings at this firm, most of them are high-end. Windermere is also a local affiliate for Christies Great Estates. With 12 experienced Realtors on board, the emphasis is on personalized boutique service. And when you're dealing in sales in the millions, it's probably expected. Most listings are in the Lake Tahoe basin but can range as far as Sacramento or Carson Valley.

HOME BUYING AND RENTAL GUIDES

Several real estate guides are available for the new-home buyer or renter in the Reno/Tahoe area. Almost every grocery and convenience store carries these free publications. Reno's daily newspaper, the *Reno Gazette-Journal,* also prints a weekly tabloid dealing with home sales. Look for real estate news in other newspapers as well, such as the *Tahoe Daily Tribune* and the *North Lake Tahoe Bonanza.*

For Rent Magazine
3550 Barron Way, Reno, NV
(775) 829-7368
This free magazine is published every two weeks and contains about 100 pages of the area's multifamily rental properties. The guide includes university and student housing, senior living, and apartment complexes all throughout Reno and Sparks. The magazine includes a map of the area's apartment complexes, a quick-check guide of all properties listed with amenities, a reader's inquiry service to mail in for more information on individual apartments, and a national relocation service.

HomeFinder
***Reno Gazette-Journal,* 955 Kuenzli Street**
Reno, NV
(775) 788-6200
www.rgj.com
HomeFinder is a weekly tabloid insert to the *Reno Gazette-Journal* that is billed as "Your weekly real estate guide." The tab is paid for by advertising from local real estate companies and is chock-a-block full of properties for sale, rentals, mobile

The Sierra Star estate in Incline Village, listed for sale at $60 million, was the eighth most expensive home on the U.S. market in 2005.

homes, land, and information on real estate loans and mortgage rates. The tabloid averages about 50 pages and is an excellent reference guide to the Reno/Tahoe area. The tab is loaded with articles on how to obtain loans, relocation tips, local mortgage company rates, and how-to tips. It has a special section that focuses on one local neighborhood and one apartment complex each week. It is probably the most comprehensive real estate guide in the area.

Homes & Land Magazine
(775) 831-8991
www.homesandland.com
This free weekly magazine is a nationwide realty guide with zoned editions for Reno, Sparks, North Shore, and South Shore Lake Tahoe. *Homes & Land* averages about 65 pages and is loaded with properties offered by local real estate companies. It has no narrative but lists about 250 residences per issue with a brief description and price. Real estate companies pay to advertise in this guide.

Premier Properties
(775) 833-3333
www.premierehomes.net
A small publication that features properties on the North Shore of Lake Tahoe and is paid for by real estate companies advertising their listings, this once-a-month magazine averages about 25 pages per issue and has zoned editions for the Nevada and California sides of the North Shore. The magazine can be found at most grocery and convenience stores along the North Shore.

Realtors Real Estate Directory
5650 Riggins Court
Reno, NV
(775) 823-8838
Printed every other week by the Reno/Sparks Association of Realtors, this magazine averages about 85 pages and is bursting with properties for sale. It is a scaled-down version of the *Multiple Listings Guide*. This publication offers one to two pages of narrative; the rest of the pages are devoted to homes for sale. The write-ups include price, house and lot dimensions, and photographs. This magazine is free and can be found at all grocery and convenience stores.

Reno Apartment Guide
102 Vine Street, Reno, NV
(775) 329-1442
www.apartmentguide.com
A monthly publication that features about 200 pages of apartments for rent throughout the Reno and Sparks areas, this magazine groups the apartment complexes by neighborhoods and contains a detailed list of prices plus the amenities associated with each complex. This free publication can be picked up at most grocery stores.

APARTMENT LIVING

Many new residents to the area prefer apartment living. You'll find a huge selection to choose from in the Reno/Sparks area, with monthly rents ranging anywhere from $400 to $1,000 and more. The choices are too numerous to list, so I suggest picking up the apartment guides previously mentioned or visiting their Web sites for specific rates and property descriptions. You can find executive transition housing in Reno at Tanamera Apartment Homes (775-852-8989) or at Marriott Residence Inn (775-853-8800).

Apartments in the Lake Tahoe area are more plentiful in Incline Village and South Shore Lake Tahoe.

SCHOOLS

For information on area schools, check the Education and Child Care chapter. To enroll your children in public school, you can consult the appropriate school district below:

Washoe County School District
425 East Ninth Street, Reno, NV
(775) 348-0200
www.washoe.k12.nv.us

Tahoe-Truckee Unified School District
11839 Donner Pass Road, Truckee, CA
(530) 582-2500
www.ttusd.org

Douglas County School District
1638 Mono Avenue, Minden, NV
(775) 782-5134
www.dcsd.k12.nv.us

Lake Tahoe Unified School District
1021 Al Tahoe Boulevard
South Lake Tahoe, CA
(530) 541-2850
www.ltusd.k12.ca.us

DEPARTMENT OF MOTOR VEHICLE INFORMATION

Within 30 days of relocating to Nevada, you must register your vehicles and renew your driver's license. And in California you need to register your vehicles within 20 days and renew your driver's license within 10. I strongly advise you to visit the DMV Web sites to be completely informed before you set out on these tasks. You can also register to vote at DMV locations in both states. Click on www.dmvstat.com for Nevada and www.dmv.ca.gov for California. You'll find full-service DMV offices at 305 Galleti Way, Sparks, NV; 555 Wright Way, Carson City, NV; and 3344 B Lake Tahoe Boulevard, South Lake Tahoe, CA. You can call their offices at (800) 777-0133 for California and (775) 684-4368 for Nevada.

TOURIST BUREAUS AND CHAMBERS OF COMMERCE

Some of the best sources of relocation information, aside from real estate agencies, are chambers of commerce and tourist bureaus. Most have prepackaged materials they are eager to send to prospective new residents. To help make your decision to relocate as informed as possible, I suggest you contact the following:

Sparks Chamber of Commerce
831 Victorian Avenue, Sparks, NV
(775) 358-1976
www.sparkschamber.org

Tahoe Douglas Chamber of Commerce and Visitors Center
195 U.S. Highway 50, Stateline, NV
(775) 588-4591
www.tahoechamber.org

North Lake Tahoe Chamber of Commerce
380 North Lake Boulevard
Tahoe City, CA
(530) 581-6900
www.mytahoevacation.com

Lake Tahoe Incline Village/Crystal Bay Visitors Bureau
969 Tahoe Boulevard, Incline Village, NV
(775) 832-1606, (800) 468-2463
www.gotahoe.com

Greater Reno/Sparks Chamber of Commerce
1 East First Street, 16th floor, Reno, NV
(775) 337-3030
www.reno-sparkschamber.org

Reno Sparks Convention and Visitors Authority
(775) 827-7600
www.visitrenotahoe.com

RETIREMENT

Silver is once again playing a hand in the economy and lifestyle of the Reno/Tahoe area. But instead of coming from the mines in Virginia City, it's arriving as a silver wave of retirees who've discovered that the area is the perfect place for their retirement. After spending their working years fighting traffic and breathing smog, they think they've died and gone to heaven in this natural mountain/desert environment. Washoe County, which includes Reno, Sparks, and Incline Village, has seen more than 23 percent growth in seniors in recent years. And as more baby boomers retire in the near future, demographers say Reno/Tahoe can expect an even greater number of retirees to make their homes here.

It's not hard to understand why so many people choose to relocate here. If they've visited before (which most have), they've probably fallen in love with the gorgeous scenery and the unlimited opportunities for recreation. And then there's the weather: four distinct seasons, all of which are relatively mild. The average high temperatures in the Reno/Sparks area range from around 90 degrees in July to 45 degrees in January. Average lows range from about 18 degrees in January to 47 degrees in July. Because they are located on the leeward side of the Sierra Nevada range, Reno and Sparks have very low humidity in summer and moderate humidity in winter. Snowfall usually runs around 27 inches a year. Lake Tahoe, however, has a colder and much wetter climate. Unless Reno experiences a winter inversion, temperatures around the lake are usually 5 to 10 degrees colder than in the leeward valleys. And even though the sun shines 274 days out of the year at the lake, annual snowfall at lake level averages 125 inches, with 300 to 500 inches falling in the surrounding mountains.

Many retirees are attracted to Nevada for financial reasons because the state has no income tax and no inheritance tax. They also find they can buy more house for their money in Nevada than in some other states, such as California. Last but not least, Reno/Tahoe is senior-friendly and welcomes newcomers with open arms.

Because they lead such busy lives, the word "retirement" is a misnomer to most Reno/Tahoe retirees. They've traded their three-piece suits for jogging outfits and are just as likely to leave home each morning with a pair of skis as a briefcase. When they're not pursuing their favorite outdoor sports or hobbies, you can find them volunteering, taking classes, or even developing new careers. They live life with gusto and seem bent on making the most of their golden years. If retirement to you means a life full of new challenges and adventures, Reno/Tahoe offers a plethora of options. In this chapter I tell you about the enriching opportunities you'll find for education, employment, entertainment, and volunteering.

If you're considering retiring in the Reno/Tahoe area, it's important to know the differences between living in the small mountain towns at Lake Tahoe and living in urban Reno or Sparks. While the small communities at the lake offer a comfortable laid-back lifestyle, they aren't large enough to provide the variety of services that are found in the Reno/Sparks area. But because Reno/Sparks are less than an hour drive away, even if you live at the lake, you can take advantage of some of the senior services in Reno/Sparks. Your best sources of information about what's offered at the lake are the senior centers I tell you about in this chapter.

In addition to having fewer services, full-time residence at Lake Tahoe can present problems in the winter because of snow removal. You should also know that some financial advantages available in Nevada are not offered by California and that housing at Lake Tahoe is usually more expensive than in Reno or Sparks. In general, the people who retire successfully at Lake Tahoe tend to be self-reliant and financially independent individuals.

To find out about senior issues and events, you can read the *Senior Spectrum* newspaper, which is available free at newsracks in the area.

SENIOR CENTERS

Aging ultimately means significant life changes for most people. When they move or retire or suffer the loss of a spouse, they are often faced with having to build new lives and to make new social connections. Senior centers provide a touchstone for many by offering opportunities to socialize and to learn with people their own age. You can enjoy a nutritious meal with newfound friends, stretch your intellectual awareness in a class or seminar, get in touch with your emotional side in a support group, find out about services designed with seniors in mind, and forget all your worries and woes with musical entertainment at Reno/Tahoe senior centers. Most businesses or organizations say they can't be all things to all people, but senior centers give it a try, with arrays of services that seem to fulfill seniors' every need. If you're new to town, there's no reason to feel disconnected. Just drop in at one of the following centers, and you'll find a whole new world of friends and activities. Reno and Sparks each have a center, and South Shore Lake Tahoe has two. The North Shore Lake Tahoe area doesn't have a center, but people living there are always welcome at any of the centers listed below.

i ***Many senior centers provide either free or low-cost transportation services. Check with the senior center closest to you to see if this service is available.***

South Lake Tahoe Senior Center
3050 Lake Tahoe Boulevard
South Lake Tahoe, CA
(530) 542-6094
www.ci.south-lake-tahoe.ca.us
www.netsierra.com

You can take classes, stop by for lunch, get help with senior resources, or just drop in to socialize at the South Lake Tahoe Senior Center. Owned by the city of South Lake Tahoe, the center is the focal point for senior activities in this area of South Shore Lake Tahoe. The welcome mat is always out for those who want to volunteer, and the center provides a variety of opportunities for getting involved. Recreational programs and activities include art workshops, quilting, water exercise, bridge, bingo, dancing, billiards, the writing club, stretch and tone classes, and Jazzercise. The center also sponsors day trips and parties, including Big Band dances. Support services include health screenings, the mature driving program, tax assistance programs, senior peer counseling, and home-delivered meals. Hours are 8:00 A.M. to 4:30 P.M. weekdays, with lunch served at noon. Call the center for information about transportation.

Sparks Senior Center
97 Richards Way
Sparks, NV
(775) 353-3110
www.co.washoe.nv.us

Like its sister center in Reno, the Sparks Senior Center is a beehive of activity. Regular events include arts and crafts, card games, pool and billiards, exercise classes, and dancing. Many of the same programs that are offered at the Reno facility are also available here (see the description below). Lunch is served weekdays at 11:30 A.M., and reservations must be made by 9:30 A.M. the same day in order to eat. The center doesn't provide transportation, but

it's easily reached by Citifare bus. The hours for this comfortable, modern facility are 8:00 A.M. to 5:00 P.M. weekdays.

Tahoe-Douglas Senior Center
U.S. Highway 50
Zephyr Cove, NV
(775) 588-5140
www.netsierra.com/tahoe-seniors
With a primary focus on social and recreational activities, Douglas County offers a limited senior program at the Tahoe-Douglas Senior Center. Because it's an all-volunteer facility, you're more than welcome to help out. Activities include arts and crafts, picnics, potlucks, day trips around the area, card games, and bingo. Hours depend upon the activities offered, so be sure to call ahead for the schedule. For a small donation, the center also offers area transportation for doctor appointments and shopping.

Washoe County Senior Services Center
1155 East Ninth Street
Reno, NV
(775) 328-2575
www.co.washoe.nv.us
A multipurpose facility sponsored by Washoe County, the Washoe County Senior Services Center is a focal point where people can obtain information, services, and access to community resources designed for older persons. When you visit the center, you're immediately aware of the high level of purposeful activity all around, from the enthusiastic exercise class in the multipurpose room to the quiet game of pool in the billiards room. The overall ambience of this large, comfortable facility is that of a club or resort, where people gather to pursue a large variety of pleasurable activities. The ongoing programs include arts and crafts, creative writing, card games, exercise classes, support groups, and a readers circle. Lunch is served weekdays from 11:30 A.M. to 12:30 P.M.

The Washoe County Library System maintains a full branch in the center, with a large selection of books (including large-print editions), paperbacks, videotapes, and newspapers. The Assistance League of Reno-Sparks sponsors the Senior Sampler Gift Shop, which sells items made by local senior crafters. And the American Association of Retired Persons (AARP) staffs an information booth in the lobby to help inform seniors of AARP programs. Other programs that are managed from the center include Benefit Assistance, Daybreak, the Homemaker Program, Home Delivered Meals, and the Senior Law Program. I tell you more about these in the "Senior Services" section of this chapter.

The center is open weekdays from 8:00 A.M. to 5:00 P.M. Programs that are federally subsidized are free, but there are charges for meals, Daybreak, and some recreational activities. The center doesn't provide transportation, but it's easily accessible by Citifare bus routes. If you're driving your own car, there's ample free parking right in front of the building.

If you're looking for an opportunity to make a difference in the community, contact Crisis Call Center at (775) 784-8085 about training to become a volunteer on their lines. Training sessions take place every other month.

EDUCATIONAL OPPORTUNITIES

Lake Tahoe Community College
1 College Drive, South Lake Tahoe, CA
(530) 541-4660
www.ltcc.cc.ca.us
One does not live by physical activity alone—most of us need opportunities to explore our intellectual side as well. Retirement offers the chance for enriching educational experiences through classes and activities we probably didn't have time for during our working years. With its

Helpful Organizations

American Association of Retired Persons (AARP), (775) 328-2506
American Cancer Society, (775) 329-0609
American Lung Association, (775) 829-5864
El Dorado County Senior Information and Referral, (530) 621-6150
Eldercare Locator, (800) 677-1116
Lend-a-Hand Senior Services, (775) 322-8414
Meals on Wheels South Lake Tahoe, (530) 573-3130
Nevada Bureau of Services to the Blind and Visually Impaired, (775) 688-1450
Nevada Division for Aging Services, (775) 688-2964
Northern Nevada Center for Independent Living, (775) 353-3599
Placer County Senior Information and Referral, (530) 889-9500, (800) 878-9222
Senior Connection, (775) 784-8090
Senior Nutrition Program El Dorado County, (530) 621-6160
Senior Nutrition Program Placer County, (530) 888-7137
Washoe Senior Options, (775) 982-5400

large variety of programs and classes, Lake Tahoe Community College is a great place to get in touch with your cerebral self. As part of the California Community College System, the school makes it affordable and easy to enroll. California residents pay just $17 per unit, and through its Good Neighbor Policy, people who've been residents of Nevada for at least one year pay $28 per unit. Enrollment is open to everyone, and courses are offered in art, business, culinary arts, computer science, health, humanities, and social sciences. (See the Education and Child Care chapter for a more detailed description of this school.)

Sierra Nevada College
999 Tahoe Boulevard
Incline Village, NV
(775) 831-1314
www.sierranevada.edu

At a cost of around $20,000 for tuition per year for full-time students, it's pricey and posh, but Sierra Nevada College (SNC) gives residents of North Shore Lake Tahoe enriching opportunities for expanding their intellectual horizons. About two-thirds of the students receive some kind of financial aid, however. There's no break for seniors (although they're welcome in all classes), but you can audit courses for no credit and pay by the credit. The only accredited four-year private liberal-arts college in Nevada, SNC offers courses in business, computer sciences, ski business and resort management, hotel management, humanities, environmental science, international studies, fine arts, and teacher education. It also sponsors The Tahoe Forum, a program that brings well-known speakers to the area. (See the Education and Child Care chapter for more details on the school.)

Truckee Meadows Community College
7000 Dandini Boulevard
Reno, NV
(775) 673-7000 (information)
www.tmcc.edu

You can pursue a degree or just take classes for enrichment through Truckee

Meadows Community College (TMCC). (See the Education and Child Care chapter for a full description of courses and programs.) But TMCC goes above and beyond for seniors in its Silver College by offering classes to Nevada residents who are age 62 years or older for just $8.00. Classes are designed especially for seniors.

For more information on classes or to register at Silver College, call (775) 829-9010. TMCC also has a satellite campus at Incline Village, Nevada. For assistance in courses offered in the North Shore Lake Tahoe region, call (775) 673-7148 or (775) 833-1809.

University of Nevada, Reno
1664 North Virginia Street, Reno, NV
(775) 784-1110 (information)
www.unr.edu, www.eldercollege.unr.edu

The best things in life are free for people age 62 and older at the University of Nevada, Reno (UNR): They don't have to pay tuition for regular university courses. If you've put off getting that first degree (or even second or third) because you didn't have the money for it, the university makes it easy for you by charging only for books and lab fees. Let your fingers do the walking through the catalog and pick from a large variety of degree and nondegree programs. (Check out the Education and Child Care chapter for more specific information.)

UNR also offers free and minimal-fee classes through its ElderCollege program. Targeted to older lifelong learners, ElderCollege provides interactive educational opportunities, with members planning and conducting classes as well as simply taking them. The annual $45 membership in ElderCollege also entitles you to university library privileges and a discount at the Lombardi Recreation facilities. For information on ElderCollege call (775) 784-8053 or visit www.eldercollege.unr.edu.

SENIOR SERVICES

Nonprofit organizations and governmental agencies in the Reno/Tahoe area offer a wealth of services designed specifically for seniors. I can't begin to list them all, but in this section I give you an overview of the kinds of programs older persons can take advantage of to enrich their retirement years.

Advocate for Elders
445 Apple Street, Suite 104, Reno, NV
(775) 688-2964
www.nvaging.net

Managed by the Nevada Division for Aging Services, the Advocate for Elders gives homebound seniors an advocate for voicing their concerns and complaints. The services are free and confidential to those who are age 60 or older. The advocates investigate allegations of elder abuse, exploitation, and neglect within care homes and nursing facilities.

Community Home-Based Initiatives Program (CHIP)
445 Apple Street, Suite 104, Reno, NV
(775) 688-2964
www.nvaging.net

As an alternative to nursing-home care, CHIP helps older persons maintain independence in their homes by providing nonmedical assistance. Attendants offer companionship in addition to help with personal care, shopping, and housekeeping.

Daybreak
1155 East Ninth Street, Reno, NV
(775) 328-2591
www.co.washoe.nv.us

Operating every day but Sunday, Daybreak is essentially an adult day-care facility. In addition to giving caregiving families a break, it helps participants overcome the social isolation that often accompanies illness. While fees are $6.00 per hour, no one is denied participation because they are unable to pay.

Home Delivered Meal and Nutrition Programs
1155 East Ninth Street, Reno, NV
(775) 328-2581
www.co.washoe.nv.us/seniorsrv
For older persons unable to take care of their own nutritional needs, the Home Delivered Meal Program is literally a lifesaver. To qualify, a person must be age 60 or older and unable to cook and prepare food or to eat at a group location. Meals are delivered weekdays at no cost, but contributions are encouraged. Washoe County Senior Services also offers meals at its two senior centers and at five additional satellite locations in the county.

Sanford Center for Aging
800 Haskell Street, Reno, NV
(775) 784-4774
www.unr.edu/sanford
Exploring innovative ideas for successful aging, the Sanford Center for Aging pursues programs in education, research, community outreach, and service. Major outreach includes the Retired and Senior Volunteer Program, wellness workshops for seniors, and the Nevada Care Connection information referral system.

Senior Law Center
1155 East Ninth Street, Reno, NV
(775) 328-2592
www.co.washoe.nv.us/seniorsrv
It's hard to imagine you can get the expertise of an attorney for free, but the Senior Law Program provides consultation and representation at no cost for residents of Washoe County who are age 60 or older. Services are limited to elder-rights law, government benefits and entitlements, consumer matters, real property and housing issues, and lifetime planning. Although clients are expected to pay only for court costs and filing fees, donations are requested.

Senior Social Services
1155 East Ninth Street, Reno, NV
(775) 328-2590
www.co.washoe.nv.us
When seniors need a little extra help with their bills each month, Washoe County Senior Social Services can help. Based upon income and age criteria, older persons are eligible for rebates on property taxes, local telephone service, sewer fees, heating costs, and TV cable fees. The program also distributes free food.

Washoe Senior Medical Group
850 Mill Street, Reno, NV
(775) 982-5420
www.washoehealth.com
As part of Washoe Health System, Washoe Senior Medical Group is a doctor's office just for people age 65 or older. The center offers comprehensive care that also includes educational and preventive information. Patients receive a free membership in Washoe Senior Options, a senior-only program that sponsors social functions, trips, and health and wellness services. For information call (775) 982-5400.

WORKING AND VOLUNTEERING

American Association of Retired Persons (AARP)
Senior Community Service Employment Program
(775) 328-2506
AARP's employment program can launch you on a second career with its counseling, training, and information and referral service. The program is free for those who are age 55 or older who also have limited income.

Foster Grandparent Program
406 Pyramid Way
Sparks, NV
(775) 358-2768
You can profoundly enrich your life as well as that of your foster grandchild in the

Foster Grandparent Program. Volunteers provide one-on-one daily attention to at-risk youth in schools, hospitals, drug treatment centers, day-care centers, and correctional institutions. You can apply if you're age 60 or older, love children, meet certain income requirements, and can volunteer 20 hours a week. Benefits include a small stipend, reimbursement of expenses, insurance, and an annual physical.

Golden Opportunity
560 Mill Street, Reno, NV
(775) 785-6106
If "retirement" means continued involvement in the world of work, Golden Opportunity can help you develop your talents, learn new skills, and find the right job to use them in. To qualify for the program, you must be age 55 or older, meet financial guidelines, and be seriously interested in working.

ProNet
1675 East Prater Way, Sparks, NV
(775) 336-5438
www.pronetreno.com
Although it's not just for seniors, I list this organization here because many older persons could benefit from its services. ProNet is a nonprofit organization that helps unemployed professionals find jobs. No-cost services include self-help networking, resources and training to assist in job hunting, and workshops and programs to develop new job skills and to improve résumés.

Retired & Senior Volunteer Program of Washoe County
401 West Second Street, Suite 101
Reno, NV
(775) 784-1807
www.unr.edu/sanford
Volunteering where you can really make a difference is one of the most rewarding experiences many older persons discover in their retirement. The Retired & Senior Volunteer Program of Washoe County (RSVP) actively recruits seniors age 55 and older for a large number of local nonprofit and public agencies. With so many to choose from, you're sure to find the position that's just right for you. The program places volunteers in schools, museums, cultural events, hospitals, social agencies, parks, and senior services. If you're newly retired and/or new to town, there's no better way to meet people with similar interests.

Senior Auxiliary Volunteer Effort (S.A.V.E.)
455 East Second Street
Reno, NV
(775) 321-8312
If you've ever wanted to be a police officer, here's your chance. Sponsored by the Reno Police Department and the Retired & Senior Volunteer Program, S.A.V.E. is open to people age 50 and older who want to help make their community a better place to live. Duties of the uniformed volunteers include checking on the vacant houses of people who are on vacation, patrolling schools and parks, visiting housebound seniors, and patrolling during daylight hours in specially marked police cars. The role of the volunteers is limited to observing and reporting.

Senior Companion Program
406 Pyramid Way
Sparks, NV
(775) 358-2322
Many older persons delay or avoid living in nursing homes by using help provided by volunteers in the Senior Companion Program. Volunteers provide assistance to frail seniors by providing transportation, escorting seniors to doctor's appointments, running errands, and simply being a friend. Volunteers are reimbursed for their expenses and receive insurance and an annual physical as a benefit. To qualify for volunteering, you must meet certain age and income requirements and agree to work 20 hours a week.

A quick way to find resources is to dial 211 on your telephone.

FUN AND FITNESS

Ballantine's Ballroom
2920 Mill Street
Reno, NV
(775) 324-1000
If you like to dance for fun and fitness, you're sure to find your comfort zone at Ballantine's Ballroom. A popular dance hangout with the older crowd, Ballantine's offers ballroom, swing, jazz, and tap lessons as well as public dancing.

Incliners
Incline Village, NV
(775) 831-0481, (775) 831-9162
With a whopping 800 members (almost 10 percent of the population of Incline Village, Nevada), the Incliners is the indisputable center of social activity for many older people living in Incline. Members meet twice a month for dinners and social events but also avidly pursue sports and hobbies together, such as tennis, golf, bike riding, and bridge. Members must be age 49 or older and be able to pay $10 in annual dues.

Incline Village Recreation Center
893 Southwood Boulevard
Incline Village, NV
(775) 832-1324
www.ivgid.org
Although Incline Village doesn't have a senior center, the recreation center provides a large variety of services especially for older residents. Seniors can stay fit, happy, and healthy by participating in activities that include the senior book club, the craft cafe, ballroom dancing, yoga, conversation cafe, and the arthritis aquacise class.

Newcomers Club of Reno/Sparks
P.O. Box 50044, Sparks, NV 89435
(775) 881-2040
www.newcomersclubofreno-sparks.org
While it's not restricted to retired people, the Newcomers Club of Reno/Sparks certainly attracts large numbers of them. With more than 800 members, the group offers an enormous variety of activities to help people adjust to a move or a transition in their lives. If you want to join the fun, you must apply for membership within two years of moving to the area. Exceptions are for those who have gone through a life change, such as retirement, divorce, or widowhood. Its motto, "There are no strangers here, only friends we have not met," seems to say it all about this popular group.

Paradise Park Activity Center
2745 Elementary Drive, Reno, NV
(775) 356-3176
www.cityofreno.com
The city of Reno offers a veritable smorgasbord of activities for seniors at the Paradise Park Activity Center, including exercise classes, quilting bees, dance workshops, and card games. The parks and recreation department also welcomes suggestions for additional activities of interest to area seniors.

Reno Singles
(775) 853-3109
www.renosingles.net
A casually organized group for people age 50-plus, Reno Singles gets together once a week for picnics, potlucks, cards, and games. The location and activities vary, so call for specific information. On this Web site you can find links to Tahoe Singles, a group at North Shore Lake Tahoe, and Sierra Singles, who cover the Carson Valley. For information on Sierra Singles call (775) 266-9536.

Sparks Recreation Department Senior Softball Leagues
(775) 353-2376
www.ci.sparks.nv.us

You may love watching your grandchildren play ball, but how about playing yourself? Dust off your mitt and join in the fun with the Senior Softball Leagues. With names like Reno Rowdies and Super Seniors, the 18 teams make up a large enthusiastic group of players that competes year-round. Sponsored by the Sparks Recreation Department, most league games take place on the Rail City's ball fields.

WHERE TO LIVE

The choices of retirement or senior housing in Reno/Tahoe run the gamut, from private residences to apartments to full-service retirement homes with assisted living and nursing care. (See the Relocation chapter for an overview of housing and locales.)

As one of the fastest growing areas in the country, it's hard to keep up with the increasing number of options. Although I can't list them all, in this chapter I give you examples of residential choices geared specifically to older persons: retirement communities and assisted-living facilities. Rates are based upon single occupancy; facilities will charge several hundred additional dollars for a second occupant. For the assisted-living facilities, rates may vary depending on individual needs. For a complete listing of retirement living options, check in local telephone books under "Retirement."

Retirement Homes

Classic Residence by Hyatt
3201 Plumas Street, Reno, NV
(775) 825-1105
www.hyattclassic.com

True to its name, Classic Residence by Hyatt is classic in every sense of the word. For retirees age 55 or older who can afford the best, it combines the ambience of an exclusive country club with the warmth of a private home. If you've stayed at Hyatt resorts or hotels, you know the level of service and the elegant accoutrements Hyatt provides.

Classic offers studio and one- and two-bedroom apartments, many with patio or balcony views of the Sierra Nevada mountains and the Washoe County Golf Course. Monthly fees include meals, weekly housekeeping, scheduled transportation, apartment maintenance, and concierge assistance, with assisted living available at additional cost. Classic even provides a moving coordinator to help with relocation details.

Amenities of the facility include the Wintergarden Lounge, library, arts and crafts studio, exercise room, beauty/barber shop, outdoor walking paths, free laundry facilities, parking, computer center, private dining room, billiards lounge, and club room. Geared to active retirees, this facility goes out of its way to offer a large variety of cultural, educational, social, and recreational outlets for residents. The facility has recently been remodeled. Call for rates.

The Fountains Senior Care, Inc.
1920 Harvard Way, Reno, NV
(775) 825-2044

Designed for carefree retirement living, the Fountains includes all the necessities for quality living in the rental payment. The rent for studio apartments and one-bedroom units includes weekly housekeeping and linen service, three daily meals, transportation, scheduled activities, and cable television. Residents can also take advantage of the on-site beauty and barber shop and the community visiting area. Since the Fountains is strictly a rental facility, residents are not required to sign leases or pay buy-in fees. Its location is especially convenient for shopping as it's right across from a large mall that has stores such as Costco, PetSmart, Office Depot, and many other small retail establishments. The facility has just been completely renovated. Call for rates.

Lakeside Manor
855 Brinkby Avenue, Reno, NV
(775) 827-3606
www.quiltedcare.com
Within easy walking distance of lovely Virginia Lake in southwest Reno, the studio apartments at Lakeside Manor include housekeeping, laundry, transportation, utilities (other than phone and cable), and meals. Residents of the manor have a full array of activities to choose from, including arts and crafts, exercise classes, local trips, social events and parties, discussion groups, card games, and billiards. The facility also has a library, a beauty salon, and free transportation service. If you're a pet owner, you'll be delighted to know the welcome mat is out for Fido or Fluffy also. Call for rates.

Odd Fellows Retirement Manor
1155 Beech Street, Reno, NV
(775) 323-1911
In a picturesque parklike setting near the University of Nevada, Reno, the Odd Fellows Retirement Manor has 118 private rooms that rent for about $900 per month. Housekeeping, meals, activities, and transportation are included. The university campus and nearby Dick Taylor Memorial Park offer enjoyable routes for daily walks.

Promenade on the River
525 Court Street, Reno, NV
(775) 786-8853
www.promenadereno.com
It would be hard to find a more elegant retirement facility than Promenade on the River. Resembling a lovely Roman villa of warm stone and tile, the building hugs a bluff overlooking the Truckee River in downtown Reno. Originally designed as upscale condominiums back in the 1980s, the facility has been remodeled to include six floors of 84 luxury apartments designed around an old-world European-style atrium. In addition to all the usual bells and whistles offered by senior living communities, Promenade also boasts a rooftop swimming pool and spa, underground parking, and concierge service. Its location in a quiet historic neighborhood close to downtown theaters and galleries is also a plus. You would think that all of this might put them in a class by themselves pricewise; however, all-inclusive monthly fees are competitive with other senior living facilities in the area.

Tahoe Senior Plaza
1109 Third Street
South Lake Tahoe, CA
(530) 542-7048
Opened in the spring of 1999, Tahoe Senior Plaza is a lovely mountain chalet with 44 one-bedroom apartments, four of which are wheelchair accessible. Because the complex is federally subsidized housing for the elderly, residents must be at least age 62 and meet certain income guidelines. Those accepted will pay rent equal to about 30 percent of their adjusted annual income. Because demand is high, it's necessary to place your name on a waiting list.

Villas of Sparks
1900 East Prater Way, Sparks, NV
(775) 359-7700
www.assisted.com
Spacious and impressive, Villas of Sparks feels just like home. Comfortable seating and lush green plants in the public areas create a cozy environment perfect for stimulating conversation or quiet reading. The rental fee includes scheduled transportation, meals, utilities, weekly housekeeping, linen service, and cable television. A full-time activities director is in charge of the large variety of outings and events offered daily to residents. There's also a library, beauty shop, and even an ice-cream parlor. Call for rates.

Assisted Living

Atria Summit Ridge
4880 Summit Ridge Drive, Reno, NV
(775) 787-3000
www.arvi.com

Atria at Summit Ridge enables residents to age in place since it offers several levels of care depending upon individual needs. Monthly fees include meals, housekeeping and linen, basic utilities, scheduled transportation, and assistance with daily activities. Residents can enjoy the beautifully landscaped courtyard, the library with its cozy fireplace, an elegant private dining room, and the activities room with a big-screen TV. Call for rates.

Lake Tahoe Guest Home
586 Glorene Avenue
South Lake Tahoe, CA
(530) 542-2383

Tucked away in a forest of beautiful pines, Lake Tahoe Guest Home is the only assisted-living facility in the Lake Tahoe area. Its personal care program is designed to assist active, healthy seniors in adjusting to a slower pace of life while maintaining their independence. Services include three meals a day, daily housekeeping, laundry service, assistance with personal care, transportation, and scheduled activities. The modern facility offers a beauty salon, recreational sitting room, and a patio for lounging. Call for government-subsidized and private-pay rates.

Wynwood of Sparks
2000 East Prater Way, Sparks, NV
(775) 359-7733
www.assisted.com

Personalized service is the trademark at Wynwood of Sparks since residents' preferences are an integral part of their care. Assistance with unscheduled needs is provided 24 hours a day by professional staff. All of the apartments in this bright, modern facility have wall-to-wall carpeting and kitchenettes. Housekeeping and laundry service plus a full array of educational and social opportunities are included. Call for rates.

HEALTH CARE AND WELLNESS 

Because Reno/Tahoe is such an attractive place to live, it's not hard to understand why many doctors choose to live here. After all, if you can choose where to practice medicine, why not select a beautiful area with unlimited opportunities for recreation? Just a glance in local telephone books will show more than 800 physicians and surgeons practicing in every field of medical specialization. Almost any medical procedure you might need is available locally except organ transplants, which are routinely done in Sacramento, California, about two hours away by car.

In addition to the hundreds of medical doctors, about 100 podiatrists and doctors of osteopathy and more than 300 dentists have hung out their shingles here. Although most of these medical personnel practice traditional medicine, alternative care, such as acupuncture and homeopathy, is also available.

But despite the large numbers of medical people who live and work here, it can sometimes be difficult to find a doctor. If you're considering relocating to Reno/Lake Tahoe I strongly recommend finding a primary care physician before you actually move here. The physician referral services listed further on in this chapter is a good place to start. Because of the strong population growth the area has experienced in recent years, the demand for doctors in some areas has exceeded the supply.

Since the Reno/Sparks area is the largest center of population, it serves the medical needs of not only its own residents but also of people living in nearby rural communities in Nevada and California. And while Lake Tahoe has a high number of doctors per person and two small hospitals, the variety of medical care available in Reno and Sparks and nearby Carson City is much greater. Although the good news is the high quality and diversity of care available, the bad news is that it costs about 20 percent more than the national average.

You might not think that an area well known for its 24-hour lifestyle would be especially conscious of health care and wellness. Statistics also paint a rather grim picture, showing high rates for suicide, smoking, and alcohol abuse, particularly in Reno and Sparks. But in spite of this, a healthy lifestyle is a priority for an increasing number of residents because they want to participate fully in the outdoor activities available in the area. Insiders also know that many people living at Lake Tahoe are sports enthusiasts who spend as much time as possible hiking, biking, and skiing.

When not exercising outside, many people stay in shape at one of the more than 30 health clubs in the area. While some clubs are fitness studios emphasizing exercise machines and individual workouts, others are full-service health centers, with lap pools, child-care facilities, racquetball and tennis courts, tanning salons, massage therapy, clothing shops, restaurants, personalized training, and a large variety of classes. And because Reno is a 24-hour city, you can work out around the clock in many of its health clubs. Before joining a club, it's a good idea to shop around, since membership packages and prices vary a lot. Check local phone books under "Health Clubs" for complete listings.

But even athletes who are in good condition occasionally have accidents and get hurt. If that happens to you, you can take some comfort in knowing that the Reno/Tahoe area has attracted a number of athletically inclined physicians who specialize in sports medicine. They understand not only the clinical aspects of sports injuries but the practical side as well, since it's likely they spend a lot of their free time hiking, biking, and skiing. If you're looking for knee reconstruction or joint replacement, just let your fingers do the walking through the Yellow Pages, where you'll find a variety of highly qualified orthopedic surgeons listed. After all, with more than 20 ski resorts in the area, they have plenty of ski-related injuries to practice on.

While the variety of available medical care reflects in part the lifestyle of area residents and visitors, the medical community is further enriched by the University of Nevada School of Medicine in Reno. Established in 1969 by the Nevada State Legislature and funded in part by the late eccentric billionaire Howard Hughes, the School of Medicine is integrated with local hospitals, clinics, and physicians. More than 900 community physicians throughout the state are involved in its mission to provide medical education and training for Nevadans. The school is also an important center of medical research, focusing on problems that affect Nevada in particular. The University of Nevada, Reno, also trains registered nurses in its Orvis School of Nursing; Truckee Meadows Community College, also in Reno, trains registered nurses as well as certified nursing assistants. The Reno/Tahoe area is also home to a number of licensed schools of massage.

In this chapter I give you a general overview of the kinds of health care offered in the Reno/Tahoe area. I tell you about the major hospitals, which are comprehensive health-care delivery systems, as well as the smaller specialty hospitals and clinics. I tell you how to find a doctor, where to get emergency care, what support groups are available, and where to get alternative medical care. And last, but not least, I tell you how to get medical attention for the family pet.

HOSPITALS

Reno

Ioannis A. Lougaris Veterans Affairs Medical Center
1000 Locust Street
(775) 786-7200
(888) 838-6256 (outpatient clinic in Minden, NV)
www1.gov.directory

Serving veterans in northern Nevada and northeastern California, the Reno Veterans Affairs Medical Center is a 62-bed general medical and surgical hospital with a 60-bed nursing-home-care unit. The VA is well known for its innovative geriatric health programs as well as research into diseases and geriatric rehabilitation. With more than 60 projects ongoing at any given time, the center conducts more research than all other hospitals in Nevada combined. The center has studied Alzheimer's, Parkinson's, kidney and cardiovascular diseases, hypertension, diabetes, and breathing disorders. The VA also offers Home Based Primary Care to veterans needing care in their home environment and Contract Adult Day Health Care, which helps delay admission to a residential care facility. Specific programs include telemedicine, a sleep apnea clinic, and treatment for Agent Orange exposure.

Renown Regional Medical Center
77 Pringle Way
(775) 982-4100

Renown South Meadows Medical Center
10101 Double R Boulevard
(775) 982-7000
www.renown.org

Formerly Washoe Medical Center, Renown Regional Medical Center is northern Nevada's oldest health-care facility. It is also Reno/Tahoe's largest and most comprehensive acute-care hospital, with the only Level II trauma center, bone-marrow transplant unit, pediatric intensive care unit, and radiation therapy program in the area. It also has centers to treat diabetes, heart disease, cancer, and substance abuse as well as dialysis, surgical, and poison centers.

Recognizing that healing has emotional as well as physical aspects, Renown encourages loved ones to become part of the health-care team with its Very Important Partners program and provides interaction with dogs through its Pet Therapy with K-9 Kare. The annual Healing Arts Festival introduces patients, visitors, and staff to a variety of healing arts, including massage therapy, visual and musical arts, and humor. The public is invited to the keynote address, usually held at the Pioneer Center for the Performing Arts. Past speakers have included best-selling spiritual authors Deepak Chopra and James Van Praagh.

Because it's a large regional complex that serves people from outlying areas as well as locals, Renown has amenities not found in all hospitals. You can rent a hotel room at the inn, enjoy tasty meals in several restaurants, and shop in the boutique, all within the medical campus. There's also covered parking, a chapel, a pharmacy, and a dry cleaners. The health resource center provides a wealth of information about health care and wellness, with 400 books and periodicals and access to computers.

If you're more comfortable in a small hospital, Renown, with its 529 licensed beds, may seem too large for you. And if you prefer a private room, Renown does not always provide one, but Saint Mary's Regional Medical Center and Northern Nevada Medical Center will. In response to the growth south of Reno, Renown opened a second acute-care hospital on Double R Boulevard with 155 beds and a full complement of medical services.

As this book went to press, construction was progressing on the $200 million expansion of the medical center. The project will add a 12-story tower for expanded patient care along with additional parking. With more than 300 additional patient rooms, the center will be one of the three largest hospitals in Nevada.

Saint Mary's Regional Medical Center
235 West Sixth Street
(775) 770-3000
www.saintmarysreno.com

The legacy of Saint Mary's Regional Medical Center was born when a group of Dominican nuns arrived in Reno in 1877 to open a school for local children. The sisters soon learned that early Reno not only lacked educational structures but needed health-care facilities as well. To help address this need they built Sisters' Hospital in 1908, which was the forerunner of Saint Mary's.

The medical center is part of Saint Mary's Health Network, a large integrated delivery system encompassing 10 health care facilities, including Saint Mary's Galena, Hospice of Northern Nevada, and Saint Mary's Family Walk-in Health Center. The network consists of 800 physicians, 2,664 employees, and more than 400 volunteers. A recent $160 million expansion at the medical center doubled its size, adding office and parking space, emergency beds, and expanded services such as a wellness center along with critical care and rehabilitation services. Because Saint Mary's is still operated by Catholic sisters, the spiritual well-being of patients is part of the healing process. The inpatient hospital rooms at the center are especially appealing, because all of them are spacious and private.

Tahoe Pacific Hospitals–Meadows
10101 Double R Boulevard
Adjacent to Washoe Medical Center South Meadows
(775) 331-1044

Tahoe Pacific Hospitals–West
235 West Sixth Street, Fifth Floor
Saint Mary's Regional Medical Center
(775) 770-7980

Tahoe Pacific Hospitals treat highly acute patients who come directly from traditional hospitals. Specializing in long-term rehabilitative care, they provide speech, occupational, physical, and recreational therapy. The two Reno facilities work closely with Saint Mary's Regional Medical Center and Washoe Medical Center.

West Hills Hospital
1240 East Ninth Street
(775) 323-0478, (800) 242-0478
www.psysolutions.com/facilities/westhills
A 95-bed private psychiatric facility, West Hills Hospital offers inpatient hospitalization and a variety of outpatient programs for people of all ages who have mental health problems. Patients work with a treatment team, consisting of a psychiatrist, social worker or counselor, psychiatric nurses, and mental health technicians. The hospital has an extensive substance abuse program that is available on either an inpatient or outpatient basis.

Willow Springs Center
690 Edison Way
(775) 858-3303
www.psysolutions.com/facilities/willowsprings
Willow Springs Center is a 74-bed residential treatment center for children and adolescents ages 5 through 17. Established in 1988, Willow Springs provides a long-term therapeutic environment for young people experiencing emotional and behavioral problems. It's affiliated with West Hills Hospital, a mental health facility also in Reno.

Sparks

Northern Nevada Adult Mental Health Services
480 Galletti Way
(775) 688-2001
www.mhds.state.nv.us
Operated by the state of Nevada, the Northern Nevada Adult Mental Health Services offers psychiatric services, day treatment, and case management. Treatment in its 74-bed adult psychiatric hospital includes diagnostic and therapeutic services. Program fees are on a sliding scale, depending upon eligibility.

Although it's outside the immediate Reno/Sparks/Lake Tahoe area, the new $118 million Carson Tahoe Regional Medical Center in Carson City offers a plethora of high-tech medical care to people living just south of Reno. For information click on www.carsontahoe.com.

Northern Nevada Medical Center
2375 East Prater Way
(775) 331-7000
www.northernnvmed.com
It's large enough to offer comprehensive medical services but small enough to add a personal touch to healing. Originally Sparks Family Hospital when it opened in 1983, Northern Nevada Medical Center (NNMC) is a 100-bed acute-care hospital on 23 acres in Sparks. It has a 24-hour emergency room and complete surgical and diagnostic services, including a comprehensive same-day surgery program.

Although it sounds like a pizza delivery system, it's the only hospital that has a "15-minute ER Guarantee," which means your emergency room visit is free if you're not seen within 15 minutes by a nurse and 60 minutes by a doctor. The center also follows up almost all cases that come through the ER with a phone call home after the patient is released from the hospital. NNMC also boasts a preadmission program designed to familiarize patients with staff and hospital procedures before treatment. Owned and operated by Universal Health Services (the third largest hospital management company in the country), NNMC is dedicated to providing quality medical care in a comfortable, accessible environment. This philosophy begins with providing all private rooms at no additional cost. Its mission also includes a long history of special events and services that promote wellness in the community. The Senior Bridges program is nationally recognized and offers complete inpatient and outpatient psychological care for people age 65 and older.

North Shore Lake Tahoe

Incline Village Community Hospital
880 Alder Avenue
Incline Village, NV
(775) 833-4100
www.tfhd.com
A division of Tahoe Forest Hospital District (which is based in Truckee, California), Incline Village Community Hospital is an eight-bed acute-care hospital. It offers 24-hour emergency care, diagnostic services, outpatient surgery, and inpatient observation. Because of its small size, the emphasis is on outpatient services. Through its Physician Finder referral system, the center provides access to more than 80 physicians who represent a wide variety of specialties. For information about these doctors, their locations, and insurance accepted, patients can call (530) 587-3769.

South Shore Lake Tahoe

Barton Memorial Hospital
2170 South Avenue
South Lake Tahoe, CA
(530) 541-3420
www.bartonmemorial.org
Barton Memorial Hospital is living testimony to what a small community can do when it works together to meet a critical need. Prior to the hospital's opening in 1963, medical care was provided by a small number of local physicians. The nearest hospitals in Reno and Carson City, Nevada, were nearly an hour away when the roads were clear and frequently were all but unreachable during periods of heavy snow. Realizing the necessity of having more accessible medical care, local residents worked to raise funds for the original 38-bed medical facility. Celebrities who regularly performed in the area even joined the effort, with the profits from Elvis Presley's benefit concert used to build the intensive care unit.

Since those first frantic fund-raising days, Barton Memorial has expanded to an 81-bed acute-care facility with a medical staff of more than 100 and a support staff of about 200. The medical complex also includes a Skilled Nursing & Rehabilitation Center with 48 beds. Services include 24-hour emergency care with a trauma room, surgery, hospice care, home health, and diagnostics. As part of its commitment to health care and wellness in the community, Barton offers a variety of special events, support groups, and health-related classes.

Barton Memorial is an attractive, modern medical facility that is a source of great pride to those living in South Shore Lake Tahoe. It continues to be a not-for-profit hospital that is owned by the community and also affiliated with Carson Valley Medical Center in Gardnerville, Nevada.

REFERRAL SERVICES

If you're new to the Reno/Tahoe area or just visiting, the easiest way to find out about local doctors is to use the referral numbers below. Also note that most hospitals keep referral lists of physicians.

Direct Doctors Plus
(800) 874-5775

Northern Nevada Medical Center
www.northernnvmed.com

Physician Finder
(530) 587-3769

Saint Mary's Health Network
(775) 770-7100

WALK-IN CLINICS

The following clinics operate with extended hours and will accept patients with no appointments.

Faster Care
3967 South McCarran Boulevard
Reno, NV

25 McCabe Drive
Reno, NV
(775) 826-9111

Saint Mary's Family Walk-In Health Center
6580 South Virginia Street, Reno, NV
(775) 853-3333

Saint Mary's Galena
18653 Wedge Parkway, Reno, NV
(775) 770-7210

Specialty Health Clinic
350 West Sixth Street, Reno, NV
(775) 322-2122

Stateline Medical Center
155 U.S. Highway 50, Stateline, NV
(775) 589-8900

Tahoe Urgent Care Medical Clinic
2130 Lake Tahoe Boulevard
South Lake Tahoe, CA
(530) 541-3277

Truckee-Tahoe Medical Group
925 North Lake Boulevard, Tahoe City, CA
(530) 581-8864

Washoe Urgent Care
975 Ryland Street, Reno, NV
(775) 982-6394

910 Vista Boulevard, Sparks, NV
(775) 982-4580

10101 Double R Boulevard, Reno, NV
(775) 982-4910

ALTERNATIVE MEDICAL CARE

It wasn't that long ago that alternative medicine, such as acupuncture and homeopathy, was viewed by many people as nothing more than treatments of last resort, used when all traditional methods of treatment had failed. But today a growing number of people rely on alternative medicine for ongoing and preventive medical care.

The Reno/Tahoe area has a number of clinics and doctors that integrate scientific and natural medicine. Some services available include homeopathy, herbology, neural therapy, chelation, hormone management, Chinese herbal medicine, sclerotherapy, trigger point therapy, and acupuncture. To find a listing of doctors and clinics, look under the subheading "Homeopathy" in the Physicians section of the SBC telephone book. You can also call the National Center for Homeopathy at (703) 548-7790 for referral and general information.

As a starting place, the following clinics and physicians offer some type of alternative medicine.

David Edwards, M.D.
615 Sierra Rose Drive, Reno, NV
(775) 828-4055

Gerber Medical Clinic
1225 Westfield Avenue, Reno, NV
(775) 826-1900

David Holt, D.O., H.M.D.
121 Washington Street, Reno, NV
(775) 324-4548

SPECIAL SERVICES AND SUPPORT GROUPS

If you need a helping hand or simply moral support, it's just a phone call away since several hundred organizations offer support services in the Reno/Tahoe area. I can't list them all, but I'll give you a sampling of what's available. If you don't find what you need, call the Crisis Call Center at (775) 784-8090; they keep a complete list of community resources.

Alzheimer's Association Northern Nevada Chapter
705 South Wells Avenue, Reno, NV
(775) 786-8061
www.alznornev.org
This association provides information, referral, support groups, and free respite care for families affected by Alzheimer's.

American Red Cross
1190 Corporate Boulevard, Reno, NV
(775) 856-1000
www.nevadaredcross.org
In addition to emergency disaster relief, the American Red Cross offers a variety of community education programs about AIDS, first aid, safety, and babysitting.

CARE Chest of Sierra Nevada
7910 North Virginia Street, Reno, NV
(775) 829-2273, (866) 206-5242
www.carechest.com
People who have no insurance benefits or adequate financial resources for medications and medical equipment can obtain them at no cost through this program.

Catholic Community Services of Northern Nevada
500 East Fourth Street, Reno, NV
(775) 322-7073
This nonprofit organization offers emergency assistance on a variety of levels: clothing, housing, transportation, and food.

Children's Cabinet, Inc.
1090 South Rock Boulevard, Reno, NV
(775) 856-6200
www.childrenscabinet.org
A highly successful organization with a large umbrella of services for children and families, Children's Cabinet is well respected for its counseling, tutoring, parenting, and substance abuse programs.

Children's Cabinet at Incline Village
948 Incline Way, Incline Village, NV
(775) 298-0004
www.cciv.org
Through a variety of programs, this nonprofit is a centralized clearinghouse of information and services for children and families in North Shore Lake Tahoe.

Crisis Call Center
(775) 784-8090, (775) 784-8085 (business), (800) 992-5757
www.crisiscallcenter.org
Established in 1966 as a suicide prevention hotline, Crisis Call Center is the longest continuously operating crisis line in the country. Highly trained volunteers answer more than 2,000 calls each month from those in need. The crisis line is staffed 24 hours a day and serves all of Nevada as well as the California area around Lake Tahoe.

Foster Grandparent Program
406 Pyramid Way, Sparks, NV
(775) 358-2768
Children and seniors lend each other a helping hand through this program. Older persons receive a stipend, transportation, and meals in exchange for providing services to children with special needs.

Gamblers Anonymous–Reno/Sparks
(775) 356-8070
Individuals with gambling problems are offered support and counseling through this program.

Gamblers Anonymous–South Lake Tahoe
(530) 573-2423
The program offers help to those addicted to gambling.

Grief Recovery Outreach Workshop (G.R.O.W.)
St. John's Presbyterian Church
1070 West Plumb Lane, Reno, NV
(775) 826-0990
www.stjohnschurch.org

Grief Recovery Outreach Workshop offers guidance, friendship, and support for those beginning the healing journey of grief. Programs are available at various times throughout fall, winter, and spring at St. John's Presbyterian Church, Washoe Medical Center, and Saint Mary's Regional Medical Center. Call for specific times and dates.

Health Access Washoe County (H.A.W.C.)
1055 South Wells Avenue, Reno, NV
(775) 329-6300
www.gbpca.org/hawc
This community health clinic provides low-cost medical services to Medicare, Medicaid, and uninsured patients.

I Can Cope
6490 South McCarran Boulevard, Suite 40
Reno, NV
(775) 329-0609
Offered by the American Cancer Society, the program offers support and counseling for individuals and families affected by cancer.

Nevada Hispanic Services, Inc.
3905 Neil Road, Reno, NV
(775) 826-1818
For the growing Spanish-speaking population, this agency provides interpretation and translation services, immigration assistance, job placement, and youth programs.

Project Restart
490 Mill Street, Reno, NV
(775) 324-2622
As its name suggests, Project Restart has a variety of programs to help at-risk people start over with training and job placement.

Reno/Sparks Gospel Mission, Inc.
145 West Third Street, Reno, NV
(775) 323-0386
www.rsgm.org
The Gospel Mission offers emergency food, clothing, and shelter to anyone who has identification and is sober. Counseling is also available through their Christian Addiction Recovery and Education (C.A.R.E.) program.

Ronald McDonald House
323 Maine Street, Reno, NV
(775) 322-4663
The house provides a home away from home for families of children who are patients in any Reno hospital.

Saint Mary's Hospice of Northern Nevada
3605 Grant Drive, Reno, NV
(775) 770-3081
Operated as part of Saint Mary's Health Network, the hospice provides medical and spiritual care for terminally ill patients and their loved ones.

Senior Daybreak
1155 East Ninth Street, Reno, NV
(775) 328-2591
This program provides day care for adults age 18 or older as an alternative to institutionalization. It offers caregivers daytime relief with nursing and social opportunities for those with disabilities.

Sexual Assault Support Services (SASS)
(775) 784-8085
www.crisiscallcenter.org
The program is a support group for survivors of sexual assault.

South Lake Tahoe Women's Center
2941 Lake Tahoe Boulevard
South Lake Tahoe, CA
(530) 544-2118
(530) 544-4444 (hotline)
www.sltwc.org
Directed at women and families in crisis, South Lake Tahoe Women's Center offers counseling, emergency services, and educational outreach.

Survivors of Suicide (SOS)
(775) 784-8085
www.crisiscallcenter.org
Individuals who have survived the suicide of a significant other can join this self-help group.

Tahoe Youth and Family Services
1021 Fremont Avenue
South Lake Tahoe, CA
(530) 541-2445
(800) 870-8937 (hotline)
www.tahoeyouth.org
Programs provided by this nonprofit include youth and family counseling, a 24-hour runaway hotline, and substance abuse counseling.

Washoe ARC
790 Sutro Street, Reno, NV
(775) 333-9272
www.warcreno.org
Formerly known as Washoe Association for Retarded Citizens (WARC), Washoe ARC evaluates, trains, and provides work opportunities for retarded persons in its thrift stores. As a highly successful advocate for the mentally retarded, it also offers family counseling and community education programs.

Washoe County Senior Law Project
1155 East Ninth Street, Reno, NV
(775) 328-2592
www.co.washoe.nv.us/seniorsrv
This project gives free legal help to those age 60 and older who are residents of Washoe County in the areas of Social Security, government benefits, Medicare, Medicaid, and landlord/tenant disputes.

PET CARE

If your pet needs medical attention, don't panic: State-of-the-art medical care is available at the many veterinary hospitals in the Reno/Tahoe area. Many clinics offer 24-hour emergency care, house calls, surgery, boarding, and even acupuncture. Some veterinarians specialize in just horses, cats, or small animals; others treat all types of pets.

Since animals (like people) don't get sick at the most convenient times, it's a good idea to have a couple of emergency numbers handy. Klaich Animal Hospital Ltd., 1990 South Virginia Street (775-826-1212), and The Animal Emergency Center, 6427 South Virginia Street (775-851-3600), provide on-call emergency care in Reno. In Incline Village, Nevada, you can call Incline Veterinary Hospital, 880 Tanager (775-831-0433), for emergency care. In the South Shore Lake Tahoe area, most veterinarians rotate emergency duty, so the answering service at any of their offices will refer you to the doctor on call. Carson-Tahoe Veterinary Hospital also has 24-hour emergency service along with one of the few pet ambulances available in the country. Equipped much like a human ambulance, it will travel throughout the Reno/Tahoe area. For information call (775) 883-8238. If you need transportation for your pet, call Pet Taxi in Reno at (775) 787-2222.

EDUCATION AND CHILD CARE

We take education seriously here in the Reno/Tahoe area, from our children in preschools to our graduate students at universities. Both California and Nevada are committed to providing each resident the opportunity to obtain a quality education, whether that student is starting kindergarten or entering a doctoral program.

Both Nevada and California have mandated high-school exit examinations, which all seniors must pass to obtain a high-school diploma. And, at the K through 8 levels, standardized tests are used by both states to evaluate student performance.

While schools in both states strive for excellence, each must cope with annual influxes of new students. Though the number of new students varies from year to year, all increases strain the already overcrowded hallways of school facilities. To help alleviate this problem, Nevada voters periodically pass bond issues to construct new schools.

As the number of students in the Reno/Tahoe area continues to grow, private educational facilities as well as charter schools become educational options for an increasing number of students. Private schools in the area serve kindergartners, elementary, middle, and high-school students. A complete list of private schools in the state of Nevada is available through the state's education Web site, listed below.

Some families prefer to homeschool their children, which is permissible as long as the curriculum is approved by the local school district.

Students moving on to the local university continue to receive wonderful educational opportunities because the University of Nevada, Reno, is ranked as one of the top 100 colleges and universities in the United States by *U.S. News and World Report* magazine. Those high-school graduates that do not go on to college have no problem finding jobs here, especially jobs in the service industry or the construction business, where advanced degrees are not needed.

This chapter begins with an overview of the public and private schools throughout the Reno/Tahoe area. Then I discuss the topic of child-care options in the area and give you a range of places to begin your search for those services that best suit you.

For more information on public and private schools in Nevada, you can visit www.doe.nv.gov or call (775) 687-9200. California's education Web site is www.cde.ca.gov; the telephone number is (916) 319-0800.

EDUCATION

Public Schools

RENO/SPARKS AND THE NEVADA SIDE OF NORTH SHORE LAKE TAHOE

Washoe County School District
425 East Ninth Street, Reno, NV
(775) 348-0200
www.washoe.k12.nv.us

The Washoe County School District (WCSD) serves more than 60,000 students. Within the Reno/Tahoe area, around 7,300 teachers, administrators, counselors, and others work in more than 90 schools. The average student/teacher ratio is 22.5 to 1 in the elementary grades, except first and second grades, where a state-mandated 16-to-1 ratio is maintained. To help remain in compliance with this state law, some first- and second-grade classrooms employ a team-teaching situation where two teachers are assigned to a class of 32 students. The middle-grade classrooms average a 26.2-to-1 student/teacher ratio, and the high schools maintain a slightly higher ratio.

WCSD is the second largest district in Nevada, with overcrowding a continual issue. To meet the challenge of maintaining a reasonable student/teacher ratio, some elementary schools have volunteered to go on a year-round singletrack or multitrack schedule.

All elementary school students are required by state law to take the TerraNova standardized test. In high school, seniors must pass state-mandated reading, writing, and math examinations to receive a high-school diploma, no matter what the student's overall grade point average is.

At the high-school level, WCSD oversees the Regional Technical Institute, which includes the Glenn Hare Occupational Center. The institute offers occupational and technical training to high-school students, including classes in electronics, computer-aided design, business systems, advanced child development, and many other occupational specialties. The WCSD also offers a magnet high-school program for juniors and seniors at a campus located at Truckee Meadows Community College (TMCC) in Reno. At TMCC, high-school students earn college credits while they finish their high-school graduation requirements.

Even though the majority of WCSD's schools are located in the Truckee Meadows, the district is responsible for one high school, one middle school, and one elementary school in Incline Village on the North Shore of Lake Tahoe.

To enroll a student in the WCSD, first contact the WCSD administration at the number listed to find out which school your home is zoned for. Then proceed to that school with the following documentation: your child's immunization record, proof of residency, and proof of the child's identity. A utility bill, a rental agreement, or a mortgage contract is acceptable as proof of residency. For child identification a birth certificate, a passport, or a baptismal certificate is sufficient. Another helpful document is a student's most recent report card to help place the student in the proper class or classes.

The WCSD provides bus service for K–12 if an elementary-aged student lives 1 mile or farther from his or her school; for middle-school students the distance stretches to 2 miles, and for high-school students it's 3 miles.

Nevada law requires that every child between the ages of 7 and 17 attend school. Kindergarten is not mandatory, but a student who does not attend kindergarten must be tested before entering the first grade.

CALIFORNIA SIDE OF NORTH SHORE LAKE TAHOE

Tahoe-Truckee Unified School District
11839 Donner Pass Road, Truckee, CA
(530) 582-2500
www.ttusd.org

The Tahoe-Truckee Unified School District (TTUSD) is responsible for schools located on the California side of North Shore Lake Tahoe, including one elementary school, one alternative school, one middle school, and one high school located in Tahoe City, California. The district is also responsible for one elementary school in Kings Beach, California. The total population of these schools is around 2,000 students. California mandates a 20-to-1 student/teacher ratio in its K–3 classrooms, and all elementary school students must take a standardized achievement test. High-school students, in order to graduate, must take an exit examination.

To enroll a student in the TTUSD, first contact the district's administration at the number listed to find out which school your home is zoned for. Then proceed to that school with the following documentation: your child's immunization record, proof of residency, and proof of the child's identity. Required immunizations may be obtained from the county's health department or from a private physician. A utility bill, a rental agreement, or a mortgage contract is acceptable proof of residency. For child identification a birth certificate or a passport is preferred. Another helpful document is a student's most recent report card to help place the student in the proper class or classes.

The TTUSD provides bus service for K–12 if a student lives within the boundaries marked for his or her school, no matter the distance from the school. California law requires that children must attend school between first grade and their 18th birthday. Kindergarten is not mandatory.

SOUTH SHORE LAKE TAHOE

Douglas County School District
1638 Mono Avenue
Minden, NV
(775) 782-5134
www.dcsd.k12.nv.us

The Douglas County School District (DCSD) is responsible for three schools on the South Shore of Lake Tahoe on the Nevada side. The district's administrative offices are located over the mountains in the tiny Nevada town of Minden, so at times students, teachers, and parents feel isolated from the rest of the school district, especially during the snow season.

The district maintains a high school, middle school, and one elementary school in Zephyr Cove, Nevada, along with 10 schools in the Carson Valley.

To enroll a student in the county's schools at the lake, proceed to your school with the following documentation: your child's immunization record, proof of residency, and proof of the child's identity. A utility bill, a rental agreement, or a mortgage contract is acceptable as proof of residency. For child identification a birth certificate, a passport, or a baptismal certificate is sufficient. Another helpful document is a student's most recent report card to help place the student in the proper class or classes.

The DCSD provides bus service for K–12 if a student lives 2 miles or farther from his or her school. Nevada law requires that every child between the ages of 7 and 17 attend school. Kindergarten is not mandatory, but a student who does not attend kindergarten must be tested before entering the first grade.

Lake Tahoe Unified School District
1021 Al Tahoe Boulevard
South Lake Tahoe, CA
(530) 541-2850
www.ltusd.k12.ca.us

The fourth school district with jurisdiction around Lake Tahoe is the Lake Tahoe Unified School District (LTUSD) of South Lake Tahoe, California. This district has the responsibility of overseeing three elementary schools, one middle school, and three high schools. The students number about 5,000, and the district employs about 200 teachers.

By California state law, the elementary schools must maintain a 20-to-1 student/teacher ratio in grades K–3, but district officials say this ratio is maintained throughout all the elementary grades.

The district's high school options are intriguing. In addition to a traditional high school, students who don't speak English can attend a Transitional Learning Center, where they are placed in small classes and given more individual time with teachers. The third school is Mt. Tallac, a continuation high school attended by a small number of students, including teen parents, who would like to obtain an alternative to a high school diploma. All three high schools are on the same campus.

To enroll a student in the LTUSD, first contact the district's administration at the number listed to find out which school your home is zoned for. Then proceed to that school with the following documentation: your child's immunization record, proof of residency, and proof of the child's identity. Required immunizations and health exams may be obtained from the county's health department or from a private physician. A utility bill, a rental agreement, or a mortgage contract is acceptable proof of residency. For child identification a birth certificate or a passport is preferred. Another helpful document is a student's most recent report card to help place the student in the proper class or classes.

The LTUSD provides bus service for K-12 if a student lives within the boundaries marked for his or her school, no matter the distance from the school. California law requires that children must attend school between first grade and their 18th birthday. Kindergarten is not mandatory.

Private Schools

About 40 private schools operate in the Reno/Tahoe area. The range of grades served by the institutions varies widely; you can find schools that only serve kindergartners, others that educate K-12, and others serving almost any grade combination between. Most of these educational facilities have religious affiliations, and only a few are large facilities. Most are smaller schools that boast low student/teacher ratios. The majority of the schools are located in the Reno/Sparks area.

Tuition costs range from a low of about $1,500 per year to a high of $8,500. The following is an alphabetical sampling of some of the leading private schools in the Reno/Tahoe area. To locate schools not listed here, refer to the Yellow Pages under "Schools/Private," or, for Nevada, visit the Web site at www.doe.nv.gov.

Bishop Manogue Catholic High School
110 Bishop Manogue Drive, Reno, NV
(775) 336-6000
www.bishopmanogue.org

The first Catholic school in the area was established in Virginia City, Nevada, in 1864.

This is the only Catholic high school in the Reno/Tahoe area. It was established in 1948 and has always had an outstanding reputation in both academics and athletics. About 650 students attend Manogue. The school employs about 31 teachers and is also known for its honors classes in English, science, math, and U.S. history. A dress code is enforced, and an entrance examination for freshmen is required. The school relocated to a new campus in south Reno in fall 2004. The new facility will initially accommodate 800 students, with eventual enrollment expected to be 1,200.

Brookfield School
6800 South McCarran Boulevard
Reno, NV
(775) 825-0257
www.brookfieldschool.com

Brookfield School is an independent private school with classes from preschool through eighth grade. The school is academically oriented and teaches French starting in first grade and Latin in grades 6, 7, and 8. It uses the LearnStar interactive learning method, the Spectra art program, and the Suzuki violin method. The school has about 200 students and 15 teachers. The school was founded in 1962 and requires an entrance examination. It is accredited by the National Independent Private School Association.

Church Academy
1205 North McCarran Boulevard
Reno, NV
(775) 329-5848

This academy, established in 1979, is a nondenominational school providing religious education to 50 students in grades K-12. The school employs three teachers who instruct in multiage classrooms.

Lake Tahoe School
995 Tahoe Boulevard, Incline Village, NV
(775) 831-5828
www.laketahoeschool.com

With David Duffield, the founder of PeopleSoft, Inc., the prime mover for LTS, the school is guaranteed to have financial as well as intellectual support from its board and parents. Situated in a new three-story building with 22 classrooms, the school provides opportunities for students to explore technology, computers, science, and performing arts. Enrollment runs around 100 students, with a student-to-teacher ratio of 6 to 1. The schedule consists of four quarters, each averaging 45 days. LTS is fully accredited for students that are prekindergarten through grade 8. Tuition is about $13,000 a year for those in K–8.

Legacy Christian Elementary School
6255 Pyramid Highway, Sparks, NV
(775) 424-1777
www.legacychristianschool.com
One of the newest Christian schools in the area, Legacy is nondenominational and offers K–12 classes on two campuses. The curriculum includes religious evangelical education, art, and athletics. About 300 students attend the two schools; 16 teachers work at the elementary site, and 12 teachers work at the middle and high school site. The school was founded in 1997. The Pyramid Highway campus serves the elementary levels; the middle and high school campus is located at 816 Holman Way in Sparks.

Little Flower School
1300 Casazza Drive, Reno, NV
(775) 323-2931
Little Flower is one of four Catholic elementary schools in the Reno/Tahoe area. The school teaches grades K–8 and has an enrollment of about 315. The students receive computer training in grades one through five, and they receive instruction in health and nutrition from nursing majors at the local university.

Mountain View Montessori School
565 Zolezzi Lane, Reno, NV
(775) 852-6162
www.mountainviewmontessori.com
This nondenominational school is affiliated with the Association Montessori International. The school teaches the self-paced Montessori curriculum to preschoolers through ninth-grade, and it has mixed-aged classes. Courses include music, art, dance, drama, chess, skiing, computers, science club, Japanese, and Spanish. Its student population of 130 is served by 10 teachers.

The annual budget for Washoe County School District runs around $335 million.

Our Lady of the Snows School
1125 Lander Street
Reno, NV
(775) 322-2773
www.ourladyofthesnows.com
This is one of the four Catholic elementary schools in the area. The school teaches grades K–8 and has an enrollment of 300. Our Lady of the Snows (OLS) boasts a hands-on science curriculum and an athletic program. And, as at most Catholic grade schools, uniforms are mandatory. OLS has a waiting list, with preference given to its parishioners.

Reno Christian Academy
2100 El Rancho Drive
Sparks, NV
(775) 331-0909
This K–10 nondenominational Christian school uses the Abeka Christ-centered, accelerated curriculum, which includes traditional classes, religion, athletics, and extracurricular activities. The school provides before- and after-school care. It was founded in 1990 and has 145 students and 18 teachers.

Safe Harbor Christian School
1881 Harvard Way
Reno, NV
(775) 329-7775
This Baptist-affiliated school provides religious education to students in grades K–8. The school is equipped with a computer lab and boasts low student/teacher ratios.

Sage Ridge School
2515 Crossbow Court
Reno, NV
(775) 852-6222
www.sageridge.org
This school opened in the fall of 1998 and is the most expensive school in the area. It serves students in grades 6 through 12. Classes are taught using an integrated, universal curriculum that stresses liberal arts combined with technology. Every student is provided with a laptop computer. Core classes at the school are 80 minutes long. The school is attended by 170 students, and more than half its teachers have master's degrees.

St. Albert the Great Catholic School
1255 St. Albert's Drive, Reno, NV
(775) 747-3392
This is the oldest and largest Catholic elementary school in the area. It was founded in 1955 and teaches 310 students in grades K–8. The school teaches the standard Catholic curriculum and boasts that, in addition to its state-of-the-art computer lab, every classroom is equipped with a computer. It has full-day kindergarten, prekindergarten, and day care. Uniforms are mandatory.

Squaw Valley Academy (SVA)
235 Squaw Valley Road
Olympic Valley, CA
(530) 583-9393
www.sva.org
The most prestigious school at Lake Tahoe, SVA is a boarding and day school that "provides a college preparatory curriculum in a structured environment" to students in grades 6 through 12. It boasts small classes and advanced placement courses. The coeducational school, which has 35 students and 13 teachers, administrators, and administrative staff, offers soccer, skiing, snowboarding, hiking, and tennis as its extracurricular activities. It was founded in 1978 and is fully accredited. Although not a ski academy, the school attracts a lot of competitive skiers and boarders.

Tahoe Montessori School
848 Glorene Avenue
South Lake Tahoe, CA
(530) 544-1818
This is one of only two schools at Lake Tahoe that uses the Montessori curriculum. The other is a preschool. This preschool through fifth-grade school offers year-round full- and part-time child care. It uses an individualized learning method and boasts a low student/teacher ratio. Summer programs are available at this nonsectarian, state-registered private school.

Charter Schools

Along with public and private schools, the Reno/Sparks area has a variety of charter schools. With smaller classes and more narrowly focused curriculums, charters often appeal to students who have not had a lot of success in traditional school settings. The schools listed below operate as autonomous educational entities that have received charters from the Washoe County School District or the state department of education.

Academy for Career Education
(775) 324-3900
www.acehighschool.org

Bailey Charter Elementary School
(775) 323-6767
www.psreno.org

Coral Academy of Science
(775) 323-2332
www.coralacademy.org

Forest Charter School
Truckee, CA
(530) 550-7205

High Desert Montessori School
(775) 624-2800

I Can Do Anything Charter High School
(775) 857-1544

Mariposa Academy of Language and Learning
(775) 826-4040

Rainshadow Community Charter High School
(775) 322-5566

Sierra Nevada Academy
(775) 677-4500

Team A (Together Everyone Achieves More Academy)
(775) 323-8555

Colleges and Universities

The state-run University and Community College System of Nevada comprises two doctoral-granting universities, four community colleges, and one environmental research facility. Of those, one university, one community college, and the research facility are located in the Reno/Tahoe area on the Nevada side. On the California side of Lake Tahoe, one community college affords students a chance at higher education.

In the private sector, five colleges offer accredited degree programs in the Reno/Tahoe area. These private colleges offer degree programs ranging from a BA in liberal arts to an MS in business administration.

PUBLIC COLLEGES AND UNIVERSITIES

Lake Tahoe Community College (LTCC)
1 College Drive, South Lake Tahoe, CA
(530) 541-4660
www.ltcc.cc.ca.us

LTCC is one of California's 106 public community colleges. Founded in 1974, the college is Lake Tahoe's only two-year college. LTCC offers 21 majors and 15 courses resulting in certificates of achievement. The majors include art, English, fine arts, physical education, humanities, natural science, culinary arts, fire science, Spanish, and criminal justice.

About 4,000 students attend the college, seeking either an associate's degree or certificates of achievement. Like most community colleges in California, LTCC offers transfer, career education, and occupational technologies programs.

The college has a child development center that is used as a lab for its Early Childhood Education programs, a theater, and a technology center. It participates in California's Golden Valley Conference in men's and women's cross-country running and women's volleyball.

LTCC recently expanded its vocational offerings by adding a nursing assistant program and a dental assistant program. It also opened a physical education facility and a culinary arts facility recently.

The college employs about 50 full-time faculty and numerous part-timers and offers both night and weekend classes to accommodate students who work (which is the majority of those who attend).

High school graduates are eligible for admission, as well as people 18 years old or older who are legal residents of the LTCC district. On special occasions, LTCC will admit students enrolled in grades 9-12 if their high school counselors recommend them.

Truckee Meadows Community College (TMCC)
7000 Dandini Boulevard, Reno, NV
(775) 673-7000 (information)
www.tmcc.edu

TMCC provides the Reno/Tahoe area with more than 50 accredited occupational and university transfer degree and certificate programs, and it has offered two-year programs ranging from casino operations to electronics technology since 1971. Enrollment at the college has grown more than 46 percent in the last five years and totals nearly 11,000 credit and noncredit students.

The Dandini campus covers 63 acres and includes an advanced technology center, library, and child-care center. The college also has a new Technical Institute, Edison Campus, and two education cen-

The oldest schoolhouse in Nevada is the Glendale School in Sparks, built in 1864. The building was used until 1958. It is now part of the Heritage Park and Museum in downtown Sparks.

ters, one at Reno Town Mall and the other in Incline Village. Classes are also held at satellite centers, giving students more than 40 different places to take TMCC classes.

The college includes English as a Second Language program, Reentry and Women's Center, distance learning facilities, state-of-the-art computer labs, Veteran's Upward Bound Program, and Community Services Offices. The Institute of Business and Industry is part of TMCC's occupational education and business partnering mission.

The average TMCC student is 31 years old, employed, and in school part-time. TMCC conducts several courses at night and on the weekends to accommodate working students.

If you are at least 18 years old and a high school graduate, you may attend TMCC, but the school's admission policies are flexible, allowing some students to attend if they are younger than 18 or to earn a GED. Juniors and seniors in high school may also apply to TMCC High School, which is a combination high school and community college.

University of Nevada, Reno (UNR)
1664 North Virginia Street, Reno, NV
(775) 784-1110 (information)
www.unr.edu

UNR is the oldest of Nevada's two universities and the only research institution. The campus was opened in 1885 as a land-grant institution and has grown from one building and 56 students to 200 acres and more than 15,000 students. Located within walking distance of downtown but secluded on a tree-covered campus, the university is supported by 10 schools and colleges offering 72 undergraduate majors, 64 master's degree programs, 33 doctoral programs, a four-year medical school, and a nationally recognized honors program.

UNR is fully accredited by the Northwest Association of Schools and Colleges and since 1991 has been ranked in the top 15 percent of America's public and private colleges. *U.S. News and World Report* always places UNR in the Top 100 schools (including Harvard and Yale) in its yearly "America's Best Colleges" issue. UNR's athletic teams receive regular regional and national attention.

UNR emphasizes a core curriculum of social sciences, natural sciences, mathematics, English, fine arts, and diversity, with additional requirements according to students' majors. The number of credits needed for graduation ranges from 124 to 134. The academic year is composed of two 15-week semesters beginning in August and ending in May. The university also offers three summer sessions. More than 96 percent of the 650 full-time faculty hold the highest degree available in their fields. Some of the colleges include College of Arts and Sciences, Business Administration, Education, Engineering, Mines, the Reynolds School of Journalism, graduate school, medical school, and continuing education. UNR is also the home of the National Judicial College and the National College of Juvenile and Family Court Justices.

Applications for admission should be received by UNR's Admissions and Records by February 1 for the fall semester and by November 1 for the spring semester. You can obtain an application packet from the Office of Admissions by calling (775) 784-4700.

PRIVATE COLLEGES AND UNIVERSITIES

Career College of Northern Nevada
1195 Corporate Boulevard, Reno, NV
(775) 856-2266
www.ccnn4u.com

This trade and technical college has 250 students and provides training in electronics, data processing, word processing, medical and legal office management, and microcomputers. It is accredited by the Accrediting Commission of Career Schools and Colleges of Technology. The college offers associate's degrees in occupational studies in electronics engineering technology and occupational studies in computerized business management.

Morrison University
10315 Professional Circle, Reno, NV
(775) 850-0700
www.morrison.edu
Morrison is a senior college, founded in 1902, which specializes in business education. The college offers undergraduate programs in accounting, computer accounting, medical, legal assistant/paralegal, office administration, computer information systems, and business management. A master's program in business administration is also available.

The school boasts that its students can earn a specialized diploma in 6 to 9 months, an associate's degree in 15 months, and a bachelor's degree in 2 to 3 years. The college is accredited by the Accrediting Council for Independent Colleges and Schools.

Sierra Nevada College
999 Tahoe Boulevard, Incline Village, NV
(775) 831-1314
www.sierranevada.edu
Sierra Nevada College (SNC) is a four-year, nonprofit, independent liberal-arts college. The coeducational college is located on the North Shore of Lake Tahoe and offers programs in more than 15 different fields from its departments of business administration, visual and performing arts, humanities and science, and teacher education.

Sierra Nevada College is best known in the area for its fifth-year teacher education program. This program prepares students for teacher certification or recertification in California and Nevada. Though no master's program for teachers is currently in place, the college is exploring this option.

The student/faculty ratio is 15 to 1. More than 95 percent of the classes have fewer than 20 students. The college is accredited by the Commission on Colleges and Northwest Association of Colleges and Schools. Its ski business and hotel, restaurant, and resort management major is one of the best in the United States.

Although SNC emphasizes academics, its alpine sports teams (the college's only athletic teams) are consistently the best in the nation. And why not, with so many ski resorts just down the road? Since 1989 the SNC men's and women's Eagles have won the U.S. Collegiate Ski and Snowboard Association Nationals almost every year.

University of Phoenix
5370 Kietzke Lane, Reno, NV
(775) 828-7722, (866) 766-0766
www.phoenix.edu
The University of Phoenix is a private bachelor's and master's degree granting institution with programs in business, management, education, computer information systems, and counseling. Calling itself "a university created just for working adults," it offers undergraduate and graduate degrees in business management, business information systems, human services, business administration, organizational management, and education supervision.

The university's mission is to meet the higher educational needs of working adults. According to its plan, students attend classes one night a week and finish a course every five to six weeks. The university is accredited by the Commission on Institutions of Higher Education of the North Central Association of Colleges and Schools.

CHILD CARE

The Reno/Tahoe area is jam-packed with things to do, places to go, and people to meet, and moms and dads sometimes must do these things without the wee ones along. An abundance of day centers provide child-care services to meet the needs of working or busy parents, however, in addition to agencies that provide babysitter referrals and handle nannies and au pairs.

Even though Nevada's business is generally a 24-hour operation, there are no child-care centers that are open all night, and only a handful of home-care facilities offer overnight care. Casinos do not have child-care facilities for visitors, but most will recommend babysitting services. The phone books for each of the geographical locations (Reno, Sparks, North Shore Lake Tahoe, and South Shore Lake Tahoe) list child-care facilities, preschools, babysitters, and nannies. But just because they are listed in the Yellow Pages doesn't mean they are licensed. So how do Insiders pick their child-care providers? Carefully, and with an emphasis on the word *licensed*.

Choosing Quality Child Care

To choose a child-care facility wisely, you must first know what distinguishes a quality program from others. According to the National Association for the Education of Young Children (www.naeyc.org), the nation's largest organization of early childhood professionals, look for these characteristics in a child-care facility:

1. Children in the program are generally comfortable, relaxed, happy, and involved in play and other activities.
2. Small groups of children are supervised by a sufficient number of adults with specialized training in first aid and early childhood development and education.
3. Adult expectations are varied appropriately for children of different ages.
4. All areas of a child's development are stressed equally.
5. The staff meets regularly to plan and evaluate the program.
6. Parents are welcome to observe, discuss policies, make suggestions, and participate in the work of the program.

Also, the association recommends asking these questions when you visit a child-care setting to help make up your mind on the facility:

1. Are they licensed?
2. Do they charge for overtime when you are late?
3. Do they provide meals and snacks?
4. What kind of disciplinary methods are used?
5. How much training and experience does the caregiver have working with children?
6. What kind of turnover does the child-care program have?
7. What will your child be doing throughout the day?
8. Can you visit your child at any time?
9. Does the caregiver have a parent contract or written policies about fees, hours, holidays, illness, and other considerations?

Finding the right caregiver can be challenging, but it is also one of the most important decisions you'll make. Be as well educated about the facilities and caregivers as possible, and visit several child-care settings before choosing one. Also, never leave a child in a setting that you haven't personally visited, and always contact your local licensing agency to ask about the complaint history of the child-care provider that you are considering.

Child Care Facilities

RULES, REGULATIONS, AND RESOURCES

On the Nevada side of the area, child-care facilities are licensed and regulated by the county upon recommendation of the state's Child Care Advisory Board and approval of the State of Nevada Division of Child and Family Services (775-684-4400; www.dcfs.state.nv.us). The Washoe County Department of Social Services (775-328-2300) is the licensing

agent for the Reno area. On the California side, policies and procedures are regulated by the state's Health and Welfare Agency, Department of Social Services, Community Care Licensing Division (916-229-4530; www.ccld.ca.gov).

Nevada

On the Nevada side of the Reno/Tahoe area, state law requires that all child-care providers be licensed, and it divides private caregiving operations into two categories. The first group is the family child-care home where a provider cares for up to six children. The second is a group child-care home where a provider cares for more than 6 but no more than 12 children. Each caregiver employee must obtain a work permit especially for child-care work from the appropriate sheriff's department. These employees must also be trained in CPR; policies, procedures, and programs of the facility; and the recognition of the symptoms of illnesses. Caregivers are also required to continue their training every year with a minimum of 12 hours related to courses in the field of developmentally appropriate practices for young children.

Several nonprofit agencies on the Nevada side of the Reno/Tahoe area provide free referral services for parents looking for child-care facilities. The Children's Cabinet (775-856-6200; www.childrens cabinet.org) provides resource and referral services to help parents in their search for child-care services. The Community Services Agency (775-786-6023; www.csa reno.org); The Division of Child and Family Services, Bureau of Services for Child Care (775-684-4421); and The Washoe County Department of Social Services (775-328-2300) will also provide you with a list of licensed child-care providers and will advise you if any complaints have been filed against a particular facility.

California

Private-family child-care homes in California are divided into two categories: small family child-care homes with up to 8 children and large family child-care homes with up to 14 children. Each child-care facility must be in strict compliance with staffing ratios and capacity restrictions. While not mandated by law, staff at these facilities are advised to get training in preventive health practices, CPR, pediatric first aid, sanitary food handling, child nutrition, caring for children with special needs, and reporting signs of child abuse. State statute requires that child-care providers receive training in prevention of infectious disease and childhood injuries. In addition to these training suggestions and requirements, all employees who have frequent and routine contact with the children must also be fingerprinted for a thorough background check. Furthermore, the facilities are under strict fire-safety rules, and the state has the right to send inspectors to large, licensed facilities at any time without notice.

The state of California's Community Care Licensing Division (916-229-4530; www.ccld.ca.gov) can tell you about any complaints lodged against day-care facilities. Several nonprofit consumer assistance groups provide information about child-care facilities on the California side of the Reno/Tahoe area. The Choices for Children Resource Agency (530-541-5848), in South Lake Tahoe, California, provides child-care referrals, parent and provider training, a resource library, and a child-care food program. In the North Shore Lake Tahoe area, the Tahoe-Truckee Community Collaborative (530-587-8322) is a free community resource for parents. Serving North Lake Tahoe and Truckee, California, as well as Incline Village, Nevada, the network provides child-care referrals, parenting support, and recreation such as after-school sports. The Sierra Nevada Children's Service (530-587-5960) also serves the North Lake and Truckee area. The Children's Cabinet in Incline Village (775-298-0004; www.cciv.org) is a centralized clearinghouse of information and direct services for children and families in the North Shore Lake Tahoe area.

Nannies and Babysitters

Local governments in the Reno/Tahoe area don't regulate nannies, nor will they refer you to any. Only two private companies work as placement agencies for nannies and au pairs: Nanny Services of Nevada (775-334-4725) and AuPairCare (800-428-7247).

Nannies generally are contracted for the traditional live-in arrangement. Even though not required by law, the more reputable nannies will be CPR-certified and licensed. Nannies' rates vary from about $10 per hour for short stays to weekly rates beginning at $300 for those who live in.

Babysitting agencies in the Reno/Tahoe area are listed in the regional Yellow Pages, but like nannies, the local governments don't regulate or refer babysitters. The laws in both California and Nevada say that a license is required when caring for more than one unrelated family's child in the sitter's home, but if a sitter goes to the child's location, no license is required.

Your ideal babysitter could be your 13-year-old next-door neighbor or a 60-year-old professional. Either way, parents should always verify qualifications and check references. Babysitting rates vary, and a small deposit may be required. It's a good idea to discuss fees and arrangements with the sitter before you commit to hiring that person for the night or day.

Latchkey and After-School Programs

The problem of finding child-care services for working parents with school-age children has been eased by a local youth watch program coordinated by various parks and recreation departments in towns and cities in the Reno/Tahoe area. These youth watch programs include: before- and after-school care for kindergartners through sixth-graders, summer programs for students in schools with traditional academic year schedules, and year-round break programs for those students in year-round schools.

Before- and after-school programs are designed to provide a fun and safe environment for children when parents have to be at work before school starts or after school ends. These latchkey programs generally give children time to do their homework, provide arts and crafts training, and include special activities such as indoor and outdoor games. Program costs and requirements vary, but generally, before- and after-school care at park and rec departments in the Reno/Tahoe area are offered on a daily basis for very reasonable rates. In Reno, for example, a child can attend the park and recreation department's before-school program for about $6.00 per day, and the after-school program for about $10.00 per day. The rates for the park and rec program in Sparks are around the same. The South Lake Tahoe and Truckee Donner parks departments both offer after-school programs.

The summer program hours vary, but most begin at 7:00 A.M. and go until 6:00 P.M. These programs also vary in cost, and some require contracts on a week-to-week basis. The South Lake Tahoe district's program offers a very affordable drop-in rate—along with a wonderful variety of activities for the kids—which makes it a great choice for residents and tourists alike. The activities offered in each summer camp are diverse but can include field trips, arts and crafts, educational programs, and special activities like bike rodeos.

Because some of the elementary

i

The Nevada Discovery Museum, a learning center for children and their families, will open in 2008 in downtown Reno. For information visit www.nvdm.org.

schools in the Washoe County School District have gone to a year-round schedule, the parks and recreation departments of Reno and Sparks have added year-round school break programs to their services. These full-day programs are for K–6 youth in year-round schools.

For more information on the programs mentioned here, contact the City of Reno Parks and Recreation Department, (775) 334-2262, www.cityofreno.com; the City of Sparks Parks and Recreation Department, (775) 353-2376, www.ci.sparks.nv.us; the City of South Lake Tahoe Parks and Recreation District (530) 542-6056, www.ci.south-lake-tahoe.ca.us; or the Truckee Donner Recreation and Parks District, (530) 582-7720, www.tdrpd.com.

Most of the private schools in the Reno/Tahoe area (see the "Education" section earlier in this chapter) have preschool or prekindergarten programs, and the majority offer before- and after-school child-care programs. Consult the individual school for specific information on programs and availability.

Also, the local YMCA can provide some services in the area of child care. (Be aware, however, that students and/or families must be members.) Contact the Sparks YMCA (775-323-9622, www.ymcasierra.org) for further details.

Another agency that can provide after-school programs is the Boys and Girls Club. These clubs are scattered around the area, and some have programs similar to the park and recreation department programs, offering games, arts and crafts, and study hours. Contact these Boys and Girls Clubs for more information: Reno/Sparks, (775) 331-3605, North Shore Lake Tahoe, (530) 546-4324; and South Shore Lake Tahoe, (530) 542-0838.

WORSHIP

Some locals say there's more praying in Reno/Tahoe casinos than in churches, but that's anybody's guess. What is clear is that the area has boasted rich religious diversity since the first pastors preached in mining camps, trading stations, and farming communities in the 1800s.

Bringing spiritual leadership to the pioneers of Reno and Lake Tahoe presented unique challenges, however. In addition to contending with the expected hardships of frontier life, the first clergy had to travel many miles to reach flocks scattered in the tiny far-flung settlements. Conditions were often less than ideal for conducting church services, since the early "towns" were sometimes nothing more than collections of tents or temporary structures. But the early preachers persevered, even offering sermons from pulpits in local saloons if necessary. When the population boomed, particularly after the discovery of silver in Virginia City, Nevada, in 1859, the first churches were constructed. And as Reno/Tahoe became more settled, representatives from a variety of denominations arrived to help "civilize" the area.

The Mormons first arrived in 1849, when a group was dispatched from Salt Lake City to develop a settlement in the Carson Valley south of Reno. Known originally as Mormon Station, the community was later renamed Genoa after the Italian town where Christopher Columbus was born. The oldest town in Nevada, Genoa was the site of the first government in what would later become the state of Nevada. (For details about the sights in this charming historic town, see the Day Trips chapter.) With more than 20 congregations, the Mormons continue to be a well-established religious group in the area.

The first Catholic church in the region was built after Father H. P. Gallagher arrived in Genoa in 1860. With around 40 parishes in the Diocese of Reno today, the Catholic church is an important part of the religious scene in Reno/Tahoe. With about 4,000 families as members, the largest congregation is at St. Therese Church of the Little Flower at 875 East Plumb Lane in Reno. A modern circular structure completed in 1978, the church is open and spacious, with lovely faceted stained-glass windows.

St. Thomas Aquinas Cathedral in Reno had humble beginnings as St. Mary's Washoe Mission. Established in 1871 as an independent parish, it was elevated to the status of cathedral in 1931 by Pope Pius XI. After fires destroyed earlier buildings, the church settled into its present home at 310 West Second Street in 1910. Constructed in Italian Renaissance style, the cathedral showcases exquisite stained-glass windows created by Hungarian artists Isabel and Edith Piczek.

The Episcopalians arrived in the area in 1859, and though less numerous than some other denominations, six churches thrive today. If you're looking for churches with a view, none is lovelier than St. John's in the Wilderness Episcopal Church at 1776 U.S. Highway 50 in Glenbrook, Nevada. Overlooking the eastern shore of Lake Tahoe, the window behind the pulpit presents an inspirational panorama of snow-dusted mountains and azure water. Trinity Episcopal Church at 200 Island Avenue in Reno also boasts a delightful setting right on the Truckee River. After services, parishioners can enjoy refreshments on the front lawn of the church while watching the river flow by, weather permitting.

The First United Methodist Church in Reno, another intriguing church on the Truckee River, dates from 1868 and has been in its present building at First and West Streets since 1926. A charming ivy-covered stone building, its lighted tower is a well-known landmark in downtown. Like many churches, First United Methodist has beautiful stained-glass windows in its sanctuary. But unlike any other church, the windows are framed by the Hosanna Arch, which contains the delicate sculptured faces of infants and children in the parish.

Along with Protestants and Catholics, people of the Jewish faith also established early religious communities. The first B'nai B'rith lodge was founded in 1862 in Virginia City, and the Chevrah B'rith Sholom in Reno in 1878. The first Jewish temple, Temple Emanu-El, was built in Reno in 1921. Today Jewish services are held in conservative Temple Emanu-El, reform Temple Sinai, and orthodox Chabad in Reno and at Temple Bat Yam in Stateline, Nevada. The North Tahoe Hebrew Congregation meets at the North Tahoe Conference Center at 8318 North Lake Boulevard in Kings Beach, California.

Bethel African Methodist Episcopal Church is the oldest African-American congregation in Nevada. Founded in Reno in 1907, it moved to its present building at 2655 North Rock Boulevard in Sparks, Nevada, in 1993. Tracing its roots to the Free African Society Church founded in 1787, Bethel AME has experienced strong growth in recent years.

With more than 200 churches and synagogues, Reno/Tahoe is diverse in religious options. Just a glance at a local phone book will show listings for every well-known denomination, such as Protestant, Catholic, and Jewish congregations, as well as some not so well known, including Baha'i, Buddhist, Eckankar, and Muslim groups. Diversity does not stop with the variety of religious communities but also extends to the languages used in the services. An increasing number of churches offer services in Spanish because of the significant number of Spanish-speaking people living in the Reno/Tahoe area. With the overall growth in population, the demand for more and larger churches has also increased. New churches are springing up to accommodate the growing number of people who want to affiliate with a religious community.

To find specific information about church services, look up "Churches" or "Synagogues" in the local telephone books, and give the congregation of your choice a call. If you don't connect with a person, most churches provide recorded messages about the times of services and activities. Church news is also printed in the Saturday edition of the *Reno Gazette-Journal* and periodically in the *Tahoe Daily Tribune*, the *North Lake Tahoe Bonanza*, and the *Tahoe World*.

RELIGIOUS UNITY AND OUTREACH

While significant differences exist among the eclectic religious groups in Reno/Tahoe, in recent years unity has become a goal for many. Some churches foster cooperation by sharing facilities, trading clergy, and holding services together.

While charity begins at home, with many religious groups reaching out to touch each other, it doesn't end there. The well-established tradition of helping those in need has expanded to include comprehensive outreach programs that fill the gaps left by governmental and nonprofit agencies. Reno/Tahoe religious congregations are involved in myriad good works, extending helping hands to the young and old, the disabled, the homeless, the hungry, and almost anyone with special needs. Virtually every religious group has organized programs that aid others in the community. They run shelters for the homeless, distribute food and clothing to the needy, offer support groups for those in crisis, and provide spiritual counseling for those in prison. If you're looking for meaningful charity work in the Reno/Tahoe area, any one of the many churches can employ you in a rewarding way.

TYING THE KNOT

Weddings have been big business in Reno/Tahoe for many years (see the History chapter for more details). Because of the exquisite scenery and the plethora of romantic locales for both the ceremony and the honeymoon, thousands of couples come to the area every year to tie the knot. And because no waiting periods or blood tests are required, it's easy to get married on the spur of the moment.

Full-service wedding chapels provide everything you need to make your wedding both romantic and legal, including the flowers, music, witnesses, minister, pictures—even a limousine to whisk you away to your wedding-night hideaway. Some chapels are small and utilitarian, while others are large and elaborate. Many resorts in the area specialize in weddings. Check with John Ascuaga's Nugget, (775) 356-3300, www.janugget.com; the Cal Neva Resort Hotel and Casino, (775) 832-4000, www.calnevaresort.com; the Hyatt Regency Lake Tahoe Resort, Spa & Casino, (775) 832-1234, www.laketahoehyatt.com; or Harrahs' Lake Tahoe, (775) 588-6611, www.harrahs.com. See the Resorts chapter for details on these properties.

The historic Thunderbird Lodge at Lake Tahoe is a romantic site for tying the knot.
TERRY BAADE

Most churches will also perform wedding ceremonies, but keep in mind that, unlike some wedding chapels, a church service can't be organized at a moment's notice.

There are plenty of choices for wedding locales, but some offer truly exceptional settings. These include:

St. John's in the Wilderness Episcopal Church (1776 U.S. Highway 50, Glenbrook, NV, 775-586-2535), featuring lovely views of Lake Tahoe; A Country Chapel (3135 Lake Tahoe Boulevard, South Lake Tahoe, CA, 530-544-4944 or 800-896-4656; www.mountainlakeweddings.com), with its charming Old Tahoe ambience; The Lakefront Wedding Chapel (3351 Lake Tahoe Boulevard, South Lake Tahoe, CA, 530-544-6119; www.lakefrontwedding.com), the only chapel right on the shore of Lake Tahoe; and the North Tahoe Conference Center, (8318 North Tahoe Boulevard, Kings Beach, CA, 530-546-7249).

If you're looking for a more exotic locale than a church or chapel, that can be arranged, too. You can get married on a yacht through Woodwind Sailing Cruises (888-867-6394 or 775-588-3000; www.sailwoodwind.com), on a paddle wheeler with Hornblower Cruises (530-541-3364; www.hornblower.com) or at Rancho San Rafael Park in Reno (775-785-4512).

Since the possibilities for a perfect wedding are endless, I can't begin to give an exhaustive list. Check local telephone books under "Wedding Chapels," "Churches," and "Wedding Consultants" for complete information. You can also log onto www.tahoeweddings.com or www.tahoesbest.com for details.

MEDIA

The roots of the media in the Reno/Tahoe area go as deep as some of the silver veins did on the Comstock Lode. At one time, more than 80 newspapers dotted the scene from Virginia City to Lake Tahoe. These newspapers constituted the first written record of the area's flamboyant history and date from 1859.

Dan De Quille and Joe Goodman are recognized as pioneer journalists on Virginia City's *Territorial Enterprise,* the same newspaper that gave Mark Twain his literary start. Alf Doten and Wells Drury gave these pioneer writers on the old *Enterprise* all the competition they could handle as rival journalists for Gold Hill's *Daily News.* Now, with only three dailies and a sprinkling of nondailies remaining, head-to-head competition in mainstream English-language newspapers is a thing of the past. But with the exploding Hispanic population in the area, competition has heated up among Spanish-language publications. In recent years several new papers have sprung up to challenge the mainstay publication *Ahora* for room on local racks.

Radio seems to be thriving in the area: 30 radio outlets crowd the airwaves between Reno and Lake Tahoe. Listeners have choices ranging from alternative rock to conservative talk and everything in between. Listeners also have the opportunity to tune in, somewhere on the AM or FM dial, almost every nationally syndicated program, from Don and Mike to G. Gordon Liddy and Rush Limbaugh.

The area's television market boasts affiliates for all the big broadcasting companies, including NBC, CBS, ABC, CW, PBS, and Fox. The local news-broadcasting stations have very competent personnel who provide the area with spirited news competition.

NEWSPAPERS

In bygone days, the Reno/Tahoe area was legendary because of its intense newspaper rivalries. Today Reno finds itself a one-paper town. The Gannett-owned *Reno Gazette-Journal* is the regional daily; it zones its local sections for the rural counties and Carson City. Even though Sparks has its own daily, the *Daily Sparks Tribune,* the small-circulation newspaper cannot compete with the much larger Gannett newspaper and doesn't try to.

South Lake Tahoe's *Tahoe Daily Tribune* is the lake's only daily newspaper, but several well-written weeklies help keep the local communities informed.

The area has only one alternative newspaper, the *Reno News & Review,* but readers can find a good assortment of out-of-area newspapers in stock at most local book and convenience stores. The *Wall Street Journal* and the *New York Times* offer home delivery, and *USA Today* can be found at almost every street corner and shopping center. And with the popularity of Internet news sites, you can get a healthy dose of news by clicking on publication Web sites.

This section is divided into daily and nondaily newspapers, with a subheading for specialty magazines and periodicals. Most of the publications can be purchased through subscriptions or at newsstands. Many of the smaller papers are free.

Dailies

Daily Sparks Tribune
1002 C Street, Sparks, NV
(775) 358-8061
www.sparkstribune-bignickel.com
This feisty little newspaper has been Spark's community newspaper since 1910

and publishes daily except Saturday and holidays. In no way does anyone see it as a rival to the bigger, more powerful *Reno Gazette-Journal;* its niche is its exhaustive coverage of Sparks.

Its small circulation (about 6,000) attests to the fact that the only readers who give a hoot about the paper are those living in Sparks's neighborhoods. The newspaper gives its readers balanced coverage of Sparks's politics, police, courts, and education, and it has a great sports section that includes good coverage of high-school athletics.

Its political leanings are best described as independent. It doggedly nips at the heels of both Republicans and Democrats and has a most diverse collection of columnists, ranging from a Christian conservative to a socialist. This diversity makes the newspaper fun to read.

The paper has been called the stepchild of the Tribune Publishing Company, which owns several other newspapers throughout the West. Its advertising staff will tell you that the only thing that keeps the *Sparks Tribune* afloat is the *Big Nickel.* The paper publishes this free tabloid every Thursday; it's a classified ad publication with a circulation of 50,000.

Reno Gazette-Journal
955 Kuenzli Street, Reno, NV
(775) 788-6200
www.rgj.com

Reno's only daily newspaper, the *Gazette-Journal* reaches about 145,000 readers Monday through Saturday and about 185,000 on Sunday. One of about 100 newspapers owned by the Gannett Co., Inc., it constantly wins awards in its parent company's yearly in-house competitions and also takes home its share of awards from the Nevada Press Association.

If someone asked a *Gazette-Journal* reader the newspaper's politics, the answer would definitely depend on which side of the political fence the reader was peeking over. The Republican readers curse the newspaper for being too liberal, and the Democratic readers call it too conservative. In reality, the newspaper is slightly left of middle-of-the-road, endorsing more Democrats than Republicans on its opinion pages.

Most criticism of the newspaper stems from the fact that it is a Gannett-owned product. *Gazette-Journal* critics condemn the newspaper for putting profit above good journalism and ridicule it for taking the path of least resistance with its editorials. Proponents of the newspaper say they like its community-oriented tradition and the way the *Gazette-Journal* concentrates on local news.

The newspaper prints a *Best Bets* tabloid insert every Thursday, covering the casino, entertainment, and nightlife scenes. On Friday it produces *Calendar,* a guide to arts and entertainment outside the casinos, including movies and the local music scene. On Saturday it distributes *HomeFinder,* a real estate guide to the area.

Tahoe Daily Tribune
3079 Harrison Avenue
South Lake Tahoe, CA
(530) 541-3880
www.tahoe.com/tribune

This newspaper, printed Monday through Friday, is Lake Tahoe's only daily. It is a member of the Swift Newspaper Group, which also owns all the weekly newspapers scattered around the lake communities. The paper is printed in the mornings, with a circulation of 9,600 Monday through Thursday and 10,500 on Friday.

In keeping with company policy, the *Daily Tribune* carries mostly local and community news. The *Daily Tribune* serves the Lake Tahoe area in El Dorado, Placer, and Alpine Counties in California and Carson, Douglas, and Washoe Counties in Nevada.

On a typical news day, the newspaper runs about five local stories on the front page and devotes one page to regional, one page to national, and one page to international news. The sports section runs Bay Area professional sports news and national sports stories but tries to cover Lake Tahoe high-school and local sports as well. The newspaper is served by the Associated Press.

Over the years, the *Daily Tribune* has become the media powerhouse of Lake Tahoe. Established in 1958, the newspaper aggressively promotes tourism to the area. Its political stand is middle-of-the-road, but it usually shies away from political controversy, concentrating instead on more feature-type stories about Lake Tahoe that visitors would enjoy.

The *Daily Tribune* also publishes *Lake Tahoe Action* (see below).

Weeklies

Ahora
743 South Virginia Street, Reno, NV
(775) 323-6811
www.ahoranews.com

Founded in 1983, this newspaper provides Reno/Tahoe's growing Spanish-speaking community with local, national, and international news printed in both Spanish and English. The oldest Spanish-language newspaper in the area, it serves more than 200,000 Hispanics in communities all over northern Nevada and California. The paper features two sections and is distributed on Friday.

Comstock Chronicle
198 North C Street, Virginia City, NV
(775) 847-0765

The *Comstock Chronicle* is the only remaining newspaper in an area that once teemed with daily newspapers. "The Voice of the Comstock" prints about 3,000 copies of its 16-page tabloid every Thursday. Though the paper concentrates on Virginia City/Gold Hill and Storey County news, with an emphasis on local politics, it also includes national news that relates to Nevada and the Comstock and has expanded its coverage of the arts. In a county that boasts only 3,500 citizens, the *Chronicle* manages to reach about two-thirds of the population.

Most of its journalists are freelancers, and the newspaper rarely uses bylines with its stories. The opinion pages and Letters to the Editor are often controversial, making this section fun to read. The *Chronicle* still exudes the feistiness that once made the *Territorial Enterprise* and the *Gold Hill Daily News* legendary.

Lake Tahoe Action
3079 Harrison Avenue
South Lake Tahoe, CA
(530) 541-3880

The *Tahoe Daily Tribune* publishes *Lake Tahoe Action,* a weekly tabloid that serves as Lake Tahoe's entertainment guide. This tab comes out on Friday and covers the entertainment happenings around the lake. Its sections include music, sports, theater, hot spots, and casino shows. It is a must-have for visitors and locals alike. *Lake Tahoe Action* has been voted the best entertainment guide in California many times by the California Newspaper Publishers Association. Circulation is about 22,000 for the free guide.

La Voz Hispana
677 Casazza Drive, Reno, NV
(775) 827-2727

La Voz Hispana (*The Spanish Voice*) is widely distributed throughout the Reno and Lake Tahoe area. Founded in 1999, the paper is all in Spanish and is printed every two weeks. Its circulation is about 6,000.

North Lake Tahoe Bonanza
925 Tahoe Boulevard, Incline Village, NV
(775) 831-4666
www.tahoe.com/bonanza

One of the four newspapers in the Lake Tahoe area owned by the Swift Newspaper Group, this newspaper reflects the community it serves and is published three times a week.

Founded in 1970, the *Bonanza* concentrates on local news, local sports, and local politics in the northern part of the basin, covering Incline Village, Crystal Bay, Kings Beach, and Tahoe Vista. The front page is more likely to have a spread on the Incline High School graduation than a hard news story of a local burglary. The opinion page is lively with Letters to the Editor, tirades on local politics, and explanations of local happenings. The newspaper has a circulation of around 7,000.

Northern Nevada Business Weekly
780 Smithridge, Suite 200, Reno, NV
(775) 770-1173
www.nnbw.biz
Although *Northern Nevada Business Weekly* takes business very seriously, its style is far from stuffy. It strives to be readable as well as informative. It's read by about 28,000 business movers and shakers each week.

Reno News & Review
708 North Center Street, Reno, NV
(775) 324-4440
www.newsreview.com/reno/home
The only alternative weekly in the Reno/Tahoe area, the *Reno News & Review* likes to take on the establishment and especially likes to badger the *Reno Gazette-Journal*. The staff maintains that its alternative voice is not beholden to the powers that be, and it covers everything, including stories that the mainstream media won't touch.

This every-Wednesday publication began in 1993 as the *Nevada Weekly* and was founded by former *Reno Gazette-Journal* reporters as an alternative source of news to the Gannett-owned Reno daily. They soon found they were not financially equipped to go up against the Gannett Company. The founders sold the weekly to Chico Community Publishing, Inc., in 1995, and it became the *Reno News & Review*, joining the publishing company's two other alternative weeklies in Chico and Sacramento, California.

The weekly tabloid is progressive, spirited, and targeted at the young-adult crowd. Stories often rake local politicians over the coals, take potshots at the establishment, and wreak havoc on corporate America. It also devotes a lot of space to the local entertainment scene.

The newspaper prints about 35,000 copies each week and has an estimated readership of 95,000. It can be found all over the Reno/Tahoe area in bright-red street racks at convenience and grocery stores, malls, gas stations, restaurants, and just about anywhere else the Generation X crowd hangs out.

The *Sierra Sun*
12315 Deerfield Drive, Truckee, CA
(530) 587-6061
www.tahoe.com/sun
Another Swift Newspaper Group product, the *Sierra Sun* concentrates on local and community news. The paper has a circulation of 6,000 and reaches about two-thirds of the population of Truckee. Stories range from the Boy Scouts' annual Pinewood Derby to opinion pieces on year-round education in local schools. It has won a number of awards from the California Newspaper Publishers Association and the Nevada Press Association for its editorial pages.

Tahoe World
395 North Lake Boulevard
Tahoe City, CA
(530) 583-3487
www.tahoe.com/world
The *Tahoe World* has the smallest circulation of the Swift Newspaper Group's weekly Lake Tahoe newspapers, but that doesn't prevent it from winning awards from the California Press Association.

The *Tahoe World* covers community and local news in Tahoe City, Kings Beach, and on the western side of the lake. Started in 1963, it reaches about 5,800 readers. Like its sister weeklies around the lake, this newspaper concentrates on keeping its readers informed of all the local happenings.

MAGAZINES AND OTHER PRINT MEDIA

Nevada Farm Bureau Agriculture & Livestock Journal
2165 Green Vista Drive, Suite 205
Sparks, NV
(775) 674-4000
This monthly tabloid provides readers with news about Nevada's agriculture and farming. Produced by the Nevada Farm Bureau and circulated to farm bureau families, the newspaper's motto is "All the News Farmers Can Use." Its circulation is about 2,100, and copies are available by subscription or from the farm bureau.

Nevada Magazine
401 North Carson Street, Suite 100
Carson City, NV
(775) 687-5416
(800) 495-3281 (subscriptions)
www.nevadamagazine.com
Nevada Magazine is published by the Nevada Department of Tourism and reaches about 80,000 readers every other month. Even though the magazine is not published in Reno or Lake Tahoe, it devotes many articles and stories to the region. The publication is the state's official guide to recreation, travel, people, history, and events in the Silver State. The best magazine for learning about the state's history, it has been published since 1936 and is available by subscription; it can also be found at magazine racks around the area. You can buy Nevada meorabilia, such as slot machines and clothing, from the magazines's online stores.

The *Nevada Rancher*
1475 Cornell Avenue, Suite 500
Lovelock, NV
(775) 273-7245
www.nevadarancher.com
Reno is at the western edge of the vast ranchlands of the Great Basin, and this tabloid covers ranching and agricultural interests in Nevada and the West. It includes livestock events, a local calendar of events, feature stories, ranching news briefs, research articles, sales reports, 4-H happenings, and Reno/Tahoe high school rodeo news. Founded in 1970, this monthly publication has a paid subscription of about 2,300 and reaches about 4,000 readers. It is available by subscription; can be picked up for free at event centers in Reno, Elko, Fallon, and other cities; and can be found in local feed and ranching stores.

Northern Nevada Family Life
KMPM Publishing
P.O. Box 6031
Sparks, NV 89432
(775) 787-3343
www.northernnevadafamily.com
Published since 1999, *Northern Nevada Family Life* is a monthly tabloid that can be picked up free at racks around the area. Typical stories have explored grandparents' rights, teenage dating, and time management. Regular features include a comprehensive calendar of family/kid-friendly events, movie reviews, an advice column, and classified ads. It usually runs around 40 pages in length.

Outlands Magazine
33 St. Lawrence Avenue, Reno, NV
(775) 324-7866
www.outlandsmagazine.com
Although the *Reno Informer* was the only gay and lesbian publication for a number of years, *Outlands* went into direct competition with it beginning in 2002. A monthly publication, the *Outlands* reaches the gay/lesbian/bisexual/transgender community in the Reno/Tahoe area as well as other parts of the West. *The Reno Informer* has recently ceased publication For more information about gay and lesbian events, click on www.arainbowplace.org.

Pet Folio
1605 Del Monte Lane, Reno, NV
(775) 827-2247
For all the latest events and products concerning pets, pick up a free copy of *Pet Folio* in newspaper/magazine racks in the

area. You'll find interesting stories written by pet psychics, veterinarians, dedicated pet owners, and retailers of pet products. If you like to get out and socialize with your pet, you won't want to miss the many activities offered especially for pets, such as the Mutt Strut at Sparks Marina Park and the free doggie swim day at Idlewild Park swimming pool.

Range
106 East Adams, Suite 201
Carson City, NV
(775) 884-2200
www.rangemagazine.com
Celebrating the cowboy spirit, *Range* magazine is an award-winning forum for issues that affect the American West. If you want to know about the people, lifestyles, lands, and wildlife of the "outback," you'll find plenty to pique your interest in this well-written publication. It's controversial, it's passionate, but it's never boring.

Reno Magazine
955 Kuenzli Street, Reno, NV
(775) 788-6326
www.renomagazine.biz
Typical of many resort and city magazines, *Reno Magazine* is a feel-good publication loaded with pretty pictures of beautiful people living in beautiful houses and eating beautiful food. Published by the *Reno Gazette-Journal* people, it first hit magazine racks in 2002. You won't find any hard-hitting journalism here, but you'll probably enjoy wallowing in the "Reno Lifestyle."

Senior Spectrum
1105 Terminal Way, Reno, NV
(775) 348-0717, (800) 253-3713
www.seniorspectrumnewspaper.com
Devoted to the senior population in the Reno/Tahoe area, this monthly newspaper is dedicated to information and entertainment for the senior community. The *Spectrum* has carried articles dealing with retirement, financial and legal advice, health and fitness, nutrition, and columns by local doctors, lawyers, and investment counselors. The newspaper also has included restaurant reviews and has featured advertisements by some companies that give seniors discounts. A monthly calendar of events is included, as well as a classified ads section and feature stories about local seniors. The newspaper began publishing in 1985.

Sunny Day Guide to Lake Tahoe
(775) 833-4311
www.sunnydayguide.com
This publication is printed for the Incline Village/Crystal Bay, North Lake Tahoe, and Tahoe/Douglas Chambers of Commerce. The small magazine is filled with feature stories about both the North Shore and the South Shore of Lake Tahoe and includes maps of the entire lake. It has a calendar of events, a casino chart, a beach chart, and a list of almost every restaurant around the lake. It has special sections on shopping, lake activities, fishing, and golfing. Almost every page offers a discount coupon to one of the many businesses around the area. The *Sunny Day Guide* is published in June and December.

Tahoe Quarterly
770 Northwood Boulevard, Suite 10
Incline Village, NV
(775) 832-3700
www.tahoequarterly.com
Like *Reno Magazine, Tahoe Quarterly* oozes a luxurious lifestyle that many people can only dream about. Filled with gorgeous photos of lovely scenery and to-die-for homes, it showcases a world of luxury and wealth. While Tahoe is much more than what is shown here, the magazine does talk about environmental and social issues occasionally. You'll find a new issue of this slick publication at newsstands every quarter, plus several special issues throughout the year.

The _Weekly_
200 Center Street
Carnelian Bay, CA
(530) 546-5995
www.tahoethisweek.com
This weekly magazine contains current

events, entertainment, recreation, and sightseeing information for Truckee and the North Shore of Lake Tahoe. Visitors and residents alike find this guide useful in planning weekends or vacations around the northern part of the lake. The circulation is about 20,000, and copies can be found at various business locations around the North Shore.

The *Wolf Pack Edge*
P.O. Box 6031, Sparks, NV 89432
(775) 787-3343
www.packedge.com
This newspaper is published monthly from September through June and is devoted to articles about athletics at the University of Nevada, Reno, and Northern Nevada High School. The publication is independently owned and is not affiliated with the university. It derives its name from a play on words using UNR's mascot and team name—the Wolf Pack. The newspaper does an outstanding job covering revenue-generating sports (football, basketball, and baseball) but also devotes a lot of ink to non-revenue-generating sports like skiing, swimming, tennis, and golf. The 1997-98 school year was its first year of publication, and it garnered a good readership; these days the paper has a print run of 25,000 copies. The paper can be found all over the area and often shares the news racks with the *Reno News & Review.*

RADIO

The first radio station hit the Reno/Tahoe airwaves in 1928, and since then radio has grown to offer every type of programming, from conservative talk to alternative rock. About 30 stations on both the AM and FM dials broadcast from Reno to the South Shore of Lake Tahoe.

The most popular stations, according to Arbitron ratings, are those with either country or news/talk formats. Following is a sampling of area stations categorized by format, but this roster is not chiseled in stone. Reno/Tahoe radio stations seem to change format and frequencies as often as two cherries pop up on the pay line of a slot machine.

ADULT CONTEMPORARY

KRNO 106.9 FM

ALTERNATIVE/CLASSIC ROCK

KDOT 104.5 FM; www.kdot.com
KLCA 96.5 FM (Alice)
KNEV 95.5 FM (Magic 95)
KODS 103.7 FM
KOZZ 105.7 FM; www.kozzradio.com
KRZQ 100.9 FM
KTHX 100.1 FM (The X)
KURK 92.9 FM
KWNZ 97.3 FM (K-Wins)

CHRISTIAN

KIHM 920 AM
KLRH 88.3 FM; www.klove.com
KRNG 101.3 FM (The Renegade)

COUNTRY

KBUL 98.1 FM; www.kbul.com
KHIT 1450 AM; www.1450khit.com
KUUB 94.5 FM; www.cubcountry.com

JAZZ

KJZS 92.1 FM; www.smoothjazzreno.com
KUNR 88.7 FM (Public radio from the UNR campus); www.kunr.org

NEWS-TALK

KBZZ 1270 AM; www.kbuzz.com
KKOH 780 AM; www.kkoh.com
KOWL 1490 AM
KRNV 101.7 FM

OLDIES

KBDB 1400 AM
KPTL 1300 AM

SPANISH

KQLO 1590 AM
KRNV 102.1 FM
KXEQ 1340 AM (La Super Q)

KXTO 1550 AM; www.kxto.com

SPORTS

KPLY 1230 AM; www.kply.com
KPTT 630 AM

TELEVISION

Reno/Tahoe television offers a variety of choices for viewers. Local TV stations that currently broadcast in the area are affiliated with ABC, CBS, Fox, NBC, PBS, CW, My TV, a public-access channel, and a Spanish-language station.

The ABC, CBS, and NBC affiliates provide news broadcasts at least four times per day, usually beginning at 6:00 A.M. This competition has been good for viewers. Each station has a bevy of reporters and camera technicians, minivans, and satellite trucks that constantly roam the area, providing excellent on-the-spot news coverage.

Azteca America provides a growing Latino population with national and local news. The addition of Sierra Nevada Cable Access Television (SNCAT) in 1997 gives the general community a place to go to produce hometown programs.

While the choices in television stations and programming can be quite mind-boggling, the options for signing up for the programming are pretty limited. Charter Communications (formerly AT&T Cable Services) is the only game in town if you want to hook up directly to a television cable provided by them. They'll sell you Charter cable and Charter digital cable. But because the complaints about Charter's poor service are legendary, many viewers have opted for Dish Network satellite dishes. You can contact Charter at (888) 954-8484. For Dish just let your fingers do the walking through the "Television Satellite" section of the Yellow Pages, where you'll find a number of companies eager to install a dish on the side of your home. Although most newspapers have some sort of printed TV guide, I wonder sometimes why they bother since they are so limited. For a complete listing of programming, refer to the guide that's on your TV screen.

The local television stations are listed in alphabetical order by station call letters.

KAME-MY, Channel 21; (775) 856-2121
KNPB-PBS, Channel 5; (775) 784-4555
KOLO-ABC, Channel 8; (775) 858-8888
KREN-CW, Channel 27; (775) 333-2727
KRNV-NBC, Channel 4; (775) 785-1210
KRXI-FOX, Channel 11; (775) 856-1100
KTVN-CBS, Channel 2; (775) 858-2222

KARZ 46 (Spanish) Azteca America
5250 South Virginia Street
Reno, NV
(775) 327-6800

SNCAT-Sierra Nevada Cable Access Television
4024 Kietzke Lane
Reno, NV
(775) 828-1211
www.sncat.org

This is Reno's community-access television station, which receives its revenue from local cable franchise fees and uses the money to help the general public produce TV programs. It offers editing, video, and producing classes, then helps students produce hometown programs. The station broadcasts city and county government meetings and also helps the local university and community college by transmitting distant learning classes, which enables students in the rural counties to attend classes by video conferencing. Programming runs 24 hours a day.

INTERNET ACCESS

Connecting to the Internet is a no-brainer; you'll find pages of listings for Internet service providers in local telephone books. High-speed access is just a phone call away, with Charter Communications (866-731-5420) providing high-speed cable and AT&T (866-831-1582) offering high-speed DSL.

INDEX

C

D

G

H

O

S

U

V

ABOUT THE AUTHOR

Born and raised in northwestern Montana, Jeanne Lauf Walpole first moved to Nevada after graduating from Washington State University in Pullman, Washington. She taught high school Spanish and geography and, together with her husband, established several family-owned casinos in Fallon, 60 miles east of Reno. After some years, the pressure of this 24-hour-a-day enterprise became grueling. They sold the business and moved to Sun Valley, Idaho, with their three sons, Chris, Scott, and Kevin. In this mountain paradise the family was able to fully indulge in their love of the outdoors. But after four years, Jeanne longed for the "real world" again.

She moved to Memphis, Tennessee, where she received her master's degree in journalism from the University of Memphis. She then returned to Reno to build a career in publishing and freelance writing.

Jeanne has written for a variety of publications and was editor of *Active Times,* a regional senior publication in Memphis, and editor/publisher of *Golden Gateways,* a travel newsletter for mature travelers. She was also a contributing writer for the book *Reno & Tahoe Country: An Illustrated History of Western Nevada.*

Community service has played an important role in her life, and she has served on numerous boards and been elected to public office. In the past several years, her commitment to those in need drew her to Crisis Call Center, where she answers calls of those in crisis and has served as president of its board of directors.

KEVIN LAUF

Her passion for travel began before she could read, as some of her earliest childhood memories are of looking at pictures in *National Geographic* magazine. She has traveled in more than 60 countries and lived in Bogota, Colombia, as a Fulbright Scholar and in Mexico City as a summer school student.

When not facing deadline, she can be found hiking or backcountry skiing with James and their dogs, Shelby and Inka.